Vasiṣṭha's Yoga

Blessing

The *Yoga Vāsiṣṭha* is a unique work of Indian philosophy. It is highly respected for its practical mysticism. The study of this great scripture alone can surely help one to attain to God-consciousness. For aspirants of the highest beatitude, the *Yoga Vāsiṣṭha* is like nectar. It is a storehouse of wisdom. Like the *Amritanubhava* of Sri Jñāneshwar, the path shown in this work is for those who are highly spiritually evolved, almost to the state of a Siddha. It expounds the highest doctrine with many stories and illustrations. Not only philosophers, but even the modern psychologists and scientists will certainly find in it something related to their own discoveries.

Most of the scriptures were narrated by God to His devotees, but the *Yoga Vāsiṣṭha* was narrated to God Himself. It is the teaching of the sage Vasiṣṭha imparted to Lord Rāma. It contains true understanding about the creation of the world. The philosophy of the *Yoga Vāsiṣṭha* is very similar to that of Kashmir Shaivism. Its main teaching is that everything is Consciousness, including the material world, and that the world is as you see it. This is absolutely true. The world is nothing but the play of Consciousness.

Abhinavagupta, the great tenth century scholar of Kashmir Shaivism, once said, "Shiva, the independent and pure Self that always vibrates in the mind, is the Parashakti that rises as joy in various sense experiences. Then the experience of this outer world appears as its Self. I do not know where this word 'saṃsāra' has come from." This is also the unparalleled philosophy of the *Yoga Vāsiṣṭha.*

In translating this monumental work, Swami Venkatesananda has worked hard to make its philosophy comprehensible to ordinary people. In doing so, he has done a great service to seekers of the Truth. Swamiji is a pure person, full of knowledge and therefore worthy of translating this work of supreme yoga.

Let this book bring true knowledge to its readers.

SWAMI MUKTANANDA

Vasiṣṭha's Yoga

SWAMI VENKATESANANDA

STATE UNIVERSITY OF NEW YORK PRESS

Published by State University of New York Press, Albany

Printed in the United States of America

For information, contact State University of New York Press, Albany, NY
www.sunypress.edu

Library of Congress Cataloging-in-Publication Data

Venkatesananda, Swami.
Vasiṣṭha's yoga / Swami Venkatesananda.
pages cm
Includes translation of: Yogavāsiṣṭharāmāyaṇa.
Includes index.
ISBN 978-0-7914-1363-0 (hc. : alk. paper)—978-0-7914-1364-7 (pbk. : alk. paper)
ISBN 978-1-4384-2284-8 (e-book)
1. Yogavāsiṣṭharāmāyaṇa—Commentaries. 2. Religious life—Hinduism. 3. Hinduism—Doctrines. I. Yogavāsiṣṭharāmāyaṇa. English. II. Title.

BL1237.32.Y633V46 1993
294.5'4—dc20 92-3160
CIP

30 29 28

Scheme of Transliteration

VOWELS: a ā i ī u ū ṛ ṝ ḷ e ai o au ṃ ḥ

CONSONANTS:

gutturals	k	kh	g	gh	ṅ
palatals	c	ch	j	jh	ñ
cerebrals	ṭ	ṭh	ḍ	ḍh	ṇ
dentals	t	th	d	dh	n
labials	p	ph	b	bh	m
semi-vowels	y	r	l	v	
sibilants	s	as in sun			
	ś	palatal sibilant			
	ṣ	cerebral sibilant—as in shun			
aspirate	h				

The above scheme does not facilitate the pronunciation of the syllable jna which occurs often in the Yoga Vāsiṣṭha as also in yoga literature (jñāna means knowledge). The j is not really pronounced as j but almost as g. It is followed by the n which partakes of the character of the guttural and the palatal n. Added to all this there is also a suggestion of y before the appropriate vowel completes the syllable.

Sātvic, rājasic and tāmasic are anglicised adjective forms of satva, rajas and tamas. Many common nouns have also been anglicised by addition of 's' for the plural.

The numbers in the margins refer to Parts and Chapters in the complete *Yoga Vasishtha*. The Roman number refers to the Part, of which there are six, and the following Arabic number designates the Chapter being summarized from that Part.

Contents

Foreword

The book, *Vasiṣṭha's Yoga*, is a translation into English accompanied by brief expositions, by Swami Venkatesananda of the Divine Life Society, Rishikesh, India, of the well-known Vedānta treatise in Sanskrit, *The Yoga Vāsiṣṭha.*

The Swami has arranged the verses of the book in such a way as to convert them into a rosary of daily thoughts throughout the year, on the lines of his two other books, already published, namely, the *Śrimad Bhāgavatam* or *The Book of God,* and *The Bhagavad-gītā* or *The Song of God.*

The *Yoga Vāsiṣṭha* has been a favourite book of spiritual seekers in India these several centuries. Its special appeal lies in its thoroughly rational approach, and in its presentation of Vedānta as a philosophy which dares, like *The Bhagavad-gītā,* to bridge the gulf between the secular and the sacred, action and contemplation, in human life, through a comprehensive and lofty spirituality. The reader will come across passages such as the verse entry II:18, highlighting the importance of reason:

> The remark of even a child is to be accepted, if it is in accordance with reason; but the remark of even Brahmā Himself, the creator of the world, is to be rejected like a piece of straw if it does not accord with reason.

It is this philosophy of a comprehensive spirituality, rational and practical, that man in the modern age needs to rescue himself from his stagnation of worldliness and put him on the high road of creative living and fulfillment.

Swami Venkatesananda, who has been working untiringly for decades to spread the life-giving message of Yoga and Vedānta in East and West, has done a great service to spiritual seekers far and wide by bringing out this translation of *The Yoga Vāsiṣṭha* in the wake of his translation of the other two great books.

The Chiltern Yoga Trust of Elgin, South Africa, deserves the silent thanks of readers for publishing these three books of the Swami and helping to broadcast far and wide the life-giving, purifying, and inspiring ideas of Eternal India, *Amat Bhārat,* in her Vedānta.

SWAMI RANGANATHANANDA

Introduction

Scholars speculate about the author of this monumental scripture and such other academic matters: may God bless them with success.

The Yoga-Vāsiṣṭha is the greatest help to the spiritual awakening and the direct experience of the Truth. This is certain. If this is what you want, you are welcome to Yoga-Vāsiṣṭha.

The text abounds in repetitions which are, however, not repetitious. If you do not like (or need) repetition, then read just this one verse:

> This world-appearance is a confusion: even as the blueness of the sky is an optical illusion. I think it is better not to let the mind dwell on it, but to ignore it. (I.3.2)

This verse occurs several times in the scripture and it seems to be the very essence of the teaching.

If that is not quite clear to you now, read the scripture. The numerous ways in which this truth is revealed will help open your mind.

It is wise to read just one page a day. The teaching is revolutionary. The biased mind does not readily accept it. After the daily reading, meditate. Let the message soak through.

****

An oft-recurring expression in this scripture is 'kākatālīya'—a crow alights on the cocoanut palm tree and that very moment a ripe cocoanut falls. The two unrelated events thus seem to be related in time and space, though there is no causal relationship.

Such is life. Such is 'creation'. But the mind caught up in its own trap of logic questions 'why', invents a 'why' and a 'wherefore' to satisfy itself, conveniently ignoring the inconvenient questions that still haunt an intelligent mind.

Vasiṣṭha demands direct observation of the mind, its motion, its notions, its reasoning, the assumed cause and the projected result, and even the observed and the observation—and the realisation of their indivisible unity as the infinite consciousness.

That is the uniqueness of this scripture which hence declares itself to be supreme:

> Except through this scripture, one cannot gain what is good, now or at any time. Therefore, for perfect realisation of the supreme truth, one should fervently investigate this scripture alone. (VI.2.103)

It is, however the teaching that is supreme, not a book or a sage. Hence, Vasiṣṭha is bold enough to say:

> If, however, one thinks it is not authoritative because it is of human origin, one can resort to the study of any other scripture dealing with self-knowledge and final liberation. (VI.2.175)

Whichever be the scripture taught by whomever and whichever be the path you choose, stop not till the psychological conditioning ceases entirely. Hence, Vasiṣṭha exhorts the seeker:

> One should study at least a small part of this scripture daily. The beauty in this scripture is that its student is not abandoned to his despair; if something is not clear in the first instance, a further study of the scripture makes it clear. (VI.2.175)

Prayer

yataḥ sarvāṇi bhūtāni pratibhānti sthitāni ca
yatrai 'vo 'paśamaṃ yānti tasmai satyātmane namaḥ (1)
jñātā jñānaṃ tathā jñeyaṃ draṣṭā darśana dṛśyabhūḥ
kartā hetuḥ kriyā yasmāt tasmai jñaptyātmane namaḥ (2)
sphuranti sīkarā yasmād ānandasyā 'ṃbare 'vanau
sarveṣāṃ jīvanaṃ tasmai brahmānandātmane namaḥ (3)

Salutations to that reality in which all the elements, and all the animate and inanimate beings shine as if they have an independent existence, and in which they exist for a time and into which they merge.

Salutations to that consciousness which is the source of the apparently distinct threefold divisions of knower, knowledge and known, seer, sight and seen, doer, doing and deed.

Salutations to that bliss absolute (the ocean of bliss) which is the life of all beings whose happiness and unfoldment is derived from the shower of spray from that ocean of bliss.

PART ONE

On Dispassion

SUTĪKṢṆA, the sage, asked the sage Agastya: I:1

O sage, kindly enlighten me on this problem of liberation—which one of the two is conducive to liberation, work or knowledge?

AGASTYA replied:

Verily, birds are able to fly with their two wings: even so both work and knowledge together lead to the supreme goal of liberation. Not indeed work alone nor indeed knowledge alone can lead to liberation: but, both of them together form the means to liberation. Listen: I shall narrate to you a legend in answer to your question. There once lived a holy man by name Kāruṇya who was the son of Agniveśya. Having mastered the holy scriptures and understood their purport, the young man became apathetic to life. Seeing this, Agniveśya demanded why Kāruṇya had abandoned the due performance of his daily duties. To which Kāruṇya replied: "Do not the scriptures declare on the one hand that one should fulfil scriptural injunctions till the end of one's life and on the other that immortality can be realised only by the abandonment of all action? Caught between these two doctrines, what shall I do, O my guru and father?" Having said this, the young man remained silent.

AGNIVEŚYA said:

My son, listen: I shall narrate to you an ancient lesson. Duly consider its moral and then do as you please. Once upon a time, a celestial nymph named Suruci was seated on a peak in the Himālayas when she saw a messenger of Indra the king of gods fly past. Questioned by her, he informed her of his mission which was as follows: "A royal sage by name Ariṣṭanemi entrusted his kingdom to his son and was engaged in breath-taking austerities in Gandhamādana hill. Seeing this, Indra asked me to approach him with a bevy of nymphs and escort the royal sage to heaven. The royal sage however wanted to know the merits and the demerits of heaven. I replied: In heaven, the best, the middling and the least among pious mortals receive appropriate rewards, and once the fruits of their respective merits have been exhausted they return to the world of mortals. The royal sage refused to accept Indra's invitation to heaven. Indra once again sent me to the royal sage with the request that he should seek the counsel of the sage Vālmīki before turning the offer down.

The royal sage was then introduced to the sage Vālmīki. He asked Vālmīki, "What is the best way to rid oneself of birth and death?" In reply, Vālmīki narrated to him the dialogue between Rāma and Vasiṣṭha.

I:2 VĀLMĪKI said:

He is qualified to study this scripture (the dialogue between Rāma and Vasiṣṭha) who feels "I am bound, I should be liberated", who is neither totally ignorant nor enlightened. He who deliberates on the means of liberation propounded in this scripture in the form of stories surely attains liberation from the repetitive history (of birth and death).

I had composed the story of Rāma earlier and I had imparted it to my beloved disciple Bharadvāja. Once when he went to the mount Meru, Bharadvāja narrated it to Brahmā, the creator. Highly pleased with this, the latter granted a boon to Bharadvāja. Bharadvāja sought a boon that "all human beings may be freed from unhappiness" and begged of Brahmā to find the best way to achieve this.

Brahmā said to Bharadvāja: "Go to the sage Vālmīki and pray to him to continue to narrate the noble story of Rāma in such a way that the listener may be freed from the darkness of nescience." Not content with that, Brahmā accompanied by the sage Bharadvāja arrived at my hermitage.

After receiving due worship at my hands Brahmā said to me: "O sage, your story of Rāma shall be the raft with which men will cross the ocean of saṃsāra (repetitive history). Hence, continue its narration and bring it to a successful completion." Having said this, the Creator instantly disappeared from the scene.

As if puzzled by the abrupt command of Brahmā, I requested the sage Bharadvāja to explain to me what Brahmā had just said. Bharadvāja repeated Brahmā's words: "Brahmā would like you to reveal the story of Rāma in such a manner that it would enable all to go beyond sorrow. I, too, pray to you, O sage: kindly tell me in detail, how Rāma, Lakṣmaṇa and the other brothers freed themselves from sorrow."

I then revealed to Bharadvāja the secret of the liberation of Rāma, Lakṣmaṇa and the other brothers, as also their parents and the members of the royal court. And, I said to Bharadvāja: "My son, if you, too, live like them you will also be freed from sorrow here and now."

VĀLMĪKI continued: I:3

This world-appearance is a confusion, even as the blueness of the sky is an optical illusion. I think it is better not to let the mind dwell on it, but to ignore it. Neither freedom from sorrow nor realisation of one's real nature is possible as long as the conviction does not arise in one that the world-appearance is unreal. And this conviction arises when one studies this scripture with diligence. It is then that one arrives at the firm conviction that the objective world is a confusion of the real with the unreal. If one does not thus study this scripture, true knowledge does not arise in him even in millions of years.

Mokṣa or liberation is the total abandonment of all vāsanā or mental conditioning, without the least reserve. Mental conditioning is of two types—the pure and the impure. The impure is the cause of birth; the pure liberates one from birth. The impure is of the nature of nescience and ego-sense; these are the seeds, as it were, for the tree of re-birth. On the other hand, when these seeds are abandoned, the mental conditioning that merely sustains the body, is of a pure nature. Such mental conditioning exists even in those who have been liberated while living: it does not lead to re-birth as it is sustained only by past momentum and not by present motivation.

I shall narrate to you how Rāma lived an enlightened life of a liberated sage: knowing this you will be freed from all misunderstanding concerning old age and death.

Upon his return from the hermitage of his preceptor, Rāma dwelt in his father's palace sporting in various ways. Desirous of touring the whole country and visiting the holy places of pilgrimage, Rāma sought the presence of his father and asked to be permitted to undertake such a pilgrimage. The king chose an auspicious day for the commencement of this pilgrimage; and on that day, after receiving the affectionate blessings of the elders of the family, Rāma departed.

Rāma toured the whole country from the Himālayas downwards, along with his brothers. He then returned to the capital to the delight of the people of the country.

I:4, 5, 6 VĀLMĪKI continued:

Upon entering the palace Rāma devoutly bowed to his father, the sage Vasiṣṭha and other elders and holy men. The whole of the city of Ayodhyā put on a festive appearance for eight days, to celebrate the return of Rāma from the pilgrimage.

For some time Rāma lived in the palace duly performing his daily duties. However, very soon a profound change came over him. He grew thin and emaciated, pale and weak. The king Daśaratha was worried over this sudden and unaccountable change in his beloved son's appearance and behaviour. Whenever he questioned Rāma concerning his health, the latter replied that there was nothing wrong. When Daśaratha asked Rāma, "Beloved son, what is worrying you?" Rāma politely replied, "Nothing, father" and remained silent.

Inevitably Daśaratha turned to the sage Vasiṣṭha for the answer. The sage enigmatically answered: "Surely, there is some reason why Rāma behaves in this manner. Even as in this world no great changes take place before the coming into being of their cause, viz., the cosmic elements, changes like anger, despondency and joy do not manifest in the behaviour of noble ones without proper cause." Daśaratha did not wish to probe further.

Soon after this, there arrived at the palace the sage Viśvāmitra of world renown. When the king was informed of the holy visit, he rushed forward to greet him. Daśaratha said: "Welcome, welcome, O holy sage! Your arrival at my humble abode makes me happy. It is as welcome to me as vision to a blind man, rain to parched earth, son to a barren woman, resurrection of a dead man, recovery of lost wealth. O sage, what may I do for you? Pray, whatever be the wish with which you have come to me, consider that wish already fulfilled. You are my worshipful deity. I shall do thy bidding."

I:7, 8, 9 VĀLMĪKI continued:

Viśvāmitra was delighted to hear Daśaratha's words and proceeded to reveal his mission. He said to the king:

"O king, I need your assistance in the fulfilment of a religious rite undertaken by me. Whenever I undertake a religious rite, the demons who are the followers of Khara and Dūṣaṇa invade the holy place and desecrate it. Under the vows of the religious rite, I am unable to curse them.

"You can help me. Your son Rāma can easily deal with these demons. And, in return for this help, I shall confer manifold blessings upon him which will bring you unexcelled glory. Do not let your attachment to your son overpower your devotion to duty. In this world the noble ones do not consider any gift beyond their means.

"The moment you say yes, that very moment I consider that the demons are dead. For, I know who Rāma is; even so does the sage Vasiṣṭha and the other holy ones in this court. Let there be no procrastination, O king: send Rāma with me without delay."

Hearing this highly unwelcome request, the king remained stunned and silent for a while and then replied: "O sage, Rāma is not even sixteen years old and is, therefore, not qualified to wage a war. He has not even seen a combat, except what goes on in the inner apartment of the palace. Command me to accompany you; command my vast army to accompany you to exterminate the demons. But I cannot part with Rāma. Is it not natural for all living beings to love their young; do not even wise men engage themselves in extraordinary activities for the love of their children; and do not people abandon their happiness, their consorts and wealth rather than their children? No, I cannot part with Rāma.

"I have heard of the mighty demon Rāvaṇa. Is he the one that causes disturbance to your religious rite? In that case, nothing can be done to help you, for I know that even the gods are powerless against him. Time and again, such powerful beings are born on this earth; and in time they leave the stage of this world."

Viśvāmitra was angry. Seeing this, the sage Vasiṣṭha intervened and persuaded the king not to back out of his promise, but to send Rāma with Viśvāmitra. "O king, it is unworthy of you to go back on your promise. A king should be an exemplar of righteous conduct. Rāma is safe in the care of Viśvāmitra, who is extremely powerful and who has numerous invincible missiles."

VĀLMĪKI continued: I:10

In obedience to the wishes of the preceptor Vasiṣṭha, the king Daśaratha ordered an attendant to fetch Rāma. This attendant returned and announced that Rāma would follow in a minute, and added "The prince seems to be dejected and he shuns company." Bewildered by this statement, Daśaratha turned to Rāma's chamberlain and wished to know the facts concerning Rāma's state of mind and health.

The chamberlain was visibly distressed and he said:

"Lord, since his return from the pilgrimage, a great change has come over the prince. He does not seem to be interested even in bathing and in the worship of the deity. He does not enjoy the company of the people in the inner apartments. He is not interested in jewels and precious stones. Even when offered charming and pleasing objects, he looks at them with sad eyes, uninterested. He spurns the palace dancers, regarding them as tormentors! He goes through the motions of eating, walking, resting, bathing and sitting like an automaton, like one who is deaf and dumb. Often he mutters to himself 'What is the use of wealth and prosperity, what is the use of adversity or of house? All this is unreal.' He is silent most of the time and is not amused by entertainment. He relishes only solitude. He is all the time immersed in his own thought. We do not know what has come over our prince, what he contemplates in his mind, nor what he is after. Day by day he gets more and more emaciated."

"Again and again, he sings to himself 'Alas, we are dissipating our life in various ways, instead of striving to reach the supreme! People wail aloud that they are suffering and that they are destitute, but no one sincerely turns away from the sources of their suffering and destitution!' Seeing all this and hearing all this, we, his humble servants, are extremely distressed. We do not know what to do. He is bereft of hope, he is bereft of desire, he is attached to nothing and he depends on nothing, he is not deluded nor demented, and he is not enlightened either. At times, however, it looks as if he is overwhelmed by suicidal thoughts spurred by the feelings of despondency: 'What is the use of wealth or of mothers and relations, what is the use of the kingdom, and what is the use of ambition in this world?' Lord, only you can find the appropriate remedy for this condition of the prince."

I:11, 12 VIŚVĀMITRA said:

If that be the case, may Rāma be requested to come here. His condition is not the result of delusion but is full of wisdom and dispassion, and it points to enlightenment. Bring him here and we shall dispel his despondency.

VĀLMĪKI said:

Thereupon, the king urged the chamberlain to invite Rāma to the court. In the meantime Rāma himself got ready to meet his father. Even from a distance he saw and saluted his father and the sages; and they saw that though young, his face shone with the peace of maturity. He bowed to the feet of the king, who embraced him, lifted him up and said to him: "What makes you so sad, my son? Dejection is an open invitation to a host of miseries." The sages Vasiṣṭha and Viśvāmitra concurred with the king.

RĀMA said:

Holy sir, I shall duly answer your question. I grew up happily in my father's abode; I was instructed by worthy teachers. Recently I went on a pilgrimage. During this period a trend of thought has taken hold of me, robbing me of all hope in this world. My heart begins to question: what do people call happiness and can it be had in the ever-changing objects of this world? All beings in this world take birth but to die, and they die to be born! I do not perceive any meaning in all these transient phenomena which are the roots of suffering and sin. Unrelated beings come together; and the mind conjures up a relationship between them. Everything in this world is dependent upon the mind, upon one's mental attitude. On examination, the mind itself appears to be unreal! But, we are bewitched by it. We seem to be running after a mirage in the desert to slake our thirst!

Sir, surely we are not bond slaves sold to a master; yet we live a life of slavery, without any freedom whatever. Ignorant of the truth, we have been aimlessly wandering in this dense forest called the world. What is this world? What comes into being, grows, and dies? How does this suffering come to an end? My heart bleeds with sorrow, though I do not shed tears, in deference to the feelings of my friends.

RĀMA continued: I:13, 14

Equally useless, O sage, is wealth which deludes the ignorant. Unsteady and fleeting, this wealth gives birth to numerous worries and generates an insatiable craving for more. Wealth is no respecter of persons: both the good and the wicked can become wealthy. However, people are good, compassionate and friendly only till their hearts are hardened by the passionate pursuit of wealth. Wealth taints the heart even of the wise scholar, a hero, a man of gratitude and a dexterous and soft-spoken person. Wealth and happiness do not dwell together. Rare is that wealthy man who does not have rivals and enemies who scandalise him. To the lotus of right action, wealth is the night; to the white-lotus of sorrow, it is the moonlight; to the lamp of clear insight, it is the wind; to the wave of enmity, it is the flood; to the cloud of confusion, it is the favourable wind; to the poison of despondency, it is the aggravating agent. It is like the serpent of evil thoughts and it adds fear to one's distress; it is destructive snow-fall to the creeper of dispassion; it is the night-fall to the owl of evil desires; it is the eclipse of the moon of wisdom; in its presence a person's good nature shrivels. Indeed, wealth seeks him who has already been chosen by death.

Even so is the life-span, O sage. Its duration is like that of a water droplet on a leaf. The life-span is fruitful only to those who have self-knowledge. We may encompass the wind, we may break up space, we may string waves into a garland, but we cannot pin our faith on the life-span. Man vainly seeks to extend his life-span, and thereby he earns more sorrow and extends the period of suffering. Only he lives who strives to gain self-knowledge, which alone is worth gaining in this world, thereby putting an end to future births; others exist here like donkeys. To the unwise, knowledge of scriptures is a burden; to one who is full of desires, even wisdom is a burden; to one who is restless, his own mind is a burden; and to one who has no self-knowledge, the body (the life-span) is a burden.

The rat of time gnaws at the life-span without respite. The termite of disease eats (destroys) the very vitals of the living being. Just as a cat intent on catching a rat looks at it with great alertness and readiness, death is ever keeping a watch over this life-span.

I:15, 16 RĀMA continued:

Holy sir, I am bewildered and scared when I contemplate the coming into being of the dreadful enemy of wisdom known as egotism. It comes into being in the darkness of ignorance, and flourishes in ignorance. It generates endless sinful tendencies and sinful actions. All suffering surely revolves around egotism (it is the 'I' who suffers); and egotism is the sole cause of mental distress. I feel that egotism is my worst disease! Spreading the net of worldly objects of pleasure, it is this egotism that traps living beings. Indeed, all the terrible calamities in this world are born of egotism. Egotism eclipses self-control, destroys virtue and dissipates equanimity. Giving up the egotistic notion that "I am Rāma" and giving up all desires, I wish to rest in the self. I realise that whatever I have done with an egotistic notion is vain: non-egotism alone is truth. When I am under the influence of egotism, I am unhappy; when I am free from egotism I am happy. Egotism promotes cravings; without it they perish. It is this egotism alone, without rhyme or reason, that has spread the net of family and social relationships, to catch the unwary soul. I think I am free from egotism; yet, I am miserable. Pray, enlighten me.

Bereft of the grace earned through the service of the holy ones, the impure mind-stuff remains restless as the wind. It is dissatisfied with whatever it gets and grows more and more restless by the day. The sieve can never be filled with water; nor can the mind ever reach the state of fulfilment however much of worldly objects one acquires. The mind flits in all directions all the time, but is unable to find happiness anywhere. Unmindful of the possibility of reaping great suffering in hell, the mind seeks pleasure here, but even that it does not get. Like the lion in a cage, the mind is ever restless, having lost its freedom yet not happy with its present state. Alas, O holy one, I am bound by the knots of craving to the net that has been spread by the mind. Even as the rushing waters of a river uproot the trees on its bank, the restless mind has uprooted my whole being. I am being wafted like a dry leaf in the wind by the mind. It does not let me rest anywhere. It is this mind alone which is the cause of all objects in the world; the three worlds exist because of the mind-stuff. When the mind vanishes the worlds vanish too.

RĀMA continued: I:17

It is really when the mind-stuff is enveloped by craving that innumerable errors arise in the darkness of ignorance thus caused. This craving dries up the good and noble qualities of the mind and heart, like sweetness and gentleness of disposition, and makes me hard and cruel. In that darkness, craving in its different forms dances like a goblin.

Though I adopt various methods to restrain this craving, the latter overpowers me in a moment and helplessly drives me astray, even as a gale carries a straw away. Whatever hope I entertain of developing dispassion and such other qualities, craving cuts that hope away even as a rat snaps a thread. And I helplessly revolve caught in the wheel of craving. Like birds caught in a net, we are unable, though we have the wings for it, to fly to our goal or abode of self-knowledge. Nor can this craving be ever appeased, even if I were to quaff nectar. The characteristic of this craving is that it has no direction: it drives me in one direction now and the very next moment it takes me away in another direction, like a mad horse. It spreads in front of us a very wide net of son, friend, wife and other relations.

Though I am a hero, this craving makes me a frightened coward; though I have eyes to see, it makes me blind; though I am full of joy, it makes me miserable; it is like a dreadful goblin. It is this dreadful goblin craving that is responsible for bondage and misfortune; it breaks the heart of man and creates delusion in him. Caught by this goblin, man is unable to enjoy even the pleasures that are within his reach. Though it appears as if the craving is for happiness, this craving leads neither to happiness nor to fruitfulness in this life; on the contrary, it involves vain effort and leads to every kind of inauspiciousness. Even when it occupies the stage called life on which several happy and unhappy situations play, this craving, like an aged actress, is incapable of performing anything good and noble and suffers defeat and discomfiture at every turn. Yet, it does not give up dancing on the stage!

Craving now ascends to the skies, now dives into the depths of the netherworld; it is ever restless. For it is based on the emptiness of the mind. In the mind the light of wisdom momentarily shines, but there is delusion the next moment. It is a wonder that sages are able to cut this with the sword of self-knowledge.

RĀMA continued: I:18

This pitiable body composed of veins, arteries and nerves is also a source of pain. Inert, it appears to be intelligent: one does not know if it is sentient or insentient, and it engenders only delusion.

Delighted with a little gratification and distressed by the least adversity, this body is indeed highly despicable.

I can only compare a tree to the body: with branches for arms, trunk for the torso, holes for eyes, fruits for head, leaves for numerous illnesses—it is a resting place for living beings. Who can say that it is one's own? Hope or despair in relation to it is futile. It is but a boat given to one for crossing this ocean of birth-and-death; but one should not regard it as one's self.

This tree which is the body is born in the forest known as saṃsāra (repetitive existence), the restless monkey (mind) plays on it, it is the abode of crickets (worries), it is constantly eaten by the insects (of endless suffering), it shelters the venomous serpent (of craving), and the wild crow (of anger) dwells on it. On it are the flowers (of laughter), its fruits are good and evil, it appears to be animated by the wind (of life-force), it supports the birds (of senses), it is resorted to by the traveller (lust or desire) for it provides the shade of pleasure, the formidable vulture (egotism) is seated on it, and it is hollow and empty. It is certainly not meant to promote happiness. Whether it lives for long or falls in a short time, it is still useless. It is composed of flesh and blood, it is subject to old age and death. I am not enamoured of it. It is completely filled with impure substances and afflicted with ignorance. How can it fulfil my hopes?

This body is the home of illness, the field for mental distress and changing emotions and mental states. I am not enamoured of it. What is wealth, what is kingdom, what is the body? All these are mercilessly cut down by time (death). At death this ungrateful body abandons the soul that dwelt in it and protected it: what hope shall I repose in it? Shamelessly it indulges again and again in the same actions! Its only certain purpose seems to be to burn in the end. Unmindful of old age and death that are common to the rich and the poor, it seeks wealth and power. Shame, shame upon those who are bound to this body, deluded by the wine of ignorance! Shame on those who are bound to this world!

I:19 RĀMA said:

Even childhood, the part of life which people ignorantly regard as enjoyable and happy, is full of sorrow, O sage. Helplessness, mishaps, cravings, inability to express oneself, utter foolishness, playfulness, instability, weakness—all these characterise childhood. The child is easily offended, easily roused to anger, easily bursts into tears. In fact, one may say boldly that the child's anguish is more terrible than that of a dying person, an aged man, a sick man or any other adult. For in childhood one's state is comparable truly to that of an animal living at the mercy of others.

The child is exposed to the countless happenings around it; they puzzle the child, confuse the child, and arouse in it various phantasies and fears. The child is impressionable and is easily influenced by the wicked: in consequence, the child is subjected to control and punishment by its parents. Childhood seems to be a period of subjection and nothing else!

Though the child may appear to be innocent, the truth is that all sorts of defects, sinful tendencies, and neurotic behaviour lie hidden and dormant in it, even as an owl lies hidden in a dark hole during the day-time. O sage, I pity those people who foolishly imagine that childhood is a happy period.

What can be worse suffering than a restless mind? And, the child's mind is extremely restless. Unless the child gets something new every day, it is unhappy. Crying and weeping seem to be the child's foremost activity. When the child does not get what it wants, it looks as if its heart is broken.

When the child goes to school, it receives punishment in the hands of its teachers; and all this adds to its unhappiness.

When the child cries, its parents, in order to pacify it, promise to give it the world; and from then on the child begins to value the world, to desire the worldly objects. The parents say "I shall give you the moon for a toy," and the child, believing their words, thinks that it can hold the moon in its hands. Thus are the seeds of delusion sown in the little heart.

Though the child feels heat and cold, it is unable to avoid it—how is it better than a tree, then? Like the animals and birds the child vainly reaches out to get what it wants; and it is fearful of every elder in the house.

RĀMA continued: I:20

Leaving this period of childhood behind, the human being goes on to the stage of youth, but he is unable to leave the unhappiness behind! There he is subjected to numerous mental modifications and he progresses from misery to greater misery, for he abandons wisdom and embraces the terrible goblin, known as lust, that resides in his heart. His life is full of desire and anxiety. They who have not been robbed of their wisdom in their youth can withstand any onslaught.

I am not enamoured of this transient youth in which shortlived pleasure is quickly followed by long-lasting suffering, and deluded by which man regards the changing to be changeless. What is worse still, it is during youth that one indulges in such actions that bring unhappiness to many others.

Even as a tree is consumed by a forest-fire, the youth's heart is consumed by the fire of lust when his beloved leaves him. However much he may strive to develop purity of heart, the youth's heart is stained with impurity. Even when his beloved is not present near him, he is distracted by the thoughts of her beauty. Such a person who is full of cravings is naturally not held in high esteem by good men.

Youth is the abode of diseases and mental distress. It can be compared to a bird whose wings are good and evil acts. Youth is like a sandstorm that disperses and dissipates one's good qualities. Youth arouses all sorts of evils in the heart and suppresses the good qualities that may exist there; it is thus the promoter of evil. It gives rise to delusion and attachment. Though youthfulness appears to be very desirable to the body, it is destructive to the mind. In youth, the man is tempted by the mirage of happiness and in its pursuit he falls into the well of sorrow. Hence I am not enamoured of youth.

Alas, even when youth is about to leave the body, the passions that had been aroused by youth burn the more fiercely and bring about one's quick destruction. He who delights in this youth is surely not a man, but an animal in human garb.

They are adorable, they are great souls and they alone are men who are not overcome by the evils of youth and who survive that stage of life without succumbing to its temptations. For, it is easy to cross a great ocean; but to reach the other shore of youth without being overcome by its likes and dislikes is indeed difficult.

I:21, 22 RĀMA continued:

In his youth, man is a slave of sexual attraction. In the body which is no more than the aggregate of flesh, blood, bone, hair and skin, he perceives beauty and charm. If this 'beauty' were permanent, there would be some justification to the imagination; but, alas, it does not last very long. On the contrary, very soon the very flesh that contributed to the attractiveness, the charm and the beauty of the beloved is transformed first into the shrivelled ugliness of old age, and later consumed by fire, or by worms, or by vultures. Yet, while it lasts this sexual attraction consumes the heart and the wisdom of the man. By this is the creation maintained; when this attraction ceases, this saṃsāra (birth-death cycle) also ceases.

When the child is dissatisfied with its childhood, youth takes over; when youth is plagued by dissatisfaction and frustration, old age overpowers it—how cruel is life. Even as wind tosses a dew-drop from a leaf, old age destroys the body. Even as a drop of poison when it enters the system soon pervades it, senility soon pervades the entire body and breaks it down, and makes it the laughing stock of other people.

Though the old man is unable to satisfy his desires physically, the desires themselves flourish and grow. He begins to ask himself, "Who am I? What should I do?" etc., when it is too late for him to change his life's course, alter his life-style, or make his life more meaningful. With the onset of senility, all the distressing symptoms of a physical break-down, like cough, white hairs, hard breathing, dyspepsia and emaciation, manifest themselves.

Perhaps, the deity presiding over death sees the white roofed head of the old man as salted melon and rushes to take it. As a flood cuts away the roots of trees standing on the river-bank, senility vigorously cuts the root of life. Death follows and carries it away. Senility is like the royal attendant who precedes the king, death.

Ah, how mysterious and how astounding it is! They who have not been overcome by enemies and who have taken their abode in inaccessible mountain-peaks—even they have been afflicted by the demoness known as senility and degeneracy.

RĀMA continued: I:23, 24

All enjoyments in this world are delusion, like the lunatic's enjoyment of the taste of fruits reflected in a mirror. All the hopes of man in this world are consistently destroyed by Time. Time alone, O sage, wears everything out in this world; there is nothing in creation which is beyond its reach. Time alone creates innumerable universes, and in a very short time Time destroys everything.

Time allows a glimpse of itself through its partial manifestation as the year, the age, and the epoch; but its essential nature is hidden. This Time overpowers everything. Time is merciless, inexorable, cruel, greedy and insatiable. Time is the greatest magician, full of deceptive tricks. This Time cannot be analysed; for however much it is divided it still survives indestructible. It has an insatiable appetite for everything—it consumes the smallest insects, the biggest mountains, and even the king of heaven! Even as a young boy plays with a ball for his pastime, Time uses the two balls known as the sun and the moon for his pastime. It is indeed Time alone that appears as the destroyer of the universe (Rudra), the creator of the world (Brahmā), the king of heaven (Indra), the lord of wealth (Kubera), and the nothingness of cosmic dissolution. It is indeed this Time that successively creates and dissolves the universe again and again. Just as even the great and mighty mountain is rooted on earth, this mighty Time is also established in the absolute being (Brahman).

Even though Time creates endless universes, it is not wearied, nor does it rejoice; it does not come, nor does it go; it does not rise, nor does it set.

Time, the gourmet, sees that the objects of this world have been ripened by the fire of the sun, and when he finds them fully ripe he consumes them! Each epoch of time is decked, as it were, by the lovely jewels of colourful beings for the pleasure of Time that wipes them all out playfully.

To the lotus of youthfulness, Time is the nightfall; to the elephant of life-span, Time is the lion. In this world there is nothing, high or low, that Time does not destroy. Even when all these are destroyed, Time is not destroyed. Just as a man after a day's activity rests in sleep, as if in ignorance, even so Time after the cosmic dissolution sleeps or rests with the creation-potential hidden in it. No one really knows what this Time is.

I:25, 26 RĀMA continued:

Besides the Time I have just described, there is another Time which is responsible for birth and death; people refer to it as the deity presiding over death.

Yet again there is another aspect of this Time, known as kṛtānta —the end of action, its inevitable result or fruition. This kṛtānta is like a dancer with niyati (the law of nature) for his wife: the two together bestow on all beings the inevitable fruit of their actions. During the course of the existence of the universe, they are indefatigable in their labour, unwinking in their vigilance and unflagging in their zeal.

When Time thus dances in this universe, creating and destroying everything, what hope can we entertain? Kṛtānta holds sway even over those whose faith is firm, and makes them restless. On account of this kṛtānta everything in this world is constantly undergoing change; there is no permanency here.

All beings in this world are tainted with evil; all relationships are bondage; all enjoyments are great diseases; and desire for happiness is only a mirage. One's own senses are one's enemies; the reality has become unreal (unknown); one's own mind has become one's worst enemy. Egotism is the foremost cause for evil; wisdom is weak; all actions lead to unpleasantness; and pleasure is sexually oriented. One's intelligence is governed by egotism, instead of being the other way round. Hence there is no peace nor happiness in one's mind. Youth is fading. Company of holy ones is rare. There is no way out of this suffering. The realisation of truth is not to be seen in anyone. No one is happy at the prosperity and happiness of others, nor is compassion to be found in anyone's heart. People are getting baser and baser by the day. Weakness has overcome strength, cowardice has overpowered courage. Evil company is easily had, good company is hard to come by. I wonder whither Time is driving humanity.

Holy one, this mysterious power that governs this creation

destroys even powerful demons, robs whatever has been considered to be eternal of its permanency, kills even the immortals—is there then any hope for simple folk like me? This mysterious being seems to dwell in all, and its individualised aspect is regarded as egotism, and there is nothing that is not destroyed by it. The entire universe is under its control; its will alone prevails here.

RĀMA continued: I:27

O sage, thus neither in childhood nor in youth nor in old age does one enjoy any happiness. None of the objects in this world is meant to give happiness to anyone. The mind vainly seeks to find such happiness in the objects of this world. Only he is happy who is free from egotism and who is not swayed by craving for sense-pleasure: but such a person is extremely rare in this world. Indeed, I do not regard him as a hero who is able to battle successfully against a mighty army; only him I consider a hero who is able to cross the ocean known as the mind and the senses.

I do not regard that as a "gain" which is soon lost: only that is a gain which is not lost—and there is no such gain available to man in this world, however hard he may struggle. On the other hand, both fleeting gains and temporary adversities come to a man even without his seeking. I am puzzled, Holy sir, that a man roams here and there seemingly busy throughout the day and is all the time engaged in selfish activity, and though he does not do one good turn during the day, he is still able to sleep at night!

Yet, even though the busy man overcomes all his earthly enemies and surrounds himself with wealth and luxury, and even when he boasts that he is happy, death creeps in upon him. How it finds him, only God knows.

In ignorance, man binds himself to wife, son and friends; he knows not that this world is like a large pilgrim centre where countless people come together fortuitously—and they whom he calls his wife, son and friends are among them.

This world is like a potter's wheel: the wheel looks as if it stands still though it revolves at a terrific speed—even so to the deluded person this world appears to be stable even though in fact it is constantly changing. This world is like a poison tree: one who comes into contact with it is knocked unconscious and stupified. All points of view in this world are tainted; all countries in the world are territories of evil; all the people of the world are subject to death; all actions are deceitful.

Many aeons have come and gone; they are but moments in time—for there is essentially no difference between an epoch and a moment, both being measures of time. From the viewpoint of the gods even an epoch is but a moment. Even so the whole earth is but a modification of the earth-element! How futile to pin our faith and our hope on it!

I:28, 29 RĀMA continued:

O Holy one! Whatever appears to be permanent or transient in this world—it is all like a dream. What is a crater today was a mountain before, what is a mountain today becomes a hole in the earth in a short while, what is a dense forest today is soon transformed into a big city, what is fertile soil now becomes arid desert. Similar is the change in one's body and in one's life-style and fortune.

This life-and-death cycle appears to be a skillful dancer whose skirt is made up of living souls, and her dancing gestures consist of lifting the souls up to heaven, hurling them down into hell, or bringing them back to this earth. All the mighty deeds, even the great religious rites that people perform here, are soon consigned to one's memory. Human beings are born as animals and vice versa; gods lose their divinity—what is unchanging here? I see even the creator Brahmā, the protector Viṣṇu, the redeemer Rudra and others inexorably going towards destruction. In this world sense-objects appear to be pleasant to one only till he remembers this inevitable destruction. Just as a child playing with earth makes different designs with a clod, the ordainer of the universe keeps creating new things and destroying them soon.

This perception of the defects of the world has destroyed the undesirable tendencies in my mind; and therefore desire for sense-pleasure does not arise in my mind, even as a mirage does not appear on the surface of water. This world and its delights appear bitter to me. I am not fond of wandering in the pleasure-gardens, I do not relish the company of girls, I do not value the acquisition of wealth. I wish to remain at peace within myself. I am constantly enquiring: "How can I wean my heart completely away from even thinking of this ever-changing phantasm called the world?" I do not long for death, nor do I long to live; I remain as I am, free from the fever of lust. What shall I do with the kingdom, pleasure or wealth, all of which are the playthings of egotism which is absent in me?

If I do not get established in wisdom now, when shall another opportunity arise? For, indulgence in sense-pleasure poisons the mind in such a way that its effects last several life-times. Only the man of self-knowledge is free from this. Therefore, O sage, I pray to thee: instruct me in such a way that I may forever be free from anguish, fear and distress. With the light of your instruction, destroy the darkness of ignorance in my heart.

RĀMA continued: I:30, 31

By reflecting on the pitiable fate of living beings thus fallen into the dreadful pit of sorrow, I am filled with grief. My mind is confused, I shudder, and at every step I am afraid. I have given up everything, but I have not established myself in wisdom; hence I am partly caught and partly freed. I am like a tree that has been cut but not severed from its root. I wish to restrain my mind but do not have the wisdom to do so.

Hence, pray tell me: what is that condition or state in which one does not experience any grief? How can one who is involved in the world and its activities, as I am, reach the supreme state of peace and bliss? What is that attitude that enables one not to be influenced by various kinds of activities and experiences? Pray tell me: how do you people who are enlightened live in this world? How can the mind be freed from lust and made to view the world both as one's own self and also as no more valuable than a blade of grass? The biography of which great one shall we study in order to learn the path of wisdom? How should one live in this world? Holy sir, instruct me in that wisdom which will enable my otherwise restless mind to be steady like a mountain. You are an enlightened being: instruct me so that I may never again be sunk in grief.

Obviously this world is full of pain and death; how does it become a source of joy, without befuddling one's heart? The mind is obviously full of impurities: how can it be cleansed and with what cleanser prescribed by what great sage? How should one live here so as not to fall a victim to the twin currents of love-and-hate? Obviously there is a secret that enables one to remain unaffected by the grief and suffering in this world even as mercury is not affected when it is thrown into the fire. What is that secret? What is the secret that counteracts the habit of the mind that is spread out in the form of this universe?

Who are those heroes who have freed themselves from delusion? And what methods did they adopt to free themselves. If you consider that I am neither fit nor capable of understanding this, I shall fast unto death.

VĀLMĪKI said:

Having said so, Rāma remained silent.

VĀLMĪKI said: I:32, 33

All those who had assembled in the court were highly inspired by the flaming words of Rāma's wisdom that is capable of dispelling the delusion of the mind. They felt as if they themselves had been rid of all their doubts and deluded misunderstanding. They drank the nectarine words of Rāma with great delight. As they sat in the court listening to Rāma's words, it appeared as though they were no longer living beings but painted figures—they were so still with rapt attention.

Who listened to Rāma's discourse? Sages like Vasiṣṭha and Viśvāmitra, the ministers, members of the royal family including king Daśaratha, citizens, holy ones, servants, caged birds, animal pets, the horses of the royal stable, and the celestials including the perfected sages and heavenly musicians. Surely, even the king of heaven and the chiefs of the nether-world listened to Rāma.

Thrilled to hear Rāma's speech, all of them acclaimed "Bravo, bravo" with one voice and this joyous sound filled the air. To felicitate Rāma, there was a shower of flowers from heaven. Everyone assembled in the court cheered him. Surely, no one but Rāma who was full of dispassion could have uttered the words that he gave expression to—not even the preceptor of the gods. We were indeed extremely fortunate to have been able to listen to him. While we listened to him, it seemed as though we were filled with the feeling that there is no happiness even in heaven.

THE PERFECTED SAGES in the assembly said:

Surely, the answers that the holy ones are about to give to the weighty and wise questions of Rāma are worthy of being heard by all beings in the universe. O sages, come, come, let us all gather in the court of king Daśaratha to listen to the answer of the supreme sage Vasiṣṭha.

VĀLMĪKI said:

Hearing this, all the sages of the world hastened to the court, where they were duly received, honoured and seated in the court. Surely, if in our heart the lofty wisdom of Rāma is not reflected, we shall indeed be the losers; whatever be our abilities and faculties, we shall thereby prove that we have lost our intelligence!

PART TWO

On the Behaviour of the Seeker

The Story of Śuka

VIŚVĀMITRA said: II:1

O Rāma, you are indeed the foremost among the wise, and there is really nothing further for you to know. However, your knowledge needs confirmation, even as the self-knowledge of Śuka needed confirmation from Janaka before Śuka could find the peace that passeth understanding.

RĀMA asked:

Holy one! Pray tell me how it was that Śuka did not find peace in spite of his knowledge, and how he found it later.

VIŚVĀMITRA said:

Listen, O Rāma. I shall duly narrate to you this soul-uplifting story of the born-sage Śuka, the son of Vedavyāsa who is now seated next to your father.

Just like you, Śuka also arrived at the truth concerning existence after deep contemplation of the evanescence of this world. Yet, because it was self-acquired knowledge, he could not positively affirm to himself "this is the truth". He had of course arrived at the state of extreme and supreme dispassion.

One day, this Śuka approached his father Vedavyāsa and asked him: "Sir, how did this diversity of world-creation come into being; and how will it come to an end?" Vedavyāsa gave a detailed answer to this question: but Śuka thought 'All this I knew already; what is new in this?' and was not impressed. Vedavyāsa also sensed this, and hence he said to Śuka: "My son, I do not know anything more than this; but there is the royal sage Janaka on earth who knows more than this. Kindly approach him."

Śuka thereupon came to Janaka's palace. Informed by the palace guards of the young Śuka's arrival, Janaka ignored him for a week while Śuka patiently waited outside. The next week Janaka had Śuka brought into the palace and waited upon by dancers and musicians. Śuka was unmoved by this, too. After this, Śuka was ushered into the royal presence, and Janaka said: "You know the truth: what else shall I tell you now." Śuka repeated the question he had asked his father, and Janaka too gave him the answer his father had given. Śuka said: "I knew this, my father told me this, the scriptures also affirm this, and now you declare the truth, and that is—this diversity arises on account of mental modifications and it will cease when they cease." Thus when his self-knowledge had been confirmed, Śuka attained peace and remained in nirvikalpa samādhi.

II:2, 3 VIŚVĀMITRA said to the assembled sages:

Like Śuka, Rāma, too, has gained the highest wisdom. The surest sign of a man of the highest wisdom is that he is unattracted by the pleasures of the world, for in him even the subtle tendencies have ceased. When these tendencies are strong, there is bondage; when they have ceased, there is liberation. He is truly a liberated sage who by nature is not swayed by sense pleasure, without the motivation of fame or other incentives. And, I pray that the sage Vasiṣṭha should so instruct Rāma that he will be confirmed in his wisdom and we, too, may be inspired. That instruction will surely become the greatest wisdom, the best of all scriptures—for it is imparted by an enlightened sage to the qualified, dispassionate student.

VASIṢṬHA said:

I shall surely accede to your request. And, O Rāma, I shall now impart to you the wisdom which was revealed to me by the divine creator Brahmā, himself.

RĀMA said:

Holy sir, kindly tell me first: why was Vedavyāsa considered not liberated, while his son Śuka was considered a liberated sage.

VASIṢṬHA said:

O Rāma, countless have been the universes that have come into being and that have been dissolved. In fact, even the countless universes that exist at this moment are impossible to conceive of. All this can immediately be realised in one's own heart, for these universes are the creation of the desires that arise in the heart, like castles built in the air. The living being conjures up this world in his heart and while he is alive he strengthens this illusion; when he passes away he conjures up the world beyond and experiences it—

thus there arise worlds within worlds just as there are layers within layers in a plantain stem. Neither the world of matter nor the modes of creation are truly real; yet the living and the dead think and feel they are real. Ignorance of this truth keeps up the appearance.

O Rāma, in this cosmic ocean of existence, beings arise here and there who are equal to others, and others who are different from yet others. This Vedavyāsa is the twenty-third in this stream of creation. He and other sages will attain embodiment and disembodiment again and again. In some they will be equal to others and in others unequal. In this embodiment Vedavyāsa is indeed a liberated sage. Such liberated sages also are embodied countless times and they assume relations with others—and sometimes they are equal to others and sometimes unequal in their learning, behaviour, etc.

Self-effort

VASIṢṬHA continued: II:4, 5

O Rāma, even as, whether there are waves or no waves, water remains water, even so whatever be the external appearance of the liberated sage, his wisdom remains unchanged. The difference is only in the eyes of the ignorant spectator.

Therefore, O Rāma, listen to what I am about to say; this instruction is sure to remove the darkness of ignorance.

In this world whatever is gained is gained only by self-effort; where failure is encountered it is seen that there has been slackness in the effort. This is obvious; but what is called fate is fictitious and is not seen.

Self-effort, Rāma, is that mental, verbal and physical action which is in accordance with the instructions of a holy person well versed in the scriptures. It is only by such effort that Indra became king of heaven, that Brahmā became the creator, and the other deities earned their place.

Self-effort is of two categories: that of past births and that of this birth. The latter effectively counteracts the former. Fate is none other than self-effort of a past incarnation. There is constant conflict between these two in this incarnation; and that which is more powerful triumphs.

Self-effort which is not in accord with the scriptures is motivated by delusion. When there is obstruction in the fruition of self-effort one should examine it to see if there is such deluded action, and if there is it should be immediately corrected. There is no power greater than right action in the present. Hence, one should take recourse to self-effort, grinding one's teeth, and one should overcome evil by good and fate by present effort.

The lazy man is worse than a donkey. One should never yield to laziness but strive to attain liberation, seeing that life is ebbing away every moment. One should not revel in the filth known as sense-pleasures as a worm revels in pus.

One who says "Fate is directing me to do this" is brainless, and the goddess of fortune abandons him. Hence, by self-effort acquire wisdom and then realise that this self-effort is not without its own end, in the direct realisation of the truth.

If this dreadful source of evil named laziness is not found on earth, who will ever be illiterate and poor? It is because laziness is found on earth that people live the life of animals, miserable and poverty-stricken.

VĀLMĪKI said: At this stage, it was time for evening prayers and the assembly broke up for the day.

II:6 VASIṢṬHA began the second day's discourse:

As is the effort so is the fruit, O Rāma: this is the meaning of self-effort, and it is also known as fate (divine). When afflicted by suffering people cry "Alas, what tragedy" or "Alas, look at my fate", both of which mean the same thing. What is called fate or divine will is nothing other than the action or self-effort of the past. The present is infinitely more potent than the past. They indeed are fools who are satisfied with the fruits of their past effort (which they regard as divine will) and do not engage themselves in self-effort now.

If you see that the present self-effort is sometimes thwarted by fate (or divine will), you should understand that the present self-effort is weak. A weak and dull-witted man sees the hand of providence when he is confronted by a strong and powerful adversary and succumbs to him.

Sometimes it happens that without effort someone makes a great gain: for example, the state elephant chooses (in accordance with an ancient practice) a mendicant as the ruler of a country whose king suddenly died without leaving an heir; this is certainly neither an accident nor some kind of divine act, but the fruit of the mendicant's self-effort in the past birth.

Sometimes it happens that a farmer's efforts are made fruitless by a hailstorm: surely, the hailstorm's own power was greater than the farmer's effort and the farmer should put forth greater effort now. He should not grieve over the inevitable loss. If such grief is justified, why should he not weep daily over the inevitability of death? The wise man should of course know what is capable of attainment by self-effort and what is not. It is, however, ignorance to attribute all this to an outside agency and to say that "God sends me to heaven or to hell" or that "an outside agency makes me do this or that"—such an ignorant person should be shunned.

One should free oneself from likes and dislikes and engage oneself in righteous self-effort and reach the supreme truth, knowing that self-effort alone is another name for divine will. We only ridicule the fatalist. That alone is self-effort which springs from right understanding which manifests in one's heart which has been exposed to the teachings of the scriptures and the conduct of holy ones.

VASIṢṬHA continued: II:7, 8

O Rāma, one should, with a body free from illness and mind free from distress, pursue self-knowledge so that he is not born again here. Such self-effort has a threefold root and therefore threefold fruit—an inner awakening in the intelligence, a decision in the mind and the physical action.

Self-effort is based on these three—knowledge of scriptures, instructions of the preceptor and one's own effort. Fate (or divine dispensation) does not enter here. Hence, he who desires salvation should divert the impure mind to pure endeavor by persistent effort —this is the very essence of all scriptures. The Holy ones emphasise: persistently tread the path that leads to the eternal good. And the wise seeker knows: the fruit of my endeavors will be commensurate with the intensity of my self-effort and neither fate nor a god can ordain it otherwise. Indeed, such self-effort alone is responsible for whatever man gets here; when he is sunk in unhappiness, to console him people suggest that it is his fate. This is obvious: one goes abroad, one appeases one's hunger, by undertaking a journey and by eating food—not on account of a fate. No one has seen such a fate or a god, but everyone has experienced how an action (good or evil) leads to a result (good or evil). Hence, right from one's childhood one should endeavor to promote one's true good (salvation) by a keen intelligent study of the scriptures, by having the company of the holy ones and by right self-effort.

Fate or divine dispensation is merely a convention which has come to be regarded as truth by being repeatedly declared to be true. If this god or fate is truly the ordainer of everything in this world, of what meaning is any action (even like bathing, speaking or giving), and whom should one teach at all? No. In this world, except a corpse, everything is active and such activity yields its appropriate result. No one has ever realised the existence of a fate or divine dispensation.

The word used in the text for fate is "daivaṃ" which also means "god".

People use such expressions as "I am impelled by fate or divine dispensation to do this" for self-satisfaction, but this is not true. For example, if an astrologer predicts that a young man would become a great scholar, does that young man become a scholar without study? No. Then, why do we believe in divine dispensation? Rāma, this sage Viśvāmitra became a Brahma-Ṛṣi by self-effort; all of us have attained self-knowledge by self-effort alone. Hence, renounce fatalism and apply yourself to self-effort.

II:9 RĀMA asked:

Lord, you are indeed the knower of truth. Pray, tell me what do people really call god, fate or daivaṃ.

VASIṢṬHA replied:

The fruition of self-effort by which one experiences the good and evil results of past action is called fate or daivaṃ by people. People also regard that as fate or daivaṃ which characterises the good and evil nature of such results. When you see that 'this plant grows out of this seed', it is regarded as an act of this daivaṃ. But I feel that fate is nothing but the culmination of one's own action.

In the mind of man are numerous latent tendencies, and these tendencies give rise to various actions—physical, verbal and mental. Surely, one's actions are in strict accordance with these tendencies, it cannot be otherwise. Such is the course of action: action is non-different from the most potent among latent tendencies, and these tendencies are non-different from the mind and the man is non-different from the mind! One cannot definitely determine whether categories like mind, latent tendencies, action and fate (daivaṃ) are real or unreal: hence, the men of wisdom have alluded to them symbolically.

RĀMA asked again:

Holy sir, if the latent tendencies brought forward from the previous birth impel me to act in the present, where is freedom of action?

VASIṢṬHA said:

Rāma, the tendencies brought forward from past incarnations are of two kinds—pure and impure. The pure ones lead you towards liberation, and the impure ones invite trouble. You are indeed consciousness itself, not inert physical matter. You are not impelled to action by anything other than yourself. Hence you are free to strengthen the pure latent tendencies in preference to the impure ones. The impure ones have to be abandoned gradually and the mind turned away from them little by little, lest there should be violent reaction. By encouraging the good tendencies to act repeatedly, strengthen them. The impure ones will weaken by disuse. You will soon become absorbed in the expression of the good tendencies, in good actions. When thus you have overcome the force of the evil tendencies then you will have to abandon even the good ones. You will then experience the supreme truth with the intelligence that rises from the good tendencies.

VASIṢṬHA continued: II:10

The cosmic order that people refer to as fate, daivaṃ or niyati and which ensures that every effort is blessed with appropriate fruition, is based on omnipresent and omnipotent omniscience (known as Brahman). By self-effort therefore restrain the senses and the mind, and with a mind that is one-pointed calmly listen to what I am going to say.

This narrative deals with liberation; listening to it with other wise seekers who are assembled here, you will realise that supreme being where there is no sorrow nor destruction. This was revealed to me by the creator Brahmā himself in a previous age.

Rāma, the omnipresent omniscience or the cosmic being shines eternally in all beings. When a vibration arises in that cosmic being, lord Viṣṇu is born, even as a wave arises when the surface of the ocean is agitated. From that Viṣṇu, Brahmā the creator was born. Brahmā began to create the countless varieties of animate and inanimate, sentient and insentient beings in the universe. And the universe was as it was before the cosmic dissolution.

The Creator saw that all living beings in the universe were subject to disease and death, to pain and suffering. In his heart there arose compassion, and he sought to lay down a path that might lead living beings away from all this. He thereupon instituted centres of pilgrimage and noble virtues like austerity, charity, truthfulness and righteous conduct. But these were inadequate; they could bestow only temporary relief from suffering on people and not final liberation from sorrow.

Reflecting thus, the Creator brought me into being. He drew me to himself and drew the veil of ignorance over my heart. Instantly I forgot my identity and my self-nature. I was miserable. I begged of Brahmā the creator, my own father, to show me the way out of this misery. Sunk in my misery I was unable and unwilling to do anything, and I remained lazy and inactive.

In response to my prayer, my father revealed to me the true knowledge which instantly dispelled the veil of ignorance that he himself had spread over me. The Creator then said to me: "My son, I veiled the knowledge and revealed it to you so that you may experience its glory; for only then will you be able to understand the travail of ignorant beings and to help them." Rāma, equipped with this knowledge, I am here and I will continue to be here till the end of creation.

II:11 VASIṢṬHA continued:

Even so in every age the Creator wills into being several sages and myself for the spiritual enlightenment of all. And, in order to ensure the due performance of the secular duties by all, Brahmā also creates kings who rule justly and wisely over parts of the earth. These kings, however, are soon corrupted by lust for power and pleasure; conflict of interests leads to wars among them which in turn give rise to remorse. To remove their ignorance, the sages used to impart spiritual wisdom to them. In days of yore, O Rāma, kings used to receive this wisdom and cherish it; hence it was known as Rāja-Vidyā, Kingly Science.

The highest form of dispassion born of pure discrimination has arisen in your heart, O Rāma, and it is superior to dispassion born of a circumstantial cause or an utter disgust. Such dispassion is surely due to the grace of God. This grace meets the maturity of discrimination at the exact moment when dispassion is generated in the heart.

As long as the highest wisdom does not dawn in the heart, the person revolves in this wheel of birth and death. Pray, listen to my exposition of this wisdom with a concentrated mind.

This wisdom destroys the forest of ignorance. Roaming in this forest one undergoes confusion and seemingly interminable suffering. One should therefore approach an enlightened teacher and by asking the right question with the right attitude, elicit the teaching. It then becomes an integral part of one's being. The fool asks irrelevant questions irreverently; and the greater fool is he who spurns the sage's wisdom. He is surely not a sage who responds to the vain questions of a foolish questioner.

O Rāma, you are indeed the best among all seekers, for you have duly reflected over the truth and you are inspired by the best form of dispassion. And I am sure that what I am going to say to you will find a firm seat in your heart. Indeed, one should positively strive to enthrone wisdom in one's heart, for the mind is unsteady like a monkey. And, one should then avoid unwise company.

Rāma, there are four gate-keepers at the entrance to the Realm of Freedom (Mokṣa). They are self-control, spirit of enquiry, contentment and good company. The wise seeker should diligently cultivate the friendship of these, or at least one of them.

II:12, 13 VASIṢṬHA continued:

With a pure heart and a receptive mind, and without the veil of doubt and the restlessness of the mind, listen to the exposition of the nature and the means of liberation, O Rāma. For, not until the supreme being is realised will the dreadful miseries of birth and death come to an end. If this deadly serpent known as ignorant life is not overcome here and now, it gives rise to interminable suffering not only in this but in countless lifetimes to come. One cannot ignore this suffering, but one should overcome it by means of the wisdom that I shall impart to you.

O Rāma, if you thus overcome this sorrow of repetitive history (saṃsāra), you will live here on earth itself like a god, like Brahmā or Viṣṇu! For when delusion is gone and the truth is realised by means of enquiry into self-nature, when the mind is at peace and the heart leaps to the supreme truth, when all the disturbing thought-waves in the mind-stuff have subsided and there is unbroken flow of peace and the heart is filled with the bliss of the absolute, when thus the truth has been seen in the heart, then this very world becomes an abode of bliss.

Such a person has nothing to acquire, nor anything to shun. He is untainted by the defects of life, untouched by its sorrow. He does not come into being nor go out, though he appears to come and go in the eyes of the beholder. Even religious duties are found to be unnecessary. He is not affected by the past tendencies which have lost their momentum: his mind has given up its restlessness, and he rests in the bliss that is his essential nature. Such bliss is possible only by self-knowledge, not by any other means. Hence, one should apply oneself constantly to self-knowledge—this alone is one's duty.

He who disregards holy scriptures and holy men does not attain self-knowledge. Such foolishness is more harmful than all the illnesses that one is subject to in this world. Hence, one should devoutly listen to this scripture which leads one to self-knowledge. He who obtains this scripture does not again fall into the blind well of ignorance. O Rāma, if you want to free yourself from the sorrow of saṃsāra (repetitive history) receive the wholesome instructions of sages like me and be free.

VASIṢṬHA continued:

In order to cross this formidable ocean of saṃsāra (repetitive history), one should resort to that which is eternal and unchanging. He alone is the best among men, O Rāma, whose mind rests in the eternal and is, therefore, fully self-controlled and at peace. He sees that pleasure and pain chase and cancel each other, and in that wisdom there is self-control and peace. He who does not see this sleeps in a burning house.

He who gains the wisdom of the eternal here is freed from saṃsāra and he is not born again in ignorance. One may doubt whether such unchanging truth exists! If it does not, one comes to no harm by enquiring into the nature of life; seeking the eternal will soften the pain caused by the changes in life. But, if it exists, then by knowing it one is freed.

The eternal is not attained by rites and rituals, by pilgrimages nor by wealth; it is to be attained only by the conquest of one's mind, by the cultivation of wisdom. Hence everyone—gods, demons, demi-gods or men should constantly seek (whether one is walking, falling or sitting) the conquest of the mind and self-control which are the fruits of wisdom.

When the mind is at peace, pure, tranquil, free from delusion or hallucination, untangled and free from cravings, it does not long for anything nor does it reject anything. This is self-control or conquest of mind—one of the four gate-keepers to liberation which I mentioned earlier.

All that is good and auspicious flows from self-control. All evil is dispelled by self-control. No gain, no pleasure in this world or in heaven is comparable to the delight of self-control. The delight one experiences in the presence of the self-controlled is incomparable. Everyone spontaneously trusts him. None (not even demons and goblins) hates him.

Self-control, O Rāma, is the best remedy for all physical and mental ills. When there is self-control, even the food you eat tastes better, else it tastes bitter. He who wears the armour of self-control is not harmed by sorrow.

He who even while hearing, touching, seeing, smelling and tasting what is regarded as pleasant and unpleasant, is neither elated nor depressed—he is self-controlled. He who looks upon all beings with equal vision, having brought under control the sensations of pleasure and pain, is self-controlled. He who, though living amongst all is unaffected by them, neither feels elated nor hates, even as one is during sleep—he is self-controlled.

II:14 VASIṢṬHA continued:

Enquiry (the second gate-keeper to liberation) should be undertaken by an intelligence that has been purified by a close study of the scripture, and this enquiry should be unbroken. By such enquiry the intelligence becomes keen and is able to realise the supreme; hence enquiry alone is the best remedy for the long-lasting illness known as saṃsāra.

The wise man regards strength, intellect, efficiency and timely action as the fruits of enquiry. Indeed kingdom, prosperity, enjoyment, as well as final liberation, are all the fruits of enquiry. The spirit of enquiry protects one from the calamities that befall the unthinking fool. When the mind has been rendered dull by the absence of enquiry, even the cool rays of the moon turn into deadly weapons, and the childish imagination throws up a goblin in every dark spot. Hence, the non-enquiring fool is really a storehouse of sorrow. It is the absence of enquiry that gives rise to actions that are harmful to oneself and to others, and to numerous psychosomatic illnesses. Therefore, one should avoid the company of such unthinking people.

They in whom the spirit of enquiry is ever awake illumine the world, enlighten all who come into contact with them, dispel the ghosts created by an ignorant mind, and realise the falsity of sense-pleasures and their objects. O Rāma, in the light of enquiry there is realisation of the eternal and unchanging reality; this is the supreme. With it one does not long for any other gain nor does one spurn anything. He is free from delusion, attachment; he is not inactive nor does he get drowned in action; he lives and functions in this world and at the end of a natural life-span he reaches the blissful state of total freedom.

The eye of spiritual enquiry does not lose its sight even in the midst of all activities; he who does not have this eye is indeed to be pitied. It is better to be born as a frog in the mud, a worm in dung, a snake in a hole, but not to be without this eye. What is enquiry? To enquire thus: "Who am I? How has this evil of saṃsāra (repetitive history) come into being?" is true enquiry. Knowledge of truth arises from such enquiry; from such knowledge there follows tranquility in oneself; and then there arises the supreme peace that passeth understanding and the ending of all sorrow.

(Vicāra or enquiry is not reasoning nor analysis: it is directly looking into oneself.)

VASIṢṬHA continued: II:15, 16

Contentment is another gate-keeper to liberation. He who has quaffed the nectar of contentment does not relish craving for sense-pleasures; no delight in this world is as sweet as contentment which destroys all sins.

What is contentment? To renounce all craving for what is not obtained unsought and to be satisfied with what comes unsought, without being elated or depressed even by them—this is contentment. As long as one is not satisfied in the self, he will be subjected to sorrow. With the rise of contentment the purity of one's heart blooms. The contented man who possesses nothing owns the world.

Satsaṅga (company of the wise, holy and enlightened persons) is yet another gate-keeper to liberation. Satsaṅga enlarges one's intelligence, destroys one's ignorance and one's psychological distress. Whatever be the cost, however difficult it may be, whatever obstacles may stand in its way, satsaṅga should never be neglected. For, satsaṅga alone is one's light on the path of life. Satsaṅga is indeed superior to all other forms of religious practice like charity, austerity, pilgrimage and the performance of religious rites.

One should by every means in one's power adore and serve the holy men who have realised the truth and in whose heart the darkness of ignorance has been dispelled. They who, on the other hand, treat such holy men disrespectfully, surely invite great suffering.

These four—contentment, satsaṅga (company of wise men), the spirit of enquiry, and self-control—are the four surest means by which they who are drowning in this ocean of saṃsāra (repetitive history) can be saved. Contentment is the supreme gain. Satsaṅga is the best companion to the destination. The spirit of enquiry itself is the greatest wisdom. And, self-control is supreme happiness. If you are unable to resort to all these four, then practise one: by the diligent practice of one of these, the others will also be found in you. The highest wisdom will seek you of its own accord. Until you tame the wild elephant of your mind with the help of these noble qualities, you cannot have progress towards the supreme, even if you become a god, demi-god or a tree. Therefore, O Rāma, strive by all means to cultivate these noble qualities.

II:17 VASIṢṬHA said:

He who is endowed with the qualities that I have enumerated thus far is qualified to listen to what I am about to reveal. You are indeed such a qualified person, O Rāma. Only he would wish to hear this who is ripe for liberation. But this revelation is capable of leading one to liberation even if one does not desire it, as a light is capable of illumining the eyes of even the sleeping person. As when the truth that a rope is a rope is seen and the fear generated by the misunderstanding that it is a snake disappears, the study of this scripture frees one from sorrow, born of saṃsāra.

This scripture consists of 32,000 couplets. The first section known as Vairāgya Prakaraṇaṃ (chapter on dispassion) imparts to one knowledge of the true nature of life in this world. Its careful study purifies the heart. This section consists of 1,500 couplets.

The next section, known as Mumukṣu Vyavahāra Prakaraṇaṃ (concerning the behaviour of a seeker of liberation) consists of 1,000 couplets. In this the qualifications of a seeker are described.

After that comes the Utpatti Prakaraṇaṃ (section on creation) which consists of 7,000 couplets. In it are found many inspiring stories which help illustrate the great truth, which is: on account of the interplay of the false ideas of 'this' and 'I', the universe which has never truly been created, appears to be.

The next is the Sthiti Prakaraṇaṃ (section on existence) and it consists of 3,000 couplets. With the help of stories again, the truth concerning the existence of this world and its substratum is revealed.

After that comes the Upaśānti Prakaraṇaṃ (section on cessation) which consists of 5,000 couplets. By listening to this, the deluded perception of the world comes to an end, leaving only a trace of ignorance.

Lastly, the Nirvāṇa Prakaraṇaṃ (section on liberation) which runs to 14,500 couplets. A study and understanding of this section destroys one's fundamental ignorance; and when all kinds of delusions and hallucinations are set at rest, there is total freedom. Though still wearing a physical body, he lives as if he is free from it, free of all cravings and desires, attachment and aversion. He is free from saṃsāra (repetitive history). Here and now, he is free from the demon known as egotism. He is one with the infinite.

VASIṢṬHA continued: II:18

One who sows the seed of the knowledge of this scripture soon obtains the fruit of the realisation of truth. Though human in origin, an exposition of truth is to be accepted; otherwise even what is regarded as divine revelation is to be rejected. Even a young boy's words are to be accepted if they are words of wisdom; else, reject it like straw even if uttered by Brahmā the creator.

He who listens to and reflects upon the exposition of this scripture enjoys unfathomable wisdom, firm conviction and unperturbable coolness of spirit. Soon he becomes a liberated sage whose glory is indescribable.

The sage of infinite vision sees in the one undivided intelligence countless universes, for he has realised the magic of Māyā or cosmic illusion. He sees the infinity in every atom, and therefore he is unattached to the rise and fall of the ideas of creation. Hence, he is ever contented with what comes unsought (which he does not reject) and he does not run after what has been taken away from him for which he does not grieve.

This scripture is easy of comprehension as it is richly embellished with a number of interesting stories. One who studies this scripture and contemplates its meaning has no need to undertake austerities, meditation or repetition of a mantra; for what is greater than liberation which is granted by a study of this scripture?

One who studies this scripture and comprehends its teaching is no longer deluded by world-appearance. When one sees that the yonder deadly snake is a life-like painting, one is no longer afraid of it. When the world-appearance is seen as an appearance it does not produce either elation or sorrow. It is indeed a great pity that even when such a scripture exists, people seek sense-pleasures which lead to great sorrow.

O Rāma, when a truth that has not been personally experienced is expounded, one does not grasp it except with the help of an illustration. Such illustrations have been used in this scripture with a definite purpose and a limited intention. They are not to be taken literally, nor is their significance to be stretched beyond the intention. When the scripture is thus studied, the world appears to be a dream-vision. These indeed are the purpose and the purport of the illustrations. Let no one of perverted intellect misinterpret the illustrations given in this scripture.

II:19, 20 VASIṢṬHA continued:

Parables have only one purpose: to enable the listener to arrive at the truth. The realisation of truth is so vital that any reasonable method used is justified, though the parables themselves may be fictitious. The parables themselves are only partly applicable to the truth thus illustrated, and only that part is to be grasped and the rest ignored. Study and understanding of the scriptures with the help of illustrations and of a qualified teacher are necessary only till one realises the truth.

Again, such study should continue till the truth is realised; one should not stop short of complete enlightenment. A little knowledge of the scripture results in confusion worse confounded. Non-recognition of the existence of supreme peace in the heart and assumption of the reality of imaginary factors, are both born of imperfect knowledge and the consequent perverted logic.

Even as the ocean is the substratum of all the waves, direct experience alone is the basis for all proofs—the direct experience of truth as it is. That substratum is the experiencing intelligence which itself becomes the experiencer, the act of experiencing, and the experience. The experiencing alone is the fact; yet, in a state of non-understanding, this experiencing seems to have a subject (the experiencer). Wisdom that is born of the spirit of enquiry dispels this non-understanding and the undivided intelligence shines in its own light. At that stage even the spirit of enquiry becomes superfluous and dissolves itself.

Even as movement is inherent in air, manifestation (as the subtle perceiving mind and the gross objects it perceives) is inherent in this experiencing intelligence. And the perceiving mind, on account of ignorance, thinks "I am such and such an object" and thence becomes that. The object is experienced only in the subject, not elsewhere!

O Rāma, till such time as this wisdom arises directly in you, take recourse to the knowledge transmitted by the great teachers. When you receive such knowledge from the great teachers, your behaviour will mirror theirs; and when thus you grow in their virtuous qualities, your wisdom will unfold within you. Wisdom and emulation of the noble behaviour of holy ones thrive on each other!

PART THREE

On Creation

ĀKĀŚA—Space or Dimension

Three important words occur in the text, which are: cidākāśa, cittākāśa and bhūtākāśa. Literally ākāśa means space and hence cidākāśa means consciousness-space, cittākāśa means mind-space and bhūtākāśa means the element space. These three concepts are thus beautifully explained by Bhagavān Ramaṇa Maharṣi:

> *"It is said that cidākāśa itself is ātma svarūpa (image of ātmā) and that we can view it only with the help of the mind. How can we see it, if the mind has subsided?" someone asked. Bhagavān said: "If the sky is taken as an illustration it must be stated to be of three varieties, cidākāśa, cittākāśa and bhūtākāśa. The natural state is called cidākāśa, the I feeling that is born from cidākāśa is cittākāśa. As that cittākāśa expands and takes the shape of all the bhūtas (elements) this is all bhūtākāśa. When the cittākāśa which is consciousness of the self ('I') does not see the cidākāśa but sees the bhūtākāśa it is said to be mano ākāśa and when it leaves mano ākāśa and sees cidākāśa it is said to be cinmaya (pure consciousness). The subsiding of the mind means, the idea of multiplicity of objects vanishes and the idea of oneness of objects appears. When that is achieved everything appears natural."*

Perhaps, a better translation for the word ākāśa is "dimension". The same infinite consciousness is known as cidākāśa, cittākāśa and bhūtākāśa viewed from the spiritual, mental (conceptual) and physical dimension respectively.

VASIṢṬHA continued: III:1

I shall now declare to you the creation and its secret. For, it is only as long as one invests the perceived object with reality that bondage lasts; once that notion goes, with it goes bondage. Here in this creation only that which is created grows, decays and then goes either to heaven or to hell, and it gets liberated.

During the cosmic dissolution the entire objective creation is resolved into the infinite being, which is variously designated as Ātmā, Brahman, Truth, etc., by the wise, to facilitate communication and dialogue. This same infinite self conceives within itself the duality of oneself and the other. Thence, mind arises, as a wave arises when the surface of the calm ocean is disturbed. But, please bear in mind that just as a bracelet of gold is but gold (and though gold exists without being a bracelet, bracelet does not exist without gold or other metal), the qualities and the nature of the created and the potentiality of creation are inherent in the creator. The mind is non-different from (has no existence independent of) the infinite self.

Even as the mirage appears to be a very real river of water, this creation appears to be entirely real. And, as long as one clings to the notion of the reality of "you" and "I", there is no liberation. Not by merely and verbally denying such a notion of existence is it obliterated: on the contrary, such denial itself becomes a further distraction.

Rāma, if the creation is in fact real then there is no possibility of its cessation: for it is an immutable law that the unreal has no real existence and the real does not cease to be. Austerity, meditation and such other practices can therefore not cause its cessation nor enlightenment. As long as the notion of creation lasts, even the contemplation (samādhi) in which there is no movement of thought (nirvikalpa) is not possible. Even if it were possible, the moment one returns from such contemplation, the creation with its sorrow arises in the mind. Movement of thought creates the notion of created objects.

Even as the essence exists in all things, as oil exists in sesame seeds, as aroma exists in flowers, the faculty of objective perception exists in the perceiver. Even as the dream-objects are experienced only by the dreamer, the objects of perception are experienced by the perceiver. Just as from a seed the sprout arises in due time, this potentiality becomes manifest as the notion of creation.

III:2 VASIṢṬHA continued:

There is a holy man named Ākāśaja (lit. born of space). He is in constant meditation and has the welfare of all at heart. He had lived for a long time, when death desired to devour him. When death approached him, it had to struggle with a fierce fire that protected the holy man. Even after fending this off, death was unable to touch him! Bewildered by this extraordinary and unprecedented event, death went to the lord Yama who presides over the destinies of mortals and questioned him: "Pray, Lord, tell me why it is that I am unable to grasp him."

Yama answered: "In fact, O death, you do not really kill anyone! Death is really caused by one's own karma (the fruition of one's own action). Hence, discover this man's fatal karma."

Even as no one can find the whereabouts of a barren woman's son, death could not discover the holy man's karma anywhere in the world. He reported this to Yama.

Yama said: "O death, this holy man Ākāśaja was truly born of space and has no karma at all. He is as pure as space. Hence he has incurred no karma which can help you grasp him or devour him. Even as a barren woman's son, this holy man is not born. He had no 'previous birth' karma either; and therefore he has no mind—hence he has not even committed a mental action which could bring him within your reach. He is nothing but a mass of intelligence. He appears to be a living being only in our eyes; in him there does not exist any such notion as can give rise to karma. Consciousness is reflected in consciousness; and the reflection assumes independence! It is a false assumption, not a real existence; and this holy man knows this truth.

"Even as liquidity is naturally present in water and emptiness in space, this holy man lives in the supreme spirit. His is a causeless manifestation: and hence he is known as self-created. He who entertains the foolish notion that 'I am this body made up of earth' is entangled in matter, and you can overpower him. Since this holy man has no such notion (and hence he is truly bodiless) he is beyond your reach.

"This holy man has never been born. He is pure consciousness that has undergone no change. In the infinite being at the beginning of an epoch there arises a vibration on account of latent ignorance: and this manifests as diverse beings, as if in a cosmic dream. Uninvolved in this, this holy man remains pure consciousness."

VASIṢṬHA said: In the Creator there is neither a seer nor an object of perception. Yet, he is known as self-created. He shines in cosmic consciousness as a painting in the mind of an artist.

VASIṢṬHA continued: III:3

In the Creator there is no memory of the past since he had no previous karma. He does not even have a physical body; the unborn is of spiritual substance. Mortal beings have two bodies, as it were, one physical and the other spiritual, but the unborn Creator has only the spiritual, since the cause that gives rise to the physical does not exist in him.

He was not created, but he is the Creator of all beings. Surely, the created (like a bracelet) is of the same substance as that of which it was created (gold). The Creator's thought being the cause of this manifold creation and the Creator himself having no physical body, the creation, too, is truly of the nature of thought, without materiality.

A throbbing arose in the Creator whose thought had spread out as the universe. This throb brought into being the subtle body (made of intelligence) of all beings. Made only of thought, all these beings only appeared to be, though they felt that that appearance was real. However, this appearance thus imagined to be real, produced realistic results or consequences, even as sexual enjoyment in a dream does. Similarly, even the Creator (the holy man of the story) though he has no body, appears to have a body.

The Creator is also of a dual nature: consciousness and thought. Consciousness is pure; thought is subject to confusion. Hence, he appears to come into being (arise), though he does not so arise. He is the intelligence that supports the entire universe, and every thought that arises in that intelligence gives rise to a form. Though all these forms are of the nature of pure intelligence, on account of self-forgetfulness of this, and of the thought of physical forms, they freeze into the physical forms, even as goblins though formless are seen to have forms on account of the perceiver's delusion.

The Creator, however, is not subject to such delusion. Hence, he is always of a spiritual nature, not materialistic. The Creator is spiritual; and even so, his creation, too, is in reality spiritual in essence. This creation is causeless. Hence, it is essentially spiritual even as the supreme being, Brahman, is. The materiality of the creation is like the castle in the air, an illusory projection of one's own mind—imaginary.

The Creator is the mind; mind or pure intelligence is his body. Thought is inherent in the mind. The object of perception is inherent in the perceiver. Who has ever discovered a distinction between the two?

III:4 VĀLMĪKI said:

At this stage the sun sped towards the western hills as if eager to meditate upon the sage's words and to illumine other parts of the earth. The assembly dispersed for prayers. The next morning all the members of the court reassembled as before.

RĀMA asked:

O Holy sage! Pray, tell me what the mind really is.

VASIṢṬHA replied:

Even as empty, inert nothingness is known as space, mind is empty nothingness. Whether the mind is real or unreal, it is that which is apprehended in objects of perception. Rāma, thought is mind; there is no distinction between the two. The self that is clothed in the spiritual body is known as mind; it is that which brings the material or physical body into existence. Ignorance, saṃsāra (repetitive history), mind-stuff, bondage, impurity, darkness and inertia are all synonyms. Experience alone is the mind; it is none other than the perceived.

This entire universe is forever non-different from the consciousness that dwells in every atom, even as an ornament is non-different from gold. Just as an ornament potentially exists in gold, the object exists in the subject. But when this notion of the object is firmly rejected and removed from the subject, then consciousness alone exists without even an apparent or potential objectivity. When this is realised, evils like attraction and repulsion, love and hate, cease in one's heart, as also the false notions of the world, you, I, etc. Even the tendency to objectify ceases; this is freedom.

RĀMA asked:

Holy sir, if the object of perception is real, then it shall not cease to be. If it is unreal, then we do not see it as unreal; so how can we overcome this?

VASIṢṬHA said:

Yet, O Rāma, we see that there are holy ones who have overcome this! External objects like space, etc., and psychological factors like "I" etc., exist only in name. In reality neither the objective universe, nor the perceiving self, nor perception as such, nor void, nor inertness exists; only one is, cosmic consciousness (cit). In this it is the mind that conjures up the diversity, diverse actions and experiences, the notion of bondage and the desire for liberation.

RĀMA asked: III:5, 6

O Holy sage! What is the source of this mind and how did it arise? Kindly enlighten me on these.

VASIṢṬHA replied:

After the cosmic dissolution and before the next epoch dawned, the entire objective universe was in a state of perfect equilibrium. There then existed the supreme Lord, the eternal, unborn, self-effulgent, who is the all and who is omnipotent. He is beyond conception and description; though he is known by various names like Ātmā etc., these are viewpoints and not the truth. He is, yet he is not realised by the world; he is within the body, too, yet he is far. From him emerge countless divinities like lord Viṣṇu, even as countless rays emerge from the sun; from him emerge infinite worlds as ripples arise from the surface of the ocean.

He is the cosmic intelligence into which countless objects of perception enter. He is the light in which the self and the world shine. He ordains the characteristic nature of every created thing. In him the worlds appear and disappear, even as a mirage appears and disappears repeatedly. His form (the world) vanishes, but his self is unchanging. He dwells in all. He is hidden and he overflows. By his mere presence, this apparently inert material world and its inhabitants are ever active. Because of his omnipresent omnipotent omniscience, his very thoughts materialise.

This supreme self cannot be realised, O Rāma, by means other than wisdom—not indeed by exerting oneself in religious practices. This self is neither far nor near; it is not inaccessible nor is it in distant places: it is what in oneself appears to be the experience of bliss, and is therefore realised in oneself.

Austerity or penance, charity and the observances of religious vows do not lead to the realisation of the Lord; only the company of holy men and the study of true scriptures are helpful, as they dispel ignorance and delusion. Indeed, when one is convinced that this self alone is real, one goes beyond sorrow, on the path of liberation.

Austerity or penance is self-inflicted pain. Of what value is charity performed with wealth earned by deceiving others—only they derive the fruits of such charity! Religious observances add to one's vanity. There is only one remedy for ignorance of the Lord—the firm and decisive renunciation of craving for sense-pleasure.

III:7 RĀMA asked:

Where does this Lord dwell, and how can I reach him?

VASIṢṬHA replied:

He who has been described as the Lord is not very far: He is the intelligence dwelling in the body. He is the universe, though the universe is not he. He is pure intelligence.

RĀMA remarked:

Even a little boy says that the Lord is intelligence: what need is there for special instruction concerning this?

VASIṢṬHA replied:

Ah, one who knows that pure intelligence is the objective universe knows nothing. Sentient is the universe, and sentient is the soul (jīva). The sentient creates the knowable and gets involved in sorrow. When there is cessation of the knowable, and the flow of attention is towards that which is not knowable (pure intelligence), then there is fulfilment and one goes beyond sorrow.

Without the cessation of the knowable, one's attention cannot be finally turned away from the knowable. Mere awareness of the involvement of the jīva in this saṃsāra is of no use. But if the supreme Lord is known, this sorrow comes to an end.

RĀMA asked:

Holy sir, please describe the Lord.

VASIṢṬHA replied:

The cosmic intelligence in which the universe as it were ceases to be, is the Lord. In him the subject-object relationship appears to have ceased, as such. He is the void in which the universe appears to exist. In him even cosmic consciousness stands still like a mountain.

RĀMA asked again:

How can we realise the Lord and realise the unreality of the universe that we have come to regard as real?

VASIṢṬHA answered: The Lord can be realised only if one is firmly established in the unreality of the universe even as the blueness of the sky is unreal. Dualism presupposes unity, and non-dualism suggests dualism. Only when the creation is known to be utterly non-existent the Lord is realised.

III:8, 9 RĀMA asked:

Holy sir, by what method is this known, and what should I know by which the knowable comes to an end?

VASIṢṬHA replied:

The wrong notion that this world is real has become deep rooted on account of persistent wrong thinking. However, it can be removed that very day on which you resort to the company of holy men and to the study of the holy scripture. Of all scriptures this Mahārāmāyaṇaṃ is best. What is found here is found elsewhere; what is not found here is not found anywhere else. However, if one does not wish to study this one is welcome to study any other scripture—there is no objection to this.

When the wrong notion is dispelled and the truth realised, that realisation so thoroughly saturates one, that one thinks of it, speaks of it, rejoices in it and teaches it to others. Such people are sometimes called Jīvanmuktas and also Videhamuktas.

RĀMA asked:

Lord, what are the characteristics of Jīvanmuktas (liberated while living) and Videhamuktas (liberated ones who have no body)?

VASIṢṬHA replied:

He who, while living an apparently normal life, experiences the whole world as an emptiness, is a Jīvanmukta. He is awake but enjoys the calmness of deep sleep; he is unaffected in the least by pleasure and pain. He is awake in deep sleep; but he is never awake to this world. His wisdom is unclouded by latent tendencies. He appears to be subject to likes, dislikes and fear; but in fact he is as free as the space. He is free from egotism and volition; and his intelligence is unattached whether in action or in inaction. None is afraid of him; he is afraid of none. He becomes a Videhamukta when, in due time, the body is dropped.

The Videhamukta is, yet is not, is not 'I' nor the 'other'. He is the sun that shines, Viṣṇu that protects all, Rudra that destroys all, Brahmā that creates; he is space, the earth, water and fire. He is in fact cosmic consciousness—that which is the very essence in all beings. All that which is in the past, present and future—all indeed is he and he alone.

RĀMA asked again:

Lord, my perception is distorted: how can I attain to that state you have indicated?

VASIṢṬHA replied:

What is known as liberation, O Rāma, is indeed the absolute itself, which alone is. That which is perceived here as 'I', 'you' etc., only seems to be, for it has never been created. How can we say that that Brahman has become all these worlds?

O Rāma, in ornaments I see only gold, in waves I see only water, in air I see only movement, in space I see only emptiness, in mirage

I see only heat, and naught else; similarly, I see only Brahman the absolute, not the worlds.

The perception of 'the worlds' is beginningless ignorance. Yet it will vanish with the help of enquiry into truth. Only that ceases to be which has come into being. This world has never really come into being, yet it appears to be—the exposition of this truth is contained in this chapter on creation.

When the previous cosmic dissolution took place, all that appeared to be before disappeared. Then the infinite alone remained; it was neither emptiness nor a form, neither sight nor the seen, and one could not say that it was, nor that it was not. It has no ears, no eyes, no tongue, and yet it hears, sees and eats. It is uncaused and uncreated; and it is the cause of everything as water is the cause of waves. This infinite and eternal light is in the heart of all: and in its light the three worlds shine, as a mirage.

When the infinite vibrates, the worlds appear to emerge; when it does not vibrate, the worlds appear to submerge: even as when a firebrand is whirled fast a fiery circle appears, and when it is held steady, the circle vanishes. Vibrating or not vibrating, it is the same everywhere at all times. Not realising it, one is subject to delusion; when it is realised all cravings and anxieties vanish.

From it is time; from it is perception of the perceivable object. Action, form, taste, smell, sound, touch and thinking—all that you know is it alone; and it is that by which you know all this! It is in the seer, sight and seen as the very seeing; when you know it, you realise your self.

III:10 RĀMA said:

Holy sir, how can it be said to be not empty, not to be illuminated and not dark? By such contradictory expressions you confuse me!

VASIṢṬHA replied:

Rāma, you are asking immature questions. Yet, I shall elucidate the correct meaning.

Even as the uncarved image is forever present in a block, the world whether you regard it as real or unreal is inherent in the absolute, which is therefore not void. Just as in a calm ocean, one cannot say that there are no waves present, the absolute is not empty of the world. Of course, these illustrations have limited application and should not be exceeded.

In truth, however, this world does not arise from the absolute nor does it merge in it. The absolute alone exists now and for ever. When one thinks of it as a void, it is because of the feeling one has that it is not void; when one thinks of it as not-void, it is because there is a feeling that it is void.

The absolute is immaterial and so material sources of light like the sun, do not illumine it. But it is self-luminous, and therefore it is not inert nor dark. This absolute cannot be realised or experienced by another; only the absolute can realise itself.

The infinite (space of) consciousness is even purer than infinite space; and the world is even as that infinite is. But, one who has not tasted capsicum does not know its taste; even so, one does not experience consciousness in the infinite in the absence of objectivity. Hence, even this consciousness appears to be inert or insentient, and the world is experienced as such too. Even as in tangible ocean tangible waves are seen, in the formless Brahman the world also exists without form. From the infinite the infinite emerges and exists in it as the infinite; hence the world has never really been created—it is the same as that from which it emerges.

When the notion of self is destroyed by the withdrawal of the fuel of ideas from the mind, that which is, is the infinite. That which is not sleep nor inert, is the infinite. It is on account of the infinite that knowledge, knower and known exist as one, in the absence of the intellect.

RĀMA said: III:11

Lord, during the cosmic dissolution, this world which is clearly seen now—where does it go?

VASIṢṬHA said:

From where does the son of a barren woman come, and where does he go? A barren woman's son has no existence, ever. Even so, this world as such has no existence, ever. This analogy baffles you only because you have taken the existence of the world for granted.

Consider this: Is there a bracelet-ness in the golden bracelet, is it not just gold? Is there a thing called sky independent of the emptiness? Even so, there is no "thing" called the world independent of Brahman the absolute. Just as coldness is inseparable from ice, what is called the world is inseparable from Brahman.

Water in the mirage does not come into being and go out of existence; even so this world does not come out of the absolute nor does it go anywhere. The creation of the world has no cause, and therefore it has had no beginning. It does not exist even now; how can it reach destruction?

If you concede that the world has not been created out of Brahman but assert that it is an appearance based on the reality of Brahman, then indeed it does not exist and Brahman alone exists. It is like dream: in a state of ignorance the intelligence within oneself appears as numerous dream-objects, all of which are nothing other than that intelligence. Even so, in what is known as the beginning of creation, such an appearance happened; but it is not independent of Brahman, it does not exist apart from Brahman, hence it does not exist.

RĀMA said:

Holy sir, if that is so, how is it that this world has acquired such a sense of reality? As long as the perceiver is, the perceived exists, and vice versa, and only when both these come to an end is there liberation. If there is a clean mirror, it reflects something or other all the time: even so in the seer this creation will again and again arise. However, if the non-existence of creation is realised then the seer ceases to be. But, such a realisation is hard to get!

VASIṢṬHA said:

Rāma, I shall presently dispel your doubts with the help of a parable. You will then realise the non-existence of creation and lead an enlightened life in this world.

III:12 VASIṢṬHA said:

O Rāma, I shall narrate to you how this creation appears to have emerged from the one pure undivided cosmic being, even as dreams appear in the consciousness of the sleeping person.

This universe is in fact the eternal effulgent infinite consciousness which generates within itself the knowable (which would be known as that which is to be) with an idea concerning its form (which is space), and with an enquiry concerning itself. Thus is space brought into being. When, after a considerable time the consciousness of creation becomes strong in the infinite being, the future jīva (living cosmic soul—also known as Hiraṇyagarbha) arises within it: and the infinite abandons, as it were, its supreme state, to limit itself as the jīva. However, even then Brahman remains the infinite, and there is no real transformation into any of these.

In space, the faculty of sound manifests itself. Then comes into being egotism which is vital to further creation of the universe, and, at the same time, the factor known as time. All this happens merely by the creative-thought inherent in the cosmic being, not as real transformations of the infinite.

By the similar exercise of the creative-thought, air is created. The Vedas come into being, too. Consciousness which is surrounded by all these is called the jīva which gives rise to all the different elements in this world.

There are fourteen planes of existence, each with its own type of inhabitants. And all these are the manifestations of the creative-thought of consciousness. Even so, when this consciousness thought 'I am light', sources of light like the sun, etc., were instantly created. Similarly water and earth were created.

All these fundamental elements continued to act on one another —as experiencer and experience—and the entire creation came into being like ripples on the surface of the ocean. And, they are interwoven and mixed up so effectively that they cannot be extricated from one another till the cosmic dissolution. These material appearances are ever changing and the reality exists unchanged; since these are all linked with consciousness, they instantly become gross physical substance, though all these are the infinite consciousness alone, which has undergone no change whatsoever.

VASIṢṬHA continued: III:13

In the supreme being there exists the vibration which is at once equilibrium and disturbance; on account of this there appear space and light and inertia, though they have not really been created. Since all this happens in consciousness, they possess the quality of the knowable; at the same time there arises the knower. It is the inherent power of consciousness to illumine all things, hence it is the cosmic knower. That consciousness itself becomes its own knowable and the knower. When such a relationship arises, the notion "I am a jīva, living soul" arises in consciousness.

By the further identification with the knowable, in the pure consciousness there arises the notion of egotism and then the faculty of discrimination or the rationalising intellect. After this the mind and the root-elements arise. These root-elements combine again and again to form the worlds. Spontaneously and also by orderly changes, all these countless forms appear and disappear repeatedly, even as cities come and go in a dream. None of these needs any instrumental or material cause like earth, water or fire. For all this is of the essential nature of consciousness, and it is this consciousness that apparently creates all these, as one creates cities in a dream. It is nothing but pure consciousness.

The five elements are the seed of which the world is the tree; and the eternal consciousness is the seed for the elements. As is the seed, so is the fruit (tree). Therefore, the world is nothing but Brahman the absolute.

In this manner has the universe been conjured up in cosmic space by cosmic consciousness with its own infinite faculties; it is not real, nor has it been really created. Though these elements have combined among themselves and created apparent materiality in the world, yet, in truth, all this is mere appearance like the forms seen in space. They owe their reality to their substratum which is cosmic consciousness which alone is real.

Do not entertain the feeling that the world of five elements is their creation: look upon the five elements themselves as the manifestation of the power inherent in consciousness absolute. It may be said that the elements such as earth etc., have arisen in consciousness like dream-objects; or it may be said that they are mere appearances ignorantly superimposed on cosmic consciousness. Such is the vision or realisation of holy men.

VASIṢṬHA continued:

Rāma, I shall now tell you how the jīva (living soul) came to dwell in this body.

The jīva thought "I am atomic in nature and stature" and so it became atomic in nature. Yet, it only apparently became so, on account of its imagination which was false. Even as one may dream that he is dead and that he has another body, this jīva which in truth had an extremely subtle body of pure consciousness, now begins to identify itself with grossness and so becomes gross.

Even as a mountain is reflected in a mirror and is seen as if it were in the mirror, the jīva reflects the external objects and activities, and soon begins to think that they are all within itself and that he is the doer of the actions and the experiencer of the experiences.

When the jīva wishes to see, eyes are formed in the gross body. Even so the skin (tactile sense), ears, tongue, nose and the organs of action are formed as a result of the appropriate desire arising in the jīva. Thus abides in the body, the jīva which has the extremely subtle body of consciousness, imagining various external physical experiences and various internal psychological experiences. Thus, resting in the unreal which however appears to be real, Brahman, now appearing to be jīva, becomes confused.

This same Brahman which has come to regard itself as a finite jīva and endowed with a physical body, apprehends the external world which on account of the veil of ignorance appears to be composed of matter. Someone thinks he is Brahmā, someone else thinks he is something else—in this manner the jīva imagines it is this or that, and so binds itself to the illusion of world-appearance.

But all this is mere imagination or thought. Even now nothing has ever been created; the pure infinite space alone exists. Brahmā the creator could not create the world as it was before the cosmic dissolution, for Brahmā attained final liberation then. Cosmic consciousness alone exists now and ever; in it are no worlds, no created beings. That consciousness reflected in itself appears to be creation. Even as an unreal nightmare produces real results, this world seems to give rise to a sense of reality in a state of ignorance. When true wisdom arises, this unreality vanishes.

III:14 VASIṢṬHA continued:

As I have already explained to you, O Rāma, this world consisting of egotism and the countless objects of experience has not been created and therefore it does not exist: what exists is Brahman, the absolute existence. Just as a wave is seen on the calm surface of the ocean when the latter is agitated, even so when the absolute 'thinks', as it were, that it is a jīva, the jīva-nature manifests itself. Just as a sleeping person appears to create diverse creatures within himself without ever abandoning his own unique and sole reality, by a mere thought or will the absolute brings into being these countless creatures without ever suffering diminution or change.

The cosmic form (Virāṭ) of this cosmic consciousness is of course of the nature of pure consciousness, uncontaminated by gross materiality. The cosmic form made of pure consciousness can be compared to an ever-lasting dream in a sleeping person in which there exist palaces and other beings.

Even the creator Brahmā is a mere thought-form in this cosmic consciousness: consciousness reflecting its own thought-forms within itself is all this apparent seer and seen, all of which are mere imaginations. All of them however exist in name only and multiply in name only. Even as the cosmic being arose in the cosmic consciousness as a cosmic thought-form, others arose from the thoughts of that cosmic being—just as one lamp is kindled from another. But all of them are non-different from that one cosmic being on account of whose thought-vibration they arose.

Brahman alone is the cosmic being (Virāṭ) and the cosmic being is all this creation, with the jīva and all the elements that constitute this creation.

RĀMA asked:

Lord, is there only one jīva that is cosmic, or are there many jīvas, or is there a huge conglomerate of jīvas?

VASIṢṬHA answered:

Rāma, there is neither one jīva nor many nor a conglomerate of jīvas. Jīva is only a name! What exists is only Brahman. Because he is omnipotent, his thought-forms materialise. One alone appears as diverse on account of ignorance; we do not experience this ignorance which disappears on enquiry even as darkness vanishes when light is brought in to look at it. Brahman alone is the cosmic (Mahājīva) soul and the millions of jīvas. There is naught else.

VASIṢṬHA continued:

By the apprehension of the perceived or the knowable, consciousness becomes jīva (the living soul) and is apparently involved in repetitive history (saṃsāra). When the false notion of a knowable apart from the knower (consciousness) ceases, it regains its equilibrium.

In an orderly and sometimes disorderly way, the one Mahājīva thus becomes individual jīva, inheriting from the previous generation the sense of duality and of individuality.

The mysterious power of consciousness which in an inexplicable and miraculous way produces this infinite diversity of names and forms (body) is known as egotism. The same consciousness, when it wishes to taste or to experience itself, becomes the knowable universe. Only immature people see in this either a real transformation or even a deluded appearance; for there is nothing other than consciousness.

The ocean is water; the waves are water; and when these waves play upon the surface of the ocean, ripples (also water) are formed. Even so with the universe. Even as the ocean might look upon and recognise the individuality of the ripples, the consciousness thinks of the individuals as independent; and thus egotism is born ('I-ness'). All this is the wonderful play of the mysterious power of consciousness—and that alone is called the universe.

When egotism has come into being, that egotism (which is non-different from consciousness) entertains notions of the various elements that constitute this universe, and they arise. In unity diversity arises. O Rāma, give up all these false notions of 'I' and 'you', by renouncing even the notions of a jīva and its own cause. When all these have gone, you will realise the truth which is in the middle between the real and the unreal. When all these 'clouds' have been dispelled, the one indivisible whole shines as it has never ceased to shine. We do not know what is real or what is false!

This consciousness is not knowable: when it wishes to become the knowable it is known as the universe. Mind, intellect, egotism, the five great elements, and the world—all these innumerable names and forms, are all consciousness alone. A man and his life and works are indistinguishable, the static and the kinetic manifestations of the same factor. Jīva and the mind etc., are all vibrations in consciousness.

VASIṢṬHA continued:

That consciousness indeed exists here, knowing "I cannot be cut, I cannot be burnt, I cannot be made wet, I cannot be dried; I am eternal, omnipresent and unchanging and unmoving." This is the truth. People like to argue and confuse others; they are indeed confused. But, O Rāma, we are beyond confusion. Changes in the unchanging are imagined by ignorant and deluded people: but in the vision of sages who have self-knowledge no change whatsoever has taken place in consciousness.

O Rāma, consciousness alone has spread itself out as space, without undergoing any change in itself. After that, consciousness alone appears as the wind that has the quality of motion. And then consciousness alone appears as fire, water, and the earth with its minerals, and also the bodies of living beings.

When the notion of an external knowable has been removed, self-knowledge arises; and when in it there is the notion of inertia or ignorance, the state of deep sleep has come to it. Hence, since consciousness alone exists at all times, it may be said that space exists and does not exist, the world exists and does not exist.

Even as heat is to fire, whiteness is to a conch-shell, firmness is to a mountain, liquidity to water, sweetness is to sugarcane, butter is to milk, coolness is to ice, brightness is to illumination, oil is to mustard seed, flow is to a river, sweetness is to honey, ornament is to gold, aroma is to a flower—the universe is to consciousness. The world exists because consciousness is: and the world is the body of consciousness. There is no division, no difference, no distinction. Hence the universe can be said to be both real and unreal: real because of the reality of consciousness which is its own reality, and unreal because the universe does not exist as universe, independent of consciousness. This consciousness is indivisible and has no parts or limbs. In it the mountain, the ocean, the earth, the rivers, etc., do not exist as such, but only as consciousness; hence there are no parts nor limbs in consciousness.

But, because of the unreality of the universe, etc., it cannot be said that their own cause, viz., the consciousness is also unreal: such a statement would only be a set of words with no meaning—for it runs counter to our experience, and the existence of consciousness cannot be denied.

(At this stage, the third evening set in: and the assembly dispersed.)

The Story of Līlā

VASIṢṬHA continued: III:15

O Rāma, even as from the waking state experience, there is no materiality in the objects seen in a dream (though while dreaming the objects appear to be solid) this world appears to be material yet in reality it is pure consciousness. There is not even a temporary or subtle river in the mirage: even so there is in no sense a real world, but only pure consciousness. Only knowledge based on ignorance clings to the notion of a world; in reality, there is no difference in the meaning of the words 'world' 'Brahman or the infinite', and 'self'. The world is as true in relation to Brahman as the dream-city is true in relation to the experience of the waking consciousness. Hence, 'world' and 'cosmic consciousness' are synonyms.

To make all this crystal clear, O Rāma, I shall now narrate to you the story of Maṇḍapa: pray, listen attentively.

Once upon a time, O Rāma, there was a king on earth called Padma. He was perfect in every respect; and by his own nature and conduct he enhanced the glory of his dynasty. He honoured religious traditions even as the ocean respects the authority of the shore. He subdued his enemies even as the sun routs darkness. Even as fire reduces hay to ashes, he destroyed evil in society. Holy men resorted to him even as gods resort to heaven. He was the abode of virtue. He made his enemies tremble on the battlefield even as a gale ruffles a creeper. He was highly learned and a master of arts. To him there was nothing impossible of achievement, even as to lord Nārāyaṇa there was no impossibility.

This king had a wife by name Līlā. She was highly accomplished as a woman and was very beautiful. It appeared as if she was goddess Lakṣmī (consort of Nārāyaṇa) incarnate on earth. She was soft-spoken, her gait was slow and graceful and her smile radiated the cool delight of moonlight. She was fair. She was sweet as honey. Her arms were soft and delicate. Her body was as pure and clear as the waters of the holy river Gaṅgā; and even as a touch of the waters of the Gaṅgā gives rise to bliss, to touch her was to experience bliss. She was highly devoted to her husband Padma and knew how to serve him and to please him.

She was one with the king and shared his joy and sorrow. She was in fact the alter ego of Padma—except that when the king became angry, she merely reflected fear.

III:16 VASIṢṬHA continued:

King Padma and the queen Līlā lived an ideal life. They enjoyed their life in every possible and righteous way. They were young and youthful like the gods, and their love for each other was pure and intense, without any hypocrisy or artificiality.

One day, the queen Līlā thought: "The most handsome king who is my husband is dearer to me than even my own life. What should I do in order that he and I may live for ever enjoying the pleasures of life? I shall immediately undertake such austerities as the holy ones would suggest in order that I may fulfil my ambition." She sought the counsel of the holy ones.

The Holy ones said to her: "O queen, austerities or penance, repetition of mantras and a disciplined life will surely bestow upon you all that it is possible for one to attain in this world; but physical immortality is not possible of attainment in this world!"

The queen pondered this advice and decided: "If I should die before my husband, then I should attain self-knowledge and be free from sorrow. But, if he should leave before me, then I shall so strive now as to obtain a boon from the gods that his jīva does not leave our palace. I shall be happy to live in it in the knowledge that he is always with me."

Thus resolved, Līlā began to propitiate the goddess Sarasvatī immediately, without even discussing this project with her husband. Once in three nights she used to eat, after devoutly worshipping the Lord, holy ones, the preceptor, the learned ones and the sages. She was utterly convinced that this penance would prove fruitful, and this conviction greatly strengthened her application to the penance undertaken. Though she did not reveal her intention to the king, she did not let her service to her husband suffer in the very least on account of this penance. After one hundred such three-nightly worship, the goddess Sarasvatī appeared before her and granted her the boons of her choice. Līlā prayed: "O Divine mother, grant me two boons: (1) when my husband departs from his body, let his jīva remain in the palace, and (2) whenever I pray to you, let me see you." Sarasvatī granted these two boons and disappeared.

Time inexorably passed. King Padma, who was mortally wounded on the battlefield, died in the palace. Queen Līlā was inconsolable with grief. When she was thus sunk in grief, an ethereal voice spoke to her.

THE ETHEREAL VOICE OF SARASVATĪ said: III:17

My child, cover the king's dead body with flowers; then it will not decay. He will not leave the palace.

(Līlā did so. Yet, she was not satisfied, and she felt like a wealthy man (who had the wealth) who had been tricked into poverty-stricken existence. She invoked goddess Sarasvatī who appeared before her and said:)

My child, why do you grieve? Sorrow, like water in mirage, is an illusion.

(Līlā asked her: Pray, tell me where my husband is.)

O Līlā, there are three types of space—the psychological space, the physical space, and the infinite space of consciousness. Of these the most subtle is the infinite space of consciousness. By intense meditation on this infinite space of consciousness, you can see and experience the presence of one (like your husband) whose body is that infinite space, even though you do not see him here. That is the infinite space which exists in the middle when the finite intelligence travels from one place to another; for it is infinite. If you give up all thoughts you will here and now attain to the realisation of oneness with all. Normally, only he who has realised the utter non-existence of the universe can experience this; but you will do so, by my grace.

VASIṢṬHA continued:

Līlā began to meditate. Immediately she entered the highest state of consciousness free from all distractions (nirvikalpa). She was in the infinite space of consciousness. There she saw the king once again, on a throne, surrounded by many kings who adored him, by many sages and holy men who chanted the Vedas, by many women, and by armed forces. She saw them but they did not see her, as one's thought-forms are visible only to oneself, not to others. She saw that the king had a youthful body. She also saw in his court very many members of the court of king Padma. She wondered: are they all dead, too!

Again, by the grace of goddess Sarasvatī, Līlā came back to her palace, and saw her attendants asleep. She woke them and asked them to request the members of the royal court to assemble at once. Messengers were quickly despatched to summon all; and very soon the royal court of king Padma was teeming with the ministers, sages, civil servants, relations, and friends. Seeing them all there, Līlā rejoiced.

III:18 VASIṢṬHA continued:

Seeing all the members of the royal court, Līlā was puzzled: she thought, 'This is strange, for these people seem to exist in two places at the same time—in that region which I saw in my meditation and here in front of me. Just as a mountain is seen both inside the mirror and outside it, this creation is seen both within consciousness and outside it. But, which of these is real and which the reflection? I must find out from Sarasvatī'. She adored Sarasvatī and saw her seated in front of her.

LĪLĀ asked:

Be gracious, O Goddess, and tell me this. That on which this world is reflected is extremely pure and undivided, and it is not the object of knowledge. This world exists both within it as its reflection and outside as solid matter: which is real and which the reflection?

SARASVATĪ asked:

Tell me first: what do you consider real and what unreal?

LĪLĀ answered:

That I am here and you are in front of me—this I consider real. That region in which my husband is now—that I consider unreal.

SARASVATĪ said:

How can the unreal be the effect of the real? The effect is the cause, there is no essential difference. Even in the case of a pot which is able to hold water whereas its cause (clay) cannot, this difference is due to the co-operative causes. What was the material cause of your husband's birth? For, only material effects are produced by material causes.

Hence, when you find no immediate cause for an effect, then surely the cause existed in the past—memory. Memory is like space, empty. All creation here is the effect of that emptiness—and hence the creation is empty, too. Even as the birth of your husband is an illusory product of memory, I see all this as the illusory and unreal effect of imagination.

I shall narrate to you a story which illustrates the dream-like nature of this creation. In pure consciousness, in a corner of the mind of the Creator, there was a dilapidated shrine covered with a blue dome. It had the fourteen worlds for rooms. The three divisions of space were holes in it. The sun was the light. In it there were little anthills (the cities), little piles of earth (mountains) and little pools of water (the oceans). This is creation, the universe. In a very small corner of it there lived a holy man with his wife and children. He was healthy and free from fear. He performed his religious and social duties well.

SARASVATĪ continued: III:19, 20

That holy man was known as Vasiṣṭha and his wife was Arundhatī (though they were different from the Vasiṣṭha and Arundhatī of legendary fame). One day when that holy man was seated on the top of a hill he saw at the foot of that hill, a colourful procession on the move, with a king riding a stately elephant, followed by an army and other royal paraphernalia. Looking at this, a wish arose in the heart of the holy man: "Indeed, the life of a king is rich and full of delight and glory. When will I ride a royal elephant like that and be followed by an army like this?"

Some time after this, the holy man grew old and then death overtook him. His wife who was highly devoted to him prayed to me and asked for the same boon that you asked for: that her husband's spirit should not leave her house. I granted her that boon.

Though that holy man was an ethereal being, on account of the power of his constant wish during the previous life-span he became a mighty king and ruled over a great empire which resembled heaven on earth. He was dreaded by his foes, he was indeed a cupid to womenfolk, he was stable and firm against temptations like a mountain, he reflected all the scriptures within himself like a mirror, he was the wish-fulfiller of everyone in need and he was the resting place of holy men: he was indeed the full moon of righteousness. (Arundhatī had also given up her body and attained reunion with her husband.) It is eight days since this happened.

Līlā, it is the same holy man who is now your husband, the king; and you are the same Arundhatī who was his wife. On account of ignorance and delusion, all this seems to take place in the infinite consciousness: you may regard all this as true or as false.

LĪLĀ asked:

O Goddess, all this seems so strange and incredible to me. It is like saying that a huge elephant is bound in the centre of a mustard seed, or that in an atom a mosquito fought with a lion, or that there is a mountain in a lotus pod.

SARASVATĪ said: My dear, I do not utter falsehood, but am telling the truth. It sounds incredible but this kingdom appears to be only in the hut of the holy man on account of his desire for a kingdom. The memory of the past is hidden, and you two have risen again. Death is but waking from a dream. Birth which arises from a wish is no more real than the wish, like waves in a mirage!

III:20, 21 SARASVATĪ continued:

Līlā, your house, you, I and all this is pure consciousness, naught else. Your house was itself in the house of the holy man Vasiṣṭha. In the space of his jīva existed the rivers and the mountains and so on. Even after the 'creation' of all this in the holy man's house, it remained as it was before. Indeed, in every atom there are worlds within worlds.

LĪLĀ asked:

O Goddess, you said that it was only eight days ago that the holy man had died; and yet my husband and I have lived for a long time. How can you reconcile this discrepancy?

SARASVATĪ said:

O Līlā, just as space does not have a fixed span, time does not have a fixed span either. Just as the world and its creation are mere appearances, a moment and an epoch are also imaginary, not real. In the twinkling of an eye the jīva undergoes the illusion of the death-experience, forgets what happened before that, and in the infinite consciousness thinks 'I am this' etc., and 'I am his son, I am so many years old', etc. There is no essential difference between the experiences of this world and those of another—all this being the thought-forms in the infinite consciousness. They are like two waves in the same ocean. Since these worlds were never created, they will never cease to be: such is the law. Their real nature is consciousness.

Even as in a dream there is birth, death and relationship all in a very short time, and even as a lover feels that a single night without his beloved is an epoch, the jīva thinks of experienced and non-experienced objects in the twinkling of an eye. And, immediately thereafter, he imagines those things (the world) to be real. Even those things which he had not experienced nor seen present themselves before him as in a dream.

This world and this creation is nothing but memory, dream: distance, measures of time like a moment and an age, all these are hallucinations. This is one kind of knowledge—memory. There is another which is not based on memory of past experience. This is the fortuitous meeting of an atom and consciousness which is then able to produce its own effects.

Liberation is the realisation of the total non-existence of the universe as such. This is different from a mere denial of the existence of the ego and the universe! The latter is only half-knowledge. Liberation is to realise that all this is pure consciousness.

LĪLĀ asked:

O Goddess, without prior hallucination how was the creation of the holy man and his wife possible?

SARASVATĪ said:

Indeed, that was due to the thought-form of Brahmā, the creator. He himself had no hidden thought-forms (memory) for before creation there was dissolution and at that time the Creator had attained liberation. At the beginning of this epoch, someone assumes the role of creator and thinks "I am the new Creator"—this is pure coincidence, even as one sees a crow alighting on a palm tree and the cocoanut falling, though these two are independent of each other. Of course, do not forget that even though all this seems to happen, there is no creation! The one infinite consciousness alone is thought-form or experience: there is no cause and effect relationship, these ('cause' and 'effect') are only words, not facts. The infinite consciousness is forever in infinite consciousness.

LĪLĀ said:

O Goddess, your words are truly enlightening. However, since I have never been exposed to them before, the wisdom is not well grounded. I wish to see the original house of the holy Vasiṣṭha.

SARASVATĪ said:

O Līlā, give up this form of yours and attain the pure spiritual insight. For only Brahman can really see or realise Brahman. My body is made of pure light, pure consciousness. Your body is not. With this body of yours you cannot even visit the places of your own imagination, then how can you enter the field of another's imagination? But if you attain the body of light, you will immediately see the holy man's house. Affirm to yourself, "I shall leave my body here and take a body of light. With that body, like the scent of incense, I shall go to the house of the holy man." Even as water mixes with water, you will become one with the field of consciousness.

By the persistent practice of such meditation, even your body will become one of pure consciousness and subtlety. For, I see even this my body as consciousness. You do not, for you see the world of matter, even as an ignorant man might mistake a precious stone for a pebble. Such ignorance arises of its own accord, but is dispelled by wisdom and enquiry. In fact, even such ignorance does not exist! There is neither unwisdom, nor ignorance; neither bondage, nor liberation. There is but one pure consciousness.

III:22, 23 SARASVATĪ said:

Dear Līlā, in dream, the dream-body appears to be real; but when there is an awakening to the fact of dream, the reality of that body vanishes. Even so, the physical body which is sustained by memory and latent tendencies is seen to be unreal when they are seen to be unreal. At the end of the dream, you become aware of the physical body; at the end of these tendencies, you become aware of the ethereal body. When the dream ends, deep sleep ensues; when the seeds of thought perish, you are liberated. In liberation the seeds of thought do not exist: if the liberated sage appears to live and to think, he only appears to do so, like a burnt cloth lying on the floor. This is, however, not like deep sleep nor unconsciousness, in both of which the seeds of thought lie hidden.

By the persistent practice (abhyāsa) egotism is quieted. Then you will naturally rest in your consciousness; and the perceived universe heads towards the vanishing point. What is called practice?

Thinking of that alone, speaking of that, conversing of that with one another, utter dedication to that one alone—this is called abhyāsa or practice by the wise. When one's intellect is filled with beauty and bliss, when one's vision is broad, when passion for sensual enjoyment is absent in one—that is practice. When one is firmly established in the conviction that this universe has never even been created, and therefore it does not exist as such, and when thoughts like "This is world, this I am" do not arise at all in one—that is abhyāsa or practice. It is then that attraction and repulsion do not arise; the overcoming of attraction and repulsion by the use of will-force is austerity, not wisdom.

(At this stage, evening set in: and the court dispersed. Early next morning the court assembled, and Vasiṣṭha continued his discourse.)

VASIṢṬHA continued:

O Rāma, Sarasvatī and queen Līlā immediately sat in deep meditation or nirvikalpa samādhi. They had risen above body-consciousness. Because they had given up all notions of the world, it had completely vanished in their consciousness. They roamed freely in their wisdom-bodies. Though it seemed that they had travelled millions of miles in space, they were still in the same 'room' but on another plane of consciousness.

VASIṢṬHA continued: III:24, 25

Holding each other's hands, Sarasvatī and Līlā, slowly ascended to far distant scenes in space. This space was intensely pure and totally empty. They rested on top of the mount Meru, the axis of the earth. They saw countless interesting sights as they proceeded away from the orbit of the moon. They roamed within huge cloud-formations in space. They entered infinite space, the womb and source of infinite beings in infinite worlds.

They saw the seven great mountains in the cosmos which were radiant like the fire of dissolution; they saw golden plains near Meru; and they saw the densest form of darkness. They saw siddhas (beings with supernatural powers); they saw crowds and crowds of demons, goblins and other spirits; they saw space vehicles come and go everywhere; they saw celestial nymphs sing and dance; they saw a variety of birds and also animals; they saw angels and gods; they saw great yogis endowed with all auspicious qualities; they saw the abode of the Creator, the abode of Śiva, and others. Like a couple of mosquitoes they roamed all these planes.

(Note: The description is graphic and detailed in the text.)

In short they saw all that was already in the mind of Sarasvatī and which Sarasvatī wanted to show to queen Līlā. It was like the lotus of the heart, with the directions for its petals, the netherworld for the mud in which it grows, held by the divine serpent which is the root.

In this lotus, they saw what is known as Jaṃbūdvīpa, in which there are very many countries and continents. It is surrounded by a salty ocean. Beyond that is Śākadvīpa, surrounded by an ocean of milk. Beyond that is Kuśadvīpa with an ocean of curd. Then Krauñcadvīpa and an ocean of ghee. Then Śālmalīdvīpa surrounded by an ocean of wine. Then Gomedadvīpa surrounded by an ocean of sugarcane juice. Then there is Puṣkaradvīpa surrounded by an ocean of sweet water. Then there is a cosmic hole. Beyond that is the Lokāloka mountain shining resplendently. Beyond that is the infinite forest, etc. Lastly there was infinite space, sheer emptiness.

(Note: Compare with the description in Bhāgavataṃ.)

Having thus seen the oceans, mountains, the protectors of the universe, the kingdom of the gods, the sky and the very bowels of the earth, Līlā saw her own house.

VASIṢṬHA continued: III:26

O Rāma, the two ladies then entered into the holy man's house. The whole family was in mourning. On account of their grief the house itself had a depressing atmosphere. By the practice of the yoga of pure wisdom Līlā had acquired that faculty by which her thoughts instantly materialised. She wished that 'These, my relations, should see me and Sarasvatī as if we are ordinary womenfolk'. They appeared so to the mourning family. But the two ladies were of supernatural radiance which dispelled the gloom that pervaded the house.

The eldest son of the departed holy couple welcomed the two ladies, taking them to be two angels of the forest! He said to them: "O angels of the forest, surely you have come here to relieve us of our grief in our bereavement. For such is the nature of divinities: they are eager to relieve the distress of others."

The two ladies asked the young man: "Tell us the cause of your sorrow which seems to afflict all these people here."

The son of the holy couple replied: "O ladies, in this very house there lived a pious man and his devoted wife, who were both devoted to a righteous life. Recently, they abandoned their children and grandchildren, their house and their cattle, and ascended to heaven. Therefore, to us this whole world appears to be empty. Look, O ladies, even the birds are crying for the departed ones. Even the gods are crying in grief (raining tears!). The trees are shedding tears every morning (the dew-drops). Abandoning this earth, my parents have surely gone away to the world of the immortals."

Hearing this, Līlā laid her hand on the young man's head: instantly he was relieved of his sorrow. Seeing this, all the others were also relieved of sorrow.

RĀMA asked:

O Holy one, why is it that Līlā did not appear to her own son as his real mother?

VASIṢṬHA replied: Rāma, he who has realised the unreality of material substances sees only the one undivided consciousness everywhere. A dreamer does not see this world, a man in deep coma may even see the other world. Līlā had realised the truth. He who has realised the truth that Brahman, the self, etc., are all one infinite consciousness—unto him where is son, friend, wife, etc.? Even her laying her hand on the young man's head was the spontaneous expression of Brahman's grace.

III:27 VASIṢṬHA continued:

Having thus blessed the family of the deceased holy man, the two ladies disappeared. The consoled members of the family returned to their abodes. Līlā turned to Sarasvatī to ask her a question: in this state, of course, their bodies were made neither of matter like earth nor psychosomatic factors like life-breath. It was like two dream-objects conversing with each other. Līlā asked Sarasvatī: "How was it that we were seen by this family of mine here, and we were not seen by my husband who was ruling a kingdom when we visited him?" Sarasvatī answered: "Then you were still clinging to your notion 'I am Līlā'; now you have overcome that body-consciousness. Till the consciousness of duality is completely dispelled, you cannot act in the infinite consciousness; you cannot even understand it, even as one standing in the sun does not know the coolness of the shade of a tree. But, now if you go to your husband, you will be able to deal with him as before."

LĪLĀ said:

O Divinity! It was here itself that my husband was the holy man and I was his wife; here again I was his queen; here he died and here again he rules now! Pray, take me where I can see him.

SARASVATĪ said:

Līlā, you and your husband have been through many incarnations, three of which you now know. In this incarnation, the king has slipped deep into the snare of worldliness and he thinks 'I am the lord, I am strong, I am happy, etc.' Though from the spiritual standpoint the whole universe is experienced here, from the physical point of view, millions of miles separate the planes. In the infinite consciousness, in every atom of it, universes come and go like particles of dust in a beam of sunlight that shines through a hole in the roof. These come and go like ripples on the ocean.

LĪLĀ reminisced: O Divinity! Since emerging as a reflection in the infinite consciousness I have had 800 births. Today I see this. I have been a nymph, a vicious human woman, a serpent, a forest tribal woman, and on account of evil deeds I became a creeper, and by the proximity of sages I became a sage's daughter; I became a king, and on account of evil deeds done then, I became a mosquito, a bee, a deer, a bird, a fish; and again I became a celestial, after which I became a tortoise, and a swan, and I became a mosquito again. I have also been a celestial nymph when other celestials (males) used to fall at my feet. Just as the scales of balance seesaw constantly I have also been caught up in the seesaw of this repetitive existence, saṃsāra.

RĀMA asked: III:28

Holy sir, how was it possible for the two ladies to travel to distant galaxies in the universe, and how did they overcome the numerous barriers on the way?

VASIṢṬHA replied:

O Rāma, where is universe, where are galaxies, where are barriers? The two ladies remained in the queen's inner apartment. It was there that the holy man Vasiṣṭha was ruling as king Vidūratha; it was he who was king Padma before. All this happened in pure space: there is no universe, no distance, no barriers.

Conversing with each other, the two ladies emerged from the room and proceeded towards a village on top of a mountain. The beauty and the glory of that mountain are indescribable. All its houses were literally covered with flowers that continually dropped from the trees. Young women slept in their rooms on beds made of clouds. The houses were illuminated by lightning.

On account of the intensity of her practice of the yoga of wisdom, Līlā had acquired full knowledge of the past, present and future. She recollected the past and said to Sarasvatī: "O Divinity, some time ago I was an aged woman and I lived here. I was devoted to righteousness in every way; but I had never practised enquiry into the nature of the self ("Who am I, what is this world?"). My husband was also a good, righteous and learned man; but, his inner intelligence had also not been awakened. We were exemplars in conduct; and by such conduct we taught others how they should live." After saying this, Līlā showed to Sarasvatī her previous dwelling, and continued: "See, this is my favourite calf. On account of my separation, it does not even eat grass and has been constantly weeping for the past eight days. In this place, my husband ruled the world. Because of his strong will power and since he was determined to be a great king soon, he had indeed become an emperor within the short span of eight days, though it looked like a long long time. Just as air moves about unseen in space, even so in the space of this house, my husband lives, unseen. Here, in the space of the size of a thumb, we imagined the kingdom of my husband to be a million square miles. O Divinity, surely both my husband and I are of pure consciousness; yet, on account of the mysterious illusory power Māyā, my husband's kingdom appears to encompass hundreds of mountains. This is truly marvellous. I wish to enter into the capital city where my husband rules. Come let us go there: for what is impossible of achievement to the industrious?"

III:29, 30 VASIṢṬHA continued:

Along with Sarasvatī, the queen Līlā rose into the sky. They went beyond the region of the pole star, beyond the realms of the sages of perfection, even beyond the realm of the gods, of Brahmā (the creator), Goloka and the realms of Śiva and of the manes and of the liberated ones. From there Līlā saw that even the sun and the moon were far below, and were barely visible. Sarasvatī said to Līlā, "Dear one, you have to go beyond even this to the very top of the head of creation; all that you have seen is just a few particles that have emanated from there." Soon they had reached this summit, for their will becomes adamantine whose consciousness is pure and unveiled.

There, Līlā saw that this creation was enveloped by layers of water, fire, air and space, and beyond that was pure consciousness. This supreme infinite consciousness is pure, peaceful, free from illusions, established in its own glory. In that Līlā saw countless creations floating like dust-particles in light. The self-projections of the jīvas dwelling in those universes gave them their forms and nature. Because of the essential nature of this infinite consciousness, all these keep arising and again arising, and by their own thought-force, return to a state of tranquillity; all this is like the spontaneous play of a child.

RĀMA asked:

What do people mean by 'above' 'below' and so on, when only the infinite is truth?

VASIṢṬHA replied:

O Rāma, just as when little ants crawl all over a round rock, what is under their feet is always 'below' and what is behind their back is always 'above'; even so people talk of these directions.

Of those countless universes, O Rāma, in some there are only plants; some have Brahmā, Viṣṇu, Rudra and others as the presiding deities, and some have none at all; in some there are only animals and birds; in some there is only an ocean; some are solid rocks; some are inhabited only by worms; some are pervaded by dense darkness; in some gods dwell; some are forever illumined. Some seem to be heading towards dissolution; some seem to be falling in space towards destruction. Since consciousness exists everywhere for ever, creation of these universes and their dissolution also goes on everywhere for ever. All these are held together by a mysterious omnipresent power. Rāma, everything exists in the one infinite consciousness; everything arises from it; it alone is everything.

VASIṢṬHA continued: III:31-40

Having seen all this, Līlā saw the inner apartment of the palace where the corpse of the king lay buried under a heap of flowers. There arose in her an intense wish to behold her husband's other life. Instantly, she broke through the summit of the universe and entered into the realm where her husband now ruled.

At the same time, a mighty king who ruled over the Sindhu region was laying a siege to her husband's kingdom. As the two ladies were coursing the space above the battlefield they encountered countless celestials who had assembled there to witness the battle and the exploits of the great heroes.

RĀMA asked:

Holy one, tell me: who is a hero among soldiers and who is a beast or a war criminal?

VASIṢṬHA replied:

O Rāma, he who fights a battle which is in accordance with the scriptural injunctions, on behalf of a righteous king of unblemished conduct, whether he dies in battle or wins, he is a hero. He who fights for an unrighteous monarch, who tortures people and mutilates their bodies, even if he dies fighting in battle, he is a beast or criminal and goes to hell. He who fights to protect the cattle, holy men, friends, or they who have taken his asylum, he is an ornament of heaven. On the other hand, they who fight for a king who delights in harassing the people (whether he be a king or not, or just a landlord), they go to hell. Only the hero who dies in battle goes to heaven; they who fight unrighteously, even if they die in battle, do not go to heaven.

O Rāma, still standing in the sky, Līlā saw the two great armies closing in on each other, ready to engage themselves in battle. (There follows a graphic description of the state of readiness of the armies, and of the different formations of the battalions, as also of the fierceness of the battle, and the gruesome scene of destruction that followed it. All these are omitted in this translation.—S.V.)

As evening set in, Līlā's husband held a council with his ministers concerning the events of the morning; and then he went to sleep.

The two ladies left the place where they stood watching the fierce battle and travelling like a breath of air, entered into the apartment where the king was asleep.

RĀMA asked:

Holy one, the body seems to be so large and heavy; how does it enter through a minute hole?

VASIṢṬHA replied:

O Rāma, indeed it is impossible for one who is rooted in the idea that he is a physical body to pass through a subtle hole or tube. It is the innermost conviction that "I am the body which is obstructed thus in its movement" that in fact manifests as such obstruction: when the former is absent, the latter is absent, too.

Just as water ever remains water and flows down, and fire does not abandon its nature of rising up, consciousness remains for ever consciousness. But, he who has not understood this does not experience its subtlety or true nature. As is his understanding so is his mind, for it is the understanding that is the mind; yet, its direction can be changed by great effort. Normally, one's actions are in accordance with one's mind, (i.e., one's understanding).

But he who knows that his body is ethereal, how can his movement be obstructed? In truth, everyone's body everywhere is pure consciousness: but on account of an idea that arises in someone's heart, there seems to be all this coming and going. For, the same infinite consciousness is also the individual consciousness (mind) and the cosmic space (material). Therefore the ethereal body can enter anything anywhere, and it goes where the wish of its heart leads.

O Rāma, everyone's consciousness is of this nature and power. In everyone's consciousness there is a different idea of the world. Death and such other experiences are like cosmic dissolution, the night of cosmic consciousness. When that comes to an end everyone wakes up to his own mental creation, which is the materialisation of his ideas, notions and delusions. Even as the cosmic being creates the universe after the cosmic dissolution, the individual creates his own world after his death.

However, divinities like Brahmā, Viṣṇu, and Śiva, as also holy sages, attain final liberation during cosmic dissolution and their creation of the next cycle is not from memory. In the case of other beings, the new creation after the death in the previous one is conditioned by the impressions left in the mind by the various experiences during that life-span.

VASIṢṬHA continued:

Immediately after death, the state in which it may be said that one is neither here nor there, when the consciousness, as it were, slightly opens the eyes though it seems not to do so—that state is known as pradhāna or the material or inert state of consciousness. It is also known as ethereal nature, unmanifest nature; and it is regarded both as sentient and insentient. It is this which is responsible both for memory and its absence, and therefore for the next birth.

When that ethereal nature becomes awakened, and when in its consciousness the ego-sense manifests itself, it gives rise to the five elements (earth, water, fire, air, and ether), space-time continuum and all the rest of the material needed for physical birth and existence. These then condense into their material counterparts. During dreaming and waking states they give rise to the feeling of a physical body. But in fact all this constitutes the ethereal body of the jīva.

When the idea 'I am the body' becomes deeply ingrained, this same ethereal body develops the physical characteristics of a body—like the eyes, etc.—though all this happens only like vibrations or movements in air. Even if all these appear to be real, they are as (un)real as the experience of sexual pleasure in a dream.

Wherever one dies, there itself that jīva sees all this happening. In that space, in that field of consciousness itself, he imagines "This is the world, this am I"; and, believing that he is born, he experiences the world which is nothing but space—he the jīva is space, too! He thinks "He is my father, she is my mother, this is my wealth, I have done this wonderful deed, alas I have sinned." He imagines "I have become a small child, and now I have become a youth," and sees all these in his heart.

This forest, known as creation, arises in the heart of every jīva. Wherever a person dies, there and then he sees this forest. In this manner, countless worlds born in the consciousness of individual jīvas have in time vanished; even so countless Brahmās, Rudras, Viṣṇus and suns have vanished. In this manner, the illusory perception of creation has taken place countless times, is taking place now, and will take place in the future. For all this is non-different from the movement of thought which, again, is not independent of the infinite consciousness. In reality, what is mental activity but consciousness, and that consciousness is the supreme truth.

III:41 VASIṢṬHA continued:

The two ladies entered the apartment of the king like two divinities, resplendent like two moons. By their grace the king's attendants were fast asleep. As they took their seats, the king awoke and beheld them. He sat down and worshipped their lotus-like feet with flowers. Sarasvatī wished that his minister should acquaint Līlā with the king's ancestry: by her will, the minister awoke.

When Sarasvatī asked the king who he was, the minister informed the ladies that he was a descendant of the great king Ikṣvāku, that his father was Nabhoratha who when the son was ten years old had entrusted the kingdom to him and retired to the forest to lead a spiritual life. The king's name was Vidūratha. Sarasvatī then blessed Vidūratha by laying her hand on his head and inspired him to recollect the facts of his own previous lives. Instantly, the king remembered everything and asked Sarasvatī:

"O Goddess, how is it that though it is hardly one day since I died, it seems that I have lived in this body a full seventy years, and how is it that I remember all the things that happened when I was young in this life-span?"

SARASVATĪ replied:

O king, at the very moment of your death and in the very place of your death, all this that you are seeing here manifested. All this is where the holy man Vasiṣṭha lived, in the village on the hill. That is his world, and in that world is the world of king Padma, and in that world of king Padma is the world that you are in. Living in it you think "These are my relations, these are my subjects, these are my ministers, these are my enemies;" you think that you are ruling, you are engaged in religious rites; you think that you have been fighting with your enemies and you were defeated by them; you think you are seeing us, worshipping us, and that you are receiving enlightenment from us; you think "I have overcome all sorrow and I enjoy supreme bliss, I shall be established in the realisation of the absolute."

All this took no time to happen, even as in no time during a dream a whole life's drama is enacted. In reality, you are unborn nor do you die. You see all this, as it were, though you do not see: for when all this is naught other than the infinite consciousness, who sees what? (VIDŪRATHA asked: Then, are not these, my ministers independent beings?) To the enlightened person there is only one infinite consciousness, and there is no notion of 'I am' or 'these are'. While Vasiṣṭha said this, another day came to an end.

SARASVATĪ continued: III:42

To an immature and childish person who is confirmed in his conviction that this world is real, it continues to be real—even as a child who believes in a ghost is haunted by it throughout his life. If a person is enamoured of the appearance of the bracelet, he does not see that it is just gold: he who sees the glory of palaces, elephants and cities does not see the infinite consciousness which alone is true.

This universe is but a long dream. The ego-sense and also the fancy that there are others, are as real as dream-objects. The sole reality is the infinite consciousness which is omnipresent, pure, tranquil, omnipotent, and whose very body and being is absolute consciousness (therefore not an object, not knowable): wherever this consciousness manifests in whatever manner, it is that. Hence when the seer fancies seeing a human being, a human being happens there. Because the substratum (the infinite consciousness) is real, all that is based on it acquires reality, though the reality is of the substratum alone. This universe and all beings in it are but a long dream. To me you are real, and to you I am real; even so the others are real to you or to me. And, this relative reality is like the reality of the dream-objects.

RĀMA asked:

Holy one, in the case of a city which appeared in one's dream, it continues to be if it is a real city: is this what you imply in your teaching?

VASIṢṬHA replied:

You are right, O Rāma. Since the dream of a city etc., is based on the real substratum of infinite consciousness, these dream-objects appear to be real. But, then there is no real difference between the waking state of consciousness and the dream state. What is real in the one is unreal in the other—hence, both these states are essentially of the same nature.

Therefore, the objects of the waking or the dreaming consciousness are equally unreal, except for the infinite consciousness on which they are all superimposed.

After having imparted this teaching to the king, Sarasvatī blessed him and said: "May all auspiciousness attend you. You have seen what is to be seen. Give us leave to go."

Vidūratha said: "Soon, O Goddess, I shall go from here, just as one goes from one dream to another in sleep. Pray, grant that my ministers and my virgin daughter may go with me." Sarasvatī granted his prayer.

III:43 SARASVATĪ said:

O king, you shall die in this war and then you will regain your previous kingdom. After your death in this body, you will come over to the previous city with your daughter and your ministers. We two shall go now as we came; and all of you will of course follow us in due course: for the nature of the motion of a horse, an elephant and a camel is different!

VASIṢṬHA continued:

Even as Sarasvatī was saying this to the king, a royal messenger rushed in to announce that the enemy forces had entered the capital and were destroying it. There was an incendiary raid in progress, and the entire city was ablaze. The two ladies, the king and his ministers moved to a window to witness that dreadful scene.

Looting of the city had commenced; and the robbers were yelling fiercely everywhere. The entire city was enveloped in dense smoke. Fire was raining from the sky. (Anti-aircraft?) missiles described 'half-moon' shaped flaming streaks in the sky. Heavy rock-like missiles (bombs) were falling on the houses, destroying them and the roads around.

The king and the others heard the pitiable cries of the citizens. Everywhere there was weeping and wailing, the heart-rending cries of women and children. Someone was crying, "O dear, this woman has lost her father, mother, brother and her little infant: though she has not perished, the tragedy of her life is burning her heart." Another shouted: "Get out of that house quickly; it is about to collapse." Yet another: "Look, bombs and weapons rain into every house." Missiles were raining like the downpour that precedes cosmic dissolution. All the trees around the houses had been burnt and the whole place looked desolate. What looked like elephants had been propelled into the air from the battlefield and they were raining fire on the city. And, there were roadblocks everywhere. Bound by attachment, men tarried in burning houses looking for their wives and children. Even women of the royal household were being dragged about by the invading soldiers. Weeping and wailing, these noble ladies did not know what to do. They cried: "Alas, who will help us in this terrible situation?" and they were surrounded by soldiers.

Such is the glory of sovereignty, kingdoms and empires.*

VASIṢṬHA continued: III:44

In the meantime, the queen arrived there. The lady-in-waiting announced her to the king. She said: "Your Majesty, all the other ladies of the harem have been violently dragged away by the enemy. From this indescribable calamity that has befallen us, only Your Majesty can redeem us."

The king bowed to Sarasvatī and excused himself, "I shall myself go to the battlefront, O Goddess, to deal with the enemy; and this, my wife, will wait upon you during that time."

The enlightened Līlā was amazed to see that the queen was a complete replica of herself. She asked Sarasvatī: "O Divinity, how is it that she is exactly what I am? Whatever I was in my own youth, she is now. What is the secret of this? Also: all these ministers, etc., who are here, are the same that were there, in our palace. If they are but a reflection or the objects of our fancy, are they sentient and are they also endowed with consciousness?"

SARASVATĪ replied:

O Līlā, whatever vision arises within oneself, that is immediately experienced. Consciousness (as subject) itself becomes, as it were, the object of knowledge. When in consciousness the image of the world arises, at that very instant, it becomes so. Time, space, duration and objectivity do not arise from matter; for then they would be material. What is reflected in one's consciousness shines outside also.

What is regarded as the real objective world experienced in the waking state is no more real than that experienced during sleep (dream). During sleep, the world does not exist; and during the waking state, the dream does not exist! Even so, death contradicts life: while living, death is non-existent, and in death, life is non-existent. Because, that which holds together either experience is absent in the other.

One cannot say that either is real, or unreal, but one can only say that their substratum alone is real. The universe exists in Brahman only as a word, an idea. It is neither real nor unreal: just as a snake-

---

* The description is astonishing and resembles modern warfare and bombing of civilians.

in-the-rope is neither real nor unreal. Even so is the existence of the jīva. This jīva experiences its own wishes. It fancies that it experiences what it had experienced before; and some others are new experiences. They are similar at times and dissimilar at times. All these experiences, though essentially unreal, appear to be real. Such is the nature of these ministers and others. Even so this Līlā exists as the product of the reflection in consciousness. Even so are you, me and all others. Know this and rest in peace.

III:45, 46 THE SECOND LĪLĀ said to Sarasvatī:

O Divinity, I used to worship Sarasvatī and she used to appear to me in my dreams. You look exactly like her: I presume that you are Śarasvatī. I humbly beg of you to grant me a boon—when my husband dies on the battlefield, may I accompany him to whichever realm he goes, in this very body of mine.

SARASVATĪ replied:

O dear lady, you have worshipped me for a long time with intense devotion: therefore, I grant you the boon sought by you.

THE FIRST LĪLĀ thereupon said to Sarasvatī:

Truly, your words never fail, your wish always comes true. Pray, tell me why you did not allow me to travel from one plane of consciousness to another with the same body.

SARASVATĪ replied:

My dear Līlā, I do not really do anything to anyone. Every jīva earns its own state by its own deeds. I am merely the deity presiding over the intelligence of every being; I am the power of its consciousness and its life-force. Whatever form the energy of the living being takes within itself, that alone comes to fruition in course of time. You longed for liberation, and you obtained it. You may consider it the fruit of your austerity or worship of the deity; but it is consciousness alone that bestows the fruit upon you—even as the fruit that seems to fall from the sky really falls from the tree.

VASIṢṬHA continued:

As they were talking among themselves like this, the king Vidūratha ascended his resplendent chariot and proceeded to the battlefront. Unfortunately, he had not assessed the relative strength of his and the enemy's forces right up to the moment he actually entered into the enemy ranks.

The two Līlās, Sarasvatī, as also the princess who had received the blessings of Sarasvatī, were watching the terrible war from their apartment in the palace.

The sky was crowded with the missiles from both the armies. The battle-cries of the warriors were heard everywhere. There was a pall of smoke and dust over the entire city.

Even as the king Vidūratha entered the ranks of the enemy, there was an intense tut-tut sound of intense crossfire. As the missiles collided, there were sounds like khut-khut, tuk-tuk, jhun-jhun.

THE SECOND LĪLĀ asked Sarasvatī: III:47-50

O Goddess, please tell me, why is it that though we are blessed by you, my husband cannot win the battle?

SARASVATĪ replied:

No doubt, I was adored by king Vidūratha for a considerable time; but he did not pray for victory in battle. Being the consciousness that dwells in the understanding of every person, I bestow upon that person that which he seeks. Whatever it be that a person asks of me, I bestow upon him that fruit: it is but natural that fire gives you heat. He had asked for liberation; and he shall attain liberation.

On the other hand, the king of Sindhu worshipped me, and prayed for victory in battle. Hence, the king Vidūratha will be slain in battle, and he will rejoin you both and in course of time will attain liberation. This king of Sindhu will win the war and will rule the country as the victorious monarch.

VASIṢṬHA continued:

As the ladies were witnessing the battle, the sun rose in the eastern horizon, as if eager to witness the concluding phase of this terrible battle. Surrounded by a thousand soldiers each, the two kings fought each other. Their missiles had several different shapes and sizes. Some of them, though they were single-headed when they left the ground, multiplied into a thousand in the air and rained literally in tens of thousands when they hit their target.

Both the kings were well matched in strength and valour: Vidūratha's was inborn, while the strength of the enemy was derived from a boon he had obtained from lord Nārāyaṇa. While they fought, their armies watched dumbfounded.

At one stage, when it looked as though Vidūratha was winning, the second Līlā was highly elated and pointed him out to Sarasvatī; but the very next moment, the enemy emerged unscathed. For every deadly missile of one the other used a countermissile. The missile that created depression was countered by one that inspired the warriors. The serpent-missile had its antidote. The water-missile was met with the fire-missile. And the Viṣṇu-missile was used by both the kings.

Both the kings lost their vehicles, and they continued to fight standing on the ground. As Vidūratha was about to ascend a new one he was cut down by the king of Sindhu. Vidūratha's body was soon brought to the palace which the pursuing enemy could not enter on account of Sarasvatī's presence.

III:51, 52 VASIṢṬHA continued:

Soon after the king Vidūratha fell, there was utter post-war confusion and chaos in the city. The king of Sindhu announced that his son would be the new ruler. There was great rejoicing among his subjects and his ministers quickly got ready for the coronation. Immediately the new administration proclaimed martial law in the new state, which restored peace and order to it.

Seeing Vidūratha fall, the second Līlā fell down unconscious. The first Līlā said to Sarasvatī: "O Goddess, see, this my husband is about to give up the ghost."

SARASVATĪ said:

Dear one, all this terrible war, this destruction and death, are as real as a dream; for there is neither a kingdom nor the earth. All this took place in the house of the holy man Vasiṣṭha on top of the hill. This palace and this battlefield and all the rest of it is nowhere but the inner apartments of your own palace. In fact, the entire universe is there. For, within the house of the holy man is the world of the king Padma; and within the palace of that king in that world is all that you have seen here. All this is mere fancy, hallucination. What is, is the sole reality—which is neither created nor destroyed. It is that infinite consciousness that is perceived by the ignorant as the universe.

Just as a whole city exists within the dreamer, the three worlds exist in a small atom; surely, there are atoms in those worlds, and each one of those atoms also contains the three worlds.

The other Līlā who fell down unconscious has already reached that world in which your husband Padma's body is lying.

LĪLĀ asked:

O Goddess, tell me: how did she go there already, and what are the people there telling her?

SARASVATĪ replied: Just as both of you are the fancied objects of the king, even so the king himself and I are dream-objects. One who knows this gives up looking for 'objects of perception'. In the infinite consciousness we have created each other in our fancy. The other youthful Līlā was indeed yourself. She worshipped me and prayed that she would never be widowed: hence, before the king Vidūratha died she left this place. Dear one, you are all individualised cosmic consciousness, but I am the cosmic consciousness: and I make all these things happen.

III:53 VASIṢṬHA continued:

O Rāma, the second Līlā who had obtained a boon from Sarasvatī rose into the sky and there met her daughter. The girl introduced herself to Līlā. And, Līlā requested her to guide her to where her husband the king was. The girl thereupon flew away with her mother.

First, they passed through the region of the clouds, then they passed through the region of air. Beyond that they went through the orbit of the sun into the starry heaven. They proceeded still further to the realms of Brahmā the creator, Viṣṇu, and Śiva, and after all that into the summit of the universe. They were able to do all this even as the coolness of ice is able to radiate from the ice-jar without breaking it. Of course, Līlā who had an ethereal body composed of materialised thought, experienced all this within herself.

Passing beyond even this universe, Līlā crossed over the oceans and other elements that envelop this universe, and entered into the infinite consciousness. In that infinite consciousness there are countless universes which do not know of one another's existence.

Līlā entered one of those universes in which lay the body of king Padma covered with a heap of flowers. She again passed through the regions of the gods (Brahmā, etc.), entered the city and the palace in which the body lay. But, alas, when she looked around she could not see her daughter—who had disappeared mysteriously. She recognised the king as her husband and thought that having died a warrior's glorious death on the battlefield he had ascended to the hero's heaven. She thought "By the grace of Sarasvatī, I have physically reached this place. I am the most blessed among persons." She began to fan the king's body.

THE FIRST LĪLĀ asked Sarasvatī: Seeing her, what did the servants of the king do?

SARASVATĪ answered: The king, the servants of the royal household and all the rest of them, are only infinite consciousness. However, since the substratum is the reflection of the infinite consciousness which is real, and since there is a conviction in the order of fanciful creation, they recognise one another. The husband says, "She is my wife" and the wife says, "He is my husband".

She could not go in her own physical body to the new realm because light cannot co-exist with darkness, and as long as there is in oneself the blind notion of ignorance, wisdom does not arise. When the wisdom concerning one's ethereal body arises, the physical body ceases to be recognised as true. This is the fruit of the boon that I granted her. The recipient of the boon thinks, "Just as you have made me think by your boon, so I am". Therefore, she thinks she has reached her husband's abode in her physical body. One may ignorantly see a snake in the rope; but the rope cannot behave like a snake.

III:54 SARASVATĪ said:

Only one who has arrived at wisdom can ascend to the ethereal realms, O Līlā, not others. This Līlā does not possess such wisdom; hence, she only fancied that she had reached the city where her husband dwelt.

THE ENLIGHTENED LĪLĀ said:

Let that be as you say, O Goddess. But, please tell me: how did the objects acquire their characteristics—like heat in fire, coolness in ice, solidity of earth? How did the world order (niyati) first arise, as also birth and death?

SARASVATĪ said:

Dear one, during the cosmic dissolution, the entire universe having disappeared, only the infinite Brahman remains in peace. This infinite being of the nature of consciousness feels 'I am' and then 'I am an atom of light'. Thus it experiences the truth of that statement within itself. It also fancies the existence within itself of the diverse creatures: and since its nature is pure and absolute consciousness, that fanciful creation appears to be a real creation, with objects of diverse characteristics in strict accord with the fancy of the infinite consciousness.

Whatever, wherever and however was conceived or fancied by the infinite consciousness during that first creation, all that has remained there and in that manner and with those characteristics even now. Thus was a definite order brought into being here.

In fact, this order is inherent in infinite consciousness. All these objects and their characteristics were potentially present in it even during the cosmic dissolution: into what else could they dissolve? Moreover, how can something become nothing? Gold that appears as bracelet cannot become formless entirely.

Thus, although all the elements of this creation are utter emptiness, yet whatever element was conceived of in the beginning with whatever characteristic, such order has persisted until now. All this is only from the relative point of view: for, the universe has not been created at all, and whatever is, is the infinite consciousness and naught else. It is the nature of appearance to appear to be real, even though it is unreal.

Such is the order (niyati) in the universe, that nothing until now has been able to alter it. It was the infinite consciousness itself that thought of all these elements within itself and it experienced them within itself, and that experience appears to have materialised.

SARASVATĪ continued:

According to the order that existed in the first creation human beings were endowed with a life-span of one, two, three or four hundred years. The shortening or the lengthening of the life-span is dependent upon the purity or impurity of the following factors—country, time, activity, and the materials used and consumed. He who adheres to the injunctions of the scriptures enjoys the life-span guaranteed by those scriptures. Thus, the person lives a long or short life and reaches its end.

THE ENLIGHTENED LĪLĀ said: O Goddess, kindly enlighten me concerning death: is it pleasant or unpleasant, and what happens after death?

SARASVATĪ said:

There are three types of human beings, my dear: the fool, one who is practising concentration and meditation, and the yogi (or intelligent one). The two latter types of human beings abandon the body by the practice of the yoga of concentration and meditation and depart at their sweet will and pleasure. But, the fool who has not practised concentration or meditation, being at the mercy of forces outside himself, experiences great anguish at the approach of death.

This fool experiences a terrible burning sensation within himself. His breathing becomes hard and laboured. His body becomes discoloured. He enters into dense darkness and sees the stars during the day. He gets dizzy. He is confused in his vision: he sees the earth as space and the sky as the solid earth. He experiences all sorts of delirious sensations—that he is falling into a well, entering into a stone, riding a fast vehicle, melting away like snow, being dragged with a rope, floating away like a blade of grass, etc. He wishes to express his suffering, but is unable to do so. Gradually, his senses lose their power; and he is unable even to think. Therefore he sinks in unwisdom and ignorance.

THE ENLIGHTENED LĪLĀ asked: Though every person is endowed with the eight limbs, why does he experience all this agony and ignorance?

SARASVATĪ replied:

Such is the order established in the beginning of creation by the infinite consciousness. When life-breath does not flow freely, the person ceases to live. But all this is imaginary. How can infinite consciousness cease to be? The person is nothing but infinite consciousness. Who dies and when, to whom does this infinite consciousness belong and how? Even when millions of bodies die, this consciousness exists undiminished.

THE ENLIGHTENED LĪLĀ said: III:55

Kindly proceed with your discourse on birth and death: listening to it again will certainly deepen my wisdom.

SARASVATĪ said:

When there is cessation of the flow of the life-breath, the consciousness of the individual becomes utterly passive. Please remember, O Līlā, that consciousness is pure, eternal and infinite: it does not arise nor cease to be. It is ever there in the moving and unmoving creatures, in the sky, on the mountain and in fire and air. When life-breath ceases, the body is said to be 'dead' or 'inert'. The life-breath returns to its source—air—and consciousness freed from memory and tendencies remains as the self.

That atomic ethereal particle which is possessed of these memories and tendencies is known as the jīva: and it remains there itself, in the space where the dead body is. And they refer to it as 'preta' (departed soul). That jīva now abandons its ideas and what it had been seeing till then, and perceives other things as in dreaming or day-dreaming.

After a momentary lapse of consciousness, the jīva begins to fancy that it sees another body, another world and another life-span.

O Līlā, there are six categories of such 'departed souls': bad, worse and worst sinners; good, better, best of virtuous ones. Of course, there are sub-divisions among these, too. (In the case of some of the worst sinners, the momentary lapse of consciousness may last a considerable time.)

The worst among the sinners undergo terrible sufferings in hell and then are born in countless living species, before they see the end of their agony. They might even exist as trees for a long time.

The middling among sinners also suffer lapse of consciousness for a considerable time; and then are born as worms and animals.

The light sinners are soon reborn as human beings.

The best among the righteous ascend to heaven and enjoy life there. Later they are born in good and affluent families on earth.

The middling among the righteous go to the region of the celestials, and return to the earth as children of brāhmaṇas, etc.

Even the righteous among the departed ones, after enjoying such heavenly pleasures, have to pass through the realms of the demi-gods to suffer the consequences of the iniquities they might have committed.

SARASVATĪ continued:

All these departed souls experience within themselves the fruition of their own past actions. At first there is the notion 'I am dead', and then 'I am being carried away by the messengers of the god of death'. The righteous among them fancy that they are taken to heaven; and the ordinary sinners fancy that they are standing in the court of the god of death where, with the help of Citragupta (the hidden record of one's deeds), they are being tried and judged for their past life.

Whatever the jīva sees, that the jīva experiences. For in this empty space of infinite consciousness there is nothing known as time, action, etc. Then the jīva fancies, 'The god of death has sent me to heaven (or hell)' and 'I have enjoyed (or suffered) the pleasures (or tortures) of heaven (or hell)', and 'I am born as animal, etc., as ordained by the god of death'.

At that moment, the jīva enters into the body of the male through the food eaten; it is then transferred to the female and delivered into this world, where it undergoes life again in accordance with the fruition of past actions. There it grows and wanes like the moon. Once again it undergoes senility and death. This goes on again and again till the jīva is enlightened by self-knowledge.

THE ENLIGHTENED LĪLĀ asked:

O Goddess, but please tell me how all this began in the very beginning.

SARASVATĪ replied:

The mountains, the forests, the earth and the sky—all these are but infinite consciousness. That alone is the very being of all, the reality in all; and hence that pure infinite consciousness appeared to become whatever form it took whenever it manifested itself. Till now it continues to be so. When the life-breath enters into the bodies and begins to vibrate the various parts of the bodies, it is said that those bodies are living. Such living bodies existed right in the beginning of creation. When those bodies into which the life-breath had entered did not vibrate, they were known as trees and plants. It is indeed a small part of the infinite consciousness that becomes the intelligence in these bodies. This intelligence, entering into the bodies, brings into being the different organs like the eyes.

Whatever this consciousness thinks it is, it takes that form. Thus, this self of all exists in all bodies, with motion as the characteristic of moving bodies, immovability as the characteristic of the immovable bodies. Thus do all these bodies continue to be even now.

SARASVATĪ continued:

When that intelligence, which is part of the infinite consciousness, fancied itself to be a tree, it became a tree; or a rock, it became a rock; or grass, it became grass. There is no distinction between the sentient and the insentient, between inert and intelligent: there is no difference at all in the essence of substances, for the infinite consciousness is present everywhere equally. The differences are only due to the intelligence identifying itself as different substances. The same infinite consciousness is known by different names in these different substances. In the same way, it is the same infinite consciousness that the intelligence identifies as the worms, ants and birds. In it there is no comparison, nor a sense of difference: just as the people living in the north pole do not know (and therefore do not contrast themselves with) the people of the south pole. Each independent substance identified as such by this intelligence exists by itself, without distinction from the other substances. Ascribing distinctions to them as 'sentient' and 'insentient' is like a frog born in a rock and a frog born outside it considering themselves different, one insentient and the other sentient!

The intelligence which is a part of the infinite consciousness is everywhere, and it is everything: whatever that intelligence thought of as itself, it became that in the very beginning of creation and so it has remained ever since.

It thought of itself as space, it thought of itself as the moving air, it thought of itself as the insentient, it thought of itself as the sentient beings. All this is nothing but the fancy of that intelligence. Such appearance is not the reality, though it appears to be real.

O Līlā, I think that now the king Vidūratha wishes to enter into the heart of the body of king Padma. He is proceeding towards it.

THE ENLIGHTENED LĪLĀ said:

O Goddess, let us also proceed in the same direction.

SARASVATĪ said:

Tuning himself to the ego-principle in the heart of Padma, Vidūratha fancies that he is proceeding to another world. Let us proceed along our own paths: one cannot tread the path of another!

III:56 VASIṢṬHA continued:

In the meantime, the life-breath left the body of the king Vidūratha even as birds abandon a tree that is about to fall. His intelligence rose into space, in an ethereal form. Līlā and Sarasvatī saw this and followed it. In a few moments, that ethereal form became conscious, when the period of post-mortem unconsciousness came to an end. And, the king fancied that he saw even the gross form which had been put together by the funeral rites performed by his relatives.

With this he travelled towards the south and reached the abode of the god of death, who declared that the king had not committed any sinful action at all and ordered his messengers to let him enter his own previous body (of Padma) which lay embalmed.

Instantly, the jīva of Vidūratha crossed over to the other universe in which Padma's body lay, and reached the palace. Obviously Vidūratha had been linked with Padma's body through the ego-sense of the latter, even as a man travelling in distant countries is still attached to the place where he has buried his treasure!

RĀMA asked:

O Holy sir, if one's relatives fail to perform the funeral rites properly, then how can that one obtain the ethereal form?

VASIṢṬHA answered:

Whether the funeral rites had been duly performed or not, if the departed one believes that they have been performed, he gets the benefit of the ethereal form. This is a well-known truth: whatever be one's consciousness, that one is. Things (objects or substances) come into being on account of one's fancy (thought or idea); and one's fancy also arises from the things. Poison turns into nectar through one's fancy (or faith); even so, an unreal object or substance becomes real when such intense faith is present. Without a cause no effect is produced anywhere at any time; and therefore there is no fancy or thought either. Hence, but for the one causeless infinite consciousness nothing whatsoever has ever arisen or been created. Rest assured of this.

If the funeral rites are performed by one's relatives with the right faith it helps the intelligence of the departed soul, unless the latter is overpoweringly vicious.

Let us return to the palace of king Padma. As I said, Līlā and Sarasvatī re-entered that beautiful palace and the room in which the embalmed body of Padma had been kept. All the royal attendants were fast asleep.

VASIṢṬHA continued: III:57

There, seated near the body of king Padma they saw the second Līlā who was devoutly fanning the king. The first Līlā and Sarasvatī saw her, but she did not see them.

RĀMA asked:

It was said that the first Līlā had temporarily left her body near the king and travelled with Sarasvatī in an ethereal body: but now the first Līlā's body is not mentioned at all.

VASIṢṬHA replied:

When the first Līlā became enlightened, the egoistic fancy of her ethereal real being abandoned its links with the gross physical form, and it melted away like snow. In fact, it was Līlā's ignorant fancy that made it appear as if she had a physical body. It was as if one dreams and thinks "I am a deer": on waking up and finding the deer missing, does one go about searching for it? In the mind of the deluded the unreal manifests itself; and when the delusion has been dispelled (like the realisation that it is rope and not snake!) there is no longer an ignorant fancy. This fanciful conviction that the unreal is real is deep-rooted by repeated imagination.

Even without destroying it, one can move from one ethereal body to another, just as in dream one can take one form after another without abandoning the previous one. The yogi's body is truly invisible, ethereal, even though it appears to be visible in the eyes of the ignorant beholder. And, it is such a beholder who, on account of his own ignorance, thinks and says, "This yogi is dead". For, where is the body, what exists and what dies? That which is—is: only delusion vanished!

RĀMA asked: Holy sir, does a yogi's physical body then become an ethereal body?

VASIṢṬHA replied:

How many times I have told you, O Rāma: yet you do not grasp it! The ethereal body alone is: by persistent fancy, it appears to be linked to a physical body. Just as when an ignorant man (who thinks he is the physical body) dies and the body is cremated, has a subtle body, even so the yogi on being enlightened while living, has an ethereal body.

The physical body is only the creation of one's ignorant fancy, and is not real. There is no difference between the body and the ignorance. To think they are two—this indeed is saṃsāra (repetitive history).

III:58 VASIṢṬHA continued:

In the meantime, Sarasvatī restrained Vidūratha's jīva from entering into the body of king Padma.

THE ENLIGHTENED LĪLĀ asked Sarasvatī:

O Goddess, from the time I sat here in contemplation till now, how much time has elapsed?

SARASVATĪ replied:

Dear one, it is a month since you entered into contemplation. During the first fifteen days, your body, on account of the heat generated by prāṇāyāma, became vaporised. Then it became like a dry leaf and fell down. Then it became rigid and cold. The ministers then thought that you had died of your own accord and cremated that body. Now, on account of your own wish you appear here in your ethereal body. In you there are no memories of past life nor latent tendencies brought forward from previous incarnation. For when the intelligence is established in the conviction of its ethereal nature, the body is forgotten, even as in youth one forgets life as a foetus. Today is the thirty-first day and you are here. Come, let us reveal ourselves to this other Līlā.

When the second Līlā saw them before her, she fell at their feet and worshipped them.

SARASVATĪ asked her: Tell us how you came here.

THE SECOND LĪLĀ replied:

When I fainted in the palace of Vidūratha, I did not know anything for some time. I then saw that my subtle body rose to the sky and was seated in an aerial vehicle which brought me here. And, I saw that Vidūratha was lying here asleep in a garden of flowers. I thought he was fatigued from battle and without disturbing him, I fan him.

Sarasvatī immediately let Vidūratha's jīva enter the body. The king at once awoke as if from slumber. The two Līlās bowed to him.

The king asked the enlightened Līlā, "Who are you, who is she, and from where has she come?"

The enlightened Līlā replied: "Lord, I am your wife in your previous incarnation and your constant companion, even as a word and its meaning are. This Līlā is your other wife; she is my own reflection, created by me for your pleasure. And, she who is seated on yonder golden throne is the goddess Sarasvatī herself. She is present here on account of our great good fortune."

Hearing this, the king sat up and saluted Sarasvatī. Sarasvatī blessed him with long life, wealth and so on, and enlightenment.

VASIṢṬHA continued: III:59, 60

After granting the desired boons to the king, Sarasvatī vanished at that spot. The king and the queen fondly embraced each other. The royal attendants who were guarding the king's body woke up and rejoiced that the king had come back to life.

There was great rejoicing in the state. People far and wide recounted for a long time how the queen Līlā returned from the other world with another Līlā as a gift to the king. The king heard from the enlightened Līlā all that took place during the previous month. He continued to rule and enjoy the blessings of the three worlds through the grace of Sarasvatī, which he had no doubt earned by his own self-effort.

Thus is the story of Līlā, O Rāma, which I have narrated in detail to you: contemplation of this story will remove from your mind the least faith in the reality of what is perceived. Truly, if only that which is true can be removed, how can one remove what is unreal? There is nothing to be removed, for all that appears to be in your eyes (the earth, etc.) is nothing but the infinite consciousness; and if something has been created even that has taken place by it, within it itself. Everything is as it is; nothing has ever been created. You may say that what appears to be is the creation of Māyā, but then Māyā itself is not real!

RĀMA said:

Lord, what a grand vision of the ultimate truth you have given me! But, Holy one, there is an insatiable hunger in me for the nectar of your enlightening words. Pray, explain to me the mystery of time: in the story of Līlā sometimes a whole life-time was spent in eight days, sometimes in one month. I am puzzled. Are there different time-scales in different universes?

VASIṢṬHA replied:

O Rāma, whatever one thinks within oneself in his own intelligence, that alone is experienced by him. Even nectar is experienced as poison by him who fancies it is poison. Friends become enemies and enemies become friends, depending upon one's inner attitude. The object is experienced by one strictly in accordance with one's inner feeling. To a suffering person a night is an epoch; and a night of revelry passes like a moment. In dream a moment is non-different from an epoch. A life-time of Manu is but an hour and a half to Brahmā; Brahmā's life-time is a day of Viṣṇu. Viṣṇu's life-span is Śiva's day. But to the sage whose consciousness has overcome limitations, there is neither day nor night.

VASIṢṬHA continued:

The yogi knows that it is one's own mentality that turns sweet things into bitter things and vice versa, and friends into enemies and vice versa. In the same way, by changing the angle of vision and by persistent practice one can develop a taste for the study of scriptures and for japa, etc., which were uninteresting earlier. For these qualities are not in the objects but only in one's own thinking: just as a sea-sick man sees the world go round, the ignorant man thinks that these qualities abide in the objects. A drunken man sees empty space where a wall stands; and a non-existent goblin kills a deluded person.

This world is nothing but a mere vibration of consciousness in space. It seems to exist even as a goblin seems to exist in the eyes of the ignorant. All this is but Māyā: for there is no contradiction between the infinite consciousness and the apparent existence of the universe. It is like a marvellous dream of a person who is awake.

O Rāma, in the autumn the trees shed their leaves; in springtime the same trees sprout new leaves which were surely within the trees themselves. Even so this creation exists all the time within the absolute consciousness. It is not seen: even as the liquidity that exists in gold is not always evident. If the creator of one epoch attains liberation and if the creator in the next epoch projects the new universe from his memory, even that memory is none other than the infinite consciousness.

RĀMA asked:

Lord, how is it that the king and also the citizens experienced the same objective facts?

VASIṢṬHA replied:

That is because the intelligence of all the jīvas is based upon the one infinite consciousness, O Rāma. The citizens, too, thought that he was their king. Thought-vibrations are natural and inherent in the infinite consciousness and they are not motivated. Even as it is natural for a diamond to sparkle, the king's intelligence thinks "I am king Vidūratha" and so do all the beings in the universe. If one's intelligence is established in this truth concerning the infinite consciousness, it reaches the supreme state of liberation. This depends upon one's own intensity of self-effort. A man is pulled in two different directions: towards the realisation of Brahman the absolute and towards the ignorant acceptance of the reality of the world. That which he strives to realise with great intensity wins! Once he overcomes ignorance, the deluded vision of the unreal is for ever dispelled.

RĀMA asked: III:61

Holy sir, please tell me briefly again: how does the delusion of the notions of 'I' and 'the world' arise in the first place, without any cause?

VASIṢṬHA replied:

As all things are equally indwelt by intelligence, so at all times in every way the uncreated is all, the self of all. We use the expression 'all things': it is only a figure of speech, for only the infinite consciousness or Brahman exists. Just as there is no division between a bracelet and gold, no division between waves and water, there is no division between the universe and the infinite consciousness. The latter alone is the universe; the universe as such is not the infinite consciousness, just as the bracelet is made of gold but gold is not made of bracelet. Just as we refer to a man and his limbs as being one and the same, we refer to the presence of the infinite consciousness as all beings, which does not imply a division in it.

In that infinite consciousness there is an inherent non-recognition of its infinite nature. That appears to manifest as 'I' and 'the world'. Just as there is an image in a marble slab, even if it has not been carved, even so this notion of 'I' and 'the world' exists in the infinite consciousness. Even as in a calm sea the waves exist in their potential state, the world exists in its potential state in the infinite consciousness: and that is known as its creation. The word 'creation' has no other connotation. No creation takes place in the supreme being or the infinite consciousness; and the infinite consciousness is not involved in the creation. They do not stand in a divided relationship to each other.

This infinite consciousness regards its own intelligence in its own heart, as it were, though it is non-different from it even as wind is non-different from its own movement. At that very moment, when there is an unreal division, there arises in that consciousness the notion of space, which, on account of the power of the consciousness, appears as the element known as space or ether. That itself later believes itself to be air and then fire. From this notion there arises the appearance of fire and light. That itself further entertains the notion of water with its inherent faculty of taste; and that itself believes itself to be the earth with its inherent faculty of smell and also its characteristic of solidity. Thus do the water and the earth elements appear to have manifested themselves.

VASIṢṬHA continued:

At the same time, the same infinite consciousness held in itself the notion of a unit of time equal to one-millionth of the twinkling of an eye: and from this evolved the time-scale right up to an epoch consisting of several revolutions of the four ages, which is the life-span of one cosmic creation. The infinite consciousness itself is uninvolved in these: for it is devoid of rising and setting (which are essential to all time-scales), and it is devoid of a beginning, middle and end.

That infinite consciousness alone is the reality, ever awake and enlightened: and with creation also it is the same. That infinite consciousness alone is the unenlightened appearance of this creation: and even after this creation it is the same always. It is ever the same. When one realises in the self by the self that consciousness is the absolute Brahman, then he experiences it as all—even as the one energy dwelling in all his limbs.

One can say that this world-appearance is real only so far as it is the manifestation of consciousness and because of direct experience; and it is unreal when it is grasped with the mind and the sense-organs. Wind is perceived as real in its motion, and it appears to be non-existent when there is no motion: even so this world-appearance can be regarded both as real and unreal. This mirage-like appearance of the three worlds exists as non-different from the absolute Brahman.

The creation exists in Brahman just as the sprout exists in the seed, liquidity in water, sweetness in milk, and pungency in capsicum; but in ignorance it appears to be different from and independent of Brahman. There is no cause for the world's existence as a pure reflection in the absolute Brahman. When there is notion of creation, the creation seems to be: and when, through self-effort, there is understanding of non-creation, there is no world.

Nothing has ever been created anywhere at any time; and nothing comes to an end either. The absolute Brahman is all, the supreme peace, unborn, pure consciousness and permanent. Worlds within worlds appear in every atom. What can be the cause and how do these arise?!

As and when one turns away from the notions of 'I' and the 'world', one is liberated: the notion of 'I am this' is the sole bondage here. They who know the infinite consciousness as the nameless, formless substratum of the universe, gain victory over saṃsāra (repetitive history).

RĀMA asked: III:62, 63

It is evident that Brahman alone exists, O Holy sage! But, then why do even these sages and men of wisdom exist in this world, as if so ordained by god—and what is god?

VASIṢṬHA replied:

There does exist, O Rāma, the power or energy of the infinite consciousness, which is in motion all the time; that alone is the reality of all inevitable futuristic events, for it penetrates all the epochs in time. It is by that power that the nature of every object in the universe is ordained. That power (cit śakti) is also known as Mahāsattā (the great existence), Mahāciti (the great intelligence), Mahāśakti (the great power), Mahādṛṣṭi (the great vision), Mahākriyā (the great doer or doing), Mahodbhavā (the great becoming), Mahāspandā (the great vibration). It is this power that endows every thing with its characteristic quality. But this power is not different from or independent of the absolute Brahman: it is as real as a pie in the sky. Sages make a verbal distinction between Brahman and the power and declare that creation is the work of that power.

The distinction is verbal, even as one speaks of the body (as a whole) and its parts. The infinite consciousness becomes aware of its inherent power, even as one becomes aware of the limbs of his body: such awareness is known as niyati (the power of the absolute that determines nature). It is also known as daiva or divine dispensation.

That you should ask me these questions is ordained by niyati; and that you should act upon my teaching is also ordained by niyati. If one says, 'The divine will feed me' and remains idle, that also is the work of niyati. This niyati cannot be set aside even by gods like Rudra. But, wise men should not give up self-effort because of this, for niyati functions only as and through self-effort. This niyati has two aspects, human and superhuman: the former is seen where self-effort bears fruit and the latter where it does not.

If one remains idle, depending upon niyati to do everything for him, he soon discovers that his life departs—for life is action. He can, by entering into the highest superconscious state, stop the breath and attain liberation: but then that is indeed the greatest self-effort!

The infinite consciousness alone appears as one thing in one place and another in another place. There is no division between that consciousness and its power, as there is no division between wave and water, limbs and the body. Such division is experienced only by the ignorant.

III:64, 65 RĀMA asked:

When the only reality is the infinite consciousness and its own inherent kinetic power, how does the jīva acquire an apparent reality in the secondless unity?

VASIṢṬHA replied:

In the mind of the ignorant alone does this terrible goblin known as jīva arise as a reflected reality or appearance. No one, not even the men of wisdom or sages can definitely say what it is: because it is devoid of any indications of its nature.

In the mirror of infinite consciousness countless reflections are seen, which constitute the appearance of the world. These are the jīvas. Jīva is like unto just a little agitation on the surface of the ocean of Brahman; or just a little movement of the flame of a candle in a windless room. When, in that slight agitation the infinitude of the infinite consciousness is veiled, limitation of consciousness appears to arise. This too is inherent in that infinite consciousness. And that limitation of consciousness is known as the jīva.

Just as when a spark from a flame comes into contact with flammable substance it bursts into an independent flame, even so this limitation of consciousness, when it is fed by latent tendencies and memories, condenses into egotism—'I'-ness. This I-ness is not a solid reality: but the jīva sees it as real, like the blueness of the sky. When the egotism begins to entertain its own notions, it gives rise to the mind-stuff, the concept of an independent and separate jīva, mind, Māyā or cosmic illusion, cosmic nature, etc.

The intelligence which entertains these notions conjures up the natural elements (earth, water, fire, air and space). Associated with these, the same intelligence becomes a spark of light, though it is the cosmic light in truth. It then condenses into countless forms—somewhere it becomes a tree, etc., somewhere a bird, etc., somewhere it becomes a goblin, etc., somewhere it becomes demi-gods, etc. The first of such modifications becomes the creator Brahmā and creates others, by thought and will. Thus the vibration in consciousness alone is the jīva, karma, god; and all the rest follows.

Creation (of the mind) is but agitation in consciousness; and the world exists in the mind! It seems to exist because of imperfect vision, imperfect understanding. It is really not more than a long dream. If this is understood, then all duality will come to an end, and Brahman, jīva, mind, Māyā, doer, action, and the world will all be seen as synonymous with the one non-dual infinite consciousness.

VASIṢṬHA continued: III:66, 67

The one never became many, O Rāma. When many candles are kindled from another, it is the same flame which burns in all candles; even so, the one Brahman appears to be many. When one contemplates the unreality of this diversity, he is freed from sorrow.

Jīva is nothing more than the limitation of consciousness; when the limitation goes, there is peace—even as for one who wears shoes the whole world is paved with leather. What is this world? Nothing but an appearance, even as a plantain stem is nothing but leaves. Even as liquor is able to make one see all sorts of phantasms in the empty sky, mind is able to make one see diversity in unity. Even as a drunkard sees a tree moving, the ignorant one sees movement in this world.

When the mind perceives duality, then there is both duality and its counterpart which is unity. When the mind drops the perception of duality, there is neither duality nor unity. When one is firmly established in the oneness of the infinite consciousness, whether he is quiet or actively engaged in work, then he is considered to be at peace with himself. When one is thus established in the supreme state, it is also known as the state of non-self or the state of knowledge of the void or emptiness.

On account of the agitation of the mind, consciousness appears to become the object of knowledge! Then there arise in the mind all sorts of false notions like 'I am born' etc. Such knowledge is not different from the mind. Hence it is known as ignorance or delusion.

To rid oneself of the disease of this saṃsāra or world-appearance, there is no remedy but wisdom or self-knowledge. Knowledge alone is the cure for the wrong perception of a snake in the rope. When there is such knowledge, then there is no craving in the mind for sense-pleasure which aggravates the ignorance. Hence, if there is craving, do not fulfil it: what difficulty is there in this?

When the mind entertains notions of objects, there is agitation or movement in the mind; and when there are no objects or ideas, then there is no movement of thought in the mind. When there is movement, the world appears to be; when there is no movement, there is cessation of world-appearance. The movement of thought itself is called jīva, cause and action; that is the seed for world-appearance. Then follows the creation of the body.

VASIṢṬHA continued:

On account of various causes, there is this movement of thought; someone is freed from this in one life-time, and someone else is freed in a thousand births. When there is movement of thought one does not see the truth; and then there is the feeling of 'I am', 'This is mine' etc.

The world-appearance is the waking state of consciousness; egotism is the dreaming state; the mind-stuff is the deep sleep state; and pure consciousness is the fourth state or uncontradicted truth. Beyond even this fourth state there is absolute purity of consciousness. One who is established in it goes beyond sorrow.

The world-appearance is said to have the absolute Brahman as its cause, in just the same way as the sky (space) is the cause of the growth of a tree (since the sky does not obstruct its growth, it promotes or causes it). In fact, Brahman is not an active causative factor; and this is revealed by enquiry. Even as one digging the solid earth finds empty space as he continues to dig, when the enquiry is continued, you will find the truth that all this is none other than the infinite consciousness.

RĀMA asked: Pray, tell me how this creation becomes so extensive.

VASIṢṬHA continued:

The vibration in the infinite consciousness is not different from that consciousness itself. From that vibration, just as the jīva becomes manifest, even so from the jīva the mind becomes manifest because the jīva thinks. The mind itself entertains the notions of the five elements and it transforms itself into those elements. Whatever the mind thinks of, that alone it sees. After this, one by one the jīva acquires the sense-organs—the tongue, the eyes, the nose, the sense of touch, etc. In this there is no causal connection between the mind and the senses, but there is the coincidence of the thought and of the manifestation of the sense-organs—just like a crow sits on a palm tree and accidentally the fruit drops from it and it appears that the crow dislodged it! Thus the first cosmic jīva came into being.

RĀMA asked: Holy sir, if ignorance is non-existent in truth, then why should one even bother about liberation or about enquiry?

VASIṢṬHA replied: Rāma, that thought should arise in its own time, not now! Flowers bloom and fruits ripen in their due time.

The cosmic jīva utters OM and by pure will creates the various objects. Just as the creator Brahmā was willed into being, even so is a worm brought into being: because the latter is caught up in impurity, its action is trivial. The distinction is illusory. In truth, there is no creation, and hence no division at all.

The Story of Karkaṭī

III:68, 69 VASIṢṬHA continued:

In connection with this, O Rāma, there is an ancient legend which I shall now narrate to you.

There once lived to the north of the Himālaya mountain a terrible demoness known as Karkaṭī. She was huge, black and dreadful to look at. This demoness could not get enough to eat, and she was ever hungry.

She thought, "If only I can eat all the people living in Jambūdvīpa-continent in one meal, then my hunger will disappear even as a mirage disappears after a heavy rain. Such a course of action is not inappropriate, since it is appropriate to preserve one's life. However, since the people of Jambūdvīpa are pious, charitable, devoted to god, and endowed with a knowledge of herbs, it is inappropriate to harass these peace-loving people. Let me engage myself in penance, for through penance is attained that which would otherwise be extremely difficult to attain."

Karkaṭī then went up one of the snow-peaks and commenced her penance, standing on one leg. She was as firm as a marble statue and did not even notice days and months pass by. In course of time, she had grown so thin that it looked as if she was a skeleton clad in transparent skin. Thus she remained for one thousand years.

After a thousand years had passed, the creator Brahmā appeared before her, pleased with her penance: by intense penance one can attain anything—even poisonous fumes are extinguished. She bowed to him mentally, and began to wonder what boon she should ask of him. "Ah, yes," she thought, "I shall request that I should become a living steel pin (Sūcikā), an embodiment of disease. With this boon I shall simultaneously enter the hearts of all beings and fulfil my desire and appease my hunger." When Brahmā said to her, "I am pleased with your penance; ask a boon of your choice," she expressed her wish.

BRAHMĀ said: So be it; you shall also be Viṣūcikā. Remaining a subtle thing, you will inflict pain on those who eat the wrong food and indulge in wrong living, by entering their heart. However, one can attain relief by the use of the following mantra:

> himādrer uttare pārśve karkaṭī nāma rākṣasī
> viṣūcikābhidhānā sānāmnā 'py anyāyabādhikā
> oṃ hrāṃ hrīṃ śrīṃ rāṃ viṣṇuśakttaye namo bhagavati
> viṣṇuśaktti ehi enāṃ hara hara daha daha hana hana paca paca
> matha matha utsādaya utsādaya dūre kuru kuru svāhā viṣūcike
> tvaṃ himavantaṃ gaccha gaccha jīvasāra candramaṇḍalam gato
> 'si svāhā

One who is proficient in this mantra should wear it on his left arm and, thinking of the moon, pass that hand over the patient who will be cured at once.

III:70 VASIṢṬHA continued:

Immediately, O Rāma, the demoness with the mountainous body began to shrink gradually to the size of a pin. She became so subtle that her existence could only be imagined. She was like the extremely subtle suṣumṇā nāḍī that links the base of the spine with the crown of the head. She was like the ālaya-consciousness described by the Buddhists. She was constantly followed by her other form known as Viṣūcikā (cholera).

Though she was extremely subtle and unseen, her demoniacal mentality underwent no change at all. She had gained the boon of her choice; but she could not fulfil her desire to devour all beings! That is because she was of the size of a needle!! How strange: the deluded ones do not have foresight. The selfish person's violent efforts to gain his selfish ends often lead to other results, even as a person is unable to see his face when he runs to the mirror puffing and panting—his own breath mists the mirror.

Significantly, again, the demoness who had a huge form gave up that body, died to it, in order to fulfil her ambition to become a needle: even death becomes desirable when one is keen on some selfish gain and when one is possessed by excessive craving.

Viṣūcikā was radiant and was as subtle as the aroma of flowers. Dependent upon the life-force of others, she was devoted to her own work.

With her twofold form of Sūcikā and Viṣūcikā, the demoness roamed the world afflicting all the people. By her own wish she had become small: indeed, people become what they intensely wish to be. Mean-minded people even pray for trivia; just as the demoness prayed to be transformed into a cruel needle. One's inborn nature is not easily counteracted even by penance.

Sūcikā entered into the physical bodies of people who, on account of previous illness had been greatly debilitated or had become obese, and transformed herself into Viṣūcikā (cholera). Sūcikā entered into the heart of even a healthy and intelligent person, and perverted his intellect. In some cases, however, she left that person when the latter underwent a healing treatment either with the aid of the mantra or with drugs.

Thus, the demoness roamed the earth for many many years.

VASIṢṬHA continued:

Sūcikā had her numerous hiding places. Among them were: dust

The demoness is perhaps the cholera virus. The connection with improper eating and living habits is interesting.

and dirt on the ground, (unclean) fingers, threads in a cloth, within one's body in the muscles, dirty skin covered with dust, unclean furrows on the palms and on other parts of the body (due to senility), places where flies abound, in a lustreless body, in places full of decaying leaves, in places devoid of healthy trees, in people of filthy dress, people of unhealthy habits, in tree-stumps caused by deforestation in which flies breed, in puddles of stagnant water, in polluted water, in open sewers running in the middle of roads, in rest houses used by travellers, and in those cities where there are many animals like elephants, horses, etc.

Being Sūcikā (a sewing needle), she wore dirty pieces of cloth thrown on the roads, sewn together; and she roamed freely in the bodies of sick people. Even as a sewing needle which has been well used by a tailor feels fatigued and falls to the ground to take some rest, as it were, Sūcikā also got tired of her destructive activity. Just as sewing (piercing) is the natural function of a needle, cruelty was the nature of Sūcikā. Just as the needle keeps on swallowing the thread that passes through it, Sūcikā continued to claim her victims.

It is seen in the world that even wicked and cruel people are sometimes moved to pity when they see others who have been poverty-stricken and miserable for a long time. Even so, Sūcikā saw the endless thread that had passed through her in the cloth (her own karma) in front of her. This worried her. She fancied that this dark cloth, which had been woven by her (as Sūcikā or sewing needle) was covering her face and that she was blindfolded. She wondered "How shall I tear this veil?" She (the needle) passed through soft cloth (good people) as also hard cloth (the wicked ones), for what fool or wicked person discriminates between what is good and what is not?

Unharmed and unprovoked by others, Sūcikā works for the destruction and death of others: bound by this thread, she is dangling perilously. Known also as Jīva-sūcikā, she moves in all beings as the life-force with the help of prāṇa and apāna, subjecting the jīva to sorrow, by causing terribly sharp pain (of gout, rheumatism) which makes one lose his mind. She enters into the feet (like a needle) and drinks blood. Like all wicked people, she rejoices in others' sorrow.

(As Vasiṣṭha was saying this, the sun set and another day came to an end. The assembly adjourned for prayers.)

VASIṢṬHA continued: III:71, 72

After living in this manner for a long long time, the demoness Karkaṭī was thoroughly disillusioned and repented her foolish desire to devour people, which entailed severe penance for a thousand years and the degraded existence as a needle (and cholera virus). She thus bewailed her own self-inflicted misfortune:

"Alas, where is my mountainous body and where is the form of a needle? Sometimes I fall into mud and filth, I am trampled upon by people. Alas, I am lost. I have no friends, no one takes pity upon me. I have no fixed abode, nor have I a body worth the name. I have surely lost my mind and my senses! The mind that is heading towards calamity first creates delusion and wickedness: and these themselves later expand into misfortune and sorrow. I am never free, ever at the mercy of others. I am in the hands of others and do what they make me do. I desired to appease the goblin of a desire to devour all; but that has led to a remedy worse than the disease, and a greater goblin has arisen. Surely, I am a brainless fool; hence, I threw away such a great and gigantic body and deliberately chose this despicable body of a virus (or a needle). Who is now going to liberate me from this miserable existence as a being smaller than a worm? The very thought of such a vicious creature as I am may not even arise in the heart of sages. Ah, when will I again be as large as a mountain and drink the blood of large beings? . . . Let me become an ascetic again and perform penance as I did before."

At once Karkaṭī abandoned all wish to devour living beings, and went to the Himālayas for doing intense penance again. Standing as if on one foot, she began her penance. The fire of penance generated smoke from the crown of her head, and that too became another Sūcikā, a helpmate. Her shadow became yet another Sūcikā, yet another friend.

Even the trees and creepers of the forest admired Sūcikā's penance and radiated their pollens for her to eat. But she would not consume anything at all. She stood firmly on her resolve. The god of heaven also sent small particles of meat to where she stood; but she would not even let them touch her. Thus she stood for seven thousand years, utterly motionless, unmoved by wind, rain, or forest-fire.

Karkaṭī's whole being became completely purified by this penance. All her sinful tendencies had been washed away by the penance and she gained the highest wisdom. The energy of her penance set the Himālayas on fire, as it were. Indra the king of heaven learnt from the sage Nārada of Karkaṭī's unprecedented undertaking.

III:73 In answer to Indra's request, SAGE NĀRADA narrated the story of Karkaṭī:

This despicable goblin Karkaṭī became a living needle embodied in a metal needle. As such she entered into the bodies of sinful people and afflicted their muscles, their joints and their blood. She entered these bodies like wind, and caused stabbing and pricking pains. She inflicted such pain on those bodies which had been nourished on impure food like meat, etc.

She also entered into the bodies of all beings like vultures, etc., and devoured the bodies of others. On account of the power of her penance she had acquired the faculty of entering into the mind and heart of all, and participating in all that the 'host' did. What is impossible to one who is invisible and subtle like the wind?

However, since she sometimes liked some beings more than others and some pleasures more than others (on account of her impure tendencies), she became bound to them and hovered over them. She roamed freely, but when there was trouble she returned to the needle-body, as ignorant people do in times of trouble.

Yet, she was not satisfied physically. Only an existential factor can undergo appropriate experiences; how can a non-existent body experience satisfaction? Thus dissatisfied, Sūcikā was miserable. In order to regain her previous body as a gigantic goblin, she began to perform penance again. She entered the body of a vulture which flew to the peak of the Himālayas where the vulture deposited the needle and flew off.

Using the solid needle as her support, Sūcikā began her penance which continues till now. O Indra, if you do not interrupt her penance, she might seek to destroy the world by the power of that penance.

VASIṢṬHA continued:

Hearing this, Indra commissioned Vāyu the wind-god to find out the exact spot where Sūcikā dwelt. Vāyu wafted through all the different planetary systems in the universe and finally entered the earth-plane and descended upon the Himālayas where, on account of its proximity to the sun, there was no vegetation and the whole area looked like an arid desert.

VASIṢṬHA continued: III:74, 75

In the Himālayas, Vāyu saw the ascetic Sūcikā standing like another peak of the mountain. As she was not eating anything at all she had become almost completely dried up. When Vāyu (wind) entered her mouth, she threw it out again and again. She had withdrawn her life-force to the crown of her head and stood as a perfect yogini. Seeing her, Vāyu was amazed and lost in wonderment. He could not even talk to her. Convinced that she was engaged in supreme penance he forthwith returned to heaven where he reported to Indra:

"Lord, in the Jambūdvīpa-continent Sūcikā is performing unprecedented penance. She does not even let wind enter her mouth! And to overcome hunger, she has turned her stomach into solid metal. Pray, get up at once and approach the creator Brahmā to appease her by granting her the desired boon. Or else, the power of her penance might burn us all up."

Thereupon, Indra went to Brahmā and in answer to his prayer, Brahmā went to where Sūcikā was engaged in penance.

In the meantime, Sūcikā had become totally pure by her penance. Only her own two other forms—her shadow, and the fire of her austerities—were witness to her penance. By coming into contact with her, even the air around her and the particles of dust near her had attained final liberation! At this time, she had gained direct knowledge of the supreme causeless cause of all by her own examination of the intelligence within her. Surely, direct enquiry into the movements of thought in one's own consciousness is the supreme guru or preceptor, O Rāma, and no one else.

Brahmā said to her, "Ask a boon" (though since she had no sense-organs, she experienced this within herself). She reflected within herself in response to this: "I have reached the realisation of the absolute; and there are no doubts or wants in me. What shall I do with boons? When I was an ignorant girl, I was haunted by the goblin of my desires; now, through self-knowledge, that ghost has been laid."

Brahmā said: "The eternal world-order cannot be set aside, O ascetic. And it decrees that you should regain your previous body, live happily for a long time and then attain liberation. You will live an enlightened life, afflicting only the wicked and the sinful, and causing the least harm—and that too only to appease your natural hunger." Sūcikā accepted what Brahmā had said and soon her needle-body grew into a mountainous body.

III:76, 77 VASIṢṬHA continued:

Though she had regained her former demoniacal form, Karkaṭī remained in the superconscious state for a considerable time, devoid of all demoniacal tendencies. She remained in the same place, seated in the lotus posture of meditation. After a period of six months she became fully aware of the outside world and her body. Immediately, she experienced hunger; for as long as the body lasts it is subject to its own physical laws, including hunger and thirst.

Karkaṭī reflected: "What shall I eat? Whom shall I devour? Destruction of other living beings for the sake of prolonging one's life is condemned by wise sages. Hence, if while not consuming such forbidden food, I have to give up this body, I see no harm in it. Unwholesome food is poison. Moreover, to an enlightened person like me, there is no distinction between physical life and death."

As she was reflecting thus, she heard an aerial voice say: "O Karkaṭī, approach ignorant and deluded people and awaken wisdom in them. This indeed is the only mission of enlightened beings. One whom you thus endeavour to enlighten but who fails to awake to truth is fit for your consumption. You shall incur no sin by devouring such an ignorant person."

Hearing this, Karkaṭī got up and descended from the mountain. She entered a dense forest where hill-tribes and hunters dwelt. Night fell over the earth.

In that region, there was a king of the hunters known as Vikram. As was his custom, this king, along with his minister, went out into the dense darkness of the night to protect his subjects by subduing robbers and dacoits. Karkaṭī saw these two brave and adventurous men who were just then offering their prayers to the tribal demi-gods of the forest.

Seeing them, Karkaṭī reflected: "Surely, these two men have come here to appease my hunger. They are ignorant and therefore a burden on earth. Such ignorant people suffer here and hereafter; suffering is the only mission in their life! Death, unto them, is a welcome release from such suffering and it is possible that after death they will awake and seek their salvation. Ah, but, it may be that they are both wise men, and I do not like to kill wise men. For, whoever wishes to enjoy unalloyed happiness, fame and long life, should by all means honour and worship good men, by giving them all that they might wish to have. Let me therefore test their wisdom. If they are wise I shall not harm them. Wise men, good men, are indeed great benefactors of humanity."

VASIṢṬHA continued: III:78

Having decided to test the king and his minister, the demoness Karkaṭī let out a piercing cry and roared. Then she shouted: "Hey you two little worms roaming this dense forest! Who are you? Tell me quick or else I shall devour you."

The king replied: "O ghost, who are you and where are you? I only hear you; let me see who you are."

Hearing this calm and cool reply of the king, the demoness felt that his answer was appropriate and made herself visible to him. The king and the minister then beheld her dreadful form, and without being perturbed in the very least, the minister said to her: "O demoness, why are you so angry? To seek food is natural to all living beings; and in performing one's natural functions one need not be bad-tempered. Even selfish ends are gained by the wise by appropriate means and proper behaviour or action, after they give up anger and mental agitation, and resort to equanimity and clear mind. We have seen thousands of insects like you and have dealt justly with them, for it is the duty of a king to punish the wicked and protect the good. Give up your anger, and achieve your end by resorting to tranquility. Such indeed is appropriate conduct—

whether one is able to achieve one's ambition or not, one should remain peaceful. Ask of us what you will have; for we have never turned a beggar away empty-handed."

Karkaṭī greatly admired the courage and the wisdom of the two men. She thought that they were not ordinary human beings but enlightened men, for the very sight of their faces filled her heart with peace. When two enlightened men meet, their hearts mingle in peace and bliss, even as the waters of two mountain streams mix at their confluence. Moreover, who but a wise man can maintain his calm while faced with almost certain death? Hence, she thought, "Let me utilise this opportunity to clear the doubts that are in my mind; for he is surely a fool who, having the company of a wise man, neglects to clear his doubts."

At her request, the minister informed her of the king's identity. Karkaṭī retorted: "O king, you do not seem to have a wise minister! A good minister makes the king wise; and as is the king so are his subjects. Lordship and equal vision accrue from the kingly science (of self-knowledge); he who does not possess this is neither a good minister nor a wise king. If you two are men not possessed of self-knowledge, then in accordance with my inherent nature, I shall devour you both. In order to determine this, I shall ask you some questions. Give me the right answers: this is the only thing I ask of you."

III:79 THE DEMONESS asked:

O king, what is it that is one and yet is many, and in which millions of universes merge even as ripples in an ocean? What is it that is pure space, though it appears to be not so? What is it that is me in you and that is you in me; what is it that moves yet does not move, that remains stationary though it is not so; what is it that is a rock though conscious and what plays wonderful tricks in empty space; what is it that is not the sun and the moon and fire and yet eternally shines; what is that atom that seems to be far and yet so near; what is it that is of the nature of consciousness and yet is not knowable; what is it that is all and yet is not any of these; what is it that, though it is the very self of all, is veiled by ignorance and is regained after many life-times of intense and persistent effort; what is it that is atomic and yet contains a mountain within it, and that transforms the three worlds into a blade of grass; what is it that is atomic and yet is immeasurable; what is it that without ever renouncing its atomic nature appears to be bigger than the biggest mountain; what is that atom in which the entire universe rests like a seed during the cosmic dissolution?

What is it that is responsible for the function of all the elements in the universe, though it does nothing at all; even as ornaments like bracelets are made of gold, of what are the seer, the sight and the seen made; what is it that veils and reveals the threefold manifestation (viz., the seer, the sight and the seen); in what is the apparent threefold division of time (the past, the present, and the future) established, even as the tree is in a seed; what is it that comes into manifestation and vanishes alternately, even as the tree comes out of the seed and the seed comes out of the tree alternately?

O king, what is the creator of this universe and by whose power do you exist and function as a king, protecting your subjects and punishing the wicked; what is it, seeing which your own vision is purified and you exist as that alone without a division?

O king, to save yourself from certain death, answer these questions. By the light of your wisdom dispel this darkness of doubt in me. He is not a wise man who is unable, when questioned, to cut at the very root of ignorance and doubt.

If, however, you are unable to uproot this ignorance in me and to answer these questions, you will appease my hunger today.

THE MINISTER replied: III:80

I shall surely answer your questions, O lady! For that to which all your questions refer is the supreme self.

That self is subtler than even space since it has no name and cannot be described; and neither the mind nor the senses can reach it or comprehend it. It is pure consciousness. The entire universe exists in the consciousness that is atomic, even as a tree exists within the seed: but, then the universe exists as consciousness and does not exist as the universe. That consciousness exists, however, because such is the experience of all, and since it alone is the self of all. Since it is, all else is.

That self is empty like space; but it is not nothingness, since it is consciousness. It is: yet because it cannot be experienced by the mind and senses, it is not. It being the self of all, it is not experienced (as the object of experience) by anyone. Though one, it is reflected in the infinite atoms of existence and hence appears to be many. This appearance is however unreal even as 'bracelet' is an imaginary appearance of gold which alone is real. But, the self is not unreal. It is not a void or nothingness: for it is the self of all, and it is the very self of one who says it is and of one who says (or thinks) it is not! Moreover, its existence can be experienced indirectly just as the existence of camphor can be experienced by its fragrance. It alone is the self of all as consciousness; and it alone is the substance that makes the world-appearance possible.

In that infinite ocean of consciousness, whirlpools known as the three worlds arise spontaneously and naturally, even as whirlpools are caused by the very nature of the running water. Because this consciousness is beyond the reach of the mind and senses, it seems to be a void; but since it can be known by self-knowledge, it is not a void. On account of the indivisibility of consciousness, I am you and you are me; but the indivisible consciousness itself has become neither I nor you! When the wrong notions of 'you' and 'I' are given up, there arises the awareness that there is neither you, nor I, nor everything; perhaps it alone is everything.

The self being infinite moves not though moving, and yet is for ever established in every atom of existence. The self does not go nor does it ever come: for space and time derive their meaning from consciousness alone. Where can the self go when all that is is within it? If a pot is taken from one place to another, the space within does not move from one place to another, for everything is for ever in space.

THE MINISTER continued:

The self which is of the nature of pure consciousness seems to be inert and insentient when it is apparently associated with inertia. In infinite space, this infinite consciousness had made infinite objects appear; though all this seems to have been done, such effect being a mere fancy, nothing has been done. Hence, it is both consciousness and inertia, the doer and the non-doer.

The reality in fire is this self or consciousness: yet, the self does not burn nor is it burnt, since it is the reality in all, and infinite. It is the eternal light which shines in the sun, the moon, and the fire, but independent of them. It shines even when these have set: it illumines all from within all. It alone is the intelligence that indwells even trees, plants and creepers, and preserves them. That self or infinite consciousness is, from the ordinary point of view, the creator, the protector and the overlord of all; and yet from the absolute point of view, in reality, being the self of all, it has no such limited roles.

There is no world independent of this consciousness: hence, even the mountains are in the atomic self. In it arise the phantasies of a moment and of an epoch: and these appear to be real time-scales, even as objects seen in a dream appear to be real at that time. Within the twinkling of an eye there exists an epoch, even as a whole city is reflected in a small mirror. Such being the case, how can one assert the reality of either duality or non-duality? This atomic self or infinite consciousness alone appears to be a moment or an epoch, near and far, and there is nothing apart from it; and these are not mutually contradictory in themselves.

As long as one sees the bracelet as a bracelet, it is not seen as gold; but when it is seen that 'bracelet' is just a word and not the reality, then gold is seen. Even so, when the world is assumed to be real, the self is not seen: but when this assumption is discarded, consciousness is realised. It is the all; hence real. It is not experienced; hence unreal.

What appears to be is but the jugglery of Māyā which creates a division in consciousness, into subject and object. It is as real as the dream-city. It is neither real nor unreal, but a long-standing illusion. It is the assumption of division that creates diversity, right from the creator Brahmā down to the little insect. Just as in a single seed the diverse characteristics of the tree remain at all times, even so this apparent diversity exists in the self at all times, but as consciousness.

KARKAṬĪ said: III:81

I am delighted with your minister's answers, O king. Now I would like to hear your answers.

THE KING said:

Your questions, O noble lady, relate to the eternal Brahman which is pure existence. It is known when the threefold modification known as waking, dreaming and deep sleep cease and when the mind-stuff is rid of all movements of thought. The extension and withdrawal of its manifestation are popularly regarded as the creation and the dissolution of the universe. It is expressed in silence when the known comes to an end, for it is beyond all expression. It is the extremely subtle middle, between the two extremes; and that middle itself has two sides. All these universes are but its playful but conscious projection. As the diversity of this universe, it seems to be divided in itself; but truly, it is undivided.

When this Brahman wishes, wind comes into being, though that wind is nothing but pure consciousness. Similarly, when sound is thought of, there is a fanciful projection of what sounds like sound: but being pure consciousness, the reality is far from what is thought of as sound and as its meaning or substance. That supreme subtle atomic being is all and is nothing; I am that yet I am not. That alone is. By its omnipotence all this appears to be.

This self can be attained by a hundred ways and means; yet, when it is attained, nothing has been attained! It is the supreme self; yet it is nothing. One roams in this forest of saṃsāra, or repetitive history, till there is the dawn of that wisdom which is able to dispel the root-ignorance in which the world appears to be real. Just as the ignorant man is attracted by the perception of water in the mirage, this world-appearance attracts the ignorant man. But the truth is that it is the infinite consciousness that perceives the universe within itself, through its own power known as Māyā. That which is seen within appears also outside, like the hallucination of one who is mad with lust.

Though the self is extremely subtle and atomic and of the essential nature of pure consciousness, by it the entire universe is wholly pervaded. This omnipresent being by its very existence inspires the world-appearance to 'dance to its tunes'. That which is thus subtler than a hundredth part of the tip of a hair is yet greater than the greatest, because of its omnipresence.

THE KING continued:

The light of self-knowledge alone illumines all experiences. It shines by its own light. What is the light by which one 'sees' (knows), if all the lights in the world from the sun onwards become inert? Only the inner light. This inner light appears to be outside and to illumine external objects. The other sources of light are indeed non-different from the darkness of ignorance and only appear to shine: though there is no essential difference between fog and cloud (both of which veil objects), it is often seen that fog seems to radiate light, while cloud seems to obscure it. The inner light of consciousness shines for ever within and without, day and night; mysteriously, it illumines the effects of ignorance without removing the darkness of ignorance. Just as the ever-luminous sun reveals its real nature with the help of night and day, even so the light of the self reveals its real nature by revealing both consciousness and ignorance.

Within the atomic space of consciousness, there exist all the experiences, even as within a drop of honey there are the subtle essences of flowers, leaves and fruits. From that consciousness all experiences expand, for the experiencing is the sole experiencer (which is consciousness). Whatever may be the particular description of the experiences, they are all encompassed in the one experiencing of consciousness. Indeed, this infinite consciousness alone is all this: and all the hands and eyes are its own, though being extremely subtle, it has no limbs. In the twinkling of an eye this infinite consciousness experiences an epoch within itself, even as in the course of a brief dream one experiences youth and old age and even death. All these objects which appear in consciousness are indeed non-different from consciousness, even as a sculpture carved of stone is nothing but stone. Just as the whole tree with all its future ramifications is in the seed, the entire universe of the past, the present and the future is contained in the atom of infinite consciousness. Therefore, though the self is neither the doer of actions nor the experiencer of experiences, it is the doer of all actions and the experiencer of all experiences: there is nothing apart from it. Within the atom of infinite consciousness the doership and the experiencer are inherent.

The world, however, has never really been created, nor does it disappear: it is regarded as unreal only from the relative point of view; from the absolute point of view it is non-different from the infinite consciousness.

THE KING continued:

Sages only speak of the inner and the outer, which are but words with no corresponding substance: it is meant to instruct the ignorant. The seer, himself remaining unseen, sees himself; and the seer does not ever become an object of consciousness. The seer is the sight only, and when the latent psychic impressions have ceased, the seer regains its pure being; when the external object is imagined, a seer has been created. If there is no subject, there is no object either: it is the son that makes a man 'father'. Again, it is the subject that becomes the object; there is no object (sight) without a subject (seer), even as without a father there is no son. Because the subject (seer) is pure consciousness, he is able to conjure up the object. This cannot be the other way round: the object does not give birth to the subject. Therefore the seer alone is real, the object being hallucination: gold alone is real, the bracelet is a name and a form. As long as the notion of bracelet lasts, the pure gold is not apprehended; as long as the notion of the object persists, the division between the seer and the seen also persists. But, just as because of the consciousness in the bracelet, gold realises its goldness, the subject (seer) manifesting as the object (the seen) realises subjectivity (consciousness). One is the reflection of the other: there is no real duality. The seer does not see himself as he sees the object: the seer sees himself as the object, and therefore does not see—though he is the reality, yet he appears to be unreal. However, when self-knowledge arises and the object ceases to be, the seer (subject) is realised as the sole reality.

The subject exists because of the object, and the object is but a reflection of the subject: duality cannot be if there is not one, and where is the need for the notion of 'unity' if one alone exists? When thus real knowledge is gained by means of right enquiry and understanding, only that remains which is not expressible in words. Of that it cannot be said that it is one or that it is many. It is neither seer nor seen, neither subject nor object, neither this nor that. Neither unity nor diversity can be truly established as the truth: for every thesis gives rise to antithesis. Yet, one is not different from 'the other': just as the wave is not other than water, bracelet is not different from gold. Even so, division is not a contradiction of unity! All this speculation concerning unity and diversity is only to overcome sorrow: that which is beyond all this is the truth, the supreme self.

VASIṢṬHA continued: III:82

After listening to these wise words of the king, Karkaṭī became tranquil, and her demoniacal nature left her. She said to them:

"O wise men, you are both fit to be worshipped by all and to be served by all. And, I have been thoroughly awakened by your holy company. One who enjoys the company of enlightened men does not suffer in this world, even as one who holds a candle in his hand does not see darkness anywhere. Pray, tell me what I can do for you."

THE KING said: "O lady, in my city many people suffer from rheumatic heart troubles. In the country there is also an epidemic of cholera. It is in order to investigate these and find a remedy for them that my minister and I came out of the palace tonight. My humble submission to you is this: do not take the life of any of my people. (Karkaṭī at once acceded to the king's request.) Now, please tell me: how shall I recompense you for your kindness and appease your hunger?"

KARKAṬĪ replied: "Once I had the intention of engaging myself in penance in the Himālayas and giving up the body. But now I have given up that idea. I shall give you my biography. Once upon a time I was a demoness of gigantic proportions. I wished to devour people and with this intention performed penance. From the creator Brahmā I obtained a boon, as a result of which I became a needle (and also the cholera virus); as such I brought untold misery to people. Brahmā, however, also evolved a mantra by which alone I am brought under control. Learn this mantra, and with its help you can enable people to get rid of rheumatic heart troubles, also leukemia and other blood illnesses. I used to spread leukemia in such a way that it was passed on by the parent to his children!"

All the three of them then went to the bank of the river where the king received the mantra from Karkaṭī; this mantra becomes effective by its repetition (japa).

The grateful KING said to Karkaṭī: "O kind lady, now you have become my guru and friend. Friendship is valued by good people. Pray, assume a gentle and smaller form, and come to my palace and live as my guest. You need not afflict good people at all. But I shall feed you with sinners and thieves."

Karkaṭī agreed. She became a charming young woman and accompanied the king to live as his guest. He entrusted thieves and other criminals and sinners to her. At night every day she resumed her demoniacal form and consumed them. During the day-time she continued to be a charming woman—the friend and guest of the king. After her meal she would often go into samādhi for a few years at a time, before returning to normal consciousness and normal life.

III:83, 84 VASIṢṬHA continued:

Thus, Karkaṭī lives even now protecting the king's descendants. She was the daughter of a demon who resembled a crab (?). Demons are of many kinds and colours (white, black, green and red); and she was of the black kind. I told you the story, however, because I remembered her questions, and the king's answers. In essence, even as the ramifications of the tree (with its leaves, flowers, fruits, etc.) extend from the seed in which there is no such diversification, the universe of diversity extends from the infinite consciousness.

O Rāma, by merely listening to my words you will be enlightened, there is no doubt in this. Know that the universe has arisen from Brahman and it is Brahman alone.

RĀMA asked: If oneness alone is the truth, why then do we say, "By this, that is attained"?

VASIṢṬHA replied:

Rāma, in the scriptures words have been used in order to facilitate the imparting of instruction. Cause and effect, the self and the Lord, difference and non-difference, knowledge and ignorance, pain and pleasure—all these pairs have been invented for the instruction of the ignorant. They are not real in themselves. All this discussion and argumentation take place only in and because of ignorance; when there is knowledge there is no duality. When the truth is known, all descriptions cease, and silence alone remains.

Then you will realise that there is only one, without beginning and without end. But as long as words are used to denote a truth, duality is inevitable; however, such duality is not the truth. All divisions are illusory.

I shall give you another illustration. Listen very carefully. By means of the potent medicine of my explanations, you will surely overcome the illness that afflicts your mind. This saṃsāra (world appearance) is nothing but the mind filled with likes and dislikes; when it is free of them, world-appearance too comes to an end. The consciousness in the mind is the seed of all substances; and the inert aspect of the mind is the cause of the illusory appearance of the world. Because of the omnipresence of consciousness, the mind takes the form of the knowable and thus becomes the seed of the universe; the mind, like a child, imagines the existence of the world. When the mind is illumined it experiences the infinite consciousness within itself. I shall presently explain to you how this subject-object division arises.

VASIṢṬHA continued: III:85

Once I asked the creator Brahmā to tell me how this universe was first created. And he gave me the following reply.

BRAHMĀ said:

My child, it is only mind that appears as all this. I shall tell you what happened to me at the beginning of this epoch. At the end of the previous epoch there was the cosmic night, and as soon as I woke at the end of that night I offered my morning prayers and looked around, wishing to create the universe. I beheld the infinite void which was neither illumined nor dark.

In my mind there was the intention to create; and in my heart I began to see subtle visions. There in my mind and with my mind I saw several seemingly independent universes. In them all I also saw my own counterparts—creators. In those universes I saw all kinds of beings, as also mountains and rivers, oceans and wind, sun and heavenly beings and the netherworld and the demons.

In all these universes I also saw scriptures and moral codes which determine good and evil and heaven and hell; as also the scriptures that lay down the path to pleasure and the path to liberation. And I saw people pursuing all these different goals.

I saw seven worlds, seven continents and also oceans and mountains, all of them inexorably heading for destruction. I saw time and its divisions, right down to days and nights. I saw the holy river Gaṅgā as it knit together the three worlds—the celestial region, the atmosphere, and the earth.

Like a castle in the air, this creation shone extensively with its sky, earth and oceans. Looking at all this I was wonderstruck and puzzled: "How is it that I am seeing all these with my mind in the great void, even though I have not seen them with physical eyes?" I contemplated this problem for a considerable time and eventually I thought of one of the suns in one of the solar systems and requested him to come to me. I asked him the question that was engaging my attention.

THE SUN replied:

O great one, being the omnipotent creator of all this you are indeed the Lord. It is the mind alone that appears as all this ceaseless and endless creative activity, which, on account of nescience, deludes one into thinking that it is real or that it is unreal. Surely, you know the truth, Lord: yet since you commanded me to answer your query, I say this.

The Story of the Sons of Indu (Ten Young Men)

III:86 THE SUN said:

O Lord of lords, near the holy mountain Kailāsa in a place known as Suvarṇajaṭa, your sons had established a colony. In that place there was a holy man known as Indu, a descendant of the sage Kaśyapa. He and his wife enjoyed every blessing except an offspring. In order to obtain this blessing they went to Kailāsa and engaged themselves in severe penance, living only on a very small quantity of water. They had resorted to the state of trees and stood unmoving.

Lord Śiva was pleased with their penance and, appearing before them, asked them to choose a boon from him. They prayed that they might beget ten worthy sons who would be devoted to God and righteousness. Lord Śiva granted the boon.

Very soon after this, the holy man's wife gave birth to ten brilliant and radiant sons. These boys grew up into young men; they had mastered all the scriptures even when they were barely seven years of age. After a considerable time, their parents abandoned their bodies and became liberated.

The ten young men were sorely distressed at the loss of their parents. One day they got together and asked themselves: "O brothers, what is the most desirable goal here, which is proper for us to aspire to and which will not lead to unhappiness? To be a king, to be an emperor, even to be Indra the god of heaven—all these are trivial, since even Indra rules heaven just for an hour and a half of the Creator's life-span. Ah, therefore, the attainment of creatorship is the best for us because of all lordships it alone will not come to an end for a whole epoch."

All the others heartily agreed with this statement. They said to themselves: "Well then, we should soon reach Brahmā-hood which is devoid of old age and death."

The eldest brother said: "Please do as I tell you to do. From now on contemplate as follows, 'I am Brahmā, seated on a full-blown lotus'." All the brothers thereupon began to meditate in the following manner: "I am Brahmā, the creator of the universe. The sages as also Sarasvatī the goddess of wisdom are within me in their personal forms. Heaven is within me, with all the celestials. Mountains, continents and oceans are within me. Demi-gods and demons are within me. The sun shines within me. Now the creation takes place. Now the creation exists. Now is the time for the dissolution. An epoch is over. The night of Brahmā is at hand. I have self-knowledge and I am liberated."

Meditating thus with all their being, they became that.

THE SUN continued: III:87, 88

Lord, after that, still deeply contemplating on their intention to be the creators of the universe, the ten holy men stood in contemplation. Their bodies had withered away and whatever was left was consumed by wild beasts. But they continued to stand there in their disembodied state, for a long long time . . . till an epoch came to a close and there was the great scorching heat of the sun and the terrible cloud-burst which destroyed everything. The holy men still continued to stand in their disembodied state, with the sole intention of becoming the creators of the universe.

At the dawn of a new creation, these men continued to stand in the same place and in the same manner and with the same intention. They became the creators. They were the ten creators whom you saw; and you saw their universes, too. Lord, I am one of the suns that shine in the universes thus created by them.

THE CREATOR asked the Sun:

O Sun, when thus the universes have been created by these ten creators, what need I do? What is there for me to do?

THE SUN replied:

Lord, you have no wishes, nor any motives of your own. Naturally, there is no need for you to do anything. What benefit do you derive from creating the universe? Creation of the universe is surely a motiveless pastime to you!

Lord, creation emerges from you who are free from the least desire or motive, just as the sun without intending to shine is reflected in a pool of water without intending to so reflect it. Just as without intending to do so, the sun causes night and day to follow each other, even so, engage yourself in the non-volitional act of creation. For, what will you gain by abandoning your natural function?

Wise men do not desire to do anything; and wise men do not desire to abandon action either.

Lord, you are viewing, with your own mental eye, this universe thus created by those holy men. One beholds with physical eyes only such objects as have been created by him in his own mind—naught else. These objects which have been created by the mind are indestructible: only those objects which have been put together with material substances disintegrate. A person is made of whatever is firmly established as the truth of his being in his own mind: that he is, naught else.

The Story of Ahalyā

III:89 THE SUN continued:

Lord, the mind alone is the creator of the world; and mind alone is the supreme person. What is done by the mind is action, what is done by the body is not action. Behold the powers of the mind: by determined thinking the sons of the holy man became creators of the universe! When one, on the other hand, thinks 'I am a little body' he becomes a mortal being. One whose consciousness is extroverted experiences pleasure and pain; the yogi, on the other hand, whose vision is introverted does not entertain ideas of pain and pleasure. In this connection there is a legend which I shall narrate to you.

In the country of Magadha there was a king named Indradyumna. Ahalyā was his wife. In that place there was also a handsome young man of loose morals known as Indra. One day during a discourse, the queen listened to the story of the seduction of the famed Ahalyā by Indra the king of heaven. As a result she conceived a great love for the young man Indra.

Ahalyā was distraught with love for Indra and with the help of one of her maids managed to have the young man brought to her. From then onwards Indra and Ahalyā used to meet each other in a secret house and enjoy themselves.

Ahalyā was so fond of Indra that she saw him everywhere. The very thought of him made her face radiant. As their love grew, their relationship became public, and it reached the king's ears.

The irate king, in an effort to break this relationship, punished them in numerous ways: they were immersed in ice-cold water, they were fried in boiling oil, they were tied to the legs of an elephant, they were whipped. Indra said to the king, laughingly:

"O king, the entire universe to me is nothing but my beloved. So it is to Ahalyā. Hence we are unaffected by all these. Sir, I am only mind; and mind alone is the individual. You can punish the body; but you cannot punish the mind nor bring about the least change in it. If the mind is fully saturated with something, whatever happens to the body does not affect the mind. The mind is unaffected even by boons and curses, even as the firmly established mountain is not moved by the horns of a little beast. . . . The body does not create the mind, but the mind creates the body. The mind alone is the seed for the body: when the tree dies, the seed does not, but when the seed perishes, the tree dies with it. If the body perishes, the mind can create other bodies for itself."

THE SUN continued: III:90, 91

Lord, the king thereupon approached the sage Bharata and pleaded that he should punish the recalcitrant couple by cursing them. And, the sage pronounced a curse upon the couple. However, they said to the sage and to the king: "Alas, you are both of little understanding. By thus cursing us you have squandered the merit acquired by penance. Your curse will surely destroy our bodies, but we shall lose nothing by that. No one can destroy the mind of others." However, the sage's curse destroyed their bodies, and on leaving those bodies, they were born together as animals and then as birds, and then as a human couple in a holy family. Till now, on account of the total love for each other, they are born together as husband and wife. Even the trees of the forest were inspired and infected by the supreme love and devotion of this couple.

Even the sage's curse could not bring about the mutation of the couple's mind. Even so, Lord, you cannot interfere with the creation of the ten sons of the holy man. But what do you lose if they are thus engaged in their own creation? Let them remain with the creations of their own mind! It cannot be destroyed by you any more than the reflection in crystal can be removed.

Lord, in your own consciousness, create the world as you like. In truth, the infinite consciousness, the mind (one's own consciousness) and the infinite space are all of one substance, pervaded by the infinite consciousness. Therefore regardless of what the young men have created, you can create as many worlds as you like!

BRAHMĀ said to Vasiṣṭha:

Having listened to this advice of the Sun, I immediately began to create the worlds as the natural expression of my own being. I requested the Sun to be my first partner in this task. Thus, he was the Sun in the creation of the young men, and the progenitor of the human race in my creation, and he played this dual role efficiently. In accordance with my intentions, he brought about the creation of the worlds. Whatever appears in one's consciousness, that seems to come into being, gets established, and even bears fruits! Such is the power of the mind. Just as the sons of the holy man gained the position of creators of the world on account of the powers of their mind, even so have I become the creator of the world. It is the mind that makes things appear here. It brings about the appearance of the body, etc. Naught else is aware of the body.

THE CREATOR BRAHMĀ said:

The individualised consciousness (mind) has in it its own manifold potentialities, even as spices have taste in them. That consciousness itself appears as the subtle or ethereal body, and when it becomes gross that itself appears to be the physical or material body. That individualised consciousness itself is known as the jīva or the individual soul, when the potentialities are in an extremely subtle state. And, when all this jugglery of the jīva ceases, that itself shines as the supreme being. I am not, nor is there anyone in this universe: all this is nothing but the infinite consciousness. Just as the intention of the young men became manifest, all this is appearance based on infinite consciousness. The young men's intention made them feel that they were the creators: even so I am.

The pure and infinite consciousness alone thinks of itself as the jīva and as the mind and then believes itself to be the body. When this dream-like fantasy is prolonged, this long dream feels like reality! It is both real and unreal: because it is perceived, it appears to be real, but because of inherent contradiction it is unreal. The mind is sentient because it is based on consciousness; when viewed as something apart from the consciousness, it is inert and deluded. When there is perception, the mind takes on the role of the object of perception: but not in reality—even as when it is perceived as such, the bracelet is seen, though the truth is that it is gold.

Because Brahman alone is all this, even what is inert is pure consciousness; but all of us, from me down to the rock, are indefinable, neither inert nor sentient. There can be no apprehension of two completely different things: only when there is similarity between the subject and object is perception possible. Concerning what is indefinable and whose existence is not certain, 'inert' and 'sentient' are only words with no substance. In the mind, the subject is believed to be sentient and the object is said to be inert. Thus, caught in delusion, the jīva hangs around. In truth, this duality itself is the creation of the mind, a hallucination. Of course, we cannot determine with certainty that such a hallucination exists, either. The infinite consciousness alone IS.

When this illusory division is not seen for what it is, there is the arising of the false egotism. But when the mind enquires into its own nature, this division disappears. There is realisation of the one infinite consciousness, and one attains great bliss.

VASIṢṬHA asked Brahmā: III:92

Lord, how is it possible that the sage's curse affected Indra's body and not his mind? If the body is non-different from the mind, then the curse should affect the mind, too. Kindly explain to me how the mind is not thus affected—or that it is affected!

THE CREATOR BRAHMĀ replied:

Dear one, in the universe, from Brahmā to a hill, every embodied being has a twofold body. Of these, the first is the mental body which is restless and which acts quickly. The second is the body made of flesh, which does not really do anything. Of these the latter is overpowered by curses and also by boons or charms: it is dumb, powerless, weak and transient like a droplet of water on lotus-leaf, and it is entirely dependent upon fate, destiny and such other factors. Mind however, is independent, though it might seem to be dependent. When this mind confidently engages in self-effort, then it is beyond the reach of sorrow. Whenever it strives, then and there it surely finds the fruition of its striving.

The physical body achieves nothing; on the other hand, the mental body gets results. When the mind dwells constantly on what is pure, it is immune to the effects of curses. The body may fall into fire or mire, but the mind experiences only that which it contemplates. This was demonstrated by Indra. It was also demonstrated by the sage Dīrghatapā who wished to perform a religious rite, but fell into a blind well while collecting the materials for it; he performed the rite mentally and derived the fruit of actual physical performance of the rite. The ten sons of the holy man were also able to achieve Brahmā-hood by their mental effort: even I could not prevent it.

Mental and physical illness, as well as curses and "evil eye" do not touch the mind that is devoted to the self, any more than a lotus flower can split a rock into two by falling on it. Hence, one should endeavour with the mind to make the mind take to the pure path, with the self make the self tread the path of purity. Whatever the mind contemplates that instantly materialises. By intense contemplation it can bring about radical change within itself, to heal itself of the defective vision in which illusions were perceived as real. What the mind does, that it experiences as truth. It makes the man who is sitting in moonlight experience burning heat; and it makes one who is in burning sun experience cool comfort!

Such is the mysterious power of the mind.

III:93 VASIṢṬHA continued:

Thus was I instructed by the creator Brahmā in days of yore and that I have conveyed to you, O Rāma.

Thus, since the absolute Brahman in its undifferentiated state pervades everything, everything is in an undifferentiated state. When that of its own accord condenses, the cosmic mind is born. In that mind there arises the intention of the existence of the different elements in their extremely subtle state: the totality of all this is the luminous cosmic person who is known as Brahmā the creator. Hence, this Creator is none other than the cosmic mind.

This Brahmā the creator sees whatever he intends to see in his own mind, for he is of the nature of consciousness. It is he (Brahmā the creator) who has wished into being this nescience which is the differentiating principle in the universe, and on account of which one confuses the self with the not-self, and it is with this factor of nescience that the Creator has caused this universe (the mountains, the blade of grass, water, etc.) to appear as one of diverse creatures. Because of this—though the entire universe is nothing but infinite consciousness—there appear to be creatures born of atomic particles and molecules.

Therefore, O Rāma, all objects and substances in this universe have emerged in Brahman the absolute, just as waves manifest in the ocean. In this uncreated universe, the mind of Brahmā the creator perceives itself as the egotism and thus does Brahmā the cosmic mind become Brahmā the creator of the universe. The power of that cosmic mind alone appears to be the diverse forces in the universe. Infinite number of diverse creatures manifest themselves in this cosmic mind and they are then known as diverse jīvas.

When these diverse jīvas arise in the infinite space of consciousness, seemingly composed of the elements, into each of the bodies consciousness enters through the aperture of life-force, and thence forms the seed of all bodies, both moving and unmoving. Thence, birth as individuals takes place, each individual being accidentally (like a crow alighting and a cocoanut falling) brought into contact with different potentialities whose expression gives rise to the law of cause and effect, etc., and thence to rise and fall in evolution. Desire alone is thereafter the cause of all this.

Rāma, such is this forest known as world-appearance; he who cuts its very root with the axe of investigation (enquiry) is freed from it. Some arrive at this understanding soon, others after a very long time.

VASIṢṬHA continued: III:94

Rāma, I shall now describe to you the divisions of beings into the best, the worst and the middling, as it happened in the beginning of this cycle of creation.

The first and foremost among the creatures are born of noble practices. They are naturally good and devoted to good deeds. They reach liberation in a few life-times. They are full of the quality of purity and light (satva). Then there are those who are full of impurity, in whom the worldly habits are strong and variegated, who will perhaps reach liberation in a thousand births—they are the least among the good. Among them there are those in whose case liberation itself is doubtful in this world-cycle: they are beings of dense darkness.

The middling type are the ones who are full of the quality of dynamism and desire (rajas). When such people are close enough to liberation that on their departure from this world they reach it, they have a mixture of rajas and satva. But when the rājasic (passionate desire) tendency is so strong that it takes a little longer to sublimate it, they are purely rājasic. But when the rājasic tendency is extremely dense, then it partakes of darkness (tamas). In the case of those from whom liberation is so remote that it is doubtful, the quality of rajas partakes of the densest darkness.

They who even after a thousand births are still in darkness unawakened, are known as beings of darkness (tamas). They may take a long time to reach liberation. But when this liberation seems to be at hand, then their tamas is mixed with satva. If they are proceeding close to liberation, then their tamas is mixed with rajas. When, even after a hundred births, liberation is another hundred births away, they are full of tamas; and if liberation is doubtful, they are in dense darkness.

(This chapter seems to suggest that satva, rajas and tamas in themselves are not obstacles to liberation, but the further modifications by wrong thought and wrong action push liberation away. —S.V.)

All these beings have arisen in the absolute Brahman when there was just a slight disturbance in its equilibrium, even as waves arise on the surface of the ocean. Even as the space in a jar, the space in a room and the space in a small hole are all integral parts of one cosmic space, all these are but the infinite being in which there are no parts. And, as they arose in it, they merge in it. Thus, by the will of the infinite Brahman all these seem to arise and then dissolve in it.

III:95 VASIṢṬHA continued:

Action and the doer of the action arose spontaneously in the supreme being at the same time, even as flower and its fragrance arise simultaneously. However, it is only in the eyes of the ignorant that the creation of the jīvas appears to be real, even as only the ignorant see blueness in the sky! To the enlightened the expressions "Jīvas are born of Brahman" and "Jīvas are not born of Brahman" are both meaningless.

Only for the sake of instruction is the dualism provisionally accepted; otherwise instruction is impossible. After having posited that jīvas are born of Brahman, it is pointed out by the teacher that since the effect is non-different from the cause, jīvas are non-different from Brahman. All these appear to be born of Brahman, even as fragrance is born of flower. And they re-enter into Brahman, even as one season 'enters' into another!

With every species of being that manifests itself in the universe is simultaneously born its natural behaviour. It is only their ignorance of their own essential nature or self which leads to such behaviour or action as to cause reaction in a later birth.

RĀMA said:

Holy sir, truly the declarations of sages whose minds are uncoloured constitute scripture. And, they who are pure at heart and in whose vision there is no division are regarded as sages. The immature person can hope to see the light of truth only with the aid of a scripture and of the knowledge of the nature of an enlightened person. Holy sir, we see in this world that the seed is born of a tree, and the tree grows from the seed. Is it then appropriate to say that without the seed of previous karma, diverse beings were born of the absolute Brahman?

VASIṢṬHA replied:

If you observe carefully, O Rāma, you will see that it is only when the mind is involved in the action that there is the extension of the action into its own fruition. Hence, mind is the seed of action. Even so, when the cosmic mind manifested itself in the absolute Brahman, at that very instant the natural tendencies of diverse beings and their behaviour were born, and the embodied beings came to be regarded as jīvas. There is no division between mind and action. Before it is projected as action it arises in the mind, with the mind itself as its 'body'. Hence, action is nothing but the movement of energy in consciousness, and it inevitably bears its own fruit. When such action comes to an end, mind comes to an end, too; and when the mind ceases to be, there is no action. This applies only to the liberated sage, not to others.

VASIṢṬHA continued: III:96

Mind is only perception; and perception is movement in consciousness. The expression of this movement is action, and fruition follows this. Mind is an intention arising in the omnipotent and infinite consciousness. It stands between the real and the unreal, as it were, but inclined towards comprehension. Though non-different from the infinite consciousness, it thinks that it is. Though non-doing, it thinks it does. Such is the mind, and these qualities are inseparable from the mind. Even so the jīva and the mind are inseparable.

Whatever the mind thinks of, the organs of action strive to materialise: hence, again, mind is action. However, mind, intellect, egotism, individualised consciousness, action, fancy, birth and death, latent tendencies, knowledge, effort, memory, the senses, nature, Māyā or illusion, activity and such other words are but words without corresponding reality: the sole reality is the infinite consciousness in which these concepts are conceived to exist. All these concepts have arisen when, by accidental coincidence (the crow dislodging the cocoanut), the infinite consciousness in a moment of self-forgetfulness viewed itself as the object of perception.

When, thus veiled by nescience, the same consciousness views diversity in an agitated state and identifies objects as such, it is known as mind. That itself when it is firmly established in the conviction of a certain perception, is known as intellect (or intelligence). When it ignorantly and foolishly identifies itself as an existent separate individual, it is known as egotism. When it abandons consistent enquiry, allowing itself to play with countless thoughts coming and going, it is known as individualised consciousness (or mind-stuff).

Whereas pure movement in consciousness is karma or action without an independent doer, when it pursues the fruition of such action, it is known as karma (action). When it entertains the notion "I have seen this before" in relation to something either seen or unseen, it is known as memory. When the effects of past enjoyments continue to remain in the field of consciousness though the effects themselves are unseen, it is known as latent tendency (or potentiality). When it is conscious of the truth that the vision of division is the product of ignorance, it is known as knowledge. On the other hand, when it moves in the wrong direction, towards greater self-forgetfulness and deeper involvement in false fancies, it is known as impurity. When it entertains the indweller with sensations, it is known as the senses (indriya). When it remains unmanifest in the cosmic being, it is known as nature. When it creates confusion between reality and appearance, it is known as Māyā (illusion). When it thinks "I am bound" there is bondage; when it thinks "I am free" there is freedom.

III:97 VASIṢṬHA continued:

The light of consciousness eclipsed by a firm conviction in the existence of the mind is indeed the mind. This mind embodies itself in diverse beings—humans, gods, demons, demi-gods and celestials. It then spreads itself out as various forms of behaviour—as also the cities and towns, etc. Such being the truth, what is the use of examining all these external appearances? It is mind alone that is the proper factor for us to examine. For when we enquire into the nature of the mind, all the created objects or all appearances are seen to be its creations; only the infinite consciousness remains as uncreated by the mind. When deeply observed, the mind is absorbed into its substratum, and when it is thus absorbed, there is supreme felicity. When the mind thus disintegrates there is liberation, and there is no more rebirth, for it was mind alone that appeared to take birth and to die. (Vicāra, usually translated 'enquiry', is 'direct observation'.)

RĀMA asked again:

Pray, Lord, how did all this take place in the pure infinite consciousness? How was it possible for the mind, which is apparently a mixture of the real and the unreal, to arise in it?

VASIṢṬHA said:

Rāma, space is threefold—the infinite space of undivided consciousness, the infinite space of divided consciousness and the physical space in which the material worlds exist. The infinite space of undivided consciousness (cid ākāśa) is that which exists in all, inside and outside, as the pure witness of that which is real and of that which appears to be. The finite space of divided consciousness (citta ākāśa) is that which creates the divisions of time, which pervades all beings and which is interested in the welfare of all beings. The physical space is that in which the other elements (air, etc.) exist. The latter two are not independent of the first, the infinite space of undivided consciousness. In fact, the others do not exist, and this division of consciousness into three is arbitrarily suggested only while instructing the ignorant. The enlightened one knows that there is only one reality—the infinite consciousness.

Rāma, when that consciousness apparently thinks "I am intelligent" or "I am inert" that is the mind. It is from this wrong notion that all the other physical and psychological factors have been imaginarily created.

The Story of the Great Forest

VASIṢṬHA continued: III:98

O Rāma, whatever might have been the origin of the mind and whatever it might be, one should constantly direct it towards liberation through self-effort. The pure mind is free from latent tendencies, and therefore it attains self-knowledge. Since the entire universe is within the mind, the notions of bondage and liberation are also within it. In this connection there is the following legend which I heard from the creator Brahmā himself. Listen to it attentively:

There was a great forest, so large that millions of square miles were like the space within an atom, in it. In it there was just one person who had a thousand arms and limbs. He was forever restless. He had a mace in his hand with which he beat himself and, afraid of the beating, he ran away in panic. He fell into a blind well. He came out of it, again beat himself and again ran away in panic, this time into a forest. He came out of it, again beat himself and again ran away in panic, this time into a banana grove. Though there was no other being to fear, he wept and cried aloud in fear. He kept running as before, beating himself as before.

I witnessed all this intuitively and with the power of my will I restrained him for a moment. I asked him, "Who are you?" But, he was sorely distressed and called me his enemy and wept aloud and then laughed aloud. Then he began to abandon his body—limb by limb.

Immediately after this, I saw another person running like the first one, beating himself, weeping and wailing. When I similarly restrained him, he began to abuse me and ran away intent on his own way of life. Like this I came across several persons. Some listened to my words and abandoning their previous way of life became enlightened. Some others ignored me or even held me in contempt. Some others even refused to come out of the blind well or the dense forest.

Such is the great forest, O Rāma: no one finds a sure resting place in it, whatever be the mode of life they may adopt. Even today you see such people in this world; and you yourself have seen such a life of ignorance and delusion. Because you are young and ignorant, you do not understand it.

III:99 VASIṢṬHA continued:

O Rāma, this great forest is not far away, nor is that strange man in a strange land! This world itself is the forest. It is a great void; but this void is seen only in the light of enquiry. This light of enquiry is the 'I' in the parable. This wisdom is accepted by some and rejected by others, who continue to suffer. They who accept it are enlightened.

The person with thousands of arms is the mind with countless manifestations. This mind punishes itself by its own latent tendencies and restlessly wanders in this world. The blind well in the story is hell and the banana grove is heaven. The dense forest of thorny bush is the life of a worldly man, with the numerous thorns of wife, children, wealth, etc. hurting him all the time. The mind now wanders into hell, now into heaven and now into the world of human beings.

Even when the light of wisdom shines on the life of the deluded mind, it foolishly rejects it, considering that that wisdom is its enemy. Then it weeps and wails in distress. Sometimes, it experiences an imperfect awakening, and it renounces the pleasures of the world without proper understanding—such renunciation itself proves to be a great source of sorrow. But, when such renunciation arises out of the fullness of understanding, of wisdom born of enquiry into the nature of the mind, the renunciation leads to supreme bliss. Such a mind may even look at its own past notions of pleasure with puzzlement. Just as the limbs of the person as they were cut away fell down and disappeared, the latent tendencies of the person who wisely renounces the world also vanish from the mind.

Behold the play of ignorance! which makes one hurt oneself out of one's own volition; and which makes one run hither and thither in meaningless panic. Though the light of self-knowledge shines in every heart, yet one wanders in this world driven by one's own latent desires. And, the mind itself intensifies this sorrow and goads one to go round in circles. By its own whims and fancies, thoughts and hopes, it binds itself. When it is visited by sorrow it despairs and becomes restless.

When one who gains wisdom preserves it for a long time and persists in the practice of enquiry, he does not experience sorrow. An uncontrolled mind is the source of sorrow; when it is thoroughly understood, the sorrow vanishes like mist at sunrise.

VASIṢṬHA continued: III:100

The individualised consciousness (the mind) has arisen in the supreme being, O Rāma: it is both different and non-different from the infinite consciousness even as a wave is different and non-different from the ocean. To the enlightened the mind is the absolute Brahman and naught else. To the unenlightened, the mind is the cause of repetitive history (saṃsāra). When dualistic concepts are used by us, O Rāma, it is only to facilitate instruction: the division is not real.

The absolute Brahman is omnipotent: and there is nothing which is outside of it. It is his own power or energy that pervades all things. In embodied beings, it is the cit-śakti (the power of consciousness or intelligence). It is motion in air, stability in earth, void in space, and it is the power of self-consciousness ('I am') in created beings. Yet all this is nothing but the power of absolute Brahman. It is the power of disintegration, the power that causes grief in the grief-stricken and the power that causes elation in the joyous; in the warrior it is valour; it is the power that triggers creation and the same power brings about the dissolution of the universe.

The jīva is at the junction of consciousness and matter; and because it is a reflection of the absolute Brahman, it is said to be in Brahman. See the entire universe and also the 'I' as the absolute Brahman, for the self (which is Brahman) is omnipresent. When that self thinks, it is known as mind. It is nothing but the power of the absolute Brahman which is non-different from Brahman: in it all this arbitrary division into 'I' and 'this' are but apparent reflections. The very reality of the mind is Brahman alone.

Here and there, now and then, this power of Brahman makes manifest one or the other of its powers. But all this manifestation is but the apparent reflection of the power of Brahman, not a real creation. Thus creation, transformation, existence and destruction are all brought about by Brahman in Brahman: it is nothing but Brahman. The instruments of action, action and the doer, birth, death and existence—all this is Brahman. Nothing else is, even in imagination. Delusion, craving, greed and attachment are non-existent; how can they exist when there is no duality? When bondage is non-existent, surely liberation is false, too.

RĀMA asked: Holy sir, you said that when the mind thinks of something it materialises. Now you say that bondage does not exist! How can these be reconciled?

VASIṢṬHA replied: O Rāma, the mind, in a state of ignorance, imagines bondage. The bondage exists only in that state of ignorance. Just as the dream-objects vanish when the dreamer wakes up, all these hallucinations known as bondage and liberation do not exist in the eyes of the enlightened.

The Story of the Three Non-existent Princes

III:101 VASIṢṬHA continued:

To illustrate this, there is an interesting legend. Kindly listen to it.

A young boy asked his nanny to tell him a story and the nanny told him the following story to which the boy listened with great attention:

Once upon a time in a city which did not exist, there were three princes who were brave and happy. Of them two were unborn and the third was not conceived. Unfortunately all their relatives died. The princes left their native city to go elsewhere. Very soon they fell into a swoon unable to bear the heat of the sun. Their feet were burnt by hot sand. The tips of grass pierced them. They reached the shade of three trees, of which two did not exist and the third was not even planted. After resting there for some time and eating the fruits of those trees, they proceeded further.

They reached the banks of three rivers; of them two were dry and in the third there was no water. The princes had a refreshing bath and quenched their thirst in them. They then reached a huge city which was about to be built. Entering it, they found three palaces of exceeding beauty. Of them two had not been built at all, and the third had no walls. They entered the palaces and found three golden plates; two of them had been broken into two and the third had been pulverised. They took hold of the one which had been pulverised. They took ninety-nine minus one hundred grams of rice and cooked it. They then invited three holy men to be their guests; of them two had no body and the third had no mouth. After these holy men had eaten the food, the three princes partook of the rest of the food cooked. They were greatly pleased. Thus they lived in that city for a long long time in peace and joy. My child, this is an extremely beautiful legend; pray remember this always, and you will grow up into a learned man.

O Rāma, when the little boy heard this he was thrilled.

What is known as the creation of the world is no more real than this story of the young boy. This world is nothing but pure hallucination. It is nothing more than an idea. In the infinite consciousness the idea of creation arose: and that is what is. O Rāma, this world is nothing more than an idea; all the objects of consciousness in this world are just an idea; reject the error (dirt) of ideation and be free of ideas; and remain rooted in truth, attain peace.

VASIṢṬHA continued: III:102

Only a fool, not a wise man, is deluded by his own ideas; it is a fool who thinks that the imperishable is perishable, and gets deluded. Egotism is but an idea based on a false association of the self with the physical elements. When one alone exists in all this as the infinite consciousness, how has what is called egotism arisen? In fact, this egotism does not exist any more than the mirage exists in the desert. Therefore, O Rāma, abandon your imperfect vision which is not based on fact; rest in the perfect vision which is of the nature of bliss and which is based on truth.

Enquire into the nature of truth. Abandon falsehood. You are ever free; why do you call yourself bound and then grieve? The self is infinite; why, how and by whom is it bound? There is no division in the self, for the absolute Brahman is all this. What then is called bondage and what is liberation? It is only in a state of ignorance that you think you experience pain, though you are untouched by pain. These things do not exist in the self.

Let the body fall or rise or let it go on to another universe; I am not confined to the body, then how am I affected by all this? The relation between the body and the self is like the relation between cloud and wind, like the relation between lotus and the bee. When the cloud is dispersed, the wind becomes one with space. When the lotus withers, the bee flies away into the sky. The self is not destroyed when the body falls. Even the mind does not cease to be until it is burnt in the fire of self-knowledge; not to mention the self.

Death is but the veiling by time and space of the ever-present self. Only foolish people fear death.

Abandon your latent tendencies even as a bird wishing to fly into the sky breaks out of its shell. Born of ignorance, these tendencies are hard to destroy, and they give birth to endless sorrow. It is this ignorant self-limiting tendency of the mind that views the infinite as the finite. However, even as sun dispels mist, enquiry into the nature of the self dispels this ignorant self-limiting tendency. In fact, the very desire to undertake this enquiry is able to bring about a change. Austerities and such other practices are of no use in this.

When the mind is purified of its past by the arising of wisdom, it abandons its previous tendencies. The mind seeks the self only in order to dissolve itself in the self. This indeed is in the very nature of the mind. This is the supreme goal, Rāma: strive for this.

At this stage, another day came to a close.

The Story of Lavaṇa

III:103, 104 VASIṢṬHA continued:

Having manifested in the infinite consciousness, the mind has by its own nature spread itself out. By its nature, again, it makes the long appear short and vice versa, and makes one's own mind appear to be distinct and vice versa. Even a little thing which it touches, it magnifies and makes its own. In the twinkling of an eye it creates countless worlds and in the twinkling of an eye it destroys them. Even as an able actor plays several roles one after the other, this mind assumes several aspects one after the other. It makes the unreal appear as real and vice versa; and on account of this it seems to enjoy and to suffer. Even that which it gets naturally it grabs with hands and feet, and as a result of this false sense of ownership, suffers the consequences.

Time as changing seasons is able indirectly to bring about changes in the trees and plants; even so, the mind makes one thing appear to be another by its powers of thought and ideation. Therefore, even time and space and all things are under the control of the mind. Depending upon its intensity or dullness, and upon the size (big or small) of the object created or influenced, the mind does what is to be done with some delay or much later: it is not incapable of doing anything whatsoever.

Pray, O Rāma, listen to another interesting legend to illustrate this.

In a country known as Uttarāpāndava, in whose forests sages dwelt and whose villages were beautiful and prosperous, there reigned a king known as Lavaṇa who was a descendant of the famous king Hariścandra. He was righteous, noble, chivalrous, charitable and in every way a worthy king. His enemies had all been conquered; and their followers could not even think of him without becoming feverish with anxiety.

One day, this king went to his court and ascended the throne. After all the ministers and others had paid their homage to him, a juggler entered the court and saluted him. He said to the king: "I shall show you something wonderful!" As he waved a bunch of peacock feathers, there entered into the court a cavalier leading an exquisitely beautiful horse. He requested the king to accept it as a gift. The juggler requested the king to ride that horse and roam freely throughout the world. The king, too, saw the horse.

Thereupon, the king closed his eyes and sat motionless. Seeing this everyone assembled in the court became silent. Absolute peace reigned in the court, as no one dared to disturb the king's peace.

VASIṢṬHA continued: III:105, 106

Rāma, after some time, the king opened his eyes and began to tremble as if in fear. As he was about to fall down, the ministers supported him. Dismayed to see them, the king asked "Who are you and what are you doing to me?" The worried ministers said to him: "Lord, you are a mighty king of great wisdom and yet this delusion has overpowered you. What has happened to your mind? Only they who are attached to the little objects of this world and the false relationships of wife, children, etc., are subject to mental aberrations, not one like you, devoted to the supreme. Moreover, only he who has not cultivated wisdom is adversely affected by spells, drugs, etc., not one whose mind is fully developed."

Hearing this, the king partly regained his composure, though upon looking at the juggler he trembled as if in fear and said to him: "O magician, what have you done to me? You have spread a net of illusion over me. Truly even the wise are overpowered by the jugglery of Māyā; even as, though I am still in this body, within a short period I experienced wonderful hallucinations." Turning to the members of the court, the king recounted his experiences during the previous hour:

"As soon as I saw this juggler wave his bundle of peacock feathers, I jumped on the horse which stood in front of me and experienced a slight mental delusion. Then I went away on a hunting expedition. The horse led me into an arid desert where nothing lived, nothing grew, where there was no water and it was bitterly cold. I experienced great grief. I spent the whole day there. Later, riding that horse again I crossed that desert and reached another which was less dreadful. I rested under a tree. The horse ran away. I rested for some time, and the sun set. Frightened, I hid myself in the bushes. The night was longer than an epoch.

"The day dawned. The sun rose. A little later, I saw a dark girl clad in black clothes carrying a plateful of food. I approached her and begged for food: I was hungry. She ignored me; I pursued her. At last, she said "I shall give you food, if you consent to marry me." I consented; survival was the first and foremost consideration then. She gave me food and later introduced me to her father who was even more dreadful to look at. Soon the three of us reached their village which was flowing with blood and flesh. I was introduced to all as that girl's husband. I was treated by them with great respect. They entertained me with dreadful stories which were a source of pain. At a diabolical ceremony, I got married to that girl."

III:107, 108 THE KING continued:

Very soon, I had become a member of the primitive tribe. My wife gave birth to a daughter, the source of more unhappiness to me. In course of time three more babies arrived. I had become a family man in that tribe. I spent many years among this tribe, suffering the agonies of a family man with a wife and children to feed and to protect. I cut firewood and often I had to sleep under a tree at night. When the weather became cold, I hid myself in the bushes in order to keep warm. Pork was my staple diet.

Time rolled on and I became old. I began to trade in meat. I took the meat to the villages on the Vindhya mountains and sold the best part of it there; what could not thus be sold at a decent profit, I cut up into bits and dried in a terribly filthy place. I would often fight with others in the tribe for a piece of meat to eat when I was afflicted with hunger. My body had become black as soot.

Thus engaged in sinful activities, my mind had also become inclined towards sin. Good thoughts and feelings had taken leave of me. My heart had shed all compassion even as a snake sheds its slough. With nets and other traps and weapons I caused untold hardship to birds and animals.

Clad only in a loin cloth I endured every inclemency of the weather. Thus I spent seven years. Bound by the ropes of evil tendencies, I grew wild with anger and used abusive words, wept in misfortunes, and ate rotten food. Thus I lived for a long time, in that place. I drifted like a dry leaf in the wind, as if my only mission in life was eating.

There was drought in the land. The air was so hot that it seemed to waft sparks of flame. The forest caught alight. Only ashes remained. People were dying of hunger. People chased after mirages thinking there was water. They mistook pebbles to be balls of meat and began to chew them.

Some had even begun to eat corpses. Some, while doing so, even chewed their own fingers which had been soaked in the blood of those dead bodies. Such was their demented state of starvation.

What was once a flourishing forest had been transformed into a huge crematorium. What was once a pleasure-grove resounded with the agonised cries of the dying.

Note: These two chapters are full of apt and graphic similes.

THE KING continued: III:109

Thus afflicted by famine, many people left the country and migrated elsewhere. Some others, deeply attached to their wives and children, perished in that land. Many others were killed by wild animals.

I, too, left the country to go away with my wife and children. At the border of the country, I found the cool shade of a tree tempting and, after putting down the little children I was carrying on my shoulders, I rested under that tree for a long time.

The youngest of my children was quite small and innocent, and therefore was the dearest to my heart. With tears in his eyes, he demanded food. Although I told him that there was no meat to eat, in his childish innocence he persisted in his demand, unable to bear his hunger. I said to him in despair, "All right, eat my flesh!" The innocent child said, without thinking, "Give me."

I was moved by attachment and pity. I saw the child was unable to endure the pangs of hunger any more. I decided that the best way to end all these miseries was to end my life. I raised a pyre with the help of the timber I found nearby. And, as I ascended that pyre, I shuddered—and I found myself in this court, being hailed and greeted by all of you.

(As the king said this, the juggler vanished.) The MINISTERS said:

Lord, he cannot be a juggler, for he was not interested in money, in a reward. Surely, some divine entity wished to demonstrate to you and to all of us the power of cosmic illusion. From all this it is clear that this world-appearance is nothing but the play of the mind; the mind itself is but the play of the omnipotent infinite being. This mind is able to fool even men of great wisdom. Else, where is the king who is well versed in all branches of learning, and where is this bewildering delusion?

Surely, this is not a juggler's trick: for a juggler performs for material gain. It is really the power of illusion. Hence, the juggler vanished without looking for a reward.

VASIṢṬHA said:

Rāma, I was there in that court at that time and so I know all this first-hand. In this manner the mind veils the real nature of the self and creates an illusory appearance with many branches, flowers and fruits. Destroy this illusion by wisdom, and rest in peace.

VASIṢṬHA continued: III:110

In the beginning, there arose a division in the supreme being or infinite consciousness, and the infinite apparently became both the observer and the observed. When this observer sought to grasp or comprehend the observed, there arose a mixture (of the reality and the apparent appearance) or a confusion. On account of this confusion, in the infinite consciousness there arises the concept of finiteness.

The finite mind then generates countless ideas within itself which weaken and veil it leading to sorrow—which the mind greatly magnifies. These ideas and these experiences leave their mark on the mind, forming the impressions or conditioning tendencies which are for the most part latent or dormant. But, when the mind is rid of these, the veil vanishes in a moment like mist at sunrise, and with it the greatest sorrow also vanishes. Till then the mind plays with all, even as little children play with fledglings and tease them.

The impure mind sees a ghost where there is just a post, and pollutes all relationships, creating suspicion among friends and making enemies of them, even as a drunken man sees that the world is revolving around him. A distressed mind turns food into poison and causes disease and death.

The impure mind (laden with the tendencies) is the cause for delusions (manias and phobias). One should strive to uproot these and discard them. What is man but the mind? The body is inert and insentient. One cannot say that the mind is inert, though one cannot say that it is sentient either. What is done by the mind is action; what is renounced by the mind is renunciation.

Mind is the whole world, mind is the atmosphere, mind is the sky, mind is earth, mind is wind, and mind is great. Only he whose mind is foolish is called a fool: when the body loses its intelligence (for example, in death) the corpse is not said to be foolish!

Mind sees: the eyes are formed. Mind hears: ears come into being. Even so with the other senses: it is the mind that creates them.

Mind decides what is sweet and what is bitter, who is friend and who is enemy. Mind decides the length of time: the king Lavaṇa experienced the period of less than an hour as if it extended to a lifetime. Mind decides what is heaven and what is hell. Hence, if this mind is mastered, everything is mastered, including the senses.

VASIṢṬHA continued:

What is more mysterious, Rāma, than that the mind is able to veil the omnipresent, pure, eternal and infinite consciousness making you confuse it with this inert physical body? The mind itself appears as wind in the moving element, lustre in the lustrous, solidity in earth and void in the space.

If 'the mind is elsewhere' the taste of food that is being eaten is not really experienced. If 'the mind is elsewhere' one does not see what is right in front of oneself. The senses are born of the mind, but not the other way round.

It is only from the point of view of fools that the body and the mind are said to be quite different; in fact, they are non-different, being mind alone. Salutations to those sages who have actually realised this truth.

The sage who has realised this is not disturbed even if the body is embraced by a woman: to him it is like a piece of wood coming into contact with the body. Even if his arms are cut off, he does not experience it. He is able to convert all sorrow into bliss.

If the mind is elsewhere, even if you hear an interesting story, you do not hear anything at all.

Just as an actor is able to portray in himself the character of different personalities, the mind is able to create different states of consciousness like waking and dreaming. How mysterious is the mind which is able to make the king Lavaṇa feel that he is a primitive tribesman! The mind experiences what it itself constructs, the mind is nothing but what has been put together by thought; knowing this, do as you please.

It is the mind indeed that, on account of persistent thinking, thinks that it is born, that it dies; and though it has no form, thinks that it is a jīva with a body etc. On account of thoughts alone does it acquire a nationality, and enjoys or suffers pleasure and pain—all of which are in the mind like oil in a seed.

He who does not allow his mind to roam in objects of pleasure is able to master it. Even as one who is bound to a pillar does not move, the mind of a noble man does not move from the reality: he alone is a human being, the others are worms. He attains to the supreme being by constant meditation.

VASIṢṬHA continued: III:111

Victory over this goblin known as mind is gained when, with the aid of one's own self-effort, one attains self-knowledge and abandons the craving for what the mind desires as pleasure. This can easily be achieved without any effort at all (even as a child's attention can be easily diverted) by the cultivation of the proper attitude. Woe unto him who is unable to give up cravings, for this is the sole means to one's ultimate good. By intense self-effort it is possible to gain victory over the mind; and then without the least effort the individualised consciousness is absorbed in the infinite consciousness when its individuality is broken through. This is easy and is easily accomplished: they who are unable to do this are indeed vultures in human form.

There is no other path to one's salvation except control over one's mind, which means resolute effort to abandon cravings in the mind. Make a firm resolve to kill the mind as it were, which is easily achieved without the least doubt. If one has not abandoned the cravings of the mind, then all the instructions of a preceptor, study of scriptures, recitation of mantras and so on are as valuable as straw! Only when one severs the very root of the mind with the weapon of non-conceptualisation, can one reach the absolute Brahman which is omnipresent, supreme peace. Conceptualisation or imagination is productive of error and sorrow; and it can be so easily got rid of by self-knowledge—and when it is got rid of there is great peace. Why does one find it so difficult?

Abandon your reliance on fate or gods created by dull-witted people, and by self-effort and self-knowledge make the mind no-mind. Let the infinite consciousness swallow, as it were, the finite mind and then go beyond everything. With your intelligence united with the supreme, hold on to the self which is imperishable.

When the mind is thus conquered by remaining completely unagitated, you will consider even the conquest of the three worlds worthless. This does not involve studying the scriptures, or rising or falling—nothing but self-knowledge. Why do you consider it difficult? If this is found difficult by someone, how does he even live in this world without self-knowledge?

One who knows the deathless nature of the self is not afraid of death. Nor is he affected by separation from friends and relations. The feelings 'This is I' and 'This is mine' are the mind; when they are removed, the mind ceases to be. Then one becomes fearless. Weapons like swords generate fear; the weapon (wisdom) that destroys egotism generates fearlessness.

III:112 VASIṢṬHA continued:

Towards whichever object the mind flows with intensity, in that it sees the fulfilment of its cravings. The cause of this movement in a particular direction is not obvious; like ripples on the surface of the ocean, such intense movement appears now here and now there, comes into being and dies. However, just as coolness is inseparable from ice, this restless movement is inseparable from mind.

RĀMA asked:

How, then, Holy sir, can this restless movement of the mind be restrained by force without causing greater restlessness?

VASIṢṬHA said:

Of course, there is no mind without restlessness; restlessness is the very nature of mind. It is the work of this restlessness of the mind based on the infinite consciousness that appears as this world, O Rāma: that indeed is the power of the mind. But, when the mind is deprived of its restlessness, it is referred to as the dead mind;

and that itself is penance (tapas) as also the verification of the scriptures and liberation.

When the mind is thus absorbed in the infinite consciousness there is supreme peace; but when the mind is involved in thoughts there is great sorrow. The restlessness of the mind itself is known as ignorance or nescience; it is the seat of tendencies, predispositions or conditioning—destroy this through enquiry, as also by the firm abandonment of contemplation of the objects of sense-pleasure.

O Rāma, mind constantly swings like a pendulum between the reality and the appearance, between consciousness and inertness. When the mind contemplates the inert objects for a considerable time, it assumes the characteristic of such inertness. When the same mind is devoted to enquiry and wisdom, it shakes off all conditioning and returns to its original nature as pure consciousness. Mind takes the very form of that which one contemplates, whether it is natural or cultivated. Therefore, resolutely but intelligently contemplate the state beyond sorrow, free from all doubts. The mind is capable of restraining itself; there is indeed no other way.

Wise men remove from their mind the manifestations of the latent tendencies or conditioning (which alone is the mind) as and when they rise: thus is nescience removed. First destroy the mental conditioning by renouncing cravings; and then remove from your mind even the concepts of bondage and liberation. Be totally free of conditioning.

VASIṢṬHA continued: III:113

The psychological tendency (or mental disposition or mental conditioning) is unreal, yet it does arise in the mind: hence it can be compared to the vision of two moons in a person suffering from diplopia. Hence this tendency should be renounced as if it were sheer delusion. The product of ignorance is real only to the ignorant person; to the wise, it is just a verbal expression (just as one speaks of the barren woman's son). Do not remain ignorant, O Rāma, but strive to be wise, by renouncing mental conditioning as you would abandon the idea that there is a second moon.

You are not the doer of any action here, O Rāma; so, why do you assume doership? When one alone exists, who does what and how? Do not become inactive, either; for what is gained by doing nothing? What has to be done has to be done. Therefore, rest in the self. Even while doing all the actions natural to you, if you are unattached to those actions, you are truly the non-doer; if you are doing nothing and are attached to that non-doership (then you are *doing* nothing) you become the doer! When all this world is like the juggler's trick, what is to be given up and what is to be sought?

The seed of this world-appearance is ignorance; without being seen as 'this is it', this ignorance has the quality of truth! The power which creates this world-appearance and keeps it revolving as the potter's wheel is kept revolving by a potter, is the psychological tendency (or mental conditioning). Like a bamboo, it is hollow and without substance. Like the waves of a river, it does not die even when it is cut asunder. It cannot be grasped. It is subtle and soft, but it has the power of a sword. Though it is perceived in its own reflection as its effects, it is not useful in one's quest of truth. On account of this conditioning, differences are seen in the objects of this creation.

Though it cannot be said to abide in a particular place, it is seen everywhere. This mental conditioning is not a manifestation of intelligence, yet being based on intelligence it has the appearance of intelligence. Though it is ever changing, it creates in oneself an illusion of permanence. Because of its proximity to the infinite consciousness, it seems to be active; and when that infinite consciousness is realised, it (the conditioning) comes to an end.

This mental conditioning dies when not fed by attachment to objects; but even in the absence of such attachment, it continues to remain as a potentiality.

VASIṢṬHA continued:

This ignorance or mental conditioning is acquired by man effortlessly and it seems to promote pleasure, but in truth it is the giver of grief. It creates a delusion of pleasure only by the total veiling of self-knowledge. Thus it was able to make the king Lavaṇa experience less than an hour as if it were of several years' duration.

This ignorance or mental conditioning is powerless to do anything, yet it seems to be very active, even as a mirror actively reflects the light of a lamp. Even as a life-like painting of a woman is unable to perform the duties of a living woman, this ignorance or mental conditioning is incapable of functioning, though it appears to be potent. It is even unable to delude the wise man, though it overpowers the stupid one even as a mirage fools animals and not an intelligent man.

This ignorance or mental conditioning has but a momentary existence: yet, since it flows on, it seems to be permanent like a river. Because it is able to veil the reality, it seems to be real: but when you try to grasp it, you discover it is nothing. Yet, again, it acquires strength and firmness on account of these qualities in the world-appearance, even as a flimsy fibre when rolled into a rope acquires great strength. This conditioning seems to grow, but in fact it does not. For when you try to grasp it, it vanishes like the tip of a flame. Yet, again, even as the sky appears to be blue, this conditioning also seems to have some kind of real appearance! It is born as the second moon in diplopia, it exists like the dream-objects, and it creates confusion even as people sitting in a moving boat see the shore moving. When it is active, it creates a delusion of the long dream of world-appearance. It perverts all relationships and experiences. It is this ignorance or mental conditioning that is responsible for the creation and perception of duality, and of division and the consequent confusion of perception and experience.

When this ignorance or mental conditioning is mastered by becoming aware of its unreality, mind ceases to be—even as when the water ceases to flow, the river dries up.

RĀMA asked:

On the other hand, Holy sir, the river seen in the mirage does not come to an end. How astonishing it is that this ignorance has blinded the whole world! This ignorance or mental conditioning thrives on the twin forces of desire and hate. Pray, tell me of the best way to ensure that this ignorance or mental conditioning may not arise at all.

RĀMA asked: III:114

Holy sir, also tell me how this dreadful darkness of ignorance disappears.

VASIṢṬHA said:

O Rāma, even as darkness disappears on turning towards light, ignorance disappears if you turn towards the light of the self. As long as there does not arise a natural yearning for self-knowledge, so long this ignorance or mental conditioning throws up an endless stream of world-appearance. Even as a shadow vanishes when it wishes to see the light, this ignorance perishes when it turns towards self-knowledge.

Rāma, it is desire that is ignorance or mental conditioning: and the coming to an end of desire is liberation. This happens when there is no movement of thought in the mind.

RĀMA asked:

O sage, you have said that when ignorance ceases to be, there is self-knowledge. What is the self (ātman)?

VASIṢṬHA replied:

O Rāma, from Brahmā the creator down to the blade of grass, all this is nothing but the self: ignorance is non-existent unreality. There is no second thing here known as the mind. In that self itself, the veil (that is also of itself) floats, creating the polarisation of subject-object; and the infinite consciousness itself is then known as the mind. This veil is an idea, an intention or a thought in that infinite consciousness. Mind is born of this idea or thought, and mind has to vanish with the help of an idea or thought, i.e., by the coming to an end of the idea or thought.

The firm conviction that 'I am not the absolute Brahman' binds the mind; and the mind is liberated by the firm conviction that 'everything is the absolute Brahman'. Ideas and thoughts are bondage; and their coming to an end is liberation. Therefore, be free of them and do whatever has to be done spontaneously.

Even as thought or idea 'sees' blueness in the sky, the mind sees the world as real. There is no blueness in the sky: the inability of the sense of sight to see beyond a certain limit appears as blueness. Even so, it is only the limitation of thought that perceives the world-appearance. This world-appearance is delusion, O Rāma: it is better not to let the very thought of it arise again in the mind.

By thinking 'I am lost' one comes to grief, and by thinking 'I am alert' one goes towards bliss.

VASIṢṬHA continued:

When the mind continually dwells on deluded or stupid ideas it becomes deluded; and when the mind continually dwells on enlightened and magnanimous ideas it is enlightened. When the thought of ignorance is sustained in the mind, ignorance is firmly established; but, when the self is realised, this ignorance is dissolved. Moreover, whatever the mind seeks to attain, that the senses strive for with all their energy.

Therefore, he who does not let his mind dwell on such thoughts and ideas, by striving to be conscious of the self, enjoys peace. That which was not in the beginning does not exist even now! That which was and therefore is now, is the absolute Brahman—contemplation of this bestows peace, for that Brahman is peace. One should not contemplate anything else at any time and in any manner anywhere. One should uproot the very hope of enjoyment with one's utmost strength, and using one's utmost intelligence.

Ignorance alone is the cause of old age and death. Hopes and attachments seem to ramify on account of the mental conditioning which is ignorance. This ramification takes the form of ideas like 'This is my wealth', 'These are my sons', etc. In this empty physical body, where is it that is called 'I'? In truth, O Rāma, 'I', 'mine' etc., have no existence at all; the one self alone is the truth at all times.

It is only in a state of ignorance that one sees a snake in the rope, not in an enlightened state. Even so, to the enlightened vision, only the infinite consciousness exists, naught else. O Rāma, do not become an ignorant man; become a sage. Destroy the mental conditioning that gives rise to this world-appearance. Why do you, like an ignorant man, consider this body as your self and feel miserable? Though the body and the self appear to exist together, they are not inseparable; when the body dies, the self does not die.

Is it not a great wonder, O Rāma, that people forget the truth that the absolute Brahman alone is, and are convinced of the existence of the unreal and non-existent ignorance? Rāma, do not let the foolish idea of the existence of ignorance take root in you; for if the consciousness is thus polluted, it invites endless suffering. Though it is unreal, it can cause real suffering! It is on account of ignorance that illusions like a mirage exist, and one sees various visions and hallucinations (like flying in the air and flying in space) and one experiences heaven and hell. Therefore, O Rāma, give up mental conditioning which alone is responsible for the perception of duality, and remain totally unconditioned. Then, you will attain incomparable pre-eminence over all!

After a few minutes of deep contemplation RĀMA asked: III:115

Holy sage! It is indeed incredible that this non-existent nescience creates such an illusion that this non-existent world appears to be very real: pray explain to me further how this is possible. Also please tell me why the king Lavaṇa underwent all sorts of sufferings. Please tell me who or what it is that experiences all these sufferings.

VASIṢṬHA replied:

O Rāma, it is not really true that consciousness is in any way related to this body. The body has only been fancied by the consciousness as if in a dream. When consciousness, clothed as it were, by its own energy, limits itself and considers itself a jīva, that jīva, endowed with this restless energy, is involved in this world-appearance.

The embodied being who enjoys or suffers the fruits of past actions and who dons a variety of bodies is known as egotism, mind and also jīva. Neither the body nor the enlightened being undergoes suffering: it is only the ignorant mind that suffers. It is only in a state of ignorance (like sleep) that the mind dreams of the world-appearance, not when it is awake or enlightened. Hence the embodied being that undergoes suffering here is variously known as the mind, ignorance, jīva, and mental conditioning, as also the individualised consciousness.

The body is insentient and hence can neither enjoy nor suffer. Nescience gives rise to heedlessness and unwisdom; hence it is nescience alone that enjoys or suffers. It is indeed the mind alone that is born, weeps, kills, goes, abuses others, etc., not the body. In all the experiences of happiness and unhappiness as also in all the hallucinations and imaginations, it is mind that does everything and it is mind that experiences all this: mind is man.

I shall narrate to you the reason for the sufferings of the king Lavaṇa. Lavaṇa was a descendant of Hariścandra. Lavaṇa thought: "My grandfather performed a great religious rite and became a great man. I should also perform the same rite." He gathered the necessary materials and the religious men and he performed the rite mentally for a whole year, (while sitting in his own garden).

Since he had thus successfully completed the religious rite performed mentally, he was entitled to its fruits. O Rāma, thus you see that mind alone is the performer of all actions and hence it is also the experiencer of all happiness and unhappiness. Therefore, guide your mind along the path to salvation, Rāma.

III:116, 117 VASIṢṬHA continued:

I myself was a witness to the scene in king Lavaṇa's court, and when they wished to know who that juggler was after he had abruptly disappeared from the court, I saw his identity through my subtle vision and found that he was a messenger of the gods. It is the tradition that Indra would send all sorts of afflictions to test the strength of anyone who engaged himself in that particular religious rite which Lavaṇa was performing mentally. The hallucinations he had were the result. The rite was performed by the mind and the hallucinations were experienced by the mind.

When the same mind is thoroughly purified, you will get rid of all duality and diversity which it creates.

Rāma, I have already narrated to you the process of cyclical creation (after the previous cosmic dissolution), and of how one comes to entertain the false notions of 'I' and 'mine'. Equipped with wisdom, he who gradually ascends the seven steps to perfection in yoga attains liberation from these.

RĀMA asked:

Holy sir, what are the seven steps you have referred to?

VASIṢṬHA replied:

O Rāma, there are seven descending steps of ignorance; and there are seven ascending steps of wisdom. I shall now describe them to you. To remain established in self-knowledge is liberation; when this is disturbed, there arises egotism and bondage. The state of self-knowledge is that in which there is no mental agitation, neither distraction nor dullness of mind, neither egotism nor perception of diversity.

The delusion that veils this self-knowledge is sevenfold: seed state of wakefulness, wakefulness, great wakefulness, wakeful dream, dream, dream wakefulness and sleep. In pure consciousness when mind and jīva exist only in name it is the seed state of wakefulness.

When notions of 'I' and 'this' arise it is known as wakefulness. When these notions get strengthened by the memory of previous incarnations, it is great wakefulness. When the mind is fully awake to its own fancies and is filled with them, it is wakeful dream. The false notions of experiences during sleep, which yet appear to be real, are dreams. In the dream wakeful state one recalls past experiences as if they are real now. When these are abandoned in favour of total inert dullness, it is sleep. These seven have their own innumerable sub-divisions.

VASIṢṬHA continued: III:118

I shall now describe to you, O Rāma, the seven states or planes of wisdom. Knowing them you will not be caught in delusion. Pure wish or intention is the first, enquiry is the second, the third is when the mind becomes subtle, establishment in truth is the fourth, total freedom from attachment or bondage is the fifth, the sixth is cessation of objectivity, and the seventh is beyond all these.

'Why do I continue to be a fool? I shall seek holy men and scriptures, having cultivated dispassion'—such a wish is the first state. Thereupon one engages in the practice of enquiry (direct observation). With all these, there arises non-attachment, and the mind becomes subtle and transparent: this is the third state. When these three are practised, there arises in the seeker a natural turning away from sense-pleasures and there is natural dwelling in truth: this is the fourth state.

When all these are well practised, there is total non-attachment and at the same time a conviction in the nature of truth: this is the fifth state. Then one rejoices in one's own self, the perception of duality and diversity both within oneself and outside oneself ceases, and the efforts that one made at the inspiration of others bear fruition in direct spiritual experience.

After this, there is no other support, no division, no diversity, and self-knowledge is spontaneous, natural and therefore unbroken: this is the seventh, transcendental state. This is the state of one who is liberated even while living here. Beyond this is the state of one who has transcended even the body (the turīyātīta).

Rāma, all these great ones who ascend these seven planes of wisdom are holy men. They are liberated and they do not fall into the mire of happiness and unhappiness. They may or may not work or be active. They rejoice in the self and do not stand in need of others to make them happy.

The highest state of consciousness can be attained by all, even by animals and by primitive men, by those who have a body and even by disembodied beings, for it involves only the rise of wisdom.

They who have reached the highest planes of consciousness are indeed great men, They are adorable; even an emperor is like a worthless blade of grass compared to them, for they are liberated here and now.

III:119 VASIṢṬHA continued:

The self ignorantly imagines an egotistic existence even as if gold forgetting its goldness might think it is a ring and weep and wail "Alas, I have lost my goldness".

RĀMA asked:

Holy sir, how can this ignorance and egotism arise in the self?

VASIṢṬHA said:

Rāma, one should ask questions concerning the reality only, not concerning the unreal. Neither goldless ringness nor limited egotism exists in truth. When the goldsmith sells the ring he weighs out the gold: for it is gold. If one were to discuss the existence of the ringness in the ring, and the finite form in the infinite consciousness, then one has to compare it with the barren woman's son. The existence of the unreal is unreal: it arises in ignorance and vanishes when enquired into. In ignorance one sees silver in the mother-of-pearl: but it cannot serve as silver even for a moment! As long as the truth that it is mother-of-pearl is not seen, the ignorance lasts. Even as one cannot extract oil from sand and even as one can obtain only gold from the ring, there are no two things here in this universe: the one infinite consciousness alone shines in all names and forms.

Such indeed is the nature of this utter ignorance, this delusion and this world-process: without real existence there is this illusory notion of egotism. This egotism does not exist in the infinite self. In the infinite self there is no creator, no creation, no worlds, no heaven, no humans, no demons, no bodies, no elements, no time, no existence and no destruction, no 'you', no 'I', no self, no that, no truth, no falsehood (none of these), no notion of diversity, no contemplation and no enjoyment. Whatever is, and is known as the universe, is that supreme peace. There is no beginning, no middle and no end: all is all at all times, beyond the comprehension of the mind and the speech. There is no creation. The infinite has never abandoned its infinity. That has never become this. It is like the ocean, but without ocean's movement. It is self-luminous like the sun, but without activity. In ignorance, the supreme being is viewed as the object, as the world. Even as space exists in space, one with space, even so what appears to be the creation is Brahman existing in Brahman, as Brahman. The notions of far and near, of diversity, of here and there are as valid as the distance between two objects in a mirror in which a whole city is reflected.

VASIṢṬHA continued: III:120, 121

The day after his hallucinatory experience king Lavaṇa thought: "I should actually go to those places that I saw in the vision; perhaps they exist in reality". Immediately, he set out with his retinue and proceeded in a southerly direction. Soon, he came across the very scenes of his vision and the type of people whom he had seen then. He met the very people whom he knew during his existence as a tribesman. He even saw his own destitute children.

He saw there an old woman who was weeping and screaming in agony: "O my beloved husband, where have you gone, leaving us all here. I have lost my beautiful daughter who had an extraordinary stroke of luck to obtain a handsome king for her husband. Where have they all gone? Alas, I have lost all of them." The king approached her, consoled her and learnt from her that she was indeed the mother of his tribal wife! Out of compassion he gave them enough wealth to meet their needs and to help them out of the drought that had stricken the whole countryside, even as he had seen the day before. He dwelt among them for some time and then returned to his palace.

The next morning, the king asked me to explain the mystery and was fully satisfied with my answer. O Rāma, thus the power of nescience is capable of creating a total confusion between the real and the unreal.

RĀMA asked:

O sage, this is indeed puzzling. How can that which was seen in a dream or a hallucination be also experienced in the reality of the waking state?

VASIṢṬHA answered:

But, O Rāma, all this is ignorance! The notions of far and near, a moment and eternity, are all hallucinations: in ignorance the real appears to be unreal, and the unreal seems to be real. The individualised consciousness perceives what it thinks it perceives, on account of its conditioning. On account of ignorance, when the notion of egotism arises, at that very moment the delusion of a beginning, a middle and an end also arises. One who is thus deluded thinks that he is an animal and experiences this. All this happens on account of accidental coincidence: just as a crow flies towards a cocoanut palm and as it alights on the tree, a fruit falls down as if the crow dislodged it—though, in fact, the crow did not! Similarly, by pure coincidence and in ignorance, the unreal seems to be real.

VASIṢṬHA continued:

In his hypnotic state, the king Lavaṇa obviously saw reflected in his own consciousness the marriage of a prince with the tribal woman, etc., and he experienced it as if it happened to him. A man forgets what he did earlier in his life even if at that time he had devoted a lot of time and energy to that action. Even so, he now thinks that he did not do what he actually did. Such discrepancies in memory are often seen.

Even as one sometimes dreams of a past incident as if it were happening now, Lavaṇa experienced in his vision some past incident connected with the tribesmen. It is possible that the people in the forests on the slopes of the Vindhyas experienced in their own minds the visions that appeared in the consciousness of Lavaṇa. It is also possible that Lavaṇa and the tribesmen saw in their own minds whatever was experienced by the other. These hallunications become reality when experienced by many, even as a statement made by very many people is accepted as true. When these are incorporated in one's life, they acquire their own reality: after all, what is the truth concerning the things of this world, except how they are experienced in one's own consciousness?

Nescience is not a real entity, even as oil in sand is not a real entity. Nescience and the self cannot have any relationship: for there can be relationship only between same or similar entities—this is obvious in everyone's experience. Thus, it is only because consciousness is infinite that everything in the universe becomes knowable. It is not as if the subject illumines the object which has no luminosity of its own, but since consciousness is all this, everything is self-luminous, without requiring a perceiving intelligence. It is by the action of consciousness becoming aware of itself that intelligence manifests itself, not when consciousness apprehends an inert object.

It is not correct to say that there is a mixture in this universe of the sentient and the inert, for they do not mix. It is because all things are full of consciousness and when this consciousness comprehends itself there is knowledge.

One may see a relationship between a tree and a rock, though they appear to be inert: but such relationship exists in their fundamental constituents which have undergone a certain kind of change to become a tree and another to become a rock. This is also seen in the sense of taste: the taste-buds in the tongue respond to the taste in the food, etc., because of their similarity in constitution.

VASIṢṬHA continued:

All relationship is therefore the realisation of the already existing unity: it is regarded as relationship only because of the previous false and deluded assumption of a division into subject and object. In fact, there is only one All, the infinite consciousness. Therefore, O Rāma, realise this universe as the infinite consciousness. It is filled with the jugglery of the power of that consciousness; yet, nothing has happened, for the full cannot be filled with more. It is filled only in the sense of a space which is filled with an imaginary city.

Only when the gold is forgotten does one see a bracelet. Bracelet is an illusory appearance of gold; even so are the illusory notions of a nation or the world and also that of repeated births. When the false notion of the bracelet is rejected, the truth of the gold is realised; and when the false notion of the subject-object is rejected, there is no ignorance to create a division. Thought alone creates all these divisions and illusions. When it ceases, creation ceases, too: then you realise that all the waves constitute one ocean, dolls are wood, pots are clay, and the three worlds are absolute Brahman.

In the middle between the sight and the seen, there is a relationship which is known as the seer. When the division between the seer, the sight and the seen is abolished, that is the supreme. When the mind travels from one country to another, between them is cosmic intelligence. Be that always. Your true nature is distinct from the limited wakeful, dreaming and sleep consciousness; it is eternal, unknowable, not inert—remain as that always. Remove dullness and be established in the truth in your heart: and then, whether you are busily engaged in activity or in contemplation, remain as that always, without cravings and hatred and without getting tangled in body-consciousness. Even as you do not busy yourself with the affairs of a future village, do not get tangled with the moods of your mind, but be established in truth. Regard the mind as a foreigner or a piece of wood or stone. There is no mind in infinite consciousness; that which is done by this non-existent mind is also unreal. Be established in this realisation.

In fact, the mind does not exist: if it did exist, now it is dead. Yet this dead mind sees all this, which is therefore false perception—be established firmly in this realisation. He who is ruled by this mind which is totally non-existent is indeed insane and feels that a thunderbolt is descending from the moon! Therefore, reject the reality of the mind from a great distance and be ever devoted to right thinking and meditation. I have investigated the truth concerning the mind for a very long time, O Rāma, and have found none: only the infinite consciousness exists.

VASIṢṬHA continued: III:122

This seemingly endless stream of ignorance can be crossed over only by the constant company of the holy ones. From such company there arises wisdom concerning what is worth seeking and what is to be avoided. Then there arises the pure wish to attain liberation. This leads to serious enquiry. Then the mind becomes subtle because the enquiry thins out the mental conditioning. As a result of the rising of pure wisdom, one's consciousness moves in the reality. Then the mental conditioning vanishes and there is non-attachment. Bondage to actions and their fruits ceases. The vision is firmly established in truth and the apprehension of the unreal is weakened. Even while living and functioning in this world, he who has this unconditioned vision does what has to be done as if he is asleep, without thinking of the world and its pleasures. After some years of living like this, one is fully liberated and transcends all these states: he is liberated while living.

Such a liberated sage is not elated at what he gets, nor does he grieve for what he has not. O Rāma, in you also the conditioning of the mind has been weakened: strive to know the truth. By attaining knowledge of the self, which is infinite consciousness, you will go beyond grief, delusion, birth and death, happiness and unhappiness. The self being one and undivided, you have no relatives and therefore no sorrow born of such false relationship. The self being one and undivided, there is nothing else worth attaining or desiring. This self undergoes no change and does not die: when the pot is broken, the space within it is not broken.

When mental conditioning is overcome and the mind is made perfectly tranquil, the illusion that deludes the ignorant comes to an end. It is only as long as this illusion (Māyā) is not clearly understood that it generates this great delusion; but once it is clearly understood, it is seen as the infinite, and it becomes the source of happiness and the realisation of the absolute Brahman. It is only for the sake of scriptural instruction that one speaks of the self, Brahman, etc., but in truth one alone is. It is pure consciousness, not embodied being. It is, whether one knows or not, whether one is embodied or without a body. All the unhappiness you see in this world belongs to the body; the self which is not grasped by the senses is not touched by sorrow. In the self there is no desire: the world appears in it without any wish or intention on its part. Thus, O Rāma, through my precepts the false notion of a creation and its existence has been dispelled. Your consciousness has become pure, devoid of duality.

PART FOUR

On Existence

VASIṢṬHA continued: IV:1

O Rāma, after the exposition of the true nature of world-creation I shall deal with the exposition of the true nature of the sustenance of this world-appearance. Only as long as the delusion of this world-appearance lasts is there this existence of the world as an object of perception. In fact, it is as real as a dream-vision; for it is produced out of nothing by no one with no instruments on nothing.

This world-appearance is experienced only like a day-dream; it is essentially unreal. It is a painting on void like the colours of a rainbow. It is like a widespread fog; when you try to grasp it, it is nothing. Some philosophers treat this as inert substance or void or the aggregate of atoms.

RĀMA asked:

It has been said that this universe remains in a seed-state in the supreme being, to manifest again in the next epoch: how can this be and are they who hold this view to be regarded as enlightened or ignorant?

VASIṢṬHA continued:

They who say that this universe exists in a seed-state after the cosmic dissolution are those who have firm faith in the reality of this universe! This is pure ignorance, O Rāma. It is a totally perverted view which deludes both the teacher and the hearer. The seed of a plant contains the future tree: this is because both the seed and the sprout are material objects which are capable of being apprehended by the senses and the mind. But, that which is beyond the reach of the mind and the senses—how can that be the seed for the worlds?

In that which is subtler than space, how can there exist the seed of the universe? When that is so, how can the universe emerge from the supreme being?

How can something exist in nothing? And if there is something called the universe in it, how is it not seen? How can a tree spring out of the empty space in a jar? How can two contrary things (Brahman and the universe) co-exist: can darkness exist in the sun? It is appropriate to say that the tree exists in the seed, because both these have appropriate forms. But in that which has no form (Brahman) it is inappropriate to say that this cosmic form of the world exists. Hence, it is pure foolishness to assume that there exists a causal relationship between Brahman and the world: the truth is that Brahman alone exists and what appears to be the world is that alone.

IV:2, 3 VASIṢṬHA continued:

Rāma, if the universe existed in a seed-state in the absolute Brahman during the cosmic dissolution, then it would need a co-operative cause for its manifestation after the dissolution. To assume that the universe manifested without such co-operative causation is to assume the existence of a barren woman's daughter. Hence, the fundamental cause itself has to be seen as the very nature of the supreme being which continues to be so even during the period after the dissolution, in what one regards as this creation. There is no cause and effect relation between the supreme being and the universe.

Millions of universes appear in the infinite consciousness (cid ākāśa) like specks of dust in a beam of light streaming into a room through a hole in the roof. But, even as such specks of dust are not to be seen in the outside sunlight itself, the world is not seen in the supreme non-dual consciousness. That is because these universes are non-different from the infinite consciousness, even as one's nature is not different from oneself.

At the conclusion of the cosmic dissolution, there arose the Creator of the universe who was nothing more than memory. The thoughts that arose from that memory constitute this world-appearance, which is no more real than a pie in the sky; for the memory from which the thoughts sprang has itself no valid basis, because all the deities of the previous world-cycle (like the creator Brahmā, etc.) had surely attained liberation. When there is no one to remember, how can memory exist?

Thus, that memory which arose in consciousness (whether of previous experiences or otherwise) appears as the world. That spontaneous world-appearance in the infinite consciousness is known as spontaneous creation. This world-appearance assumed a certain ethereal form which is known as the cosmic person.

In one small atom all the three worlds appear to be, with all their components like space, time, action, substance, day and night. In that there are other atoms in which there are such world-appearances, just as there is a figure in an uncarved marble slab and that figure (which is marble) has a figure in its limbs and so on ad infinitum. Hence, O Rāma, in the eyes of both the enlightened and the ignorant, the vision does not vanish: to the enlightened this is Brahman at all times, and to the ignorant it is always the world! In utter void, you see what is regarded as 'distance'; in the infinite consciousness, you see what is regarded as 'creation'. Creation is just a word, without corresponding substantial reality.

The Story of Śukra

VASIṢṬHA continued: IV:4, 5, 6

O Rāma, the only way to cross this formidable ocean of world-appearance is the successful mastery of the senses. No other effort is of any use. When one is equipped with the wisdom gained by study of the scriptures and the company of sages, and has his senses under his control, he realises the utter non-existence of all objects of perception.

Rāma, mind alone is all this: and when that is healed, this jugglery of world-appearance is also healed. This mind alone by its thinking faculty conjures up what is known as the body: no body is seen where the mind does not function! Hence, the treatment of the psychological illness known as perception of objects is the best of all treatment in this world. The mind creates delusion, the mind produces ideas of birth and death; and, as a direct result of its own thoughts, it is bound and it is liberated.

RĀMA asked:

O Holy sage, kindly tell me: how does this enormous universe exist in the mind?

VASIṢṬHA replied:

O Rāma, it is like the universes created by the brāhmaṇa boys. Again, it is like the hallucinations suffered by the king Lavaṇa. There is another illustration. It is the story of the sage Śukra which I shall presently narrate to you.

A long time ago, the sage Bhṛgu was performing intense penance on the peak of a mountain. His son Śukra was a young man at that time. While the father sat motionless in meditation, the young son attended to the father's needs. One day, this young man beheld in the sky a beautiful flying nymph. His mind was disturbed with desire for her; so was her own mind disturbed when she saw the radiant young Śukra.

Intensely overcome by desire for the nymph, Śukra closed his eyes and (mentally) pursued her. He reached heaven. There he saw the radiant celestial beings, gods and their consorts, the celestial elephant and horses. He saw the creator Brahmā himself as also the other deities who govern this universe. He saw the siddhas (perfected beings). He listened to celestial music. He visited the celestial gardens in heaven. Finally, he saw the king of heaven, Indra himself, seated in all his majesty, waited upon by incomparably beautiful nymphs. He saluted Indra. Indra, too, got up from his throne and greeted the young sage Śukra and begged him to stay in heaven for a long time. Śukra also consented to do so.

IV:7, 8, 9 VASIṢṬHA continued:

Śukra had completely forgotten his previous identity. After spending some time in the court of Indra, Śukra roamed the heaven and soon discovered the whereabouts of the nymph he had seen. When they looked at each other they were overcome by desire for each other, for wish-fulfilment is the characteristic of heaven.

Śukra wished for the darkness of night to envelop the pleasure-garden where he met the nymph. So it was dark. Śukra then entered the beautiful rest house in that garden: the nymph followed. She pleaded, "Great one, I am tormented by desire for you. Only the dull-witted deride love, not the wise ones. Even the lordship of the three worlds is nothing compared to the delight of the company of the loved one. Hence, pray, give me shelter in your heart." Saying so, she collapsed on his chest.

Śukra spent a very long time with that nymph, roaming at will in heaven. He lived with that nymph for a period equal to eight world-cycles.

After this length of time, as if his merit had been exhausted, Śukra fell from heaven, along with that nymph. When their subtle bodies fell on earth, they became dew-drops which entered food-grains which were eaten by a holy brāhmaṇa, from whom his wife received their essence. Śukra became their son. He grew up there. The nymph had become a female deer, and Śukra begot through her a human child. He became greatly attached to this son. Worries and anxieties caused by this child soon aged Śukra, and he died longing for pleasures.

On account of this Śukra became the ruler of a kingdom in the next birth and he died to that embodiment longing for a life of austerity and holiness. In the next birth he became a holy man.

Thus, after passing from one embodiment to another and enduring all manner of destinies Śukra practised intense austerity, standing firm on the bank of a river.

Thus contemplating while seated in front of his father, Śukra spent a long time. His body had become extremely emaciated. In the meantime the restless mind created scene after scene of successive life-spans, birth and death, ascent to heaven and descent to earth and the peaceful life of a hermit. He was so immersed in these that he regarded them as the truth. The body had been reduced to skin and bone, for it had been assailed by the inclemencies of every type of weather. It appeared terribly frightening even to look at. Yet, it was not consumed by carnivorous beasts, as it stood right in front of the sage Bhṛgu who was engaged in deep meditation, and as Śukra himself had endowed it with psychic strength through the practice of yogic discipline.

VASIṢṬHA continued: IV:10

After a hundred celestial years of contemplation, the sage Bhṛgu got up from his seat. He did not see his son, Śukra, in front of him, but saw the dried up body. The body appeared hideous, an abode of worms which, dwelling in the eye-sockets, had multiplied very fast indeed. Deeply concerned with what he saw, and without really reflecting over the natural course of events, Bhṛgu was filled with rage and resolved to curse Time for thus causing the untimely death of his son.

Time (or Death) instantly approached the sage in physical form. Time had a sword in one hand and a noose in the other. He had impenetrable armour. He had six arms and six faces. He was surrounded by a host of his servants and messengers. He was radiant with the flames of destruction that emanated from his body and from the weapons he held in his hands.

Calmly and in an unfaltering voice, TIME thus addressed Bhṛgu:

O sage, how is it that such a wise sage as you are contemplates such unworthy conduct? Wise men are not upset even when they are offended; yet, you have lost your balance of mind even though no one has offended you! You are indeed an adorable person, and I am one of those who strictly adhere to the appropriate mode of behaviour; hence I salute you—not with any other motive.

Do not waste your merit in useless exhibition of your power to curse! Know that I am unaffected even by the fires of cosmic dissolution; how childish of you to hope to destroy me with your curse!

I am Time: and I have destroyed countless beings, nay, even the gods who preside over this universe. Holy one, I am the consumer and you are our food: this indeed is ordained by nature. This relationship is not based on mutual likes or dislikes. Fire by its very nature flames upward, and water naturally flows down: food seeks the consumer, and created objects seek their end. This is how it has been ordained by the Lord: in the self of all, the self dwells as itself. To the purified vision there is neither a doer nor an enjoyer; but to the unpurified vision which sees division, such a division seems to exist.

You are indeed a knower of truth and you know that there is neither doership nor non-doership here. Creatures come and go like flowers on trees, their causation is naught else than conjecture. All these are attributed to time. This can be considered real or unreal. For, when the surface of the lake is agitated, the reflection of the moon seems to be agitated. This can be considered both true and false.

TIME continued:

Do not give way to anger, O sage: that is surely the path to disaster. For, what will be will be. Realise this truth. We are not swayed by vanity; we are naturally inclined to the fulfilment of our natural functions. Such indeed is the nature of wise ones. What has to be done has to be done by wise men here, remaining egoless and unselfish as if in deep sleep: do not let this be violated.

Where is your wisdom, your greatness and your moral courage? O sage, though you know the path to blessedness, why do you act like a fool? Surely, you know that the ripe fruit falls to the ground; ignoring this, why do you think of cursing me?

Surely, you know that everyone has two bodies, the one physical and the other mental. The physical body is insentient and seeks its own destruction; the mind is finite but orderly—but that mind is disturbed in you! The mind makes the body dance to its tunes, bringing about successive changes in it, like the child playing with mud. Mental actions alone are actions; its thoughts cause bondage and its own pure state is liberation. It is the mind that creates the body with all its limbs. Mind itself is both the sentient and the insentient beings; all this endless diversity is nothing but mind. Mind itself in its function as determination is known as the intellect and in its function as identification is known as the ego-sense. The physical body is only physical matter; yet the mind deems it as its own. Yet, if the mind turns towards the truth, it abandons its identification with the body and attains the supreme.

O sage, while you were engaged in contemplation, your son went far, far away in his own fancy. He left here the body which was 'the son of Bhṛgu' and rose up to the heaven. There in heaven he enjoyed the celestial nymphs. In course of time, when his merit had been exhausted by such enjoyment, he fell down on the earth like ripe fruit, along with the nymph. He had to leave his celestial body in heaven. He fell on earth to be born with a physical body. Here on earth he had to undergo a series of births. He was, successively, a brāhmaṇa boy, a king, a fisherman, a swan, again a king, a great yogi with psychic powers, a celestial demi-god, the son of a sage, a king again, and again the son of a sage, and on account of evil deeds he became a hunter, a king, and then as worms and plants, a donkey, a bamboo, a deer in China, a snake, a bird, and once again a demi-god, and now once again he has become the son of a brāhmaṇa known as Vasudeva. He is well read in the scriptures and is at present engaged in penance on the bank of the holy river Samaṅga.

VASIṢṬHA continued: IV:11

Encouraged by Yama (Time), the sage Bhṛgu thereupon entered into the eye of wisdom in order to behold the life of his son. In an instant, he saw in his own intelligence the entire story of his son's transmigration. Wonderstruck at what he saw, he re-entered his own body.

Completely devoid of all attachment to his son, BHṚGU said:

Lord, you are indeed the knower of the past, present and future, whereas we are of little understanding. This world-appearance which though unreal appears to be real, deludes even the heroic man of wisdom. Surely, all this is within you, and only you know the true form of this phantom created by the imaginations of the mind.

This son of mine is not dead: yet, taking him to be dead I became agitated. I thought that my son had been taken away from me before his time arrived. Lord, though we understand the course of earthly events, we are moved to joy and sorrow by what we consider as good fortune and misfortune.

In this world, anger impels man to do what should not be done, but tranquillity enables one to do what should be done. As long as there exists the delusion of world-existence, so long the distinction between appropriate and inappropriate action is valid. It is inappropriate that we should be agitated by your natural function, which is to cause the apparent death of beings here.

By your grace, I have seen my son again, and I realise that mind alone is the body and it is the mind that conjures up this world-vision.

TIME said:

Well said, O sage; truly mind is the body; it is the mind that 'creates' the body by mere thoughts, just as the potter makes a pot. It creates new bodies and brings about the destruction of what exists, and all this by mere wish. It is surely obvious that within mind exist the faculties of delusion or hallucination, dreaming and irrational thought, which create a pie in the sky. Even so it creates the appearance of the body within itself; but the ignorant man with a gross physical vision sees the physical body as different from and independent of the mind.

The three worlds (of waking, dream and sleep) are nothing but the expression of the faculties of the mind: this expression can be considered neither real nor unreal. When the mind conditioned by the perception of diversity 'sees', it sees the diversity.

TIME continued:

The mind itself gets involved in this world-appearance by entertaining countless notions (like 'I am weak, unhappy, foolish, etc.'). When the understanding arises that all this is but the false creation of the mind, I am what I am—then the peace of the supreme arises in one's consciousness.

The mind is like a vast ocean with infinite variety of creatures within it, on the surface of which ripples and waves of different sizes rise and fall. The small wave thinks it is small; the big one that it is big. The one that is broken by the wind thinks it has been destroyed. One thinks it is cold, another that it is warm. But all the waves are but the water of the ocean. It is indeed true to say that there are no waves in the ocean; the ocean alone exists. Yet, it is also true that there are waves!

Even so, the absolute Brahman alone exists. Since it is omnipotent, the natural expression of its infinite faculties appears as the infinite diversity in this universe. Diversity has no real existence except in one's own imagination. 'All this is indeed the absolute Brahman'—remain established in this truth. Give up all other notions. Even as the waves, etc. are non-different from the ocean, all these things are non-different from Brahman. Even as in the seed is hidden the entire tree in potential, in Brahman there exists the entire universe for ever. Even as the multicoloured rainbow is produced by sunlight, all this diversity is seen in the one. Even as the inert web emanates from the living spider, this inert world-appearance has sprung from the infinite consciousness.

Even as the silk-worm weaves its cocoon and thus binds itself, the infinite being fancies this universe and gets caught in it. Even as an elephant effortlessly breaks loose from the post to which it is tied, the self liberates itself from its bondage. For, the self is what it considers itself to be. In fact, there is neither bondage nor liberation for the Lord. I do not know how these notions of bondage and liberation have come into being! There is neither bondage nor liberation, only that infinite being is seen: yet the eternal is veiled by the transient, and this is indeed a great wonder (or a great illusion).

The moment this mind manifested in the infinite consciousness, there also arose the notions of diversity, and these notions exist in the infinite consciousness. On account of this, there appear to exist in this universe the various deities and the innumerable species of creations—some long-lived, some short-lived, some big and some small, some happy and some unhappy. All these living entities are but notions in the infinite consciousness: some consider themselves ignorant and bound, others are free from ignorance and liberated.

TIME continued: IV:12, 13

O sage, gods, demons and human beings are non-different from this cosmic ocean of consciousness known as Brahman: this is the truth, all other assertions are false. They (the gods, etc.) entertain false notions (like 'I am not the absolute') and thus superimpose upon themselves impurity and the feeling of downfall. Even they dwell forever in this cosmic ocean of consciousness; yet considering themselves separated from Brahman, they are deluded. Though they are for ever pure, they superimpose impurity on themselves and this is the seed of all their actions and their consequences, viz., happiness, unhappiness, ignorance and enlightenment.

Of these beings, some are pure like Śiva and Viṣṇu, some are slightly tainted like men and gods, some are in dense delusion like trees and shrubs, some are blinded by ignorance like worms, some wander far far from wisdom and some have reached the state of enlightenment and liberation, like Brahmā, Viṣṇu and Śiva.

Though revolving thus in the wheel of ignorance and delusion, when one steps on to the wisdom concerning the supreme truth he is instantly redeemed.

Of these, neither they who are like the trees firmly rooted in delusion, nor they who have utterly destroyed their delusion need engage themselves in the enquiry into the scriptures. The scriptures themselves have been produced by enlightened beings for the guidance of those who have been awakened from the slumber of ignorance after their evil nature and its expressions have ceased to be, and whose intellect naturally seeks such scriptural guidance.

O sage, it is only the mind that experiences pleasures and pain in this world, not the physical body of beings. In fact, the physical body is nothing but the fruit of the fancy of the mind; the physical body is not an existential fact independent of the mind. Whatever your son willed in his own mind, that he experiences; we are not responsible for this. All beings here in this world obtain only those actions which spring from the storehouse of their own potentialities and predispositions: no one else is responsible for those actions, no superhuman being or god.

Come, let us go to where your son is engaged in penance, after momentarily enjoying the pleasures of the heaven.

(Saying thus, Yama (Time) caught hold of Bhṛgu and led him away. . . . While the sage Vasiṣṭha said this the eighth day came to a close and the assembly dispersed.)

IV:14 VASIṢṬHA continued:

O Rāma, the sage Bhṛgu and the deity presiding over Time proceeded towards the bank of the river Samaṅga. As they were descending the Mandara mountain they saw beautiful forests inhabited by perfected and enlightened sages. They saw mighty elephants in rut. They saw other perfected sages who were being playfully pelted with flowers by celestial nymphs. They saw Buddhist (or enlightened) monks roaming the forest. Then they descended onto the plains dotted with villages and cities. Very soon, they had reached the bank of the river Samaṅga.

There, the sage Bhṛgu saw his son, who had another body and whose nature was different from what it was before, who was of a peaceful disposition and whose mind was established in the tranquility of enlightenment, though he was deeply reflecting the destiny of living beings in the universe. This radiant young man appeared to have reached total quiescence of mind in which the play of thoughts and counter-thoughts had ceased. He was absolutely pure, like a crystal that is not interested even in reflecting what is around it! There was no thought in his mind of either 'this is to be obtained' or 'this is to be avoided'.

Time pointed out this young man and said to Bhṛgu: "This is your son". Śukra heard the words "Get up" and gently opened his eyes. Seeing the two radiant beings standing in front of him, he greeted them appropriately and seated them on a rock. In soft and sweet words, he said: "O Divine beings, I am truly blessed to behold both of you! By your very presence before me the delusions of my mind have been destroyed: delusions which are not destroyed either by the study of scriptures, or by austerities, or by wisdom or by knowledge. Even a shower of nectar is not so blissful as the sight of holy ones. The very earth trodden by your feet is holy."

The sage Bhṛgu said to him: "Recollect yourself, for you are not an ignorant person!" Śukra was instantly awakened to the memory of his previous existence, which he beheld with his eyes closed for a brief period.

ŚUKRA said:

"Behold, I have passed through countless embodiments and

through countless experiences of pain and pleasure, wisdom and delusion. I have been a cruel king, a greedy trader and a wandering ascetic. There is no pleasure that I have not enjoyed, no action I have not performed, no unhappiness or happiness I have not endured. Now I wish for nothing, nor do I wish to avoid anything: let nature take its course. Come, father, let us go to where the previous body stands, dried up."

VASIṢṬHA continued: IV:15

Soon they arrived at the place where the body of Śukra, the son of Bhṛgu, lay in an advanced condition of decay. Looking at this, Śukra wailed: "Ah, look at this body which was admired and adored by even celestial nymphs; it is now the abode of worms and vermin. The body which was smeared with sandal-paste is now covered with dust. O body! You are now known as a corpse and you are truly frightening me. Even wild beasts are afraid of your dreadful appearance. Totally devoid of sensations, this body remains in a state of utter freedom from thoughts and ideas. Freed from the goblin of the mind, it remains unaffected by even natural calamities. Rid of the frolics of the restless monkey known as the mind, this tree of the body has fallen uprooted. It is indeed good fortune that I am able to see this body, liberated from sorrow, in this dense forest."

RĀMA asked: Holy sir, even though as you have just said Śukra had passed through countless embodiments, why is it that he bemoaned the fate of the body which was born of Bhṛgu?

VASIṢṬHA replied:

Rāma, it is because all the other bodies were the hallucinations of this original body, which was that of Śukra the son of sage Bhṛgu. Soon after creation at the end of the previous dissolution, on account of the will of the infinite consciousness, the jīva or the living soul which became the food that entered the body of the sage Bhṛgu, was later born as Śukra. It was in that embodiment that this soul had all the rites and rituals appropriate to the birth of a brāhmaṇa boy.

Why did Śukra (now known as Vasudeva) bemoan that body? Whether one is wise or ignorant, as long as the body lasts its functions continue unaltered according to its nature. And the embodied person functions as it is appropriate in the world, either attached or unattached. The difference between the two lies in their mental dispositions: in the case of the wise these are liberating and in the case of the ignorant these are binding. As long as there is the body, so long shall pain be painful and pleasure pleasant: but the wise are not attached to either. Rejoicing in joy and suffering in suffering, the great ones appear to behave like the ignorant, though in fact they are enlightened. He whose sense-organs are freed but whose organs of action are restrained is liberated; he whose sense-organs are bound but whose organs of action are free and unrestrained is in bondage. The wise behave appropriately in society though inwardly they are free of all need to conform. O Rāma, renounce all cravings and longings and do what needs to be done, in the realisation that you are ever the pure infinite consciousness.

IV:16 VASIṢṬHA continued:

Hearing the young ascetic Vasudeva mourning the fate of his previous body, Time (or Death) intervened and said to Śukra:

TIME (or DEATH) said:

O son of Bhṛgu! Abandon this body of yours and re-enter your other body, even as a king re-enters his kingdom. With that other body of Śukra, once again engage yourself in penance and then become the spiritual preceptor of the demons. At the end of the epoch, you will give up that body, never to become embodied again.

Having said this, Time vanished at that very place.

Thereupon, Śukra abandoned the body of Vasudeva in which he had performed intense penance on the bank of the river Samaṅga and re-entered the decayed body of Śukra, the son of the sage Bhṛgu. At that very moment, the body of Vasudeva fell down like an uprooted tree and became a corpse. The sage Bhṛgu sprinkled the body of Śukra with the holy water from his own water-pot, uttering sacred hymns which had the power to revive that body, clothing it with flesh, etc. Instantly, that body became youthful and radiant as it was before.

Śukra got up from the meditative posture and seeing his father, the sage Bhṛgu, standing in front of him, fell prostrate at his feet. Bhṛgu was delighted to see his son thus resurrected from the dead and fondly embraced him, smiling happily all the while. The feeling of affection at the thought, "This is my son" overcame even the sage Bhṛgu; this is natural as long as there is body-consciousness. Both of them rejoiced at this happy re-union.

Both Bhṛgu and Śukra then performed the funeral rites of the body of the brāhmaṇa boy Vasudeva; for thus do the men of wisdom honour social customs and traditions.

Both of them then shone with the radiance of the sun and the moon. They who were surely the spiritual preceptors of the whole universe roamed the world. Established firmly in the knowledge of the self, they remained unmoved by the changes that took place in the time and in the environment. In course of time, Śukra became the spiritual preceptor of the demons; and his father Bhṛgu became one of the sages of highest wisdom.

Such is the story of the sage Śukra; who on account of his infatuation with a nymph, wandered in countless wombs.

RĀMA asked: IV:17

Holy sir, why does not the wish of others materialise as the wish of Śukra materialised in his ascent to heaven, etc.?

VASIṢṬHA replied:

Śukra's mind was pure, since that was his first embodiment; that mind was not loaded with the impurities of other previous embodiments. That mind is pure in which all cravings are in a state of quiescence. Whatever that pure mind wishes, that materialises. What happened in this respect to Śukra is possible for everyone else.

The world exists in each jīva in a seed state and becomes manifest like the tree sprouting from the seed. The world is thus falsely fancied by each individual. The world neither arises nor sets; all this is nothing but the fancy of the deluded mind. Within each one there is a fancy world. Even as one's dreams are unknown to others, one's world is unknown to others. There are goblins and demi-gods and demons, all of which are embodiments of delusion. Even so have we come into being, O Rāma, out of pure thought-force, and consider the false to be real. Such indeed is the origin of creation in the infinite consciousness. Materiality is not factual though it is perceived in emptiness. Everyone thus fancies his own world; when this truth is realised, the world thus fancied comes to an end. This world exists only in appearance or imagination and not because one sees the material substances. It is like a long dream or a juggler's trick. It is the post to which the mind-elephant is tied.

The mind is the world, the world is the mind; when one is realised as not true, both of them vanish! When the mind is purified it reflects the truth, and the unreal world-appearance vanishes. The mind is purified by persistent contemplation of truth.

RĀMA asked:

How did the succession of births, etc., arise in the mind of Śukra?

VASIṢṬHA replied:

Śukra had been taught by his father Bhṛgu concerning the succession of births, and this teaching had conditioned Śukra's mind which conjured up the expansion of such conditioning. Only when the mind is totally purified of all conditioning does it regain its utter purity; that pure mind experiences liberation.

VASIṢṬHA continued: IV:18

The diversity that is seen in this creation, O Rāma, is but an appearance of diversity. Evolution or involution has the one infinite consciousness as its source and as its goal. During evolution, there seems to be an apparent diversity in the one infinite consciousness, in accordance with the notions that appear in that consciousness. Some of these notions intermingle, thus producing infinite variety in this diversity. Some do not thus intermingle. But, in fact, all these notions appear in every atom of existence and these atoms exist independent of one another. The totality is known as the absolute Brahman.

Each individual sees only those objects which are rooted in his own mind. When the ideas in the mind do not bear fruits, there is a change in the mind; there follows a succession of births to suit these psychological changes. It is this psychological connection that creates the conviction in the reality of birth and death, and in the reality of the body. When this conviction is given up, there is the cessation of embodiment.

It is only because of forgetfulness of truth that the confusion arises that the unreal is real. By the purification of the life-force (prāṇa) and by the knowledge of that which is beyond this prāṇa or life-force, one gains knowledge of all that is to be known concerning the activities of the mind as well as the basis for the succession of births.

The self of all living beings passes through three states: waking, dreaming and deep sleep. They have nothing to do with the body. (Even this is based on the assumption of the existence of living beings in the one self, which is not the truth.) The wise man who goes beyond the deep sleep state (which is pure consciousness) returns to the source: but the fool who does not is caught up in the life-cycle.

Since the consciousness is infinite, one is led from one life-cycle to another, even beyond the world-cycle. Such creations are endless, one appearing within another like the barks of a plantain stem. Of course, it is unwise to compare Brahman the absolute with anything.

One should enquire into that which is truly the uncaused cause of all substances, which is yet beyond all such causation: this alone is worth enquiring into, for this alone is the essential. Why enquire into the non-essential?

VASIṢṬHA continued:

O Rāma, the tree in a seed grows out of it after destroying the seed: but Brahman creates this world without destroying itself—the tree (world) appears even when the seed (Brahman) is as it is. Hence, it is impossible to compare the incomparable Brahman with anything whatsoever; whereas the tree, etc. are definable material substances, Brahman is nameless and formless being. It is Brahman alone that becomes what appears to be of a different nature; yet, from another point of view, it does not so become, for it is eternal and changeless.

One cannot therefore posit anything concerning Brahman: it is not possible to say that it has not become all this, nor is it possible to say that it has become all this.

When the self is seen as an object, the seer is not seen (realised); as long as the objective universe is perceived one does not realise the self. When you see the mirage as water, you do not perceive the rising hot-air; but, when you perceive the hot-air, you do not see water in the mirage! When one is truth, the other is not.

The eyes which perceive all the objects of the world, do not see themselves. As long as one entertains the notion of objectivity, the self is not realised. Brahman is as subtle and pure as space. It cannot be realised by any effort whatsoever. As long as one sees what is seen with the inner feeling that they are objects of perception (himself being their separate seer or subject), the realisation of Brahman is far indeed.

It is only when the division between the seer and the seen is given up, only when the two are 'seen' as of one substance, that the truth is realised. There is no object which is totally of a different nature from the subject. Nor can the subject (self) be seen as if it were an object! In fact, the subject (self) alone appears to the sight as the seen (object): there is no other object of perception here. If again the subject or the self alone is all this, then surely it is not even the subject or the seer! There is no division in such a vision.

Just as sugar becomes diverse sweetmeats without ever losing its natural sweetness, this infinite consciousness or Brahman visualises itself as all this infinite diversity without ever divesting itself of its essential nature. There is no limit whatsoever to the manifestation of this infinite consciousness.

VASIṢṬHA continued:

Each jīva experiences within itself whatever and however it has given rise to within itself with the help of its own life-force. O Rāma, behold with the eye of your inner wisdom the truth that in every atom of existence there are countless world-appearances. In everyone's mind, in the very space, in every rock, in the flame of fire and in water there exist countless world-appearances; even as oil exists in sesame seed. It is when the mind becomes absolutely pure that it becomes pure consciousness, and therefore one with the infinite consciousness.

This world-appearance is but a long dream which manifests everywhere, being the imagination of Brahmā the creator and all others. The objects thus born in the Creator's dream migrate from dream to dream, from embodiment to embodiment—thus generating the illusory solidity of this world-appearance. This dream-like appearance is yet true during the period of the dream itself.

Within every atom is the potential experience of every kind, even as a seed contains within itself the different aspects of the tree (flowers, leaves, fruits, etc.) Within every atom of existence, there is the infinite consciousness: hence, it is indivisible. Therefore, give up all your notions of diversity or unity. Time, space, action (or motion) and matter are all but different aspects of the one infinite consciousness: and consciousness experiences them within itself, whether it happens to be the body of the creator Brahmā or that of a worm.

An atom of consciousness, when it attains to the fully grown state of a body, experiences its own faculties. Someone perceives the objects spread out as if outside because the infinite consciousness is omnipresent. Others behold everything within, evolving and devolving alternately. Some go from one dream-experience to another, wandering in this world-appearance.

The rare few realise that the world-appearance seen within themselves is illusory, except as the one infinite consciousness which alone is ever true. On account of this consciousness, the world appears in the jīva: and there are jīvas within jīvas, ad infinitum. It is when one thus experiences the truth, that he is freed from illusion. At the same time, one's craving for pleasure is thinned out. This is the only proof of wisdom. A painted pot of nectar is not nectar, nor a painted flame fire, and a painting of a woman is not a woman: wise words are mere words (ignorance) not wisdom, unless they are substantiated by the absence of desire and anger.

IV:19 VASIṢṬHA continued:

The very seed for all jīvas, which is the absolute Brahman, exists everywhere; and within the jīvas there are countless other jīvas. All this is because the entire universe is totally permeated with the infinite consciousness.

Upon their appearance as the jīvas, whatever type of contemplation they adopt, they soon become of the same nature. They who are devoted to the gods, reach the gods; they who adore the demi-gods, attain the demi-gods. They who contemplate the absolute Brahman, become Brahman. Hence, one should resort to that which is not limited, conditioned or finite.

By contemplating the form of the nymph, Śukra was bound; and when he realised the purity of his self which is infinite consciousness, he was instantly liberated.

RĀMA asked:

Holy sir, pray tell me of the true nature of the waking and the dreaming states. What constitutes the waking state, and how does dream, or delusion in the waking state, arise?

VASIṢṬHA said:

That state which endures is known as the waking state; and that which is transient is the dream state. During the period of even the dream, it takes on the characteristic of the waking state; and when the waking state is realised to be of a fleeting nature, it gets the characteristic of dream. Otherwise, the two are the same.

When the life-force in the body stirs, the various organs of thought, word and deed perform their functions. They flow towards their objects of perception in accordance with the deluded notions that prevail in the mind. This life-force perceives diverse forms within the self. Since this perception seems to be of an enduring nature, it is known as the waking state.

But, when the life-force (jīva-cetanā) is not thus diverted by the mind and body, it remains rooted in peace within the heart. There is no movement of consciousness in the nerves of the body nor does the life-force activate the senses. However, that consciousness which is awake even in deep sleep and which is also the light that shines in waking and dreaming, is the transcendental consciousness, turīya.

When again the seeds of ignorance and delusion expand, there arises the first thought—which is the thought 'I am'. Then, one perceives thought-forms within the mind in dreams. At this time the external sense-organs do not function, but the inner senses function and there is perception within oneself. This is the dream state. When the life-force again activates the sense-organs, once again there is wakefulness.

VASIṢṬHA continued: IV:20, 21

I have described the states of the mind just to enable you to understand the nature of the mind: it has no other use. For, mind takes on the form of that which it intensely contemplates. Existence, non-existence, gaining and renouncing—all these are no more than moods of the mind.

RĀMA asked:

If mind is all this, Lord, how does it ever get tainted?

VASIṢṬHA replied:

It is a beautiful question, Rāma, but not the proper time to ask: when you have listened to what I have to say, you will surely find the answer to this question with the utmost clarity.

That the mind is impure, is the experience of everyone who strives for liberation. Depending upon one's particular point of view, everyone describes it differently.

Just as air coming into contact with different flowers takes on their scent, so mind entertaining different notions takes on those moods, creates bodies suitable to them and, as the energy activating the senses, enjoys the fruition of its own notions. It is the mind, again, that provides the fuel for the functioning of the organs of action. Mind is action and action is mind—the two are like the flower and its scent. The conviction of the mind determines the action and the action strengthens the conviction.

Mind is everywhere devoted to dharma, wealth, pleasure and freedom: but everyone has a different definition of these and is convinced that that definition is the truth. Even so, the followers of Kapila, the Vedāntins, the Vijñānavādins, the Jainas and others assert that theirs is the only path to liberation. Their philosophies are the expressions of their experiences which are the fruit of their own practice, which is in accordance with the convictions in their mind.

Rāma, bondage is none other than the notion of an object. This notion is Māyā, ignorance, etc. It is the cataract that blinds one to the sun of truth. Ignorance raises a doubt; doubt perceives—that perception is perverted. In darkness when one approaches even a lion's empty cage, he is afraid. Even so, one ignorantly believes he is imprisoned in this empty body. The notions of 'I' and 'the world' are but shadows, not truth. Such notions alone create 'objects': these objects are neither true nor false. A mother who considers herself a housekeeper behaves like one; a wife who considers herself her husband's mother behaves like one for the time being. Therefore, Rāma, abandon the notions of 'I' and 'this' and remain established in the truth.

IV:22 VASIṢṬHA continued:

He who acquires wisdom through self-enquiry and possesses the following qualifications enjoys clarity of self-knowledge even as water becomes clear when a piece of alum is thrown into it.

His mind is undisturbed by modifications. His being has been transmuted. Having attained what is worth attainment, viz., self-knowledge, he has abandoned the very notion of objectivity. Since the seer alone sees, he does not regard any other factor as the seer (subject). He is fully awake in the supreme truth; hence he is totally asleep, as it were, in the world-appearance. His dispassion being pervasive, he is disinterested in pleasure and its opposite. His cravings have ceased, even as the restlessness of rivers ceases on their entering the ocean. He has cut the net of world-appearance even as a mouse cuts the snare.

It is only when the mind has become devoid of all attachment, when it is not swayed by the pairs of opposites, when it is not attracted by objects and when it is totally independent of all supports, that it is freed from the cage of delusion. When all doubt comes to rest and when there is neither elation nor depression, then the mind shines like the full moon. When the impurities of the mind have ceased to be, there arise in the heart all the auspicious qualities, and there is equal vision everywhere. Even as darkness is dispelled by the rising sun, the world-illusion is dispelled when the sun of infinite consciousness arises in the heart. Such wisdom as is capable of gladdening the hearts of all beings in the universe manifests and expands. In short, he who has known that which alone is worth knowing transcends all coming and going, birth and death.

Even the gods Brahmā, Viṣṇu, Indra and Śiva are sympathised with and assisted by the holy ones in whom self-knowledge has arisen through self-enquiry or direct observation.

When there is absence of egoism, there is no confusion in the mind when that mind functions naturally. Just as waves rise and fall in the ocean, the worlds arise and vanish: this deludes the ignorant, but not the wise. The space in a pot does not come into being when the pot is brought in, nor is it destroyed when the pot is broken: he who knows that such is the relationship between his body (pot) and the self (space) is not influenced by praise and censure.

This glamorous world-appearance haunts one only as long as one does not engage oneself in enquiry into the nature of the self. When wisdom arises, delusion sets.

VASIṢṬHA continued:

O Rāma, he sees the truth who sees the body as a product of deluded understanding and as the fountain-source of misfortune, and who knows that the body is not the self.

He sees the truth who sees that in this body pleasure and pain are experienced on account of the passage of time and the circumstances in which one is placed; and that they do not pertain to him.

He sees the truth who sees that he is the omnipresent infinite consciousness which encompasses within itself all that takes place everywhere at all times.

He sees the truth who knows that the self, which is as subtle as the millionth part of the tip of a hair divided a million times, pervades everything.

He sees the truth who sees that there is no division at all between the self and the other, and that the one infinite light of consciousness exists as the sole reality.

He sees the truth who sees that the non-dual consciousness which indwells all beings is omnipotent and omnipresent.

He sees the truth who is not deluded into thinking that he is the body which is subject to illness, fear, agitation, old age and death.

He sees the truth who sees that all things are strung in the self as beads are strung on a thread, and who knows 'I am not the mind'.

He sees the truth who sees that all this is Brahman, neither 'I' nor 'the other'.

He sees the truth who sees all beings in the three worlds as his own family, deserving of his sympathy and protection.

He sees the truth who knows that the self alone exists and that there is no substance in objectivity.

He is unaffected who knows that pleasure, pain, birth, death, etc., are all the self only.

He is firmly established in the truth who feels: "What should I acquire, what should I renounce, when all this is the one self?"

Salutations to that abode of auspiciousness, who is filled with the supreme realisation that the entire universe is truly Brahman alone, which remains unchanged during all the apparent creation, existence and dissolution of the universe.

IV:23 VASIṢṬHA continued:

Rāma, he who treads the superior path, though he dwells in this body which functions as the potter's wheel does by past momentum, is untainted by the actions that might be performed. In his case, the body exists for his pleasure and for the liberation of his soul; he does not experience unhappiness in it.

To the ignorant, this body is the source of suffering; but to the enlightened man, this body is the source of infinite delight. While it exists the wise man derives from it great pleasure and the delight of enlightenment; and when its life-span comes to an end he does not regard it as a loss at all. Hence, to the enlightened person the body itself is a source of infinite delight. And, since it transports him in this world in which he roams freely and delightfully, the body is regarded as a vehicle of wisdom. Since it is through the body that the wise man derives the different sense-experiences and gains the friendship and affection of others, to him it is a source of gain. The enlightened man reigns happily while dwelling in the city known as the body, even as Indra the king of heaven dwells in his city.

The body does not subject the wise man to the temptations of lust and greed, nor does it allow ignorance or fear to invade him. The intelligence that governs the wise man's body is not drawn out by the excitement which the ignorant call pleasure, but it rests within in a state of contemplation.

The embodied being comes lightly into contact with the body while it lasts but is untouched by it once it is gone, even as air touches a pot which exists, but not one that does not exist.

Just as the most deadly poison which was drunk by lord Śiva did not harm him but enhanced his charm, the varied actions and enjoyments of an enlightened person do not bind him to the cycle of birth and death. Just as if you know someone is a thief and deal with him with that knowledge, he becomes your friend, when you enjoy the objects knowing their true nature, they give you joy. The wise man who is rid of all doubts and in whom there is no image of self, reigns supreme in the body.

Therefore one should abandon all cravings for pleasure and attain wisdom. Only the mind that has been well disciplined really experiences happiness. The captive king, when freed, is delighted with a piece of bread; the king who has not been subjected to captivity does not enjoy as much, even should it be the annexation of another kingdom. Hence, the wise man grinds his teeth and strives to conquer his mind and senses: such conquest is far greater than conquest of external foes.

The Story of Dāma, Vyāla and Kaṭa

VASIṢṬHA continued: IV:24, 25

O Rāma, in the great empire known as dreadful hell, evil actions roam like mighty elephants in rut. The senses which are responsible for these actions are equipped with a formidable magazine of cravings. Hence, these senses are hard to conquer. These ungrateful senses destroy the body, their own abode and support.

However, one who is equipped with wisdom is able to restrain craving without injuring the being even as a noose restrains the elephant without harming its being. The bliss enjoyed by the wise man who has his senses under control is incomparably superior to the enjoyment of a king who rules over a city built with brick and mortar. The former's intelligence grows in clarity as his craving for sense-pleasure is worn out. However, the craving disappears completely only after the supreme truth has been seen.

To the wise, the mind is an obedient servant, good counsellor, able commander of the senses, pleasing wife, protecting father and trustworthy friend. It impels him in good actions.

Rāma, be established in truth and live in freedom in a mindless state. Behave not like the demons Dāma, Vyāla and Kaṭa, whose story I shall presently narrate to you.

In the netherworld there was a mighty demon known as Saṃbara. He was a pastmaster in the art of magic. He created a magic city with a hundred suns on the horizon, walking and talking beings made of gold, swans carved in precious stones, ice-cold fire and his own celestial bodies. He was a terror to the gods of heaven.

When he was asleep or away from his city, the gods took advantage of the situation and killed his army. Enraged, the demon invaded the heaven. The gods, afraid of his magic powers, hid themselves. He could not find them. But, they managed to kill his forces at opportune moments. In order to protect his forces, the demon created three other demons: Dāma, Vyāla and Kaṭa.

These three had had no previous incarnation and hence they were free from every type of mental conditioning. They had no fear, doubt or other predispositions; they did not flee before the enemy, they were not afraid of death; they did not know the meaning of war, victory or defeat. In fact, they were not independent jīvas at all; they were merely the robot-like working projections of the demon Saṃbara. Their behaviour was like that of one who has eradicated all latent tendencies or conditioning but has not attained enlightenment. The demon Saṃbara was delighted that his army had invincible protectors.

IV:26, 27 VASIṢṬHA continued:

The demon Saṃbara despatched his invulnerable army, protected by the three new demons, to fight with the gods. The army of the gods, too, got ready to fight. The demons were unarmed and they were engaged in hand-to-hand combat with the gods. A fierce battle ensued. Later they fought with all kinds of terrible missiles, destroying all the cities, villages, caves, animals and others. Each side alternately enjoyed victory and suffered defeat.

The three principal demons looked for the principal gods, but they could not be found. The demons went back to Saṃbara to report to him. The gods prayed to the creator Brahmā, who appeared before them at once, and begged him to find a way to destroy the three demons.

BRAHMĀ said:

O gods, Saṃbara cannot be killed now. He will be killed after a hundred years, by lord Viṣṇu. It is wise for you to retreat from battle, as if defeated by the three demons. In due course, on account of their engagement in this war, the ego-sense will arise in them. Then they will be subjected to psychological conditioning and develop latent tendencies. Just now, these three demons are utterly devoid of the ego-sense and its adjuncts (conditioning and tendencies).

They in whom the ego-sense ('me') and its counterpart (the tendencies) do not exist, know neither desire nor anger. They are invincible. He who is bound by the ego-sense ('me') and by the conditioning of the mind, even if he is regarded as a great man or a man of great learning, can be defeated even by a child.

In fact, the notions of 'I' and 'mine' are the eager receptacles which receive sorrow and suffering. He who identifies the body with the self sinks in misery; he who even envisions the self as the omnipresent being overcomes sorrow. To the latter, there is nothing in the three worlds which is not the self and which is to be desired.

He whose mind is conditioned can be defeated: in the absence of such conditioning even a mosquito becomes immortal. The conditioned mind experiences suffering; when rid of the conditioning, it experiences delight. Conditioning or craving weakens a person. Hence, you need not feel anxious to fight these three demons. Do what you can to create in them the feelings of 'I' and 'mine'. Since they are ignorant creatures of the demon Saṃbara they will easily fall for this bait. Then they can be easily defeated by you all.

VASIṢṬHA continued: IV:28, 29, 30

Having said thus, the creator Brahmā vanished. The gods rested in their abodes for a while, in preparation for a fresh onslaught on the demons. The renewed fighting between the armies of the gods and the demons was even more fierce than the previous one. There was terrible destruction everywhere.

This continued involvement in fighting generated in the three demon-leaders the basic notion of 'I am'. Even as a mirror reflects an object held close to it, one's behaviour reflects as the ego-sense in one's consciousness. However, if this behaviour is 'held at a distance' from consciousness and there is no identification with such behaviour, the ego-sense does not arise.

Once this ego-sense arose, there quickly followed the desire for the prolongation of life in the body, acquisition of wealth, health, pleasure, etc. These desires greatly debilitated their personalities. Then there arose confusion in their minds, which in turn gave rise to feelings of 'This is mine' and 'This is my body'. All these inevitably resulted in inefficiency and inability to do their own work. They were greatly attached to eating and drinking. Objects gave them feelings of pleasure and thus robbed them of their freedom. With the loss of freedom, their courage also went and they experienced fear. They were terribly worried at the very thought, "We shall die in this war".

The gods took advantage of this situation and began to attack these demons. The three demons who were possessed by fear of death fled.

When the demon-army saw that their invincible protectors had fled before the invading gods, they were thoroughly demoralised; the demons fell by the thousands.

When the demon Saṃbara heard that his army had been routed by the gods, he was furious. Referring to the three invincible demons,

Dāma, Vyāla and Kaṭa, he demanded: "Where have they gone?" Afraid of his wrath, these three demons took refuge in the nethermost world.

There, the servants of the god of death, Yama, gave them refuge and also three girls to marry. They lived in the netherworld for a long time. One day they were visited by Yama himself, without his paraphernalia. They failed to recognise and honour him. Angered, Yama despatched them to the most dreadful hells. After suffering there and after a number of incarnations in different subhuman species, they now live as fish in a lake in Kashmir.

IV:31 VASIṢṬHA continued:

Thus you see the disastrous results that arise from non-wisdom. You see how the invincible demons were utterly defeated and disgraced on account of their ego-sense, which gave rise to fear in their hearts. The deadly creeper of worldliness sprouts from the seed of the ego-sense. Therefore, O Rāma, abandon this ego-sense with all the strength that lies within; and by being established in the conviction: 'I is nothing', be happy. The one infinite consciousness, which is of the nature of pure bliss, is eclipsed by the shadow of the ego-sense.

Though the demons Dāma, Vyāla and Kaṭa were really free from the cycle of birth and death, on account of their ego-sense they had to be subjected to birth and death. They of whom even the gods were afraid are today miserable fish in a lake in Kashmir.

RĀMA asked:

Holy sir, Dāma, Vyāla and Kaṭa were unreal, having been produced by the magic of Saṃbara. How was it that they became real entities like us?

VASIṢṬHA replied:

Rāma, just as the demons Dāma and others were unreal and the products of magic, even so are we and all the gods and others. All these notions of 'I' and 'you', O Rāma, are unreal. That you and I are seen to be real entities does not alter the truth; even if a dead person appears before you now, he is still dead!

However, it is unwise to declare the truth ('Brahman alone is real') to the ignorant. For, the reality of the world-appearance, which has become deep-rooted in the heart of the ignorant, will not be dispelled except through intense enquiry into the purport of the scriptures. One who declares: "This world is unreal; Brahman alone is real" to such ignorant people is laughed at. However well you explain to them that 'All this is Brahman', the ignorant cannot comprehend it any more than a corpse can walk. That truth can be experienced only by the wise.

O Rāma, neither we nor these demons are real. The reality is the one infinite consciousness which does not undergo any change. In that infinite consciousness there arise the notions of yourself, myself, these demons etc., and they are invested with reality because the perceiving consciousness is real. Where this consciousness is 'awake' as it were, there such notions arise; and where it is 'asleep', there such notions are dissolved. Yet, in the infinite consciousness there are no such states as awake and asleep. It is but pure consciousness. Realise this and be free from sorrow and fear caused by division.

RĀMA asked: IV:32

O Holy sage, pray, tell me, when and how will the three demons attain liberation?

VASIṢṬHA replied:

Rāma, when they listen to the narration of their story and are reminded of their own essential nature as pure consciousness, they will be liberated.

In course of time, there will arise a city named Adhiṣṭhāna in the middle of the country known as Kashmir. In the centre of that city there will be a hill whose peak will be known as Pradyumna. On top of that hill there will be a skyscraper. In a corner of that building the demon Vyāla will be born as a sparrow.

In that building, a king known as Yaśaskar will reside. The demon Dāma will be born as a mosquito and reside in a hole in one of the pillars of that palace.

Elsewhere in that city there will be a palace known as Ratnāvalīvihāra which will be inhabited by the state minister known as Narasiṃha. The demon Kaṭa will be born as a bird (myna) and live in that palace.

One day that minister, Narasiṃha, will recite the story of the three demons Dāma, Vyāla and Kaṭa. Listening to it, the myna will be enlightened. It will recall that its original personality was but a magical creation of the demon Saṃbara; this recollection will free it from the magic of Saṃbara. The demon Kaṭa will thus attain nirvāṇa (liberation).

Other people will recount this story and the sparrow will also attain liberation after listening to it. Thus will the demon Vyāla attain liberation.

In the same way, the mosquito-demon Dāma will also listen to this story and will also attain liberation.

Such is the story, O Rāma, of the three demons Dāma, Vyāla and Kaṭa, who, on account of their ego-sense and their cravings, fell into hell. All this is nothing more than the play of ignorance and delusion.

In fact, it is the pure consciousness that entertains the impure notion of 'I am', playfully as it were, and without ever renouncing its essential nature as consciousness, experiences the distorted image of itself within itself. Even though this distorted image is truly unreal, the ego-sense ('I am') believes it to be real and gets deluded.

VASIṢṬHA continued:

O Rāma, they who are established in the state of liberation, as pointed out by the scriptures, surely cross this ocean of world-appearance as their consciousness flows towards the self. But, they who are caught in the net of polemics, which are only productive of sorrow and confusion, forfeit their own highest good. Even in the case of the path shown by the scriptures, only one's direct experience leads one along the safest way to the supreme goal.

What else is left of a greedy man except a handful of ashes? But, he who looks upon the world as less valuable than a blade of grass never comes to grief. He who has fully realised the infinite is protected by the cosmic deities. Hence, one should not set foot on the wrong path even in times of great distress. He who has earned a good reputation through a virtuous life gains whatever has not been gained and is rid of misfortune. Only he can be considered a human being who is not complacent with his own virtue, who is devoted to the teaching he has heard and who strives to tread the path of truth: others are animals in human disguise. He who is filled with the milk of human kindness is surely the abode of the lord Hari (who is said to dwell in the ocean of milk).

Whatever has to be enjoyed has already been enjoyed, whatever has to be seen has been seen: what else is there new in this world which a wise man should seek? Hence, one should be devoted to one's duty as ordained by the scriptures, having given up all craving for pleasure. Adore the saints: this will save you from death.

Adhering to the injunctions of the scriptures one should patiently wait for perfection which comes in its own time. Arrest the downward trend by studying this holy scripture for liberation. Enquire constantly into the nature of truth, knowing that 'this is but a reflection'. Do not be led by others; only animals are led by others. Wake up from the slumber of ignorance. Wake up and strive to end old age and death.

Wealth is the mother of evil. Sense-pleasure is the source of pain. Misfortune is the best fortune. Rejection by all is victory. Life, honour and noble qualities blossom and attain fruition in one whose conduct and behaviour are good and pleasant, who is devoted to seclusion and who does not crave for the pleasures of the world, which lead to suffering.

VASIṢṬHA continued: IV:33

O Rāma, every zealous effort is always crowned with fruition. Hence, do not abandon right effort. Surely, it is necessary to weigh the worthiness of the end-result before plunging into zealous effort of any sort. If you carefully investigate in this manner you will surely discover that self-knowledge alone is capable of utterly destroying all pain and pleasure by their very roots; hence zealous effort should be directed towards self-knowledge alone. Get rid of all notions of objectivity created by the pleasure-seeking desire within you. Is there any happiness which is untainted by unhappiness?

Both the absence of restraint and the practice of restraint are indeed one in the absolute Brahman and there is no real division between them; yet, the practice of restraint bestows great joy and auspiciousness upon you. Hence, resort to self-restraint and give up ego-sense. Enquire into the nature of truth and seek the company of the wise. They indeed are good and wise men who live in accordance with the scriptural injunctions and in whom greed, delusion and anger decrease day by day.

In the company of the wise, self-knowledge arises; and at the same time the notion of the reality of the objects of perception as such wanes and eventually vanishes. When the world as object of perception thus fades away, only the supreme truth exists and the jīva or the individual personality is absorbed in it, as it does not find any object worth clinging to. The world as an object was never created, nor does it exist as such now, nor will it ever be so: it is only the one supreme being that exists at all times as the sole reality.

Thus have I explained to you in a thousand ways the essential unreality of the world-as-an-object-of-perception. It is nothing but the pure space of consciousness: in it there is no division which could be referred to as 'This is the truth' and 'This is not real'. The wonderful manifestation of that infinite consciousness alone is regarded as the world, naught else. In it, the divisions like subject and object and substance and shadow are unwarranted arbitrary assumptions like the distinction made between the sun's rays and sunlight: in truth, only the indivisible and unmodified consciousness exists. When in accordance with its own nature it closes and opens its eyes, as it were, there is what is known as dissolution and creation of the universe.

VASIṢṬHA continued:

When it is not rightly understood, the 'I' appears to be an impure notion in the infinite consciousness; but, when the 'I' is rightly understood, its meaning is seen as the infinite consciousness. When its own reality is seen it does not appear as the ego-sense any more, but as the one infinite reality. In fact, there is no distinct entity as 'I'.

When this truth is revealed to one with a pure mind, his ignorance is at once dispelled; but others cling to their own false notion like a child clinging to the notion of the existence of a ghost.

When the 'I' as a separate entity is thus known to be false, how can one believe in the other notions (of heaven, hell, etc.) that are related to it? Craving for heaven and even for liberation arises in one's heart only as long as the 'I' is seen as an entity. As long as the 'I' thus remains, there is only unhappiness in one's life. And, this notion of the 'I' cannot be got rid of except through self-knowledge. When one is possessed by this ghost of 'I-ness', no scriptures, no mantras, nothing enables one to get rid of it.

Only by the constant remembrance of the truth that the self is a pure reflection in the infinite consciousness does 'I-ness' cease to grow. The world-appearance is a juggler's trick; all subject-object relationship between it and me is foolish—when this understanding takes root, 'I-ness' is uprooted. When it is seen that it is the 'I' that gives rise to the notion of a 'world', both of them cease in peace.

However, the higher form of 'I-ness' which gives rise to the feeling 'I am one with the entire universe; there is nothing apart from me', is the understanding of the enlightened person. Another type of 'I-ness' is when one feels that the 'I' is extremely subtle and atomic in nature and therefore different from and independent of everything in this universe: this, too, is unobjectionable, being conducive to liberation. But the 'I-ness' that has been described earlier on is one which identifies the self with the body: this is to be abandoned firmly. By the persistent cultivation of the higher form of 'I-ness' the lower form is eradicated.

Having kept the lower 'I-ness' in check, one should resort to the higher form of 'I-ness', persistently generating in oneself the feeling: 'I am the All' or 'I am extremely subtle and independent'. In due course even this higher form of 'I-ness' should be completely abandoned. Then one may either engage oneself in all activity or remain in seclusion: there is no fear of downfall for him.

The Story of Bhīma, Bhāsa and Dṛḍha

IV:34 VASIṢṬHA continued:

O Rāma, after Saṃbara had been deserted by the three demons Dāma, Vyāla and Kaṭa, he realised that they had foolishly entertained egoistic notions and had thus come to grief. Hence, he resolved to create more demons, but this time with self-knowledge and wisdom, so that they might not fall into the same trap of ego-sense.

Saṃbara thereupon created by his own magic power three more

demons known as Bhīma, Bhāsa and Dṛḍha. They were omniscient, they were endowed with self-knowledge, they were full of dispassion and sinless. They regarded the whole universe as of no more value than a blade of grass.

They began to fight with the army of the gods. In spite of fighting for a considerable time, the ego-sense did not arise in them. Whenever the ego-sense raised its head, they subdued it with self-enquiry ('Who am I'). They were therefore free from fear of death, devoted to appropriate action in the present, free from all attachment, devoid of the feeling 'I did this', intent on doing the work allotted to them by the master Saṃbara, free from desire and from aversion and endowed with equal vision. The army of the gods was quickly defeated by them. The gods fled to lord Viṣṇu for refuge. At his command, they took up their abode in another region.

After this, lord Viṣṇu himself had to fight with the demon Saṃbara: slain by the Lord the demon instantly reached the abode of Viṣṇu. Lord Viṣṇu also liberated the three demons Bhīma, Bhāsa and Dṛḍha, who, when the body fell, became enlightened, as they had no ego-sense.

O Rāma, the conditioned mind alone is bondage; and liberation is when the mind is unconditioned. The conditioning of the mind drops away when the truth is clearly seen and realised; and when the conditioning has ceased one's consciousness is made supremely peaceful, as when the flame of a lamp is put out. To realise that 'The self alone is all this, whatever one may think of anywhere' is clear perception. 'Conditioning' and 'mind' are but words without corresponding truth: when the truth is investigated they cease to be meaningful—this is clear perception. When this clear perception arises, there is liberation.

Dāma, Vyāla and Kaṭa illustrate the mind that is conditioned by the ego-sense; Bhīma, Bhāsa and Dṛḍha illustrate the mind that is free from conditioning or ego-sense. O Rāma, do not be like the former, but be like the latter. That is the reason why I narrated this story to you, my dear and highly intelligent disciple.

VASIṢṬHA continued: IV:35

O Rāma, they are the true heroes who have brought under control the mind which is dominated by ignorance and delusion. Such control of the mind is the only way by which one can remedy the sufferings of this world-appearance (or the cycle of birth and death) and the endless chain of tragedy. I shall declare to you the quintessence of all wisdom: listen and let it perfume your whole life. Bondage is the craving for pleasure; and its abandonment is liberation. Hence, look upon all the pleasure-centres in this world as poison fumes.

Blind abandonment is undesirable: enquire deeply and seriously into the nature of sense-pleasures and abandon all craving for them. Then you can live happily.

By the cultivation of auspicious qualities, as all wrong knowledge gradually ceases, the mind becomes desireless, free from the pairs of opposites, restlessness, fear and delusion. Thereby the mind rests in a state of peace and bliss. It is then unpolluted by the ego-sense, evil thoughts and feelings, attachment and sorrow.

Then, the mind gets rid of its violent son known as doubt and its wife known as craving. Ironically, the awakened mind brings about the cessation of those very things (like thoughts and desires) which promoted its growth. Pursuing the enquiry into its real nature, the mind abandons its identification even with the body. The ignorant mind expands; but on the awakening of wisdom, the same mind ceases to be mind.

Mind alone is this universe. Mind is the mountain-range. Mind is the space. Mind is god. Mind alone is friend and foe. When the consciousness forgets itself, and undergoes modification and psychological conditioning, it is known as the mind, which gives rise to birth and death. This is known as jīva, being that part of the infinite consciousness which has assumed the character of an object of this consciousness, just a little enveloped by the psychological conditioning. It is this jīva that moves away from the truth of the infinite consciousness and by sinking deeper and deeper into the conditioning becomes involved in the world-appearance.

Of course, the self is neither the jīva, nor the body, nor its components. The self is, like space, independent of all these.

VASIṢṬHA continued:

O Rāma, the mind itself is the jīva; the mind experiences what it itself has projected out of itself. By that it is bound. It is the state of the mind that determines the nature of the re-incarnation of the jīva.

One who wishes to be a king dreams that he has become king. What one intensely wishes for he obtains sooner or later. If the mind is impure, its effects are also impure; if it is pure, its products are pure too. The noble man engages himself in noble spiritual pursuits even in straitened circumstances.

There is neither bondage nor liberation in truth. The infinite thinks 'I am the body' and this thought acts as bondage. When one realises that all these are false, he shines as the infinite consciousness. When the mind has been purified by pure thoughts and actions, it takes on the nature of the infinite, even as a pure cloth takes on a colour easily.

When in a pure mind there arise concepts and notions of a body, scriptural knowledge and dispassion, etc., the world-appearance comes into being. When the mind gets involved in the external objective universe it moves away from the self. But, when the mind gives up the subject-object relationship it has with the world, it is instantly absorbed in the infinite.

The mind has no existence apart from the infinite consciousness: it did not exist in the beginning, it will not exist in the end and so it does not now! One who thinks that it does exist holds sorrow in his hand. He who knows that this world is the self in reality goes beyond that sorrow, and this world gives him both joy and liberation.

The mind is naught but ideas and notions: who will grieve when such a mind comes to an end! The reality is consciousness which is the middle, between the seer and the object; this reality is veiled by the mind and revealed when the mind ceases.

When the mind's conditioning ceases, then ignorance, craving, desires and aversions, delusion, stupidity, fear and ideations come to an end; purity, auspiciousness and goodness arise. One enjoys the delight of self-knowledge.

He who has an intelligence that has been rendered pure by the destruction of all inner impurities, has his heart illumined by the light of the self obtained through enquiry into the self; seeing the worthlessness of birth and death, he dwells without fear or anxiety in the city which is the body.

RĀMA asked: IV:36

Lord, the infinite consciousness is transcendental; pray, tell me how this universe exists in it.

VASIṢṬHA replied:

O Rāma, this universe exists in the infinite consciousness just as future waves exist in a calm sea; non-different in truth but with the potentiality of an apparent difference. The infinite consciousness is unmanifest, though omnipresent, even as space, though existing everywhere, is unmanifest. Just as the reflection of an object in crystal can be said to be neither real nor entirely unreal, one cannot say that this universe which is reflected in the infinite consciousness is real nor unreal. Again, just as space is unaffected by the clouds that float in it, this infinite consciousness is unaffected and untouched by the universe that appears in it. Just as light is not seen except through the refracting agent, even so the infinite consciousness is revealed through these various bodies. It is essentially nameless and formless, but names and forms are ascribed to its reflections.

Consciousness reflecting in consciousness shines as consciousness and exists as consciousness; yet, to one who is ignorant (though considering oneself as wise and rational) there arises the notion that there has come into being and there exists something other than this consciousness. To the ignorant this consciousness appears as the terrible world-appearance; to the wise the same consciousness appears as the one self. This consciousness alone is known as pure experiencing; and it is thanks to it that the sun shines and all beings enjoy life here.

This consciousness is not created, nor does it perish; it is eternal and the world-appearance is superimposed on it, even as waves in relation to the ocean. In that consciousness, when it is reflected within itself, there arises the 'I am' notion which gives rise to diversity. As space, the same consciousness enables the seed to sprout; as air, it draws the sprout, as it were; as water, it nourishes it; as earth, it stabilises it; and as light, the consciousness itself reveals the new life. It is the consciousness in the seed that in due course manifests as the fruit.

This consciousness alone is the different seasons and their characteristics. It is on account of this consciousness that the entire universe exists as it does supporting an infinite number of beings, till the time of the cosmic dissolution.

IV:37 VASIṢṬHA continued:

Thus, this world-appearance comes and goes as the very nature of the infinite consciousness. Being non-different from the infinite consciousness this world-appearance has a mutual causal relationship with it—arises in it, exists in it and is absorbed in it. Though like the deep ocean it is not agitated, yet it is agitated like the waves appearing on the surface. Even as one who is intoxicated sees himself as another person, this consciousness, becoming conscious of itself, considers itself as another.

This universe is not real, nor is it unreal: it exists in consciousness, yet it does not exist (independently) in consciousness. Though appearing to be an addition to consciousness, it does not exceed consciousness. The relationship is like ornaments and gold.

This self, the supreme Brahman, which permeates everything, is that which enables you to experience sound, taste, form and fragrance, O Rāma. It is transcendental and omnipresent; it is non-dual and pure. In it there is not even a notion of another. All these diversities like existence and non-existence, good and evil, are vainly imagined by ignorant people. It matters not whether this imagination is said to be based on the not-self or the self itself.

Since there is nothing other than the self, how can there be desire for another? Hence, notions like 'This is desirable' and 'This is undesirable' do not touch the self. Since the self is desireless and because the doer (the instrument of action) and the action itself are also non-dual, it does not get involved in action. Since that which exists and that in which it exists are identical, one cannot even say it is. Since in it there is no desire whatsoever, there is no notion of inaction in it.

There is naught else, O Rāma. You are the very existence of this absolute Brahman. Therefore, free yourself from all notions of duality and live an active life. What have you to gain by doing all kinds of actions again and again? And, what will you gain by desiring to be inactive? Or, by adhering to scriptures? O Rāma, rest in peace and purity like the ocean when it is not agitated by wind. That self, by which everything is completely permeated, is not to be gained by travelling far and wide. Do not let your mind wander among the objects of the world. You yourself are the supreme self, the infinite consciousness; you are naught else!

VASIṢṬHA continued: IV:38

O Rāma, the sense of doership (the notion 'I do this') which gives rise to both happiness and unhappiness, or which gives rise to the state of yoga, is fictitious in the eyes of the wise; to the ignorant, however, it is real. For, what is the source of this notion? This notion arises when the mind, spurred by the predisposition, endeavours to gain something; the resultant action is then attributed to oneself. When the same action leads to the experience of its fruition, the notion 'I enjoy this' arises. The two notions are in truth the two faces (phases) of the same notion.

Whether one is engaged in action or not, whether one is in heaven or in hell, whatever may be the psychological conditioning, that itself is experienced by the mind. Hence, to the ignorant and conditioned person there is the notion 'I do this' whether he is doing something or doing nothing; but such a notion does not arise in the enlightened or unconditioned. When the truth concerning this is known the conditioning is weakened and thenceforth the wise man, even while acting in this world, is not interested in the fruits of those actions. He lets actions happen in his life, without attachment to those actions; and whatever be the results of those actions, he regards them as non-different from his own self. But such is not the attitude of one who is immersed in the mental states.

Whatever the mind does, that alone is action: hence, the mind alone is the doer of actions, not the body. The mind alone is this world-appearance; this world-appearance has arisen in it and it rests in the mind. When the objects as well as the experiencing mind have become tranquil, consciousness alone remains.

The wise declare that the mind of the enlightened is neither in a state of bliss nor devoid of bliss, neither in motion nor static, neither real nor unreal, but between these two propositions. His unconditioned consciousness blissfully plays its role in this world-appearance as if in a play. Since it is the mental conditioning (which exists in the ignorant) which determines the nature of the action and of the experience, and since it is absent in the enlightened, the latter is ever in bliss. His actions are non-actions. Hence he does not incur merit nor demerit. His behaviour is like that of a child; and even if he appears to be in pain, he is not. He is totally unattached to this world-appearance and to the actions of the mind and the senses. He does not even entertain the notion of liberation, nor that of bondage. He sees the self and self alone.

IV:39 VASIṢṬHA continued:

Rāma, the absolute Brahman being omnipotent, his infinite potencies appear as this visible universe. All the diverse categories like reality, unreality, unity, diversity, beginning and end exist in that Brahman. Like waves on the sea, the jīva also appears in Brahman self-limited by individualised consciousness: this jīva later undergoes progressively denser conditioning, functions in accordance with that conditioning and experiences the consequences of such action.

RĀMA asked: Lord, Brahman is free from sorrow; and yet that which has emerged from it, as a lamp kindled from another lamp, is the universe which is full of sorrow. How is this possible?

VĀLMĪKI said: Hearing this question, Vasiṣṭha contemplated thus for a while: Obviously, Rāma's understanding is not efficient because there is impurity in his mind. Yet, if he is not enabled fully to understand the truth, his mind will not find rest. As long as the mind is swayed by thoughts of pleasure or happiness, so long is it unable to comprehend the truth. If the mind is pure, then it instantly comprehends the truth. Hence, it is declared that he who declares 'All this is Brahman' to one who is ignorant or half-awakened, goes to hell. Hence, a wise teacher should encourage his students first to be established in self-control and tranquillity. Then the student should be properly examined before the knowledge of the truth is imparted to him. Then,

VASIṢṬHA said:

You will discover the truth for yourself whether Brahman is free from sorrow or not. Or, I shall help you understand this in course of time. For the present, understand this:

Brahman is omnipotent, omnipresent and the indwelling presence in all. This Brahman, through the indescribable power known as Māyā, has brought this creation into being. This Māyā is capable of making the unreal appear as the real, and vice versa, even as the empty void of space appears to be blue in colour.

Behold Rāma: you see such infinite diversity of creatures in this world itself. That is the manifestation of the infinite potencies of the Lord. Embrace tranquility; he who is at peace within himself beholds the truth. When the mind is not at peace, the world appears to be a confusion of diversity. But in fact, this universe is an apparent manifestation of the infinite potencies of the Lord. Just as where there is light there is natural visibility, even so on account of the omnipotence of the Lord, this world-appearance has arisen as his very nature. However, simultaneously with this world-appearance, ignorance has also come into being, on account of which there is sorrow. Give up this ignorance and be free.

VASIṢṬHA continued: IV:40

O Rāma, this entire creation of world-appearance is but an accidental manifestation of the intention of the omnipotent conscious-energy (cit-śakti) of the infinite consciousness or Brahman. The intention itself condenses and thus gives rise in the mind to the substance thus intended. Immediately the mind reproduces the substance as if in the objective field. At this stage, there is a notion of this creation having factually abandoned its fundamental and true nature as the infinite consciousness.

This infinite consciousness apparently sees within itself a pure void: and the conscious-energy (cit-śakti) thereupon brings space into existence. In that conscious-energy there arises an intention to diversify: this intention itself is then regarded as the creator Brahmā, with his retinue of other living creatures. Thus have all the fourteen worlds appeared in the space of infinite consciousness, with their endless variety of beings—some immersed in dense darkness, some very close to enlightenment and others fully enlightened.

In this world, O Rāma, among the many species of living beings only the human beings are fit to be instructed into the nature of truth. Even among these human beings many are obsessed by sorrow and delusion, hate and fear. All this I shall presently deal with in great detail.

But all this talk about who created this world and how it was created is intended only for the purpose of composing scriptures and expounding them: it is not based on truth. Modifications arising in the infinite consciousness or organisation of the cosmic being, do not really take place in the Lord, though they appear to do so. There is naught but the infinite consciousness, even in imagination! To think of that being the creator and the universe as the created, is absurd: when one lamp is kindled from another, there is no creator-creature relationship between them—fire is one. Creation is just a word, it has no corresponding substantial reality.

Consciousness is Brahman, the mind is Brahman, the intellect is Brahman, Brahman alone is the substance. Sound or word is Brahman and Brahman alone is the component of all substances. All indeed is Brahman; there is no world in reality.

Just as when the dirt is removed the real substance is made manifest, just as when the darkness of the night is dispelled the objects that were shrouded by the darkness are clearly seen, even so when ignorance is dispelled truth is realised.

IV:41 RĀMA asked:

Lord, how could there be even an intention to diversify in the infinite consciousness?

VASIṢṬHA said:

O Rāma, there is no contradiction in my statements. You will see the beauty of the truth in my statements when you attain the vision of truth. Descriptions of creation, etc., are given in the scriptures for the purpose of instructing disciples: do not let your mind be coloured by them. When you realise that which is indicated by the words, then naturally you will abandon the jugglery of words.

In the infinite consciousness itself there is neither an intention nor the veil of delusion. But, that itself is before you as the world.

This can be realised only when ignorance comes to an end. Ignorance will not cease except with the help of instruction which rests in the use of these words and descriptions. This ignorance seeks to destroy itself and hence seeks the light of true knowledge. Weapons are destroyed by other weapons, dirt cleans dirt, poison cures poison and enemies are destroyed by other enemies: even so this Māyā rejoices when it is destroyed! The moment you become aware of this Māyā, it vanishes.

This ignorance or Māyā veils the truth and creates this diversity; but it does not know its own nature, and that is strange. As long as one does not enquire into its nature, it rules; the moment there is enquiry into its nature, it ceases.

This Māyā does not exist in truth. So long as this truth is not directly experienced by you, you will have to accept my word for it. He who knows that Brahman alone is the truth, he is liberated. All other points of view are intended to bind a person to ignorance.

This ignorance will not go away without self-knowledge. And, self-knowledge arises only when the scriptures are studied deeply. Whatever may be the origin of this ignorance, surely, even that exists in the self. Hence, O Rāma, do not enquire into 'How has this ignorance arisen'; but enquire into 'How shall I get rid of it'. When this ignorance or Māyā has ceased to be, then you shall know how it arose. You will realise that this ignorance is not a real entity. It arises only in a state of unwisdom. Not a single person, whether he is a great scholar or a hero, has been spared by this ignorance! This ignorance is the source of all sorrow: uproot and destroy it.

VASIṢṬHA continued: IV:42

I shall again declare to you the way in which the one infinite consciousness has come to appear as the jīva and all the rest of it. You see in the ocean that it is tranquil in places and agitated in other places. Even so, the infinite consciousness seems to embrace diversity in some places, though it in itself is non-dual. It is natural for the omnipotent infinite consciousness to manifest in all its infinite glory.

This manifestation of the omnipotence of infinite consciousness enters into an alliance with time, space and causation which are indispensable to the manifestation. Thence arose the infinite names and forms. But all these apparent manifestations are in reality non-different from the infinite consciousness. That aspect of this infinite consciousness which relates itself to the manifestation of the names and forms and thus to time, space and causation is known as the 'knower of the field', or the witness consciousness. The body is the field; that which knows this field inside out and in all its aspects is the knower of the field or witness consciousness.

This witness consciousness becomes involved in the latent predispositions and develops the ego-sense. When this ego-sense generates notions and intentions within itself, it is known as the intellect. As the thinking instrument, it is known as the mind. When the intelligence gets further modified or perverted, it becomes the senses. All of these constitute the body. Just as a fruit undergoes various changes in size, colour, etc., as it matures, the same consciousness undergoes these apparent changes as the ignorance grows deeper and denser.

The foolish person then abandons all right thinking or enquiry into the truth and voluntarily embraces ignorance as bliss. Caught in its own trap of various activities, and of identification of oneself as their doer, he undergoes endless suffering which is self-imposed and self-willed. O Rāma, in this world the cause of all misfortunes is only the mind which is full of sorrow and grief, desire and delusion. Forgetful of self-knowledge, it generates desire and anger, evil thoughts and cravings which throw the person into the fire of sense-objects. O Rāma, rescue this mind from the mire of ignorance.

O Rāma, he indeed is a demon in human form who is not distressed by the impure state of the mind caused by alternating good and evil thoughts, and who is subjected to old age, death and despair.

IV:43 VASIṢṬHA continued:

This incidental manifestation of the power of the infinite consciousness appears as the millions of species of beings in this universe. These countless beings are caught up in their own mental conditioning. They are found in every country and in every place in the universe, and they are in every conceivable kind of situation.

Some of them are part of the new creation in this epoch, others are more ancient. Some have incarnated just a couple of times, others have had countless incarnations. Some are liberated. Others are sunk in dreadful suffering. Some are celestials, some are demigods, and others are the deities presiding over this manifest universe. Some others are demons, others are goblins. Some are members of the four castes of human beings, and others are members of primitive uncivilised tribes.

Some of them are in the form of herbs and grass; others appear as roots, fruits and leaves. Some are in the form of creepers, and some are living as flowers. Some are the kings and their ministers, clad in royal robes; others are clad in rags and bark of trees, either because they are anchorites or they are beggars.

Some are snakes and others are insects; others are animals like lions, tigers, etc. Some are birds, others are elephants and donkeys.

Some are prosperous; others are in adverse circumstances. Some are in heaven, others are in hell. Some are in the region of the stars, others are in holes of dying trees. Some live amongst liberated sages; others are already liberated sages who have risen above body-consciousness. Some are endowed with enlightened intelligence; some are extremely dull.

O Rāma, just as in this universe there are countless beings of various species, in other universes, too, there are similar beings, with different bodies suited to those universes.

But, all of them are bound by their own mental conditioning. These beings roam this universe sometimes uplifted, sometimes degraded; and death plays with them as with a ball. Bound to their own countless desires and attachments and limited by their own mental conditioning, they migrate from one body to another. They will continue to do so, till they perceive the truth concerning their own self which is infinite consciousness. After attaining this self-knowledge, they are liberated from delusion and they do not return to this plane of birth and death any more.

IV:44 VASIṢṬHA continued:

However, all this creation takes place only as in a dream. This creation is not real; it merely appears to be so. He who has eradicated ignorance totally and in whom every form of conditioning has ceased is a liberated sage: though he seems to be aware of this dream known as world-appearance, in reality he does not see it as the world. This world-appearance is naturally conceived of in all the jīvas at all times, till the jīva attains liberation. In every jīva, therefore, the body exists potentially—not in all its physical substantiality, but as a thought and as an intention.

I shall describe to you once again how the creator Brahmā arose in the infinite consciousness and you will see from that account how the infinite beings arose similarly in that consciousness. The infinite consciousness which is devoid of time, space and causation playfully assumes these. Thus the cosmic person comes into being; this cosmic person is also the cosmic mind and cosmic life.

This cosmic person intends to experience sound; and space is brought into being, with the transmission of sound as its character. It intends to experience touch; air is created. These are unseen and subtle. Wishing to see, this cosmic person brings fire into being, and this fire expands into the numerous sources of light. It intends to experience taste as well as coolness to counteract fire; water comes into being. And, lastly, by its mere wish to smell, earth with its faculty of smell comes into being.

This cosmic person with all its faculties is still extremely subtle and undivided. It apparently abandons that and perceives itself as infinite sparks in space. It thinks of itself as each one of these sparks; the ego-sense arises. This ego-sense also has intelligence inherent in it, and it conceives of a body for itself with the help of the five cosmic elements I have already mentioned. This body it regards as gross, physical and material, and so it becomes.

This cosmic person is the Brahmā. He appears to create all these countless beings; and he himself protects them. He first arose in the infinite consciousness: but apparently overcome by self-limitation and forgetfulness of the infinite nature, as in foetal sleep, he identifies himself with the body, fueled and maintained by the life-force (prāṇa) and composed of material substances. When he begins to enquire into his origin, his true nature is revealed to him; and he is liberated from self-limitation.

VASIṢṬHA continued: IV:45

O Rāma, though this universe seems to exist, nothing really exists as the universe. It is but the appearance or reflection of the infinite consciousness, which alone is the reality. In that consciousness the creation appears as if in a dream. Hence, only the reality in which it appears is real: and that is the infinite void. You see the world because the eyes (or the other senses) perceive the world: and in the same way, if you think or believe or know that it exists, that is because your mind thinks so. And that mind has brought this body into being for its own dwelling.

All the powers that are inherent in the mind and by which this world has been brought into being are found in the infinite consciousness. Hence, the sages have declared that the mind is omnipotent. All these gods, demons and humans have all been conjured up by the mind; when the mind ceases to entertain such notions, they shall cease to be, even as a lamp without fuel.

The wise man who knows that all the objects in the world are unreal does not consider them objects of pleasure to be pursued. He who runs after the objects created by his own mind surely comes to grief. This world-appearance has come into being on account of desire; it will cease only when desire ceases to arise (not when you turn against or hate it). When this world-appearance has been dissolved nothing whatsoever has really been destroyed.

If an unreal appearance has vanished, what does one lose? If it is utterly unreal, then how can it even be destroyed; and why does one grieve over the unreal loss? Or, if it were real, then no one could destroy it or make it unreal; from this point of view this world is nothing but Brahman, the eternal truth. In which case, is there any room for sorrow at all?

Similarly, that which is unreal cannot grow or flourish; for what does one rejoice? What does one desire then? When all this is indeed the one infinite consciousness, what does one renounce?

That which was non-existent in the beginning, and that which shall cease to be in the end, is not real in the middle (in the present), either. That which exists in the beginning, and in the end, is the reality in the present, too. See that 'all this is unreal, including myself' and there will be no sorrow in you: or, see that 'all this is real, including myself' and sorrow will not touch you either.

(As the sage said this, the ninth day came to an end, and the assembly dispersed.)

IV:46 VASIṢṬHA continued:

Knowing that the entire universe including one's wealth, wife, son, etc. are nothing but the creation of the jugglery of the mind, one does not grieve when they are lost, nor does one feel elated when they prosper. On the other hand, it may be proper to feel unhappy when they prosper; for such prosperity may intensify one's ignorance. Hence, that which generates attachment and craving in the fool, generates detachment and cool indifference in the wise.

The nature of the wise person is not to desire those experiences which one does not effortlessly obtain, and to experience those which have already arrived. If one is able to wean the mind away from craving for sense-pleasure by whatever means, one is saved from being drowned in the ocean of delusion. He who has realised his oneness with the entire universe, and who has thus risen above both desire 'for' and desire 'against', is never deluded.

Therefore, O Rāma, realise that self or infinite consciousness which permeates and therefore transcends both the unreal and the real: and, then, neither grasp nor give up whatever is inside or outside. The wise sage who is established in such self-knowledge is free from any sort of colouring or mental conditioning or self-limitation: he is like the sky or space which is totally free from being tainted by anything that happens within it.

Let your mind not entertain a feeling of 'mine-ness' in any of the objects of the senses: then, whether you are active or inactive, you will not be sunk in the mire of ignorance. When your heart does not taste sense-pleasures as sweet and desirable, then you have known all that there is to be known, and you are saved from this cycle of birth and death. He who is not attracted by the pleasures of either this world or of heaven (whether or not there is body-consciousness in him) is liberated, even if he does not specifically desire or strive for such liberation.

O Rāma, in this ocean of ignorant mental conditioning, he who has found the raft of self-knowledge is saved from drowning; he who has not found that raft is surely drowned. Therefore, O Rāma, examine the nature of the self with an intelligence as sharp as the razor's edge; and then rest established in self-knowledge.

Live as the sages of self-knowledge live. They know the infinite consciousness and the world-appearance: hence, they do not relish nor renounce activity in this world. You, too, have attained self-knowledge, Rāma, and you are at peace.

VASIṢṬHA continued: IV:47

O Rāma, in the past there have been millions of Brahmās, Śivas, Indras, and Nārāyaṇas: however, even the creations of these gods were but the jugglery of Māyā! These creations were sometimes from Brahmā; others were ascribed to Śiva or Nārāyaṇa or the sages. Again, sometimes Brahmā was born of a lotus, at others he rose from the waters or from an egg or from space. In some universes Brahmā is the supreme deity, in others it is the Sun, Indra, Nārāyaṇa or Śiva. In some universes the earth is filled with trees, in others with people or with mountains. Somewhere the earth is of mud or clay, elsewhere it is rocky or golden or coppery. One may count the rays of the sun; but it is impossible to count the number of universes that exist. This creation is beginningless. In this 'city of Brahman' (which is the infinite consciousness or the consciousness in the space of one's heart) these universes arise and vanish again and again. But these are different from the one infinite consciousness.

These creations, whether they are gross or subtle, whether established or disintegrating, are all garlands of the subtle elements which have all arisen from the infinite space of consciousness. Sometimes, space gets established first, and the Creator is said to be born of space; at other times, air gets established first, and at other times, fire, water or earth; and the Creator gets an appropriate title. From this Creator's body there arise 'words' like brāhmaṇa (a priest) etc., and these words become 'living beings' with appropriate designations.

Of course, all this is unreal, like the creations seen in a dream. Hence the question "How did all this arise in the one infinite consciousness?" is immature and childish. The creation appears to take place on account of the intentions of the mind. This is certainly a mystery and a wonder.

I have described all this to you only as an illustration of the truth. However, in this creation, there is no such order or sequence. This creation is nothing but the creation of the mind; this is the truth, the rest is but a fanciful description. On account of the succession of the creation and dissolution of this universe a time-scale is conceived of, from a moment to an aeon. But this universe is for ever present in consciousness just as sparks are ever present in a red-hot iron. In the pure vision of an enlightened person, however, all this is Brahman alone, not a world-appearance. The repetition (creation and dissolution) of infinite number of universes, with the infinite variety of creators in them, is nothing but the fanciful perception of the ignorant and the deluded.

The Story of Dāśūra

IV:48 VASIṢṬHA continued:

O Rāma, they who are busy with the diverse affairs in this world in pursuit of pleasure and power do not desire to know the truth which they obviously do not see. He who is wise but who has not completely controlled the pleasure-seeking tendencies of his senses, sees the truth and sees the illusion. And, he who has clearly understood the nature of the world and of the jīva and who has firmly rejected the world-appearance as the reality, he is liberated and is not born again. The ignorant strive for the welfare of the body and not of the self: be not like the ignorant, O Rāma, but be wise.

To illustrate this, I shall now narrate to you an interesting legend. In the country known as Magadha which had an abundance of pleasure-gardens, there lived a sage by name Dāśūra. He was engaged in breath-taking penance. He was a great ascetic who had no interest at all in worldly pleasures; and he was learned, too.

He was the son of another sage known as Śaraloma. But, as ill-luck would have it, he lost both his parents when he was young. The deities of the forest took pity on this orphan who was inconsolable in his grief, and they said to him:

O wise boy! You are the son of a sage; why do you weep like an ignorant fool? Do you not know the evanescent nature of this world-appearance? Young one, such is the very nature of this world-appearance: things come into being, they exist for a while, and they are then destroyed. Whatever being there appears to be, from the relative point of view, (even if that being is called Brahmā, the creator) is subject to this inevitable end. There is no doubt about this. Hence, do not grieve over the inevitable death of your parents.

The young man's sorrow was ameliorated. He got up and performed the funeral rites of his parents. Then, he began to lead a rigorously religious life, hemmed in on all sides with do's and don'ts. Since he had not yet realised the truth, he was immersed in the performance of the rituals with all their injunctions and prohibitions. All this created in him a feeling that the whole world is full of impurities. He sought to live in an unpolluted place. A tree-top, he decided! Wishing to live on a tree-top, he performed a sacred rite during which he cut off and offered his own flesh into the sacred fire. Soon, the fire-deity himself appeared before him and announced, "You will surely attain the wish which has already appeared in your heart."

After accepting the ascetic's worship, Fire disappeared.

VASIṢṬHA continued: IV:49, 50, 51

The sage then saw in front of him a huge Kadamba tree which had a majestic appearance. It seemed to wipe with its hands (its foliage) the tears (raindrops) of his beloved sky. It had actually covered the space between heaven and earth with the thousands of its arms (branches) and it stood like the cosmic form of the Lord, with the sun and the moon for his eyes. Laden with flowers, it rained them on the holy and divine sages who traversed the sky. And the bees that dwelt on it sang a song of welcome to those sages. (The detailed description of the tree is graphic and beautiful.—S.V.)

The sage ascended this tree which stood like a pillar linking heaven and earth. He sat on the topmost branch of the tree. For a brief moment, he let his eyes roam in all the directions. He had a vision of the cosmic being. (The detailed description given in chapter 50 of what he saw is also interesting.—S.V.)

Because he had taken his abode on the Kadamba tree he had come to be known as Kadamba-dāśūra. He commenced his austerities sitting on the top of that tree. He had been accustomed to the ritualistic performances enjoined in the Vedas, and so he engaged himself in their performance, but this time mentally. Yet, such is the power of such mental performance, it purified the sage's mind and his heart, and he attained pure wisdom.

One day, he beheld in front of him a nymph clad in flowers. She was extremely beautiful. The sage asked her: "O beautiful lady, with your radiance you can overpower even Cupid. Who are you?" She replied: "Lord, I am a deity of the forest. In this world nothing is unattainable to one who resorts to the presence of an enlightened sage like you. I have just been to attend a festival in the forest, where I met several other goddesses of the forest, each one of them with her offspring. I was the only one among them who had no children. Hence, I am unhappy. However, when you are in this forest, why should I be unhappy? Grant me a son or I shall reduce myself to ashes." The sage picked up a creeper and handing it to her said: "Go. Just as this creeper will produce flowers in a month, you too, will give birth to a son." The grateful goddess went away.

She returned to the sage, after twelve years, with a son of that age. She said: "Lord, this is your son. And, I have instructed him in all branches of learning. I pray that you may instruct him in self-knowledge: for who will let his son grow into a fool?" The sage accepted to do so and the goddess went away. From that day, the sage began to instruct the young man in all branches of self-knowledge.

IV:52 VASIṢṬHA continued:

During this period I was myself going over that very tree and heard the sage's instructions to his son.

DĀŚŪRA said:

I shall illustrate what I wish to say concerning this world, with a story. There lives a mighty king named Khottha who is capable of conquering the three worlds. The deities presiding over the worlds faithfully honour his commands. No one can even catalogue his innumerable deeds which were productive of both happiness and unhappiness. His valour could not be challenged by anyone using any weapon whatsoever, or even by fire, any more than one can hit space with a fist. Even Indra, Viṣṇu and Śiva could not equal him in his enterprises.

This king had three bodies which had completely engulfed the worlds: and they were respectively the best, the middling and the least. This king arose in space and got established in space. There in space, the king built a city with fourteen roads and three sectors. In it were pleasure gardens, beautiful mountain-peaks for sports, and seven lakes with pearls and creepers in them. In it there were two lights which were hot and cold and whose light never diminished.

In that city the king created several types of beings. Some were placed above, others in the middle and yet others below. Of them some were long-lived and others short-lived. They were covered with black hair. They had nine gates. They were well-ventilated. They had five lamps, three pillars, and white supporting wooden poles. They were soft with clay-plastering. All this was created by the Māyā or illusory power of the king.

Here, the king besports himself, with all the ghosts and goblins (which are afraid of enquiry or investigation) that had been created to protect the mansions (the different bodies). When he thinks of moving he thinks of a future city and contemplates migrating to it. Surrounded by the ghosts, he runs fast to the new abode after leaving the previous one, and occupies the new city built in the fashion of a magic creation. In that again when he contemplates destruction, he destroys himself. Sometimes he wails, "What shall I do? I am ignorant, I am miserable". Sometimes he is happy, at others pitiable.

Thus, he lives and conquers, goes, talks, flourishes, shines and does not shine: my son, thus this king is tossed in this ocean of world-appearance.

DĀŚŪRA continued: IV:53

Thus has been illustrated the creation of the universe and of man. Khottha, who arose in the great void, is none but a notion or an intention. This notion arises in the great void of its own accord and dissolves in the great void of its own accord, too. The entire universe and whatever there is in it is the creation of this notion or intention, and naught else. In fact, even the trinity (Brahmā, Viṣṇu and Śiva) are the limbs of that notion. That intention alone is responsible for the creation of the three worlds, the fourteen regions and the seven oceans. The city built by the king is nothing but the living entity, with his different organs and their characteristics. Of the different kinds of beings thus created, some (the gods) are in a higher region and the others are in lower realms.

Having built this imaginary city, the king placed it under the protecting care of ghosts: these ghosts are the ahaṃkāra (ego-principle). The king thenceforth sports in this world, in this body. In a moment he sees the world in the waking state; and after some time he abruptly shifts his attention to the world within which he enjoys in his dreams. He moves from one city to another, from one body to another, from one realm to another.

After many such peregrinations, he develops wisdom, getting disillusioned with these worlds and their pleasures, and reaches the end of his wandering by the cessation of all notions.

In one moment he seems to enjoy wisdom, whilst the very next moment he is caught up in pleasure-seeking, and in an instant his understanding gets perverted, just as in the case of a little child. These notions are either like dense darkness (and give rise to ignorance and births in the lower orders of creation) or pure and transparent (and give rise to wisdom, drawing one close to the truth) or impure (and give rise to worldliness). When all such notions cease, then there is liberation.

Even if one engages oneself in every other sort of spiritual endeavour, and even if one has the gods themselves as one's teachers, and even if one were in heaven or any other region, liberation is not had except through the cessation of all notions. The real, the unreal and the admixture of these two are all but notions and naught else; and notions themselves are neither real nor unreal. What then shall we call real in this universe? Hence, my son, give up these notions, thoughts and intentions. When they cease, the mind naturally turns to what is truly beyond the mind—the infinite consciousness.

IV:54 THE YOUNG MAN asked:

Father, please tell me how this saṅkalpa (notion, thought, idea, concept) arises and how it grows and ceases.

DĀŚŪRA replied:

My son, when, in the infinite consciousness, the consciousness becomes aware of itself as its own object, there is the seed of ideation. This is very subtle. But soon it becomes gross and fills the whole of space, as it were. When consciousness is engrossed in this ideation it thinks the object is distinct from the subject. Then the ideation begins to germinate and to grow. Ideation multiplies naturally by itself. This leads to sorrow, not to happiness. There is no cause for sorrow in this world other than this ideation!

This ideation or notion has really come into being by sheer coincidence (the crow alights on the palm tree, and the fruit falls to the ground, without any causal connection). But this unreal non-substance is yet able to grow! Your birth, therefore, is unreal; your existence, surely, is unreal too. When you know this and realise this, the unreality ceases.

Do not entertain ideas. Do not hold onto the notion of your existence. For it is only by these that the future comes into being. There is no cause for fear in the destruction of all ideation. When there is no thought, notion or ideation ceases. My son, it is easier to cease to entertain notions, than it is to crush a flower that lies on the palm of your hand. The latter demands effort; the former is effortless. When thus all notions cease, there is great peace, and sorrow is destroyed to its very root. For everything in this universe is but an idea, a notion, a concept: it has different names like the mind, the living soul or jīva, intelligence and conditioning—there are no real substances corresponding to these words. Hence, remove all thought. Do not waste your life and effort in other endeavours.

Already as the notions weaken, one is less affected by happiness and unhappiness, and knowledge of the unreality of the objects prevents attachment. When there is no hope, there is neither elation nor depression. The mind itself is the jīva when it is reflected in consciousness; and mind itself builds castles in the air, stretching itself, as it were, into the past, the present and the future. It is not possible to comprehend the ripples of ideation; but this much can be said: sense-experiences multiply them, and when these are given up, they cease to be. If these notions are real, like the blackness of coal, then you cannot remove them; but that is not so. Hence they can be destroyed.

VASIṢṬHA continued: IV:55, 56

Hearing the sage's words, I descended upon that Kadamba tree. For a considerable time the three of us discussed self-knowledge, and I awakened in them the supreme knowledge. Then I took leave of them and went away. O Rāma, this is meant to illustrate the nature of the world-appearance; and therefore, this story is as true as the world itself!

Even if you believe that this world and yourself are real, then be it so: rest firmly in your own self. If you think that this is both real and unreal, then adopt the appropriate attitude to this changing world. If you believe that the world is unreal, then be firmly established in the infinite consciousness. Similarly, whether you believe that the world has had a creator or not, let it not cloud your understanding.

The self is devoid of the senses; hence though the doer of everything, he is as if inert. One enjoys a life-span of just a hundred years: why does the immortal self run after the sensual pleasures during this brief period? If the world and its objects are real, even then it does not stand to reason that the conscious self should seek the inert objects! And of course if they are not real, nothing but unhappiness can result from their pursuit.

Give up the desires of your heart. You are what you are in this world: knowing this, sport in this world. In the very presence of the self all activities take place in this world, just as in the very presence of a lamp there is light. The lamp has no intention to shine: even so, the self does not intend to do anything and yet everything happens in its very presence. You may adopt one or the other of the two attitudes: (1) I am the omnipresent being that does nothing, and (2) I am the doer of all actions in this world. In both cases you will arrive at the same state of perfect equanimity, which is immortality. You will be free from likes and dislikes, attraction and aversion. You will be rid of foolish feelings like "Someone served me", or "Someone else hurt me". Hence, O Rāma, you may feel, "I am not the doer, I do not exist" or "I am the doer, and I am everything": or enquire into the nature of the self ('Who am I') and realise "I am not any of this that is attributed to me". Rest established in the self which is the highest state of consciousness, in which the best among the holy men who know of this state ever dwell.

IV:57 RĀMA asked:

Holy sage, how does this unreal world exist in the absolute Brahman: can snow exist in the sun?

VASIṢṬHA said:

Rāma, this is not the right time for you to ask this question, for you will not be able to comprehend the answer now. Love stories are uninteresting to a little boy. Every tree bears its fruits in due season; and my instruction will also bear fruit in good time. If you seek your self with the self by your own self effort, then you will clearly find the answer to your question. I discussed the question of doership and non-doership in order that the nature of the mental conditioning or ideation may become evident.

Bondage is bondage to these thoughts and notions: freedom is freedom from them. Give up all notions, even those of liberation. First, by the cultivation of good relationships like friendship, give up tendencies and notions which are gross and materialistic. Later, give up even such notions as friendship, even though continuing to be friendly, etc. Give up all desires and contemplate the nature (or notion) of cosmic consciousness. Even this is within the realm of ideation or thought. Hence, give this up in due course. Rest in what remains after all these have been given up. And, renounce the renouncer of these notions. When even the notion of the ego-sense has ceased, you will be like the infinite space. He who has thus renounced everything from his heart, he indeed is the supreme Lord, whether he continues to live an active life or whether he rests in contemplation all the time. To him neither action nor inaction is of any use. O Rāma, I have examined all the scriptures and investigated the truth; there is no salvation without the total renunciation of all notions or ideas or mental conditioning.

This world of diverse names and forms is composed of the desirable and the undesirable! For these people strive, but for self-knowledge no one strives. Rare are the sages of self-knowledge in the three worlds. One may be an emperor of the world or the king of heaven; but all these are only composed of the five elements! It is a pity that people indulge in such colossal destruction of life for these petty gains. Shame on them. None of these engages the attention of the sage, because he is equipped with self-knowledge. He is established in that supreme seat to which the sun and the moon have no access (the suṣumnā?). Hence, the sage of self-knowledge is not enamoured of the gains or the pleasures of the entire universe.

Kaca's Song

VASIṢṬHA continued: IV:58

In this connection, O Rāma, I remember an inspiring song sung by the son of the preceptor of the gods, Kaca. This Kaca was established in self-knowledge. He lived in a cave on the mount Meru. His mind was saturated with the highest wisdom and hence it was not attracted by any of the objects of the world composed of the five elements. Feigning despair, Kaca sang this meaningful song. Pray listen to this.

KACA said: What shall I do? Where shall I go? What shall I try to hold? What shall I renounce? This entire universe is permeated by the one self. Unhappiness or sorrow is the self. Happiness is the self, too. For all desires are but empty void. Having known that all this is the self, I am freed from all travail. In this body, within and without, above and below, everywhere—here and there—there is only the self and self alone and there is no non-self. The self alone is everywhere; everything exists as the self. All this is truly the self. I exist in the self as the self. I exist as all this, as the reality in all everywhere. I am the fullness. I am the self-bliss. I fill the entire universe like the cosmic ocean.

Thus he sang. And, he intoned the holy word OM which resounded like a bell. He had merged his entire being in that holy sound. He was neither inside anything nor outside anything. This sage remained in that place totally absorbed in the self.

VASIṢṬHA continued: IV:59

What else is there in this world, O Rāma, except eating, drinking and sex: hence, what is there in this world that a wise man would find worthy of seeking? This world of five elements, and the body composed of flesh, blood, hair and all the rest of it, are considered real by the ignorant, and they exist for his entertainment. The wise see in all this an impermanent and unreal but terrible poison.

RĀMA asked:

By the destruction of all notions when the mind regains the state of the Creator himself, how does the notion of the world arise in it?

VASIṢṬHA continued:

Rāma, the first-born Creator on arising from the womb of the infinite consciousness uttered the sound 'Brahmā': hence he is known as Brahmā, the creator. This Creator first entertained the notion of light, and light came into being. In that light he visualised his own cosmic body, and this came into being—from the brilliant sun to the diverse objects that fill the space. He contemplated the same light as of infinite sparks, and all these sparks became diverse beings. Surely, it is the cosmic mind alone that has become this Brahmā and all the other beings. Whatever this Brahmā created in the beginning is seen even today.

This unreal world has acquired substantiality on account of the persistence of the notion of its existence. All the beings in this universe sustain it by their own notions and ideas.

After creating the universe by his own thought-force, the Creator reflected thus: "I have created all this by the power of a little agitation in the cosmic mind. I have had enough of it. It will now perpetuate itself. Let me rest." Contemplating thus, Brahmā the creator rested —rested in his own self in deep meditation.

Then, out of compassion for the created beings, the Creator revealed the scriptures which treat of self-knowledge. Once again he became absorbed in the knowledge of his own self which is beyond all concepts and descriptions. This indeed is the highest 'state of the Creator' (brāhmī-sthiti).

From there on, created beings acquired the character of the things with which they associated. By associating with the good they became good, and those who associated with the worldly, became worldly. Thus one gets bound to this world-appearance; and thus one is liberated too.

IV:60, 61 VASIṢṬHA continued:

After the creation of the world-appearance, it (this world-appearance) became like a water-pot in which the living creatures keep coming up and going down into the blind-well, with the 'desire to live' as the binding rope. These living beings that arose in the ocean of infinite consciousness like waves and ripples entered into the physical space; and when the elements like air, fire, water and earth were evolved they became involved in them. Then the cycle of birth and death began to revolve.

The jīvas come down, as it were, riding the rays of the moon, and enter into the plants and herbs. They become the fruits, as it were, of those plants; the fruits are ripened by the light of the sun. Then they are ready to incarnate. The subtle notions, ideas and mental conditioning are dormant even in the unborn being; at birth, the veil that covered them is removed.

Some of these beings are born pure and enlightened (sātvika). Even in their own previous births they had turned away from the lure of sensual pleasures. But the nature of the others, who are born merely to perpetuate the cycle of birth and death, is a mixture of the pure, the impure, and the dark. There are others whose nature is pure with just a slight impurity; they are devoted to the truth and are full of noble qualities—rare are such people who are devoid of the darkness of ignorance. Other people are enveloped by the darkness of ignorance and stupidity—they are like rocks and hills!

Those beings in whom purity is preponderant with just a slight impurity (the rājasa-sātvika people) are ever happy, enlightened and do not grieve nor despair. They are unselfish like trees, and like them, they live to experience the fruition of past actions without committing new ones. They are desireless. They are at peace within themselves and they do not abandon this peace even in the worst calamities. They love all, and look upon all with equal vision. They do not drown in the ocean of sorrow.

By all means one should avoid drowning in the ocean of sorrow and engage oneself in the enquiry into the nature of the self: "Who am I, how has this world-illusion arisen?" One should thus abandon egoism in the body and attraction to the world. Then one will realise that there is no division in space, whether or not a building stands in space. The same consciousness that shines in the sun also dwells as the little worm that crawls in a hole on this earth.

VASIṢṬHA continued: IV:62

O Rāma, one who is wise and who is capable of enquiring into the nature of truth should approach a good and learned person and study the scripture. This teacher should be free from craving for pleasure and he should also have had direct experience of the truth; and with his help, one should study the scripture and by the practice of the great yoga, one can reach the supreme state.

O Rāma, you are indeed a spiritual hero and an abode of good qualities. You are free from sorrow. You have reached the state of equanimity. Give up all delusion through the highest form of intelligence. When you are free from all concern about the objects of the world, you will be established in non-dual consciousness, and that is final liberation. There is no doubt about this. And, sages of self-knowledge will follow your noble example.

Rāma, only a person who is intelligent like you, who is good-natured and equal-visioned like you, and who sees only what is good, is entitled to the vision of wisdom which I have described here.

O Rāma, as long as you are embodied, live without being swayed by likes and dislikes, attraction and aversion, in conformity with the standards of the community in which you live, but without any desires and cravings. Constantly seek to discover the supreme peace, as the holy ones do.

It is by emulating the example of the holy ones that one makes progress towards the supreme state. Whatever be one's nature here in this life, that alone he obtains after leaving this life-span. But he who exerts seriously now is able to overcome such predispositions and exalt himself from the states of darkness and stupidity (tamas) and impurity (rajas). It is by the exercise of one's wisdom that one can ascend from these other states to the state of purity and enlightenment (satva).

It is only by intense self-effort that one obtains a good embodiment. There is nothing that intense self-effort cannot achieve. By the practice of brahmacarya (continence or whole-souled devotion to Brahman), courage and endurance, and dispassion, and by intelligent practice based on common-sense, one obtains that which one seeks to obtain, self-knowledge.

Rāma, you are already a liberated being: live like one!

PART FIVE

On Dissolution

VĀLMĪKI said: V:1, 2

The people (including the gods, demi-gods and sages and the members of the royal court) listened to sage Vasiṣṭha's words of wisdom with total attention. The emperor Daśaratha and his ministers had for the time being abandoned their royal preoccupations and pleasures, intent on absorbing the teachings of the sage. At noon, the conches gave the time-signal and the assembly rose for the midday interval. In the evening the congregation was given leave to retire for the day, and as the kings and the princes rose to leave the court, their dazzling ornaments illumined it. The court itself appeared to be a miniature universe.

When the assembly had thus dispersed, the king Daśaratha duly worshipped the sages and received their blessings. After this, Vasiṣṭha gave leave to the princes, Rāma and his brothers, to retire for the day. They too, fell at the sage's feet and received his blessings.

When night fell, all except Rāma retired to bed. But, Rāma could not sleep.

RĀMA contemplated the illuminating words of the sage Vasiṣṭha thus:

What is this world-appearance? Who are all these different kinds of people and other beings? How do they appear here, from where do they come and where do they go? What is the nature of the mind and how does it attain quiescence? How did this Māyā (cosmic illusion) arise in the first place and how does it come to an end? Again, is such an end to this illusion desirable or undesirable? How has limitation entered into the infinite self?

What exactly are the means that the sage Vasiṣṭha has prescribed for the conquest of the senses and the mind? They are surely the sources of sorrow. It is impossible to abandon enjoyment of pleasure, and it is not possible to end sorrow without abandoning such enjoyment: this indeed is a problem. But, since the mind is the crucial factor in all this, surely if the mind once tastes the supreme peace, freed of all world-illusion, it will not abandon that and run after sense-pleasure.

Oh, when will my mind be pure and when will it rest in the supreme being? When will my mind rest in the infinite even as a wave is re-absorbed in the ocean? When will I be free of all craving? When will I be blessed with equal vision? When will I be rid of this terrible fever of worldliness?

O mind, will you really remain firmly established in the wisdom revealed by the great sages? O my intellect, you are my friend: contemplate the teachings of sage Vasiṣṭha in such a way that we shall both be saved from the miseries of this worldly existence.

V:3, 4 VĀLMĪKI continued:

When the day dawned, Rāma and the others got up and performed their morning religious functions and went over to the residence of the sage Vasiṣṭha. The sage himself had by then concluded his own dawn prayers and was in deep meditation. When he rose, he and the others ascended a chariot and drove to the palace of king Daśaratha. As they entered the royal court, the king walked three paces to receive them with due honour.

Soon after this, all the other members of the assembly (the gods, the demi-gods, the sages and others) entered the assembly and took up their respective places.

Opening the day's proceedings, DAŚARATHA said:

O blessed Lord, I hope you have thoroughly recovered from the strain of yesterday's discourse. For our part, we feel highly elevated by the words of supreme wisdom that you uttered yesterday. Surely, the words of enlightened sages dispel the sorrows of all beings and bestow bliss upon them. They drive away the impurities caused in us by our own evil deeds. The evil tendencies like craving, greed, etc., are weakened by your wisdom. Our deluded belief in the reality of this world-appearance is also provided with a powerful challenge.

O Rāma, only that day on which such sages are worshipped can be regarded as fruitful; the other days are of darkness. This is your best opportunity: enquire and learn from the sage that which is worth learning.

VASIṢṬHA said:

O Rāma, have you deeply contemplated the teachings I have

communicated to you? Did you reflect over them during the night and have you inscribed them on the tablet of your heart? Do you remember that I said to you that the mind is man? Do you remember what I said about the creation of this universe in all its details? For it is only by frequent remembrance of such teachings that they attain clarity.

RĀMA said:

Lord, I have indeed done just that. Giving up sleep, I have spent the whole night meditating upon your enlightening words, endeavouring to see the truth that the words pointed to. Thus have I enshrined that truth in my heart. Who will not bear your teachings on his head, knowing that they confer the highest bliss on him? At the same time, they are extremely sweet to hear, they promote every type of auspiciousness and they bring us the incomparable experience.

Hence, O Lord, I pray: resume your most excellent discourse.

VASIṢṬHA said: V:5

O Rāma, kindly listen to this discourse on the dissolution of the universe and the attainment of supreme peace.

This seemingly unending world-appearance is sustained by impure (rājasa) and dull (tāmasa) beings, even as a superstructure is sustained by pillars. But it is playfully and easily abandoned by those who are of a pure nature, even as the slough is effortlessly abandoned by a snake. They who are of a pure (satva) nature and they whose activities (rajas) are based on purity and light (satva) do not live their life mechanically, but enquire into the origin and the nature of this world-appearance. When such enquiry is conducted with the help of the right study of scriptures and the company of holy ones, there arises a clear understanding within oneself in which the truth is seen, as in the light of a lamp. Not until this truth is perceived by oneself for oneself through such enquiry is the truth seen truly. O Rāma, you are indeed of a pure nature: therefore, enquire into the nature of the truth and the falsehood, and be devoted to the truth. That which was not in the beginning and which will cease to be after a time, how can that be regarded as truth? That alone can be regarded as the truth which has always been and which will always be.

Birth is of the mind, O Rāma: and growth is mental, too. And, when the truth is clearly seen, it is mind that is liberated from its own ignorance. Hence, let the mind be led along the path of righteousness by the prior study of the scriptures, company of the holy ones and the cultivation of dispassion. Equipped with these, one should resort to the feet of a master (guru) whose wisdom is perfected. By faithfully adhering to the teachings of the master, one gradually attains to the plane of total purity.

Rāma, behold the self by the self through pure enquiry, even as the cool moon perceives the entire space. One is tossed around over the waters of this illusory world-appearance like a piece of straw only as long as one does not get into the secure boat of self-enquiry. Even as particles of sand floating in water settle down when the water is absolutely steady, the mind of the man who has gained the knowledge of the truth settles down in total peace. Once this knowledge of the truth is gained, it is not lost: even if a piece of gold has lain in a heap of ashes, the goldsmith finds no problem seeing it. When the truth has not been known, there may be confusion: but once it is known there can be no confusion. Ignorance of the self is the cause of your sorrow; knowledge of the self leads to delight and tranquility.

VASIṢṬHA continued:

Resolve the confusion between the body and the self, and you will be at peace at once. Even as a nugget of gold fallen into mud is never spoiled by the mud, the self is untainted by the body. I repeat, with uplifted arms I proclaim, "The self is one thing and the body is another, even as the water and the lotus", but no one listens to me! As long as the inert and insentient mind pursues the path of pleasure, so long this darkness of world-illusion cannot be dispelled. But, the moment one awakens from this and enquires into the nature of the self, this darkness is dispelled at once. Hence, one should constantly endeavour to awaken the mind which dwells in the body in order that one may go beyond the process of becoming—for such becoming is fraught with sorrow.

Even as the sky is not affected by the dust-particles floating in it, the self is unaffected by the body. Pleasure and pain are falsely imagined to be experienced by oneself, even as one falsely thinks that 'the sky is polluted by dust'. In fact, pleasure and pain are neither of the body nor of the self which transcends everything; they belong only to ignorance. Their loss is no loss. Neither pleasure nor pain belong to anyone: all indeed is the self which is supreme peace and infinite. Realise this, O Rāma.

The self and the world are neither identical nor are they different (dual). All this is but the reflection of the truth. Nothing but the one Brahman exists. 'I am different from this' is pure fancy: give it up, O Rāma. The one self perceives itself within itself as the infinite consciousness. Therefore, there is no sorrow, no delusion, no birth (creation), nor creature: whatever is, is. Be free from distress, O Rāma. Be free of duality; remain firmly established in the self, abandoning even concern for your own welfare. Be at peace within, with a steady mind. Let there be no sorrow in your mind. Rest in the inner silence. Remain alone, without self-willed thoughts. Be brave, having conquered the mind and the senses. Be desireless, content with what comes to you unsought. Live effortlessly, without grabbing or giving up anything. Be free from all mental perversions and from the blinding taint of illusion. Rest content in your own self. Thus, be free from all distress. Remain in an expansive state in the self, like the full ocean. Rejoice in the self by the self, like the blissful rays of the full moon.

VASIṢṬHA continued: V:6, 7

O Rāma, he who knows that all the activities merely happen because of the mere existence of consciousness—even as a crystal reflects the objects around it without intending to do so—is liberated. They who, even after taking this human birth, are not interested in such non-volitional activity, go from heaven to hell and from hell to heaven again.

Some there are who are devoted to inaction, having turned away from or suppressed all action; they go from hell to hell, from sorrow to sorrow, from fear to fear. Some are bound by their tendencies and intentions to the fruits of their own actions; and they take birth as worms and vermin, then as trees and plants, then as worms and vermin again. Others there are who know the self; blessed indeed are they, they have carefully enquired into the nature of the mind and overcome all cravings: they go to higher planes of consciousness.

He who has taken birth for the last time now, is endowed with a mixture of light (satva) and a little impurity (rajas). Right from birth he grows in holiness. The nobler type of knowledge enters into him with ease. All the noble qualities like friendliness, compassion, wisdom, goodness and magnanimity seek him and take their abode in him. He performs all appropriate actions, but is not swayed if their results appear to be gain or loss, nor does he feel elated or depressed. His heart is clear. He is much sought after by the people.

Such a one, who is full of all the noble qualities, seeks and follows an enlightened master who directs him along the path of self-knowledge. He then realises the self which is the one cosmic being. Such a liberated one awakens the inner intelligence, which has been asleep so far: and this awakened intelligence instantly knows itself to be the infinite consciousness. Becoming constantly aware of the inner light, such a blessed one instantly ascends into the utterly pure state.

Such is the normal course of evolution, O Rāma. However, there are exceptions to this rule. In the case of those who have taken birth in this world, two possibilities exist for the attainment of liberation. The first is: treading the path indicated by the master, the seeker gradually reaches the goal of liberation. The second is: self-knowledge literally drops into one's lap, as it were, and there is instant enlightenment.

I shall narrate to you an ancient legend which illustrates the second type of enlightenment. Please listen.

The Story of King Janaka

V:8 VASIṢṬHA continued:

O Rāma, there is a great monarch whose vision is unlimited, who rules over the Videha territory: he is known as Janaka. To those who seek his aid, he is a cornucopia. In his very presence the heart-lotuses of his friends blossom: he is like unto a sun for them. He is a great benefactor to all good people.

One day he went to a pleasure-garden where he roamed freely. While he was thus roaming, he heard the inspiring words uttered by certain holy, perfected ones. Thus did the

PERFECTED SAGES sing:

We contemplate that self which reveals itself as the pure experience of bliss when seer (the experiencer) comes into contact with the object (the experience), without a division or conceptualisation.

We contemplate the self in which the objects are reflected non-volitionally, once the divided experience (predicate) of subject-object and the intention or volition that created this division have all ceased.

We contemplate that light that illumines all that shines, the self that transcends the twin concepts of 'is' and 'is not' and which therefore is 'in the middle' of the two sides, as it were.

We contemplate that reality in which everything exists, to which everything belongs, from which everything has emerged, which is the cause of everything and which is everything.

We contemplate the self which is the very basis of all language and expression, being the alpha and the omega, which covers the entire field from 'a' to 'ha' and which is indicated by the word 'aham' ('I').

Alas, people run after other objects, foolishly giving up the Lord who dwells in the cave of one's own heart.

He who, having known the worthlessness of the objects still remains bound at heart to them, is not a human being!

One should strike down every craving with the rod of wisdom, whether that craving has arisen or is about to rise in the heart.

One should enjoy the delight that flows from peace. The man whose mind is well-controlled is firmly established in peace. When the heart is thus established in peace, there arises the pure bliss of the self without delay.

VASIṢṬHA continued: V:9

Having heard the words of the sages, king Janaka became terribly depressed. With the utmost expedition, he retraced his steps to the palace. Quickly dismissing all his attendants, he sought the seclusion of his own chamber. In a mood of intense anguish,

KING JANAKA said to himself:

Alas, alas, I am helplessly swinging like a stone in this world of misery. What is the duration of a life-span in eternity: yet, I have developed a love for it! Fie on the mind. What is sovereignty even during a whole life-time? Yet, like a fool, I think I cannot do without it! This life-span of mine is but a trivial moment—eternity stretches before and after it. How shall I cherish it now?

Ah, who is that magician who has spread this illusion called the world and thus deluded me? How is it that I am so deluded? Realising that what is near and what is far is all in my mind, I shall give up the apprehension of all external objects. Knowing that all the busy-ness in this world leads only to endless suffering, what hope shall I cherish for happiness? Day after day, month after month, year after year, moment after moment, I see happiness comes to me bearing sorrow and sorrow comes to me again and again!

Whatever is seen or experienced here is subject to change and destruction: there is nothing whatsoever in this world which the wise would rely on. They who are exalted today are trodden under foot tomorrow: O foolish mind, what shall we trust in this world?

Alas, I am bound without a cord; I am tainted without impurity; I am fallen, though remaining at the top. O my self, what a mystery! Even as the ever-brilliant sun suddenly faces a cloud floating in front of him, I find this strange delusion mysteriously floating towards me. Who are these friends and relatives, what are these pleasures? Even as a boy seeing a ghost is frightened, I am deluded by these fanciful relatives. Knowing all such relatives as cords that bind me to this old age, death, etc., I still cling to them. Let these relatives continue or perish: what is it to me? Great events and great men have come and gone, leaving just a memory behind: on what shall one place reliance even now? Even the gods and the trinity have come and gone a million times: what is permanent in this universe? It is vain hope that binds one to this nightmare known as world-appearance. Fie on this wretched condition.

KING JANAKA continued:

I am like an ignorant fool deluded by the goblin known as the ego-sense which creates the false feeling "I am so-and-so". Knowing full well that Time has trampled under foot countless gods and trinities, I still entertain love for life. Days and nights are spent in vain cravings, but not in the experience of the bliss of infinite consciousness. I have gone from sorrow to greater sorrow, but dispassion does not arise in me.

What shall I regard as excellent or desirable, seeing that whatever one cherished in this world has passed away, leaving one miserable. Day by day people in this world grow in sin and violence, hence day by day they experience greater sorrow. Childhood is wasted in ignorance, youth is wasted in lusting after pleasures and the rest of one's life is spent in family worries: what does a stupid person achieve in this life?

Even if one performs great religious rites, one may go to heaven —nothing more. What is heaven, is it on earth or in the netherworld, and is there a place which is untouched by affliction? Sorrow brings happiness, and happiness brings sorrow on its shoulders! The pores of the earth are filled by the dead bodies of beings: hence it looks solid!

There are beings in this universe whose winking is of the duration of an epoch. What is my life-span in comparison? Of course there appear to be delightful and enduring objects in this world, but they bring with them endless worries and anxieties! Prosperity is truly adversity, and adversity may be desirable depending upon the effect upon the mind. Mind alone is the seed for this delusion of world-appearance; it is the mind that gives rise to the false sense of 'I' and 'mine'.

In this world which appears to have been created, even as the fruit of cocoanut-palm might appear to have been dislodged by a crow which coincidentally happens to alight on the tree at that moment, sheer ignorance generates feelings like 'this I should have' and 'this I should reject'. It is better to spend one's time in seclusion or in hell than to live in this world-appearance.

Intention or motivation alone is the seed for this world-appearance. I shall dry up this motivation! I have enjoyed and suffered all kinds of experiences. Now I shall rest. I shall not grieve any more. I have been awakened. I shall slay this thief (the mind) who has stolen my wisdom. I have been well instructed by the sages: now I shall seek self-knowledge.

V:10 VASIṢṬHA continued:

Seeing the king thus seated engrossed in deep contemplation, his bodyguard respectfully approached him and said: "Lord, it is time to consider your royal duties. Your Majesty's handmaiden awaits your pleasure, having prepared your perfumed bath. The holy priests await your arrival in the bath chamber, to commence the chanting of the appropriate hymns. Lord, arise and let what has to be done be done; for noble men are never unpunctual or negligent."

But the king ignored the bodyguard's words and continued to muse:

What shall I do with this court and the royal duties, when I know that all these are ephemeral? They are useless to me. I shall renounce all activities and duties and I shall remain immersed in the bliss of the self.

O mind, abandon your craving for sense-pleasures so that you may be rid of the miseries of repeated old age and death. Whatever be the condition in which you hope to enjoy happiness, that very condition proves to be the source of unhappiness! Enough of this sinful, conditioned, pleasure-seeking life. Seek the delight that is natural and inherent in you.

Seeing that the king was silent, the bodyguard became silent, too. THE KING once again said to himself:

What shall I seek to gain in this universe, on what eternal truth in this universe shall I rest with confidence? What difference does it make if I am engaged in ceaseless activity or if I remain idle? Nothing in this world is truly enduring in any case. Whether active or idle, this body is impermanent and ever-changing. When the intelligence is rooted in equanimity, what is lost and how?

I do not long for what I do not have, nor do I desire to abandon what has come to me unsought. I am firmly established in the self; let what is mine be mine! There is nothing that I should work for, nor is there any meaning in inaction. Whatever is gained by action or by inaction is false. When the mind is thus established in desirelessness, when it does not seek pleasure, when the body and its limbs perform their natural functions, action and inaction are of equal value or meaning. Hence, let the body engage itself in its natural functions; without such activity, the body will disintegrate. When the mind ceases to entertain the notions 'I do this' 'I enjoy this' in regard to the actions thus performed, action becomes non-action.

VASIṢṬHA continued: V:11

Reflecting thus, king Janaka rose from his seat as the sun rises in the horizon and began to engage himself in the royal duties, without any attachment to them. Having abandoned all concepts of the desirable and the undesirable, freed from all psychological conditioning and intention, he engaged himself in spontaneous and appropriate action—as if in deep sleep, though wide awake. He performed the day's tasks, including the adoration of the holy ones; and at the conclusion of the day he retired to his own seclusion to spend the night in deep meditation, which was easy and natural to him. His mind had naturally turned away from all confusion and delusion, and had become firmly established in equanimity: and when he rose in the morning,

KING JANAKA thus reflected in his own mind:

O unsteady mind! This worldly life is not conducive to your true happiness. Hence, reach the state of equanimity. It is in such equanimity that you will experience peace, bliss and the truth. Whenever you create perverse thinking in yourself, out of your wantonness, it is then that this world-illusion begins to expand and spread out. It is when you entertain desire for pleasure that this world-illusion sprouts countless branches. It is thought that gives rise to this network of world-appearance. Hence, abandon this whim and fancy and attain to equanimity. Weigh in the balance of your wisdom, the sense pleasures on one side and the bliss of peace on the other. Whatever you determine to be the truth, seek that. Give up all hopes and expectations, and freed from the wish to seek or to abandon, roam about freely. Let this world-appearance be real or unreal, let it arise or set: but, do not let its merits and demerits disturb your equanimity. For, at no time do you have a real relationship with this world-appearance: it is only because of your ignorance that such a relationship has appeared in you. O mind, you are false, and this world-appearance is also false: hence there is a mysterious relationship between you two—like the relationship between the barren woman and her son. If you think that you are real and that the world is unreal, how can a valid relationship exist between the two? On the other hand, if both are real, where then is the justification for exultation and sorrow? Hence, abandon sorrow and resort to deep contemplation. There is naught here in this world which can lead you to the state of fullness. Hence, resolutely take refuge in courage and endurance, and overcome your own waywardness.

V:12 VASIṢṬHA continued:

Having reached the understanding already described, Janaka functioned as the king and did all that was necessary, without getting befuddled, and with a great strength of mind and spirit. His mind was not distracted by royal pleasures. In fact, he moved about as if he were continually in a state of deep sleep.

From then on, he was interested neither in accumulating nor in rejecting anything: without any doubt or confusion, he lived in the present. His wisdom was uninterrupted and his intelligence did not become clouded again by impurities. The light of self-knowledge (cid-ātmā) arose in his heart, free from the least taint of impurity and sorrow, even as the sun rises on the horizon. He beheld everything in the universe as existing in cosmic power (cid-śakti). Endowed with self-knowledge he saw all things in the self which is infinite. Knowing that all that happens happens naturally, he neither experienced elation nor suffered depression and remained in unbroken equanimity. Janaka had become a liberated one while still living (jīvan-mukta).

Janaka continued to rule the kingdom, without his self-knowledge setting or rising again on account of the influence of the evil or the good prevalent around him. Remaining for ever in the consciousness of the infinite, he experienced the state of non-action, even though he appeared to others to be ever busy in diverse actions. All his tendencies and intentions had ceased to be: hence, though he appeared to be active, he was really in a state of deep sleep all the time.

He did not brood over the past, nor did he worry over the future: he lived in the present moment, smiling happily all the time.

Janaka attained whatever he did by dint of his own enquiry. Similarly, one should pursue the enquiry into the nature of truth till one reaches the very limits of such enquiry. Self-knowledge or knowledge of truth is not had by resorting to a guru (preceptor) nor by the study of scripture, nor by good works: it is attained only by means of enquiry inspired by the company of wise and holy men. One's inner light alone is the means, naught else. When this inner light is kept alive, it is not affected by the darkness of inertia.

VASIṢṬHA continued:

Whatever sorrows there may be that seem to be difficult to overcome are easily crossed over with the help of the boat of wisdom (the inner light). He who is devoid of this wisdom is bothered even by minor difficulties. But, he who has this wisdom, even if he is alone and helpless in this world and even if he is unlearned in the scriptures, easily crosses the sea of sorrow. Even without the help of another the man of wisdom accomplishes his work. He who is without wisdom does not—nay, even his capital is lost. Hence, one should constantly endeavour to gain this inner light or wisdom, even as one who aspires for fruits exerts constant effort in his garden. Wisdom is the root which, when thus constantly nourished, yields the good fruits of self-knowledge.

The effort and the energy that are directed by the people in worldly activities should first be directed to the gaining of this wisdom. One should first destroy the dullness of wit which is the source of all sorrow and calamities and which is the seed for this huge tree of world-appearance. And, whatever is gained in heaven or in the netherworld or by empires here, is gained by wisdom here and now. By wisdom is this ocean of world-appearance crossed over, not by charity nor by pilgrimage nor by austerities. Those men who are endowed with divine virtues here gained them through wisdom. Even kings have gained their throne through wisdom: wisdom is surely the path to heaven as well as to supreme good or liberation.

It is by wisdom alone that a meek scholar wins in a contest against a powerful adversary. Wisdom or the inner light is like the legendary precious stone, O Rāma, which bestows on its owner whatever he wishes to have. He who has this wisdom reaches the other shore of this world-illusion easily; he who does not have this wisdom drowns in world-illusion. When one's intelligence and understanding are properly guided by this inner light, one reaches the other shore; if not, one is overcome by obstacles.

Defects, desires and evils do not even approach that man of wisdom whose mind is undeluded. Through wisdom (in the inner light) the entire world is clearly seen as it is; neither good fortune nor misfortune even approach one who has such clear vision. Even as the dense dark cloud that veils the sun is dispersed by wind, the darkness of ego-sense which veils the self is dispelled by wisdom (inner light). He who seeks to be established in the highest state of consciousness, should first purify his mind by the cultivation of wisdom or by the kindling of the inner light, even as one who desires foodgrains tills the field.

V:13 VASIṢṬHA continued:

O Rāma, thus do enquire into the nature of the self, even as Janaka did. Then you will reach, without any obstacle whatsoever, that realm of the knowers of what is to be known. Again and again, one should overcome the enemies known as the senses: and then the self attains self-satisfaction by its own endeavour. When thus the infinite self is realised, sorrow comes to an end—even the seeds of delusion are destroyed, the shower of misfortunes ceases and the perception of evil ends. Hence, O Rāma, be like Janaka, and realise the self in the inner light. Be an excellent person.

If one engages oneself in constant self-enquiry and sees the ever-changing nature of the world, in due time, one will attain self-knowledge like Janaka. Neither god, nor rites and rituals (or any action) nor wealth nor relatives are of any use in this; to those who are afraid of the world-illusion, self-effort as self-enquiry alone is capable of bringing about self-knowledge. Pray, do not follow the teachings of those deluded ones who depend upon gods, various rites and routine actions, and such other perverse practices. This ocean of world-appearance can be crossed only when you are firmly established in supreme wisdom, when you see the self with the self alone and when your intelligence is not diverted or coloured by sense-perceptions.

Thus have I narrated to you how king Janaka attained self-knowledge as if by an act of grace which caused the knowledge to drop from heaven, as it were. One who cultivates the wisdom that Janaka had will experience the inner light in his own heart, and the ignorant fancy of world-illusion will be instantly dispelled. When the limited and conditioned feeling "I am so-and-so" ceases, there arises consciousness of the all-pervading infinite. Hence, O Rāma, like Janaka, you too abandon the false and fanciful notion of the ego-sense within your own heart. When this ego-sense is dispelled the supreme light of self-knowledge will surely shine in your heart. This ego-sense alone is the densest form of darkness: when it is dispelled, the inner light shines by itself. He who knows 'I am not', 'Nor does the other exist', 'Nor is there non-existence', and whose mental activity has thus come to a standstill, is not engrossed in acquisitiveness. O Rāma, there is no bondage here other than craving for acquisition and the anxiety to avoid what one considers undesirable. Do not succumb to such anxiety and do not let acquisition of what is considered desirable be your goal: giving up both these attitudes, rest in what remains.

VASIṢṬHA continued:

They in whom the twin-urges of acquisition and rejection have come to an end do not desire anything nor do they renounce anything. The mind does not reach the state of utter tranquility till these two impulses (of acquisition and of rejection) have been eliminated. Even so, as long as one feels 'this is real' and 'this is unreal' the mind does not experience peace and equilibrium. How can equanimity, purity or dispassion arise in the mind of one who is swayed by thoughts of 'this is right', 'this is wrong' 'this is gain', 'this is loss'? When there is only one Brahman (which is forever one and the many) what can be said to be right and what wrong? As long as the mind is swayed by thoughts of the desirable and the undesirable there cannot be equanimity.

Desirelessness (absence of all expectations), fearlessness, unchanging steadiness, equanimity, wisdom, non-attachment, non-action, goodness, total absence of perversion, courage, endurance, friendliness, intelligence, contentment, gentleness, pleasant speech —all these qualities are natural to one who is free from the instincts of acquisition and rejection: and even those qualities are non-intentional and spontaneous.

One should restrain the mind from flowing downward, even as the flow of a river is blocked by the construction of a dam. After having firmly abandoned all contact with external objects turn the mind within and reflect over everything within yourself, even while engaged in various activities. With the help of this sharp sword of wisdom, cut through this net-work of conditioning (which throws up cravings, intentions, motivations, acceptance and rejection) which alone is the cause of this stream of world-appearance.

Cut down the mind with the mind itself. Having reached the state of purity, remain established in it right now. Cut the mind down with the mind and dismiss the thought of the mind which thus negates the mind: thus will you have finally destroyed the world-appearance. When thus the world-appearance has been eliminated, delusion will not arise again and the mind will not create the world-appearance again either. Though appearing to function in this world, be firmly rooted in the awareness of the unreality of all this and thus give up all hopes and expectations. Rooted in equanimity, doing whatever happens to be the appropriate action in each given situation and not even thinking about what has thus befallen you unsought, live a non-volitional life here. Even as the Lord may be said to be both the doer and the non-doer of all actions here, you, too, live non-volitionally—doing yet not doing what has to be done.

VASIṢṬHA continued:

You are the knower of all, the self. You are the unborn being, you are the supreme Lord; you are non-different from the self which pervades everything. He who has abandoned the idea that there is an object of perception which is other than the self, is not subjected to the defects born of joy and grief. He is known as a yogi who is freed from attraction and aversion, to whom a clod of earth and a nugget of gold are of equal value and importance, and who has given up all the tendencies which confirm the world-appearance. Whatever he does, whatever he enjoys, whatever he gives and whatever he destroys, his consciousness is free and therefore equanimous in pain and pleasure. Doing whatever has to be done without the division into the desirable and the undesirable, he who engages himself in action does not drown in it.

He who is confirmed in his conviction that the infinite consciousness alone exists, is instantly freed from thoughts of pleasure and is therefore tranquil and self-controlled. The mind is by nature inert: it borrows intelligence from the consciousness which it pursues in order to gain the ability to experience. The mind thus comes into contact with whatever has been brought into being by the power or energy of consciousness (cit-śakti). Thus, the mind exists by the grace of consciousness, as it were; and it entertains various thoughts on account of its perception of this universe. The consciousness alone is its light: otherwise, how does the inert mind function intelligently?

They who are well versed in the scriptures declare that the fictitious movement of energy in consciousness is known as the mind. And, the expressions of the mind (like the hissing of the snake) are known as thoughts or ideas. Consciousness minus conceptualisation is the eternal Brahman the absolute; consciousness plus conceptualisation is thought. A small part of it, as it were, is seated in the heart as the reality. This is known as the finite intelligence or individualised consciousness. However, this limited consciousness soon 'forgot' its own essential conscious nature and continued to be, but inert. It then became the thinking faculty with reception and rejection as its inherent tendencies. In fact, it is the infinite consciousness alone that has become all this: but until it awakes to its infinite nature, it does not know itself in self-knowledge. Hence, the mind should be awakened by means of enquiry based on scriptures, dispassion and control of the senses. This intelligence when it is thus awakened shines as Brahman the absolute; or else it continues to experience this finite world.

VASIṢṬHA continued:

When this inner intelligence is not awakened, it does not really know or understand anything: and what appears to be known through the thoughts is of course not the reality. These thoughts themselves derive their value from consciousness, even as a receptacle derives its scent from the incense kept in it. On account of this borrowed intelligence thought is able to know a minute fragmented fraction of this cosmic consciousness. The mind blossoms fully only when the light of the infinite shines upon it.

Otherwise, though appearing to be intelligent, thought is unable to comprehend anything really, even as the granite figure of a dancer does not dance even when requested to do so. Can a battle-scene painted on a canvas generate the roar of the fighting armies? Can a corpse get up and run? Does the figure of the sun carved on a rock dispel darkness? Similarly, what can the inert mind do? Even as the mirage appears to be flowing water only when the sun shines, the mind appears to be intelligent and active only because of the inner light of consciousness.

Ignorant people misconstrue the movement of life-force to be the mind: but in fact it is nothing more than the prāṇa or life-force. But, in the case of those whose intelligence is not fragmented or conditioned by thoughts, it is surely the radiance of the supreme being or self. The intelligence that identifies itself with certain movements of life-force in the self (by entertaining notions of 'this am I', 'this is mine') is known as the jīva or the living soul. Intelligence, mind, jīva, etc., are names which are used even by wise men: such entities are not real, however, from the absolute point of view. In truth, there is no mind, no intelligence, no embodied being: the self alone exists at all times. The self alone is the world; the self alone is time and also the evolutionary process. Because it is extremely subtle it seems not to exist, though it exists. While appearing to be a reflection or appearance, it is also realised to be the truth: but the self is beyond all these descriptions and its truth can only be experienced directly in self-knowledge.

When the inner light begins to shine, the mind ceases to be—even as when there is light, darkness vanishes. On the other hand, when consciousness is objectified in an effort to experience the objects of the senses, the self is forgotten, as it were, and there arise thoughts concerning the creatures of the mind.

VASIṢṬHA continued:

A thought arising in the supreme being is known as individual consciousness; when this consciousness is freed from thought and individuation, there is liberation. The seed or the sole cause for this world-appearance is but the arising of a thought in the infinite consciousness, which gave rise to the limited finite individual consciousness. When consciousness thus moved away from its utterly quiescent state and became tainted, as it were, from thought, the thinking faculty arose and, with it, the mind thought of the universe.

O Rāma, by the control of the life-force the mind is also restrained: even as the shadow ceases when the substance is removed, the mind ceases when the life-force is restrained. It is because of the movement of the life-force that one remembers the experiences one had elsewhere; it is known as mind because it thus experiences movements of life-force. The life-force is restrained by the following means: by dispassion, by the practice of prāṇāyāma (breath-control) or by the practice of enquiry into the cause of the movement of the life-force, by the ending of sorrow through intelligent means and by the direct knowledge or experience of the supreme truth.

It is possible for the mind to assume the existence of intelligence in a stone. But the mind does not possess the least intelligence. Movement belongs to the life-force which is inert: intelligence or the power of consciousness belongs to the self which is pure and eternally omnipresent. It is the mind that fancies a relationship between these two factors: but such fancy is false and hence all knowledge that arises from this false relationship is also false. This is known as ignorance, as Māyā or cosmic illusion, which gives rise to the dreadful poison known as world-appearance.

This relationship between the life-force and consciousness is imaginary; if it is not so imagined, there can be no world-appearance! The life-force, by its association with consciousness becomes conscious and experiences the world as its object. But all this is as unreal as the experience of a ghost by a child: the movement within the infinite consciousness alone is the truth. Can this infinite consciousness be affected by any finite factor? In other words, can an inferior entity overwhelm a superior one? Hence, O Rāma, in truth there is no mind or finite consciousness: when this truth is clearly understood, that which was falsely imagined as the mind comes to an end. It appeared to be because of imperfect understanding; when this misunderstanding ceases, the mind also ceases to be.

VASIṢṬHA continued:

This mind is inert and is not a real entity: hence it is for ever dead! Yet, beings in this world are killed by this dead thing: how mysterious is this stupidity!! The mind has no self, no body, no support and no form; yet, by this mind is everything consumed in this world. This indeed is a great mystery. He who says that he is destroyed by the mind which has no substantiality at all, says in effect that his head was smashed by the lotus-petal. To say that one can be hurt by the mind which is inert, dumb and blind is like saying that one is roasted by the heat of the full moon. The hero who is able to destroy a real enemy standing in front of him is himself destroyed by this mind which does not even exist.

What is the power of that which has been put together by thought, whose very existence is false and which is found to be non-existent when its existence is enquired into?

Stupidity and ignorance alone are the sources of all sorrow in this world; this creation has been brought about only by ignorance and stupidity. In spite of knowing this, it is indeed strange that this unreal and false non-entity is sought to be strengthened by living beings.

This world-illusion can be compared to the imagination of the hero who thinks that he is bound by the invisible chains that issue from the eyes of his enemy and that he is harassed by the invisible army created by the mere thought of the enemy. This world thus conjured up by the non-existent mind is also destroyed by another equally non-existent mind. This illusory world-appearance is none other than the mind. He who is unable to understand the true nature of the mind is also unfit for being instructed in the truth expounded in the scripture. The mind of such a person is unable to grasp the subtle truth of the teaching expounded in this scripture: it seems to be satisfied with the illusory world-appearance. Such a mind is full of fear: it is afraid of the melodious sound of the veena and it is even afraid of a sleeping relative. It is frightened by hearing someone shout aloud and flees that spot. The ignorant man is completely overcome by his own deluded mind.

A man is burnt by his own mind which is in his heart, which is as virulent as poison though it is mixed with just a little happiness. He does not know the truth, for, he is foolishly deluded by the mind! This indeed is a great mystery.

V:14 VASIṢṬHA continued:

My teachings are not meant for those, O Rāma, whose intelligence has been silenced by a firm faith in the reality of this illusory world and the consequent striving for the pleasures of this world. What foolish man will endeavour to show a colourful forest to one who refuses to see? Who will strive to educate that man, whose nose has been eaten away by leprosy, in the delicate art of distinguishing different perfumes? Who will instruct the drunkard in the subtleties of metaphysics? Who will make enquiries concerning village affairs from a corpse lying in the crematorium: and if a fool does just this, who can dissuade him from such foolish attempt? Even so, who can instruct that ignorant person who finds it difficult to govern the mind which is dumb and blind?

In fact the mind does not exist: and hence, rest assured that it has all the time been conquered. He who finds it difficult to overcome the non-existent mind suffers from the effects of poison he has not taken. The wise man sees the self all the time; and he knows that all movement arises from the movement of the life-force; he knows, too, that the senses perform their respective functions. What then is known as the mind? All motion belongs to life-force and all consciousness belongs to the self, and the senses have each their own power: which is the one that binds them all together? All these are indeed aspects of the one infinite omnipotent consciousness: diversity is a word without substance. How does even the idea of diversity arise in you?

What indeed is the jīva (individual soul) but a word which has befuddled the intelligence of people? Even the finite or individualised consciousness is an unreal fancy: what can it do! Seeing the fate of the ignorant people who are suffering because the mind that they have fancied into existence veils the truth which alone exists, I am filled with pity.

In this world fools are born only to suffer and perish. Every day millions of animals are killed throughout the world; every day millions upon millions of mosquitoes are killed by the wind; every day in the oceans the big fish eat the small ones—what is there to grieve? The stronger animal kills and eats the weaker animal in this world; from the smallest ant to the greatest of divinities, all are subject to birth and death. Every moment countless beings die and countless others are born, totally regardless of whether people like it or not, whether they rejoice or grieve. Hence, it were wiser neither to grieve nor to rejoice over the inevitable!

VASIṢṬHA continued:

O Rāma, he who comes forward to remove the sorrow of people of perverted intelligence is endeavouring to cover the sky with a small umbrella. They who behave like beasts cannot be instructed, for they are being led like animals by the rope of their own mind. Indeed, even stones shed tears, looking at those ignorant people who sink in the mire of their own mind, whose actions spell their own doom. Hence, the wise man does not attempt to teach those who have not overcome their own mind and are therefore miserable in every way. On the other hand, the wise do endeavour to remove the sorrow of those who have conquered their mind and who are therefore ripe to undertake self-enquiry.

The mind is not, O Rāma: do not unnecessarily imagine its existence. If you imagine its existence then it destroys you, like a ghost. As long as you have forgotten your self, so long does this imaginary mind exist. Now that you have realised that the mind waxes large by the continued affirmation of its existence, abandon such thinking.

When objectivity arises in your consciousness, the latter becomes conditioned and limited: that is bondage. When objectivity is abandoned, you become mind-less: that is liberation. Coming into contact with the qualities of nature is conducive to bondage; abandoning them is the road to liberation. Knowing this do whatever you please. Realising 'I am not' and 'this is not' remain firm and unmoved, like the infinite space. Abandon the impure thought which creates a duality of self–world. In the middle between the self as the seer and the world as the seen, you are the seeing (sight): always remain in this realisation. Between the experiencer and the experience you are the experiencing: knowing this remain in self-knowledge.

When, abandoning this self you think of an object, then you become the mind (subject) and thus become the subject of unhappiness. That intelligence which is other than self-knowledge is what constitutes the mind: that is the root of sorrow. When it is realised that 'All this is but the self' there is no mind, no subject, no object and no thinking. When you think 'I am the jīva' etc., the mind arises and with it sorrow. When you know 'I am the self, the jīva and such other things do not exist', the mind ceases to be and there is supreme bliss. In the light of the truth that 'All this universe is the self alone', the mind does not exist. Only so long as this serpent of mind is in the body is there fear; when it is removed by the practice of yoga, where is the cause for fear?

V:15 VASIṢṬHA continued:

When the self, self-forgetfully, identifies itself with the objects seen and experienced and is thus impurified, there arises the poison of craving. This craving intensifies delusion. Gods like Śiva, etc., may be able to cope with the fires of cosmic dissolution; but it is impossible for anyone to deal with the consuming fire of craving. Whatever terrible sufferings and calamities there are in the world are all the fruits of craving, O Rāma. Remaining unseen and subtle, this craving is yet able to consume the very flesh, bone and blood of the body. In a moment it seems to subside, the next moment it is in an expanded state. Afflicted by it, man becomes pitiable, weak, lustreless, mean, deluded, miserable and fallen.

When this craving has ceased, one's life-force is pure and all divine qualities and virtues enter one's heart. The river of craving flows only in the heart of the unwise person. Even as an animal falls into a trap (a blind well) on account of its craving for food (the bait), a man following the trail of his craving falls into hell. Even the worst blindness of senility is mild in comparison to the blinding delusion which craving brings about in one's heart in the twinkling of an eye.

Craving makes one cringe and become 'small': even lord Viṣṇu became a dwarf when he decided to beg. Hence, this craving which is the source of all sorrows and which destroys the lives of all beings should be renounced from a great distance.

Yet, it is on account of craving that the sun shines on earth, the wind blows, the mountains stand and the earth upholds living beings; all the three worlds exist only on account of craving. All the beings in the three worlds are bound by the rope of craving. It is possible to break even the strongest rope in this world, but the rope of craving is hard to break.

Therefore, O Rāma, give up craving by giving up thinking or conceptualisation. The mind cannot exist without thinking or conceptualisation. First, let the images of 'I', 'you' and 'this' not arise in the mind, for it is because of these images that hopes and expectations come into being. If you can thus refrain from building these images, you will also be counted as a man of wisdom. Craving is non-different from the ego-sense. Ego-sense is the source of all sins. Cut at the very root of this ego-sense with the sword of wisdom of the non-ego. Be free from fear.

RĀMA said: V:16

Lord, you instruct me to abandon the ego-sense and the craving that it gives rise to. If I abandon the ego-sense, then surely I should also give up this body and all that is based on the ego-sense. For, the body and the life-force rest on the support of the ego-sense. When the root (the ego-sense) is cut, then the tree (the body, etc.) will fall. How is it possible for me to abandon the ego-sense and yet live?

VASIṢṬHA replied:

Rāma! The abandonment of all notions, conditioning and conceptualisation is said to be of two kinds: one is based on knowledge or direct realisation and the other is based on contemplation. I shall describe them to you in detail.

One should become aware of one's deluded notion in which one thinks that 'I belong to these objects of the world and my life depends upon them. I cannot live without them and they cannot exist without me, either.' Then by profound enquiry, one contemplates 'I do not belong to these objects, nor do these objects belong to me'. Thus abandoning the ego-sense through intense contemplation, one should playfully engage oneself in the actions that happen naturally, but with the heart and mind ever cool and tranquil. Such an abandonment of the ego-sense and the conditioning is known as the contemplative egolessness.

When there is knowledge or direct experience of the non-dual truth, one abandons the ego-sense and conditioning, and entertains no feeling of 'This is mine' even with regard to the body—this is known as direct realisation of egolessness.

He is liberated even while living who playfully abandons the ego-sense through the contemplative method. He who uproots this ego-sense completely by the direct experience is established in equanimity: he is liberated. Janaka and others like him follow the contemplative method. Others who have the direct experience of egolessness are one with Brahman and have risen beyond body-consciousness. However, both of them are liberated and both have become one with Brahman.

He is considered a liberated sage who is not swayed by the desirable and the undesirable, who lives in this world and functions though inwardly totally untouched by the world, as if he is in deep sleep.

(As the sage Vasiṣṭha said this, another day came to an end. The assembly dispersed.)

VASIṢṬHA continued: V:17

O Rāma, they who have gone above body-consciousness are

beyond description, too: I shall therefore describe to you the nature of those who are liberated while living.

The desire that arises in the course of one's natural functions devoid of craving is that of a liberated sage. But that desire which is bound up with craving for external objects is conducive to bondage. However, when all ego-based notions have ceased in one's heart, the attention that is directed naturally is also the nature of the liberated sage. That which is afflicted by contact with external objects is the craving conducive to bondage; the non-volitional desire which is unaffected by any object is liberation. That desire which existed even before contact with the objects, exists even now and for ever: it is natural, therefore sorrowless and free from impurity. Such a desire is regarded by the wise as free from bondage.

'I want this to be mine'. When such a craving arises in one's heart, it gives rise to impurity. Such a craving should be abandoned by a wise person by all means at all times. Give up the desire that tends to bondage and the desire for liberation too. Remain still like the ocean. Knowing that the self is free from old age and death, let not these disturb your mind. When the whole universe is realised as illusory, craving loses its meaning.

The following four types of feelings arise in the heart of man: (1) I am the body born of my parents, (2) I am the subtle atomic principle, different from the body, (3) I am the eternal principle in all the diverse perishable objects in the world, and (4) the 'I' as also the 'world' are pure void like space. Of these the first is conducive to bondage and the others to freedom. The desires that are related to the first cause bondage; desires that are concomitant to the other three do not cause bondage.

Once the realisation that 'I am the self of all' has arisen, one does not again fall into error or sorrow. It is this self alone which is variously described as the void, nature, Māyā, Brahman, consciousness, Śiva, Puruṣa, etc. That alone is ever real; there is naught else. Resort to the understanding of non-duality, for the truth is non-dual; however, action involves duality and hence functions in apparent duality—thus, let your nature partake of both duality and non-duality. The reality is neither duality (for it is the mind that creates division) nor unity (for the concept of unity arises from its antithesis of duality). When these concepts cease, the infinite consciousness alone is realised to be the sole reality.

V:18 VASIṢṬHA continued:

The liberated sage who is disinterested in the events of the past, present and future looks at the state of the world with amusement. Constantly engaged in appropriate action, established in the happy medium between two extreme and opposite points of view, he dwells unremittingly, rejecting every form of conditioning or intention. He rests in the supreme state of plenitude; hence he is not agitated or excited by the events of this world. In all hostilities he is in the neutral position; yet endowed with compassion and consideration for all, he remains unaffected by the world-appearance. If he is spoken to, he answers simply and suitably; if not spoken to, he is silent; he seeks nothing and he hates nothing. Thus he is not afflicted by the world. He says what is good for all, and when questioned he explains his views convincingly. He knows what is appropriate and what is inappropriate. He is aware of the point of view of other people. He is firmly established in the supreme state; remaining calm and cool in his own heart, he looks at the state of the world amusedly. Such is the state of the sages who have reached liberation while yet living in this world.

We are unable to expound the philosophy of the fools who have not controlled their own mind and who are immersed in the mire of sense-pleasure. They are only interested in sexual pleasures and in the acquisition of material wealth. We are also unable to expound the path of rituals and routines which bestow all kinds of rewards in the shape of pain and pleasure.

O Rāma, live in this world with unlimited vision, having firmly rejected all limitation. Inwardly be free from all desires and hopes; but outwardly do what has to be done. Examine everything and seek only that which is not limited or finite: and, live in this world constantly contemplating the infinite. Without entertaining any hope in your heart, yet living as if you are full of hopes, live in this world with your heart calm and cool, behaving outwardly like everyone else. Inwardly give up all notions of 'I am the doer', yet engage yourself in all activities outwardly. Thus live in this world, O Rāma, completely free from the least trace of the ego-sense.

There is no bondage and therefore there is no liberation, in truth. This world-appearance is essentially unreal and is of the nature of a juggler's trick. The omnipresent, infinite self can never be bound; so how is it to be liberated? All this confusion arises on account of the ignorance of the truth: when the truth is known this confusion vanishes, like the imaginary snake in the rope.

VASIṢṬHA continued:

You are a wise man, O Rāma: be firmly established in egolessness and remain unpolluted like space. When the ego is non-existent, how can notions like 'These are my relatives' arise? The self is not involved in such notions, nor in notions of pleasure and pain, good and evil. Be free from fear and delusion caused by world-appearance.

To one who is unborn there are no relatives, or sorrow caused by such relatives!

If you realise that you have been someone before, you are someone now and you will be someone later on, and if you realise that this is true even of all these relatives, you will be free from delusion. If you feel that you were before, you are now, but that you will not be hereafter—even then you need not grieve, for that is the end of this world-appearance. Hence, it is foolish to grieve here in this world; it is better to be happy at all times and to be ever engaged in appropriate actions. However, O Rāma, yield neither to exultation nor to sorrow, but remain in a balanced state of mind. You are the eternal infinite light, pure and extremely subtle.

This world-appearance exists; later it will vanish and reappear: but this is only for the ignorant, not for the enlightened. This world-appearance has sorrow for its nature: ignorance expands and aggravates it. But you are wise, O Rāma, therefore be happy. Illusory appearance is none other than illusion; dream is none other than a dream! All this is the power of the omnipotent and the appearance is just the appearance.

Who is a relative here and to whom, and who is an enemy to whom: by the wish of the Lord of all beings, all are all to all at all times! This river of relationship is flowing on constantly. What is on top proceeds towards the bottom, and what is below rises up, like the cartwheel. They who are in heaven later go to hell; and they who are in hell go to heaven. They go from one species to another, from one part of the universe to another. The brave become cowards and cowards become brave. There is nothing in this universe which is unchanging, O Rāma. They who were relatives go away after a while. Friend, foe, relative, stranger, I, you—are words without corresponding substance. 'He is friend' and 'He is not a relative'—such thoughts arise in a mean person: in the magnanimous person such distinction does not arise. O Rāma, all beings are your relatives, for in this universe there does not exist absolute unrelatedness. The wise know that 'There is nowhere where I am not' and 'That is not which is not mine': thus they overcome limitation or conditioning.

The Story of Puṇya and Pāvana

V:19 VASIṢṬHA continued:

O Rāma, in this connection there is an ancient legend which I shall narrate to you.

In the continent known as Jambūdvīpa there is a great mountain known as Mahendra. In the forests on the slopes of that mountain many holy men and sages lived. They had in fact brought down onto that mountain the river Vyoma Gaṅgā (or Ākāśa Gaṅgā) for their bath, drinking, etc. On the bank of this river there lived a holy man named Dīrghatapā who was, as his name implies, the very embodiment of ceaseless austerity.

This ascetic had two sons named Puṇya and Pāvana. Of these Puṇya had reached full enlightenment, but Pāvana, though he had overcome ignorance, had not yet reached full enlightenment and hence he had semi-wisdom.

With the inexorable passage of invisible and intangible time, the sage Dīrghatapā (who had freed himself from every form of attachment and craving) had grown in age and, even as a bird flies away from its cage, abandoned the body and reached the state of utter purity. Using the yogic method she had learnt from him, his wife, too, followed him.

At this sudden departure of the parents Pāvana was sunk in grief and he wailed aloud inconsolably. Puṇya, on the other hand, performed the funeral ceremonies but remained unmoved by the bereavement. He approached his grieving brother, Pāvana.

PUṆYA said: Brother, why do you bring this dreadful sorrow upon yourself? The blindness of ignorance alone is the cause of this torrential downpour of tears from your eyes. Our father has departed from here along with our mother to that state of liberation or the highest state, which is natural to all beings and is the very being of those who have overcome the self. Why do you grieve when they have returned to their own nature? You have ignorantly bound yourself to the notions of 'father' and 'mother'; and yet you grieve for those who are liberated from such ignorance! He was not your father, nor was she your mother, nor were you their son. You have had countless fathers and mothers. They have had countless children. Countless have been your incarnations! And, if you wish to grieve over the death of parents, why do you not grieve for all those countless beings unceasingly?

Noble one, what you see as the world is only an illusory appearance. In truth there are neither friends nor relatives. Hence, there is neither death nor separation. All these wonderful signs of prosperity that you see around you are tricks, some of which last for three days and others for five days! With your keen intelligence enquire into the truth: abandon notions of 'I', 'you' etc., and of 'He is dead', 'He is gone'. All these are your own notions, not truth.

PUṆYA continued: V:20

These false notions of father, mother, friend, relative, etc., are swept aside by wisdom as dust is swept away by wind. These relatives are not based on truth, they are but words! If one is thought of as a friend, he is a friend; if he is thought of as the other, he is the other! When all this is seen as the one omnipresent being, where is the distinction between the friend and the other?

Brother, enquire within yourself—this body is inert and it is composed of blood, flesh, bones, etc.; what is the 'I' in it? If you thus enquire into the truth, you will realise that there is nothing which is you nor anything which is 'I': what is called Puṇya or Pāvana is but a false notion.

However, if you still think 'I am', then in the incarnations past you have had very many relatives. Why do you not grieve for their death? You had many swan relatives when you were a swan, many tree relatives when you were a tree, many lion-relatives when you were a lion, many fish-relatives when you were a fish. Why do you not weep for them? You were a prince, you were a donkey, you were a peepul tree and then a banyan tree. You were a brāhmaṇa, you were a fly and also a mosquito, you were an ant. You were a scorpion for half a year, you were a bee, and now you are my brother. In these many other embodiments you have taken birth again and again countless times.

Even so, I have had very many embodiments. I see them all, and your embodiments too, through my subtle intelligence which is pure and clear-visioned. I was a bird, a crane, a frog, a tree, a camel, a king, a tiger—and now I am your elder brother. For ten years I was an eagle, for five months I was a crocodile and for a hundred years I was a lion: now I am your elder brother. I remember all these and many more embodiments I have passed through in a state of ignorance and delusion. In all these embodiments there were countless relatives. Whom shall I mourn? Considering this, I do not grieve.

All along this path of life relatives are strewn like dry leaves on a forest path. What can be the proper cause for grief or joy in this world, brother? Let us therefore abandon all these ignorant notions and remain at peace. Abandon the notion of the world which arises in your mind as the 'I'. And, be still, neither going up nor falling down! You have no unhappiness, no birth, no father, no mother: you are the self and naught else. The sages perceive the middle path, they see what is at the moment, they are at peace, they are established in witness consciousness: they shine like a lamp in darkness, in whose light events happen (without the lamp being involved).

V:21 VASIṢṬHA continued:

Thus instructed by his brother, Pāvana was awakened. Both of them remained as enlightened beings, endowed with wisdom and direct realisation. They roamed the forest doing what they pleased but without blemish. In course of time they abandoned their embodiment and attained final liberation, as a lamp without fuel.

Craving is the root of all sorrow, O Rāma: and the only intelligent way is to renounce all cravings completely and not to indulge them. Even as fire burns all the more fiercely when fed with fuel, thoughts multiply by thinking: thoughts cease only by the extinction of thinking. Hence, ascend the chariot of non-thinking and with a compassionate and limitless vision behold the worlds sunk in sorrow. Arise, O Rāma.

This indeed is the Brāhmic state—pure, free from craving and from illness. Attaining this even one who has been a fool is freed from delusion. He who roams the earth with wisdom as his friend and awareness as the female companion, does not become deluded.

There is nothing of value in the three worlds, nothing that one may wish to have which cannot be had by the mind free from craving. They who are cured of the fever of craving do not subject themselves to the successive rise and fall inherent in embodied existence. The mind attains fulfilment only by utter dispassion, not by filling it with desires and hopes. To those who are devoid of any attachment or craving, the three worlds are as wide as the footprint of a calf and a whole world-cycle is but a moment. The coolness of the ice-pack on top of the Himālayas is nothing compared to the coolness of the mind of the sage free from craving. The light of the full moon is not as bright nor is the ocean as full nor the face of the goddess of prosperity as radiant as the mind free from craving.

When all the desires and hopes which are like the branches of the tree of the mind are cut down, the mind resumes its own nature. If you resolutely deny refuge to these hopes and cravings in your mind, then there is no fear for you. When the mind is free from movements of thought (which are motivated by hopes or cravings) then it becomes no-mind: and that is liberation. The thinking that is brought about by hopes and cravings is known as 'vṛtti' (movement of thought); when hopes and cravings are given up, there is no vṛtti either. When the aggravating cause is removed, the effect ceases to be. Hence, for restoring peace to the mind, remove the disturbing cause, which is hope or craving.

The Story of Bali

VASIṢṬHA continued: V:22

Or, O Rāma, bring about a transmutation of the mind even as king Bali did. I shall narrate to you the story of Bali, listening to which you will gain knowledge of the eternal truth.

In another part of the world (jagat) there is what is known as Pātāla (the netherworld). In it are found extremely beautiful demonesses, strange reptiles with many heads, demons with enormous bodies, huge elephants, places which are heavily polluted and where a terrible 'kaṭa-kaṭa' noise constantly fills the air, caves or deep mines full of precious gems, places which have been hallowed or sanctified by the dust of the divine feet of the sage Kapila (California is regarded by some to be Kapila-araṇya, the forest inhabited by Kapila!) and places sanctified by lord Hāṭakeśvara who is adored by celestial damsels.

The demon-king Bali, son of Virocana, ruled over this region. The Lord of the universe, Śrī Hari, himself was the protector of this king; hence, even the king of heaven, Indra, adored him. By the heat of the very radiance of this king Bali, the oceans got dried up, as it were. His eyes were so powerful that by a mere look he could move mountains. Bali ruled for a very long time over the netherworld.

In course of time, intense dispassion overcame king Bali and he began to enquire thus:

How long should I rule over this netherworld, how long shall I wander in the three worlds? What shall I gain by ruling over this kingdom? When all that is in the three worlds is subject to destruction, how can one hope to enjoy happiness through all this?

Again and again, the same disgusting pleasures are experienced and the same acts are repeated day after day in this world: how is it that even a wise man is not ashamed of this? The same day and the same night, again and again, life in this world revolves like a whirlpool.

Doing all this every day, how can one reach that state in which there is cessation of this repetitive existence? How long should we continue to revolve in this whirlpool and of what use is it?

While he was thus reflecting, he remembered:

Ah, I remember what my father Virocana once told me. I had asked him: "Father, what is the destination of this world-appearance or repetitive existence? When will it come to an end? When will the delusion of the mind cease? Gaining what shall one attain total satisfaction, seeing what shall one seek naught else? I see that it is impossible to attain this by means of experience of the worldly pleasures or actions. For, they only aggravate the delusion! Pray, tell me the means by which I shall rest for ever in supreme peace."

V:23 VIROCANA said to Bali:

My son, there is a vast realm, wide enough to engulf the three worlds. In it there are no lakes, no oceans, no mountains, no forests, no rivers, no earth, no sky, no winds, no moon, no gods, no demons, no demi-gods, no vegetation, no heaven, no high and low, no words; not me, nor the gods like Viṣṇu. Only one is there and that is the supreme light. He is omnipotent, omnipresent, he is all—and he remains silent, as if inactive. Prompted by him, the king, his minister does everything—what has not been he brings about and what is, he alters. This minister is incapable of enjoying anything, nor does he know anything: though ignorant and insentient he does everything for the sake of his master, the king. The king remains alone, established in peace.

BALI asked:

Father, what is that realm which is free from psychosomatic illnesses? Who is that minister and who is that king? The story is wonderful and unheard-of. Kindly explain all this to me in detail.

VIROCANA replied:

All the gods and demons put together and even a force many times their strength can not even challenge the minister. He is not Indra the king of the gods, nor the god of death, nor the god of wealth, nor a god nor a demon whom you can easily conquer. Though it is believed that the god Viṣṇu killed the demons, it was indeed this minister who destroyed them. In fact, even the gods like Viṣṇu were overpowered by him and made to take birth here. Cupid derives his power from this minister. Anger derives its power from him, too. It is because of his wish that there is unceasing conflict between good and evil here.

This minister can only be defeated by his own master, the king; by no one else. When in due course of time there arises such a wish in the heart of the king, this minister can be easily defeated. He is the most powerful in all the three worlds; and the three worlds are but his exhalation! If you have the ability to conquer him, then, indeed, you are a hero.

When the minister arises, the three worlds are manifested, even as the lotus blossoms when the sun rises. When he retires, the three worlds become dormant. If you can conquer him, with your mind utterly one-pointed and completely free of delusion and ignorance, then you are a hero. If he is conquered, then all the worlds and everything in them are conquered. If he is not conquered, then nothing is conquered, even if you think you have conquered this or that in this world.

Hence, my son, in order to attain absolute perfection and eternal bliss, strive with all your might and in every possible manner, whatever be the difficulties and obstacles, to conquer that minister.

V:24 BALI asked: Father, by what effective means can that powerful minister be conquered?

VIROCANA replied:

Though this minister is almost invincible, my son, I shall tell you how to conquer him. He is overcome in a moment if one grasps him by means of intelligent action; in the absence of such intelligent action, he burns everything like a venomous snake. One who approaches him intelligently, plays with him as one plays with a child and playfully subdues him; such a one beholds the king and is established in the supreme state. For, once the king is seen, the minister comes completely under one's control; and when the minister is under one's control, the king is seen clearly. Until the king is seen, the minister is not really conquered; and until the minister is conquered, the king is not seen! When the king is not seen, the minister plays havoc and spreads sorrow; then the minister is not conquered, the king remains unseen. Therefore, one's intelligent practice has to be simultaneously twofold: to behold the king and to subdue the minister. By intense self-effort and by steady practice, you can gain both these and then you will enter that region and never again experience sorrow. That is the region inhabited by holy men who are forever established in peace.

My son, I shall now make all this explicit to you! The region I have referred to is the state of liberation, which is the end of all sorrow. The king there is the self who transcends all other realms and states of consciousness. The minister is the mind. It is the mind that has made all this world, like a pot from clay. When the mind is conquered, everything is conquered. Remember that the mind is almost invincible, except through intelligent practice.

BALI asked: Father, kindly tell me what intelligent practice will enable me to conquer the mind.

VIROCANA replied:

The very best intelligent means by which the mind can be subdued is complete freedom from desire, hope or expectation in regard to all objects at all times. It is by this means that this powerful elephant (the mind) can be subdued. This means is both very easy and extremely difficult, my son: it is very difficult for one who does not engage himself in serious practice, but very easy for one who is earnest in his effort. There is no harvest without sowing: the mind is not subdued without persistent practice. Hence, take up this practice of renunciation. Until one turns away from sense-pleasure here, one will continue to roam in this world of sorrow. Even a strong man will not reach his destination if he does not move towards it. No one can reach the state of total dispassion without persistent practice.

VIROCANA continued:

Only by right exertion can dispassion be attained; there is no other means. People talk of divine grace or fate; but in this world we perceive the body, not a god. When people speak of god they imply what is inevitable, what is beyond their control and the events of natural order. Even so, whatever brings about total equanimity and the cessation of joy and sorrow is also referred to as divine grace. Divine grace, natural order and right self-exertion, all of them refer to the same truth; the distinction is due to wrong perception or illusion.

Whatever the mind conceives of through right self-exertion comes to be in its fruition, and when the mind apprehends such fruition there is experience of joy, etc. The mind is the doer, and whatever it conceives of the natural order (niyati) creates and manifests. The mind is also able to run counter to the natural order; hence it may even be said that mind is the prompter of the natural order.

Even as wind moves in space, the jīva (the individual) functions in this world, doing what has to be done within the natural order, though such action appears to be selfish or egotistic. Prompted by nature, he seems to move or stand still—both of which are mere expressions or false superimpositions, even as the movement of trees on a mountain-top makes it look as if the peak is swaying.

Hence, as long as there is mind there is neither god nor a natural order; when the mind has ceased to be, let there be whatever is!

BALI asked:

Lord, tell me, how can the cessation of craving for pleasure be firmly established in my heart?

VIROCANA said:

My son, self-knowledge is the creeper that yields the fruit of cessation of craving for pleasure. It is only when the self is seen that the highest form of dispassion becomes firmly rooted in the heart. Hence, one should simultaneously behold the self through intelligent enquiry, and thereby get rid of the craving for pleasure.

When the intelligence is still unawakened, one should fill two quarters of the mind with enjoyment of pleasure, one part with study of scriptures and the other with service of the guru. When it is partially awakened, two parts are given over to the service of the guru and the others get one part each. When it is fully awakened, two parts are devoted to service of the guru and the other two to the study of scriptures, with dispassion as the constant companion.

VIROCANA continued:

Only when one is filled with goodness is one qualified to listen to the exposition of the highest wisdom. Hence, one should constantly endeavour to educate the mind with purifying knowledge, and nourish the mind with the inner transformation brought about by the study of scriptures. When the mind has thus been transformed, it is able to reflect the truth without distortion. Then without delay one should endeavour to see the self. These two—self-realisation and cessation of craving—should proceed hand in hand, simultaneously.

True dispassion does not arise in one by austerity, charity, pilgrimage, etc., but only by directly perceiving one's own nature. And, there is no means for direct self-realisation except right self-exertion. Hence, one should give up dependence upon a god or fate and by right self-exertion firmly reject the seeking of pleasure. When dispassion matures, the spirit of enquiry arises in oneself. The spirit of enquiry strengthens dispassion. The two are interdependent, even as the ocean and the clouds are. These two and also self-realisation are all intimate friends and always exist together.

Hence, first of all, one should abandon all dependence on extraneous factors (like god) and, grinding one's teeth and with intense right self-exertion, cultivate dispassion. One may, however, earn wealth without violating local traditions and customs and without defying one's relatives, etc. One should utilise this wealth to acquire the company of good and holy men endowed with noble qualities. Such company of holy men generates dispassion. Then there arises the spirit of enquiry, knowledge and the study of scriptures. By stages, one reaches the supreme truth.

When you turn completely away from the pursuit of pleasure, then you attain to the supreme state through the means of enquiry. When the self is completely purified, then you will be firmly established in the supreme peace. You will never again fall into the mire of conceptualisation which is the cause of sorrow. Though you continue to live, you will remain freed from all hopes and expectations. You are pure! Salutations to you, O embodiment of auspiciousness!!

In accordance with the prevailing social tradition, acquire a little wealth; and with that acquire the company of saints, and adore them. By their company you will gain contempt for the objects of pleasure. And by the right enquiry you will gain self-knowledge.

V:25, 26 BALI said to himself:

Luckily, I remembered all that my father said to me. Now that craving for pleasure has ceased in me, I shall attain to the state of tranquility which is like nectar. I am really and truly tired of repeatedly earning wealth, fulfilling my desires and enjoying sexual pleasures. Delightful is the state of peace; in utter inner tranquility all pleasures and pains cease to be of value.

Life is one continuous round of repetitive experiences; nothing new is ever experienced. I shall give up everything and with my mind completely withdrawn from the pursuit of pleasure, I shall remain happily established in the self. This universe is but the creation of the mind: what is lost by abandoning it?

Enough of even this repentance! For, the important thing in a cure is the immediate treatment of the illness. 'Who am I?' 'What is all this?' I shall submit these questions to my guru Śukra.

VASIṢṬHA continued:

Having thus resolved, Bali contemplated the guru of the demons, Śukra. On account of the infinite consciousness he was established in, Śukra was omnipresent and knew that his disciple needed his presence. Instantly, he materialised his body in front of the king Bali.

In the immediate presence of the guru, Bali shone with a special radiance. He received the guru with due honours and worshipped the guru's feet with great devotion. Then,

BALI asked Śukra: Lord, it is the reflection of your own divine radiance that prompts me to place this problem before you. I have no desire for pleasure; and I wish to learn the truth. Who am I? Who are you? What is this world? Please tell me all this!

ŚUKRA replied: I am on my way to another realm, O Bali: but I shall give you in a few words the very quintessence of wisdom. Consciousness alone exists, consciousness alone is all this, all this is filled with consciousness. I, you, and all this world, are but consciousness. If you are humble and sincere, you will gain everything from what I have said; if not, an attempt at further explanation will be like pouring oblations into a heap of ashes (i.e., useless; the oblations are meaningful only when poured into the sacred fire). The objectivity (conceptualisation) of consciousness is known as bondage and the abandonment of such objectivity is liberation. Consciousness minus such objectivity is the reality of everything: this is the conviction of all philosophies. When you are established in this vision, you will also attain the infinite consciousness. I shall now depart to do the work of the gods; for as long as this body lasts, one shall not abandon appropriate action.

After Śukra left, BALI reflected thus: V:27

What my preceptor said to me was indeed correct and appropriate. Surely, all that is is consciousness and there is naught else. It is when that infinite consciousness entertains the concept 'This is sun' that the sun is distinguished from darkness: it is consciousness that distinguishes light from darkness. It is consciousness that cognises earth as earth, the directions in space as such directions and the whole world as the world. If consciousness did not recognise a mountain, would it exist as a mountain?

Consciousness itself is all this: including the senses, the body, the desires that arise in the mind, whatever is within and whatever is outside, space and even changing phenomena. It is indeed on account of that consciousness that I am able to come into contact with the objects and experience them, not because of the body itself. Regardless of the body, I am consciousness, which is the self of the entire universe.

Since consciousness exists one without a second, who is my friend and who is my enemy? Even if the head of the body known as Bali is cut off, does the infinite consciousness lose its head? Even hate and other such qualities are but modifications of consciousness. Hence, again, there is neither hate nor attachment, neither mind nor its modifications—since the consciousness is infinite and absolutely pure, how can perversions arise in it? Consciousness is not its name, it is but a word! It has no name.

I am the eternal subject free from all object and predicate. I salute that omnipresent consciousness which is free from the tempting concept of objects, and hence eternally free. I salute myself which is the consciousness free of the subject-object division, which acts appropriately without division and which is the light which is reflected in all appearances. I am that consciousness in which the craving for experience has ceased. I am limitless like space; I am untouched by happiness, unhappiness and the like. Let them therefore do what they like to me, for I am non-different from them. Movement of energy in one substance is neither loss nor gain. When consciousness alone is everything, thoughts or its expansions do not make that consciousness expand or contract. Hence, I shall continue to be active till I reach absolute quiescence in the self.

VASIṢṬHA continued:

Having thus reflected, Bali, uttering the sacred word OM and contemplating its subtle significance, remained quiet. Freed from all doubts, from perception of objects and without the division between thinker, thought and thinking (meditation, meditator and the object of meditation), with all intentions and concepts quietened, Bali remained firmly established in the supreme state with a mind in which all movement of thought had ceased, like a lamp in a windless place. Thus he lived for a considerable time.

V:28, 29 VASIṢṬHA continued:

All the demons (followers or subjects of the king Bali) rushed to the palace and surrounded the king who was seated in deep contemplation. Unable to understand the mystery, they thought of their preceptor, Śukra. They beheld Śukra in front of them. Śukra saw that Bali was in a super-conscious state. He said to the demons, with a smile radiating joy:

"It is indeed wonderful, O demons, that this king Bali has attained such perfection by dint of his own resolute enquiry. Let him remain established in his own self. The mental activity that gives rise to the perception of the world has ceased in him: hence do not try to talk to him. When the dark night of ignorance comes to an end, the sun of self-knowledge arises: such is his state now. In course of time he himself will come out of that state, when the seed of world-perception begins to sprout in his consciousness. Hence, go about doing your work as before: he will return to world-consciousness in a thousand years from now."

Hearing this, the demons returned to their posts of duty and carried on the work of the realm. After a thousand celestial years of such contemplation, the king Bali was awakened by the music of the celestials and divinities. A supernatural light that radiated from him illumined the entire city.

Even before the demons could reach him again, BALI reflected thus:

It was indeed a wondrous state in which I remained for a brief moment. I shall continue to remain in that state: what have I to do with the affairs of the external world? Supreme peace and bliss reign in my own heart now.

(In the meantime, the demons rushed to where he sat; after looking at them, Bali continued to reflect thus:)

I am consciousness and in me there does not exist any perversion. What is there for me to acquire or to abandon? What fun: I long for liberation, but who has bound me, when and how! Why do I long for liberation then? There is no bondage and no liberation: what shall I gain by meditation or by not meditating? Freed from delusion of meditation and non-meditation, let be what has to be: there is neither gain nor loss to me. I do not desire either meditation or non-meditation, neither joy nor non-joy, I do not desire the supreme being or the world. I am neither alive nor dead; I am neither real nor unreal. Salutations to myself, the infinite being! Let this world be my kingdom, I shall be what I am: let this world be not my kingdom, I shall be what I am. What have I to do with meditation and what have I to do with the kingdom? Let be what has to be. I belong to none and none belongs to me. There is absolutely nothing that has to be done by what is known as me; then why should I not do that action which is natural?

Thus having reflected, the king Bali turned his radiant gaze towards the assembled demons, even as the sun gazes upon a lotus.

VASIṢṬHA continued:

King Bali thereafter ruled the kingdom, doing everything spontaneously without premeditation. He worshipped the brāhmaṇas, gods and the holy ones. He treated his relatives with deference. He rewarded his servants amply and gave in charity more than what they who sought it had expected. He fondly sported with the womenfolk.

The wish to perform a sacred rite rose in his heart. Quickly he assembled the men and materials needed for it. He conducted the rite in the appropriate manner. It was during this rite that lord Viṣṇu, wishing to snatch the rulership of the three worlds from Bali and bestow it upon Indra, took the form of a dwarf and cheated Bali into giving away the rulership of the world to Viṣṇu in charity.

O Rāma, this Bali will be the next Indra; hence he dwells in the netherworld (to which he had been sent by lord Viṣṇu himself) as a liberated and enlightened sage, awaiting the time when he shall rule the heaven. He is totally unconcerned whether he is visited by prosperity or adversity. His consciousness does not experience elation or depression in happiness or unhappiness. He had ruled the three worlds for billions of years; but now his heart is at rest. Once again he will rule the three worlds as Indra for a very long time.

But, he is not excited at the prospect of becoming Indra; nor was he depressed when he lost his position and was hurled into the netherworld. He welcomes whatever comes to him unsought and is at peace within himself.

Thus have I told you the story of king Bali, O Rāma. Gain such a vision as he had and enjoy supreme felicity. Abandon the desire for the essenceless and useless sense-pleasure in this world. The attractive objects that tempt you here do not deserve your admiration any more than rock-figures seen at a distance. Establish your mind, which flits from one thing to another, firmly in your heart.

You are the light of consciousness, O Rāma; in you are the worlds rooted. Who is your friend and who is other? You are the infinite. In you are all the worlds strung like beads of a rosary. That being which thou art is neither born nor does he die. The self is real; birth and death are imaginary. Enquire into the nature of all the illnesses that beset life, and live without craving. You are the light and the Lord, Rāma: and this world appears to be in that light. It has no real and independent existence.

Formerly, you had repeatedly entertained the wrong notions of the desirable and the undesirable: give up these too. Then you will enjoy equanimity: and the wheel of birth will come to a halt. In whatever the mind tends to sink, retrieve it from it and direct it towards the truth. Thus will the wild elephant of the mind be tamed. Do not be led astray by the long-winded empty statements of the wicked self-appointed teachers who have no direct experience: you will surely attain enlightenment by listening to my discourse.

The Story of Prahlāda

VASIṢṬHA continued: V:30, 31

O Rāma, I shall narrate to you another story which illustrates the path to enlightenment which is free from obstacles.

In the netherworld there was a mighty demon-king known as Hiraṇyakaśipu. He had wrested the sovereignty of the three worlds from Indra (Hari?). He ruled the three worlds. He had many sons. Among them was the famous Prahlāda who shone like a brilliant diamond among jewels.

The demon-king who thus enjoyed the lordship of the three worlds, the blessing of a mighty army and good children, became proud and arrogant. His aggressive ways and his rule of terror greatly worried the gods who prayed to the creator Brahmā to find a way out of their predicament. In answer to their prayer, the lord Hari assumed the form of Narasimha and destroyed the demon-king. Narasimha's body was enormous and powerful. He had sharp and dreadful teeth and nails. His ear-rings were like fire-brands. His abdomen was mountainous. He had powerful arms which could shake the whole creation. His breath rocked mountains. The hairs on his body were like tongues of flames. His very limbs were terrible missiles. Unable to endure the fiery gaze of Narasimha, the demons fled in all directions. The inner apartments of the palace had been reduced to ashes.

Prahlāda whose life had been spared performed the funeral rite of his fallen relations. He consoled the wounded ones. Stunned by the magnitude of the destruction, he and the others who remained alive stood immobile for a while.

PRAHLĀDA mused: Who is there to help us now: the very seeds of the demon-families have been destroyed by Hari. Alas, our enemy has swiftly reached the peak of military victory. The gods who used to bow down humbly to the feet of my father have occupied our realm. My own relations have become lustreless, unemployed, without enthusiasm, destitute and miserable. The demons who were strong and powerful once, are weak and timid now like the gods: indeed, mysterious is the destiny. A timid deer when it is taken into a strange village, takes fright at the sound of a falling leaf: even so the demonesses, who have seen the valour of the enemy, panic at anything.

The gods have taken back the wish-fulfilling tree. Even as the demons delighted to look at the faces of the goddesses before, the gods delight to look at the demonesses now. The demi-goddesses and others who enjoyed life in the inner apartments of the demons have escaped and have gone away to the forests of the mount Meru and live like birds of the forest. My own mothers (the queens) are the very images of grief. Alas, my father's fan serves Indra now. By the grace of Hari, we have been subjected to incomparable and inexpressible adversity, the very thought of which makes us miserable and desperate.

PRAHLĀDA continued to muse:

Even as the snowclad peaks of the Himālayas are never subjected to the scorching heat of the sun, the gods who live in the shade of the protection of Viṣṇu are not subjected to oppression. Even as a little monkey seated on the branch of a tree annoys a powerful dog standing on the ground, these gods enjoying the security of the protection of Viṣṇu harass the demons.

It is Viṣṇu that protects the whole universe and upholds it. Even if Viṣṇu abandons the use of weapons, no one can face him (Narasimha did not use conventional weapons). He alone is the refuge of all beings in this world, therefore by all means one should take refuge in him—there is no other way. No one is superior to him and he alone is the cause of the creation, preservation and dissolution of the universe. From this very moment I shall also be devoted to Viṣṇu and live as if filled with his presence. The holy mantra 'Namo Nārāyaṇāya' dedicated to him is capable of bestowing every blessing on the devotee: may it never leave my heart.

However, one who is not Viṣṇu does not derive any benefit by worshipping Viṣṇu. One should worship Viṣṇu by being Viṣṇu. Hence I am Viṣṇu. He who is known as Prahlāda is none other than Viṣṇu: there is no duality. Viṣṇu's vehicle Garuḍa now bears me. His insignia adorn my limbs. Lakṣmi, his consort, is standing next to me. All the divine splendour of Viṣṇu has become mine.

The conch, the discus, the mace and sword which are the symbols that are invariably associated with Viṣṇu are with me now. The lotus that bears on it the creator Brahmā springs from my navel. The entire universe which repeatedly appears and disappears is in my abdomen.

My colour is now the colour of Viṣṇu, which is blue. I am dressed in the yellow garment of Viṣṇu. I am Viṣṇu. Who can be my enemy and who can challenge me now? Since I am Viṣṇu, he who is hostile to me has surely reached the end of his life-span. These demons who stand in front of me find it difficult or impossible to endure the dazzling brilliance that radiates from me. And those gods are really singing my own praise, as I am Viṣṇu.

I have transcended all sense of duality and therefore I have myself become Viṣṇu. He in whose abdomen ever abides the three worlds, he who subdues all evil forces in the universe and he who dispels the anxieties and fears of all—he am I and I salute him.

VASIṢṬHA continued: V:32, 33

Having thus transfigured himself into the very image of Viṣṇu, Prahlāda thought of worshipping Viṣṇu. He thought, "Here stands another Viṣṇu who is also seated on his vehicle Garuḍa, who is endowed with all the divine qualities and powers, who bears all the insignia relative to the status of Viṣṇu. I shall now worship him according to the tradition relating to such worship, but mentally."

Having thus resolved, Prahlāda mentally worshipped Viṣṇu, with all the materials ordained by tradition and scriptural injunctions. After this he also worshipped Viṣṇu with external rites and rituals. Upon completion of this worship, Prahlāda rejoiced.

From that time, Prahlāda worshipped Viṣṇu in that manner every day. Seeing him and following his example, all the demons in the kingdom also became staunch devotees of Viṣṇu. And, the rumour spread like wild fire in heaven that the demons who had till lately been enemies of Viṣṇu, had suddenly become his devotees! The gods in heaven were bewildered: how could demons become devotees! They quickly approached Viṣṇu and asked him.

THE GODS said:

Lord, what is this mystery? The demons are your traditional enemies. That they should turn into your devotees appears to be unreal and a trick. Where is the diabolical nature of the demons; and where is devotion to you which arises only during the last incarnation of a jīva? Good and divine qualities just do not go with these demons: it sounds so incongruous. Surely, the qualities of a being are always in accordance with the fundamental nature of that being. To hear that these demons have become your devotees overnight is almost painful. If it were said that they had gradually evolved into higher states of being, cultivated good qualities and then become your devotees, we could very well understand it. But that someone who has been of wicked disposition has all at once become your devotee, is incredible.

THE LORD replied:

O gods, do not suffer doubt and despair. Prahlāda has become my devotee. This is indeed his last birth and he deserves to be liberated now. The seeds of his ignorance have been burnt; he will not be born any more. It is meaningless and painful to hear that a good man has become evil-minded. It is appropriate and good to hear that one who has had no good qualities has become good. Prahlāda's change is for your good. (Alternative meaning: It is improper to say that one who is limited and conditioned became unconditioned: but it is true to say that the unconditioned being without qualities appears to be conditioned.)

VASIṢṬHA continued:

After thus reassuring the gods, Viṣṇu disappeared. And, the gods returned to their respective abodes. They became friendly towards Prahlāda.

Every day Prahlāda thus worshipped the lord Viṣṇu by thought, word and deed. As the immediate fruit of such worship, all the noble qualities like wisdom and dispassion grew in him. He did not seek pleasure; even his mind did not contemplate pleasure. Having abandoned craving for pleasure, his mind was dangling without support. Lord Viṣṇu came to know of the state of Prahlāda. He travelled along the netherworld to where Prahlāda was worshipping him. Seeing that lord Viṣṇu himself had come to the palace, Prahlāda rejoiced even more and worshipped Viṣṇu again.

PRAHLĀDA prayed:

I take refuge in the Lord in whom the three worlds rejoice, who is the supreme light which destroys the darkness of every kind of ignorance and impurity, who is the refuge of the helpless destitute, who alone is the Lord whose refuge is worth seeking, the unborn, the surest security. You are radiant like the blue lotus or the blue jewel; your body is blue like the zenith of the clear winter sky; and you hold your divine insignia in your hands—I take refuge in you. I take refuge in him whose voice is the truth (the holy scriptures), whose navel-lotus is the seat of Brahmā the creator and who dwells in the hearts of all beings. I take refuge in him the radiance of whose nails sparkles as the stars in the heaven, whose sweet smiling face is the moon, in whose heart there is a jewel from which rays emanate and flow as the holy river Gaṅgā and who is clad in the pure autumnal sky. I take refuge in him in whom this extensive universe rests without diminution, who is ever unborn and unchanging, whose body is composed of all the auspicious qualities and who rests on a banyan leaf. I take refuge in him who has goddess Lakṣmi at his own side, the beauty of whose body is like the beauty of the setting sun. I take refuge in the Lord who is like the sun unto the lotus of the three worlds, who is like a lamp unto the darkness of ignorance, who is of the nature of infinite consciousness, and who destroys the suffering and distress of all beings in the universe.

THE LORD said: V:34

O Prahlāda, you are an ocean of good qualities and you are indeed the jewel among the demons. Ask of me any boon of your choice which is conducive to the cessation of the sorrow of birth.

PRAHLĀDA said:

Lord, you are the indweller of all beings and you grant the fruition of all our wishes. Pray, grant me that boon which you consider to be limitless and infinite.

THE LORD said:

Prahlāda, may you be endowed with the spirit of enquiry till you rest in the infinite Brahman, so that all your delusions might come to an end and you may attain the highest fruit (blessing).

VASIṢṬHA continued:

Having said thus, the Lord disappeared. Prahlāda concluded his worship and after singing hymns in praise of the Lord, began to reflect in the following manner.

PRAHLĀDA contemplated:

The Lord had commanded "Be continually engaged in enquiry"; hence, I shall engage myself in enquiry into the self. What am I who speaks, walks, stands and functions on this elaborate stage known as the world—I should find this out to begin with.

Surely, I am not this world which is outside and which is inert, composed of trees, shrubs and mountains. Nor am I the body which was born on account of the movement of the life-breath, and which seems to live for a very brief moment. I am not sound (word or name or expression) which is apprehended by the inert substance known as the ear, which is but a momentary movement of air and which is devoid of form and devoid of existence. I am not the sense or experience of touch, which is also momentary and which is able to function only on account of the infinite consciousness. Nor am I the sense of taste based on the ever changing and restless tongue ever devoted to its objects. I am not the sense of sight (or form) which too is momentary and which is but a perversion of the understanding of the seer. Nor am I the sense of smell, which is an imaginary creation of the nose and which has an indeterminate form.

Hence, I am devoid of all these imaginary qualities. I have nothing whatsoever to do with the functions of these senses. I am pure consciousness. I am peace beyond thought.

PRAHLĀDA continued to contemplate:

I am the all-pervading reality which is devoid of objectivity and therefore percepts and concepts. I am pure consciousness. It is by this consciousness that all things, from a little pot to the mighty sun, are perceived. Ah, I now recollect the truth that I am the self which is omnipresent, in which there is no conceptualisation. It is by that self that all the senses and their experiences are made possible, for it is the inner light. It is because of that inner light that these objects acquire their apparent substantiality.

It is thanks to that inner light of consciousness, which is utterly free from all modifications, that the sun is hot, the moon is cool, the mountain is heavy and water is liquid. It is the cause of all the effects that manifest as this creation, but it is itself uncaused. It is on account of that inner light of consciousness that the characteristic nature of the diverse objects arises. Because it is formless and because it is the cause of all effects, this universe has arisen in it, with all its diversity. It alone is the cause of the manifestation of the trinity (Brahmā the creator, Viṣṇu the preserver and Śiva the redeemer); but it is not itself caused.

I salute this self which is its own light, free from the duality of knower and known, subject and object. In it exist all things of this universe; and into it they enter. Whatever this inner self thinks of, that happens everywhere—apparently as an external reality. When thought of by this consciousness, these things seem to come into being; when thought of as non-existent, they reach their end. Thus, all these infinite objects appear in the limitless space of consciousness. They appear to grow and they appear to diminish, even as a shadow seems to grow and to diminish in the light of the sun.

This self or inner light of consciousness is unknown and unseen: it is attained by those who have purified their heart. But by the holy ones it is seen in the supremely pure cosmic space (dimension) of consciousness.

This self exists in an undivided state in the three worlds—from Brahmā the creator to the blade of grass, as the infinite and self-luminous consciousness. It is one, without beginning and end; it exists as the all, as the inner experiencing of all mobile and immobile beings.

PRAHLĀDA continued to contemplate:

The one self, which is the sole experiencing, is therefore the experiencer in all: hence the self is said to have a thousand hands and a thousand eyes. With this beauteous body of the sun, this self which is 'I' roams the space, as also in the body of air. It is the same with the self embodied as the deity holding the conch, discus, mace, etc., who is adored in this world. It was this self or 'I' that was born as the one who is ever seated in the lotus (the creator Brahmā). It is the self again that shall dissolve this creation or withdraw it from manifestation at the end of the world-cycle.

The self referred to as the I embodied in Indra protects the world. I am woman, I am man, I am the youth, I am the senile old man; and on account of embodiment, I am apparently born here. I am the omnipresent. From the ground of the infinite consciousness I raise trees and plants, being present in them as their very essence. Even as clay in the hands of a playful child, this world-appearance is pervaded by me for my own delight. The world derives its reality from the self (me), it functions in and through me and when I abandon it or cease to comprehend it, it ceases to have any reality. For, this world exists in me, the self or infinite consciousness, even as a reflection seems to exist in a mirror.

I am the fragrance in flowers, I am the radiance in flowers and leaves, I am the light in the radiance and even in that light I am the experience. Whatever mobile and immobile beings exist in this universe, I am their supreme truth or consciousness free from conceptualisation. I am the very essence in all things in the universe. Just as butter exists in milk and just as liquidity exists in water, even so as the energy of consciousness I exist in all that exists. This world-appearance of the past, the present and the future exists in the infinite consciousness without the distinction of objectivity. This omnipresent, omnipotent cosmic being is the self which is indicated by the 'I'. This cosmic kingdom known as the universe has come to me unsought and is pervaded by me. As the self or the infinite consciousness I pervade the entire universe, even as the one cosmic ocean pervades the cosmos after the cosmic creation has been dissolved. Even as a lame (incapacitated) aquatic creature finds the cosmic ocean is without limits, I find no end to the extent of myself, which is infinite. This world-appearance is like a dust-particle in the infinite consciousness: it does not satisfy me, even as a tiny fruit does not appease an elephant's hunger. Hence, the form which began to expand in the house of the creator Brahmā even now continues to expand.

PRAHLĀDA continued to contemplate:

Truly, it was but the infinite consciousness that existed: how has this finite, limited ego-sense arisen in it, without any justification and support? What has given rise to the delusion which expresses itself in statements like 'This is you' and 'This I am'? What is this body and what is bodilessness, who lives and who is it that dies? Surely, my ancestors were of little understanding in that they abandoned this infinite consciousness and roamed this little earth. What comparison is there between the vision of the infinite and this fearful vanity known as worldly glory, which is full of dreadful desires and cravings? This vision of the infinite consciousness is pure and is of the nature of supreme peace: and it is surely the very best among the visions that are possible in this universe.

I salute my own self which is the indweller in all beings, which is the consciousness freed from objectivity or conceptualisation and which is the intelligence in all beings. I am the unborn in whom the world-appearance has vanished. I have gained what is worth gaining. I have triumphed and I live triumphantly. I find no delight in reigning over a kingdom, abandoning this supreme felicity of cosmic consciousness. Fie upon those wicked demons who revel in the filth of this worldly life.

Alas, how foolish and ignorant of my father to have remained satisfied and pleased with this physical existence! What has he gained by living a long life and by reigning over this little mud-ball called the earth? The delights of even countless such worlds is nothing compared to the bliss of the self. He who has nothing but has this self-knowledge has everything. He who abandons this and seeks other things is not a man of wisdom. What comparison is there between this mortal physical existence (like the arid desert) and the bliss of enlightenment (like a delightful pleasure-garden)? The sovereignty of the world as also all things in the three worlds exist in consciousness: why do people not experience the truth that there is nothing outside of consciousness?

Everything, everywhere and at all times is easily obtained through consciousness which is omnipresent and undifferentiated. The light that shines in the sun and the moon, the energy that animates the gods, the intrinsic characteristic of the mind and the elements, the qualities and the faculties that exist in nature (like that in space which permits aircraft to move in it) and the infinite variety of the manifestations of energy and intelligence are all the expansions and the functions of the one cosmic consciousness, which in itself is undivided and unmodified. Even as the sun shines on all things without distinction, this cosmic consciousness illumines all things without distinction, instantly and spontaneously as the very self of all things in the universe.

PRAHLĀDA continued to contemplate:

The infinite consciousness simultaneously pervades the three periods of time and experiences the infinite worlds. It envelops all, it sees all; and because it is undisturbed and unmodified, it alone remains at all times. This consciousness experiences simultaneously what is sweet and what is bitter; it is tranquil and at peace. Because this consciousness is in itself free from all modifications (concepts and percepts), and because it is subtle and experiences all things at the same time, it is ever at peace and homogeneous, even while apparently experiencing the diversity of diverse phenomena.

When the apparently transformed becoming resorts to or rests on that being which has not undergone any modification, the former is freed from sorrow: and when what is is seen by what is not (or by the mind in which there is no movement of thought) that which is, abandons its wickedness.

When consciousness abandons the perception of the three modes of time, when it is freed from the bondage of objectivity or conceptualisation, it rests in utter tranquility. It is as if it were unreal, because it is beyond description: hence some people declare that the self does not exist. Whether there is the self (Brahman) or not, that which is not subject to dissolution is the supreme liberation.

On account of the modification (thought), this consciousness is apparently veiled and is not realised. They who are sunk in the mire of attraction and repulsion are unable to reach this realisation. They are caught in the net of thoughts. Such have been my ancestors. On account of their desire and hate and the deluded perception of duality, they lead the life of vermin.

He in whom the ghosts of cravings and hostility have been laid and the mirage of ignorant thinking and psychological perversion has been dispelled by the cloud of true inner awakening, he alone lives. For, how can there arise concepts and percepts in the infinite consciousness which alone is?

I salute the self! Salutations to myself—the undivided consciousness, the jewel of all the seen and the unseen worlds! You have indeed been reached very soon! You have been touched, you have been gained, you have been realised, you have been raised above all kinds of perversions: you are what you are. Salutations to you. Salutations to you—my self, Śiva, the Lord of lords, the supreme self.

I salute the self which rejoices in its own body, being established in itself, in full control of itself, utterly freed from the veil of self-imposed ignorance (thoughts and concepts).

PRAHLĀDA continued to contemplate: V:35

OM is the one non-dual consciousness devoid of all perversion. Whatever there is in the universe is the one self. Even within this body composed of flesh and blood, etc., it is the intelligence that shines, as it does in and through light-sources such as the sun, etc. It makes the fire hot and it tastes the nectarine sweetness: it experiences all sense-experiences, as it were. Standing, it is not stationary; going, it does not move; at rest it is ever busy; dynamic, it is unaffected. In the past, present and in the future, here, there and everywhere, it is ever the same in all apparent modifications. Utterly fearless and uninhibited, it is this consciousness that brings into manifestation and sustains the infinite variety of beings, from Brahmā the creator to the blade of grass. It is ever dynamic and active; yet it is more inactive than a rock and it is more unaffected by such activity than even the space.

It is this self or consciousness that activates the mind even as wind rustles the leaves; it makes the senses function as the rider guides the horse. Though the self is the lord of this body, it is ever engaged in diverse actions as if it were a slave.

This self alone is to be sought, adored and meditated upon. It is by resorting to it that one crosses this world-appearance with its cycle of birth and death and delusion. It is very easily accessible, it can be easily won over like a good friend, for it dwells in the heart-lotus of every one. It is attained in one's own body, without even the need to call upon it: it manifests itself and reveals itself even if it is contemplated for an instant. Though it is the Lord of all and is endowed with all excellences, one who adores it is free from arrogance and pride.

This self dwells in all bodies even as fragrance resides in flowers. It is not realised by all because no one enquires into the truth concerning the self. If it is realised through self-enquiry, there is instant experience of supreme bliss and one gets an undying vision of truth: all fetters drop away, all enemies are quelled and cravings do not agitate the mind. When it is seen, everything is seen; when it is heard, everything is heard; when it is touched, everything is touched—for the world is because it is. It is awake even when one sleeps, it goads the unwise into wakefulness, it removes the distress of the suffering and bestows all desired objects. In this creation, it exists as if it is a jīva (living entity); it appears to enjoy the pleasures; and it seems to expand in the objects of this world.

Yet, in all bodies, it exists as the self, experiencing itself in utter tranquility. It is the one sole and cosmic reality in the whole universe.

PRAHLĀDA continued to contemplate:

This self is the emptiness in space. It is the motion in all things moving. It is the light in all things luminous. In all liquids it is taste. It is solidity in earth. It is heat in fire. It is coolness in the moon. It is the very existence of the worlds. Even as all these characteristic qualities exist in the corresponding substances, even so it exists as Lord in the body. Just as existence exists everywhere and just as time exists at all times, this self exists in all bodies, with all the physical and psychological faculties.

This self is the eternal existence. It enlightens even the gods. I, the self, alone am: in me there is no percept or concept. Even as space is unaffected by the dust-particles floating in it, even as a lotus is untainted by water, even so I am not affected by anything. Let the body be subjected to happiness or unhappiness: how is the self affected by it? Just as the flame of a lamp (though the wick itself is made of threads) cannot be bound by a piece of thread, the self which exceeds or transcends all material existence is not bound by such materiality. What relationship can exist between us (the self) and the cravings which spring from notions of existence and non-existence and from the senses? Who or what binds the space and by whom is the mind bound?

Even if the body is cut into a hundred pieces, the self is not injured; even if the pot is pulverised, the space within it is not destroyed. Even if this goblin mind which exists only as a word and not as a reality, ceases to be, what do we lose? Formerly, there was a mind which consisted of notions of happiness and unhappiness: but now that all such notions have ceased to be, where is my mind? Which fool would entertain such notions as 'One enjoys another', 'One grasps another', 'One sees another', 'One suffers a calamity'? Nature alone enjoys, the mind grasps or comprehends, suffering belongs to the body, the wicked person is a fool: but in one who has attained liberation there is none of these. I neither entertain craving for pleasure, nor do I wish to get rid of it. Whatever comes, let it come; whatever goes, let it go. Let notions of diverse experiences either arise or set in the body: I am neither in them nor they in me.

For so long I have been enslaved by the dreaded enemy known as ignorance who robbed me of my wealth of wisdom. But now, by the grace of lord Viṣṇu and through my own excellent self-effort, I have attained that wisdom. By the magic-spell of self-knowledge this goblin ego-sense has been expelled. Rid of the destitution of delusion, I remain as the supreme Lord. All that is worth knowing is already known, all that is worth seeing has been seen; I have now attained that beyond which there is naught to be attained.

PRAHLĀDA continued to contemplate:

Luckily for me, the deadly serpent of craving for sense-pleasure has been left far behind and all delusions and hopes have been quietened. I have attained the plane of supreme truth. The Lord who is the self, has been seen by me by means of singing hymns, salutations, prayer, peace of mind and disciplined living. By the grace of lord Viṣṇu the realisation of the supreme being is firmly established in my heart.

Till now I was harassed by ignorant limitations and delusions. The forest of ignorance has numerous anthills inhabited by deadly snakes in the form of sense-cravings, many blind-holes known as death and many forest-fires of sorrow; in it roam the thieves of violence and greed, as also the most deadly enemy of ego-sense. Now I am free of that by the grace of lord Viṣṇu as also by my own self-effort; and my intelligence has been fully awakened. In the light of that awakened intelligence I do not perceive an entity which can be called ego-sense, even as one does not see darkness when the sun has arisen. Now that the goblin of ego-sense has been laid, I remain at peace within myself.

When the truth is seen and the ego-sense has been dispelled, where is room for delusion, sorrows, hopes, desires and mental distress? Heaven and hell, as also delusions concerning liberation, exist only as long as the ego-sense exists: pictures are painted on canvas, not on empty sky! When the intelligence is freed from the cloud of ego-sense and from the thunderstorm of cravings, it shines with the light of self-knowledge, even as the sky shines during the autumnal full-moon night.

O self free from the mire of ego-sense, salutations to you. O self in whom the fearsome senses and all-consuming mind have attained quiescence, salutations to you. O self in whom the lotus of bliss has fully blossomed, salutations to you. O self whose two wings are consciousness and its reflection, and who dwells in the lotus of the heart, salutations to you. O self, the sun that dispels the darkness of ignorance in the heart, salutations to you. O self, the promoter of supreme love and the sustainer of all things in the universe, salutations to you.

Even as steel cuts the steel-beam which has been heated, I have subdued the mind with its own purified state. I have cut asunder cravings, ignorance and foolishness by their opposites. Egolessly, my body functions with its inherent energy. The past tendencies, mental conditioning and limitations have been completely destroyed. I begin to wonder: how was it that for such a long time I was caught up in the trap of the ego-sense! Freed from dependency, from habits of thought, from desires and cravings, from deluded belief in the existence of the ego, from the colouring of pleasure-seeking tendency and from revelry—my mind has reached a state of utter quiescence. With this, all sorrow has come to an end and the light of supreme bliss has dawned!

V:36 PRAHLĀDA continued to contemplate:

At last, the self which is beyond all states or modes of consciousness has been realised. O self! fortunately you have been realised;

salutations to you. I salute you, I embrace you: who but you is my friend and relative in the three worlds? You alone destroy, you alone protect, you give, you praise and you move: now, O self, you have been seen and attained—what will you do now and where will you go? By your reality are all the worlds pervaded, you alone are seen everywhere, O self: where will you run to now?

Between us stood the great wall of ignorance from beginningless time. Now that that wall has collapsed you are seen to be not distant at all. Salutations to the self, who has fully accomplished what needs to be accomplished, the real doer of all actions, the Lord, the eternal and the ever-pure being. Salutations to Viṣṇu, to Śiva, and to Brahmā the creator. O self, the distinction between you (the self) and me is verbal, like the distinction between the word and the substance it refers to; the distinction is unreal and imaginary, like the verbal distinction between the wave and the water in the wave. In truth, you alone are spread out as the infinite variety of created objects that appear to be in this world.

Salutations to the seer, the experiencer. Salutations to the one that creates, to the one that unfolds and expands as all things. Salutations to that which is the inner reality of all. Salutations to the omnipresent. Alas, on account of your identification with the embodiment, you, O self, had, as it were, forgotten your own nature. Hence, you had to undergo endless suffering in repeated births, experiencing external perceptions without self-knowledge. This external world is nothing more than earth, wood and rock: O self, there is no reality in all this other than you. Attaining self-knowledge, one does not long for aught else.

Now, Lord, you have been seen and reached. Hereafter you will not be deluded again: salutations to you. Lord, how is it that the self which is the very light of the eyes and which fills the whole body as the innate intelligence, is not seen or experienced? How is it that that intelligence which functioning as the sense of touch and experiencing all other objects is itself not realised? How can that intelligence be distant from oneself—which as the intelligence in the sense of hearing, hears and produces goose-pimples? How is it that one does not taste the sweetness of that intelligence which experiences the sweetness or otherwise of the objects placed before it? How is it that one does not directly experience the presence of that intelligence which enjoys the sense of smell? How is it that the self whose glory is sung by the scriptures and who is knowledge or wisdom itself forgets itself? O self, now that you have been realised, the sense-pleasures that I revelled in before are no longer worthy of my attention!

PRAHLĀDA continued to contemplate:

O self, it is your own light of purity that shines in the sun; your nectarine coolness that radiates through the moon. The heaviness of the mountains is derived from you, as also the speed of the wind. Because of you the earth is firm and space is empty. Luckily, you have been realised by me: luckily, I have become yours. Luckily, O Lord, there is no distinction between you (the self) and me—you are I, I am you. Whatever is referred to as you (the self) or as I, whichever be the root and whichever be the branch, to that I offer my salutations again and again. Salutations to my self which is infinite and egoless: salutations to the formless self.

You (self) dwell in 'me' in a state of equilibrium, as pure witness consciousness, without form and without the divisions of space and time. The mind gets agitated, the senses begin to stir and the energy begins to expand, setting in motion the twin-forces of prāṇa and apāna (two modifications of the life-force). Drawn by the power of desires, the driver (mind) carries away the body made up of flesh and blood, bone and skin. However, I am pure consciousness, not dependent upon the body or anything else: let this body rise or fall, in accordance with the desires that move it.

In course of time the ego-sense arises and in course of time the ego-sense ceases to be, even as the universe dissolves at the end of the cosmic cycle. But, after a long time of such cyclic (birth and death) existence in this creation, I have attained the state of peace and rest, even as the whole cosmos comes to rest at the end of its own cyclic existence. Salutations to you, myself, who is transcendental and who is all: salutations to all of them that speak of us!

The supreme self being the witness-consciousness is utterly unaffected by the faults of the experiences related to it. The self is all in all everywhere and exists in everything, even as fragrance exists in flowers and oil in sesame seeds. O self, you destroy, you protect, you give, you roar and you function here, although you are completely free from ego-sense: indeed this is a great wonder. Being the light of the self, I open my eyes, as it were, and the universe comes into being; and I close my eyes and the universe ceases to be. You, O self, are the supreme atom in which the entire universe exists already, even as the great banyan tree exists potentially in the tiny banyan seed. Even as cloud formations in the sky often resemble horses, elephants and other animals, you yourself, O self, appear in the cosmic space as the infinite variety of objects. Free from being and non-being, the self exists as being and non-being and also the diverse beings, one distinct and separate from the other, as it were.

PRAHLĀDA continued to contemplate:

Abandon vanity, anger, impurity and violence: for great souls are not overcome by such base qualities. Remember past sorrow again and again; and with a cheerful attitude of mind enquire 'Who am I?', 'How could all this happen?' and be free from all that. All that is past is past and all the sorrows and anxieties that burnt you have ceased to be. Today, you are the sovereign of this city known as the body; and even as one cannot get hold of the sky with his fist, sorrow is not able to lay its hand upon you. Now, you are the master of your senses and your mind; and you enjoy the greatest delight.

Lord, O self, you are ever asleep, as it were: you are apparently awakened by your own energy for the purpose of becoming aware of the experiences being undergone. It is in fact that energy which comes into contact with the object of such experiences: but on account of such awareness, you assume such experiences to yourself. They who have, through the exercise of the life-forces, reached 'the aperture of Brahmā' at the crown of the head, perceive every moment what is past and what will be in the future in the city of Brahmā the creator.

O self, you are the fragrance in the flower known as the body; you are the nectar in the moon known as the body; you are the essence in the herb known as the body; you are the coolness in the ice known as the body. Just as there is butter in milk, there is friendship or attachment in the body. You dwell in this body even as fire dwells in wood. You are the light in all luminous objects; you are the inner light that makes knowledge of objects possible. You are the strength of the elephant known as mind. You are both the light and the heat of the fire of self-knowledge.

Speech terminates in you, O self! It reappears somewhere else. Even as different ornaments are fashioned out of gold, all the countless objects of creation have been fashioned out of you: the distinction is verbal. 'This is you,' 'This is I,'—such expressions are used when you yourself adore yourself or describe yourself for your own delight. Even as a huge forest-fire might momentarily assume various forms though it is but a single flame, even so your non-dual being appears to be all these diverse objects in this universe. You are the string on which all these worlds are strung. You are the ground of truth in which all these worlds abide. The worlds are for ever potentially present in you: and by you they are made manifest, as the flavour of foodstuff is made manifest by cooking. However, though these worlds seem to exist, they will cease to be if you are not! You are their reality. Even this body will fall down lifeless like a log of wood. Happiness and sorrow collapse when they approach you, even as darkness disappears when it approaches light. However, the experience of happiness etc., is made possible only because of the light of awareness derived from you.

PRAHLĀDA continued to contemplate:

Pleasure and pain, happiness and unhappiness owe their existence to you, O self: they are born of you and they lose their identity when their non-existence independent of you is realised. Even as an optical illusion comes into being and vanishes in the twinkling of an eye, the illusory experiences of pain and pleasure appear and disappear in the twinkling of an eye. They appear in the light of awareness and they disappear when they are perceived as non-different from that awareness: they are born the moment they die and they die the moment they are born—who is the perceiver of all this mystery?

Everything is thus ever-changing all the time: how then can such momentary causes produce tangible and stable results? Waves may look like flowers, but can one string them into a garland? If it is credible to think that one can expect stable effects to accrue from such an unstable cause as the fleeting phenomena, then it should be possible to string lightnings into a luminous garland and wear it as an ornament! O self, you enjoy pleasure and pain as if they were real, while you perceive and receive them through the consciousness of a wise person, without ever abandoning the state of utter equanimity. But, what your experiences are when the same thing happens in the heart of an unwise or unawakened person, it is impossible for me to describe! O self, you are in truth non-attached, free from all desires and hopes, you are one and homogeneous without any parts, you are devoid of ego-sense: and you assume the doership of actions and you appear to experience the diversity, whether this is really true and factual or unreal and fictitious.

Hail, hail to you, O self who has manifested as this limitless universe. Hail to the self which is supreme peace. Hail to you, O self, who is beyond the reach of the scriptures. Hail to you, O self, who is the basis and the goal of all scriptures. Hail to you, O self, who is born and who dwells in all creatures. Hail to you, O self, who is unborn. Hail to you, O self, who undergoes change and destruction. Hail to you, O self, that is unchanging and indestructible. Hail to you, O self, that is existence: hail to you, O self, that is non-existence. Hail to you, O self, that is conquerable, that can be attained. Hail to you, O self, that is invincible and beyond reach.

I am delighted. I am in a state of utter equilibrium and of supreme peace. I stand unmoving. I have reached self-knowledge. I am the victor. I live to conquer. Salutations to myself; salutations to you.

As long as you, O my self, exist as the pure untainted reality, where is bondage, where is misfortune, where is good fortune, where is birth or death? I shall rest for ever in supreme peace.

VASIṢṬHA continued: V:37, 38

After thus contemplating, Prahlāda entered into the state in which there is no mental modification at all, but where there is supreme bliss, undisturbed by the movement of thought. He sat where he was, like a statue.

A very long time passed in this manner. The demons tried their best to disturb him: they could not. A thousand years went by. The demons concluded that he was dead.

Anarchy prevailed in the netherworld. Hiraṇyakaśipu was dead; and his son remained dead to the world. No one else ascended the throne. The demons roamed the country freely, guided solely by their whims and fancies. There was utter disorder and the strong overpowered the weak, even as in the ocean the big fish swallow the small ones.

In the meantime, the protector of the universe lord Viṣṇu who was reclining on his serpent-couch in the ocean of milk contemplated the state of the universe. In his own mind he saw the heaven and the earth and satisfied himself that everything was in order in those regions. Then, he saw the state of the netherworld. He perceived that Prahlāda was deeply immersed in the transcendental state of consciousness. Freed from harassment by the demons, the gods in heaven enjoyed a run-away prosperity. Seeing this,

LORD VIṢṆU thought:

Since Prahlāda is immersed in the transcendental state of consciousness, the leaderless demons have lost their power. In the absence of a threat from the demons, the gods in heaven have nothing to fear and hence nothing to hate. If they have nothing to fear or hate, they will soon rise to the transcendental state of consciousness, beyond the pairs of opposites, and attain liberation! Then, the earthlings will find religious rites to be meaningless, since there are no gods to propitiate. This universe, which ought to exist till the natural cosmic dissolution, will thus abruptly cease to be. I do not see any good in this: hence, I think that the demons should continue to live as demons. If the demons function as the enemies of the gods, religious and righteous actions shall prevail in this creation: and thus will this creation continue to exist and flourish, not otherwise.

Hence, I shall presently go to the netherworld and re-establish it as it should be. If Prahlāda shows no interest in ruling that realm,

I shall appoint someone else in his place. Surely, this is the last incarnation of Prahlāda and he shall live in this embodiment till the end of this world-cycle. Such is the world-order. Hence, I shall go to the netherworld and roar to awaken Prahlāda. I shall persuade him to rule the realm whilst enjoying the consciousness of liberation. Thus shall I be able to sustain this creation till its natural dissolution.

V:39 VASIṢṬHA continued:

Thus resolved, lord Viṣṇu quickly reached the netherworld. In his radiance the demons gained new strength and vitality; but dazzled by his divine light they ran away. Viṣṇu approached where Prahlāda was seated, and roared aloud "Noble one, wake up!" and at the same time blew his conch. Hearing this the demons fell down and the gods rejoiced.

The life-force began to vibrate in the crown of Prahlāda's head. The life-force then spread throughout his body. The senses gained energy and they began to apprehend their respective objects. The mind began to function. The nāḍīs (nerves?) began to vibrate. The mind began to become aware of its physical encasing, the body. Prahlāda was fully awake to his surroundings and gazed upon the Lord.

LORD VIṢṆU said to Prahlāda:

Remember, O Prahlāda, your identity as such, and as the ruler of the netherworld. You have nothing whatsoever either to acquire or to reject: arise. You have to remain in this body till the end of this world-cycle: I know this as inevitable, as I know the law of this world-order. Hence, you have to rule this realm here and now as a sage liberated from all delusion.

The time for cosmic dissolution is not yet: why do you vainly wish to abandon this body? The signs, symptoms and events that naturally precede such natural cosmic dissolution are not yet seen: why do you vainly wish to abandon this body?

I exist. All this world and the creatures in it exist. Hence, do not think of abandoning your body yet.

He is fit to die who is sunk in ignorance and sorrow. He who grieves, thinking "I am weak, miserable, stupid" etc., is fit to die. He who is swayed by countless desires and hopes and he whose mind is restless is fit to die. He who is subject to the pairs of opposites like happiness and unhappiness, who is attached to this body, who is distressed physically and mentally, whose heart has dried up through the fires of lust and anger, is fit to experience death. People regard that as death when one abandons the body!

Living is appropriate to one whose mind is well controlled by his self-knowledge and who is aware of the truth. He should live who does not entertain notions of egoism and who is unattached to anything, who is free from likes and dislikes and has a calm mind, whose mind has reached the state of no-mind. It is proper that he should live who is established in the perception of the truth and who functions here as if playfully, who is inwardly neither elated nor depressed by external events, who is free from the desire to acquire or to reject. He, hearing of whom or listening to whom, people experience great joy—life alone is appropriate to him, and not death.

THE LORD continued: V:40

The functioning or the existence of the body is known as the state of living, according to the people; and the abandonment of the body in order to get another body is known as death. You are free from these two notions, O Prahlāda: to you what is death and what is life! I was only using the popular notions to explain myself to you: in truth, you neither live nor die. Even though you are in the body, since you do not have the body, you are bodiless. You are the observer which is immaterial intelligence: just as, though air exists in space it is not attached to space, and hence it is free from spatial limitation. Yet, in a manner of speaking you are the body since you experience sensations through the body, even as, in a manner of speaking, space is responsible for the growth of a plant in as much as space does not arrest such growth.

You are enlightened. What is a body or embodiment to you? It is only in the eyes of the ignorant that even your form exists. At all times you are the all, you are the supreme inner light of consciousness: what is body or bodilessness to you and what can you hold or abandon? Whether it is springtime or the day of cosmic dissolution, they are nothing to one who has transcended the notions of being and non-being. For, in all conditions, he is firmly established in self-knowledge. Whether all the beings in the universe live or perish, or they prosper, he remains firmly established in self-knowledge.

The supreme Lord dwells in the body, undying when the body dies and unchanging when the body changes. When you have given up the false notions 'I belong to the body' or 'The body belongs to me', then there is no meaning in expressions like 'I shall give it up' or 'I shall not give it up', 'I have done this', and 'I shall do this now'.

Enlightened men, though they be constantly engaged in activity, do nothing: it is not by means of inaction that they reach the state of non-action! This very fact of non-action frees you from experiences: for there is no harvest where there is no sowing. When thus both the notions of 'I do' and 'I experience' have ceased, there remains only peace; when that peace is firmly grounded, there is liberation.

To such an enlightened person what is there to acquire or to renounce? For it is only when the notions of subject and object have ceased that there is liberation. Such enlightened persons (as you are) live in this world as if they are for ever in a state of deep sleep. Likewise, O Prahlāda, perceive this world as if you are half asleep! Enlightened beings do not exult in pleasure nor grieve in pain; they function non-volitionally even as a crystal reflects the objects placed near it without intending to do so. They are fully awake in self-knowledge, but they are asleep, as it were, in relation to the world; they function in this world like children, without ego-sense and all the rest of its retinue. O Prahlāda, you have reached the plane of Viṣṇu; rule the netherworld for a world-cycle, which is equal to a day in the life of the creator Brahmā.

V:41 PRAHLĀDA said:

Lord, I was really overcome by fatigue and I took rest for a brief moment. By your grace, I have attained to the realisation in which there is no distinction between contemplation and non-contemplation. You were seen by me for a long time within myself: luckily, you are now seen in front of me. I have experienced the truth of the infinite consciousness within myself, in which there is no sorrow, no delusion, no concern with dispassion, no desire to abandon the body and no fear of this world-appearance. When the one single reality is known, where is sorrow, where is destruction, what is body, what is world-appearance, what is fear or its absence? I was in that state of consciousness which spontaneously arose in me.

'Oh I am disgusted with this world and I shall abandon it,' such thoughts arise only in the ignorant. Only the ignorant think that there is sorrow when there is body and that there is no sorrow once the body is abandoned. 'This is pleasure', 'this is pain', 'this is', 'this is not'—only the mind of the ignorant swings like this, not of the wise. Notions of 'I' and the 'other' exist only in the minds of the ignorant who have left wisdom far behind. 'This is to be acquired' and 'This is to be abandoned', such thoughts arise only in the minds of the ignorant. When everything is pervaded by you, where is 'another' which can be acquired or abandoned? The entire universe is pervaded by consciousness: what is to be acquired and what abandoned?

I was naturally enquiring of myself in myself, and rested just for a moment without any notions of being or non-being, of acquisition or rejection. I have attained self-knowledge now: and I shall do whatever pleases you. Pray, accept my worshipful adoration.

After receiving Prahlāda's worship, LORD VIṢṆU said to him:

Arise, O Prahlāda: I shall presently anoint you king of the netherworld while the gods and the sages who are here sing your glories. (After thus crowning him king of the netherworld, he continued:) Be thou ruler of the netherworld as long as the sun and the moon shine. Protect this realm without being swayed by desire, fear or hate and looking upon all with equal vision. Enjoy the royal pleasures and may all prosperity attend you: but act in such a way that neither the gods in heaven nor the humans on earth are unduly agitated or worried. Engage yourself in appropriate action, without being swayed by thoughts and motives. Thus will you not be bound by actions. O Prahlāda, you know everything already; what need have you to be instructed? From now the gods and the demons will live in friendship; the goddesses and the demonesses will live in harmony. O king, keep ignorance at a great distance from you and live an enlightened life, ruling this world for a very long time to come.

VASIṢṬHA continued: V:42

Having said thus, lord Viṣṇu left the realm of the demons. By the grace and with the blessings of the Lord, the gods in heaven, the demons in the netherworld and the humans on earth lived happily, without distress.

Thus I have narrated to you, O Rāma, the auspicious story of Prahlāda, which is capable of destroying all the impurities of one's heart. They who contemplate this narrative will soon attain a higher state of consciousness, even if they have been very wicked and sinful. Even a simple investigation of this narrative will destroy all sins; but if the investigation is of a yogic nature, surely it will lead to supreme realisation. Sin is only ignorance and it is destroyed by enquiry; hence one should never abandon enquiry.

RĀMA asked:

How was it, O Lord, that Prahlāda who was in the highest state of non-dual consciousness was awakened by the conch-sound?

VASIṢṬHA replied:

O Rāma, liberation is of two kinds—'with body' and 'without body'. That state of liberation in which the mind is totally unattached to anything (neither to actions involving acquisitions nor to renunciation) and in which there is no craving at all, is known as 'liberation with body'. That itself is known as 'liberation without body' when the body drops.

In the case of the 'liberation with body', all the tendencies and mental conditioning are like fried seeds incapable of giving rise to future embodiment: but there still remains the conditioning of such purity, expansiveness and self-knowledge, though even this conditioning is unintentional and non-volitional (as in a sleeping person). As long as this trace remains, the sage who is 'liberated with body' can be awakened to world-consciousness even after a hundred years of inward contemplation. Such was the state of Prahlāda and hence he 'awoke' to the sound of the conch.

Moreover, lord Viṣṇu is the self of all and whatever notion arises in him materialises immediately. His manifestation is uncaused, but it has the sole purpose of creating the infinite creatures in this universe. By the attainment of self-knowledge, lord Viṣṇu is realised; and by the adoration of lord Viṣṇu, self-realisation is attained.

O Rāma, reach the vision which Prahlāda had and engage yourself in ceaseless enquiry: you will reach the supreme state. This world deludes one only as long as the sun of self-enquiry does not arise in one's heart. When one obtains the grace of the self and of lord Viṣṇu, he is not troubled by the ghost of this illusory world-appearance.

V:43 RĀMA asked:

Holy sir, you said that Prahlāda attained enlightenment by the grace of lord Viṣṇu. If everything is achieved by self-effort, why was he not able to attain enlightenment without Viṣṇu's grace?

VASIṢṬHA replied:

Surely, whatever Prahlāda attained was through self-effort, O Rāma, not otherwise. Viṣṇu is the self and the self is Viṣṇu: the distinction is verbal. It was the self of Prahlāda that generated in itself devotion to Viṣṇu. Prahlāda obtained from Viṣṇu, who was his own self, the boon of self-enquiry; and through such enquiry attained self-knowledge. At times one attains self-knowledge through self-enquiry undertaken through self-effort; at times this self-effort manifests as devotion to Viṣṇu who is also the self, and thus one attains enlightenment.

Even if one worships Viṣṇu for a long time with great devotion, he does not bestow enlightenment on one who is not wise with self-knowledge. Thus, the foremost means for self-knowledge is self-enquiry; grace and such other factors are secondary means. Hence, attain mastery over the senses and by whole-souled spiritual practice lead the mind along the path of self-enquiry. Resort to self-effort and cross this ocean of world-appearance and reach the other shore.

If you think that lord Viṣṇu can be seen without self-effort, why do the birds and beasts not get uplifted by him? If it is true that the guru can spiritually uplift one without the need for self-effort, then why does a guru not so uplift a camel or a bull. No, nothing whatsoever is gained with the help of god or guru or wealth or other means, but only by self-effort at a complete mastery of the mind. What cannot be attained by the resolute practice of self-mastery coupled with uncolouredness (freedom from every form of mental conditioning) cannot be attained by any other means in the three worlds.

Hence, adore the self by the self, worship the self by the self, behold the self by the self, and be firmly established by the self in the self. The cult of devotion to Viṣṇu has been founded with the intention of possibly inducing those people who have turned away from the study of scriptures, from self-effort and from self-enquiry, to do something good. Determined and persistent self-effort is considered the best: in its absence, other forms of worship are prescribed. If there is complete mastery of the senses, of what use is worship; and if there is no mastery of the senses, of what use is worship? Without self-enquiry and the consequent inner tranquility, neither devotion to lord Viṣṇu nor self-knowledge is possible. Hence, resort to self-enquiry and the practice of cessation of distraction and thus adore the self: if you are successful in this, you have attained perfection; if not, you are no more than a wild donkey.

VASIṢṬHA continued:

Just as you perform worship of lord Viṣṇu and others, why do you not worship your own self? Lord Viṣṇu in fact dwells as the innermost being of all: they are surely the worst among men who, abandoning the indweller, seek Viṣṇu outside. The Lord's primary dwelling is the heart-cave of all beings: that is his eternal body. The form that is seen with the conch, discus, mace etc., is the secondary form of the self. He who abandons the primary truth and runs after the secondary aspects is like one who throws away a proven remedy and struggles in vain to effect a cure by other means. He who is unable to contemplate with one-pointed attention the indwelling self and who is therefore unable to attain wisdom of the self, might engage himself in the worship of the external form of lord Viṣṇu. By the very effort involved in such practice the mind will gradually become purified and uncoloured. In the course of time when this practice is continued with intelligence and wisdom, there arises joy and peace in the heart and one attains maturity and ripeness for self-knowledge. In fact, this fruition that I have mentioned is derived from the self: the worship of lord Viṣṇu (as it is called) is but an excuse for it.

Whatever boons or blessings are obtained from lord Viṣṇu are in fact obtained from the self alone by one who practises enquiry into the nature of the self. All these different practices and all the blessings that seem to accrue from them are all based on the understanding and the mastery of one's own mind, even as the earth is the basis for all the diverse foodstuff. In fact, even for ploughing the soil or turning a rock there is no way but the mastery of one's own mind!

One may revolve on the wheel of birth and death for a thousand lifetimes: this will not cease till one has fully mastered the mind and till that mind has come to a state of supreme peace and equanimity. No one in the three worlds, not even the gods or the members of the trinity, can save a man from the torments of a wayward mind.

Hence, O Rāma, abandon all the illusory appearances of objective phenomena, whether they appear to be within you or outside you. Contemplate the sole reality of consciousness for the cessation of repeated birth. Taste the pure consciousness (which is, in truth, the very essence of all that exists) by resolutely renouncing objectivity of consciousness (all the concepts and percepts) and contemplating the changeless consciousness which is infinite. You will surely cross this river of world-appearance and rebirth.

The Story of Gādhi

V:44 VASIṢṬHA continued:

O Rāma, this cycle of birth and death is an interminable one; this Māyā ceases only by the mastery of one's own heart (mind), not otherwise. To illustrate this, there is a legend which I shall presently narrate to you.

In this world there is a region known as Kosala. In it there was a brāhmaṇa known as Gādhi. He was very learned and the very embodiment of dharma. Right from his very childhood he was filled with the spirit of renunciation and dispassion. Once this brāhmaṇa went away to the forest in order to practise austerity. Desiring to behold Viṣṇu, he entered the water of a river and there began to recite various mantras, which soon completely purified his being.

After a period of eight months, LORD VIṢṆU appeared there and said to him: "Ask of me the boon of your choice."

The BRĀHMAṆA said: "Lord, I wish to behold your own illusory power (Māyā) which deludes all beings and keeps them in ignorance."

LORD VIṢṆU said: "You will behold my Māyā and then you will at once abandon the illusory perception of objects."

After lord Viṣṇu disappeared, Gādhi rose from the water. He was highly pleased. For several days thereafter Gādhi engaged himself in various holy activities, constantly immersed in the bliss which had resulted from his vision of lord Viṣṇu.

One day, he went to the river for his bath, still meditating upon the words of lord Viṣṇu. While he immersed himself in the water, he beheld himself dead and mourned by all. His body had fallen and his face had become pale and lifeless.

He saw himself surrounded by very many relatives who were all weeping and wailing aloud; they were inconsolably grief-stricken. His wife was shedding tears as if a dam had been breached, and she had caught hold of his feet. His mother, beside herself with grief, had caught hold of his face and was weeping bitter tears and crying aloud. He was surrounded by a number of grief-stricken relatives.

He saw himself lying silent, as if asleep or in deep meditation; he was taking a long rest, as it were. He listened to all the weeping and wailing of the relatives and wondered "What does all this mean?"; he was curious about the nature of friendship and relationship.

Soon the relatives carried his body away to the crematorium. After the performance of the funeral rites, they placed the body on the funeral pyre. They set the pyre alight and soon the body of Gādhi was consumed by the fire.

VASIṢṬHA continued: V:45

O Rāma, Gādhi, who still remained immersed in the river, then saw that he was in the region known as Bhūtamaṇḍalaṃ as a foetus in the womb of a tribal woman. He was surrounded by filth and flesh in the body of that woman. In course of time, he was born as her son. For a time he wallowed in his own excreta. He was dark in colour like his parents. He was well-beloved in the family.

Soon he grew up into a robust young man. He was a good hunter. He got married to a tribeswoman. He roamed the forest freely. He led a nomadic life, sometimes sleeping under a tree, sometimes hiding himself in the bushes and sometimes making a cave his abode. And, he became a father. His children were as violent and wicked as he was.

He had a large family. He had numerous relations and friends. He grew old. He did not die, but one by one he lost all his friends and relatives to death. Disgusted, he left his native realm and wandered away to foreign lands. Aimlessly he wandered in many countries.

One day, while thus wandering from one place to another, he entered a kingdom which was obviously very rich and prosperous. He was walking along the main road of the capital city of this kingdom. He saw in front of him a huge royal elephant which had been richly caparisoned.

This royal elephant had a mission. The king who ruled over that kingdom had just died without an heir. In accordance with the custom, the royal elephant had been commissioned to find a suitable successor. It was looking for a suitable person, even as a jeweller might look for a precious gem.

The hunter looked at the elephant for some time with a mixture of curiosity and wonder. The elephant picked him up with its trunk and quickly placed him on its own back. At that very moment there arose in that city a tumultuous sound of drums and bugles. The people everywhere exclaimed in great joy "Long live the king". The elephant had chosen the king.

Very soon, the hunter was surrounded by the members of the royal court. The beautiful women of the court surrounded him and began to dress him and adorn him with princely garments and jewels. They garlanded him; they applied various unguents and perfumes. The hunter shone as a radiant king. And they crowned him while he was seated on a throne on the back of that very elephant. Thus a tribesman and hunter became the king of Kīrapura! Thereafter he enjoyed all the royal pleasures and privileges.

By and by, the very nature of his position taught him the art of ruling the kingdom: he became a well-known king named Gavala.

V:46 VASIṢṬHA continued:

Gavala, the king, devoutly served by the maids of the palace and by his ministers, had totally forgotten his humble origin. Thus eight years passed. And, he ruled the kingdom justly and wisely, with compassion and purity.

One day he roamed out of his inner apartments alone, and unadorned with regal dress and royal insignia: people who are conscious of their excellence ignore external adornments. Outside the palace he saw a group of tribesmen who were singing familiar songs. Quietly he joined them and also began to sing with them.

An aged tribesman recognised him and rising from the crowd addressed him: "O Kaṭanja! Does the king of this place bestow good gifts and presents upon you in recognition of your musical accomplishments? Ah, I am delighted to see you: who will not rejoice to meet an old friend again?" Gavala ignored this: but the ladies of the royal household and the members of the court, who were watching from a distance, were shocked. The king quickly returned to the palace.

But, the royal servants and the members of the court had not recovered from the shock of the realisation that their king was an unworthy tribesman, whom they would not even knowingly touch. They began to avoid him; they treated him as if he were a putrid corpse.

Thus neglected by his ministers, servants and the ladies-in-waiting who used to adorn him, Gavala began to appear in his real form—as a dark and ugly tribesman, hideous to look at, like a crematorium.

Even the citizens avoided him and ran away at his very sight. He felt utterly lonely though he was living in the palace, surrounded by the people; he felt like a destitute person though he was king. Even if he tried to talk to them, the people would not respond or answer him!

The leaders of the community held counsel among themselves and began to talk, "Alas, we have been polluted by the touch of this tribesman who lives on the flesh of dogs. There is no expiation for this pollution, other than death. Let us raise a huge pyre and throw our sullied bodies into it and thus purify our souls." Having decided thus, they gathered firewood with which they built a huge funeral pyre. One by one they threw themselves into it. With all the elders thus having ended their lives, there was disorder and anarchy in the city.

The king Gavala reflected: "Alas, all this was brought about by me! Why should I continue to live: death is preferable to life. For one who is dishonoured by the people death is better than life." Thus resolved, the king Gavala calmly offered his body, too, into the fire. As fire began to consume the limbs of Gavala, Gādhi, who was reciting prayers immersed in the water of the river, regained his consciousness.

(At this stage, evening set in. Another day came to an end.)

VASIṢṬHA continued: V:47

Thereafter, Gādhi had become freed from the illusory vision he had. Once again he regained his consciousness that 'I am Gādhi'. He completed his religious rite and got out of the river. He continued to wonder, 'Who am I? What did I see? And how?' He concluded that because he was fatigued his mind had obviously played some tricks on him. Even as he walked away from the place, he was still contemplating the vision and enquiring into the nature of the parents, the friends and the people he had seen in that vision. He thought, "Surely, all that was illusory, for I do not perceive anything now!"

After some days, another brāhmaṇa visited him; and Gādhi duly entertained the honoured guest. During the course of their conversation, GĀDHI asked the guest: "Sir, why do you look so tired and worn-out?" the GUEST answered: "Holy one, I shall tell you the truth! There is a kingdom in the north known as Kīra. I spent a month there, being lavishly entertained by the citizens. I heard an extraordinary story from them. They said, "A tribesman ruled this kingdom for eight years. After that his identity became known. On account of him very many brāhmaṇas of this place perished." When I heard that, I too felt polluted and hence I went to the holy place known as Prayāga and engaged myself in severe austerity and prolonged fasting. I am breaking this prolonged fast only today."

The guest spent the night with Gādhi and left the following day.

GĀDHI contemplated further: "That which I saw in a hallucination, my guest saw as a factual event! Ah, I should verify the story for myself." Having thus resolved, Gādhi quickly proceeded first to the place known as Bhūtamaṇḍala. Men of highly evolved consciousness can, by appropriate self-effort, attain even what they mentally visualise: Gādhi thus saw, after reaching the destination, whatever he had seen in his vision.

There he saw a village which had been deeply impressed in his consciousness. He saw the very house of the tribesman (himself) and he saw the very objects which were used by him. The house was in a very bad shape. He saw there skeletons of animals whose flesh had been eaten by the family: for some time he saw that dreadful place which looked truly like a cemetery. From there he went to the nearby village and asked the villagers: "Do you know anything about that tribesman who lived in yonder house?"

The VILLAGERS replied: "Holy sir, of course we know. There was a dreadful-looking and fierce tribesman in that house who lived up to a ripe old age. When he had lost all his kinsmen he went away and became a king of Kīra and ruled for eight years. He was found out and as a result many people died and he too killed himself. Pray, why do you ask about him? Was he related to you or do you think you are somehow related to him?" Hearing this, Gādhi was greatly puzzled.

V:48 VASIṢṬHA continued:

Gādhi recognised several objects and places connected with his 'life' in that village—where he lay intoxicated, where he slept, where he ate, the dress he wore, etc. From there Gādhi travelled to the Kīra kingdom. He went to the capital city and there he enquired of the citizens: "Was this country ruled by a tribesman some time ago?" They replied enthusiastically, "Oh, yes: and he ruled for eight years, having been chosen by the royal elephant! When his identity was discovered, he committed suicide. It was twelve years ago."

Just then he beheld the king come out of the palace with his retinue: and the king was disguised lord Viṣṇu! Seeing all this, he wondered: this indeed is the kingdom of Kīra which I ruled not so long ago, which I see now as if it happened in a past birth! He asked himself, "It was like a dream: yet, it appears in front of me in the wakeful state! Alas, I am surely caught in the net of some sort of hallucination. I remember now that Lord Viṣṇu had granted me the boon that I would see his Māyā. Surely, this is it." He left the city at once and went to a mountain-cave nearby and there performed intense austerity.

Soon, lord Viṣṇu appeared before him and asked him to choose any boon he liked. GĀDHI asked the Lord: "The hallucination that I had as in a dream, how is it also seen in the wakeful state?"

The LORD said:

O Gādhi! That which you see now is an illusion: it is truly naught but the self, but perceived by the mind which has not been purified and which has not realised the truth. There is nothing outside the self: just as the tree is in the seed, all this is already in the mind and the mind sees it as if it is outside. It is the mind alone that perceives all this now, visualises all this as if in the future and remembers all this as if in the past. It is the mind alone that is experienced as dream, illusion, illness, etc. In the mind are countless 'events' like flowers on a tree in full bloom. And, just as an uprooted tree bears no flowers, the mind freed of percepts and concepts is freed from rebirth etc.

Is it any wonder that the mind which contains countless thought-forms should be able to manifest the idea "I am a tribesman"? Even so, the same mind manifests other ideas like "I have a brāhmaṇa-guest who told me the story, etc." and "I am going to Bhūtamaṇḍalam" and "I am in Kīra kingdom now". All this was but hallucination! Thus, O Holy one, you have seen both forms of illusion: the one which you yourself thought was illusion and the other which you think is reality—both of which are hallucination in truth. You entertained no guest, and you did not go anywhere! All this, too, was but hallucination. You have really not been to Bhūtamaṇḍalam or the Kīra kingdom—all these were also illusions. Arise, O sage, engage yourself in whatever action is appropriate here: for without such activity, one does not attain what is worthy in this life!

VASIṢṬHA continued: V:49

In order to reassure himself, Gādhi once again went over to Bhūtamaṇḍalam etc. Once again he heard the same stories from the people over there. Once again, he adored lord Viṣṇu, who once again appeared before him. GĀDHI asked the Lord: "Lord, I roamed for six months in the two realms and heard the same stories which the people there narrate as true. Pray, clear this confusion."

THE LORD said:

O Gādhi, these incidents are reflected in your mind, though they took place unrelated to you, even as there appears to be a coincidental connection between the crow alighting upon a cocoanut tree and a cocoanut falling to the ground. Hence, they narrate the same story which you believe to be yours! Such coincidence is not uncommon: sometimes the same illusion is perceived by many. Sometimes many people have the same dream: several people experience the same hallucination and many drunkards may all of them simultaneously experience that the world is revolving around them. Several children play at the same game.

Such confusion may arise in the minds of people in regard to time, too. Time is a concept of the mind. Time is related to certain phenomena in a mutual causal relationship.

(Lord Viṣṇu disappeared, and Gādhi contemplated for a long time. Once again he prayed and the Lord appeared before him. GĀDHI prayed to him: "Lord, I am utterly confused by your Māyā. Pray remove this confusion by appropriate means." And the Lord said:)

Whatever you saw in the Bhūtamaṇḍalam and Kīra were possibly true. The tribesman known as Kaṭanja was indeed born some time ago. He lost his kinsmen and became king of Kīra. All this was reflected in your consciousness. Even as the mind sometimes forgets what it actually experienced, it also thinks it has experienced what it has never seen. Just as one sees dreams and visions, one experiences hallucinations even during the wakeful state. Though Kaṭanja lived several years ago, it appeared to be in the present in your consciousness.

'This I am'—such a concept does not arise in the person who has self-knowledge but only in the mind of an ignorant person. 'I am the all'—knowing thus the knower of truth does not drown in sorrow; he does not grasp finite objects productive of sorrow. Hence, he is not swayed by joy and sorrow.

Because you are not fully enlightened your mind clings to the illusion of objective perception, of concepts. This Māyā is spread out in all directions: he who remains established in the centre is free from delusion. Get up and meditate intensely for ten years.

(Gādhi engaged himself in intense meditation thereafter and attained self-realisation. After that, he lived as a liberated sage, free from fear and sorrow.)

V:50 VASIṢṬHA continued:

This cosmic illusion (Māyā) creates great delusion and is of the nature of disequilibrium. It is extremely difficult to understand it. What comparison is there between a hallucination which lasts for the brief duration of an hour's dream, and a whole life-time as a tribesman with all the varied experiences? Again, how can we relate what is seen in that hallucination and what is seen 'in front of our eyes'? Or, what is truly unreal and what has really undergone a factual transformation? Hence, I tell you, O Rāma, this cosmic illusion leads the unwary mind into endless difficulties.

RĀMA asked: But, O Holy sir, how can one restrain this wheel of cosmic illusion which revolves with such tremendous force?

VASIṢṬHA replied:

O Rāma, the mind is the hub around which this vicious cycle revolves, creating delusion in the minds of the deluded. It is by firmly restraining that hub through intense self-effort and keen intelligence, that the whole wheel is brought to a standstill. When the hub's motion is stopped, the wheel does not revolve: when the mind is stilled, illusion ceases. One who does not know this trick and does not practise it, undergoes endless sorrow; the moment the truth is seen, behold! the sorrow comes to an end.

The disease of the perception of this world-illusion is not cured except through the mastery of the mind which is its only remedy. Hence, O Rāma, abandon all other activities like pilgrimage, gifts and austerities, and bring the mind under your control for your ultimate good. This world-appearance abides in the mind, even as there is space within the pot; if the pot is broken, the illusory division of space vanishes; and if the mind ceases to be, the concept of a world within the mind also ceases to be. Even as an insect trapped within the pot attains freedom of movement when the pot is broken, you will also enjoy freedom when the mind ceases to be, along with the world-illusion contained in it.

Live in the present, with your consciousness externalised momentarily but without any effort: when the mind stops linking itself to the past and to the future, it becomes no-mind. If from moment to moment your mind dwells on what is and drops it effortlessly at once, the mind becomes no-mind, full of purity. It is only as long as the mind continues to be agitated that it experiences the diversity of its own projection or expansion, even as rain falls only as long as there are clouds. And, it is only as long as the infinite consciousness limits itself into the finite mind, that such agitation and expansion take place. If consciousness ceases to be the finite mind, then know that the very roots of cyclic world-illusion (of birth and death) are burnt and there is perfection.

VASIṢṬHA continued:

Consciousness free from the limitations of the mind is known as the inner intelligence: it is the essential nature of no-mind, and therefore it is not tainted by the impurities of concepts and percepts. That is the reality, that is supreme auspiciousness, that is the state known as the supreme self, that is omniscience—and that vision is not had when the wicked mind functions. Where there is mind, there flourish hopes and desires, and there arise the experiences of pain and pleasure. The consciousness which has been awakened to the truth does not fall into concepts and percepts: therefore, even though it seems to undergo various psychological experiences, it does not give rise to the world-illusion and the cycle of world-appearance.

In the case of those who have been awakened through the study of scriptures, company of holy men and unceasing and vigilant practice of truth, their consciousness has reached the pure state of non-objectiveness. Hence, one should forcefully uplift one's mind from the state of ignorance and vacillation and apply it to the study of scriptures and to the company of holy sages.

The self alone is the sole aid for the realisation of the supreme self or the infinite consciousness. It is one's own self that strives to abandon one's own sorrow; and for this the realisation of one's own self by oneself is the only course.

Hence, O Rāma, while yet remaining active in this world (talking, taking and leaving, etc.) be without the mind and realise that you are pure consciousness. Abandon notions such as 'This is mine', 'That is he', 'This I am' and be established in the consciousness of undivided oneness. As long as the body lasts, consider the present and the future with an equanimous consciousness. Be for ever established in the consciousness of the self in all states—youth, manhood and old age, pleasure and pain, in the waking, dream and sleep states. Abandon the impurity of objective perception, hopes and desires: remain established in self-knowledge. Give up notions of auspicious and inauspicious happenings, give up visions of the desirable and undesirable: know that you are the essence of consciousness. Realise that subject, object and actions do not touch you: remain as pure consciousness without any disturbance in it. Know 'I am the all' and live in the waking state as if in deep sleep. Be freed from conditions known as duality and non-duality: and remain in a state of equilibrium which is a state of pure consciousness and freedom. Realise that this cosmic consciousness is indivisible into 'I' and 'the other'; thus remain firm and unshakable.

VASIṢṬHA continued:

Cut off all the fetters of desire and hope solely with the intelligence that is unlimited and which is endowed with patience and perseverance, and go beyond dharma and adharma. When one is firmly rooted in self-knowledge, even the worst of poisons turns into immortalising nectar. It is only when this self-knowledge is overpowered by ignorance that the delusion of world-appearance arises in the mind; but when one is firmly established in self-knowledge—which is infinite, unlimited and unconditioned—then the delusion or ignorance that gave rise to world-appearance comes to an end. Then, the light of your wisdom will radiate in the four directions, throughout the world.

To one who thus drinks the nectar of immortality in the shape of self-knowledge, the delights of sense-pleasures become painful. We resort to the company of only those who have attained self-knowledge; the others are donkeys in human garb. Even as elephants move with long strides, the sages who have reached the higher states of consciousness rise to the highest states of consciousness. They have no external help at all and no sun illumines their path: self-knowledge alone is their light. In fact, the sun and the worlds become non-objects of perception to them who have gone beyond the realm of objective perception and knowledge, even as lamps lose their luminosity while the midday sun shines.

The sage of self-knowledge (the knower of truth) is supreme amongst those who are radiant, glorious, strong, great and endowed with other characteristics which are considered marks of excellence. These sages shine in this world like the sun, the fire, the moon, and the stars all put together. On the other hand, they who have not attained self-knowledge are worse than worms and insects.

The ghost of delusion afflicts one only as long as self-knowledge does not arise in him. The ignorant man is for ever sorrowful, though he roams everywhere to get rid of it. He is truly a walking corpse. Only the sage of self-knowledge is a living sentient being. Even as when dense clouds form in the sky the sun's light is veiled, when the mind becomes gross with impurities and ignorance, the light of self-knowledge is veiled. Therefore, one should abandon craving for pleasures (those that have been experienced in the past and others that have not yet been experienced but for which one craves) and thus gradually weaken the mind by the abandonment of a taste for them. By the cultivation of a false relationship with what is not self, (the body and those related to it such as wife, son, family, etc.) the mind becomes gross. The notions of 'I' and 'mine' make the mind dense and ignorant. This is further aggravated by old age, sorrow, ambitions, psychological distress, efforts to acquire and to abandon, attachments, greed, lust for wealth and sex and by the enjoyment of sense-pleasures, all of which are based on ignorance and delusion.

VASIṢṬHA continued:

O Rāma, this mind is like a tree which is firmly rooted in the vicious field known as the body. Worries and anxieties are its blossoms; it is laden with the fruits of old age and disease; it is adorned with the flowers of desires and sense-enjoyments; hopes and longings are its branches; and perversities are its leaves. Cut down this deadly poisonous tree, which looks as unshakable as the mountain, with the sharp axe known as enquiry.

O Rāma, this mind is like an elephant which roams the forest known as the body. Its vision is clouded by delusion; it has entered into the one (conditioned and ignorant) side; it is incapable of resting in its own self-bliss; it is violent; though it wishes to perceive the truth which it hears from wise men, it is caught up in the perception of diversity and it is conditioned by its own concepts of pleasure and pain; it is endowed with the fierce tusks of lust, etc. O Rāma, you are a lion among princes! Tear this elephant to pieces by your sharp intelligence.

O Rāma, this mind is like a crow which dwells in the nest of this body. It revels in filth; it waxes strong by consuming flesh; it pierces the hearts of others; it knows only its own point of view which it considers as the truth; it is dark on account of its ever-growing stupidity; it is full of evil tendencies; and it indulges in violent expressions. It is a burden on earth, O Rāma: drive it far, far away from yourself.

O Rāma, this mind is like a ghost. It is served by the female goblin known as craving; it rests in the forest of ignorance; it roams in countless bodies out of delusion. How can one attain self-knowledge if one does not lay this ghost with the help of wisdom and dispassion, the grace of the guru, self-effort, chanting of mantras, etc.?

O Rāma, this mind is like a venomous serpent which has killed countless beings; destroy this with the help of the eagle of the appropriate contemplative formula or instruction.

O Rāma, this mind is like a monkey. It roams from one place to another, seeking fruits (rewards, pleasures, etc.); bound to this world-cycle it dances and entertains people. Restrain it from all sides if you wish to attain perfection.

O Rāma, this mind is like a cloud of ignorance: dispel it by the repeated renunciation of all concepts and percepts.

Even as a terrible weapon is encountered and destroyed by a more powerful weapon, tranquilise the mind with the help of the mind itself. For ever abandon every form of mental agitation. Remain at peace within yourself like a tree freed from the disturbance caused by monkeys.

The Story of Uddālaka

V:51 VASIṢṬHA continued:

O Rāma, do not take your stand on concepts and percepts of the mind, which are subtle and sharp; the mind has been put together by time and it has gained great strength in course of time. Bring it under control by wisdom, before time fells this creeper known as the body. By devoutly contemplating my words you will attain supreme bliss.

I shall narrate to you, O Rāma, how the sage Uddālaka of yore attained the supreme vision of truth.

In a corner of the earth, there is a great mountain known as Gandhamādana. On one of its peaks there was a great tree. In that region there lived the sage Uddālaka. Even while he was a young boy he aspired to attain supreme wisdom through his own effort. Of course, then he was of little understanding and he had a restless mind, though he had a pure heart. He engaged himself in austerities, in the study of scriptures and so on, and there arose wisdom in him.

While sitting alone one day, the SAGE UDDĀLAKA reflected thus:

What is liberation, which is said to be the foremost among the objects to be attained, upon attaining which one does not experience sorrow and is not born again? When shall I rest permanently in that state? When will the mental agitations caused by desires and cravings cease? When will I be freed from thoughts like 'This I have done' and 'This I should do'? When will my mind cease to undergo perversities though living in relationship here, even as the lotus though lying on water is not tainted by it? When will I, with the help of the boat of supreme wisdom, cross to the other shore of liberation? When will I be able to look upon the diverse activities of people with the playfulness of a child? When will the mind attain utter quiescence? When will the illusory division between the subjective and the objective experiences cease through the experience of the infinite consciousness? When will I be able to behold this concept, known as time, without being involved in it? When will I, living in a cave with a mind in utter tranquility, remain like a rock in a state in which there is no movement of thought at all?

Thus reflecting, Uddālaka continued his practice of meditation. But his mind continued to be agitated. Some days, however, his mind abandoned external objects and remained in a state of purity. At other times it was greatly disturbed. Greatly distressed by such changing moods, he roamed the forest. One day he reached a lonely spot in the forest which had not been visited by anyone else. There he saw a cave which appeared to be most conducive to the attainment of the state of utter tranquility and peace. It was delightful in every way with beautiful creepers and flowers around it, with a moderate climate, and it shone as if it had been carved out of an emerald.

VASIṢṬHA continued: V:52

Uddālaka entered that delightful cave and sat in a meditative posture. Intent on attaining the state of mind without the least movement of thought, he concentrated his attention on the latent tendencies in the mind, and

UDDĀLAKA reflected thus within himself:

O mind, what have you to do with this world-appearance? Wise men do not come into contact with what is called pleasure which turns into pain later on. He who abandons the supreme peace that lies within and goes in search of sense-pleasure, abandons a delightful garden and goes into a field of poison-herbs. You may go where you like; you will never taste supreme peace except through perfect quiescence. Hence, abandon all hopes and desires. For, all these seemingly wondrous objects of the nature either of being or of non-being, are not meant for your happiness.

Do not perish like the deer which is trapped by the sound of music and bells, nor like the male elephant which is trapped with the help of the female elephant, nor like the fish whose sense of taste leads it to its death in the hook, nor like the moth which is attracted by the sight of a flame and perishes in it, nor like the bee whose sense of smell leads it to the flower, trapped in which it is destroyed when the flower folds up for the night.

O foolish mind, all these perish being subjected to just one sense-craving (the deer by the sense of hearing, the bee by the sense of smell, the moth by the sense of sight, the elephant by the sense of touch, and the fish by the sense of taste): but you are a victim to all the five temptations; how can you have happiness? Just as the silk-worm spins its cocoon and gets caught in it, you have woven the web of your own concepts and are caught in it. If you can get rid of all that, attain purity, overcome even the fear of life and death and thus attain to total equanimity, you have achieved the greatest victory. On the other hand, if you cling to this ever-changing phenomenon called the world, you will surely perish in sorrow.

Why do I instruct you thus, O mind: for, if one investigates the truth he discovers that there is no such thing called mind! Mind is but a product of ignorance; when ignorance wears out, then the mind wears out, too. Hence, you are in the process of being worn out. It is unwise and foolish to instruct one who is in the process of disintegrating! Since, day by day you are becoming weaker and weaker, I renounce you; wise men do not teach one who is to be abandoned.

O mind, I am the egoless infinite and homogeneous consciousness; I have nothing to do with you who are the cause of the ego.

UDDĀLAKA continued to contemplate thus:

The infinite self cannot possibly be squeezed into the mind, any more than an elephant can be squeezed into a wood-apple fruit.

The consciousness that, through the process of self-limitation, is confined to finitude (and therefore to concepts and percepts) is known as the mind: this is the result of ignorance and hence I do not accept this. The ego-sense is only a child's concept and it is believed in by one who does not investigate the truth.

I have carefully investigated, I have observed everything from the tips of my toes to the top of my head: and I have not found anything of which I could say, 'This I am'. Who is 'I'? I am the all-pervading consciousness which is itself not an object of knowledge or knowing and is free from selfhood. I am that which is indivisible, which has no name or change, which is beyond all concepts of unity and diversity, which is beyond measure (small and big) and other than which naught else is. Hence, O mind, I abandon you who are the source of sorrow.

In this body in which there is flesh, blood, bone, etc., who says 'This I am'? Motion is the nature of energy, thinking is inherent in consciousness, old age and death are natural to the body—who says 'This I am'? This is the tongue, these are ears, this is nose, this is motion and these are eyes—who says 'This I am'? I am none of these, nor am I you, O mind, nor these concepts: I am but the infinite consciousness, pure and independent. 'I am all this' or 'There is no I'—both are expressions of the same truth; naught else is truth.

Alas, for so long I have been victimised by ignorance: but, luckily, I have discovered that which robbed me of self-knowledge! I shall never more be the victim of ignorance. Even as the cloud sitting on top of a hill does not belong to the hill, though I seem to be associated with sorrow I am independent of it. In the absence of self-knowledge, there arose ego-sense: but now, I am free of ego-sense. Let the body, the senses and so on be, or perish—I have nothing to do with them. The senses (the eyes, etc.) exist in order to come into contact with their own objects for their own sake: who is the I that is deluded into thinking 'This is I', or 'I see', etc.? These eyes, etc. see or experience, their objects naturally, without being impelled to do so by previous conditioning. Hence, if actions are performed spontaneously without mental conditioning, their experience will be pure and free from memories of past happiness or unhappiness. Hence, O senses, perform your functions without being hampered by memory. This memory or mental conditioning is not a fact, in truth: it is non-different from and not independent of the infinite consciousness. It can therefore be easily dispelled, merely by not reviving it in consciousness. Hence, O mind, abandon this perception of diversity and realise the unreality of your own independence from the infinite consciousness: that is liberation.

V:53 UDDĀLAKA continued to reflect thus:

In reality, consciousness cannot be conditioned: it is unlimited and is subtler than the subtlest atom, hence beyond the influence of mental conditioning. The mind rests in the ego-sense and the reflected consciousness in the senses; and from this there arises the illusion of self-limitation of consciousness. When this is experienced and thought of again and again, the ego-sense and the illusion of self-limitation acquire a false validity. But, I am consciousness which is untouched by any of these.

Let the body continue to live in a world brought into being by its ignorant activities, or let it abandon it: I am consciousness unaffected by any of these. Consciousness, being infinite and all-pervading, has no birth, no death, nor is it possessed by anyone. It has nothing to gain by 'living' as a separate entity, since it is all-pervading. Birth and death are mental concepts: they have nothing to do with the self. Only that which entertains notions of the ego-sense can be grasped and bound: the self is free from the ego-sense and is therefore beyond being and non-being.

The ego-sense is vain delusion, the mind is like a mirage and the objects of the world are inert substances: who is it that says 'I am'? The body is an aggregate of flesh, blood, etc., the mind vanishes on enquiry into its nature, self-limitation of consciousness and such other concepts are insentient (non-sense)—what is the ego? The senses exist and are engaged in self-satisfying activity all the time; the substances of the world are the substances of the world—where is the ego? Nature is nature and its qualities interact on one another (like the sight and light, hearing and sound, etc.); and what is rests in itself—where is the ego?

The self, which is consciousness, exists as the supreme self of all, everywhere in all bodies at all times. Who am I, what am I made of, what is my form, made by whom: and what shall I acquire and what shall I reject? There is thus nothing which can be called 'I' and which undergoes being and non-being: when there is no ego-sense in truth, how can that ego-sense be related, and to whom? When thus it is realised that there is no relationship at all, then the false notion of duality vanishes. Thus, whatever there is is the one cosmic being (Brahman or the self); I am that reality, why do I suffer in delusion? When one alone exists as the pure omnipresent being, how can there even arise something known as the ego-sense? There is no substantiality in any substance in truth, the self alone exists: or, even if one assumes the substantiality to be real, there is no relationship between that and the self. The senses function as senses, the mind exists as mind, the consciousness is untouched by these—what is relationship and how does it come into being? Just because they exist side by side, it is not right to assume a relationship: a stone and an iron rod may lie side by side, totally unrelated to each other.

UDDĀLAKA continued to reflect:

It is only when this false ego-sense has arisen that the perverse notions 'This is mine' and 'That is his' arise. And, when it is seen that all these are tricks of the false ego-sense, these unreal notions cease to be. There is in truth naught else but the self; hence I realise that all this is the one cosmic being or Brahman. The delusion known as ego-sense is like the blueness of the sky: it is better not to entertain that notion once again, but to abandon it. After having abandoned the very root of the ego-sense, I rest in the self which is of the nature of peace.

The ego-sense is the source of endless sorrow, suffering and evil action. Life ends in death and death leads to birth and what is is disrupted by its own end—such notions entertained by the ego-sense lead to great sorrow. The anxiety caused by thoughts like 'I have got this now', 'I shall get that too' burns the ignorant. 'This is' and 'That is not'—such notions cause restlessness in the egotist. But if the ego-sense ceases to be then the illusory world-appearance does not germinate again and all cravings come to an end.

This universe has surely come into being without any valid cause for its creation: how can one accept the truth of a creation which had no cause or purpose? From time immemorial, all these bodies have been inherent in the cosmic being, even as pots are for ever inherent in clay. Even as ocean exists in the past, present and future as ocean and the same water temporarily assumes the form of a wave, all this is for ever the cosmic being at all times. It is only a fool that entertains a feeling 'This I am' in relation to that temporary appearance known as the body, etc.

In the same way, the mind was consciousness in the beginning and it will be consciousness again in the end (after its nature and function as mind have ceased), why is it then called differently in the middle (now)?

All these phenomena seem to have a transient reality, like dream-experiences, visions in a state of delirium, hallucinations of a drunkard, optical illusions, psychosomatic illness, emotional disturbances and psychotic states. But, O mind, you have conferred a permanent reality upon them, even as a lover suffers from the very imagination of his beloved's separation. But, of course, this is not your fault; it is my fault that I still cling to the notion that you, my mind, is a real entity. When I realise that all these phenomena are illusory appearances, then you will become no-mind and all the memories of sense-experiences, etc., will come to an end. When consciousness realises itself and abandons its self-limiting mental conditioning, the mind is freed from its colouring and rests in its essential nature, which is consciousness. When the mind, gathering to itself all its limbs, offers itself into the fire of pure consciousness, it is purified and attains immortality.

UDDĀLAKA continued to contemplate:

When the mind perceives the body as distinct from it, abandons its own conditioning (the concepts) and recognises its own transient nature, it is victorious. Mind and body are each other's foes: hence supreme happiness follows their destruction. For, when they come together there is a host of suffering on account of their mutual conflict.

The mind gives birth to the body through its own thought-force: and throughout the body's life-time the mind feeds it with its (the mind's own) sorrow. Thus tortured by sorrow the body wishes to destroy the mind, its own parent! There is no friend nor enemy in this world: that which gives us pleasure is considered our friend and that which causes pain is our enemy!

When thus the mind and the body are constantly engaged in mutual destruction, how can one have happiness? It is by the destruction of the mind that there can be happiness; hence the body tries every day (in deep sleep) to destroy the mind. However, until self-knowledge is attained, one unwittingly promotes the strength of the other and they seem to function together for a common purpose—even as water and fire, though opposed to each other, work together for a common cause (e.g., cooking).

If the mind ceases to be, then the body ceases to be, too, on account of the cessation of thought-force and mental conditioning: but the mind does not cease to be when the body dies. Hence, one should strive to kill the mind. Mind is like a forest with thought-forms for its trees and cravings for its creepers: by destroying these, I attain bliss. When the mind is dead, whether the body (composed of flesh, blood, etc.,) exists or not does not matter to me. That I am not the body is obvious: for the corpse does not function!

Where there is self-knowledge, there is neither mind nor the senses, nor the tendencies and habits (the concepts and percepts). I have attained that supreme state. I have emerged victorious. I have attained liberation (nirvāṇa). I have risen above all relationships with the mind, body and the senses, even as the oil pressed out of the seeds has no relation with the seeds. To me now the mind, body and the senses are playthings. Purity, total fulfilment of all desires (hence, their absence), friendliness to all, truthfulness, wisdom, tranquility and blissfulness, sweetness of speech, supreme magnanimity, lustrousness, one-pointedness, realisation of cosmic unity, fearlessness, absence of divided-consciousness, non-perversity—these are my constant companions. Since at all times everything everywhere happens in every manner, in me there is no desire or aversion towards anything, whether pleasant or unpleasant. Since all delusion has come to an end, since the mind has ceased to be and all evil thoughts have vanished, I rest peacefully in my own self.

VASIṢṬHA continued: V:54

The sage Uddālaka then sat down in the lotus posture, with his eyes half-closed, in meditation. He uttered the holy word OM which bestows the highest state. He intoned OM in such a way that its vibrations filled his whole being right up to the crown of his head. As the first part of his practice, he exhaled his breath completely. It was as if his life-force had abandoned the body and was roaming in the space (dimension) of pure consciousness. The fire that arose from his heart burnt the whole of his body. (All this, Uddālaka practised without the violence involved in Haṭha Yoga: for Haṭha Yoga gives rise to pain.)

With the second utterance of the holy word OM, he reached the state of equilibrium and there happened in him a spontaneous retention of the breath (life-force) without agitation or vibration. The life-force stood still, as it were, neither outside, nor inside, neither below nor above. After reducing the body to ashes, the fire burnt itself out and vanished; only the pure ashes were visible. It was as if the very bones had turned into camphor which was being burnt in adoration. The ashes were blown by a powerful wind and dispersed in space. (All this happened without the violence of Haṭha Yoga: for Haṭha Yoga gives rise to pain.)

In the third stage, when the holy word OM reached its culmination or tranquility, there arose the inhalation of breath (the drawing in of the life-force). During this stage the life-forces, which were in the very centre of the nectar of consciousness, spread out in space as a cool breeze. These forces reached the region of the moon. There they spread out as auspicious rays which thereupon rained on the ashes that remained of the body.

Instantly, there arose from the ashes a radiant being with four arms like lord Viṣṇu. Uddālaka shone like a divinity, his whole being transmuted into a divinity. The life-force filled the inner kuṇḍalinī which was spread out like a spiral. Uddālaka's body had thus been completely purified. Then he, who was already seated in the lotus posture, made the posture firm, 'tied up' his senses and proceeded to make his consciousness absolutely free from the least movement of thought. With all his strength he restrained his mind from distraction. His half-closed eyes were still and motionless. With his mind established in inner silence, he equalised the movement of the twin life-forces, prāṇa and apāna. He withdrew his inner senses from contact with their objects, even as oil is separated from the seed. Thereupon he became directly aware of the mental conditioning created by past experiences, and unconditioned the awareness and made it pure. Then, he firmly closed his rectum and the other outlets to the body (the eyes, etc.). With his life-force and awareness thus prevented from externalisation by perfect discipline, he held his mind in his heart.

VASIṢṬHA continued:

Uddālaka's mind had attained absolute tranquility and no distraction could afflict it. Directly he beheld in his heart the darkness of ignorance that veiled the light of self-knowledge. With the light of knowledge that arose in him, he dispelled even that darkness. He then beheld the light within. However, when that light dimmed, the sage experienced sleep. But, the sage dispelled the dullness of sleep, too. Once the drowsiness of sleep had been dispelled, the mind of the sage threw up diverse brilliant forms. The sage cleared his consciousness of these visions. Then he was overcome by a great inertia, like one intoxicated. He got over that inertia, too. After this, his mind rested in another state which was different from all these so far described. After resting for a while in this state, however, his mind awoke to the experience of the totality of existence. Immediately after this, he experienced pure awareness. This awareness, which till then had been associated with other factors, had now regained its purity and independence: even as when the muddy water in an earthen pot has completely evaporated, the mud becomes an integral part of the pot made of the same substance. Even as the wave merges in the ocean and becomes one and non-different from it, the consciousness abandoned its objectivity and regained its absolute purity. Uddālaka was enlightened. He enjoyed the supreme bliss that gods like Brahmā enjoy. His state was beyond description. He was one with the ocean of bliss.

Soon, Uddālaka beheld great sages in that infinite consciousness. He ignored them. He continued with the experience of supreme bliss. He attained the state of 'one liberated while living'. He beheld the gods and the sages, and he even beheld the members of the trinity. He went beyond even that state. He was completely transmuted into bliss itself and hence he had gone beyond the realm of bliss. He experienced neither bliss nor non-bliss. He became pure consciousness. He who experiences this even for a moment is disinterested even in the delights of heaven. This is the supreme state, this is the goal, this is the eternal abode. He who rests in this is not again deluded and is no longer caught in the subject-object relationship. He is fully awakened and never again entertains the notion of objectivity or conceptualisation. Of course this is not an 'attainment'.

Uddālaka remained for six months in this state, vigilantly avoiding the temptation of psychic powers. Even sages and gods adored him. He was invited to ascend to heaven: he declined the invitation. Totally freed from all desires, Uddālaka roamed as a sage liberated while living. Often he would spend days and months in meditation in the caves of mountains. Though at other times he engaged himself in the ordinary activities of living, he had reached the state of perfect equilibrium. He looked upon all with equal vision. His inner light shone at all times, never rising and never setting. With all notions of duality totally at rest, he lived devoid of body-consciousness, established in pure being.

In answer to Rāma's question concerning pure being, VASIṢṬHA V:55
said:

When the mind has ceased to be because of the total absence of the notions of material existence, consciousness exists in its own nature as consciousness: and that is known as pure being. When consciousness devoid of notions of objectivity merges in itself losing its separate identity, as it were, it is pure being. When all external (material) and internal (notional) objects merge in consciousness, there is pure being of consciousness. This is the supreme vision which happens to all liberated ones, whether they seem to have a body or they are without one. This vision is available to one who has been 'awakened', to one who is in a state of deep contemplation and to a man of self-knowledge; it is not experienced by the ignorant person. Sages and the members of the trinity are established in this consciousness, O Rāma. Having reached this state of consciousness, Uddālaka lived for some time.

In course of time, in his mind there arose the wish, "Let me drop this embodiment". He went to a mountain-cave and seated himself in the lotus posture, with his eyes half-closed. He closed off the nine apertures of the body, by pressing his heel against the rectum, etc. He withdrew the senses into his heart. He restrained his life-force (prāṇa). He held his body in a state of perfect equilibrium. He pressed the tip of his tongue against the root of his palate, his jaws were slightly parted from each other. His inner vision was directed neither inward nor outward, neither above nor below, neither in substantiality nor void. He was established in pure consciousness and he experienced pure bliss within himself. He had reached the consciousness of pure being, beyond the state of bliss. His whole being had become absolutely pure.

Uddālaka remained in this totally pure state for some time, like a painted picture. Gradually, day by day, he attained perfect quiescence; he remained in his own pure being. He had risen above the cycle of birth and death. All his doubts were set at rest; perverse thoughts had ceased; all impurities of the heart had been washed away; he had attained that state of bliss which is beyond description, in which one regards even the joy of the king of heaven as worthless. Thus, his body remained for a period of six months.

After that, one day several goddesses led by Pārvati arrived at that spot in response to the prayers of a devotee. That goddess, worshipped by the gods themselves, saw the body of Uddālaka which had been dried by the scorching rays of the sun and quickly placed it on the crown of her head.

Such is the glorious story of the sage Uddālaka, O Rāma, which awakens the highest wisdom in the heart of one who takes shelter in its shade.

V:56 VASIṢṬHA continued:

O Rāma, living like this, constantly enquiring into the nature of the self, attain peace. This state of consciousness can be attained by the cultivation of dispassion, the study of scriptures, the instructions of a guru and by the persistent practice of enquiry. But, if the awakened intelligence is keen and sharp, you will attain it even without the other aids.

RĀMA asked: Holy sir, some there are who rest in self-knowledge, who are enlightened and yet engage themselves in activities; and there are others who isolate themselves and practise contemplation (samādhi). Of these who is the better?

VASIṢṬHA replied:

Rāma, that is samādhi (contemplation or meditation) in which one realises the objects of the senses as not-self, and thus one enjoys inner calmness and tranquility at all times. Having realised that the objects are related only to the mind and therefore constantly resting in inner peace, some are engaged in activity while others live in isolation. Both of them enjoy the bliss of contemplation. If the mind of one who appears to be in samādhi is distracted, he is a mad man: on the other hand, if the mind of one who appears to be a mad man is free from all notions and distraction, he is enlightened and he is in unbroken samādhi. Whether he is engaged in activity or he lives in isolation in a forest, in enlightenment there is no distinction. The mind which is free from conditioning is not tainted even while it is engaged in activity. The non-action of the mind is known as quiescence (samādhāna); it is total freedom, it is blessedness.

The difference between contemplation and its absence is indicated by whether or not there is movement of thought in the mind: hence make the mind unconditioned. The unconditioned mind is firm, and that in itself is meditation, freedom and peace eternal. The conditioned mind is the source of sorrow; and the unconditioned mind is a non-actor and attains to the supreme state of enlightenment. Hence one should work to remove all mental conditioning. That is known as contemplation or samādhi in which all the desires and hopes concerning the world have ceased and which is free from sorrow, fear and desire, and by which the self rests in itself.

Mentally renounce all false identification of the self with objects here: and then live where you like, either at home or in a mountain-cave. To that householder whose mind has attained utter quiescence his house itself is the forest. If the mind is at peace and if there is no ego-sense, even cities are as void. On the other hand, forests are like cities to him whose heart is full of desires and other evils. The distractions of the mind subside in deep sleep; enlightenment attains enlightenment—do as you please.

VASIṢṬHA continued:

He who sees the self as the transcendent being or as the immanent being (as the self of all) is established in equanimity. He in whom likes and dislikes have ceased, to whom all beings are the same and who perceives the world in the wakeful state as if he perceives objects in a dream, he is established in equanimity and lives in a forest even while living in a village. He who moves about with his consciousness turned in upon itself views a city or a village as a forest.

He who has attained inner tranquility and peace finds peace and tranquility everywhere in the world. He whose mind is agitated and restless finds the world full of restlessness. For, what one experiences within, that alone he experiences outside. In fact, the sky, the earth, the air and the space, the mountains and the rivers are all parts of the inner instrument (mind); they only appear to be outside. All these exist like the tree in the seed and they are externalised like the scent of a flower. Truly, there is nothing either inside or outside: whatever the consciousness conceives of, in whatever manner, appears so. Thus the self alone is all this, within and without.

He who is filled with inner delight, who is not swayed by exultation or sorrow and who performs actions merely with his physical body, he is established in equanimity. He is pure as the sky, he is free from desires, his actions are appropriate and spontaneous; and in relation to exultation and sorrow he behaves as if he is made of wood or clay. He is at peace, he sees all as his own self, he considers others' possessions as dirt—naturally and not through fear: he alone sees the truth.

The ignorant man does not realise the unreality of the objects (big or small), because he has not realised the reality.

He who has attained the state of pure being is never sullied, whether he lives or dies, at home or elsewhere, in luxury or mendicancy, whether he enjoys and dances, or he renounces everything and isolates himself on a mountain, whether he wears expensive creams and scents or he wears matted locks or falls into the fire, whether he commits sins or performs virtuous deeds, whether he dies or lives till the end of the world-cycle. For he does nothing. It is only the conditioned mind that is tainted, because of its ego-sense and the notions attached to it. When all notions have ceased and wisdom has arisen, the impurities of the mind are removed, naturally.

The enlightened sage stands to gain nothing by either doing anything or by not doing anything. Even as a tree does not spring from a stone, desires do not appear in the life of a sage. Should they arise at times, they instantly vanish like writings on water. The sage and the entire universe are non-different from each other.

V:57 VASIṢṬHA continued:

O Rāma, the infinite consciousness becomes aware of the pungency of the chili: and this gives rise to the ego-sense, with all its differentiation in time and space. The infinite consciousness becomes aware of the savour in salt; and that gives rise to the ego-sense with all the differentiation which seems to exist in time and space. The infinite consciousness becomes aware of the sweetness in sugarcane; and thereby arises the awareness of its particular characteristic. Similarly, the infinite consciousness, being the indwelling omnipresence, becomes aware of the nature of a rock, a mountain, a tree, of water, of space and thus self-consciousness or individuality arises.

Thus the natural combination of atomic particles and molecules (which is indwelt by consciousness) apparently acts as a dividing wall, thus giving rise to the divisions of 'I', 'you' etc., and these then appear to be outside of consciousness as its object. In fact, all these are but reflections in the consciousness which, becoming aware of them within itself, bestows upon them their apparent individuality. Consciousness tastes itself, the awareness being non-different from consciousness: and that appears to give rise to the ego-sense, etc., naught else. The crystal of this infinite consciousness reflects its own light of consciousness which is present in all these combinations of atomic particles: and they then gain an apparent self-consciousness and think 'I am', etc.

In reality, because the inner awareness in all these combinations is non-different from the infinite consciousness, there is no subject-object relationship between them: hence one does not experience the other, gain the other, or change or modify the other. O Rāma, all that I have said above is but a play of words to help your comprehension: there is no such thing as 'I' or 'the world' (the combination of atomic particles, etc.). There is neither mind nor an object of knowledge nor the world-illusion. Just as water acquires the appearance of a whirlpool with a personality of its own, consciousness seems to give the appearance of 'I' etc., within itself. But consciousness is consciousness only, whether it thinks of itself as lord Śiva or as a little jīva!

All this diversity of 'I', 'you' etc., and of the material substances, arises for the satisfaction of the ignorant: whatever the ignorant person imagines in the infinite consciousness that alone he sees. In the light of awareness, life is seen as consciousness; when it is regarded as life, life appears to be no more than life! There is in reality no essential distinction between life and consciousness. In the same way, there is no real and essential distinction between the individual (jīva) and the cosmic being (Śiva). Know all this to be undivided and indivisible infinite consciousness.

The Story of Suraghu

VASIṢṬHA continued: V:58

In this connection, O Rāma, pray listen to an interesting legend.

In the Himālaya mountain-range there is a mountain known as Kailāsa. At the foot of that mountain there lived a hill-tribe known as Hemajaṭa (yellow-haired). Suraghu was their king. He was strong, powerful and wise; he was endowed with self-knowledge and he was highly accomplished in poesy and literary art. Fatigue was unknown to him. He was just in his rule, blessing and punishing those who deserved to be thus blessed and punished. In all this activity, however, his spiritual vision became obscured.

Suraghu began to reflect within himself: "People undergo a lot of suffering on my account. Their suffering is truly my suffering. I should bestow riches upon them: they will rejoice, even as I would rejoice if I became wealthy. Their joy is my joy. Alas, by alternately blessing and punishing the people, I am myself alternately enjoying and suffering." Thinking thus, the king was greatly distressed.

One day, the sage Māṇḍavya came to visit the king. Suraghu

welcomed the sage, bowed to him, worshipped him and asked: "Lord, I am tormented by the anxieties that the blessing and the punishment that I inflict upon my subjects will return to me. Please help me gain equal vision and save me from prejudice and partiality."

MĀṆḌAVYA said:

All mental weaknesses come to an end by self-effort based on the wisdom which arises in one who is firmly rooted in self-knowledge. The distress of the mind is got rid of by enquiry into the nature of the self. One should enquire in one's own mind, "What are these moods and modes and feelings that arise within me?" By such enquiry, your mind expands. When you realise your true nature by such enquiry, you are not disturbed by exultation and depression. The mind abandons the past and the future, and thus its fragmented functioning. Then you experience supreme peace. When you are in that state of tranquility, you take pity on all those who revel in great wealth and secular power. When you have gained self-knowledge and when your consciousness has infinitely expanded, your mind no longer falls into the cesspool of this world, even as an elephant does not enter a puddle. It is only the little mind that seeks little pleasure and power.

The mind abandons everything when the vision of the supreme is gained. Hence, one should resolutely renounce everything till the supreme vision is gained. Not till one renounces everything is self-knowledge gained: when all points of view are abandoned, what remains is the self. This is true even of life in this world: one does not get what one desires unless the obstacle to it is removed. It is even more so in self-knowledge.

V:59 When the sage Māṇḍavya had departed after saying this, SURAGHU contemplated thus:

What is it that is known as 'I'? I am not the Meru, the Meru is not mine. I am not the hill-tribe, nor the hill-tribe mine. This is merely called my kingdom: I abandon that notion. Now, the capital city is left. I am not this city nor is it mine. That notion, too, is abandoned. Even so I abandon the notions of family relationship—wife, sons, etc.

Let me enquire into this body. I am not the inert substances like flesh and bones—nor am I the blood, nor the organs of action. All these are inert substances, but I am sentient. I am not the enjoyments, nor do they belong to me; this intellect and the sense-organs are not me, nor are they mine—they are inert and I am sentient. I am not the mind which is the root-cause of this ignorant cycle of birth and death. I am not the faculty of discrimination nor am I the ego-sense, these being notions that arise in the mind.

Now, what is left? What remains is the sentient jīva. But, it is involved in subject-object relationship. That which is the object of knowledge or comprehension is not the self. Thus do I abandon that which is knowable—or the object. What now remains is the pure consciousness which is free from the shadow of doubt. I am the infinite self, for there is no limit to this self. Even the gods like Brahmā the creator, Indra the king of gods, Yama the god of death, Vāyu the god of wind and all the countless beings are strung on this infinite consciousness.

This cit-śakti (omnipotent consciousness) is free from the defect of objectivity. It is beyond being and non-being, though it is the reality in all being. It pervades all beings in the universe. It is the beauty in all, it is the light of all. It is the essence of all forms and all modifications: yet it is beyond all these. At all times it is all in all. It is itself spread out as these fourteen planes of existence: even the notion concerning this universe is nothing but this omnipotent consciousness.

False are the fragmented notions of pain and pleasure, for this omnipotent consciousness is omnipresent and infinite. That is the self, when I am awakened; when I am deluded that itself becomes the king. It is by its grace that the body, the mind, etc. function. It is by its power that everything in the whole universe dances to its tunes. How foolish of me to have experienced distress at having to bless and punish! I have been awakened, I have seen all that there is to be seen, I have attained all that is worth attainment. What are all these: pain and pleasure, happiness and sorrow, blessing and punishment? All this is pervaded by Brahman. Where is the justification for grief and delusion; who does what? It is but the infinite consciousness that exists. Salutations to you, O beautiful god, salutations to the infinite self!

VASIṢṬHA continued: V:60, 61

By such enquiry, Suraghu attained to the supreme state of consciousness. Never again did he grieve; but from that time onwards he performed his work ever remaining in a balanced state of mind. Compassionate, yet not uncontemptuous; not avoiding the pairs of opposites and not jealous; neither intelligent nor non-intelligent; neither motivated nor non-motivated—he lived with equal vision and inner calmness. He had realised that 'All this is but the diverse manifestation of consciousness': he was therefore peaceful in both pain and pleasure, having attained to the fullness of understanding.

Thus he ruled in this world for a considerable time, and then of his own accord discarded his body. He attained oneness with the infinite consciousness. O Rāma, live and rule the world thus with an enlightened mind.

RĀMA asked: But, O Lord, the mind is so unsteady. How can one reach the state of perfect equanimity?

VASIṢṬHA continued:

O Rāma, a dialogue which is relevant to this problem took place between that very king Suraghu and the sage Parigha. Listen to it.

There was a king in Persia named Parigha who was a close friend of the king Suraghu. Once, there was a great famine in the kingdom of Parigha. Sorely distressed at heart at the very sight of his people's suffering and seeing that all his attempts at bringing relief to them proved fruitless, Parigha went away to the forest, unbeknownst to his people, to perform austerities. He lived on dried leaves and earned the name Parṇāda. After a thousand years of penance and contemplation, he attained self-knowledge. Thereafter he roamed the three worlds freely.

One day, he met the king Suraghu whom he had known before. The two enlightened kings duly worshipped each other. After that, PARIGHA asked Suraghu: "Even as you attained self-knowledge through the instructions of the sage Māṇḍavya, I reached it through the grace of the Lord earned by penance. Pray tell me: is your mind at perfect rest now? Are your subjects living in peace and prosperity? Are you firmly established in dispassion?"

SURAGHU replied:

Who can truly understand the course of the divine will? You and I had been separated by a great distance so far; but now we have been brought together. What is impossible for the divine? We have been truly blessed by your holy visit. By your very presence in our midst, we have all been rid of all sins and defects and I feel that all prosperity stands in front of us in your form. Company of good and holy men is indeed equal to the supreme state of liberation.

V:62, 63 PARIGHA said:

O king, all actions that are performed by one who is firmly established in equanimity are productive of joy, not those done by others. Are you established in that state of supreme peace in which no thoughts or notions arise in your mind, and which is known as samādhi?

SURAGHU said:

Holy sir, please tell me this: why is only that state of mind which is free from thoughts and notions called samādhi? If one is a knower of truth, whether he be engaged in constant action or in contemplation, does his mind ever lose the state of samādhi? No. The enlightened ones are for ever in samādhi, even though they engage themselves in the affairs of the world. On the other hand, one whose mind is not at peace does not enjoy samādhi by merely sitting in the lotus posture.

Knowledge of truth, Lord, is the fire that burns up all hopes and desires as if they are dried blades of grass: and that is known by the word samādhi—not simply remaining silent! That is known as the state of samādhi in which there is eternal satisfaction, clear perception of what is, egolessness, not being subject to the pairs of opposites, freedom from anxiety and from the wish to acquire or to reject. From the very moment of the dawn of self-knowledge, the state of samādhi becomes permanent in the sage: he does not lose it, neither is it interrupted, even for a moment. Even as time does not forget to move on, the man of self-knowledge does not forget the self. Even as a material object is forever material, the sage of self-knowledge is for ever a sage of self-knowledge.

Hence, I am always awakened, pure, at peace within myself and in a state of samādhi. How can it be otherwise? How can there be anything other than the self? When at all times and in all ways the self alone is all in all, how can there be a state other than samādhi? And what can be termed samādhi?

PARIGHA said: Surely, O king, you have attained total enlightenment. You shine, radiant with bliss, with peace, with sweetness and with purity. In you there is no ego-sense, desire or aversion.

SURAGHU continued: O sage, there is indeed nothing which is worth desiring or renouncing. For as long as these things are seen as objects, they are nothing but concepts, percepts and notions. When nothing is worth acquiring, it follows that nothing is worth renouncing. Good and evil, great and small, worthy or unworthy are all based on the notion of desirability. When desirability has no meaning, the others do not arise at all. There is truly no essence in all that is seen in this world—the mountains, the oceans, the forests, the men and women and all the objects. Hence there is no desire for them. When there is no desire, there is supreme peace at heart.

VASIṢṬHA continued: V:64

After thus considering the illusory nature of the world-appearance and after mutually worshipping each other, Suraghu and Parigha continued to engage themselves in their respective duties. Be firmly established in this wisdom and discard the impure notion of ego-sense from your heart. When the pure heart contemplates the infinite space (dimension) of consciousness which is the source of all bliss and which is within easy reach of all, it rests in the supreme self. The mind that is thus devoted to the infinite consciousness, which is introverted and which is filled with self-knowledge, is not affected by sorrow.

Even if you engage yourself in the activities relating to your daily life and even if likes and dislikes arise in you, your inner being will never become impure. Even as light alone can remove darkness, the knowledge that this world is the creation of ignorance is the only remedy for its ills. Once this knowledge has arisen, the ignorant perception of the world as something real ceases once and for all. Thereafter, even if you engage yourself in activity, you are unattached to it and therefore not tainted by it, even as the eyes of fish are not affected by sea-water. You will never again experience delusion.

Only on those days on which the light of self-knowledge shines brightly in one's heart does one live truly. All one's actions are full of bliss on those days. They alone are friends—scriptures and days that generate in one's heart true dispassion and also self-knowledge. O Rāma, rescue your jīva from this dreadful mire of world-appearance. Once you have realised the truth concerning it, you will never again return to this mire.

O Rāma, the company of holy sages will provide you with the knowledge of the means to attain self-knowledge. Hence, one should not live in such places where such company is not available. In the company of sages, the mind of the seeker becomes quiescent at once. One should uplift oneself and not revel in the mire of ignorance. The wise man should constantly enquire into the nature of the world, the self, etc. In this neither wealth nor friends, nor relations, nor scriptures are of any help; only the pure mind which is constantly engaged in self-enquiry and which is endowed with dispassion enables one to cross this ocean of ignorance.

The very moment one looks upon the body as an inert substance, one attains self-knowledge. When the darkness of ignorance or ego-sense is dispelled, the light of self-knowledge shines. That state of self-knowledge or perfect enlightenment is beyond description. Just as the sweetness of sugar is known only by direct experience, the nature of enlightenment is known only by direct experience. When the mind and the ego-sense cease, this self-knowledge arises. It is reached by the practice of yoga, it is comparable in some respects to deep sleep: but it is truly incomparable, indescribable.

The Story of Bhāsa and Vilāsa

V:65, 66 VASIṢṬHA continued:

O Rāma, so long as one does not subdue the mind with the mind, one cannot attain self-knowledge; and as long as one entertains the false notions of 'I' and 'mine', so long sorrow does not come to an an end, even as the sun in a painting never sets. There is a legend that illustrates this truth. I shall now narrate it to you.

There is a great mountain which is as high as the three worlds put together. On its peaks dwell the gods, in the middle dwell human beings and at its base dwell the beings of the netherworld. It is known as Sahya. It contains everything, as it were. On it there is the hermitage of the sage Atri. In it there dwelt two sages known as Bṛhaspati and Śukra, each of whom had a son, known as Vilāsa and Bhāsa respectively. The two boys grew up into young men. They were very greatly attached to each other and were inseparable.

In course of time, the two elder sages, Bṛhaspati and Śukra, left this world. Grief-stricken, the two young men performed the appropriate funeral rites. On account of the loss of their fathers they felt disinterested in property, wealth, etc., and both of them thereupon went away to the forest, each in a different direction, to lead a nomadic life. After a considerable time, once again they met each other.

VILĀSA said to his friend Bhāsa:

What a delight to meet you again, O my dearest friend. Tell me what you have been doing since we parted. Did your austerities bear fruit? Has your mind rid itself of the burning fever of worldliness? Have you attained self-knowledge? Tell me: are you well and happy?

BHĀSA replied:

I consider myself extremely fortunate to see you again, my very dear friend and brother. However, how can we who are wandering in this world-appearance ever be well and happy unless and until we attain the highest wisdom, until the psychological perversions cease? Until we cross this ocean of world-cycle, how can we be well and happy? Until the hopes and desires born of the mind have been completely destroyed, how can we be well and happy?

Until we attain self-knowledge, we shall return again to this plane of birth and death to undergo childhood, youth, manhood, old age and death again and again, we shall engage ourselves in the same essenseless actions and experiences. Cravings destroy wisdom. Lost in satisfying sensual appetites, life ebbs away fast. The mind falls into the blind well of sense-pleasure. It is a wonder how and why this body, which is an excellent vehicle to take us to the other shore of self-knowledge, falls into the mire of worldliness! In the twinkling of an eye this little ripple known as the mind assumes terrible proportions. Man foolishly ascribes to the self the sorrow and the sufferings that do not touch it in the least, and becomes miserable.

VASIṢṬHA continued: V:67

Thus conversing with each other and enquiring into the nature of the world, they soon attained the supreme wisdom. Hence, O Rāma, I tell you that there is no way other than self-knowledge for the cutting asunder of bondage and for crossing this ocean of illusion. To the enlightened person this ocean of sorrow is like a little puddle. He views the body as a spectator looks at a distant crowd. Hence he is not affected by the pains that the body is subjected to. The existence of the body does not diminish the omnipresence of the self any more than waves diminish the fullness of the ocean.

What is the relationship of a swan, a rock or a piece of wood to the water which surrounds them? Even so, the supreme self has no relationship with this world-appearance. A falling tree seems to raise waves on the water: similar is the experience by the self of the pleasure and pain that appear on the body. Even as by its proximity to water, wood is reflected in the water, the body is reflected in the self. But even as a rock falling into the water does not injure the water nor is injured by it, even so when the body comes into contact with other material substances (such as wife, children, or material objects) there is no injury or pain to anyone.

The reflection of an object in the mirror can be said to be neither real nor unreal; it is indescribable: even so the body which is reflected in the self is neither real nor unreal, but is indescribable. The ignorant person accepts as real whatever he sees in this world; not so the wise one. Even as a piece of wood and the water in which it is reflected have no real relationship, the body and the self have no real relationship. Moreover, there is in fact no duality where such relationship could exist. One infinite consciousness alone exists without subject-object division. In this, diversity is imagined and that which is untouched by sorrow believes itself to be miserable, even as one who thinks he sees a ghost sees a ghost! On account of the power of thought this imaginary relationship assumes the force of reality. The self is ever untouched by pain and pleasure; but thinking itself to be the body, it undergoes the experiences of the body. The abandonment of this ignorant belief is liberation.

They who are not thus overcome by false identification or attachment are freed at once from sorrow. It is this conditioning that is the seed of old age, death and delusion; when it ceases, one goes beyond the ocean of delusion. The conditioned mind creates bondage even in ascetics; the unconditioned mind is pure even in a householder. The mind that is thus conditioned is bondage; liberation is freedom from conditioning (inner contact, attachment or identification). This inner contact (which presupposes fictitious division) alone is the cause for bondage and liberation. Actions performed by the unconditioned are non-action; the conditioned mind acts even while outwardly refraining from it. Action or non-action is in the mind; the body does nothing. Hence, one should resolutely abandon this false inner division.

RĀMA asked: V:68

What is conditioning, O Lord, and how does it cause bondage; and what is liberation and how is it attained?

VASIṢṬHA continued:

Conviction in the reality of the body in one who has abandoned the distinction between the body and the self is known as conditioning. He who believes that the infinite self is limited and therefore seeks pleasure, thus gets bound. He who enquires, 'All this is indeed the self, what do I desire and what should I renounce?' is established in the unconditioned state of liberation. He who knows 'I am not, nor is there another' or, 'Let these be or not be' and does not seek pleasure, is liberated. He is not addicted to inaction nor does he get lost in the results of action; he is not given to exultation or to depression. He renounces the fruits of actions by his mind (not by action!). It is by the rejection of the conditioning that bondage is got rid of and the highest good gained. Conditioning is the cause of all sorrow.

Conditioning can be illustrated by the following examples: (1) the donkey is led by the master's rope and, afraid, it carries a heavy burden; (2) the tree rooted to the ground bears heat, cold, wind and rain; (3) the worm lies in a hole in earth, biding its time; (4) the hungry bird rests on the branch of a tree, fearful of predators; (5) the tame deer peacefully goes about grazing and falls a prey to the hunter's shot; (6) numerous people are born again and again as worms and insects; (7) the countless creatures arise and fall in this creation like waves on the surface of the ocean; (8) the weak human beings who, unable even to move about, die again and again; (9) those shrubs and creepers which derive their nourishment from the earth and grow on earth; and (10) this very world-illusion which is like a river that carries in its stream the countless sorrows and sufferings. All these are the expansions of conditioning.

Conditioning (or inner contact, attachment or self-limitation) is of two kinds: the adorable and the sterile or barren. The sterile or barren conditioning is seen everywhere in fools: the adorable conditioning is seen among those who know the truth. That conditioning which exists in the minds of those who are ignorant of self-knowledge, which arises from things like the body and which is conducive to repeated birth and death, that is barren and sterile. The other form of conditioning, which is found in adorable beings who have self-knowledge, arises from the realisation of true wisdom; this enables one to avoid birth and death.

(The adorable conditioning recognises 'natural' limitations, e.g., the eyes and the ears, etc. are limited in their perception. The fool's is self-imposed conditioning and he regards the infinite self to be identical with the physical body. The word used in the text, viz. samsaktti is usually translated 'attachment'. However, attachment implies division and duality which is limitation of the infinite and conditioning of the unconditioned.)

VASIṢṬHA continued:

The god who holds in his hands the conch, the discus, etc., protects the three worlds, on account of the 'adorable conditioning'. It is thanks to the same type of conditioning that the sun shines and the cosmic body of the Creator continues to direct this vast creation. And, lord Śiva, too, shines as a divinity on account of this type of conditioning. The gods that sustain this world and function in various ways are endowed with their faculties by this adorable conditioning or self-limitation.

On the other hand, under the influence of the sterile or barren conditioning, the mind falls a prey to the desire for pleasure in the deluded belief that such experience is delightful.

Even the functioning of the cosmic elements is due to conditioning. And it is because of it that the gods in heaven, the humans on earth and the demons in the netherworld arise and fall, like waves on the ocean. Even as in the ocean the big fish eat the small ones, all these countless beings feed upon one another and are helplessly blown around in space on account of their conditioning. And, the stars in space move in their own orbits because of conditioning. Now rising, now setting, now bright, now dark (and said to have several spots or defects), the moon continues to revolve around the earth and is not abandoned because of conditioning.

O Rāma, behold this mysterious creation brought into being by who-knows-who in response to the mental concepts of beings. This universe has been conjured up in empty space merely by mental conditioning: it is not a reality. And in this universe, craving for pleasure gnaws at the very vitals of all beings who are attached to the world, the body, etc. No one can count their number any more than the number of particles of sand along the ocean beaches. The Creator of this universe has brought this universe into being, as it were, only in response to the mental conditioning of these countless beings. These beings are indeed excellent dry fuel for the flaming fire of hell here. Whatever suffering is found in this world, know that it is meant only for these beings. Even as rivers flow rapidly towards the ocean, suffering flows towards those who are mentally conditioned. This whole creation is thus pervaded by ignorance. However, if one cuts asunder this craving for pleasure, the limitation of mental conditioning yields to a great expansion. Mental conditioning (or attachment to the finite and the perishable) is burning pain to the limbs, O Rāma: but infinite expansion (or devotion to the infinite) is the magic cure for the burning pain. That mind which is unattached to anything, which is established in the peace of infinite expansion, is conducive to delight. He who stands rooted in self-knowledge is liberated here and now.

(In this chapter the real significance of 'conditioning' is brought out, though the word used again is saṃsaṅgaṃ which may also be translated as 'contact' or 'attachment'. It is 'identification' or 'conditioning' that is really implied.)

VASIṢṬHA continued: V:69, 70

O Rāma, doing what is appropriate, at all times, the mind should not be attached to the action, the thoughts or the object. Neither should it be attached to the heavens above, nor what is below nor in the other directions. It should not be bound to external relations, to the natural movement of the inner senses, nor to the life-force. The mind should not rest in the head, inside the palate, between the eyebrows, at the tip of the nose or in the mouth or eyes. It should not repose either in the darkness or in the light or even in the cave of the heart. The states of wakefulness, dream and sleep should not hold it and even the wide, pure space should not be its home. Unattached to the spectrum of colours, to movement and steadiness, to the beginning, the middle, the end and elsewhere, the mind should not rest either at a distance or nearby, in front, in objects or in the self. Sense experiences, the deluded state of happiness, concepts and percepts should have no hold over the mind.

The mind should rest in pure consciousness as pure consciousness, with just a little externalised movement of thought, as if aware of the utter vanity of the objects of this world. When thus all attachments have been snapped, the jīva becomes no-jīva: whatever happens thereafter happens—whether activity or inactivity. In such a state of non-attachment the jīva is not bound to the fruits of action. Or, abandoning even that state of a little comprehension of the objects, let the jīva rest in supreme peace.

Such a liberated person, whether he appears to others to be engaged in activity or not, is for ever free from sorrow and fear. All the people love and adore him. Even if in the eyes of others he appears to be agitated, within himself he is firmly rooted in wisdom. His consciousness is ever uncoloured by happiness and unhappiness. He is not distracted by the glamour of the world. Having attained self-knowledge, he lives in constant contemplation as it were; and therefore he is unattached to anything in the universe. Having risen above the pairs of opposites, he appears to be as if in deep sleep even in the wakeful state.

That state in which the mind is freed from its characteristic movement of thought and in which there is only the experience of peace, is known as 'deep sleep in wakefulness'. He who is in it lives a non-volitional life, freed from every type of mental distraction or distress, unconcerned with a short or a long life. When this same state of 'deep sleep in wakefulness' matures, it is known as turīya or the fourth state. Firmly established in that, the sage perceives the universe as if it is a cosmic playground and life in it is a cosmic dance. Utterly freed from sorrow and fear and from delusion of world-appearance, he who is established in the turīya does not fall into error once again. He is forever immersed in bliss. He goes even beyond this to the great, inexpressible state of supreme bliss. That is considered the state beyond even turīya—incomprehensible and indescribable.

V:71 VASIṢṬHA continued:

It may be possible to put into words the state of one who is liberated while yet living, which is the state known as turīya or 'deep sleep in wakefulness', or the state of total freedom. The state beyond that (which is the state of those who have transcended body-consciousness) is not for words to describe. This is the 'state beyond the turīya'. O Rāma, strive to reach that.

But first be established in the state of 'deep sleep in wakefulness'. Remain unconcerned about the existence or otherwise of the body, knowing that the body is but a product of illusion. You are a man of wisdom, O Rāma; and you have reached inner awakening. The mind of the man of self-knowledge does not take the downward path. Only the pure consciousness exists here: hence, let not the notions of 'I am so-and-so', 'This is mine' arise in you. Even the word 'self' is used only in order to communicate; the truth is beyond all these descriptions. There is no duality, there are no bodies and therefore there are no relationships among them; there are no shadows in the sun! Though I am speaking to you while assuming the apparent duality, in truth there is no such division.

Even as there is no relationship between light and darkness, there can be no relationship between the body and the embodied. When the truth is known, the erroneous perception vanishes. The self is consciousness—pure eternal, self-luminous and free from change; the body is impermanent and impure. How can there exist a relation between the two? The body is enlivened by the life-force or by the other elements; this body can have no relationship whatsoever with the self. Thus, even if the two (self and body) are regarded as two distinct realities, there can be no relationship between them: but, if this duality is unreal, then such thinking itself becomes irrelevant. Let this truth be firmly established in you; there is no bondage nor liberation at any time for anyone anywhere.

It is clear that all this is but the one infinite self or consciousness. If you lend ear to concepts like 'I am happy or unhappy' or 'I am ignorant', then they will bring you endless sorrow. The body came into being because of wind (life-breath), it exists because of it, its speech is caused by it and all the senses function because of it: the intelligence in it is but the indivisible consciousness. That infinite consciousness alone is spread out everywhere as space, etc., and the latter are reflected in the consciousness, and this reflection has come to be known as the mind. When the mind abandons its body-cage and flies away, it experiences the self which is consciousness. Where there is fragrance there is flower; where there is mind there is consciousness. But, the mind alone is the cause for the appearance of the world: since the consciousness is omnipresent and infinite, though it is the ultimate cause, it is not the cause of the world-appearance. Hence, truly, the cause for this world-appearance is non-investigation into the nature of reality—ignorance. Even as a lamp instantly removes darkness, the light of self-knowledge dispels the darkness of ignorance instantly. Hence one should enquire into what is known as jīva or mind or the inner psychological factor.

RĀMA asked:

Holy sir, how have these concepts and categories come to be firmly accepted? Pray enlighten me.

VASIṢṬHA continued:

All this is indeed the self. However, even as waves rise in the ocean, the diversity known as the universe arises in the mind. Here and there, the self appears to be kinetic self. Elsewhere, the self remains in a static state. The static are inert substances like rock, and the kinetic substances are humans etc. In all these, the omnipotent self entertains the notion of ignorance and therefore remains as if ignorant. The infinite thus clothed in ignorance, is known as the jīva—who is like the trapped elephant in this world-appearance.

Because it lives, it is known as jīva. Because of its egoistic notion, it is known as the ego. Because it discriminates and determines, it is known as the buddhi or the discriminating faculty. Because of its ability to form concepts and percepts, it is known as the mind. Being natural, it is called nature. It itself is known as the body, because it changes. It is known as consciousness, because its nature is consciousness.

The supreme self which alone is the truth is right in the middle between the inert and the intelligent: that alone creates diversity and is known by all these diverse names. But, all these categories have been invented by men of perverse intellect for the pleasure of polemics and for the confusion of ignorant men.

Thus, O Rāma, it is this jīva alone which is the cause of this world-appearance: what can this deaf and dumb body do? If the body perishes the self does not perish, even as if a leaf falls the tree does not perish. Only the deluded person thinks otherwise.

On the other hand, if the mind perishes, everything perishes, and there is final liberation. The man who wails "I am dying, I perish", is foolishly clinging to a false concept. He goes on experiencing the world-illusion in some other place or time. The jīva that dwells in mental conditioning abandons one body and goes looking for another, even as a monkey abandons one tree in a forest and jumps on to another. Thereafter, in a moment, it abandons that too, and seeks yet another, in another part of space and in another period of time. Just as a nanny takes the baby from one place to another in order to distract it, this mental conditioning (or the psychological habit or tendency) takes the jīva here and there. Thus tied to the rope of mental conditioning, the jīva goes through repeated birth in various species, enduring interminable suffering.

(As the sage Vasiṣṭha said this, another day came to an end and the assembly dispersed for their evening prayers.)

V:72 VASIṢṬHA continued:

O Rāma, you are not born when the body is born, nor do you die when it dies. To think that the space within the jar came into being when it was made and the space perishes with the jar is sheer foolishness. Moreover, the indwelling consciousness is free from notions of the desirable and the undesirable in relation to the body, mind and senses. The indwelling consciousness seems to come into contact with these even as travellers meet in an inn or logs of wood meet and part in a stream: meeting and parting do not cause happiness or unhappiness to the consciousness. Why then do people exult or grieve in these circumstances?

The self on account of its ignorant self-limitation as the mind becomes as if tainted by the objects of the world; but, the same self when it is awakened to its true nature abandons its ignorant delusion and regains its self-knowledge. Then, the mind sees the body as if from a great height. Recognising the body as an aggregate of the elements, it transcends body-consciousness and becomes enlightened.

Such an enlightened person is untainted by worldliness or ignorance even while acting in this world. He is neither attracted nor repelled by anything in the world. He knows "What is known as 'I' and what is known as 'the world' in the three periods of time are but the expansion of the conjunction between pure experiencing and the experience itself." Whether the object of experiencing be real or unreal, it is entirely dependent upon the experiencing: how then do joy and sorrow arise? The false is false, the truth is the truth; a mixture of these two is of course false! Be not deluded. Abandon false perception and behold the truth; you will never again be deluded.

All that is, is but the expansion of the relationship between pure experiencing and its experience. That experience is truly the delight of self-bliss. It is pure experiencing itself. Hence it is known as Brahman the absolute. That delight which arises in the contact of this pure experiencing with experience is the highest: to the ignorant, it is worldliness, and to the wise it is liberation. This pure experiencing is itself the infinite self: when it is bent towards objects, it is bondage, but when it is free, it is liberation. When such experiencing is free from decay or curiosity, it is liberation. When such experiencing is freed from even this contact (the subject-object relationship), then the world-appearance ceases entirely. Then arises the turīya consciousness or 'deep sleep in wakefulness'.

The self is neither this nor that; it transcends whatever is the object of experiencing here. In the unlimited and unconditioned vision of the knower of truth, all this is but the one self, the infinite consciousness, and there is nothing which can be regarded as the not-self. The substantiality of all substances is none other than the self or the infinite consciousness.

VASIṢṬHA continued: V:73

O Rāma, there is another attitude by which you will also gain divine insight and remain firmly established in self-knowledge. And that is as follows:

'I am the space. I am the sun. I am the directions, above and below. I am the gods. I am the demons. I am all beings. I am darkness. I am the earth, the oceans, etc. I am the dust, the wind, the fire and all this world. I am omnipresent. How can there be anything other than me?'

By adopting this attitude you will rise beyond joy and sorrow.

Both these attitudes are conducive to liberation: one is 'I am the extremely subtle and transcendent self' and the other is 'I am all and everything'. There is another attitude with regard to the 'I', and that is 'I am this body': this attitude is the source of endless sorrow. Abandon all these three attitudes, O Rāma, and remain as pure consciousness. For, though the self is transcendental and though it is omnipresent, the self alone is the light in all things in the world, though they are in fact false.

This self-knowledge is not gained by explanations and descriptions, nor by the instructions of others. At all times, everything is known only by direct experience. Whatever is experienced and known here in this world, all that is the self, the consciousness devoid of the duality of the experiencing and the experience. It is the self alone that exists everywhere at all times, but because of its extreme subtlety, it is not experienced. In all beings, it is the jīva. All activities take place in the light of the sun, but if the activities cease, the sun does not suffer loss: even so, it is on account of the self that the body, etc., function, but if the body, etc., perish, the self does not suffer loss. The self is not born, nor does it die; it does not acquire, nor does it desire; it is not bound, nor is it liberated—the self is the self of all at all times.

That (self) is unconditioned by time, space, etc.; how does it become bound? When there is no bondage, what is liberation? Such is the glory of the self. But on account of ignorance of the nature of the self, people weep and wail here. Abandon these two false concepts, viz., that of bondage and that of liberation, and live an enlightened life here. There is no liberation in the sky or on earth or in the netherworld; liberation is but a synonym for pure mind, correct self-knowledge and a truly awakened state. The complete absence of all desires and hopes is liberation. Until one reaches this true inner awakening or self-knowledge, one considers oneself bound and strives for liberation. Abandon these wrong notions of bondage and liberation and become 'a man of supreme renunciation', O Rāma. Then live a very long life and rule the whole world.

V:74 VASIṢṬHA continued:

The self playfully seeing a body entertains the notion that it has become the body. All these that constitute the world-illusion come into being like a mirage in the desert. This illusion spreads out like waves in the ocean, assuming various names like mind, the faculty of discrimination, the ego-sense, the latent tendencies and the senses. The mind and the ego-sense are not in fact two but one and the same: the distinction is verbal. The mind is the ego-sense and what is known as the ego-sense is the mind. Only ignorant people think that one is born of the other, even as ignorant people might say that whiteness is born of snow.

Thus of the mind and the ego-sense—if one ceases the other ceases to be. Hence, instead of entertaining the notion of bondage and that of liberation, abandon all cravings and through wisdom and dispassion, bring about the cessation of the mind. If even the wish, "May I be liberated" arises within you, the mind is revived; and the mind entertaining other notions creates a body. Then there arise other concepts like 'I do this', 'I enjoy this' and 'I know this'. All these concepts are unreal like a mirage in the desert. However, since their unreality is not realised, the illusion attracts the mind even as the mirage deludes and attracts an animal. But, if it is realised as an illusion it does not attract the mind, even as a mirage does not delude one who knows it to be a mirage. Just as a lamp utterly dispels darkness, the knowledge of truth completely uproots concepts and conditioning.

When one sincerely questions, 'This body is but inert substance; why should one seek pleasure for its sake?', all cravings drop away. When thus the cravings drop away, one experiences great bliss and supreme peace within oneself. The sage of self-knowledge attains courage and stability and shines in his own glory. He enjoys supreme satisfaction in himself. He is enlightened and this inner light shines brightly within him. He beholds the self as self of all, omnipresent, the Lord of all and formless, yet pervading all forms.

Remembering the past when he was swayed by lust, he laughs at his own past ignorance. He is far from evil company, freed from mental distress, but firmly established in self-knowledge. He is glorified by all, he is sought by all, he is applauded by all, but he remains indifferent. He neither gives nor does he take, he does not insult or praise anyone, he does not rejoice or grieve. He is a sage liberated while living, who has abandoned all motivated actions, who is free from conditioning and who has given up all desires and hopes. O Rāma, abandon all desires and remain at peace within yourself. No delight in the world is comparable to the delight that will fill your heart when you completely abandon all desires and hopes. Not in kingship, nor in heaven, nor in the company of the beloved one does one experience such delight as when one is free from hope.

VASIṢṬHA continued:

He who is endowed with desirelessness (hope-lessness) treats the whole world as if it were the footprint of a calf, the highest mountain as the stump of a felled tree, space as a small box and the three worlds as a blade of grass. He laughs at the activities of the worldly-minded persons. How can we compare such a person, and to what? How can anyone disturb his equanimity when he is totally free from thoughts like "I wish this had happened to me"? O Rāma, it is desire or hope that makes one revolve, bound to the wheel of world-illusion.

When you perceive the truth that the self alone is all this and that diversity is just a word without substance, you will become totally free from desire or hope. Such a hero who is endowed with supreme dispassion drives away the goblin of illusion by his very presence. He is not pleased by pleasure, he is not troubled by troubles. Attractions do not distract him any more than wind can uproot a mountain. The twin-forces of attraction and aversion do not even touch him. He looks upon all with equal vision.

Free from the least attachment he enjoys whatever comes to him unsought, even as the eyes perceive their objects without desire or hate. Such experiences do not therefore produce either joy or sorrow in him. Even though he appears to be engaged in the performance of appropriate actions in this world, his consciousness is not distracted in the least. Whatever may befall him in accordance with the laws of time, space and causation, whether it is pleasant or unpleasant, he remains inwardly undisturbed.

Even as a rope which had been mistaken for a snake does not frighten one who has seen that it is a rope and not a snake, illusion once dispelled does not return and self-knowledge once attained is never lost. Can one restore to the tree the fruit that has fallen from it?

The knower of truth regards even the most beautiful woman as a painted image; that is the truth, for both of them are made of the same substance (earth, water, etc.) When thus the truth is seen, desire to possess does not arise in the heart. Even as a woman who has a lover goes about doing her housework with her heart absorbed in contemplation of that lover, the enlightened sage functions in this world while his consciousness is firmly established in the truth. In both these cases it is impossible for anyone to prevent such behaviour, i.e., make the woman forget her lover or make the sage forget the truth.

The enlightened sage knows that his self is not cut when the body is cut, does not weep when the eyes shed tears, is not burnt when the body is burnt, and is not lost when everything is lost. Whatever may befall him, whether he is destitute or affluent, whether he lives in a palace or in a forest—he is inwardly undisturbed.

V:75 VASIṢṬHA continued:

Very many such liberated beings exist in the universe, O Rāma. I shall give you a few instances. Janaka the emperor, your own ancestor the emperor Dilīpa, the first ruler of the world Manu, emperor Māndhātā who engaged himself in wars, the demon-kings Bali, Namūci, Vṛtra (who even fought with the king of gods Indra), Prahlāda and Saṃbara, the preceptors of the gods and demons, as also the trinity (who are involved in the creation, preservation and dissolution of the universe), sages like Viśvāmitra and Nārada, as well as the deities presiding over natural elements like fire and air.

There are thousands of others, O Rāma, who exist in the universe and who are liberated. Some of them are sages, others are kings, others shine as stars and planets, others are divinities and others are demons. O Rāma, there are liberated beings even among worms and insects; and there are stupid fools among the gods. The self is in all; it exists as the all everywhere at all times and in all ways. The self alone is the Lord and all the divinities. There is void (space) in substances and substantiality in the void or space. What is inappropriate appears to be appropriate on enquiry. People are righteous because they are afraid of the consequences of sin. Even what is not leads to what is!—the contemplation of the space or void leads to the attainment of the supreme truth! What is not comes into being, guided by time and space. On the other hand, what appears to be strong and powerful reaches its own destruction. Thus perceiving the truth, O Rāma, abandon joy and sorrow, grief and attachment. The unreal appears to be real and the real appears to be unreal: hence give up hope and hopelessness and attain equanimity.

In this world, O Rāma, liberation is at hand at all times everywhere. By their own self-effort millions of beings have attained liberation. Liberation is either easy or difficult depending upon one's wisdom or unwisdom; hence, O Rāma, kindle the lamp of wisdom in yourself. By the vision of the self is sorrow beheaded.

There have been countless beings in this world who have attained self-knowledge and liberation while yet living: like the emperor Janaka. Therefore, do thou become liberated here and now. The attainment of inner peace by utter non-attachment to anything here is known as liberation; this is possible whether the body exists or not. He who is freed from all attachments is liberated. One should wisely and intelligently exert oneself to attain this liberation; one who does not exert cannot even jump over the footprint of a calf. Hence, O Rāma, resort to spiritual heroism, to right exertion, and by the right self-enquiry strive to reach the perfection of self-knowledge. For one who thus strives, the entire universe is like the footprint of a calf.

VASIṢṬHA continued: V:76, 77

All these worlds, O Rāma, appear in Brahman the absolute; but they are apprehended as an independent substantial reality on account of ignorance or non-wisdom. Such an erroneous notion ceases on the arising of wisdom. Erroneous perception makes all this appear as 'the world': right perception brings about the cessation of this error. Rāma, this error is not dispelled except by right exertion with the right attitude and wisdom. Fie on that person, O Rāma, who though such possibility of overcoming this error exists, remains sunk in the mire of world-illusion. Blessed are you, Rāma, that the right spirit of enquiry has already manifested in your heart. When the truth is realised through such enquiry, strength, intelligence and radiance increase.

The sage who has realised the truth and who is liberated from error here and now beholds this world as he would in deep sleep, without the least craving. He does not apprehend with his inner intelligence even those objects and experiences which seek him unsought: for his own heart is withdrawn into itself. He has no hopes for the future and he does not recall the past, nor does he even live in the present; and yet he does all. Asleep, he is awake; awake, he sleeps. He does all, yet he does nothing. Inwardly having renounced everything though outwardly he appears to be busy, he is ever in a state of equilibrium. His actions are entirely non-volitional.

The sage is unattached to anything or anybody. Hence, his behaviour appears to be devout to the devout and harsh to the harsh. He is a child among children, old man among old men, hero among heroes, youth among youth and sorrowing among the sorrowful. His soft and sweet words are full of wisdom. He has nothing to gain from noble deeds, yet he is noble; he has no longing for pleasure and hence is not tempted by it. He is not attracted to bondage or even to liberation. The net of ignorance and error having been burnt by the fire of wisdom, the bird of his consciousness flies away to liberation.

He is not elated when his efforts bear fruit; nor is he worried if they do not. He appears to take and to abandon with the playfulness of a child. He is not surprised if the moon shines hot or the sun shines cool. Knowing that the self which is the infinite consciousness can bring all these about, he is not surprised even by such wondrous phenomena. He is not timid and he is not given to outbursts of anger.

Knowing that beings are constantly born and that they die constantly, he does not give way to joy or grief. He knows that the world arises in his own vision, even as the dream-objects arise when one dreams, and hence all these objects are of momentary existence. Therefore, he does not feel any justification for either pity or joy. When all such concepts like pleasure and pain, desirable and undesirable cease, all notions in the mind cease. Error does not arise again, even as oil is not obtained from burnt seed.

VASIṢṬHA continued: V:78

O Rāma, just as when a firebrand is swung around, an illusory circle of fire is formed, there is an illusory appearance of the world due to the vibration that arises in consciousness. Vibration and consciousness are inseparably one like the whiteness of snow, the oil in the sesame seed, the fragrance of the flower and the heat of fire. Their description as distinct categories is an error. Mind and movement of thought are inseparable; and the cessation of one is the cessation of both.

O Rāma, there are two ways in which this cessation can be achieved: one is the way of yoga which involves the restraint of the movement of thought, and the other is the way of knowledge which involves the right knowledge of truth.

In this body, that energy (lit. air) which circulates in the energy-channels (nādī lit. means 'channel of motion', not necessarily a nerve though for convenience it may be called so) is known as prāṇa. In accordance with its diverse functions in the body, it is also known by the names apāna, etc. This prāṇa is indistinguishably united with the mind. In fact, the consciousness that tends towards thinking, on account of the movement of prāṇa, is known as the mind. Movement of thought in the mind arises from the movement of prāṇa; and movement of prāṇa arises because of the movement of thought in consciousness. They thus form a cycle of mutual dependence, like waves and movement of currents in water.

The wise ones declare that the mind is caused by the movement of prāṇa; and hence by the restraint of the prāṇa, the mind becomes quiescent. When the mind abandons the movement of thought, the appearance of the world-illusion ceases. The movement of prāṇa is arrested at the moment when all hopes and desires come to an end in one's heart through the earnest practice of the precepts of the scriptures and sages, and by the cultivation of dispassion in previous life-spans or through endeavouring to practise contemplation or meditation and reaching a stage of devotion to a single truth in a single-minded way.

The movement of prāṇa is also arrested by the effortless practice of inhalation, etc., without strain, in seclusion, or the repetition of the sacred OM with the experience of its meaning, when the consciousness reaches the deep sleep state. The practice of exhalation, when the prāṇa roams in space without touching the limbs of the body, of inhalation, leading to the peaceful movement of prāṇa, and of retention, bringing it to a standstill for a long time, all lead to the arrest of the movement of prāṇa. Likewise the closure of the posterior nares by the tip of the tongue as the prāṇa moves towards the crown of the head, the practice of meditation where there is no movement of thought, the holding of the consciousness steadily at the point twelve inches from the tip of the nose, the entering of the prāṇa into the forehead through the palate and upper aperture, the fixing of the prāṇa at the eyebrow centre, the sudden cessation of the movement of thought, or cessation of all mental conditioning through meditation on the space in the heart-centre over a long period of time, all these lead to this arrest of the movement of prāṇa.

RĀMA asked: Lord, what is the heart that is spoken of by you?

V:79 VASIṢṬHA continued:

O Rāma, two aspects of the 'heart' are spoken of here: one is acceptable and the other is to be ignored. The heart that is part of this physical body and is located in one part of the body may be ignored! The heart which is acceptable is of the nature of pure consciousness. It is both inside and outside and it is neither inside nor outside. That is the principal heart and in it is reflected everything which is in the universe, and it is the treasure-house of all wealth. Consciousness alone is the heart of all beings, not the piece of flesh which people call the heart! Hence, if the mind, freed of all conditioning, is gathered into pure consciousness, the movement of prāṇa is restrained.

By any one of these methods, propounded by the various teachers, the movement of prāṇa can be restrained. These yogic methods bring about the desired results if they are practised without violence or force. When one is firmly established in such practice with simultaneous growth in dispassion and when the mental conditioning comes under perfect restraint, there is fruition of the restraint of the movement of prāṇa.

During the practice one may use the eye-brow centre, the palate, the tip of the nose, or the top of the head (twelve inches from the nose); thus the prāṇa will be restrained. Again, if by steady and persistent practice the tip of the tongue can touch the uvula, the movement of prāṇa will be restricted. Surely, all these practices appear to be distractions; but by their steady practice, one reaches the absence of distractions. It is only by such steady practice that one is freed from sorrow and experiences the bliss of the self. Hence, practise yoga. When through practice the movement of prāṇa is restrained, then nirvāṇa or liberation alone remains. In it is all; from it is all; it is all; it is everywhere: in it this world-appearance is not, nor is this from it, nor is the world-appearance like it! He who is firmly established in it is liberated while living.

He whose mind is firmly established in peace through the practice of yoga has the right vision of the truth. To see that the supreme self is without beginning and without end, and that these countless objects are in fact the self and no other, is the right vision. Erroneous vision leads to rebirth; right vision ends rebirth. In it there is no subject-object (knower-knowable) relationship; for the self (consciousness) is the knower, knowledge and the knowable, too, and the division is ignorance. When this is directly seen there is neither bondage nor liberation. When the sage rests in his own self, with his intelligence firmly established in the inner self, what pleasures can bind him in this world?

VASIṢṬHA continued: V:80

One who engages himself in enquiry is not tempted by distractions. The eyes but see: the notions pleasant, unpleasant, etc. arise, not in the eyes, but elsewhere—it is even so with the other senses. Hence, the sense-functions are not evil. If egoistic thought is linked to these sense-functions (which arise and cease in a moment) there is mental agitation.

O eyes! The objects of your experience arise and fall, and they are but appearances. Do not let your gaze linger on them, lest the eternal indwelling consciousness suffer mortality. Be an onlooker that you truly are. O mind! Countless scenes are seen by the eyes in accordance with their natural function; why do you get involved in them? Even if these scenes are reflected in the mind and recognised by it, why do you respond to these as the ego-sense? There is, without doubt, an intimate relationship between the eyes and their objects; but why do you offer yourself as their support and then endeavour to apprehend them? Truly, scene, sight and mind are unrelated, like the face, mirror and reflection: yet, somehow the illusory notion arises that 'I see this'. Ignorance is the wax in which these are sealed to one another; but self-knowledge is the fire in whose heat this wax melts away!

Indeed, it is through repeated thinking, that this ignorant relationship is strengthened; but I shall now destroy it through right enquiry. When ignorance is destroyed, such illusory relationship between scene, sight and mind will never again arise. The mind alone provides the senses with their intelligence; hence this mind should be destroyed. O mind, why do you vainly get agitated through the five senses? Only he who thinks 'It is my mind' is deluded by you. You do not exist, O mind. I do not care whether you stay or you go from me. You are unreal, inert, illusory. Only a fool is harassed by you, not a wise man. This understanding puts an end to the darkness of ignorance. Get out of this body, O ghost, along with your cravings and your emotions like anger. O mind, I have slain you today because I have realised that you never did exist in truth.

For a very long time, this ghost of a mind generated countless evil notions like lust, anger, etc. Now that that ghost has been laid, I laugh at my own past foolishness. The mind is dead; all my worries and anxieties are dead; the demon known as ego-sense is dead, too: all this has been brought about through the mantra of enquiry. I am free and happy now. All my hopes and desires have gone. Salutations to my own self! There is no delusion, no sorrow, no I, no other! I am not the self, nor am I someone else, I am the all in all: salutations to my own self! I am the beginning. I am the consciousness. I am all the universes. There are no divisions in me. Salutations to my own self alone! That which is omnipresent equally in all, to that subtle indwelling omnipresence, that self, salutations!

V:81 VASIṢṬHA continued:

O Rāma, thus having reflected, the wise man should proceed further in the following manner:

"When the self (consciousness) alone is all this and when the mind has been cleansed with this understanding, what is mind—mind is surely non-existent. Whether it is unseen, or it is not-mind, or it is an illusory appearance, this much is certain—either it does not exist or it is mere illusion. Now that both wickedness and delusion have ceased, I do not see what the mind is.

"All my doubts have ceased. I am without the fever of agitation. Whatever I am, I am—but without craving. When the mind ceases to be, the craving ceases to be too. When the mind is dead and the craving is dead, delusion has vanished and egolessness is born. Hence I am awakened in this state of wakefulness. When there is only one truth and diversity has no reality at all, what shall I investigate?

"I am the eternal self that is omnipresent and subtle. I have reached that state of reality which is unreflected in anything, which is beginningless and endless and which is utterly pure. Whatever is and whatever is not, the mind and the inner reality are all the one infinite consciousness, which is supreme peace beyond comprehension and by which all this is pervaded. Let the mind continue to be or let it die. What is the sense in enquiring into all this, when the self is established in utter equanimity? I remained in a conditioned state as long as I was foolishly engaged in this enquiry. Now that through this enquiry I have reached the unconditioned being, who is the enquirer?

"Such thoughts are utterly useless, now that the mind is dead; they may revive this ghost known as the mind. Hence I abandon all these thoughts and notions; contemplating the OM, I shall remain in the self, in total inner silence."

Thus should a wise man investigate the nature of the truth at all times, whatever he may be doing. On account of such investigation, the mind remains established in itself, freed of all agitation but performing its natural functions.

The Holy ones with unconditioned consciousness live and function here, freed from pride and delusion, with their heart ever rejoicing, their countenance shining with a divine radiance and performing their natural actions.

The above line of enquiry was adopted by the sage Samvarta who himself described it to me once upon a time.

The Story of Vītahavya

VASIṢṬHA continued: V:82

There is another mode of enquiry which was adopted by the sage Vītahavya. This sage used to roam the forests in the mountain ranges known as Vindhyas. At one stage, he became totally disenchanted with the affairs of the world which create delusion: and through the contemplation which is free from all perverse notions and thoughts, he abandoned the world as a worn-out illusion. He entered his hermitage, seated himself in the lotus posture and remained firm like a mountain-peak. Having withdrawn the senses and having turned the attention of the mind upon itself, he began to contemplate as follows:

How fickle is my mind! Even if it is introverted, it does not remain steady but gets agitated in a moment like the surface of the ocean. Tied to the senses (like the sight) it bounces again and again like a ball. Having been nourished by the senses, the mind grasps the very objects it has given up; and like a demented person, it runs after the very things from which it has been restrained. It jumps from one object to the other like a monkey.

I shall now consider the character of the five senses through which the mind thus gets distracted. O senses, has the time not yet arrived for you all to attain self-knowledge? Do you not remember the sorrow that followed your pursuit of pleasure? Then, give up this vain excitement. Truly, you are inert and insentient: you are the avenue through which the mind flows out to reach objective experience. I am your Lord, I am consciousness and I alone do all these as the pure intelligence. You, O senses, are false. There is no connection whatsoever between you and the consciousness which is the self. In the very light of the consciousness which is non-volitional, you function, even as people perform various actions in the light of the sun. But do not entertain the false notion, O senses, that 'I am intelligent', for you are not. Even the notion 'I am alive' that you entertain falsely is conducive only to sorrow.

There is nothing but consciousness which is beginningless and endless. O wicked mind, what then are you? The notions that arise in you, viz., 'I am the doer' and 'I am the enjoyer' which appear to be great rejuvenators, are in fact deadly poisons. Do not be so deluded, O mind; you are neither the doer of anything nor are you the experiencer in truth. You are inert and your intelligence is derived from some other source. How are pleasures related to you? You yourself do not exist; how do you have relations? If you realise that 'I am but pure consciousness', then you are indeed the self. Then how does sorrow arise in you when you are the unlimited and unconditioned consciousness?

VĪTAHAVYA continued to contemplate:

O mind, I shall gently bring home to you the truth that you are indeed neither the doer nor the experiencer. You are indeed inert; how can a statue made of stone dance? If your intelligence is entirely dependent upon the infinite consciousness, then may you live long in that realisation. However, what is done with the intelligence or the energy of another, is considered to be done by the latter. The sickle harvests with the energy of the farmer; and hence the farmer is said to be the harvester. Similarly, though it is the sword that cuts, the man who wields the sword is the killer. You are inert, O mind; your intelligence is derived from the infinite consciousness. That self or the infinite consciousness knows itself by itself, experiences itself in itself by itself. The Lord endeavours to enlighten you continuously, for the wise should thus instruct the ignorant in a hundred ways. The light of the self alone exists as consciousness or intelligence; that itself has come to be known as the mind. If you realise this truth, you will instantly be dissolved.

O fool, when you are in truth the infinite consciousness, why do you grieve? That is omnipresent, that is the all: when you realise it, you become the all. You are not, the body is not: the one infinite consciousness alone exists and in that homogeneous being the diverse concepts of 'I' and 'you' appear to exist. If you are the self, then the self alone exists, not you! If you are inert, but different from the self, then you do not exist either! For the self or the infinite consciousness alone is all; there is naught else. There is no possibility for the existence of a third thing, apart from the consciousness and the inert substance.

Hence, O mind, you are neither the doer nor the experiencer. You have been used as a channel of instruction by the wise ones in their communication with the ignorant. But, in fact, that channel is unreal and inert; the self alone is the reality. If the farmer does not use the sickle, can it harvest? The sword has no power to kill either. O mind, you are neither the doer nor the experiencer: hence grieve not. The Lord (consciousness) is not like you; hence do not grieve for him! He does not gain anything by either doing or not-doing. He alone pervades all; there is naught else. Then, what shall he do and what shall he desire?

You have no relationship to the self, except as the fragrance to a flower. Relationship exists only between two independent beings of similar nature when they strive to become one. You, O mind, are ever agitated; and the self is ever at peace. There can thus be no relationship between you two. If, however, you enter into the state of samādhi or utter equanimity, you will remain firmly established in consciousness, without the distraction of diversity, without the notions of either many or one, and realise that there is but one self, the infinite consciousness, which shines as these countless beings.

VĪTAHAVYA continued to contemplate: V:83

O senses, I feel that you have all been dispelled by the light of my admonitions, for you are born of the darkness of ignorance. O mind, surely your emergence as an appearance is for your own grief! See how when you exist, countless beings get deluded and they enter into this ocean of sorrow with all its prosperity and adversity, illness, old age and death; how greed gnaws at all the good qualities and destroys them; how lust or desire distracts and dissipates their energy.

O mind, when you cease to be, all the good and noble qualities blossom. There is peace and purity of heart. People do not fall into doubt and error. There is friendship which promotes the happiness of all. Worries and anxieties dry up. When the darkness of ignorance is dispelled, the inner light shines brightly. Mental distraction and distress cease, just as when the wind ceases to agitate its surface, the ocean becomes calm. There arises self-knowledge within and the realisation of truth puts an end to the perception of the world-illusion: infinite consciousness alone shines. There is an experience of bliss not granted to the ignorant who are full of desires. Even as new shoots may arise from burnt leaves, a new life may emerge from this. However, he who would avoid entanglement in delusion once again, rests in self-knowledge constantly. Such are the fruits of your absence, O mind, and there are countless others. O mind, you are the support of all our hopes and desires; when you cease to be, all these hopes and desires cease. You can now choose either to be one with the reality or to cease to be an independent entity.

Your existence as identical with the self and non-different from it, is conducive to happiness, O mind. Hence, be firmly rooted in the realisation of your non-existence. Surely, it is foolish to neglect happiness. If you exist as the inner being or consciousness, who will wish for your non-existence? But, you are not a real entity; hence your happiness is delusion. You were not real, you came into being through ignorance and delusion, but now through enquiry into your nature and that of the senses and self, you have once again ceased to be. You exist as long as one does not undertake this enquiry. When the spirit of enquiry arises, there is total equanimity or homogeneity. You were born of the ignorance which is the absence of wisdom and discrimination. When this wisdom arises, you cease to be. Hence, I salute wisdom! O mind, you were awakened by many means. Now that you have lost the false characteristic of a mind, you exist as the supreme being or the infinite consciousness, freed from all limitation and conditioning. That which arose in ignorance perishes in wisdom. In spite of yourself, O good mind, this enquiry has arisen in you; this is surely for the attainment of bliss. There is indeed no mind, no mind: the self alone exists, it alone is, there is naught else. I am that self; hence there is naught other than me in the universe. I am the infinite consciousness whose kinetic state alone appears as the universe.

V:84 VASIṢṬHA continued:

After this enquiry, the sage Vītahavya remained in a state of total quiescence (samādhi) and even his prāṇa did not move. His consciousness was neither fixed within nor did it perceive objects outside. His eyes were softly focused around the nose. With his body held erect, he appeared to be a living statue. He lived thus for three hundred years, without abandoning his body. His samādhi was undisturbed by the countless natural disturbances or by those caused by human and subhuman beings. Thus he spent three hundred years as if it were an hour. The body which was reflected in the consciousness was protected by it.

After this period, his mind began to move in his heart and there arose in it notions of a creation. Then he spent a hundred years as a sage in mount Kailāsa. For a hundred years he was a demi-god. Then he ruled as Indra, the king of heaven, for a period of five world-cycles.

RĀMA asked: How was it possible to interfere with the time-table of gods like Indra, O Holy one?

VASIṢṬHA replied:

The energy of the infinite consciousness is omnipresent; and it manifests as whatever it likes wherever it likes. Whatever wherever and however this consciousness conceives the order, so does it become. Thus he saw all this in his own heart, which was free from all conditioning. On account of his attainment of the infinite consciousness, therefore, these notions apparently arose in it non-volitionally. After this, he served as an attendant of lord Śiva for a whole epoch. All this the liberated sage Vītahavya experienced.

RĀMA asked: If such is the experience of Vītahavya, a liberated sage, then it seems as if bondage and liberation exist even for a sage!

VASIṢṬHA replied:

O Rāma, for the liberated sages this world exists in all its purity, peace and perfection as Brahman, the infinite: how can there be bondage and liberation for them? Since Vītahavya had become one with the infinite consciousness, he experienced the experiences of all, and he does so even now!

RĀMA asked: If the creation of the sage was fictitious and imaginary, how were the embodied beings in it conscious and sentient?

VASIṢṬHA replied: If the creation of Vītahavya was fictitious, O Rāma, so is this! That and this are both pure infinite consciousness, their appearance being the result of the delusion of the mind. In truth, neither that creation existed nor does this exist. Brahman alone exists in the three periods of time. Only till this truth is realised does the world appear to be a solid reality.

RĀMA asked: V:85

Lord, please tell me how Vītahavya revived his body in the cave.

VASIṢṬHA continued:

The sage had realised the infinite consciousness; and he knew that the mind, called Vītahavya, was but a trick of the infinite consciousness. While he was a servant of lord Śiva, he once thought of seeing that body of Vītahavya. When he thought thus, in his own consciousness he saw all the other embodiments that he had had—some of them had come to an end and others were still functioning. And, he saw the body known as Vītahavya sunk like a worm in mud.

Seeing it thus, he reflected: "Surely, this body of mine is devoid of life-force and is therefore unable to function. I shall now enter the solar orbit and with the help of the solar power known as piṅgalā I shall enter that body. Or, shall I abandon it; for, what have I to do with the body of Vītahavya? On the other hand, this body is neither worth reviving nor worth abandoning. It is the same to me, whether the body is abandoned or it is revived. Seeing that this body has not decomposed and returned to the elements, I shall enter into it and function for a while."

The sage's subtle body then entered into the orbit of the sun. Reflecting on the purpose of the sage's entry into his orbit and the appropriate action concerning that purpose, the sun ordained his own energy to execute the task. The subtle body of the sage thereupon saluted the sun.

The energy of the sun led the way and, as ordained by the sun, it entered the region of the Vindhya after descending from the solar orbit. It descended right where the body of the sage was lying covered in mud, in order to raise it. Following it, the subtle body of Vītahavya also entered that body. That body was instantly revived. Vītahavya thereupon bowed to the solar energy, piṅgalā, who returned the salutation.

Piṅgalā returned to the solar orbit and the sage proceeded towards the lake for his bath and ablution. Having had his bath and having worshipped the sun, the sage resumed his life as before. He lived an enlightened life, with friendliness, balanced mind, peace, compassion and joy.

V:86 VASIṢṬHA continued:

In the evening the sage once again entered the forest with which he was familiar, for the practice of intense meditation. He thought "I have already realised the falsity of the senses; any further enquiry concerning them will be a contradiction." Having abandoned all vain imagination ('This is' and 'This is not'), he sat in the lotus posture again and in him arose the knowledge 'I am established in the consciousness of total equanimity. Awake, I remain as if in sleep. Established in the transcendental state of consciousness, I shall continue to be, till the body drops away.'

Thus resolved, he meditated for six days, which passed as if in a moment. After that he lived a long time as a liberated sage. He was free from exultation and sorrow. At times, he would address his mind thus: "O mind, look how blissful you are, now that you are in a balanced state! Remain like that all the time."

He would address his senses as follows: "O senses! The self does not belong to you, nor do you belong to the self. May you all perish! Your cravings have ceased. You will no longer be able to rule me. The error of your existence arose from ignorance of the self, even as the non-perception of the rope gives rise to the erroneous perception of a snake. All these errors exist in the darkness of non-wisdom and in the light of wisdom they vanish.

"O senses! You are different from the self, the doer of actions is different from all these, the experiencer of experiences is again different and the infinite consciousness is again different from all these—what is whose error and how does it arise? It is like this:

trees grow in the forest, ropes are made of other fibres with which the timber is bound together, the blacksmith fashions axe, etc. With all these the carpenter builds a house for his own livelihood, not because he wants to build a house! Thus in this world all things happen independently of one another and their coincidence is accidental—like the ripe cocoanut falling coincidentally when a crow alights on it, making ignorant people feel that the crow dislodged the cocoanut. Who is to blame for all these? When this truth is known, error remains error, knowledge becomes clear knowledge, the real is real, the unreal is unreal, what has been destroyed is destroyed and what remains remains."

Thus reflecting and established in this knowledge, the sage lived in this world for a very long time. He was established in that state which is totally free from ignorance and error, and which ensures that he would not be born again. Whenever there was contact with the objects of the senses, he resorted to the peace of contemplation and enjoyed the bliss of the self. His heart was free from attraction and aversion even when all manner of experiences came to him unsought.

VASIṢṬHA continued:

Once, the sage Vītahavya felt inclined to abandon his body and to ensure that he would never again return to embodiment. He resorted to a cave on the Sahya mountain, sat in the lotus posture and

VĪTAHAVYA said this within himself:

O attraction, abandon your force of attraction. O hate, abandon hatred. You have played long enough with me. O pleasures, salutations to you; you have indeed sustained me all these years and even made me forget the self. O sorrow, salutations to you; you spurred me on my quest for self-knowledge and it is by your grace that I have attained this self-knowledge; hence you are indeed the bestower of delight.

O body, my friend, permit me to go to my eternal abode of self-knowledge. Such indeed is the course of nature; everyone has to abandon the body at some time or the other. O body, my friend, you have been my relation for a long time. I abandon you now. You yourself have brought on this separation by nobly leading me to the realisation of the self. How wonderful! In order to enable me to attain self-knowledge, you have destroyed yourself.

O mother craving! Give me leave to go; you are now left alone to wither away, because I have reached the state of supreme peace. O lust! In order to conquer you, I befriended your enemy dispassion; forgive me. I proceed to freedom; bless me. O merit! Salutations to you, for you rescued me from hell and led me to heaven. Salutations to demerit, the source of pain and punishment. Salutations to delusion under which I laboured for a long time and which is not seen by me even now.

O cave, the companion of samādhi (meditation), salutation to you. You have given me shelter when I was tormented by the pains of worldly existence. O staff, you have been my friend too, protecting me from snakes, etc., and you have saved me from falling into a pit, etc. Salutations to you.

O body, return to the elements of which you are composed. Salutations to activities like bathing; salutations to all the activities in this world. Salutations to the life-forces (prāṇa) that have been my companions. Whatever I did in this world was done only with you, through you and because of your energy. Pray, return to your own source, for now I shall merge in the infinite consciousness (Brahman). All things that come together in this world have to part one day or the other. O senses, return to your own sources, the cosmic elements.

I shall now enter into the self by the self indicated by the culmination of the OM-sound—as a lamp without fuel. I am free from all the activities of this world and from all notions of perceptions and experiences. My heart is established in the peace indicated by the resonance of the OM. Gone are delusion and error.

V:87, 88 VASIṢṬHA continued:

With all the desires in the mind utterly silenced and having well grounded himself in the plane of non-dual consciousness, sage Vītahavya uttered the holy word OM. Contemplating the esoteric significance of the OM, he perceived the error of confusing the reality with the appearance. By the total abandonment of all concepts and percepts, he renounced the three worlds. He became utterly quiescent, as when the potter's wheel comes to rest. By the utterance of the OM he dispelled the webs of sense-organs and their objects, even as wind disperses scent. After this, he pierced the darkness of ignorance. He beheld the inner light for just a split second, but renounced that too immediately. He transcended both light and darkness. There remained just a trace of thought-form; this, too, the sage cut asunder in the twinkling of an eye, through the mind. Now the sage remained in the pure infinite consciousness, not modified in the least; it was like the state of consciousness of the just-born infant. He abandoned all objectivity of consciousness and even the slightest movement of consciousness. He crossed the state known as 'paśyantī' and reached the deep sleep consciousness. He continued beyond that, too, and reached the transcendental or turīya consciousness. It is a state of bliss that is not its description, which is both the 'is' and the 'is not', both something and not-something, light and darkness. It is full of non-consciousness and (objectless) consciousness, it can only be indicated by negation (not this, not this). He became that which is beyond description.

That state is the void, Brahman, consciousness, the Puruṣa of the Sāṅkhya, Īśvara of the yogi, Śiva, time, Ātman or self, non-self, the middle, etc., of the mystics holding different views. It is that state which is established as the truth by all these scriptural viewpoints, that which is all—in that the sage remained firmly established.

When the sage had thus become one with the infinite consciousness, the body decomposed and the elements returned to their respective source.

Thus have I told, O Rāma, the auspicious story of the sage Vītahavya. Reflect over it. Whatever I have said to you and whatever I shall say to you now is born of direct perception, direct experience and deep contemplation.

Meditate upon this, O Rāma, and attain wisdom. Liberation is attained only by wisdom or self-knowledge. Only through such wisdom does one go beyond sorrow, destroy ignorance and attain perfection.

What has been described as Vītahavya is only a notion in our mind; so am I and so are you. All these senses and the whole world are nothing but the mind. What else can the world be, O Rāma?

RĀMA asked: Lord, why do we not see many of these liberated V:89
sages traversing the sky now?

VASIṢṬHA replied: Flying in the sky and other powers are natural to some beings, O Rāma. The extraordinary qualities and faculties which are observed in this world are natural to those beings—not to the sages of self-knowledge. Supernatural faculties (like flying in the air) are developed by even those who are devoid of self-knowledge or liberation, by the utilisation of certain substances or by certain practices. All this does not interest the man of self-knowledge who is utterly content in himself. They who, in pursuit of pleasures, acquire these powers tainted by ignorance, are surely full of ignorance; the sages of self-knowledge do not adopt such a course.

Whether one is a knower of truth or ignorant of it, powers like flying in the air accrue to one who engages himself in some practices. But the sage of self-knowledge has no desire to acquire these. These practices bestow their fruit on anyone, for such is their nature. Poison kills all, wine intoxicates all, even so these practices bring about the ability to fly, etc., but they who have attained the supreme self-knowledge are not interested in these, O Rāma. They are gained only by those who are full of desires; but the sage is free from the least desire for anything. Self-knowledge is the greatest gain; how does the sage of self-knowledge entertain any desire for anything else? In the case of Vītahavya, however, he did not desire these powers; they sought him unsought.

RĀMA asked: How is it that worms and vermin did not destroy Vītahavya's body when it lay abandoned in the cave? And, how was it that Vītahavya did not attain disembodied liberation in the first place?

VASIṢṬHA replied: O Rāma, the ignorant man's body is composed and decomposed on account of the states of his mental conditioning; in the case of one who has no such conditioning, there is no momentum for decomposition. Again, the mind of all beings responds to the qualities of the object with which it comes into contact. When a violent creature comes into contact with one who has reached utter equanimity, it also becomes temporarily equanimous and tranquil, though it may return to its violence when this contact is lost. Hence, too, Vītahavya's body remained unharmed. This applies even to material substances like earth, wood, etc., for consciousness pervades all. Since Vītahavya's consciousness did not undergo any change, no change happened to his body. Since there was no movement of prāṇa in it, even decomposition could not take place. The sage is independent and free to live or to abandon the body. That he did not abandon the body at one time and did so later is purely coincidental; it may be related to his karma, etc., but in truth he is beyond karma, beyond fate, and devoid of mental conditioning. Again, it is like the crow dislodging the ripe cocoanut—purely coincidental.

V:90 VASIṢṬHA continued:

When the mind of Vītahavya had become unattached and totally free through the practice of enquiry, there arose in him noble qualities like friendliness, etc.

RĀMA asked:

When the mind has been dissolved in Brahman the absolute, in whom do qualities like friendliness arise?

VASIṢṬHA answered:

O Rāma, there are two types of 'death of the mind'. One is where the form of the mind remains and the other is where even the form ceases to be. The former happens when the sage is still alive; and the latter happens when he is disembodied. The existence of the mind causes misery; and its cessation brings joy. The mind that is heavily conditioned and caught in its own conditioning brings about repeated births. Such a mind brings unhappiness. That which regards as 'my own' the qualities that are beginningless is the jīva. It arises in the mind which has no self-knowledge and which is therefore unhappy.

As long there is mind, there is no cessation of sorrow. When the mind ceases, the world-appearance also ceases to be. The mind is the seed for misery.

I shall now describe how the mind ceases to be. When both happiness and unhappiness do not divert a man from his utter equanimity, then know that his mind is dead. He in whom the notions 'This I am' and 'This I am not' do not arise thus limiting his consciousness—his mind is dead. He in whom the very notions of calamity, poverty, elation, pride, dullness and excitement do not arise—his mind is dead and he is liberated while living.

The very nature of the mind is stupidity. Hence, when it dies purity and noble qualities arise. Some wise men refer to 'the pure mind' as that state of utter purity that prevails in a liberated sage in whom the mind is dead. Such a mind of the liberated sage is, therefore, full of noble qualities like friendliness, etc. The existence (sattā) of such natural goodness in a liberated sage is known as satva, purity, etc. Hence, this is also called 'death of the mind where form remains'.

The death of the mind where even the form vanishes pertains to the disembodied sage. In the case of such a mind, no trace is left. It is impossible to describe it in a positive way: in it there are neither qualities nor their absence, neither virtues nor their absence, neither light nor darkness, no notions at all, no conditioning, neither existence nor non-existence. It is a state of supreme quiescence and equilibrium. They who have risen beyond the mind and the intelligence, they reach that supreme state of peace.

RĀMA asked: V:91

Lord, what is the seed of this fearful tree known as the mind and what is the seed of that seed and so on?

VASIṢṬHA replied:

Rāma, the seed for this world-appearance is the body within, with all its notions and concepts of good and evil. That body has a seed, too, and that is the mind which flows constantly in the direction of hopes and desires, and which is also the repository of notions of being and non-being and the consequent sorrow. The world-appearance arises only in the mind, and this is illustrated by the dream state. Whatever is seen here as the world is but the expansion of the mind, even as pots are transformations of clay.

There are two seeds for the tree known as the mind which carries within it innumerable notions and ideas: first, movement of prāṇa (life-force) and second, obstinate fancy. When there is movement of prāṇa in the appropriate channels, then there is movement in consciousness and mind arises. Again, it is the movement of prāṇa alone, when it is seen or apprehended by the mind, that is seen as this world-appearance which is as real as the blueness of the sky. The cessation of the movement of prāṇa is the cessation of the world-appearance too. The omnipresent consciousness is 'awakened', as it were, by the movement of prāṇa. If this does not happen, then there is supreme good.

When consciousness is 'awakened' thus, it begins to apprehend objects, ideas arise and thence sorrow. On the other hand, if this consciousness rests in itself, as if fast asleep, then one attains what is most desirable and that is the supreme state. Therefore, you will realise the unborn state of consciousness if you either restrain the movement of prāṇa in your own psychological ground (of concepts and notions), or refrain from disturbing the homogeneity in consciousness. It is when this homogeneity is disturbed and the consciousness experiences diversity that the mind arises, and the countless psychological conditions spring up into activity.

In order to bring about quiescence of the mind, the yogi practises prāṇāyāma (restraint of the movement of the life-force), meditation and such other proper and appropriate methods. Great yogis regard this prāṇāyāma itself as the most appropriate method for the achievement of tranquility of the mind, peace, etc.

I shall now describe to you the other viewpoint, that of the men of wisdom, born of their direct experience: they declare that the mind is born of one's obstinate clinging to a fancy or deluded imagination.

VASIṢṬHA continued:

When, obstinately clinging to a fancy, and therefore abandoning a thorough enquiry into the nature of truth, one apprehends an object with that fancy—such apprehension is described as conditioning or limitation. When such fancy is persistently and intensely indulged in, this world-appearance arises in consciousness. Caught up in his own conditioning, whatever the person sees he thinks that to be real and gets deluded. And on account of the intensity of the conditioning and the fancy, he discards his own nature and perceives only the world-illusion. All this happens only to the unwise person. That, whose perception is thus perverted, is known as mind. When this mind is confirmed in its perverted perception, it becomes the seed for repeated birth, old age and death.

When notions of the desirable and undesirable do not arise, then the mind does not arise and there is supreme peace. These alone constitute the form of the mind—conception, imagination, thought and memory. When these are absent, how does a mind exist? When one, established in non-becoming, contemplates that which has not changed into becoming and when one thus perceives what is as it is, then the mind becomes no-mind. When the psychological conditioning or limitation is not dense, when it has become transparent, one becomes a liberated sage who apparently lives and functions by past momentum (even as a potter's wheel rotates after the initial impulse has been withdrawn), but he will not be born again. In his case, the seed has been fried, as it were, and will not germinate into world-illusion. When the body falls, he is absorbed into the infinite.

Of the two seeds for this world-illusion (viz., movement of prāṇa and clinging to fancy), if one is got rid of the other also goes away; for the two are interdependent. The mind creates the world-illusion and the mind is created by the movement of prāṇa in one's own conditioning. Again, this movement of prāṇa also takes place because of the mental conditioning or fancy. Thus this vicious circle is completed; one feeds the other, one spurs the other into action. Motion is natural to prāṇa and when it moves in consciousness, mind arises; then the conditioning keeps the prāṇa in motion. When one is arrested, both fall.

The psychological conditioning or limitation alone is the source of untold pain and sorrow and it is the root of ignorance: but when it comes to an end, the mind falls with it instantly. Even so, by the restraint of the movement of prāṇa (life-force) the mind comes to a standstill, without perceiving the world that dwells within it.

VASIṢṬHA continued:

Rāma, the notion of an object (of knowledge, of experience) is the seed for both movement of prāṇa and for the clinging to a fancy, for it is only when such desire for experience arises in the heart that such movement of prāṇa and mental conditioning take place. When such desire for experience is abandoned, both these cease instantly.

Of course, the indwelling consciousness is the seed for this desire for experiencing: for without that consciousness the desire for such experience will not arise at all. However, it has no object of experience either outside or inside; for it is the consciousness itself that, on account of a movement of thought within itself, desires to experience itself as an object. Just as a man dreams of his own death or of his travel abroad, even so this consciousness, by its own cleverness, experiences itself as an object. When such experience takes place, this world-appearance results, O Rāma. When this truth is realised, the illusion ceases to be.

What is the truth? That all this is nothing but the one infinite consciousness and that there is naught else besides. Whatever is seen and whatever is unseen, all that is the infinite consciousness—thus should the wise one realise, so purifying his vision. Unpurified vision perceives the world; purified vision perceives the infinite consciousness and that itself is liberation. Hence, O Rāma, strive to eradicate the desire for experience. Get rid of idleness. Free yourself from all experiences.

RĀMA asked:

Lord, how can these two be reconciled? Can I seek freedom from all experiences and freedom from inactivity at the same time?

VASIṢṬHA replied:

He who has no desire or hope for anything here, nor entertains a wish to rest in inactivity, such a one does not exist as a jīva; he is neither inactive nor does he seek to experience. He who does not lean towards experience or perception of objects, though he is engaged in ceaseless activity, he is neither inactive nor does he do anything or experience anything. The objective experiences do not touch the heart at all: hence, he whose consciousness is not inactive is a liberated sage here and now.

Freed from all conditioning, fully established in the state of unmodified consciousness, the yogi remains like a child or a dumb person: in him there is bliss, like the blueness of the sky. This bliss is not an experience, but the very nature of consciousness. Hence, it does not act as a disturbance, but remains integrated in the consciousness. There is freedom from all experiences. At the same time, the yogi is constantly engaged in action: hence, there is freedom from inactivity.

VASIṢṬHA continued:

However difficult it may be to reach this state, Rāma, strive for it and cross this ocean of sorrow.

This desire for experience arises as a thought in consciousness; and by the repetition of this thought, it gains strength. Thus having brought about the illusory creation within itself, consciousness leads itself to its own liberation. Whatever it conceives of, that materialises. Thus having bound itself, having subjected itself to sorrow (like the silkworm with the cocoon) in due course of time it attains to liberation, because its nature is infinite consciousness. What is seen as the universe is nothing but pure consciousness, O Rāma.

Pure existence alone is the seed for this infinite consciousness. They are inseparable like the sun and his rays. However, this pure existence has two aspects: one, diversity, and second, unity. That which is described as 'this' and 'that', 'I' and 'you' is known as diversity. When this diversity is abandoned and there is pure existence, it is regarded as unity. When diversity is abandoned and unity prevails, there is also non-experience: and hence unity is not a 'thing' nor an object of experience. This unity is therefore eternal and imperishable.

Hence, O Rāma, abandon all forms of division—division in terms of time or of parts or of substance—and rest in pure existence. These divisions are conducive to the arising of concepts. They are non-different from the pure consciousness; what is more, they are not facts as such. Contemplation of division does not lead to purity of vision.

Pure existence alone without any division in it is the seed for all these that we have discussed thus far: and there is no seed for this pure existence. It is the cause of everything and it is itself uncaused. In it are all these reflected. All the diverse experiences are experienced in this pure existence, even as diverse tastes are tasted by the one tongue. An infinite number of universes are born, exist and dissolve in it; and they come into mutual relationship in it.

That pure existence is heaviness in all heavy things; that is lightness in all that is light. That is grossness and that alone is subtlety. It is first among the first, last among the last. It is the light of the luminous and the darkness of the dark. It is substantiality of all substances and it is the space, too. It is nothing and it is everything; it is and it is not. It is seen and it is unseen. That I am and that I am not.

O Rāma, therefore, by every means in your power, strive to get established in that supreme state and then do what is appropriate. They who reach that state, which is pure and undecaying and which is the truth of one's own self, attain to supreme peace. By reaching it, you will for ever be freed from the fear of this worldy existence.

RĀMA asked: V:92

Holy sir, kindly tell me, how may one quickly destroy all these seeds of distraction and reach the supreme state?

VASIṢṬHA said:

These seeds of sorrow, O Rāma, can be destroyed, each by the destruction of the previous one. But, if you can at one stroke cut off all mental conditioning and by great self-effort rest in the state of pure existence (if you rest in that state even for a second) in no time you will be established in it. If however you wish merely to find your foothold in pure existence, you can achieve it, by even greater effort. Similarly, by contemplating the infinite consciousness, too, you can rest in the supreme state: but that demands greater effort.

Meditation is not possible on objects of experience: for they exist only in consciousness or the self. But if you strive to destroy the conditioning (the concepts, notions, habits, etc.), then in a moment all your errors and illnesses will vanish. However, this is more difficult than the ones described earlier. For, until the mind is free from the movement of thought, cessation of conditioning is difficult, and vice versa; and unless the truth is realised, the mind does not cease to function, and vice versa. Yet, again, until the conditioning ceases, the unconditioned truth is not realised, and vice versa. Since realisation of truth, cessation of the mind and the ending of conditioning are interwoven, it is extremely difficult to deal with them individually and separately.

Hence, O Rāma, by every means in your power, renounce the pursuit of pleasure and resort to all the three simultaneously. If all these are simultaneously practised for a considerable time, then they become fruitful, not otherwise. O Rāma, this world-appearance has been experienced as truth for a very long time: and it needs persistent practice of all these three simultaneously to overcome it.

Wise ones declare that the abandonment of conditioning and the restraint of prāṇa are of equal effect: hence, one should practise them simultaneously. Prāṇa is restrained by the practice of prāṇāyāma and the yoga āsana, as taught by the guru, or by other means. When desires, aversions and cravings do not arise in the mind even though their objects are seen in front, then it is to be inferred that mental conditioning has weakened; thence wisdom arises, further weakening the conditioning. Then the mind ceases.

It is not possible to 'kill the mind' without proper methods. Knowledge of the self, company of holy men, the abandonment of conditioning and the restraint of prāṇa—these are the means to overcome the mind. Ignoring these and resorting to violent practices like Haṭha Yoga, austerities, pilgrimage, rites and rituals are a waste of time. Self-knowledge alone bestows delight on you. A man of self-knowledge alone lives. Hence, gain self-knowledge, O Rāma.

V:93 VASIṢṬHA continued:

If one has achieved even a little bit of control over the mind by self-enquiry, such a person has attained the fruit of his life. For that self-enquiry will expand in his heart. When such enquiry is preceded by dispassion and has attained stability by practice, all the noble qualities resort to it naturally. Ignorance and its retinue do not bother one who is fully established in self-enquiry and who sees what is, without distortion. When he has found his foothold in the spiritual ground, he is not overcome by the robbers known as sense-pleasures.

But, sense-pleasures do overcome one who is not so established. He who is not constantly engaged in self-enquiry and is not thus constantly conscious of the self, he alone is considered a dead man. Hence, O Rāma, carry on this enquiry constantly. This enquiry reveals the truth by dispelling the darkness of ignorance. Knowledge of the truth in its turn drives away all sorrow. Along with knowledge arises the experience of it. But when the inner light, kindled by a proper study of the scriptures and enquiry into their truth, illumines both knowledge and the experience of it, their total identity is realised. This inner light itself is regarded as self-knowledge by the holy ones: and the experience of it is an integral part of self-knowledge and non-different from it. He who has self-knowledge is for ever immersed in the experience of it. He is liberated while living and lives like an emperor of the world.

Such a sage is not distracted by the diverse experiences he may apparently be subject to, whether they are regarded by others as pleasant or unpleasant. He is not bound or overcome by pleasure nor is there a craving for pleasure in him. He is completely satisfied in his own self. He is not attached to anything or anybody; and he has no enmity or hatred in his heart. Nor is he frightened by the roar of an enemy or the roar of a lion in the forest. He does not rejoice when he visits a garden nor is he distressed if he happens to travel in a desert. Inwardly ever free, yet he engages in doing constantly whatever actions may be appropriate for the moment. His attitude towards both a murderer and a philanthropist is the same. In his cosmic vision all things great and small appear to be the same, for he knows that the entire universe is nothing but pure consciousness.

He who acts without attachment, merely with the organs of action, is not affected by anything, neither by joy nor by sorrow. His actions are non-volitional. He sees not, though eyes see; he hears not, though ears hear; he touches not, though the body touches. Surely, attachment (contact, association) is the cause for this world-illusion; it alone creates objects. Attachment causes bondage and endless sorrow. Therefore, holy ones declare that the abandonment of attachment is itself liberation. Abandon attachment, O Rāma, and be a liberated sage.

RĀMA asked: Lord, kindly tell me what is this attachment?

VASIṢṬHA replied:

Attachment is that, O Rāma, which makes the conditioning of the mind more and more dense, by repeatedly causing the experiences of pleasure and pain in relation to the existence and the non-existence of the objects of pleasure, thus confirming such association as inevitable and thus bringing about an intense attachment to the objects of pleasure. In the case of the liberated sage, however, this conditioning is freed from the experiences of joy and sorrow: hence it is purified, i.e., the conditioning is weakened if not destroyed. Even if it exists in an extremely weakened state till the death of the body, the actions that spring from such a weakened and so pure conditioning do not result in rebirth.

On the other hand, the dense conditioning which exists in the unwise is itself known as attachment. If you abandon this attachment which causes perverse notions in you, the actions that you may spontaneously perform here will not affect you. If you rise beyond joy and sorrow and therefore treat them alike, and if you are free from attraction, aversion and fear, you are unattached. If you do not grieve in sorrow, if you do not exult in happiness and if you are independent of your own desires and hopes, you are unattached. Even while carrying on your activities here, if you do not abandon your awareness of the homogeneity of the truth, you are unattached. If you have gained self-knowledge and if, endowed with equal vision, you engage yourself in spontaneous and appropriate action in the here and now, you are unattached.

By effortlessly remaining established in non-attachment, live here as a liberated sage without being attracted by anything. The liberated sage lives in the inner silence, without pride or vanity, without jealousy and with his senses fully under his control. Even when all the objects of the world are spread out in front of him, the liberated sage, who is free from cravings, is not tempted by them, but engages himself in mere natural actions. Whatever is inevitable and appropriate, he does; his joy and delight, however, he derives from within: thus he is freed from this world-appearance. Even as milk does not abandon its colour when it is boiled, he does not abandon his wisdom even when it is severely tested by terrible calamities. Whether he is subjected to great pain or he is appointed the ruler of heaven, he remains in a balanced state of mind.

Hence, O Rāma, engage yourself constantly in self-enquiry and rest firmly established in self-knowledge. You will never again be subjected to birth and bondage.

(Vicāra in the preceding pages has been translated 'enquiry' or 'self-enquiry'. That is the popular translation. However, the word really means efficient movement of one's inner intelligence—'car' in sanskrit is 'to move'. It should not be confused with intellectual analysis. It is direct observation or 'looking within'.)

PART SIX

On Liberation

BHAGAVĀN RAMAṆA MAHARṢI said:

Cidābhāsa is the feeling of the self which appears as the shining of the mind. The one becomes three, the three becomes five and the five becomes many; that is, the pure self (satva which appears to be one) becomes through contact three (satva, rajas and tamas) and with those three the five elements come into existence, and with those five, the whole universe. It is this which creates the illusion that the body is the self. In terms of the sky (ākāśa) it is explained as being divided into three categories as reflected in the soul; the boundless world of pure consciousness, the boundless world of mental consciousness and the boundless world of matter (cidākāśa, cittākāśa and bhūtākāśa). When mind (citta) is divided into its three aspects, namely mind, intuition and maker of the 'I' (manas, buddhi and ahaṃkāra), it is called the inner instrument or antaḥkaraṇa. Karaṇaṃ means upakaraṇaṃ. Legs, hands and other organs of the body are called bāhyakaraṇa or outer instruments, while the senses (indriyas) which work inside the body are antaḥkaraṇas or inner instruments. That feeling of the self or shining mind which works with these inner instruments is said to be the personal soul or jīva. When the mental consciousness which is a reflection of the tangible aspect of pure consciousness, sees the world of matter, it is called mental world (mano ākāśa), but when it sees the tangible aspect of pure consciousness, it is called total consciousness (cinmaya). That is why it is said, "The mind is the cause of both bondage and liberation for man." That mind creates many illusions.

If the secret truth mentioned above is ascertained by self-enquiry, the multiplicity resolves itself into five, the five into three, and the three into one. Suppose you have a headache and you get rid of it by taking some medicine, you then remain what you were originally; the headache is like the illusion that the body is the self; it disappears when the medicine called self-enquiry is administered.

It is true that it is only possible for mature minds, not for immature ones. For the latter, repetition of a mantra under one's breath (japa), worship of images, breath-control (prāṇāyāma), visualising a pillar of light and similar yogic and spiritual and religious practices have been prescribed. By those practices, people become mature and will then realise the self through the path of self-enquiry.

VĀLMĪKI said: VI.1:1

The sage Vasiṣṭha had concluded the teaching contained in the upaśama prakaraṇaṃ and he uttered the words, "O Rāma, you have heard the upaśama prakaraṇaṃ; now hear the section dealing with liberation." All the kings and the sages who were seated in the court were deeply absorbed in the great Vasiṣṭha's discourse; with their attention totally riveted on his words and gestures, they appeared more like figures in a painting than actual living human beings. In fact, it seemed that even the sun, the air, the birds and the beasts—the entire nature was absorbed in intently listening to the sage's discourse with their souls absorbed in the sublime exposition of the nature of the innermost self.

As the sun was about to set the palace suddenly resounded with drums and trumpets. For a few moments this sound drowned the voice of the sage Vasiṣṭha. When the sound of the drums, trumpets and conches died down, the sage asked Rāma the following question.

VASIṢṬHA said:

I have thus provided you with a net woven with words which are indicative of the highest truth: tie down the bird of your mind with this net and let the mind then rest in your heart. Thus shall you attain self-knowledge. O Rāma, have you absorbed this truth imparted by me, although it is mixed with varied expressions and illustrations, even as the proverbial swan is able to separate milk from water when these are mixed together and to drink the milk alone?

You should contemplate this truth again and again, from beginning to end, reflect upon it and you should march along this path now, O noble one. Though engaged in diverse activities, you will not be bound if your intelligence is saturated with this truth; otherwise, you will fall, even as an elephant falls from the cliff. Again, if you conceptualise this teaching for your intellectual entertainment and do not let it act in your life, you will stumble and fall like a blind man.

In order to reach the state of perfection or liberation taught by me you should live a life of non-attachment, doing what is appropriate in every situation as it reaches you. Rest assured that this is the vital factor in the teachings of all scriptures.

Given leave to depart, all the kings and the sages of the assembly left for their abode. They contemplated Vasiṣṭha's teachings and discussed it among themselves, spending only a couple of hours in pleasant and deep sleep.

VI.1:2 VĀLMĪKI continued:

Very soon the darkness of the night began to recede even as mental conditioning recedes with the approach of the awakening of the inner intelligence. Shafts of light from the eastern horizon illumined the eastern and the western peaks.

Rāma, Lakṣmaṇa and all the others awoke at that auspicious hour and performed their morning religious duties. Then they proceeded swiftly to the hermitage of the sage Vasiṣṭha. They offered him appropriate worship, prostrated at his feet and followed him to the royal court. The audience packed the court; but there was pin-drop silence. The space in the court was again filled with celestial beings and sages who had attained perfection. All of them took their allotted seats as on the previous days. Rāma devoutly gazed at the face of the sage Vasiṣṭha.

VASIṢṬHA said:

Rāma, do you remember what I have so far said to you, the words which are capable of awakening a knowledge of truth or self-knowledge? I shall once again declare to you how perfection can be permanently established.

By resorting to dispassion (the unconditioned mind) and a clear understanding of the truth, this ocean of saṃsāra (bondage to life and death) can be crossed: hence engage yourself in such endeavour. When the truth is clearly perceived and when its misunderstanding has been completely abandoned, upon the dissolution of all the latent tendencies or mental conditioning, the sorrowless state is reached.

The one infinite absolute existence or cosmic consciousness alone is and it is not affected by the concepts of time and space, nor is it subject to polarity or division. The infinite alone exists and has somehow assumed duality. However, when in fact the infinite cannot thus be divided, how can such duality come into being? Knowing this, be free of the ego-sense and rejoice in the self.

There is no mind, no ignorance, no individual soul: these are all concepts that arose in the creator Brahmā. Whatever objects there may be, whatever may be the mind and its desires—all that is indeed the one cosmic consciousness. That one alone shines in the nether-world, on earth and in heaven as consciousness.

As long as the concepts born of ignorance persist, as long as there is perception of that which is not the infinite and as long as there is hope in the trap known as the world, so long one entertains notions of mind, etc. As long as one considers the body as the 'I' and as long as the self is related to what is seen, as long as there is hope in objects with the feeling 'this is mine', so long will there be delusion concerning mind, etc.

VASIṢṬHA continued:

The illusory notion of the existence of the mind, etc., persists only as long as the sublime realisation of the truth is not experienced through the company of the wise, who are totally unattached, and as long as wickedness has not been weakened. As long as the experience of this world as a reality has not been shaken by the energy derived from the clear perception of the truth, so long the existence of the mind etc., seems to be self-evident. Such a notion continues as long as there is blind dependence, on account of craving for objective experience, and as long as there are wickedness and delusion as a consequence.

But in the case of one who is not attracted by pleasure, whose heart is cool because of its purity and who has shattered the cage of desires, cravings and hopes, the deluded notion of the existence of the mind ceases to be. When he sees even his body as the deluded experience of a non-entity, how can a mind arise in him? He who has the vision of the infinite and into whose heart the world-appearance has merged, does not entertain the deluded notion of a jīva, etc.

When incorrect perception has come to an end and when the sun of self-knowledge arises in the heart, know that the mind is reduced to naught. It is not seen again, even as burnt dry leaves. The state of mind of the liberated ones who are still living and who see both the supreme truth and the relative appearance, is known as satva (transparency). It is improper to call it the mind: it is really satva. These knowers of truth are mindless and are in a state of perfect equilibrium: they live their life here playfully. They behold the inner light all the time, even though they seem to be engaged in diverse actions. Concepts of duality, unity or such others do not arise in them, for there are no tendencies in their heart. The very seed of ignorance is burnt in the state of satva and it does not again give rise to delusion.

O Rāma, you have reached that state of satva and your mind has been burnt in the fire of wisdom. What is that wisdom? It is that the infinite Brahman is indeed the infinite Brahman, the world-appearance is but an appearance whose reality is Brahman. The appearance (for instance, your body as 'Rāma') is insentient, is unreal; its reality is the reality of its substratum which is consciousness. Why then do you grieve? However, if you feel that all this is consciousness, there need not arise in you the notions of diversity. Recollect your essential nature as the infinite consciousness. Abandon the notions of diversity. You are what you are: nay, not even that as a concept but beyond it you are the self-luminous being. Salutations to you, O cosmic being that is infinite consciousness.

VI.1:3 VASIṢṬHA continued:

You are that ocean of consciousness in which there appear countless waves and ripples which are known as universes. You are indeed beyond the states of being and non-being, both of which are mere concepts of the mind. Rise beyond such conditioning and therefore beyond all duality. How can tendencies and limitations exist in you? All such concepts ('This is a latent tendency or limitation' and 'This is a jīva or the living soul') arise in consciousness: how then are they different from consciousness and if they are not, how can we say that they arise in consciousness?

That which is known as Rāma is in truth the magnificent and infinite ocean of consciousness in which numerous universes appear and disappear like ripples and waves. Remain in a state of total equanimity. You are like the infinite space. Fire is inseparable from heat, fragrance from the lotus, blackness from collyrium, whiteness from snow, sweetness from sugar-cane and light from a luminary. Even so experiencing is inseparable from consciousness. Even as waves are inseparable from the ocean, even so the universes are inseparable from consciousness.

Experiencing is non-different from consciousness, the ego-sense is non-different from experiencing, the jīva is non-different from ego-sense and the mind is non-different from the jīva (non-different or inseparable). The senses are non-different from the mind, the body is non-different from the senses, the world is non-different from the body and there is nothing but this world. This catalogue of dependent categories has existed for a very long time; yet this has neither been set in motion by anyone, nor can we say whether it has existed for a very long or very short time. The truth is, O Rāma, all this is naught else but the self-experiencing of the infinite.

There is emptiness in the empty, Brahman pervades Brahman, the truth shines in the truth and fullness fills fullness. The wise man, though functioning in this world, does nothing, for he seeks nothing. Even so, O Rāma, remain pure at heart like space, but outwardly engage yourself in appropriate action; in situations which could provoke exultation or depression, remain unaffected by them like a log of wood. He who is friendly even to one who is about to murder him, is a seer of truth. Adoration of one who has not thus risen above likes and dislikes (rāga and dveṣa) is futile effort. Only he who is free from egoistic or volitional activity and who is utterly non-attached to anything here is liberated; even if he should destroy the world, he does nothing.

He in whom all concepts and habitual tendencies have ceased has overcome all mental conditioning and bondage. He is like a lamp which is not fed with oil.

VASIṢṬHA continued: VI.1:4, 5

O Rāma, the mind, the intellect and the ego-sense, as also the senses, are all devoid of independent intelligence: where then do the jīva and all the rest of it reside? Even as the moon is one yet it appears to be two or more on account of defective vision or agitation in the reflecting medium, the self (inner intelligence or consciousness) is one, but appears to be many on account of the agitation caused by the thoughts.

Just as night comes to an end when darkness recedes, ignorance comes to an end when the poison of craving for pleasure ceases. This deadly virus of craving for pleasure is instantly cured by the magic formula of scriptural declarations. At the very instant when wickedness or foolishness comes to an end, the mind with all its retinue vanishes, even as pearls scatter when the connecting thread is broken. Hence, O Rāma, they who abandon the scriptures have chosen to live as worms and vermin for their own self-destruction.

When wind subsides, the surface of the lake becomes calm once again: when agitation caused by ignorance ceases, the unsteadiness of the eyes caused by infatuation for wife and other objects of pleasure ceases. Obviously, O Rāma, you have reached that steadiness. You have listened intently to my words: and on account of that the veil of ignorance has been lifted in you. Even ordinary human beings are profoundly influenced by the words of their family preceptor: how then can it be different in one who possesses an expanded vision, as you do?

RĀMA said:

Lord, by listening to your words of wisdom, the world which appears to be outside has lost its substantiality and my mind has ceased. I rest in supreme peace. I perceive the world as it is, as the infinite consciousness infinitely displayed before me. All my doubts have been dispelled. I am free from attraction and resistance. I am established in nature, I am well (svasthah: I rest in the self) and I am happy, I am Rāma in whom the worlds find their refuge. Salutations to me, salutations to you. The mental conditioning has vanished. The mind has come to an end. I see the self as the all-in-all. When I think of the past I smile at the foolish ideas of duality I used to entertain. All this, thanks to the effect of your nectarine words of spiritual counsel. While still living in this world I am also in the world of light. Thanks to the rays of light that emanate from your illumined heart in the form of words of supreme wisdom, I am immersed in supreme bliss here and now.

VI.1:6 VASIṢṬHA continued:

O Rāma, you are dear to me: hence I declare the truth to you once again. Listen attentively. Listen, though for doing so, you have to assume the existence of diversity. Your consciousness will expand. And, the truth that I shall expound will save from sorrow even they who are not fully awakened.

When one is ignorant, one entertains the wrong notion that the body is the self; his own senses prove to be his worst enemies. On the other hand, he who is endowed with self-knowledge and knows the truth enjoys the friendship of his senses which are pleased and contented; they do not destroy him. He who has nothing but disgust for the physical body and its functions does not surely indulge it and thus invite suffering.

The self is not affected by the body, nor is the body in any way related to the self. They are like light and darkness. The self, which transcends all modifications and perversions, neither comes into being nor does it vanish. Whatever happens, happens to this body which is inert, ignorant, insentient, finite, perishable and ungrateful: let it happen. But, how can this body ever comprehend (through the senses or the mind) the eternal consciousness? For, when either is seen as the reality the other ceases to be. When thus their nature is totally different, how can their experience of pain and pleasure be the same? When they do not and cannot have any relationship whatsoever, how can they exist together? When either arises the other ceases, even as when the day dawns the darkness of night ceases to be. Self-knowledge can never become self-ignorance; even as the shadow can never become hot.

Brahman, which is the reality, can never become unreal even when one is aware of diversity; nor can the body ever acquire the nature of the infinite consciousness. Though the self is omnipresent, it is unaffected by the body, even as the lotus is not affected by water. Hence, even as space is not affected by the movement of air within it, this infinite self is not affected by conditions known as old age, death, pleasure and pain, existence and non-existence which pertain to the body. Even though all these bodies are seen by deluded understanding, they are all in the infinite consciousness alone even as waves appear on the ocean. The diversity and the perversity of the appearances belong to the reflecting medium: the truth or the infinite self is not affected by all this, even as the sun is not affected by the diversity and the agitation that its reflection undergoes in several mirrors or other reflecting media.

When the truth concerning the self is thus seen, the notion of self-ignorance vanishes instantly.

VASIṢṬHA continued:

Correct understanding of the body and the intelligence that dwells in the body enables one to understand the entire creation in its material and its spiritual aspects, as easily as one sees objects illumined by a lamp. It is only when there is not this right understanding that deluded and wrong notions rise and flourish within one's heart—notions which are utterly devoid of substance. Befuddled by these wrong notions which arise in the absence of the light of true knowledge, one is constantly and restlessly carried hither and thither like a blade of grass in wind.

In the absence of the 'taste' (direct knowledge) of the cosmic intelligence, the senses endeavour to apprehend their objects and vainly imagine that such contact gives rise to meaningful experience! Surely, the infinite and inexhaustible intelligence (consciousness) dwells in all these: however on account of the absence of self-knowledge, it appears to be ignorant of itself and therefore limited and finite.

The life-force and its retinue function here merely to provide energy for the movements inherent in living, not with any other motive. In the absence of self-knowledge, all the talking and roaring which people indulge in are like the sound produced by a gun! They inevitably proceed towards destruction and do not lead to salutary results. Fools enjoy the fruits of their labour, not knowing that they are resting and sleeping on a rock that is burning hot.

Keeping company with such fools is like sitting in a forest on a tree which is about to be felled. Whatever you do for the sake of such people is like beating the air with a rod. What is given to them is thrown into mud, and to converse with them is as meaningful as the dog barking at the sky.

Ignorance of the self is the source of all troubles and calamities. Tell me, O Rāma, is there a single trouble that does not spring from ignorance of the self? This entire creation is pervaded by ignorance which sustains it. One who is ignorant is visited again and again by terrible sorrow and rarely by pleasure. Sources of sorrow like body, wealth and wife do not cease in the case of one who is ignorant of the self. For there is no end to the ignorance of one who firmly believes that the body is the self: how can true self-knowledge arise in him? As long as such ignorance rules the fool falls again and again. His sorrow is unceasing. Even the cool rays of the moon are experienced as poisonous fumes by him. The portals of hell are wide open, eager to receive such a fool.

VASIṢṬHA continued:

It is only in the eyes of the fool that the poisonous creeper (woman) bears the blossoms of restless eyes and pearl-like smiling teeth. For only in the heart of the wicked grows the dreadful tree of infatuation providing an abode for countless birds (sinful tendencies). In the forest of his vicious heart rages the fire of hate. His mind is flooded with jealousy giving rise to the growth of the weeds of destructive criticism of others; the only lotus his heart knows is envy, which is sought by the bees of endless worry.

Death is meant only for such vicious fools. Birth and childhood lead to youth, youth leads to old age, and old age ends in death—and all these are repeatedly experienced by the ignorant. The ignorant man is like a pot tied to the rope known as the world, with which he is now lowered into the blind well of saṃsāra and now lifted up. This very ocean of world-appearance is like the footprint of a calf to the wise and an unfathomable and endless sea of sorrow to the ignorant. Even as a caged bird is unable to find freedom, the ignorant man devoted to the fulfilment of his appetites is unable to find release from bondage. His mind, which is befuddled with apparently countless tendencies and conditioning, is unable to see clearly the revolving wheel of life and death.

In order to capture and to hold in bondage the ignorant person, his own infatuation spreads out throughout the world a whole network of illusory relationships. With a small piece of flesh (the eyes) the foolish man sees a little particle of earth which he regards as mountains, lakes, forests and cities. Ignorance is a mighty tree which has spread its branches in all directions, creating countless leaves of illusory objects. On that tree dwell numerous birds (like ever so many experiences of pleasure of the ignorant). Births are its leaves, actions are its buds, merit and demerit are the fruits, wealth and auspiciousness are its flowers.

This ignorance is like the moon which rises when the sun of wisdom has set; repeated births are the rays of the moon; and this ignorance is the lord of defects and imperfection. Tendencies and habits are the nectarine rays showered by this moon; the birds of hope and desire drink of this nectar. In the darkness of ignorance, the fool thinks he experiences pleasure or happiness in the objects of this world.

The external appearance of sweetness in the objects is caused by ignorance. For all these objects have a beginning and an end, they are limited, they are perishable.

VASIṢṬHA continued: VI.1:7

They whom you regard here as radiant women decked with pearls and other jewels are but the creation of your own delusion: they are the ripples that arise in the ocean of lust. It is this delusion that sees attractiveness and seductive qualities in what is but a modification of flesh, fat, skin, etc., and even makes them appear charming; and it is on account of such delusion that their breasts are described as golden pots and their lips as the source of nectar, etc.

It is on account of delusion that one seeks wealth and prosperity which are sweet in the beginning to the dull-witted, which are the cause of the pairs of opposites (happiness and unhappiness, pleasure and pain, success and failure) in the middle and which come to an end very soon. From the pursuit of prosperity arise countless branches of pleasure and numberless branches of unhappiness.

This delusion flows like a river from beginningless time and it is muddied and darkened by useless actions and their reactions. It gives rise to repeated births and it swells more and more on account of the bitter reactions or the consequences of actions calculated to bring pleasure or happiness.

Such actions are like an ill-wind that raises a cloud of dust whose particles are physical and mental illness, old age and the various relationships. All these lead to death (or the passage of time) which has an insatiable and voracious appetite and which consumes all the worlds when they are ripe, as it were.

Youth is haunted by the goblins of worries and anxieties which dance when the wisdom-moon does not shine; and youth proceeds towards denser darkness of delusion. One's tongue (the faculty of speech) is overworked in the service of the common and uncultured folk here and it grows debilitated.

In the meantime, poverty spreads its thousands of branches

yielding the fruits of unhappiness and hard labour. Yet, greed which is empty and insubstantial and which is destructive of one's own spiritual elevation, continues to proclaim victory in the darkness of delusion.

Stealthily the cat of senility catches the mouse of youth.

This creation is essenceless; yet, it gains a false reality. It even grows the fruits of dharma (righteous living) and artha (pursuit of prosperity). This world enveloped by the sky and endowed with the eyes of the sun and the moon is upheld by the delusion of its substantiality. In the lake of this world-appearance lilies known as bodies blossom and they are resorted to by the bees known as life-forces.

VASIṢṬHA continued:

The decadent concept of the world-existence lies imprisoned in the senses, bound by self-limitation and conditioning and by the powerful thread of hopes and desires. This world-appearance is like a delicate creeper which constantly trembles in the wind of the movement of prāṇa or life-force and which constantly sheds all kinds of beings, abandoning them to their destruction.

There are many noble people who have risen above the quagmire of this hell known as world-existence and, devoid of all doubt, rejoice for a little while. There are the divine beings who dwell like lotuses in the blue expanse of the firmament.

In this creation, actions are like the lotus which is polluted by vain desire for the fruits of such actions, which is caught in the net of psychological conditioning and which is endowed with the perfume of dynamism. But, this world-appearance is like a little fish which comes into being in this finite space and which is soon swallowed by the obstinate and invincible old vulture known as kṛtānta (the end or conclusion of action). Yet, diverse scenes arise and cease day after day, as ripples and waves appear and disappear on the surface of the ocean. The potter known as time keeps all these revolving like the potter's wheel. Innumerable forests known as creation have been reduced to ashes by the forest-fire known as time. Such is the state of this creation. But since the ignorant are bound fast to their own false notions, neither the transiency of the world nor the hard blow they suffer in their life is able to awaken them.

This psychological conditioning or self-limitation persists during the whole world-cycle, like the body of the chief of the gods, Indra. As if by accident, in the midst of all this there occur divine manifestations in whom the purest nature is revealed.

Whereas the immobile creatures stand contemplating the mystery of time, as it were, the mobile creatures swayed by the twin-forces of attraction and repulsion, love and hate, and afflicted by the terrible illness known as pleasure and pain, old age and death, become debilitated and decadent. Among the latter, the worms and vermin silently and patiently endure the fruits of their own past evil actions, contemplating them, as it were, all the time. But the imperceptible time (or death) which is beyond even contemplation devours all and everything.

VASIṢṬHA continued:

The trees stand, the very picture of misery, having to endure cold, wind and heat, yet laden with flowers and yielding fruits. Caught in the lotus known as this world, beings like bees hum restlessly all the time.

This whole universe is, as it were, the begging-bowl of Kālī (suggestive of the feminine of kāla which means time and death!), the goddess whose nature is action, motion. This Kālī constantly seeks to fill the bowl with all the creatures of this world and to offer them again and again to her lord.

This universe can be compared to an aged woman. The darkness of self-ignorance is her hair. The sun and the moon are her restless eyes. Her internal and external nature include the gods Brahmā, Viṣṇu, Indra, the earth, the mountains, etc. The truth concerning Brahman the absolute is the treasure-chest hidden in her chest. Her mother is the consciousness-energy (or, she is the mother known as consciousness-energy). She is extremely agitated and inconstant like a cloud. The stars are her teeth. Dawn and dusk are her lips. The lotus is her palm. The sky is her mouth. The seven oceans are her pearl-necklace. She is clad in the garment of the blue firmament. The pole is her navel. The forests are the hair on her body. This aged woman is born again and again: she dies again and again.

All this takes place in the light of consciousness. In this there are gods who are created within the twinkling of an eye by the creator Brahmā; and there are beings who are destroyed by the very act of Brahmā closing his eyes. In that supreme consciousness, there are Rudras who commence and conclude thousands of time-cycles within the twinkling of an eye. And there are other deities who within the twinkling of an eye create and destroy deities like Rudra! Surely, such manifestation is infinite. What is impossible for the infinite consciousness to bring about in infinite space? However, all these are but imagination which is a manifestation of ignorance. All prosperity and all adversity, childhood, youth, old age and death, as also suffering, what is known as being immersed in happiness and unhappiness and all the rest of it: all these are the extensions of the dense darkness of ignorance.

VI.1:8 VASIṢṬHA continued:

O Rāma, I shall now narrate to you how this creeper known as ignorance creeps in all directions. This creeper flourishes in the forest known as world-appearance and it is rooted in the mountain of consciousness. The three worlds are its body; and the entire universe is its skin. Pleasure and pain, being and non-being, wisdom and ignorance are its roots and fruits. When that ignorance entertains the notion of pleasure, pleasure is experienced; when it entertains the notion of pain, pain is experienced. When the notion of being prevails there is being; when the notion of non-being prevails there is non-being. That ignorance expands by means of ignorance, and yields greater ignorance; when it seeks wisdom, it feeds on wisdom and grows into wisdom in the end.

This creeper of ignorance is made manifest in its various pastimes and psychological states or modes. Somewhere at some time it falls on (comes into contact with) wisdom and is purified; but it gets attached again. It is the source of all emotions and sense-experiences. Its sap is the memory of past experiences. Vicāra or enquiry into the nature of the self is the termite that eats it away. The stars and the planets that shine in the firmament are the flowers of this creeper.

This creeper is shaken by the mind. It is resorted to by the birds of notions. The deadly snakes of the senses encircle it. The python of prohibited action dwells in it. It is illumined by the light of the heaven. It is filled with the livelihood of living beings. It contains other things, too: all those things that delude the foolish, all those things that promote wisdom, and an infinite variety of living beings. In it are they who are born, who are about to be born, who are dead and who are about to die. It is sometimes partially severed; it is elsewhere completely uncut (in the case of the totally immature persons); but it is impossible to destroy it altogether. The past, present and future are in it. It is a deadly creeper which makes one senseless; but it dies when it is resolutely examined.

This creeper itself is manifest as all these: the stars and the planets, the living beings, the plants, the elements, heaven and earth, the gods as well as the worms and vermin. Whatever there is in this universe is pervaded by this ignorance. When it is transcended you will attain self-knowledge.

VI.1:9 RĀMA asked:

Lord, I am puzzled by your statement that even the gods like Viṣṇu and Śiva are part of this ignorance or avidyā. Pray explain that statement further.

VASIṢṬHA replied:

The truth or existence-consciousness-bliss absolute is beyond thought and understanding, it is supreme peace and omnipresent, it transcends imagination and description. There arises naturally in it the faculty of conceptualisation. This self-understanding is considered to be threefold: subtle, middling and gross. The intellect that comprehends these three regards them as satva, rajas and tamas. The three together constitute what is known as prakṛti or nature. Avidyā or ignorance is prakṛti or nature, and it is threefold. This is the source of all beings; beyond it is the supreme.

These three qualities of nature (satva, rajas and tamas) are subdivided again into three each, i.e., the subtle, middling and gross of each of these. Thus you have nine categories. These nine qualities constitute the entire universe.

The sages, the ascetics, the perfected ones, the dwellers of the netherworld, the celestials, the gods—these are the sātvic part of ignorance. Among these the celestials and the dwellers of the netherworld form the gross (tamas), the sages form the middling (rajas) and the gods Viṣṇu, Śiva, etc. form the sātvic part. They who come under the category of satva are not born again: hence they are considered liberated. They exist as long as this world lasts. The others (like the sages) who are liberated while living (jīvanmukta) shed their body in course of time, reach the abode of the gods, dwell there during the period of the existence of the world and then they are liberated. Thus this part of avidyā or ignorance has become vidyā or self-knowledge! Avidyā arises in vidyā just as ripples arise in the ocean; and avidyā dissolves in vidyā just as ripples dissolve in the water.

The distinction between the ripples and the water is unreal and verbal. Even so, the distinction between ignorance and knowledge is unreal and verbal. There is neither ignorance here nor even knowledge! When you cease to see knowledge and ignorance as two distinct entities, what exists, alone exists. The reflection of vidyā in itself is considered avidyā. When these two notions are abandoned what remains is the truth: it may be something or it may be nothing! It is omnipotent, it is more empty than space and yet it is not empty because it is full of consciousness. Like the space within a pot, it is indestructible and everywhere. It is the reality in all things. Just as a magnet makes iron filings move by its very presence, it causes cosmic motion, without intending to do so. Hence, it is said that it does nothing at all.

VASIṢṬHA continued: VI.1:10

Thus, all this world-appearance with all the mobile and immobile beings in it is naught whatsoever. Nothing has really become physical or material. If conceptualisation, which gives rise to notions of being and non-being, is eliminated then it is realised that all these jīvas (the individual souls), etc., are empty expressions. All the relationships that arise in one's heart on account of ignorance are seen to be non-existent. Even when the rope is mistaken for a snake, no one can be bitten by that snake!

It is absence of self-knowledge that is known as ignorance or delusion. When the self is known one reaches the shores of limitless intelligence. When consciousness objectifies itself and regards itself as its own object of observation, there is avidyā or ignorance. When this subject-object notion is transcended, all the veils that envelop the reality are removed. The individual is nothing more than the personalised mind. Individuality ceases when that mind ceases; it remains as long as the notion of a personality remains. So long as there is a pot there is also the notion of a space enclosed within or confined to that pot; when it is broken, the infinite space alone is, even where the pot-space was imagined before.

RĀMA asked: Lord, please tell me how this cosmic intelligence becomes things like insentient rocks.

VASIṢṬHA replied:

In these substances like rocks, consciousness remains immobile having abandoned the thinking faculty but not having been able to reach the state of no-mind. It is like the state of deep sleep, far away from the state of liberation.

RĀMA asked again:

But, if they exist as in a state of deep sleep without any concepts or percepts, I think they are close to liberation!

VASIṢṬHA replied:

Mokṣa, liberation or the realisation of the infinite is not existence as an immobile creature! Liberation is attained when one arrives at the state of supreme peace after intelligent inquiry into the nature of the self and after this has brought about an inner awakening. Kaivalya or total freedom is the attainment of pure being after all mental conditioning is transcended consciously and after a thorough investigation. The wise ones say that one is established in pure being or Brahman only after one has investigated the nature of the truth as expounded in the scriptures, in the company and with the help of enlightened sages.

VASIṢṬHA continued:

As long as psychological limitation and conditioning remain in the heart, even in their subtle 'seed' state, it should be regarded as the deep sleep state; it gives rise to rebirth, even if a state of tranquility is experienced and even when the mind appears to be self-absorbed. It is an inert state and is the source of unhappiness. Such is the state of the insentient and immobile objects like rocks, etc. They are not free of self-limitation (vāsanā) but self-limitation is hidden and latent in them even as flowers are latent in seeds (which sprout, grow and yield flowers) and pots in clay. Where the seed of vāsanā (self-limitation, conditioning or tendency) exists, that state is like deep sleep; it is not perfection; when all vāsanās are destroyed and even the potentiality of the vāsanā does not exist, that state is known as the fourth (beyond waking, dream and deep sleep) and transcendental state. It brings about perfection. Vāsanā, fire, debt, disease, enemy, friendship (or glue), hate and poison—all these are bothersome even if a little residue is left after their removal.

On the other hand, if all the vāsanās have been completely removed, then one is established in the state of pure being; whether such a one is alive or not, he is not again afflicted by sorrow. The cit-śakti (energy-consciousness) lies in immobile creatures, etc., as latent vāsanā. It is this cit-śakti that determines the nature of each object; it is the fundamental characteristic of the very molecules of each object.

If this is not realised as ātma-śakti (the energy of the self or infinite consciousness) it creates the delusion of world-appearance; if it is realised as the truth, which is infinite consciousness, that realisation destroys all sorrow. The non-seeing of this truth is known as avidyā or ignorance; such ignorance is the cause of the world-appearance which is the source of all the other phenomena. Even as the arising of the first thought disturbs sleep and ends it, the slightest awakening of inner intelligence destroys ignorance. When one approaches darkness with light in hand, wishing to behold it, the darkness vanishes; when the light of enquiry is turned on ignorance, ignorance disappears. When one begins to enquire: "What is 'I' in this body composed of blood, flesh, bone, etc.?" at once ignorance ceases to be. That which has a beginning has an end. When all things that have a beginning are ruled out, what remains is the truth which is the cessation of avidyā or ignorance. You may regard it as something or as no-thing: that is to be sought which IS when ignorance has been dispelled. The sweetness one tastes is not experienced by another: listening to someone's description of the cessation of avidyā does not give rise to your enlightenment. Each one has to realise it. In short, avidyā is the belief that 'There exists a reality which is not Brahman or cosmic consciousness'; when there is the certain knowledge that 'This is indeed Brahman', avidyā ceases.

Discourse on Brahman

VI.1:11 VASIṢṬHA continued:

Again and again I repeat all this, O Rāma, for the sake of your spiritual awakening; the realisation of the self does not happen without such repetition (or, spiritual practice). This ignorance, known as avidyā or ajñāna, has become dense by having been expressed and experienced by the senses in thousands of incarnations, within and outside this body. But, self-knowledge is not within the reach of the senses. It arises when the senses and the mind, which is the sixth sense, cease.

O Rāma, live in this world firmly established in self-knowledge, even as king Janaka lives having known what there is to be known. In his case the truth is realised all the time whether he is active or not, whether he is awake or not. Lord Viṣṇu incarnates in this world and takes on embodiment fully established in this self-knowledge. Even so, lord Śiva remains established in self-knowledge; and lord Brahmā, too, is established in self-knowledge. Be established in self-knowledge, O Rāma, as they are.

RĀMA asked:

Lord, pray tell me what is the nature of the self-knowledge in which all these great ones are established.

VASIṢṬHA replied:

Rāma, you know this already. Yet, in order to make it abundantly clear, you are asking about it again.

Whatever there is and whatever appears to be the world-jugglery, is but the pure Brahman or the absolute consciousness and naught else. Consciousness is Brahman, the world is Brahman, all the elements are Brahman, I am Brahman, my enemy is Brahman, my friends and relatives are Brahman, Brahman is the three periods of time, for all these are rooted in Brahman. Even as the ocean appears to be expanded on account of the waves, Brahman seems to be expanded on account of the infinite variety of substances. Brahman apprehends Brahman, Brahman experiences or enjoys Brahman, Brahman is made manifest in Brahman by the power of Brahman himself. Brahman is the form of my enemy who displeases me who am Brahman: when such is the case, who does what to another?

The modes of the mind like attraction and repulsion, likes and dislikes have been conjured up in imagination. These have been destroyed by the absence of thoughts. How then can they be magnified? When Brahman alone moves in all which is Brahman and Brahman alone unfolds as Brahman in all, what is joy and what is sorrow? Brahman is satisfied with Brahman, Brahman is established in Brahman. There is neither 'I' nor another!

VASIṢṬHA continued:

All the objects in this world are Brahman. 'I' am Brahman. Such being the case, both passion and dispassion, craving and aversion, are but notions. Body is Brahman, death is Brahman, too: when they come together, as the real rope and the unreal imaginary snake come together, where is the cause for sorrow? Similarly, body is Brahman and pleasure is Brahman; where is the cause of rejoicing when body experiences pleasure? When, on the surface of the calm ocean, waves appear to be agitated, the waves do not cease to be water! Even when Brahman appears to be agitated (in the world-appearance), its essence is unchanged and there is neither 'I'-ness nor 'you'-ness. When the whirlpool dies in the water, nothing is dead! When the death-Brahman overtakes the body-Brahman, nothing is lost.

Water is capable of being calm and of being agitated: even so Brahman can be quiescent and restless. Such is its nature. It is ignorance or delusion that divides the one into 'This is sentient jīva' and 'This is insentient matter': the wise ones do not hold such erroneous views. Hence, to the ignorant the world is full of sorrow; to the wise the same world is full of bliss, even as to the blind man the world is dark and to one who has good eyesight the world is full of light.

When the one Brahman alone pervades all, there is no death nor is there a living person. The ripples play on the surface of the ocean, they are neither born nor do they die! Even so do the elements in this creation. 'This is' and 'This is not'—such deluded notions arise in the self. These notions are not really caused nor do they have a motivation, even as a crystal reflects different-coloured objects without a motivation.

The self remains itself even when the energies of the world throw up endless diversities on the surface of the ocean of consciousness. There are no independent entities in this world known as 'body' etc. What is seen as the body and what are seen as notions, the objects of perception, the perishable and the imperishable, the thoughts and feelings and their meaning—all these are Brahman in Brahman the infinite consciousness. There is duality only in the eyes of the deluded and ignorant. The mind, the intellect, the ego-sense, the cosmic root-elements, the senses and all such diverse phenomena are Brahman only: pleasure and pain are illusions (they are words without substance). Even as a single sound produced amongst hills echoes and re-echoes into diversity, the one cosmic consciousness experiences multiplicity within itself, with the notions 'This is I' and 'This is mind' etc. The one cosmic consciousness sees diversity within itself even as a dreamer dreams of diverse objects within himself.

VASIṢṬHA continued:

When gold is not recognised as such, it gets mixed up with the earth; when Brahman is not thus recognised, the impurity of ignorance arises. The knower of Brahman declares that such a great one is himself the Lord and Brahman; in the case of the ignorant the non-recognition of the truth is known as ignorance. (Or, it is the opinion of the knowers of Brahman that the very same Lord or supreme being is regarded as ignorance in the ignorant.) When gold is recognised as such it 'becomes' gold instantly; when Brahman is recognised as such it 'becomes' Brahman instantly.

Being omnipotent, Brahman becomes whatever it considers itself to be without any motivation for doing so. The knowers of Brahman declare that Brahman is the Lord, the great being which is devoid of action, the doer and the instrument, devoid of causal motivation and of transformation or change.

When this truth is not realised, it arises as ignorance in the ignorant, but when it is realised, the ignorance is dispelled. When a relative is not recognised as such, he is known as a stranger; when the relative is recognised, the notion of stranger is instantly dispelled.

When one knows that duality is illusory appearance, there is realisation of Brahman the absolute. When one knows 'This is not I', the unreality of the ego-sense is realised. From this arises true dispassion. 'I am verily Brahman'—when this truth is realised the awareness of the truth arises in one, and all things are then merged in that awareness. When such notions as 'I' and 'you' are dispelled, the realisation of the truth arises and one realises that all this, whatever there is, is indeed Brahman.

What is the truth? 'I have nothing to do with sorrow, with actions, with delusion or desire. I am at peace, free from sorrow. I am Brahman'—such is the truth. 'I am free from all defects, I am the all, I do not seek anything nor do I abandon anything, I am Brahman'—such is the truth. 'I am blood, I am flesh, I am bone, I am the body, I am consciousness, I am the mind also, I am Brahman'—such is the truth. 'I am the firmament, I am space, I am the sun and the entire space, I am all things here, I am Brahman'—such is the truth. 'I am a blade of grass, I am the earth, I am a tree-stump, I am the forest, I am the mountain and the oceans, I am the non-dual Brahman'—such is the truth. 'I am the consciousness in which all things are strung and through whose power all beings engage themselves in all their activities; I am the essence of all things'—such is the truth.

This is certain: all things exist in Brahman, all things flow from it, all things are Brahman; it is omnipresent, it is the one self, it is the truth.

VASIṢṬHA continued:

The truth which is omnipresent and which is pure consciousness devoid of objectivity, is referred to variously as consciousness, self, Brahman, existence, truth, order and also as pure knowledge. It is pure and in its light all beings know their own self. I am the Brahman which is pure consciousness after its own appearance as the mind, the intellect, the senses and all other such notions have been negated. I am imperishable consciousness or Brahman in whose light alone all the elements and the entire universe shine. I am the consciousness or Brahman, sparks from whom arise continually radiating reflected consciousness throughout the universe. Even when seen by a pure mind it is expressed in silence. Though it appears to be in contact with the ceaseless experiences of the ego-sense of countless beings who thus derive the delight that is of Brahman, yet it is beyond the reach of these and untouched by them. For, though it is truly the ultimate source of all happiness and delight, it is of the nature of deep sleep (devoid of diversity), peaceful and pure. In subject-object relationship and the consequent experience of pleasure the bliss of Brahman is infinitesimally experienced.

I am the eternal Brahman free from the wrong notions of pleasure and pain, etc., and therefore pure; I am the consciousness in which there is true and pure experiencing. I am that pure consciousness in which the pure intelligence functions without thought-interference. I am that Brahman which is the intelligent energy that functions in all the elements (earth, water, fire, etc.). I am the pure consciousness which manifests as the characteristic taste, etc., of the different fruits.

I am the changeless Brahman which is realised when both elation at having gained what one desires and depression at not having gained it are transcended. When the sun shines and the objects of the world are seen in that light, I am the pure consciousness that is in the middle between these two, and which is the very self of the light and of the illumined object. I am that pure consciousness or Brahman which exists unbroken in the waking, dream and deep sleep states and which is therefore the fourth or the transcendental truth.

Even as the taste of the juice of sugarcane cultivated in a hundred different fields is uniform and same, even so the consciousness indwelling all beings is the same—that consciousness I am. I am that conscious energy (cit-śakti) which is larger than the universe and yet subtler than the minutest atomic particle and therefore invisible. I am the consciousness that exists everywhere like butter in milk, and whose very nature is experiencing.

VASIṢṬHA continued:

Even as ornaments made of gold are only gold, I am the pure consciousness in the body. I am the self that pervades all things within and without. I am that consciousness which reflects all experiences without itself undergoing any change and which is untouched by impurity.

I salute that consciousness which is the bestower of the fruits of all thoughts, the light that shines in all luminaries, the supreme gain; that consciousness pervades all the limbs, ever awake and alert, vibrates constantly in all substances and is ever homogeneous and undisturbed as if it were in deep sleep though wide awake. That consciousness is the reality that bestows the individual characteristic on each and every substance in the universe and though within all and so nearest to all, is far on account of its inaccessibility to the mind and the senses. Continuous and homogeneous in waking, dreaming, deep sleep and in the fourth (transcendental) state of consciousness, it shines when all thoughts have ceased, when all excitements have ceased and when all hate has ceased. I salute that consciousness which is devoid of desire and ego-sense and cannot be divided into parts.

I have attained that consciousness which is the indweller of all; and yet though all, is beyond diversity. It is the cosmic net in which the infinite number of beings are caught like birds; in it all these worlds manifest, though in fact, nothing has ever happened. That consciousness is of the nature of being and non-being and the resting place of all that is good and divine. It plays the roles of all beings and it is the source of all affection and peace, though it is forever united and liberated. It is the life of all living beings, the uncreated nectar that cannot be stolen by anyone, the ever existent reality. That consciousness which is reflected in sense-experiences is yet devoid of them and cannot be experienced by them. In it all beings rejoice, though it itself is pure bliss beyond all joy; like the space but beyond space; glorious yet devoid of all expansions and glory. Though seemingly it does all, it does nothing.

All this is 'I' and all this is mine. But I am not and I am not 'other than I'. I have realised this. Let this world be an illusion or substantial. I am free from the fever of distress.

VI.1:12, 13 VASIṢṬHA continued:

Established in this realisation of the truth, the great sages lived for ever in peace and equanimity. They were free from psychological predisposition and hence they did not seek nor reject either life or death. They remained unshaken in their direct experience like another Meru-mountain. Yet, they roamed the forests, islands and cities, they travelled to the heavens as if they were angels or gods; they conquered their enemies and they ruled as emperors—they engaged themselves in diverse activities in accordance with scriptural injunctions as they realised that such was appropriate conduct. They enjoyed the pleasure of life; they visited pleasure gardens and were entertained by celestial damsels. They duly filfilled the duties of the household life. They even engaged themselves in great wars. They retained their equanimity even in those disastrous situations where others would have lost their peace and balanced state of mind.

Their mind had fully entered the state of satva or divinity and was therefore utterly free from delusion, from egoistic notion ('I do this') and from the desire for achievement, though they did not reject such achievement or the rewards for their actions. They did not indulge in vain exultation when they defeated their enemies nor did they give way to despair and grief when they were defeated. They were engaged in natural activities, allowing all actions to proceed from them non-volitionally.

Follow their example, O Rāma. Let your personality (ego-sense) be egoless and let appropriate actions spontaneously proceed from you. For the infinite indivisible consciousness alone is the truth; and it is that which has put on this appearance of diversity, which is neither real nor unreal. Hence live completely unattached to anything here. Why do you grieve as if you are an ignoramus?

RĀMA said:

Lord, by your grace I am fully awakened to the reality. My delusion has vanished. I shall do as you bid me to do. Surely, I rest peacefully in the state of one who is liberated even while living. Pray, Lord, tell me how one reaches this state of liberation by the restraint of the life-force (prāṇa) and by the annihilation of all self-limitations or psychological conditioning.

VASIṢṬHA continued:

They call it yoga which is the method by which this cycle of birth and death ceases. It is the utter transcendence of the mind and it is of two types. Self-knowledge is one type; restraint of the life-force is another. However, yoga has come to mean only the latter. Yet, both the methods lead to the same result. To some self-knowledge through enquiry is difficult; to others yoga is difficult. But my conviction is that the path of enquiry is easy for all, because self-knowledge is the ever-present truth. I shall now describe to you the method of yoga.

The Story of Bhuśuṇḍa

VI.1:14, 15 VASIṢṬHA continued:

In the infinite and indivisible consciousness there is a mirage-like world-appearance in one corner, as it were. The creator Brahmā, who is the apparent cause for this world-appearance, dwells there. I am his mind-born son. Once when I was in the heaven of Indra, I heard from sages like Nārada the stories of long-lived beings. In the course of this discussion, the great sage Śātātapa said:

"In one corner of the mount Meru there is a wish-fulfilling tree known as Cūta, whose leaves are made of gold and silver. On that tree there dwells a crow known as Bhuśuṇḍa who is utterly free from all attraction and aversion. There is none on earth or in heaven who has lived longer than he has. He is not only long-lived but he is also an enlightened and peaceful person. If any of you can live as he lives, that shall be regarded as a highly laudable and meritorious life."

I heard these words. I was greatly inspired. Soon I set out to meet this Bhuśuṇḍa. Instantly I reached that peak of the mount Meru where Bhuśuṇḍa lived. The mountain was radiant, comparable to the lustre of the yogi who through the practice of yoga has 'opened' the psychic portal at the crown of the head and at the upper end of the nāḍī known as the suṣumnā (it is also known as Meru). The peak reached right up to heaven.

There I saw the tree known as Cūta whose flowers and leaves were radiant like jewels. It was a heaven-scraping tree. The celestials who dwelt on it filled the atmosphere with their songs. Perfected sages who could assume any form they liked also dwelt on it. It was an enormous tree of immeasurable dimensions.

I saw the different types of birds that dwelt on that tree. I saw the famous swan which is the vehicle for the creator Brahmā. I saw the bird Śuka which is the vehicle of the fire-god and which was learned in the scriptures. I saw the peacock which is the vehicle of the god Kārtikeya. I also saw the bird known as Bharadvāja, as also other birds. And at a great distance on that tree I saw crows. Among them I saw the great Bhuśuṇḍa who sat there in utter tranquility and peace. He was beautiful, radiant and peaceful.

This was the famous Bhuśuṇḍa the long-lived. He had lived through several world-cycles. He remembered even those who lived aeons ago. He remained silent. He was free from I-ness and mineness. He was the friend and relation of all.

VI.1:16, 17 VASIṢṬHA continued:

I descended right in front of Bhuśuṇḍa. He knew that I was Vasiṣṭha and welcomed me appropriately. By his mere thought-force he materialised flowers with which he worshipped me. He made me sit near him. Bhuśuṇḍa then said to me:

"I consider it a great blessing that after a long time you have given us your darśan (visit). Bathed in the nectar of your darśan (presence and company), we have been renewed like a good tree. You are the greatest among those who are worthy of adoration: and you have come here only as a result of my accumulated merit. Pray tell me the immediate reason for this visit. Surely, in your heart there shines the light of self-knowledge kindled by continuous and intense enquiry into the nature of this unreal world-appearance? What is the purpose of your visit? Ah, by the very sight of your blessed feet, I have divined your purpose. You have come here in pursuit of your enquiry into the secrets of extreme longevity. Yet, I would love to hear the purpose from your own lips."

I replied as follows? "You are truly blessed in that you enjoy the supreme peace all around you, in that you are endowed with the highest wisdom (self-knowledge) and in that you are not caught in the net of illusion known as world-appearance. Pray enlighten me in regard to a few facts concerning yourself.

"In what clan were you born? How did you acquire the knowledge of that which alone deserves to be known? What is your age now? Do you remember anything concerning the past? Who is it that ordained that you shall be long-lived and that you shall live on this tree?"

BHUŚUṆḌA replied:

Since you ask these questions concerning me, O sage, I shall duly answer them. Pray listen attentively. The story I am about to narrate is so inspiring that it will destroy the sins of those who relate it and those who listen to it.

Having said this, O Rāma, Bhuśuṇḍa began the following narration. His words were grave and polite. They had power for he had risen beyond all desires and the pursuit of pleasure. His heart was pure for it had reached its own fulfilment. He was fully aware of the birth and the extinction of the creations. His words were sweet. He had the dignity of the creator Brahmā himself. His words were like nectar. And he commenced his discourse which follows.

BHUŚUṆḌA said: VI.1:18

In this universe there is a great divinity known as Hara who is the god of gods and who is adored by all the gods in heaven. His consort occupies one half of his body. The holy river Gaṅgā flows from his matted locks. On his head also shines the radiant moon. A deadly cobra encircles his neck, apparently deprived of its poison by the nectar that flows from the moon. His sole adornment is the sacred ash which is smeared all over his body. He dwells in cemeteries or cremation grounds. He wears a garland of skulls. His amulets and bracelets are snakes.

By a mere glance he destroys the demons. He is devoted to the welfare of the entire universe. Hills and mountains which seem to be forever immersed in meditation are the symbols which represent him. His lieutenants are goblins that have heads and hands like razors and that have faces like a bear, a camel, a mouse, etc. He is radiant with three eyes. These goblins bow down to him. And, the female deities who feed on the beings in the fourteen worlds dance in front of him.

These female deities are also endowed with faces resembling various animals. They dwell on the peaks of mountains, in space, in different worlds, in crematoriums and in the bodies of embodied ones. Of these female deities eight are principal ones: they are Jayā, Vijayā, Jayantī, Aparājitā, Siddhā, Rakttā, Alaṃbusā and Utpalā. All the others follow these eight deities. Of these, the seventh Alaṃbusā is the most famous. Her vehicle is the crow which is extremely powerful and which is blue in colour.

Once upon a time all these female deities assembled in space. They duly worshipped the divinity known as Tumburu (which is one of the aspects of Rudra) and engaged themselves in left-handed ritual which reveals the supreme truth. They adored Tumburu and also the deity known as Bhairava and they began to perform various rites intoxicated, as they were, by wine. Soon they began to discuss an important question: how is it that the Lord of Umā (Hara) treats us contemptuously? They made up their mind thus: "We shall demonstrate our prowess in such a way that he does not do so hereafter." They overwhelmed Umā by their magic powers and separated her from her lord Hara. All the female deities sang and danced in ecstasy. Some drank, some sang, some laughed, some roared, some ran, some fell and some ate flesh. These intoxicated deities began to create disorder in the whole world.

VI.1:19 BHUŚUṆḌA continued:

While the deities were thus besporting and celebrating, their vehicles, too, got themselves intoxicated and began to dance. All the female swans danced along with the crow (Caṇḍa) which was Alaṃbusā's vehicle. While these female swans were thus dancing, there arose in them the desire to mate. One by one, all the swans mated with the crow, as they were all drunk. Soon they became pregnant.

When the celebrations were over, all the deities went over to the lord Hara (Śiva): they offered him the body of Umā which they had converted into food by their magic power. The Lord knew the truth and was annoyed with the deities. And, they re-created Umā as she was before and offered her to the Lord, who regained his consort. All the deities returned to their respective abodes. The swans which were the vehicles of Brāhmī informed her of everything that happened.

The goddess Brāhmī said to them: "Since you are all big with child, you will not be able to perform your duties. Hence, for some time go where you please." Having said this, the goddess sat in deep contemplation.

The swans laid twenty-one eggs at the proper time and they were soon hatched. Thus twenty-one of us were born in the family of Caṇḍa the crow. Along with our mothers, we adored the goddess Brāhmī. By her grace we attained self-knowledge and liberation. We then approached our father who fondly embraced us all. All of us then worshipped the goddess Alaṃbusā.

Caṇḍa said: "Children, have you gone beyond the dragnet known as the world-appearance after having cut the shackles of vāsanā or mental conditioning? Or else, come let us adore the goddess by whose grace you will attain the highest wisdom."

We replied: "Father, we have gained the knowledge that is worth gaining, by the grace of the goddess Brāhmī. We seek a secluded and excellent place to dwell."

Caṇḍa said: "There is an excellent mountain in the world known as Meru which is the support for the fourteen worlds and for all the beings that dwell in them. All the gods and sages dwell on it. On it is the wish-fulfilling tree. On one of its branches I once built a nest, while the goddess Alaṃbusā was in deep meditation. It is beautiful and excellent in every way. Children, go to that nest and live in it. You will never encounter any hindrance."

In accordance with our father's instructions all of us came here and took up our abode in that nest.

BHUŚUṆḌA continued: VI.1:20

There was a world in days of yore which is not far beyond our memory, for we witnessed it ourselves.

VASIṢṬHA asked: What happened to your brothers, for I see only you here?

BHUŚUṆḌA continued:

A very long time has passed, O sage, and in course of time my brothers abandoned their physical existence and ascended to the heaven of lord Śiva. Indeed, even long-lived persons who may be holy and saintly and strong are consumed in course of time by Time (or death).

VASIṢṬHA asked again: How is it that you have remained

unaffected by the heat and the cold and the wind and the fire?

BHUŚUṆḌA continued:

Truly, to be embodied as a crow held in contempt by the people is not a happy state, though the Creator has amply provided for the survival of even the humble crow. But, we have remained immersed in the self, happy and contented: hence we have survived in spite of ever so many calamities. We have remained firmly established in the self, having abandoned vain activities that are but torment of the body and the mind. To this physical body there is misery neither in life nor in death; hence we remain as we are, not seeking anything other than what is.

We have seen the fate of the worlds. We have mentally abandoned identification with the body. Established in self-knowledge and remaining on this tree I see the passage of time. Through the practice of prāṇāyāma I have risen above the division of time. Hence, I am at peace within my heart and I am not affected by the events of the world. Let all beings vanish or let them come into existence; we have no fear at all. Let all these beings enter into the ocean known as Time (or death); but we are seated on the shores of that ocean and are therefore unaffected. We neither accept nor reject; we appear to be but we are not what appears to be. Thus do we remain on this tree.

Though we engage ourselves in diverse activities, we do not get drowned in mental modifications and we never lose contact with the reality.

Lord, that nectar for which the gods churned the ocean is inferior to the nectarine blessing that flows from the very presence of sages like you. I consider nothing more praiseworthy than the company of sages who are free from all cravings and desires. Holy one, even though I have already attained self-knowledge, I consider that my birth has been truly fulfilled, in that today I have seen you and I have enjoyed your company.

VI.1:21 BHUŚUṆḌA continued:

This wish-fulfilling tree is not shaken by the various natural calamities nor by the cataclysms caused by living beings. There have been several of the latter when demons have tried to destroy or overwhelm the earth, as also when the Lord has intervened and rescued the earth from the grip of the demons. During all these this tree has remained unaffected. Even the flood and the scorching heat of the sun attendant upon cosmic dissolution have not succeeded in shaking this tree. On account of this, we who dwell on this tree have also escaped harm: evil overtakes one who lives in an unholy place.

VASIṢṬHA asked:

But, at the end of the life of the cosmos, when everything is dissolved, how have you managed to survive?

BHUŚUṆḌA replied:

During that period, O sage, I abandon this nest, even as an ungrateful man abandons his friend. Then I remain united with cosmic space, totally free from all thoughts and mental modifications. When the twelve cosmic suns pour unbearable heat upon this creation, I practise the vāruṇī-dhāraṇā and remain unaffected. (Varuṇa is the lord of waters: vāruṇī dhāraṇā is contemplation of Varuṇa.) When the wind blows with such force as to uproot even mountains, I practice the pārvatī-dhāraṇā and remain unaffected. (Parvata is mountain and pārvatī dhāraṇā is contemplation of the mountain.) When the whole universe is flooded with the waters of cosmic dissolution, I practise vāyu-dhāraṇā and remain unaffected. (Vāyu is wind and vāyu dhāraṇā is contemplation of the wind.) Then I remain as if in deep sleep till the beginning of the next cosmic cycle. When the new Creator begins to create a new cosmos, I resume my abode in this nest.

VASIṢṬHA asked:

Why is it that others are not able to do what you have done?

BHUŚUṆḌA replied:

O sage, the will of the supreme being cannot be transgressed: it is his will that I should be like this and that the others should be as they are. One cannot fathom nor measure what has to be. In accordance with the nature of each being, that which is to be comes to be. Therefore, in accordance with my thought-force or conception, this tree is found in every world-cycle at this place in this manner.

VASIṢṬHA asked:

You enjoy such longevity as would suggest that you have attained final liberation! And you are wise, brave and you are a great yogi. Pray, tell me what extraordinary events you remember, relating to this and the previous world-cycles.

BHUŚUṆḌA said:

I remember that once upon a time there was nothing on this earth, no trees and plants, not even mountains. For a period of eleven thousand years the earth was covered by lava. In those days there was neither day nor night below the polar region: for in the rest of the earth neither the sun nor the moon shone. Only one half of the polar region was illumined.

Then demons ruled the earth: they were deluded, powerful and prosperous. The earth was their playground.

Apart from the polar region, the rest of the earth was covered with water. And then for a very long time, the whole earth was covered with forests, except the polar region. Then there arose great mountains, but without any human inhabitants. For a period of ten thousand years, the earth was covered with the corpses of the demons.

At one time, the gods who used to roam the skies had vanished from sight on account of fear. And the earth had become more like a single mountain! I remember many such events: but let me narrate to you what is important.

During my life-time I have seen the appearance and disappearance of countless Manus (the progenitor of the human race). At one time the world was devoid of the gods and the demons, but was one radiant cosmic egg. At another time, the earth was populated by brāhmaṇas (members of the priest-class) who were addicted to alcohol, śūdras (servant-class) who ridiculed the gods, and by polyandrous women. I also remember another epoch when the earth was covered with forests, when the ocean could not even be imagined and when human beings were spontaneously created. At another time there was neither mountain nor earth; the gods and the sages dwelt in space. At another time there were neither the gods nor the sages, etc.; darkness prevailed everywhere.

First there arose the notion of creation. Then light and the division of the universe arose. Then one after the other the diverse beings were created, as also the stars and the planets.

I saw that during one epoch it was lord Viṣṇu (generally considered the protector) who created the universe, during another it was Brahmā who created the universe and in another it was Śiva who became the creator.

VI.1:22 BHUŚUṆḌA continued:

Of course I remember sages like you, goddesses like Gauri, demons like Hiranyāksa, kings like Śibi, of the recent past and of a bygone age. O sage, this is the eighth time you have taken birth as sage Vasiṣṭha, and this is the eighth time we meet each other. At one time you were born of space, at another of water, at another of wind, at another of a mountain and then of fire.

Whatever is happening in the present creation has happened exactly in the same manner during three previous creations. But I remember the events of ten such creations. (NOTE: Then follows a list of major world-events all of which were not repeated all the time in every creation, accounting for the differences in the number of times Bhuśuṇḍa witnessed them. A few of them are reproduced here to illustrate this.) In every age there have been sages who propounded the truth and revealed the Vedas. There have been Vyāsas who wrote down the legends (or prehistoric tales). And, time and again Vālmīki composed the sacred Rāmāyaṇa. In addition to that, a sacred book of wisdom which contains your instructions to Rāma has also been recorded by a sage known as Vālmīki: originally it was of one hundred thousand verses. In this age, too, it will again be recorded by Vālmīki for the twelfth time. There was an equally great scripture known as 'Bharata' which has been forgotten.

In order to destroy the demons, lord Viṣṇu takes birth again and again as Rāma: he will be born in this age for the eleventh time. And, lord Viṣṇu will incarnate as Kṛṣṇa for the sixteenth time.

However, all this is illusory appearance; the world as such is not a reality. It seems to be real to the deluded mind. It arises and it ceases in the twinkling of an eye like ripples on the ocean. The three worlds were similar during some epochs and in other epochs they were utterly dissimilar. On account of all these differences, in every age I have new friends, new relatives, new servants and new dwellings. Sometimes I dwell in the Himālayas, at other times in the Malaya mountains and at other times, on account of inherited tendencies, I take my abode here in this nest.

Even the directions change from age to age. Because I alone have survived even the night of the creator Brahmā I know the truth about these changes. Depending upon the position of the poles and the movements of the stars, the sun and the moon, the directions (north, east, etc.) are determined. When these change, the directions change. But, I know that this world is neither real nor unreal. The only reality is the movement of energy within the cosmic consciousness. This, on account of deluded understanding, appears as this creation and disappears: such delusion also causes confusion of relationships and duties. In some ages the son behaves like the father, friend like an enemy and man like woman. Sometimes in 'the dark age' people behave as if 'the golden age' prevails and vice versa.

VASIṢṬHA asked: VI.1:23

O Bhuśuṇḍa, how is it that your body has not been consumed by death?

BHUŚUṆḌA replied:

O sage, you know everything, yet you ask this question in order to cultivate the eloquence of your servant. I shall answer your question; for obedience is the best form of worshipping saints.

Death does not wish to kill one who does not have rāga-dveṣa (attraction and aversion) nor false notions and mental habits. Death does not wish to kill one who does not suffer from mental illness, who does not entertain desires and hopes which give rise to anxieties and worry, who is not poisoned by greed, whose body and mind are not burnt by the fire of anger and hate, who is not churned and ground by the mill of lust, who is firmly established in the pure awareness of Brahman the absolute and whose mind is not distracted like a monkey.

O sage, these evils do not even approach one whose heart has found the state of utter quiescence and tranquility. Nor do illnesses of the body and the mind affect him. His awareness neither rises nor sets either in deep sleep or in the waking state. He whose mind and heart are established in supreme peace is not touched by the blinding evils born of lust and hate. He neither seeks nor does he spurn, neither gives up nor gathers, though he is constantly engaged in appropriate action. None of the evil forces afflict him. All joy and happiness and all auspicious qualities flow towards him.

Hence, O sage, one should remain firmly established in the imperishable and eternal self which is free from nescience and from all seeking. One should slay the ghost of duality or division and fix the heart on the one truth, which alone is sweet in the beginning, in the middle and in the end.

Neither in the company of the gods and demons, nor of the celestial artistes nor heavenly damsels, is there to be found permanent joy. One cannot find what is eternally good either in heaven or on earth or even in the netherworld—nowhere in this creation. All activities are beset with physical and mental illness and many forms of unhappiness: the eternal good is not found in them. Such eternal good is not to be found in any of the activities of any of the senses, for their experiences are tainted by a beginning and thus an end.

Neither the sovereignty of the whole world nor the attainment of the form of a god, neither the study of scriptures nor engaging oneself in the work of others, neither listening to nor reciting stories, neither longevity nor death, neither heaven nor hell is comparable to the state of the mind of a holy one.

VI.1:24 BHUŚUṆḌA continued:

The best of all states, O sage, is indeed the vision of the one infinite consciousness. Even the contemplation of the self which is infinite consciousness banishes sorrow, terminates the long-dream vision of the world-appearance, purifies the mind and the heart, and dispels worries and misfortunes. That contemplation of the self is devoid of mentation. It is easy for the like of you; it is rather difficult for the like of me.

But this contemplation of the self has comrades, as it were, that closely resemble such contemplation; among them is the contemplation of the life-force or prāṇa, which enables one to overcome sorrow and to promote auspiciousness. I have adopted this contemplation.

It is that contemplation of prāṇa that has bestowed longevity and also self-knowledge on me. I shall now describe it to you.

Lord, look at this enchanting body which is supported by three pillars (the three bodies or the three nāḍīs?) and endowed with nine gates, and which is protected by the egosense which has eight consorts (the puryaṣṭaka) and several relatives (the root elements).

Enclosed right in the middle of this body are the subtle idā and piṅgalā. There are three lotus-like wheels. These wheels are composed of bones and flesh. When the vital air wets the wheels, the petals or the radii of these lotus-like wheels begin to vibrate. The vital airs expand on account of their expansion. These nāḍīs thereupon radiate above and below. Sages call these vital airs by different names—prāṇa, apāna, samāna, etc., on account of their diverse functions. These functions derive their energy from the central psychic centre which is the heart-lotus.

That energy which thus vibrates in the heart-lotus is known as prāṇa: it enables the eyes to see, the skin to feel, the mouth to speak, the food to be digested and it performs all the functions in the body. It has two different roles, one above and one below, and it is then known as prāṇa and apāna respectively. I am devoted to them, which are free from fatigue, which shine like the sun and the moon in the heart, which are like the cart-wheels of the mind which is the guardian of the city known as the body, which are the favourite horses of the king known as egosense. Being devoted to them I live as if in deep sleep, for ever in homogeneous consciousness.

He who adores the prāṇa and the apāna thus is not reborn in this world again and he is freed from all bondage.

BHUŚUṆḌA continued: VI.1:25

Prāṇa is constantly in motion inside and outside the body: prāṇa is that vital air which is established in the upper part. Apāna is similarly and constantly in motion inside and outside the body, but it dwells in the lower part. Pray, listen to the practice of the extension or the control of this life-force, which is conducive to the welfare of one who is awake or asleep.

The efflux of the vital force centred in the heart-lotus, of its own accord and without effort, is known as recaka or exhalation. The contact with the source of the prāṇic force which is located downward to the length of twelve 'fingers', in the heart-lotus, is known as pūraka or inhalation.

When the apāna has ceased to move and when the prāṇa does not arise and move out of the heart (and till these begin to happen) it is known as kumbhaka (retention as of a filled pot). There are said to be three points for the recaka, kumbhaka and pūraka: (1) outside (the nose); (2) from below the place known as dvādaśānta (above or in front of the forehead at a distance of twelve fingers); (3) the source of prāṇa (heart-lotus).

Pray listen to the natural and effortless movement of the life-force at all times. The movement of the vital air up to the extent of twelve fingers from oneself constitutes recaka. That state in which the apāna-force remains in the dvādaśānta, like the unfashioned pot in the potter's clay, should be known as external-kumbhaka.

When the outgoing air moves up to the tip of the nose, it is known as recaka. When it moves up to the extent of the dvādaśānta it is known as external-recaka. When the movement of prāṇa has ceased outside itself and as long as the apāna does not rise, they call it external-kumbhaka. When, however, the apāna flows inwards, without the prāṇa rising within, they call it internal-kumbhaka. When the apāna rises in the dvādaśānta and attains internal expansion, it is known as internal-pūraka. He who knows these kumbhakas is not born again.

Whether one is going or standing, awake or asleep, these vital airs—which are naturally restless—are restrained by these practices. Then whatever he does or eats, he who knows these kumbhakas is not the doer of those actions. In a very few days he attains the supreme state. He who practises these kumbhakas is not attracted by external objects. They who are endowed with this vision—whether they are stationary or moving (active or inactive)—are not bound: They have attained that which is worthy of being attained.

BHUŚUṆḌA continued:

When the impurity of one's heart and mind have been destroyed by thus being devoted to prāṇa and apāna, one is freed from delusion, attains inner awakening and rests in one's own self even while doing whatever has to be done.

Lord, prāṇa arises in the lotus of the heart and terminates at a distance of twelve finger-breadths outside the body. Apāna arises in the dvādaśānta (twelve finger-breadths from the body) and terminates in the lotus of the heart. Thus apāna arises where prāṇa terminates. Prāṇa is like a flame and it goes up and out; apāna is like water and it goes down towards the heart-lotus.

Apāna is the moon which protects the body from outside; prāṇa is

---

Note: Dvādaśāntam suggests a magnetic field around the body twelve finger-widths all round. This magnetic field is also composed of prāṇa-apāna.

like the sun or the fire and promotes the body's internal welfare. Prāṇa generates heat in the heart-space every moment, and after producing this heat it generates heat in the space in front of the face. Apāna, which is the moon, nourishes the space in front of the face and then it nourishes the space in the heart.

If one is able to reach that space where the apāna unites with the prāṇa, he does not grieve any more, nor is he born again.

In fact, it is only prāṇa that undergoes a modification and appears as apāna, after abandoning its burning heat. And then, the same prāṇa, having abandoned the coolness of the moon, gains its nature as the purifying fire of the sun. The wise ones enquire into the nature of prāṇa as long as it does not abandon its solar nature to become lunar. One who knows the truth concerning the rising and the setting of the sun and the moon in one's own heart, is not born again. He who sees the Lord, the sun, in one's heart, sees the truth.

In order to attain perfection one does not prevent nor protect external darkness, but one strives to destroy the darkness of ignorance in the heart. When the external darkness goes, one is able to see the world; but when the darkness of ignorance in the heart is dispelled, there arises self-knowledge. Hence one should strive to behold the prāṇa and the apāna, whose knowledge bestows liberation.

Apāna terminates in the heart where prāṇa arises. Where prāṇa is born, there apāna perishes; where apāna takes birth, there prāṇa ceases. When prāṇa has ceased to move and when apāna is about to rise one experiences external-kumbhaka; rooted in this one does not grieve any more. When apāna has ceased to move and when prāṇa has arisen just a little, one experiences internal-kumbhaka; rooted in this one does not grieve any more.

BHUŚUṆḌA continued:

If one practices kumbhaka (suspension of breath) after exhaling the prāṇa to a distance farther from where the apāna rises (the twelve fingerbreadth distance), he is not subject to sorrow any more. Or, if one is able to see the space within oneself where the inhaled breath turns into the impulse for exhalation, he is not born again. By seeing where the prāṇa and the apāna terminate their motions and by holding fast to that state of peace, one is not subject to sorrow again.

If one keenly observes the place and the exact moment at which the prāṇa is consumed by the apāna, he does not grieve. Or, if one keenly observes the place and the exact moment at which the apāna is consumed by prāṇa, his mind does not arise again. Therefore, behold that place and that moment at which prāṇa is consumed by apāna and apāna is consumed by prāṇa inside and outside the body. For that precise moment at which the prāṇa has ceased to move and the apāna has not begun to move, there arises a kumbhaka which is effortless: the wise regard that as an important state. When there is effortless suspension of breath, it is the supreme state. This is the self, it is pure infinite consciousness. He who reaches this does not grieve.

I contemplate that infinite consciousness which is the indwelling presence in the prāṇa but which is neither with prāṇa nor other than prāṇa. I contemplate that infinite consciousness which is the indwelling presence in the apāna but which is neither with apāna nor other than apāna. That which IS after the prāṇa and the apāna have ceased to be and which is in the middle between prāṇa and apāna—I contemplate that infinite consciousness. I contemplate that consciousness which is the prāṇa of prāṇa, which is the life of life, which alone is responsible for the preservation of the body; which is the mind of the mind, the intelligence in the intellect, the reality in the egosense. I salute that consciousness in which all things abide, from which they emerge, which is all and everywhere and which is all in all and eternal; which is the purifier of all and whose vision is most meritorious. I salute that consciousness in which prāṇa ceases to move but apāna does not arise and which dwells in the space in front (or, at the root) of the nose. I salute the consciousness which is the source for both prāṇa and apāna, which is the energy in both prāṇa and apāna and which enables the senses to function. I salute that consciousness which is in fact the essence of the internal and the external kumbhakas, which is the only goal of the contemplation of prāṇa, which enables the prāṇa to function and which is the cause of all causes. I take refuge in that supreme being.

VI.1:26 BHUŚUṆḌA continued:

By the regular and systematic practice of prāṇāyāma as described by me, I have gained the state of purity and I am not disturbed even when the mount Meru (or the north pole) is shaken. This state of samādhi or total equanimity is not lost whether I am walking or standing, whether I am awake, asleep or dreaming. With my vision turned upon the self, I rest in the self, with the self in all conditions of life, whatever changes may take place in the world or in the environment. Thus have I lived right from the time of the previous cosmic dissolution.

I do not contemplate either the past or the future: my attention is constantly directed to the present. I do what has to be done in the present, without thinking of the results. Without considerations of being or non-being, desirable and undesirable, I remain in the self: hence I am happy, healthy and free from illness.

My state is the fruit of contemplation of the moment of union of the prāṇa and the apāna (when the self is revealed); I do not entertain vain notions like, "I have obtained this and I shall gain that, too." I do not praise nor do I censure anyone (neither myself nor others) or anything at any time; my mind does not exult on gaining what is considered good nor does it become depressed on obtaining what is considered evil; hence my state of happiness and health. I embrace the supreme renunciation, having renounced even the desire to live; thus my mind does not entertain cravings but is peaceful and balanced. I behold the one common substratum in all things (a piece of wood, a beautiful woman, a mountain, a blade of grass, ice and fire and space) and I am not worried by thoughts like, "What shall I do now?" nor "What shall I get tomorrow morning?" I am not bothered by thoughts of old age and death, or by longing for happiness, nor do I regard some as "mine" and others as "not-mine". I know that everything at all times, everywhere, is but the one cosmic consciousness. These are the secrets of my state of happiness and health. I do not think, "I am the body," even while engaged in physical activity as I know this world-appearance to be illusory and live in it as if fast asleep. I am disturbed neither by prosperity nor by adversity when they are granted to me, as I regard them with equal vision (even as I look upon both my arms as arms). Whatever I do is untainted by desire or the mud of ego-sense; thus I do not lose my head when I am powerful or go begging when I am poor; I do not let hopes and expectations touch me and even when a thing is old and worn out I look upon it with fresh eyes as if it were new. I rejoice with the happy ones and share the grief of the grief-stricken, for I am the friend of all, knowing I belong to none and none belongs to me. I know that I am the world, all the activities in it and its intelligence. This is the secret of my longevity.

VASIṢṬHA said: VI.1:27, 28

Thereupon I said to Bhuśuṇḍa, "Marvellous indeed is this, your autobiography, O Lord. Blessed indeed are they who can behold you. You are like a second creator. Rare indeed are people like you. I have earned great merit by seeing you. May you continue to be blessed. Give me leave to depart."

O Rāma, on hearing this Bhuśuṇḍa worshipped me and, in spite of my remonstrances, accompanied me for some distance holding my hand tightly in a gesture of friendship. Then we parted. and parting of friends is indeed a difficult event. All this was in the previous (Kṛta) age and now it is Tretā-age.

Such is the story of Bhuśuṇḍa, O Rāma: you too, practise the prāṇāyāma described by Bhuśuṇḍa and endeavour to live like him.

RĀMA asked: Lord, by the rays of light shed by you the gloom of darkness has vanished. We are all spiritually awakened, we are delighted, we have entered into our own self, we are your own replica, as it were, having known what there is to be known.

In that inspiring account of Bhuśuṇḍa that you narrated, you made mention of a body which has three pillars, nine gates, etc. Pray tell me: how did it arise in the first place, how does it exist and who dwells in it?

VASIṢṬHA said:

O Rāma, this house known as the body has not been made by anyone in fact! It is only an appearance, like the two moons seen by one suffering from diplopia. The moon is really only one, the duality is optical illusion. The body is experienced to exist only when the notion of a physical body prevails in the mind; it is unreal, but since it appears to be when the notion arises, it is considered both real and unreal. Dreams are real during the dream-state, though they are unreal at other times; ripples are real when they are seen to exist, not at other times. Even so the body is real when it is experienced as a real substance. It is only an illusory appearance, even though it appears to be real.

The notion of 'I am this body' arises in relation to what is truly a piece of flesh with bones, etc., because of a mental predisposition; it is an illusion. Abandon this illusion. There are thousands of such bodies which have been brought into being by your thought-force. When you are asleep and dreaming, you experience a body in it: Where does that body arise or exist? While day-dreaming, you imagine you are in heaven, etc.: where is that body? When all these have ceased, you engage yourself in diverse activities, playing different roles: where is the body with which you do these? When you besport with your friends and enjoy their company in self-forgetful delight, where does that body abide? Thus, O Rāma, the bodies are but the products of the mind: hence they are regarded as real and unreal. Their conduct is determined by the mind, they are non-different from the mind.

VASIṢṬHA continued:

'This is wealth', 'This is body' and 'This is a nation'—all these are notions, O Rāma, which are the manifestation of the energy of the mind and which are otherwise illusory. Know this to be a long dream, or a long-standing hallucination, or day-dreaming, or wishful thinking. When, by the grace of God or the self you attain awakening, you will then see all this clearly. The existence of a world independent of you or the mind is but the jugglery of the mind, it is nothing but the recognition of a notion as if it were a substance.

I remarked that I was born of the mind of the Creator: even so the world arises in the mind as a notion. In fact, even the Creator is but a notion in the cosmic mind; the world-appearance, too, is a notion in the mind. These notions gain strength in the mind by being invested repeatedly with the mantle of truth and, therefore, they arise again and again, creating the illusory world-appearance with them.

If a man resolutely seeks the source of the notions, he realises consciousness; otherwise he experiences the illusory world-appearance again and again. For by continually entertaining notions such as 'This is it', 'This is mine' and 'This is my world' such notions assume the appearance of substantiality. The permanency of the world is also an illusion: in the dream-state what is really a brief moment is experienced by the dreamer as a life-time. In a mirage only the illusory 'water' is seen and not the substratum: even so, in a state of ignorance one sees only the illusory world-appearance but not the substratum. However, when one has shed that ignorance, the illusory appearance vanishes. Even the man who is normally subject to fear is not afraid of an imaginary tiger; the wise man who knows that this world is naught but a notion or imagination is unafraid of anything. When one knows that the world is nothing but the appearance of one's self, of whom need he be afraid? When one's vision is purified by enquiry, one's deluded understanding concerning the world vanishes.

It is by clear perception and understanding that one's nature is purified and then it does not become impure again. What is that right understanding? It is to realise that this world is nothing but the reflection (and therefore appearance) of pure consciousness and thus it is neither real nor unreal. Birth, death, heaven, knowledge and ignorance are all reflections of consciousness. I, you, the ten directions and all this, are consciousness: such is right understanding. When there is right understanding the mind does not arise nor does it set, but it attains supreme peace. It does not indulge in praise and censure, in exultation and depression, but it is ever cool and rests in truth.

VASIṢṬHA continued:

When one realises that death is inevitable to all, why will he grieve over the death of relatives or the approach of one's own end? When one realises that everyone is sometimes prosperous and otherwise at other times, why will he be elated or depressed? When one sees that living beings appear and disappear like ripples on the surface of consciousness, where is the cause for sorrow? What is true is always true (what exists always exists) and what is unreal is ever unreal; where is the cause for sorrow?

The 'I' is not, was not and will never be. The body has risen from a mysterious delusion and appears to exist. Where is the cause for sorrow? When there is right understanding of the truth that even if the body is real, 'I' is different from it and that 'I' is but the reflection of the infinite consciousness, there is no sorrow.

Hence, one should not pin one's faith, hope and aspiration on that which is unreal; for such hope is bondage. O Rāma, do thou live in this world without entertaining any hope. What has to be done has to be done and what is inappropriate should be given up. Live happily and playfully in this world without considerations of desirable and undesirable.

The infinite consciousness alone exists everywhere at all times. What appears to be is but an appearance. When the appearance is realised as appearance, that which IS, is realised. Either realise that 'I am not and these experiences are not mine' or know that 'I am everything': you will be free from the lure of world-appearance. Both these attitudes are good: adopt the one that suits you. You will be freed from attraction and aversion (rāga-dveṣa).

Whatever there is in the world, in the firmament and in heaven is attained by one who has destroyed the twin forces of attraction and aversion. Whatever the ignorant man does prompted by these forces leads him to instant sorrow. One who has not overcome these forces, even if he is learned in the scriptures, is indeed pitiable and despicable. His conversations are 'I have been robbed by another' or 'I have abandoned wealth and pleasure'. Wealth, relatives and friends come and go; the wise one does not seek them nor abandon them. That which has a beginning and an end is not worthy of the attention of the wise. In this world someone produces something (like a daughter) and someone else (like the bridegroom) enjoys it; who is deceived by this?

O Rāma, for your spiritual awakening I declare again and again: this world-appearance is like a long dream. Wake up, wake up. Behold the self which shines like a sun. You are indeed awakened by this shower of nectarine words: you have nothing to do with birth, sorrow, sin and delusion. Abandon all these notions and rest in the self.

VI.1:29 VASIṢṬHA, who suddenly became silent when he found that Rāma was completely absorbed in the self, resumed his discourse after an interval and after Rāma had returned to normal consciousness:

O Rāma, you are thoroughly awakened and you have gained self-knowledge. Remain forever in this exalted state; do not get involved in this world-appearance. This wheel of world-appearance (the wheel of birth and death of all things) has ideas, thoughts or notions for its hub. When these are arrested the world-appearance ceases, too. If one uses his will-force to arrest the wheel, it continues to revolve if the distractions caused by thoughts do not cease. Hence, one should restrain the hub (the thoughts and notions) having resort to supreme self-effort, strength, wisdom and commonsense. What is not achieved by such concerted action is not achieved by any other means. Hence, one should abandon the false dependence on divine intervention which is in fact the creation of the immature childish mind and, with one's intense self-effort, one should gain mastery over the mind.

This world-appearance commenced with the thought-force of the Creator. But, it is false. In it these bodies born of the natural characteristics of various elements wander about. Hence, one should never again entertain the notion that the body exists and that pleasure and pain are factual states.

The ignorant man who thinks he is suffering and whose face is streaming constantly with tears, is worse than a painting or a statue, for the latter is free from experience of sorrow! Nor is the statue subject to illness and death. The statue is destroyed only when someone destroys it, but the human body is certainly doomed to die. If the statue is well protected and preserved it lasts a long time in good condition: but even when well protected and preserved, the human body decays from day to day and does not remain in good condition. Hence the statue is better than the body created by thoughts and notions. Who will entertain any hopes based on such a human body?

The body is worse than even the body one dreams about. The dream body is created by a short-lived notion (the dream) and hence it is not subjected to long-standing sorrow; but the wakeful body is the product of long-standing ideas and notions and hence it is tormented by long-standing sorrow for a long time. Whether you think that the body is real or unreal, it is certain that it is the product of thoughts and notions. Hence, there need be no sorrow in relation to it.

Even as when a statue is broken, no life is lost, when the body born of thoughts and notions is dead, nothing is lost. It is like the loss of the second moon when one is cured of diplopia. The self which is infinite consciousness does not die nor does it undergo any change whatsoever.

VASIṢṬHA continued:

O Rāma, a man riding the merry-go-round sees the world whirling in the opposite direction: even so, man whirling on the wheel of ignorance thinks that the world and the body are revolving. The spiritual hero, however, should reject this: this body is the product of thoughts and notions entertained by an ignorant mind. The creation of ignorance is false. Hence, even if the body seems to be active and doing all kinds of actions it is still unreal, even as the imaginary snake in the rope is for ever unreal. What is done by an inert object is not done by it; though appearing to do, the body does nothing.

The inert body does not entertain any desire (to motivate its actions) and the self (which is the infinite consciousness) has no such desire either; hence there is in truth no doer of action but only the witnessing intelligence. Even as a lamp in a windless place shines spontaneously and naturally, being a lamp, thus should one remain the self in all conditions. Even as the sun, resting always in himself and in his own essential nature constantly engages himself in the affairs of the day, you too, resting in your own self engage yourself in the affairs of the state.

Once the deluded notion that this false body is a reality has arisen, then like a ghost imagined by a little boy, there arises the goblin of egosense or the mind. This false mind or egosense then roars aloud in such a way that even great men, frightened by it, withdraw themselves in deep meditation. He who however lays the ghost known as the mind (or egosense) in the body, dwells without fear in the void known as the world.

It is strange that even now people live considering the self to be the body created by the illusory ghost known as the mind. They who die while they are yet in the grip of the ghost known as the mind, their intelligence is ignorance! He who trusts in the house haunted by the ghost known as mind and lives in it is a goblin and he is indeed deluded, for that house (the body) is impermanent and unstable. Hence, O Rāma, give up this subservience to the ghost known as egosense and rest in the self without bestowing a second thought on the egosense.

They who are under the evil influence of the ghost known as egosense are deluded and in fact they have neither friends nor relatives. A deed done with the intelligence overpowered by the egosense is poisonous and it yields the fruit of death. The fool who is devoid of wisdom and courage and who is wedded to the egosense is already dead. He is like the firewood ready to be consigned into the fire known as hell.

Let this ghost known as egosense rest in or depart from the body. Do not let your mind even look at it, O Rāma!

VASIṢṬHA continued:

When the egosense is stripped of its coverings, ignored and

abandoned by the awakened intelligence, it is incapable of doing you any harm. The self is infinite consciousness. Even if the ego-sense dwells in this body, how is the self affected?

O Rāma, it is impossible to catalogue the calamities that visit one who is under the influence of the mind. All this weeping and wailing 'Alas, I am dead', 'Alas, I am burning' that one hears in this world—all this is nothing more than the play of the egosense. However, even as the all-pervading space is not polluted by anything, the self which is omnipresent is not affected by the egosense.

Whatever a man does with the body is really done by the ego-sense with the help of the reins known as inhalation and exhalation. The self is indirectly regarded as the cause of all this, even as space is indirectly responsible for the growth of plants inasmuch as it (the space) does not prevent the plant from extending into space. Even as a lamp is considered responsible for the vision of an object, the self is regarded as responsible for the actions of the body, mind, etc., which function in the light of the self. Otherwise, there is no connection whatsoever between the inert body and the conscious self. It is only because of the energy of the self (prāṇa) which is constantly vibrating, creating agitation everywhere, that the mind is confused with the self.

You are the self, O Rāma, not the mind. What have you to do with the mind? Abandon this delusion. The goblin-mind residing in the body has nothing to do with the self, yet it quietly assumes 'I am the self'. This is the cause of birth and death. This assumption robs you of courage. Give up this ghost, O Rāma, and remain firm. Neither scriptures nor relatives nor even the gurus or preceptors can protect the man who is utterly overpowered by the ghost known as the mind. On the other hand, if one has laid this ghost, the guru, the scriptures and relatives can easily aid him, even as one can easily rescue an animal from a mud-puddle. They who have laid this ghost are the good people who render some service to this world. Hence, one should uplift oneself from this ignorance, by laying this ghost known as egosense. O Rāma, do not wander in this forest of worldly existence like an animal in human garb. Do not wallow in this mud known as family-relationship for the sake of this impermanent body. The body was born of someone, it is protected by the egosense and in it happiness and sorrow are experienced by someone else: this indeed is a great mystery.

Even as the essential nature of a pot and that of a piece of cloth are non-different, even so the essential nature of the mind and that of the infinite consciousness are non-different. In this connection, I shall narrate to you the teaching that was imparted to me by lord

Śiva himself: the vision revealed in that teaching will destroy even the greatest delusion.

Description of the Lord

VASIṢṬHA continued:

There is the abode of lord Śiva known as Kailāsa. I lived there for some time, worshipping lord Śiva and practising austerities. I was surrounded by the perfected sages in whose company I used to discuss the truths of the scriptures.

One evening I was engaged in the worship of lord Śiva. The entire atmosphere was filled with peace and silence. In that forest the darkness was so dense that it appeared to be solid enough to be cut with a sword.

At that time I saw a great light in the forest. With the external sight I saw that light and with my insight I enquired into its nature. I saw that it was lord Śiva himself who was walking along holding his consort Pārvatī with one hand. In front of him walked his vehicle Nandi, making way for the Lord. I made the divine presence known to the disciples assembled around me and proceeded to where the Lord was.

I saluted the Lord and offered him due worship. I remained for a considerable time feasting my eyes on the divine vision. Lord Śiva then said to me: "Is your austerity proceeding satisfactorily, without any obstacles? Have you attained that which is worthy of attainment and have your internal fears ceased?"

In response, I said to the Lord: "Supreme Lord, they who are fortunate to be devoted to thee find nothing difficult of attainment and they do not experience fear at all. Everyone in the world salutes and prostrates to those who are devoted to you and who constantly remember you.* Only they are countries, they are cities, they are directions and mountains, where people who are solely and wholeheartedly devoted to you dwell. Your remembrance is the fruit of merits acquired in the past births and it is also the guarantee of still more blessedness in the future. Your constant remembrance, O Lord, is like the pot of nectar and is the ever-open door to liberation. Lord, wearing the precious and radiant jewel of your remembrance I have trampled under foot all the calamities that might otherwise torment me in the future.

"Lord, though by your grace I have reached the state of self-

---

* Only they deserve to be taken notice of as countries, cities, etc., where the Lord's devotees dwell.

fulfilment, I am eager to know more about one thing. Pray enlighten me. What is the method of worshipping the Lord which destroys all sins and promotes all auspiciousness?"

THE LORD said:

Do you know who 'god' is? God is not Viṣṇu, Śiva or Brahmā; not the wind, the sun or the moon; not the brāhmaṇa or the king; not I nor you; not Lakṣmī nor the mind (intellect). God is without form and undivided (not in the objects); that splendour (devanam) which is not made and which has neither beginning nor end is known as god (deva) or lord Śiva which is pure consciousness. That alone is to be worshipped; and that alone is all.

If one is unable to worship this Śiva then he is encouraged to worship the form. The latter yields finite results but the former bestows infinite bliss. He who ignores the infinite and is devoted to the finite abandons a pleasure-garden and seeks the thorny bush. However, sages sometimes worship a form playfully.

Now for the articles used in the worship: wisdom, self-control and the perception of the self in all beings are the foremost among those articles. The self alone is lord Śiva who is fit to be worshipped at all times with the flowers of wisdom.

(I asked the Lord: "Pray tell me how this world is transmuted into pure consciousness and also how that pure consciousness appears as the jīva and other things". The LORD continued:)

Indeed only that cid-ākāśa (the infinite consciousness), which alone exists even after the cosmic dissolution, exists even now, utterly devoid of objectivity. The concepts and notions that are illumined by the consciousness within itself shine as this creation, on account of the movement of energy within consciousness, precisely as dreams arise during sleep. Otherwise, it is totally impossible for an object of perception to exist outside of the omnipresent infinite consciousness.

All these mountains, the whole world, the firmament, the self, the jīva or the individuality and all the elements of which this world is constituted—all these are naught but pure consciousness. Before the so-called creation when only this pure consciousness existed, where were all these (heaven, etc.)? Space (ākāśa), supreme or infinite space (paramākāśam), absolute space (brahmākāśam), creation, consciousness—are mere words and they indicate the same truth even as synonyms do. Even as the duality experienced in dream is illusory, the duality implied in the creation of the world is illusory. Even as the objects seem to exist and function in the inner world of consciousness in a dream, objects seem to exist and function in the outer world of consciousness during the wakeful state. Nothing really happens in both these states. Even as consciousness alone is the reality in the dream state, consciousness alone is the substance in the wakeful state too. That is the Lord, that is the supreme truth, that you are, that I am and that is all.

VI.1:30 The LORD continued:

The worship of that Lord is true worship and by that worship one attains everything. He is undivided and indivisible, non-dual and not fashioned or created by activity; he is not attained by external efforts. His adoration is the fountain-source of joy.

The external worship of a form is prescribed only for those whose intelligence has not been awakened and who are immature like little boys. When one does not have self-control, etc., he uses flowers in worship; such worship is futile, even as adoring the self in an external form is futile. However, these immature devotees derive satisfaction by worshipping an object created by themselves; they may even earn worthless rewards from such worship.

I shall now describe to you the mode of worship appropriate to enlightened people like you. The Lord fit to be worshipped is indeed the one who upholds the entire creation, who is beyond thought and description, who is beyond the concepts of even the 'all' and the 'collective totality'. He alone is referred to as 'God' who is undivided and indivisible by space and time, whose light illumines all the objects, who is pure and absolute consciousness. He is that intelligence which is beyond all its parts, which is hidden in all that is, which is the being in all that is and which robs all that is of their being (i.e., which veils the truth). This Brahman is in the middle of being and non-being, it is God, and the truth that is indicated as 'OM'. It exists everywhere like the essence in a plant. That pure consciousness which is in you, in me and in all the gods and goddesses alone is God. Holy one, even the other gods endowed with form are indeed nothing but that pure consciousness. The entire universe is pure consciousness. That is God, that 'all' I am; everything is attained from and through him.

That God is not distant from anyone, O Holy one, nor is he difficult to attain: he is for ever seated in the body and he is everywhere like space. He does everything, he eats, he holds everything together, he goes, he breathes, he knows every limb of the body. He is the light in which all these limbs function and all the diverse activities take place. He dwells in the cave of one's own heart. He transcends the mind and the five senses of cognition; therefore he cannot be comprehended nor described by them—yet for the purpose of instruction, he is indicated as 'consciousness'. Hence, though it appears as though he does everything, he does nothing. That consciousness is pure and seemingly engages itself in the activities of the world to the same extent as the spring does in the flowering of trees.

The LORD continued:

Somewhere this consciousness functions as space, somewhere as a jīva, somewhere as action, somewhere as substance and so forth, but without intending to do so. Even as all the 'different' oceans are but one indivisible mass of water, this consciousness, though described in different ways, is but one cosmic mass of consciousness. In the body, which is like a lotus, it is the same consciousness that imbibes the experience which is like honey gathered by the restless mind which is like the bee. In this universe all these various beings (the gods, the demons, mountains, oceans and so forth) flow within this infinite consciousness even as eddies and whirlpools appear in the ocean. Even the wheel of ignorance, which causes the wheel of life and death to revolve, revolves within this cosmic consciousness whose energy is in constant motion.

It was consciousness, in the form of the four-armed Viṣṇu, that destroyed the demons, even as a thunderstorm equipped with the rainbow quenches the heat that rises from the earth. It is consciousness alone which takes the form of Śiva and Pārvatī, of Brahmā the creator and the numerous other beings. This consciousness is like a mirror which holds a reflection within itself, as it were, without undergoing any modification thereby. Without undergoing any modification in itself, this consciousness appears as all these countless beings in this universe.

The infinite consciousness is like a creeper. It is sprinkled with the latent tendencies of countless jīvas. Desires are the buds. Past creations are the filaments. The sentient and the insentient beings are parts of the creeper. The one appears as many, but it has not become many.

It is by this infinite consciousness that all this is thought of, expressed and done. It is the infinite consciousness alone which shines as the sun. It is the infinite consciousness which appears as the bodies which are in fact inert and which come into contact with one another and derive various experiences. This consciousness is like the typhoon which is unseen in itself but in which sand-particles and dust rise and dance as if by themselves. This consciousness casts a shadow in itself, as it were, and that is regarded as tamas or inertia.

In this body, thoughts and notions generate action in the light of this very consciousness. Surely, but for this consciousness even an object which is immediately in front of oneself cannot be experienced. The body cannot function nor exist but for this consciousness. It grows, it falls, it eats. This consciousness creates and maintains all the movable and the immovable beings in the universe. The infinite consciousness alone exists, naught else exists. Consciousness alone has arisen in consciousness.

VASIṢṬHA continued:

Thereupon I asked the Lord: "If this consciousness is omnipresent, how then does one become insentient and inert in this world? How is it possible that one who is endowed with consciousness loses consciousness?"

The LORD applauded the question and replied:

The omnipresent consciousness, which is all in all, exists in this body both as the changing and as the unchanging and unmodified one. Just as a woman dreams herself to be another with another as her husband in that dream, the same consciousness believes itself to be of another nature. Just as the same man when he is under the influence of uncontrollable rage behaves completely differently, even so consciousness assumes another aspect and functions differently. By stages, it becomes insentient and inert.

Consciousness thus becomes its own object, creating space and then air and their respective qualities. At the same time, it evolves within itself time and space, and becomes a jīva followed by individualised finite intellect and mind. From this arises the cyclic world-appearance and notions like 'I am an untouchable', etc. The infinite consciousness itself thus becomes apparently inert, just as water becomes crystal. Thereafter the mind becomes deluded, entertains cravings, falls a prey to lust and anger, experiences prosperity and adversity, suffers pain and pleasure, clings to hope, endures terrible suffering and is filled with likes and dislikes that perpetuate the delusion. Thoroughly deluded, it goes from error to error, from ignorance to greater ignorance.

In childhood, this deluded consciousness is totally dependent on others, in youth it runs after wealth and is filled with worry, in old age it is sunk in sorrow and in death it is led by its own karma. In accordance with that karma, it is born in heaven or in hell, in the netherworld or on earth as human, subhuman or inanimate being. It is the same consciousness that appears as Viṣṇu, Śiva, Brahmā and others. It is the same consciousness that functions as the sun, the moon, the wind, the factors that cause changes in seasons, day and night. It is the same consciousness that is the life-force in seeds and the characteristics of all material substances. This consciousness which is conditioned by self-limitation is afraid of itself! Such is the truth concerning the jīva-consciousness. It is also known as karma-ātmā (the self that is caught in the wheel of action and reaction).

Behold the power of ignorance and inertia! Merely by the forgetfulness of one's own true state, the consciousness undergoes great troubles and sorrows and experiences pitiable downfall.

The LORD continued: VI.1:31

Consciousness thinks (feels or imagines) falsely 'I am unhappy' even as a demented woman might think she is miserable. Just as one who is not dead wails aloud "Alas, I am dead", and when she is not lost she weeps "Alas, I am lost", on account of perverse understanding, even so the consciousness falsely imagines it is miserable or limited. Such imagination is irrational and unfounded. Due to the false assumption of the egosense the consciousness thinks that the world-appearance is indeed real. It is the mind alone that is the root-cause of experiencing the world as if it were real; but it cannot be truly considered such a cause since there can be no mind other than pure consciousness. Thus, if it is realised that the perceiving mind itself is unreal, then it is clear that the perceived world is unreal too.

Even as there is no oil in a rock, in pure consciousness the diversity of sight, seer and scene, or of doer, act and action, or of knower, knowledge and known does not exist. Similarly, the distinction between 'I' and 'you' is imaginary. The distinction between the one and the many is verbal. All these do not exist at all even as darkness does not exist in the sun. Opposites like substantiality and unsubstantiality, void and non-void are mere concepts. On enquiry, all these disappear and only the unmodified pure consciousness remains.

Consciousness does not truly undergo any modification nor does it become impure. The impurity itself is imaginary; imagination is the impurity. When this is realised, the imagination is abandoned and impurity ceases. However, even in those who have realised this, the impurity arises unless the imagination is firmly rejected. By self-effort this imagination can be easily rejected: if one can drop a piece of straw, one can with equal ease also drop the three worlds! What is it that cannot be achieved by one's self-effort?

This infinite consciousness, which is unmodified and non-dual, can be realised by one in the single self-luminous inner light. It is pure and eternal, it is ever-present and devoid of mind, it is unmodified and untainted, it is all the objects. In fact, it is non-moving consciousness which exists as if witness to all, even as light shines but shining is not its action. While pure, this consciousness appears to be tainted; in inert material it is non-inert energy. It is omnipresent without being divided by the particulars constituting the all.

This infinite consciousness, which is devoid of concepts and extremely subtle, knows itself. In self-forgetfulness this consciousness entertains thoughts and experiences peception, though all this is possible because of the very nature of the infinite consciousness: even as one who is asleep is also inwardly awake!

The LORD continued:

By identification with its own object, consciousness seems to reduce itself to the state of thinking or worrying: even as impure gold looks like copper until it is purified, when it shines like gold. By self-forgetfulness on the part of the infinite consciousness the notion of the universe arises, but this unreality ceases when there is self-knowledge.

When consciousness becomes aware of itself within itself, the egosense arises. With just a little movement though, this egosense (which in truth is nothing other than consciousness) falls down as a rock rolls down the mountainside. However, even then it is consciousness alone that is the reality in all forms and all experiences. The movement of the vital airs brings about vision within and an object which is apparently outside. But the experiencing of sight (the seeing itself) is the pure (supreme) consciousness! The apparently inert vital air which is the tactile sensation comes into contact with its object and there is the sense of touch. But the awareness of the tactile sensation is again pure consciousness. In the same way it is the vital air (prāṇa) that enables the nose to smell the scents which are modifications of the same energy, while the awareness of the smell is pure consciousness. If the mind is not associated with the sense of hearing, no hearing is possible. Again, it is pure consciousness that is the experience of hearing.

Action springs from thought, thought is the function of the mind, mind is conditioned consciousness, but consciousness is unconditioned! The universe is but a reflection in consciousness (like the scenery reflected in a crystal ball) but consciousness is not conditioned by such reflection. Jīva is the vehicle of consciousness, egosense is the vehicle of jīva, intelligence of egosense, mind of intelligence, prāṇa of the mind, the senses of prāṇa, the body of the senses and motion is the vehicle of the body. Such motion is karma. Because prāṇa is the vehicle for the mind, where the prāṇa takes it the mind goes. But when the mind is merged in the spiritual heart, prāṇa does not move. And if the prāṇa does not move, the mind attains a quiescent state. Where the prāṇa goes the mind follows it, even as the rider goes where the vehicle goes.

The reflection of consciousness within itself is known as puryaṣṭaka. Mind alone is puryaṣṭaka, though others have described it more elaborately (as composed of the five elements, the inner instrument—mind, buddhi, egosense and citta—prāṇa, the organs of action, the senses, ignorance, desire, and karma or action). It is also known as the liṅga-śarīra, the subtle body. Since all these arise in consciousness, exist in consciousness and dissolve in consciousness, that consciousness alone is the reality.

The LORD said: VI.1:32

But for the mind and prāṇa the body is an inert mass. Just as a piece of iron moves in the presence of a magnet, even so the jīva moves in the very presence of consciousness which is infinite and omnipresent. The body is inert and dependent; it is made to function by the consciousness which believes itself to be similar to the vital airs (prāṇa). Thus, it is the karma-self or the active self (karmātmā) that keeps the body in motion. It is, however, the supreme self itself that has ordained both the mind and the prāṇa as the promoters of life in the body. It is the consciousness itself, assuming inertia, which rides the mind as the jīva.

Once this limitation is established, then other consequences follow. They are the physical and mental diseases! This is like waves first arising on the surface of the ocean and then creating ripples and so forth. The consciousness as jīva becomes dependent, having abandoned the self-knowledge as consciousness. Labouring under a thick veil of ignorance, it is foolishly unable to recognise the harm that it has brought upon itself, even as a drunkard wielding a sword cuts his own leg. However, even as the drunkard can soon become sober, this consciousness can soon regain self-knowledge.

When the mind is divested of its support, it remains alone in the self. When the puryaṣṭaka (the subtle body) is rid of all its supports, it attains a state of quiescence and falls motionless. When consciousness, on account of objectification, becomes deluded, the latent psychological tendencies become active; identifying with these, consciousness forgets its essential nature.

When the lotus of the heart unfolds, the puryaṣṭaka functions; when that lotus folds, the puryaṣṭaka ceases to function. As long as the puryaṣṭaka functions in the body, the body lives; when it ceases to function, the body dies. This cessation can be caused by some form of inner conflict between the impurities and inner awakening. If only pure vāsanās or tendencies fill one's heart all conflicts cease and there are harmony, liberation and longevity. Otherwise, when the puryaṣtka ceases to function, the body dies and the subtle body chooses another suited to fulfil the hidden vāsanās. Due to these vāsanās, the puryaṣṭaka forges new links with the new subtle body, forgetting its nature as pure consciousness. However, since consciousness is infinite and omnipresent, the mind riding the puryaṣṭaka roams everywhere. Bodies are taken up and abandoned by the jīva even as trees sprout new leaves and discard old ones. Wise men do not set any store by these changes.

VI.1:33 In response to Vasiṣṭha's questions: (i) in the infinite consciousness how did duality arise and (ii) how does that duality which has been strengthened by aeons of confirmation, cease, the LORD continued:

Since that omnipresent infinite consciousness alone is present at all times, diversity (duality) is absurd and impossible. The concept of one arises when there is a concept of two and vice versa: when the diversity is realised as of consciousness, the diversity is also that! The cause and effect are one in their essence. This essence is indivisible. Consciousness being its own object, is consciousness at all times; the modifications are but vain thinking. (To assert that there are waves UPON the surface of the ocean is like saying 'Mountains made of water float upon the surface of the ocean'. Are the waves outside the ocean?) Consciousness alone is 'that', 'this' and 'in the middle' (the factor that perceives the modification). It is the one infinite consciousness that is variously known as Brahman, truth, god, Śiva, void, one and supreme self.

That which is beyond all these forms and states of consciousness, that which is the supreme self, that which is indicated by the pure 'I'—that is not for words to describe. That which is perceived here is itself indivisible. When this consciousness invests itself with a secondary vision (upanayana also means the sacred thread of vedic learning!) then it perceives duality. It is bound by its own ignorant imagination. This imagination gives rise to substantiality, and the experience of objects gives rise to the confirmation of the reality of that object. The egosense gains credence thereafter and is firmly established, assuming the role of the doer of actions and the experiencer of other experiences. Thus, what was accidental coincidence to begin with soon becomes an established fact.

Belief in the existence of the goblin creates it. Belief in the duality (diversity) establishes it. When the non-dual being is known, the duality vanishes instantly. Belief (or imagination) gave rise to diversity; when that belief is dropped, diversity goes. Thought, imagination or belief gives rise to sorrow; to abandon such thinking is not painful! It is feeding these thoughts and beliefs that has brought about this sorrow; and this comes to an end by not entertaining those thoughts and beliefs: where is the difficulty in this? All thoughts and beliefs lead to sorrow, whereas no-thought and no-belief are pure bliss. Therefore, with the help of the fire of wisdom, vaporise the waters of your beliefs and become peaceful, supremely blissful. Behold the one infinite consciousness.

It is only as long as the king remains forgetful of the fact 'I am king' that he is miserable. Once he regains that knowledge, that sorrow vanishes. Even as after the rainy season, when the winter season has set in, the sky is unable to collect clouds to veil itself, once the infinite consciousness is realised, the clouds of ignorance are banished for ever.

The LORD said: VI.1:34

Thus does the universe exist as both real and unreal; the divine, being free of duality, unites them, transcends them and is therefore both of them. Manifest consciousness is the universe, and the unmanifest universe is consciousness. By entertaining the notion 'I am this', consciousness is bound; by this very knowledge it is freed. Objectification (or conceptualisation) leads to self-forgetfulness. However, even in the state of diversity and activity, consciousness is truly undivided. For it is only that supremely peaceful Brahman that is apparently manifest as the universe through the instrumentality of the mind and its three modes (satva, rajas and tamas, or waking, dreaming and sleeping).

When, however, the mind is destroyed by the mind, the veil is rent asunder and the truth of the world-jugglery is seen, the notion of world-appearance and the existence of a jīva are destroyed. The mind is then clear, having given up repeatedly reviving the notions of objective perception. This state is known as 'paśyantī'. Then the mind which is pure abandons conjuring up images of objects. It attains a state like deep sleep or the consciousness of homogeneity, thus going beyond the possibility of birth again. It rests in supreme peace. This is the first state.

Now listen to the second state. Consciousness devoid of mind is all-light, free from darkness and beautiful like space. The infinite consciousness frees itself totally from all modification or duality and remains as if in deep sleep or as a figure in uncut marble. It abandons even the factors of time and space and transcends both inertness and motion; it remains as pure being beyond expression. It transcends the three states of consciousness and remains as the fourth or the state of undivided infinite consciousness.

Now comes the third state. This is beyond even what is termed 'Brahman', 'the self', etc. It is sometimes referred to as turīya-atīta (beyond the fourth or turīya state). It is supreme and ultimate. It defies description, for it is beyond the practices which are described by those who undertake them.

O sage, remain for ever in that third state. That is the real worship of the Lord. Then you will be established in that which is beyond what is and what is not. Nothing has been created and there is nothing to vanish. It is beyond the one and the two. It is the eternal, beyond the eternal and the transient; it is pure mass of consciousness. In it there is no question of diversity. It is all, it is supreme blessedness and peace, it is beyond expression. It is purest OM. It is transcendent. It is supreme.

(VĀLMĪKI said: "Having said this, the lord Śiva remained in silent and deep contemplation for some time.")

Deva Pūjā

VI.1:35 After thus remaining immersed in himself for some time, the LORD opened his eyes and continued:

O sage, abandon the habit of apprehending the objects with your mind. The knowers of that (self) have seen what is worth seeing. What more is there to be seen or not to be seen? Behold the self. Be a sword which sunders what is regarded as peace and what is regarded as restlessness. Or, resorting to just a little extroversion of attention, listen to what I am going to say to you. Nothing is gained by merely keeping quiet!

This body is kept alive and active by the life-force or prāṇa. Without that life-force the body is inert. The energy that moves the body is prāṇa. The intelligence that experiences through all this is consciousness. This consciousness is formless and purer than even the sky. When the relationship between the life-force and body ceases, only the life-force is separated from the body. Consciousness, which is purer than space, does not perish.

A pure mirror reflects what is in front of it, but the reflection is not seen if the mirror is covered with dirt. Even so, though the body is seen, when the prāṇa has left the body the intelligence does not reflect the objects.

The consciousness though infinite and omnipresent is able to become aware of the movement of the mind and the body. When this defect of objectification (conceptualisation) is removed, that itself shines as the supreme being. It is itself the creator Brahmā, Viṣṇu, Śiva, Indra, the sun, the moon and the supreme Lord. Some of these divinities like Brahmā, Viṣṇu and Śiva are not deceived by the cosmic illusion. They are indeed parts of the infinite consciousness sharing its true nature: like red-hot iron which shares the nature of fire. However, none of these has actually been created by the infinite consciousness and none of these exists apart from it. These are no more than notions—some notions being more dense than the others. It is impossible to describe the extent of such notions which have arisen in ignorance.

In a manner of speaking, the supreme being (the infinite consciousness) is the father of Brahmā, Viṣṇu, Śiva and others. That infinite consciousness alone is fit to be adored and worshipped. However, there is no use inviting it for the worship; no mantras are of any use in its worship for it is immediate (closest, one's own self) and hence does not need to be invited. It is the omnipresent self of all. The realisation of this infinite consciousness (which is totally effortless) is alone the best form of worship.

The LORD said: VI.1:36

Thus, they say that lord Rudra is the pure, spontaneous self-experience which is the one consciousness that dwells in all substances. It is the seed of all seeds, it is the essence of this world-appearance, it is the greatest of actions. It is the cause of all causes and it is the essence in all beings, though in fact it does not cause anything nor is it the concept of being, and therefore cannot be conceived. It is the awareness in all that is sentient, it knows itself as its own object, it is its own supreme object and it is aware of infinite diversity within itself.

It is consciousness in all experiences but it is pure and unconditioned. It is absolute truth and therefore not truth as a concept. It is not limited to the definitions of truth or falsehood. It is in fact the very end (terminus) of the supreme truth or the primordial reality. It is pure absolute consciousness, naught else.

Yet, it itself becomes coloured with desire or attraction for pleasure. It itself becomes the experiencer of pleasure, the pleasure-experience and the impurity or taint caused by it. Though it is like the sky, unconditioned and undivided, soon it becomes limited and conditioned. In this infinite consciousness there have been millions of mirages known as world-appearance and there will also arise millions more mirages known as world-appearance. Yet, nothing really has come into being independent of the infinite consciousness: light and heat seem to come out of fire but they are not independent of fire.

This infinite consciousness can be compared to the ultimate subatomic particle which yet hides within its heart the greatest of mountains. It encompasses the span of countless epochs, but it does not let go of a moment of time. It is subtler than the tip of a single strand of hair, yet it pervades the entire universe. No one has seen its limits or boundaries.

It does nothing, yet it has fashioned the universe. Sustaining the entire universe, it does nothing at all. All substances are non-different from it, yet it is not a substance; though it is non-substantial it pervades all substances. The cosmos is its body, yet it has no body. It is the eternal 'now', yet it is the tomorrow (morning). Often apparently meaningless sounds become meaningful and are regarded as meaningful while communicating with one another: even so that infinite consciousness is and is not. It is even what it is not. All these statements about what is and what is not are based on logic, and the infinite consciousness goes beyond truth, beyond logic.

VI.1:37 The LORD continued:

It is this infinite consciousness that makes the seed sprout with the help of earth, water, time, etc., and become food. It makes flowers blossom and makes the nose smell their fragrance. In the same way, it is able to create and sustain the substances in the world and their corresponding sense-organs, with the help of suitable means which are also brought into being by the same consciousness. The energy of this consciousness is able to create the entire universe and then, entertaining the notion 'This is not', reduces everything to a state of void.

This apparent creation is but a reflection of consciousness within itself, which has apparently acquired a body in course of time. The trinity is the manifestation of—and also is—that cosmic power or energy that determines 'So it shall be, and it shall not be otherwise.' Yet, consciousness does not create anything; it is like a lamp that illumines the room in which actions take place.

VASIṢṬHA asked:

Lord, what are energies of this Śiva (consciousness) and what are their powers and their activities?

The LORD replied:

The supreme being is formless, and yet the following five are its aspects—will, space, time, order (or destiny) and the cosmic unmanifest nature. It has countless powers or energies or potencies. Chief among them are knowledge, dynamics, action and non-action.

All these are but pure consciousness; because they are called the potencies of consciousness, they are apparently regarded as distinct from consciousness, though in fact they are not.

This entire creation is like a stage on which all these potencies of consciousness dance to the tune of time. The foremost among these is known as 'order' (the natural order of things and sequences). It is also known as action, desire or will-to-do, time, etc. It is this potency that ordains that each thing should have a certain characteristic—from the blade of grass to the creator Brahmā. This natural order is free from excitement but not purified of its limitation: that (the natural order) is what dances a dance—drama known as the world-appearance. It portrays various moods (compassion, anger, etc.), it produces and removes various seasons and epochs, it is accompanied by the celestial music and the roaring of the oceans, its stage is illumined by the sun and the moon and the stars, it actors and actresses are the living beings in all the worlds—such is the dance of the natural order. The Lord who is the infinite consciousness is the silent but alert witness of this cosmic dance. He is non-different from the dancer (the cosmic natural order) and the dance (the happenings).

The LORD continued: VI.1:38

Such is the Lord who is fit to be worshipped constantly by holy ones. It is he indeed who is worshipped by wise men in various ways and in various forms such as Śiva, Viṣṇu, etc. Now listen to the ways in which he is to be worshipped.

First of all, one should abandon the body-idea (the notion that 'I am this body'). Meditation alone is true worship. Hence one should constantly worship the Lord of the three worlds by means of meditation. How should one contemplate him? He is pure intelligence, he is as radiant as a hundred thousand suns risen together, he is the light that illumines all lights, he is the inner light, the limitless space is his throat, the firmament is his feet, the directions are his arms, the worlds are the weapons he bears in his hands, the entire universe is hidden in his heart, the gods are hairs on his body, the cosmic potencies are the energies in his body, time is his gate-keeper and he has thousands of heads, eyes, ears and arms. He touches all, he tastes all, he hears all, he thinks through all though he is beyond thinking. He does everything at all times, he bestows whatever one thinks of or desires, he dwells in all, he is the all, he alone is to be sought by all. Thus should one contemplate him.

This Lord is not to be worshipped by material substances but by one's own consciousness. Not by waving of lamps nor lighting incense, nor by offering flowers nor even by offering food or sandal-paste. He is attained without the least effort; he is worshipped by self-realisation alone. This is the supreme meditation, this is the supreme worship: the continuous and unbroken awareness of the indwelling presence, inner light or consciousness. While doing whatever one is doing—seeing, hearing, touching, smelling, eating, moving, sleeping, breathing or talking—one should realise one's essential nature as pure consciousness. Thus does one attain liberation.

Meditation is the offering, meditation is the water offered to the deity to wash his hands and feet, self-knowledge gained through meditation is the flower—indeed all these are directed towards meditation. The self is not realised by any means other than meditation. If one is able to meditate even for thirteen seconds, even if one is ignorant, one attains the merit of giving away a cow in charity. If one does so for one hundred and one seconds, the merit is that of performing a sacred rite. If the duration is twelve minutes, the merit is a thousandfold. If the duration is of a day, one dwells in the highest realm. This is the supreme yoga, this is the supreme kriyā (action or service). One who practises this mode of worship is worshipped by the gods and the demons and all other beings. However, this is external worship.

VI.1:39 The LORD continued:

I shall now declare to you the internal worship of the self which is the greatest among all purifiers and which destroys all darkness completely. This is of the nature of perpetual meditation—whether one is walking or standing, whether one is awake or asleep, in and through all of one's actions. One should contemplate this supreme Lord who is seated in the heart and who brings about, as it were, all the modifications within oneself. One should worship the 'bodha-liṅgaṃ' (the manifest consciousness or self-awareness) which sleeps and wakes up, goes about or stands, touches what is to be touched, abandons what should be abandoned, enjoys and abandons pleasures, engages in varied external activities, lends value to all actions and remains as peace in the vital organs in the body (deha-liṅgaṃ in the text may also refer to the three 'liṅgaṃs' associated with the psychic centres). This inner intelligence should be worshipped with whatever comes to one unsought. Remaining firmly seated in the stream of life and its experiences after having bathed in self-knowledge, one should worship this inner intelligence with the materials of self-realisation.

One should contemplate the Lord in the following manner: he is the light illumined by the solar force as well as the lunar force, he is the intelligence that eternally lies hidden in all material substances, he is the extrovert awareness that flows through the bodily avenues on to the external world, he is the prāṇa that moves in one's face (nose), he transforms contacts of the senses into meaningful experiences, he rides the chariot composed of prāṇa and apāna, he dwells in secret in the cave of one's heart. He is the knower of the knowable and the doer of all actions, the experiencer of all experiences, the thinker of all thoughts. It is he who knows all parts or limbs thoroughly, who is recognised by being and non-being and who illumines all experiences.

He is without parts but he is the all, he dwells in the body but he is omnipresent, he enjoys and does not enjoy, he is the intelligence in every limb. He is the thinking faculty in the mind. He rises in the middle of prāṇa and apāna. He dwells in the heart, in the throat, in the middle of the palate, the middle of the eyebrows and at the tip of the nose. He is the reality in all the thirty-six elements (or metaphysical categories), he transcends the internal states, he is the one that produces the internal sounds, and he brings into being the bird known as mind. He is the reality in what is described as imagination and non-imagination. He dwells in all beings as oil dwells in the seed. He dwells in the heart-lotus and again he dwells throughout the body. He shines as pure consciousness. He is immediately seen everywhere, for he is the pure experiencing in all experiences, who apparently polarises himself when apprehending the objects of such experiences.

The LORD continued:

One should contemplate that the Lord is the intelligence in the body. The various functions and faculties in the body serve that intelligence as consorts serve their lord. The mind is the messenger who brings and presents to the Lord the knowledge of the three worlds. The two fundamental energies, viz., the energy of wisdom (jñāna śakti) and the energy of action (kriyā śakti), are the consorts of the Lord. Diverse aspects of knowledge are his ornaments. The organs of action are the gates through which the Lord enters the outside world. 'I am that infinite self which is indivisible; I remain full and finite,' thus the intelligence dwells in the body.

He who contemplates in this manner is equanimity itself, his behaviour is equanimous, guided by equal vision. He has reached the state of natural goodness and inner purity and he is beautiful in every aspect of his being. He worships the Lord who is the intelligence that pervades his entire body.

This worship is performed day and night perpetually, with the objects that are effortlessly obtained, and are offered to the Lord with a mind firmly established in equanimity and in the right spirit (for the Lord is consciousness and cares only for the right spirit). The Lord should be worshipped with everything that is obtained without effort. One should never make the least effort to attain that which one does not possess. The Lord should be worshipped by means of all the enjoyments that the body enjoys, through eating, drinking, being with one's consort and such other pleasures. The Lord should be worshipped with the illnesses one experiences and with every sort of unhappiness or suffering one experiences. The Lord should be worshipped with all of one's activities, including life and death and all of one's dreams. The Lord should be worshipped with one's poverty and prosperity. The Lord should be worshipped even with fights and quarrels as well as with sports and other pasttimes, and with the manifestations of the emotions of attraction and aversion. The Lord should be adored with the noble qualities of a pious heart—friendship, compassion, joy and indifference.

The Lord should be worshipped with all kinds of pleasures that are granted to one unsought, whether those pleasures are sanctioned by the scriptures, etc., or forbidden by them. The Lord should be worshipped with those which are regarded as desirable and others which are regarded as undesirable, with those that are considered appropriate and others that are considered inappropriate. For this worship, one should abandon what is lost and one should accept and receive what has been obtained without effort.

The LORD continued:

One should engage oneself in this worship at all times, established in supreme equanimity in regard to all the percepts whether they be pleasant or unpleasant. One should regard everything as good and auspicious (or one should regard everything as a mixture of good and evil). Realising that everything is the one self, one should worship the self in this spirit. One should look with equal vision upon that which is pleasant and beautiful through and through and that which is unendurably unpleasant. Thus should one worship the self.

One should abandon the divisive notions of 'This I am' and 'This I am not' and realise that 'All this is indeed Brahman', the one indivisible and infinite consciousness. In that spirit one should worship the self. At all times, in all forms and their modifications, one should worship the self in and through all that one obtains. One should worship the self after having abandoned the distinction between the desirable and the undesirable, or even while relying on such a distinction (but using them as the materials for the worship).

Without craving and without rejecting, that which is effortlessly and naturally obtained may be enjoyed. One should not get excited or depressed when faced with insignificant or significant objects, just as neither sky nor space is so affected by the diverse objects that exist and grow in it. One should worship the self, without psychological perversion, with every object that is obtained purely on account of the coincidence of the time, place and activity—whether they are popularly known as good or as not-good.

In this procedure for the worship of the self, whatever article has been mentioned as being necessary for the worship is of the same nature as all others, though the expressions used are different. Equanimity is sweetness itself and this sweetness is beyond the senses and the mind. Whatever is touched by that equanimity instantly becomes sweet, whatever its description or definition may be. That alone is regarded as worship which is performed when one is in a state of equanimity like that of space, when the mind has become utterly quiescent without the least movement of thought, when there is effortless absence of perversity. Established in this state of equanimity, the wise man should experience infinite expansion within himself while carrying out his natural actions externally without craving or rejection. Such is the nature of the worshipper of this intelligence. In his case, delusion, ignorance and egosense do not arise even in dream. Remain in this state, O sage, experiencing everything as a child does. Worship the Lord of this body (the intelligence that pervades it) with all that is brought to you by time, circumstance and environment, and rest in supreme peace, devoid of desire.

The LORD continued: VI.1:40

Whatever you do and whenever you do it (or refrain from doing it) —all that is worship of the Lord who is pure consciousness. By regarding all that as the worship of the self who is the Lord—he is delighted.

Likes and dislikes, attraction and aversion are not found in the self independent of its essential nature; they are mere words. Even the concepts indicated by words like 'sovereignty', 'poverty', 'pleasure', 'pain', 'one's own' and 'others', are in fact worship of the self, for the conceiving intelligence is the self. Knowledge of the cosmic being alone is the proper worship of the cosmic being.

It is that self or cosmic consciousness alone which is indicated by expressions like 'this world'. Oh, what a mysterious wonder it is that the self which is pure consciousness or intelligence somehow seems to forget its own nature and comes to regard itself as the jīva (the individual). In fact, in that cosmic being which is the reality in everything, there is not even the division into worshipper, worship and the worshipped. It is impossible to describe that cosmic being which supports the entire universe without division; it is impossible to teach another concerning it. And, we do not consider them worthy of being taught by us, who consider that god is limited by time and space. Hence, abandoning all such limited concepts, abandoning even the division between the worshipper and the worshipped (Lord), worship the self by the self. Be at peace, pure, free from cravings. Consider that all your experiences and expressions are the worship of the self.

(In reply to Vasiṣṭha's request for a fuller explanation of Śiva, Brahman, self; why they are so called and how such differences arose, the Lord continued:)

The reality is beginningless and endless and it is not even reflected in anything: that is the reality. However, since it is not possible to experience it through the mind and the senses, it is even regarded as if it were non-being.

(In reply to Vasiṣṭha's question. "If it is beyond the mind, how is it realised?" the LORD replied:)

In the case of the seeker who is eager to attain freedom from ignorance and who is therefore equipped with what is termed 'sātvic avidyā' (subtle ignorance), this sātvic avidyā, with the help of what are known as scriptures, removes the ignorance, just as a washerman removes dirt with the help of another form of dirt (soap). By this catalytic action the ignorance is removed, the self realises the self and the self sees the self on account of its own self-luminous nature.

VI.1:41 The LORD continued:

When a child is playing with charcoal, his hands become black. If he washes his hands but immediately plays again with charcoal, his hands become black again. However, if he does not handle charcoal again after washing, his hands can remain clean. Even so, if one enquires into the nature of the self and at the same time refrains from those actions that promote avidyā or ignorance, the darkness of ignorance vanishes. However, it is only the self that becomes aware of the self.

Do not look upon this diversity as the self. Do not entertain the feeling that self-knowledge is the result of the teaching of a preceptor. The guru or the preceptor is endowed with the mind and the senses; the self or Brahman is beyond the mind and the senses. That which is attained only after the other ceases, is not attained with its help while it still exists. However, though the instructions of a preceptor and all the rest of it are not really the means for the attainment of self-knowledge, they have come to be regarded as the means for it.

The self is not revealed either by the scriptures or by the instructions of a preceptor, and the self is not revealed without the instructions of a preceptor and without the help of the scripture. It is revealed only when all these come together. It is only when the scriptural knowledge, instructions of a preceptor and true discipleship come together that self-knowledge is attained.

That which IS after all the senses have ceased to function and all notions of pleasure and pain have vanished is the self or Siva which is also indicated by expressions like 'that', 'truth' or 'reality'. However, that which IS when all these cease to be exists even when all these are present, like the limitless space. Out of their compassion for the ignorant deluded ones, in an effort to awaken them spiritually and to awaken in them a thirst for liberation, the redeemers of the universe (known as Brahmā, Indra, Rudra and others) have composed scriptures like the vedas and the purāṇas (the legends). In these scriptures they have used words like 'consciousness', 'Brahman', 'Śiva', 'self', 'Lord', 'supreme self', etc. These words may imply a diversity, but in truth there is no such diversity.

The truth indicated by the words like 'Brahman', etc., is indeed pure consciousness. In relation to it even the limitless space is as gross and substantial as a great mountain. That pure consciousness appears to be the knowable object and gives rise to the concept of intelligence or consciousness, though, being the innermost self it is not an object of knowledge. On account of a momentary conceptualisation, this pure consciousness gives rise to the egosense ('I know').

The LORD continued:

This egosense then gives rise to the notions of time and space. Endowed with the energy of the vital air, it then becomes jīva or the individual. The individual thenceforward follows the dictates of the notions and slips into dense ignorance. Thus is the mind born in conjunction with the egosense and the different forms of psychological energy. All these together are known as the 'ātivāhika' body, the subtle body which moves from one plane to another.

After this, the substances (the objects of the world) corresponding to the subtle energies of the ātivāhika body were conceived of, and thus were the various senses (sight, touch, hearing, taste and smelling), their corresponding objects and their connecting experiences brought into being. These together are known as the puryaṣṭaka and in their subtle state they are also known as the ātivāhika body.

Thus were all these substances created; but nothing was created in fact. All these are but apparent modifications in the one infinite consciousness. Even as dream-objects are within oneself, all these are non-different from the infinite consciousness. Even as when one dreams those objects, they seem to become the objects of one's perception, all these, too, appear to be objective realities.

When the truth concerning them is realised, all these shine as the Lord. However, even that is untrue, for all these have never become material substances or objects. On account of one's own notions of their being substances which one experiences, they appear to have a substantiality. Thus, conjuring up a substantiality, the consciousness sees the substantiality.

Conditioned by such notions it seems to suffer. Conditioning is sorrow. But conditioning is based on thoughts and notions (or sensual and psychological experiences). However, the truth is beyond such experience and the world is an appearance like a mirage! In that case, what is psychological conditioning, who conditions what and who is conditioned by such conditioning? Who drinks the water of the mirage? Thus, when all these are rejected, the reality alone remains in which there is no conditioning, naught conditioned. It may be styled the being or the non-being, but it alone is. Mental conditioning is illusory non-being, like a ghost; when it is laid, the illusion of creation also vanishes. He who takes this egosense and this mirage known as creation to be real, he is unfit to be instructed. Preceptors instruct only a man endowed with wisdom, not foolish men. The latter pin their faith and hope on the world-appearance, like the ignorant man who bestows his daughter in marriage to the man seen only in his dream!

VI.1:42 The LORD continued:

The jīva perceives all these elements as constituting its body in the void, even as the dreaming person perceives diverse objects within the inner void. This is true even today; the cosmic consciousness or the cosmic being perceives the universe of diversity within itself even as the dreamer perceives diversity within himself.

The jīva thinks of itself as Brahmā, Viṣṇu, etc., but all this is nothing more than thought-form. However, this thought-form conceives and perceives other thought-forms and experiences them. The sole reality in all these percepts is the primary concept known as the egosense, which arises the very instant consciousness conceives of an object within itself and thinks it perceives it (obviously as its object). That instant itself is the epoch and all the multiples and divisions of epochs. In every atom of existence this drama of self-veiling and self-knowledge is enacted all the time, all of which is nothing more than thought-form created by cosmic consciousness. Yet, nothing is created by or in cosmic consciousness, for it remains unchanged and unmodified.

The mountain seen in a dream only appears to exist in time and space. It does not occupy any space nor does it take time to appear and disappear. Even so is the case with the world. In whatever manner the omnipotent deity comes into being, in exactly the same manner a worm also comes into being within the twinkling of an eye. From the lord Rudra down to the blade of grass, all the beings one sees in the universe have come into being in the same manner, whether they are micro-organisms or colossal personalities.

If one thus enquires into the nature of this saṃsāra (world-appearance), the perception of diversity disappears simultaneously with the dawn of self-knowledge or god-realisation. If the real nature of the infinite consciousness is allowed to slip even for one-half of a hundredth part of a second, then all these unfortunate illusory creations take place. By the expression 'Brahman' the wise sages indicate that state in which one remains forever firmly established in the infinite consciousness. When this is disturbed one entertains the notion of the world as real, and this gives rise to an endless sequence of diversity—gods, demons, humans and subhumans, plants and worms. However, if one does not slip from that state of cosmic consciousness, one realises that the truth is ever-present everywhere.

VASIṢṬHA said:

O Rāma, having said thus, lord Śiva received my adoration and after blessing me, departed with his consort, Pārvatī. Having imbibed his teaching, I abandoned my previous mode of worship and commenced the worship of the omnipresent non-dual self.

VASIṢṬHA continued: VI.1:43

O Rāma, the unreal jīva perceives the unreal world on account of the unreal influence of the unreality. In all this what can be considered as real and what as unreal? An imaginary object is imaginatively described by someone; and one understands in one's own imagination and imagines that he understands it. Just as liquidity is in liquids, motion in wind, emptiness in space, even so is omnipresence in the self.

From the time the Lord instructed me, I have been performing the worship of the infinite self. By the grace of such worship, though I am constantly engaged in various activities I am free from sorrow. I perform the worship of the self, who is undivided though apparently divided, with the flowers of whatever comes to me naturally and whatever actions are natural to me.

To come into relationship (to possess and to be possessed) is common to all embodied beings; but the yogis are forever vigilant, and such vigilance is the worship of the self. Adopting this inner attitude and with a mind utterly devoid of any attachment, I roam in this dreadful forest of saṃsāra (world-appearance). If you do so, you will not suffer.

When great sorrow (like the loss of wealth and relations) befalls you, enquire into the nature of truth, in the manner described. You will not be affected by joy or sorrow. You now know how all these things arise and how they cease, and you also know the fate of the man who is deluded by them, who does not enquire into their real nature. They do not belong to you; you do not belong to them. Such is the unreal nature of the world. Do not grieve.

Dear Rāma, you are pure consciousness which is not affected by the illusory perception of the diversity of creation. If you see this, how will notions of the desirable and the undesirable arise in you? Realising thus, O Rāma, remain established in the turīya (transcendental) state of consciousness.

RĀMA said:

Lord, I am free from the dirt of duality. I have realised that all this is indeed Brahman. My intelligence has been purified, rid of doubts and desires and even questions. I do not desire heaven nor do I dread hell. I remain established in the self. By your grace, O Lord, I have crossed this ocean of saṃsāra (world-appearance). I have realised the fullness of direct self-knowledge.

VI.1:44 VASIṢṬHA continued:

That is not considered action, O Rāma, which you perform merely with the organs of action, with an unattached mind. The delight derived from sensual experience is fleeting. A repetition of that experience does not afford a repetition of the same delight. Who but a fool will entertain desire for such a momentary joy? Moreover, an object gives you pleasure only when it is desired. So the pleasure belongs to the desire—hence give up desire or craving.

If in the course of time, you attain to the experience of that (the self), do not store it in your mind as a memory or egosense to be revived as desire once again. For, when you rest on the pinnacle of self-knowledge, it is unwise to fall into the pit of egosense again. Let hopes cease and let notions vanish, let the mind reach the state of no-mind while you live unattached. You are bound only when you are ignorant. You will not be bound if you have self-knowledge. Hence, strive by every means to remain vigilant in self-knowledge.

When you do not engage yourself in sense-experiences and also when you experience whatever comes to you unsought, you are in a state of equanimity and purity, free from latent tendencies or memories. In such a state, like the sky, you will not be tainted even by a thousand distractions. When knower, known and knowledge merge in the one self, the pure experiencer does not once again generate a division within.

With the slightest movement in the mind (when the mind blinks) the saṃsāra (world-appearance) arises and ceases. Make the mind unwinking (free from movement of thought) by the restraint of the prāṇa and also the latent tendencies (vāsanā). By the movement (blinking) of prāṇa, the saṃsāra arises and ceases; by diligent practice make the prāṇa free from such movement. By the rise and cessation of foolishness (ignorance), self-binding action arises and ceases; restrain it by means of self-discipline and the instructions of the preceptor and the scriptures.

This world-illusion has arisen because of the movement of thought in the mind; when that ceases the illusion will cease, too, and the mind becomes no-mind. This can also be achieved by the restraint of prāṇa. That is the supreme state. The bliss that is experienced in a state of no-mind, that bliss which is uncaused, is not found even in the highest heaven. In fact, that bliss is inexpressible and indescribable and should not even be called happiness! The mind of the knower of the truth is no-mind: it is pure satva. After living with such no-mind for some time, there arises the state known as turīya-atīta (the state beyond the transcendental, or the turīya state).

The Story of the Wood-apple

VASIṢṬHA continued: VI.1:45

In this connection, O Rāma, there is an instructive parable which I shall presently narrate to you.

There is a wood-apple fruit which is immeasurably large and which does not decay nor perish though it has existed for countless aeons. It is the source and support of the nectar of immortality and indestructibility. It is the abode of sweetness. Though it is most ancient, it is ever new, like the new moon. It is the very centre or heart of the universe, it is unmoving and it is not shaken even by the forces of cosmic dissolution. This wood-apple fruit, which is immeasurably large, is the original source of this creation.

Even when it is fully ripe, it does not fall from its place. It is for ever fully ripe but it does not become overripe. Even the creator Brahmā, Viṣṇu, Rudra and the other gods do not know the origin of this wood-apple fruit. No one has seen the seed nor the tree on which this fruit grows. The only thing that can be said about it is that this fruit exists, without beginning, without middle and without end, without change and without modification. Even within this fruit there is no diversity; it is completely full without emptiness. It is the fountain-source of all joys and delights, from the delight of an ordinary man to that of the highest of divinities. Thus, this fruit is none other than the manifestation of the energy of infinite consciousness.

This energy of the infinite consciousness, without even for a moment abandoning its own true nature, has manifested this creation, as it were, by merely willing it in its own intelligence. In fact, even this (i.e., that it willed so) is not really true! The egosense that is implied in such willing is itself unreal; but out of this have proceeded all the elements and their corresponding subjective senses. In truth, that energy of the infinite consciousness itself is space, time, natural order, expansion of thought, attraction and repulsion, I-ness, you-ness and it-ness, above, below, the other directions, the mountains, the firmament and the stars, knowledge and ignorance—all, whatever is, was and will ever be. All that is nothing but the energy of the infinite consciousness.

Though it is one, it is conceived of as diverse beings; it is neither one nor many. It is not even it! It is established in reality. It is of the nature of supreme, all-inclusive peace. It is the one immeasurably great cosmic being or self. It is (cosmic) energy of the nature of (cosmic) consciousness.

The Story of the Rock

VI.1:46 VASIṢṬHA continued:

There is yet another parable, O Rāma, to illustrate this further. I shall now narrate that to you.

There is a great rock which is full of tenderness and affection, which is obvious and ever clearly perceived, which is soft, which is omnipresent and eternal. Within it countless lotuses blossom. Their petals sometimes touch one another, sometimes not, sometimes they are exposed and sometimes they are hidden from view. Some face downwards, some face upwards and some have their roots intertwined. Some have no roots at all. All things exist within it though they do not.

O Rāma, this rock is indeed the cosmic consciousness; it is rocklike in its homogeneity. Yet within it, all these diverse creatures of this universe appear to be. Just as one conceives or imagines different forms within the rock, this universe is also ignorantly imagined to exist in this consciousness. Even if a sculptor 'creates' different forms in the rock, it is still rock: even so in the case of this cosmic consciousness which is a homogeneous mass of consciousness. Even as the solid rock contains potentially diverse figures which can be carved out of it, the diverse names and forms of the creatures of this universe exist potentially in cosmic consciousness. Even as rock remains rock, carved or uncarved, consciousness remains consciousness whether the world appears or not. The world-appearance is but an empty expression; its substance is naught but consciousness.

In fact, even these manifestations and modifications are but Brahman, the cosmic consciousness—though not in the sense of manifestation or modification. Even this distinction—modification in the sense of modification, or any other sense—is meaningless in Brahman. When such expressions are used in relation to Brahman, the meaning is quite different, like water in the mirage. Since the seed does not contain anything other than the seed, even the flowers and the fruits are of the same nature as the seed: the substance of the seed is the substance of subsequent effects, too. Even so, the homogeneous mass of cosmic consciousness does not give rise to anything other than what it is in essence. When this truth is realised, duality ceases. Consciousness never becomes un-consciousness. If there is modification, that too is consciousness. Hence, whatever there may be, wherever and in whatever form—all this is Brahman. All these exist forever in their potential state in the mass of homogeneous consciousness.

VASIṢṬHA continued: VI.1:47

Time, space and other factors in this so-called creation (which is in truth another aspect of the same consciousness) are none other than consciousness. When it is realised that all these are but thoughts and notions and that the self is one and indivisible, how then are these regarded as unreal? In the seed there is nothing but the seed—no diversity. At the same time there is the notion of potential diversity (of flowers, fruits) supposedly present in the seed. Even so, cosmic consciousness is one, devoid of diversity; yet the universe of diversity is said to exist only in notion.

The stone is single; the notion of numerous lotuses arises only in relation to that single stone. Even so the notion of diversity arises in consciousness without causing diversity. But just as water in mirage is and is not simultaneously, even so is diversity in relation to the infinite consciousness. All this is indeed Brahman, the infinite consciousness. Even as the notion of the existence of lotuses in the stone does not destroy the stone, Brahman is unaffected by world-appearance which exists as the very nature of Brahman in Brahman. There is no essential difference in truth between Brahman and the world: they are synonyms. When the reality is thus seen, Brahman alone is seen.

Even as all that is seen as water in the world is naught but hydrogen and oxygen gases, even so the world-appearance is but Brahman alone. The one consciousness appears as the mind, the mountains, etc., even as the multicoloured feathers and the wings of the peacock are present in the egg of the peacock. This power or faculty is potentially present in the infinite consciousness. Whatever is now seen as the diverse objects of the universe, if it is seen with the eye of wisdom (the eye that is wisdom), then only Brahman or the infinite consciousness will be seen. For that is non-dual though apparently diverse, just like the notion of diversity in the fluid in the peacock's egg. The notion of Brahman and the world is therefore both dual and non-dual. That which is the substratum for all these notions of unity and diversity—that is the supreme state.

The infinite consciousness pervades the entire universe, and the universe exists in the infinite consciousness. The relationship is one of diversity and non-diversity—just as the numerous parts of the peacock are in the one egg-substance. Where is the diversity in all this?

VI.1:48 VASIṢṬHA continued:

All these—the egosense and the space, etc.—have acquired the nature of real substances though they have not been created at all. Where nothing has arisen (been created) there everything is seen. Even so, the sages, gods and the perfected ones remain in their transcendental consciousness, tasting the bliss of their own nature. They have abandoned the illusion of duality of the observer and the object, and the consequent movement of thought. Their gaze is fixed and unwinking.

Though these sages are active here, they do not entertain the least notion of illusory existence. They are firmly rooted in the abandonment of the relationship between the knower and the known (subject and object). Their life-force is not agitated. It is as if they were painted pictures; their mind does not move, even as the mind of painted figures does not move. For, they have abandoned the conceptualising tendency of the consciousness.

They engage themselves in appropriate activity by a little movement of thought in consciousness (even as the Lord does). However, such movement of thought and the experiencing of the contact of the observer with the object also produce great joy in them. Their consciousness is absolutely pure, purified of all images (concepts and notions).

Such a state of purity of the self, the true nature of the infinite consciousness, is not a vision (an experience of the mind and the senses). It is incapable of being taught. It is not very easy nor is it far distant or impossible. It is attained by direct experience alone.

That alone exists, naught else: neither the body nor the senses and life-force, neither the mind nor the storehouse of memory or latent tendencies, neither the jīva nor even a movement in consciousness, neither consciousness nor the world. It is neither real nor unreal nor something in-between, neither void nor non-void, neither time nor space nor substantiality. Free from all these and free from a hundred veils in the heart, one should experience the self in all that is seen.

It is neither the beginning nor the end. Because it is ever present everywhere, it is taken for something else. Thousands are born and thousands die: but the self which is everywhere, inside and outside, is not affected. It remains in all these bodies, etc., as if it were just a little different from the infinite.

Though radiantly engaged in diverse activities, remain free from the sense of I-ness and mine-ness. For whatever is seen in this world is Brahman, free from characteristics and qualities; it is eternal, peaceful, pure and utterly quiescent.

RĀMA asked: If Brahman does not undergo any modification at VI.1:49
all, how does this world-appearance, which is and is not real, arise in it?

VASIṢṬHA replied:

True modification, O Rāma, is a transformation of a substance into another; like the curdling of milk, in which case the curd cannot once again return to its milk-state. Such is not the case with Brahman which was unmodified before the world-appearance and which regains its unmodified state after the world-disappearance. Both in the beginning and in the end, it is unmodified homogeneous consciousness. The momentary and apparent modification in this is but a mild disturbance of consciousness, not a modification at all. In that Brahman there is neither a subject nor an object of consciousness. Whatever a thing is in the beginning and in the end, that alone it is. If it appears to be something else in the middle, that appearance is regarded as unreal. Hence, the self is the self in the beginning and in the end and therefore in the middle, too! It never undergoes any transformation or modification.

RĀMA asked again: In that self which is pure consciousness, how does this mild disturbance arise?

VASIṢṬHA replied:

I am convinced, O Rāma, that that infinite consciousness alone is real and that there is no disturbance at all in its nature. We use words like 'Brahman' just for the sake of communication or instruction, not to raise notions of one and two. You, I and all these things are pure Brahman: there is no ignorance at all.

RĀMA asked again: But at the end of the previous section, you exhorted me to enquire into the nature of this ignorance!

VASIṢṬHA replied:

Yes, at that time you were still not fully awakened. Such expressions as 'ignorance', 'jīva', etc., have been invented as aids to instructing the unawakened. One should use commonsense and suitable aids (yuktti also commonly means 'trick') to awaken the seeker before imparting the knowledge of the truth. If one declares, "All this is Brahman" to an unawakened person, it is like a man petitioning a tree for relief from his suffering. It is by suitable aids that the unawakened is awakened. The awakened is enlightened by the truth. Thus, now that you are awakened, I declare the truth to you.

You are Brahman, I am Brahman, the whole universe is Brahman. Whatever you are doing, realise this truth at all times. This Brahman or the self alone is the reality in all beings, even as clay is the real substance in thousands of pots. Even as wind and its movement are non-different, consciousness and its internal movement (energy) which causes all these manifestations are non-different. It is the seed of notion falling on the soil of consciousness that gives rise to apparent diversity. If it does not so fall, mind does not sprout.

VI.1:50 RĀMA said:

What is to be known is known, what is to be seen is seen, we are all filled with the supreme truth, thanks indeed to the nectarine wisdom of Brahman, imparted by you. This fullness is filled with fullness. Fullness is born from fullness. Fullness fills fullness. In fullness fullness is ever established. However, for the further expansion of awareness, I ask again: pray bear with me. The sense-organs are obviously present in all: yet how is it that the dead person does not experience sensations, though while living he experienced their objects through those organs?

VASIṢṬHA continued:

Apart from the pure consciousness there are neither the senses, nor the mind, nor even their objects. It is that consciousness alone which appears as the objects in nature and as the senses in the person. When that consciousness has apparently become the subtle body (puryaṣṭaka), it reflects the external objects.

The eternal and infinite consciousness is indeed free of all modifications; but when there arises the notion of 'I am' in it, that notion is known as the jīva. It is that jīva that lives and moves in this body. When the notion of 'I' arises (ahaṃbhāvanā), it is known as egosense (ahaṃkāra). When there are thoughts (manana), it is known as mind (manas). When there is awareness (bodha), it is intelligence (buddhi). When seen (dṛś) by the individual soul (indra) it is known as the sense (indriya). When the notion of body prevails it appears to be body; when the notion of object prevails it appears to be the diverse objects. However, through the persistence of these notions, the subtle personality condenses into material substantiality. The same consciousness thereafter thinks 'I am the body', 'I am the tree', etc. Thus self-deluded it rises and falls, until it attains a pure birth and is spiritually awakened. Then by being devoted to the truth, it attains self-knowledge.

I shall now tell you how it perceives the objects. I said that on account of the notion of 'I am', consciousness abides as jīva in the body. When its senses descend upon similar bodies outside itself, there is contact between the two and there is desire to know (to become one with) them. When there is this contact the object is reflected within oneself and the jīva perceives this reflection, though it believes that the reflection is outside! The jīva knows only this reflection, which means it knows itself. This contact is the cause of the perception of external objects; hence it is possible only in the case of the ignorant one whose mind is deluded and not in the case of the liberated sage. Of course, since the jīva (which is but a 'notion') and all the rest of it are inert and insentient, the reflection thus seen and experienced is in fact an optical illusion or intellectual perversion. The self is all-in-all all the time.

The Story of Arjuna

VASIṢṬHA continued: VI.1:51

Just as the cosmic body (composed of the intelligence-energy and the cosmic elements) or the first puryaṣṭaka (cosmic subtle body) arose in the infinite consciousness as a notion, all the other bodies (puryaṣṭaka) also arise in the same manner. Whatever the jīva (which is the puryaṣṭaka or the subtle body) conceives of while still in the womb, that it sees as existent. Just as in the macrocosm the cosmic elements evolve, even so in the microcosm the senses corresponding to those elements evolve. Of course, they are not actually created. These expressions and descriptions are used merely for the sake of instruction. These ideas which are used in instruction are dispelled by the enquiry which they initially promote and prompt.

Even when you observe this ignorance very carefully and keenly you do not see it: it vanishes. The unreal is rooted in unreality. We only talk of water in the mirage. The water in the mirage, being unreal, has never been water at all. In the light of truth, the reality of all things is revealed, and delusion or illusory perception vanishes.

The self is real. Jīva, puryaṣṭaka (the subtle body) and all the rest of it are unreal, and the enquiry into their nature is no doubt enquiry into their unreality! It is in order to instruct one in the real nature of the unreality that such expressions as 'jīva', etc., are used.

This infinite consciousness has, as it were, assumed the nature of the jīva, and oblivious of its true nature it experiences whatever it thinks of as being. Even as, to the child the unreal ghost it visualises at night is truly real, the jīva conceives of the five elements which it sees as existing. These are nothing but notions of the jīva; however, the jīva sees them as if they are outside it. It thinks that some are within and others are outside of it. And so it experiences them.

Knowledge is inherent in consciousness, even as void is in space. However, consciousness now believes knowledge to be its own object. The diverse objects are limited by time and space which are themselves but the notional division in consciousness brought about by this division (of consciousness and knowledge as subject and object) within itself. Such division does not exist in the self, which transcends time and space.

However, the infinite consciousness with the knowledge inherent in it conceives of diverse creatures. Such is its power, which no one can challenge. The inert space is unable to reflect itself within itself. But because its nature is infinite consciousness, Brahman reflects itself within itself and conceives of itself as a duality, though it is bodiless.

VASIṢṬHA continued:

Whatever this consciousness thinks of, that it sees as existing; its concepts and notions are never barren. In a golden bracelet, there are these two—gold and bracelet, one being the reality (gold) and the other being the appearance (of bracelet). Even so, in the self there are both consciousness and the notion of material (inert) substantiality. Since consciousness is omnipresent, it is ever present in the mind in which the notion arises.

The dreamer dreams of a village which occupies his mind and in which he lives for the time being; a little later he dreams of another situation and he thinks he lives there. Even so, the jīva goes from one body to another; the body is but the reflection of the notion entertained by the jīva. The unreal (body) alone dies and it is the unreal that is born again apparently in another body. Just as in the dream one experiences things seen and unseen, even so in the dream of the jīva it experiences the world and even sees what is to come in the future.

Even as an error of yesterday can be rectified and turned into a good action by self-effort today, the habits of the past can be overcome by appropriate self-effort. However, the notion of jīva-hood and of the existence and functioning of the eyes, etc., cannot be abolished except by the attainment of liberation. Till then, they become alternately latent and patent.

A notion entertained by consciousness appears as the body. It has a corresponding subtle body (ātivāhika, which is also known as puryaṣṭaka) composed of mind, intellect, egosense and the five elements. The self is formless, but the puryaṣṭaka roams in this creation in sentient and insentient bodies until it purifies itself, lives as if in deep sleep and attains liberation. The subtle body exists all the time, during dreams and during sleep. It continues to exist in insentient 'bodies' (like inanimate objects) as if it were in deep sleep. All these are also experienced in this (human) body. Its deep sleep is inert and insentient, its dream-state is the experience of this creation, its waking state is truly the transcendental (turīya) consciousness; and the realisation of the truth is liberation. The state of liberation-while-living is itself the turīya consciousness. Beyond that is Brahman which is turīya-atīta (beyond turīya). In every atom of existence there is naught else than the supreme being; wherever the world is seen, that is but an illusory world-appearance. This illusion, and therefore bondage, is sustained by psychological conditioning. Such conditioning is bondage and its abandonment is freedom. Dense and heavy conditioning is existence as inert objects, middling conditioning as animals and thin conditioning as humans. But enough of perception of division: the whole universe is but the manifestation of the energy of infinite consciousness.

VASIṢṬHA continued: VI.1:52

What is known as this saṃsāra (world-appearance) is but the original dream of the jīva (the first person). The dream of the jīva is not like the dream of a person: the former's dream is experienced as the wakeful state. Hence it is that the wakeful state is considered a dream. The jīva's long dream is instantly materialised, though it is unreal and unsubstantial. The jīva goes from one dream to another within that dream; and as this misconception of the dream as the reality becomes denser, it is experienced as if it were real and the real is ignored as unreal. Be wise and live like Arjuna who will become enlightened through the Lord's instruction.

The entire universe appears in the one ocean of cosmic consciousness; in that universe dwell fourteen types of beings. This universe has already had Yama, Candra, Surya and others as its presiding deities. They have established the tenets of right conduct. However, when the people become predominantly sinful, Yama the god of death sometimes engages himself in meditation for some years, during which the population increases and explodes.

The gods, frightened by this population explosion, resort to various devices to reduce it. All this has happened again and again countless times. The present ruler (Yama) is Vaivasvata. He, too, will have to perform meditation for some time. When, on account of that the population of the earth will multiply very fast, all the gods will appeal to lord Viṣṇu to come to their aid. He will incarnate as lord Kṛṣṇa, along with his alter ego named Arjuna.

His elder brother will be Yudhiṣṭhira or the son of Dharma, who will be the embodiment of righteousness. His cousin, Duryodhana will fight a duel with Bhīma, Arjuna's brother. In this battle between cousins 18 divisions of armed forces will be killed; and thus will Viṣṇu dispose of the burden on the earth.

Kṛṣṇa and Arjuna will play the roles of simple human beings. When Arjuna sees that the armies on both sides are composed of his own kinsmen, he will become despondent and will refuse to fight. At that time, lord Kṛṣṇa will instruct him in the highest wisdom and bring about a spiritual awakening in him. He will tell Arjuna: "This (self) is neither born nor does it die; it is eternal and is not killed when this body is killed. He who thinks that it kills or that it is killed, he is ignorant. How, why and by whom is this infinite being, which is one without a second and which is subtler than space, destroyed? Arjuna, behold the self which is infinite, unmanifest, eternal and which is of the nature of pure consciousness and untainted. You are unborn and eternal!"

VI.1:53 The LORD continues to instruct Arjuna:

Arjuna, you are not the killer; give up this vain egotistic notion. You are the self which is devoid of old age and death. He who is free from egosense and whose intelligence is not attached to anything, he does not kill nor is he bound even if he destroys the whole world. Hence abandon the wrong notions of 'This I am' and 'This is mine'. It is only because of these wrong notions that you think 'I am destroyed,' and suffer. It is only the egotistic and ignorant person who thinks 'I do this', whereas all this is done by the different aspects of the one self or infinite consciousness.

Let the eyes see, let the ears hear, let the skin feel, let the tongue taste. Where is the 'I' in all this? Even when the mind continues to entertain various notions, there is naught which can be identified as 'I'. Whereas all these factors are involved in an action, the 'I' assumes doership and then suffers. The yogis perform action merely by their mind and senses, for self-purification. He who is polluted by the egosense, whether he is a learned scholar or one superior even to that, he indeed is a wicked man. On the other hand, he who is free from the egosense and from the sense of possession and who is equanimous in pleasure and pain, he is not bound whether he does what is approved or what is forbidden.

Hence, O Arjuna, your duty now as a warrior, though it involves violence, is proper and noble. The performance of action appropriate to you—even if it is despicable and unrighteous—is the best. By its due performance become immortal here. Even a fool's natural action is noble in his case. How much more is this valid in the case of a good man! Engage yourself in action, established in the spirit of yoga and unattached to the action; thus you shall not be bound.

Be at peace, even as Brahman is peace. And make your action of the nature of Brahman. Thus doing everything as an offering unto Brahman, you will instantly become Brahman. The Lord dwells in all. By performing all your actions as an offering unto him, shine as the Lord adored by all. Become a true sanyāsi (renunciate) by firmly abandoning all thoughts and notions; thus you shall liberate your consciousness.

The cessation of all thoughts and notions or mental images and the cessation of heavy psychological conditioning are the supreme self or Brahman. Striving towards this end is known both as yoga and as wisdom (jñāna); the conviction that Brahman alone is all, including the world and the 'I', is known as 'offering everything to Brahman' (Brahmārpaṇaṃ).

The LORD instructs Arjuna:

Brahman is empty within and empty without (undifferentiated and homogeneous). It is not an object of observation, nor is it different from the observer. The world-appearance arises in it as an infinitesimal part of it. Because the 'world' is in fact only an appearance, it is in reality emptiness, void and unreal. Mysteriously, there arises in all this a feeling 'I' which is infinitesimal compared even to the world-appearance! The infinite is undivided by any of this, yet it appears to be divided on account of this 'I'-feeling. Even as the 'I' is non-different from the infinite consciousness, even so material objects like a pot and living beings like a monkey are non-different from one another. Who would like to hang on to this 'I'? Why not cling to the infinite consciousness, which alone appears as all this by its own mysterious energy? Such an understanding, and the consequent absence of craving for the enjoyment of the fruits of one's natural activities, is known as 'renunciation' (sanyāsa). Renunciation is renunciation of hopes and aspirations. When one feels the presence of the Lord in all appearances and modifications and when one abandons all delusion of duality, that is regarded as surrender to the Lord, or offering of self and all to the Lord.

I am hope, I am the world, I am action, I am time, I am the one and I am also the many. Hence, saturate your mind with me, be devoted to me, serve me, salute me. Thus constantly united with me, and with me as your supreme goal, you will reach me.

I have two forms, O Arjuna: the ordinary and the supreme. The ordinary form is that which is endowed with hands, etc., and with the conch, the discus, the mace, etc. The supreme form is without beginning and without end, one without a second. It is known variously as Brahman, self, supreme self, etc. As long as one is not fully awakened spiritually, one should worship the common form. By such worship one is spiritually awakened and one will know the supreme form, knowing which he will not be born again.

I consider that you have been awakened by my instructions. Behold the self in all and all in the self, remaining for ever firmly established in yoga. He who is thus established is not born again though he may continue to perform his natural actions here. The concept of unity is used to cancel the concept of the many; the concept of self (infinite consciousness) is used to cancel the conceptualisation of unity. The self can neither be conceived of as existence or non-existence, it is what it is.

The inner light that shines as pure experiencing in all beings, that alone is the self which is indicated by the word 'I': this is for certain.

The LORD continues to instruct Arjuna:

The pure experience of taste that exists in all substances in the world is the self. The faculty of experiencing that exists in all creatures, that is the omnipresent self. It exists in all even as butter exists in milk.

Even as in a collection of a thousand pots there is space within and outside of all the pots, undivided and indivisible, even so the self exists pervading all beings in the three worlds. Even as in a necklace of pearls the connecting thread may remain invisible, even so this self connects all and keeps all together, itself remaining invisible. That truth or reality is known as the self which pervades all things right from Brahmā the creator to the blade of grass.

In that Brahman there is a little manifestation which is also Brahman: and that is known here as the I-am-ness and the world on account of ignorance and delusion. When all this is but the one self, O Arjuna, what is the meaning of expressions like 'This is killed' and 'He kills' as also 'good', 'not good', 'unhappiness' etc.? He who knows that the self is the witness of all these changes and that the self is unchanged and unaffected by these changes, he knows the truth.

Though I use expressions suggestive of diversity, the reality is nondual. All these comings and goings, creation and dissolution, are non-different from the self. The self is the very nature of the totality of existence, even as hardness is the characteristic of a rock and liquidity the nature of waves.

He who sees the self in all and all in the self and he who sees that the self is non-doer (being non-dual), he sees the truth. Just as gold is the reality in all the ornaments made of gold, whatever be their shape and size; just as water is the reality in all the waves and ripples on the ocean, whatever be their shape or size, even so the supreme self or the infinite consciousness alone is the reality in what appears to be a world of diverse creatures.

Why then do you vainly grieve? What is there in all these changing phenomena that your heart should be devoted to? Thus questioning themselves, the liberated ones roam this world in total freedom and in perfect equilibrium. Their desires having turned back on themselves (desires), their delusion having been shed, unattached to anything but firmly established in self-knowledge, freed from all sense of duality known as happiness and unhappiness, the sages reach the supreme state.

The LORD continues to instruct Arjuna: VI.1:54

Hear again what I am going to tell you. I say this to you for your own good because you are dear to me.

Endure whatever pleasure and pain, heat and cold you are subjected to; they come and go. They do not pertain to the self which is beginningless and endless and which is free from parts. Sense-experience is born of the delusion of contact with the illusory elements. He who knows this and is undisturbed, is earmarked for liberation. When the self alone exists, where is room for pleasure and pain to arise? As the supreme self alone is omnipresent, pleasure and pain do not exist. The unreal has no existence and the real does not cease to be.

The self does not rejoice in pleasure nor does it grieve in pain! It is the inert mind that, dwelling in the body, experiences pain. If the body decays, the self is not affected. There is no such thing as body, etc., nor is there an entity known as pain, etc., independent of the self. Then, what is experienced by whom? Hence, one who is fully awakened is free from such delusion. Even as the delusion of a snake in the rope vanishes upon right understanding, even so the delusion of body, etc., and sorrow, etc., vanishes upon spiritual awakening. Right understanding or spiritual awakening is, that the universal Brahman is neither born nor does it die.

Destroy the forces of delusion like pride, sorrow, fear, desire as also pain and pleasure. Such pairs of opposites are illusory. Be established in oneness. You are the single ocean of consciousness. Pain and pleasure, gain and loss, victory and defeat are born of ignorance. Hence remain unaffected by them. Whatever you do, eat, offer in worship and give—all that is the self. Whatever your inner being is, that you shall certainly attain. Hence, in order to attain the realisation of Brahman, fill your entire being with Brahman.

He who sees action in inaction and inaction in action, he is wise and he accomplishes all. Be not attached to the fruits of action nor to inaction. Attachment is real 'doership'; it is also 'non-doership' (one may egotistically think 'I do' or 'I do not do'). Both these are aspects of foolishness: hence abandon foolishness. Abandon the concept of diversity even while being engaged in diverse actions. You are not the doer of actions. He is regarded as a wise man whose actions are burnt in the fire of self-knowledge and are therefore free from desire. He who restrains the physical organs but indulges in mental experience of pleasure is a hypocrite. But he who, restraining the senses by the mind, works with his physical body, free from attachment, he is a superior person. He in whose heart the desires that arise are turned upon themselves as rivers flow into the ocean, he is at peace, not the man of desire.

VI.1:55 The LORD continues to instruct Arjuna:

Without renouncing aught and without the egotistic feeling 'I enjoy' or 'I suffer', one should remain in an equanimous state in all natural situations. Do not entertain the feeling of 'This is self or consciousness' towards what is not-self (non-consciousness). When the body perishes, nothing is lost. The self is never lost! The self is by definition the indestructible and infinite consciousness. Never let even the thought 'The self is perishable' enter your mind. What perishes, what changes is naught other than the notions 'This is lost' and 'This has been gained'. The self which is eternal and infinite does not cease to be the reality, and the unreal has no existence whatsoever. The self that pervades all everywhere is imperishable. The bodies have an end, but the self (the infinite consciousness) is eternal. The self or the infinite consciousness is one and non-dual. What remains when all sense of duality has been abandoned, that is the self, that is the supreme truth.

ARJUNA asks:

Then, O Lord, what is known as death, and what are known as heaven and hell?

The LORD replies:

The jīva or the living soul or personality lives in the net woven by the elements (earth, water, fire, air and space) and also by the mind and the intellect. And that jīva is dragged by the latent tendencies (past impressions, memory, etc.), imprisoned as it is in the cage known as the body. In course of time the body gets old; the jīva gets out of that body even as juice from a leaf when pressed. Taking with it the senses and the mind it leaves the body and goes forth, even as scent leaves its source and goes. The jīva's body is none other than the vāsanā or the residual impressions gained in the body. When the jīva has left the body it becomes inert: it is then known as 'dead'.

Wherever it roams in space, the jīva, which is of the nature of prāṇa or life-force, sees whatever forms are conjured up by its previous vāsanās or impressions. These previous impressions are destroyed only by intense self-effort. Even if the mountains were pulverised and the worlds dissolved, one should not give up self-effort. Even heaven and hell are but the projection of these impressions or vāsanās.

This vāsanā arose in ignorance and foolishness, and it ceases only on the dawn of self-knowledge. What is jīva except vāsanā or mental conditioning, which again is vain imagination or thought-form? He who is able to abandon this vāsanā while yet living in the body in this world is said to be liberated. He who has not abandoned vāsanā is in bondage, even if he is a great scholar.

The LORD continues to instruct Arjuna: VI.1:56

Thus abandoning mental conditioning, be a liberated soul. Be calm and cool within and give up sorrow caused by relationship. Abandon even the least doubt concerning old age and death, have vision as expansive as the sky, be free from attraction and hence from aversion, too. Whatever action is natural to you, do that. Nothing perishes here. This is the nature of a liberated sage. It is only the fool who thinks, 'I shall do this now' and 'I shall abandon this now'.

The senses of a liberated sage are naturally and firmly established in his own heart. It is the mind (heart) that paints the picture known as the three worlds on the canvas of the omnipresent being. The mind creates fragmentation and division. In fact there is no such fragmentation, but the fragmentation that is observed in this creation is but the mind's own painting. Space is absolute emptiness. However, in the mind the world-appearance rises and falls in the twinkling of an eye! Since the self (on which the world is painted by the mind) pervades the whole creation, creation appears to be real. But, on right inquiry, it dissolves in the self.

Neither do 'they' exist nor do you exist. Why then do you grieve? In pure space there is no action or motion, for such motion or action is itself void. Hence, pure space is untainted by such concepts as time, action, etc. All this is only in the mind whose idea is spread as these images. The pure space is empty. That space cannot be divided at any time.

Now that fancied creation has been dissolved, O Arjuna. It came into being by momentary delusion. It is unreal; yet, the mind is capable of creating this fantasy in a moment. It (the mind) makes a moment appear like an epoch, it makes a little look like very much, it makes the unreal appear real instantly: thus has this delusion arisen. It is that momentary delusion that seems to have remained as the illusion known as the world, which in the eyes of the ignorant is an undeniable and solid reality.

However, since this world-appearance is based on the reality of the infinite consciousness, arguments concerning its real or unreal nature are of little consequence. It is indeed a great wonder that this world of diversity appears in the indivisible infinite consciousness. Yet, it is no more than the painting of a dancer, with all the phenomena as the different parts and the gods and the demons and other beings as her limbs. All these are indeed nothing but their substratum which has never undergone any change. It is the infinite, indivisible consciousness.

VI.1:57, 58 The LORD continues to instruct Arjuna:

This indeed is a great wonder: first there appears the picture and then there arises fragmentation. The picture exists only in the mind. Whatever is done is done by emptiness in emptiness (space); emptiness dissolves in emptiness; emptiness enjoys emptiness; emptiness pervades emptiness. Whatever appears to be is pervaded by vāsanās (psychological conditioning or mental image). The world-appearance is illusory. It exists in Brahman as an image exists in a mirror—intangible and without holes (breaks) and divisions—being non-different from Brahman. Even what is known as vāsanā is essentially based on the infinite consciousness and non-different from it.

He who is not free from the bonds of vāsanā is firmly bound to its illusion. Even if one is left with just a trace of this vāsanā or mental conditioning, it will soon grow into a mighty forest of saṃsāra (world-appearance or cycle of birth and death). But, if through constant endeavour this seed of vāsanā is burnt by the fire of correct understanding and self-knowledge, then that burnt seed will not give rise to further bondage. One whose vāsanās are thus burnt does not get lost in pain and pleasure; he lives in this world as a lotus leaf in water.

ARJUNA says:

Lord, my delusion is gone. I have attained an awakening of intelligence through your grace. I am free from all doubts. I shall do thy bidding.

The LORD concludes his teaching:

If the mental modifications are pacified, then the mind is at peace. Satva arises. Then the consciousness is freed from the object. There is pure inner consciousness. It is all and it is omnipresent. It is pure and free from movement of thought. It is transcendental. It is not attained unless all the vāsanās have been purified. Even as heat melts snow, this pure consciousness dissolves ignorance and dispels it. That which is everything in the universe, that which is devoid of everything in the universe, that which is inexpressible, that which is the supreme truth—by what name can it be called?!

VASIṢṬHA continued:

When the Lord will thus instruct Arjuna, the latter will remain silent for a few moments and then will say: "Lord, in the light of the sun of your admonitions, the lotus of the intelligence in my heart has fully unfolded." Having said this, Arjuna will instantly pick up his weapons and engage himself in the conduct of the war, as if in a play.

VASIṢṬHA continued: VI.1:59

Equip yourself with such an attitude, O Rāma, and remain unattached, endowed with the spirit of renunciation and with the realisation that whatever you do or you experience is an offering to the omnipresent being, Brahman. Then you will realise the truth, and that is the end of all doubts.

That is the supreme state, it is the guru of all gurus, it is the self, it is the light that illumines the world from within. It is the reality in all substances, that which endows the substances with their essential characteristic. The notion of 'world' arises only when the spirit of enquiry is absent. But, 'I' am before the world was. How then do the notions of world, etc., bind me? He who has thus realised the truth is free from all beginnings and all ends. He who is thus equipped with the spirit of non-duality (as if he is in deep sleep, though awake) is not disturbed though actively engaged in life. Such a person is liberated here and now.

What appears to be the world here is truly the magic (the work) of the infinite consciousness. There is no unity here, nor is there duality. My instructions, too, are of the same nature! The words, their meaning, the disciple, the wish (or the effort of the disciple) and the guru's ability in the use of the words—all these are also the play of the energy of the infinite consciousness! In the peace of one's own inner being, consciousness vibrates and the world-vision arises. If that consciousness does not vibrate, there will be no world-vision.

The mind is but the movement in consciousness. The non-realisation of this truth is world-vision! Non-realisation of this truth intensifies and aggravates the movement of thought in consciousness. Thus a cycle is formed. Ignorance and mental activity are perpetuated by each other.

When the inner intelligence is awakened, the craving for pleasure

---

NOTE: The very essence of the Bhagavad Gita is found in these chapters—and many verses are quoted verbatim.

ceases: this is the nature of the wise. In him this cessation of craving for pleasure is therefore natural and effortless. He knows that it is the energy of the self that experiences the experiences. He who, in order to please the public, refuses to experience what is to be experienced, he indeed beats the air with a stick! One attains self-knowledge by sometimes using appropriate means.

Desire for liberation interferes with the fullness of the self; absence of such desire promotes bondage! Hence, constant awareness is to be preferred. The sole cause for bondage and liberation is the movement in consciousness. Awareness of this ends this movement. The egosense ceases the very moment one observes it, for it has no support any longer. Then who is bound by whom or who is liberated by whom?

VI.1:60 VASIṢṬHA continued:

Such is the nature of the supreme being which is the infinite consciousness. They who are endowed with macrocosmic forms like Brahmā the creator, Viṣṇu and Śiva, are established in that supreme being; and they function here as the lords or kings of the world. Established in it, the perfected sages roam the heavens. Having attained it, one does not die nor does one grieve. The sage who dwells even for the twinkling of an eye in that pure being, which is of the nature of the illimitable and infinite consciousness and which is also known as the supreme self, is not again afflicted even though he continues to engage himself in the activities of this world.

RĀMA asked:

When the mind, the intellect and the egosense have all ceased to function, how does that pure being or infinite consciousness appear here?

VASIṢṬHA continued:

Brahman, which dwells in all bodies and experiences experiences—eats, drinks, speaks, gathers and destroys, but is free from the division of consciousness and its awareness. That which is omnipresent and which is without beginning and end and which is pure, unmodified, undifferentiated being—that is known as existence (vastu-tattvam) or reality.

That exists as space in space, as sound in sound, as touch in touch, as skin in skin, in taste as taste, in form as form, in the eyes as sight, in smell as smell, in scent as scent, in the body as strength, in earth as the earth, in milk as milk, in wind as wind, in fire as fire, in intelligence as intelligence, in mind as mind, in the egosense as egosense. It rises as citta or mind in the mind. It is tree in the tree. It is immobility in the immovable and mobility in the moving beings. It is insentience in the insentient and intelligence in the sentient. It is the divinity of gods and humanity in human beings. In animals it is bestial nature and in worms it is wormhood. It is the very essence of time and the seasons. It is dynamism in action and order in order. It is existence in the existent and death in the perishable. It is childhood, youth and age and also death.

It is undivided and indivisible, for it is the very essence of all things. Diversity is unreal, though it is real in the above sense (that the diversity is conceived of and pervaded by the infinite consciousness). Realise: "All this is pervaded by me for I am omnipresent and devoid of body and such other limitation" and dwell in peace and supreme happiness.

VĀLMĪKI said:

As the sage Vasiṣṭha said this, the day came to an end and the assembly dispersed for their evening prayers.

RĀMA asked: VI.1:61

O sage, even as the cities, etc., that we see during our dream are unreal, the world which is the dream of Brahmā, the creator, is in fact unreal and illusory. But how is it that it has acquired solid firmness in our vision?

VASIṢṬHA replied:

The very first creation of Brahmā is observed by us even today as if it were real! Because consciousness is infinite, the creation of jīva also takes place everywhere. This creation is no doubt born of ignorance and the belief in creation destroys true perception. Though this creation is unreal, yet on account of the emergence of the ego-sense it appears to be solidly real. The dreamer does not realise the evanescence of the objects seen in the dream; even so, it is in the case of this cosmic dream of the Creator. The dream partakes of the characteristic of the dreamer. That which is born of the unreal must be unreal, too. Hence, though this world appears to be real, as it is born of the unreal concept (the dream of the Creator), it should be firmly rejected.

In the self which is the infinite consciousness this creation appears but momentarily. During that moment itself the illusory notion that it is of a very long duration arises. The creation then appears to be solidly real. Even as this universe exists as a dream in the consciousness of the Creator, it is experienced as a long period in the consciousness (dream) of all the beings who are the dream-objects of the Creator.

Whatever is seen in whatever form in that dream, that it becomes. Surely, when the mind is in a demented or confused state, there is nothing in this world which that mind cannot experience. For even in this world so many extraordinary phenomena are seen: fire burns in the middle of water, water remains suspended in the sky, living beings are found in the heart of a rock, insentient machines function in different ways. One can also see what is obviously unreal, even as it is possible for one to dream one's own death.

There is naught which is real nor is there aught which is unreal; all is made possible everywhere in this dream known as creation! Just as one who is immersed in the dream sees the dream as utterly real, one who is immersed in this creation thinks that it is utterly real. Just as one goes from one dream to another, one goes from one delusion to another delusion and thus experiences this world as utterly real.

The Story of the Hundred Rudras

VI.1:62 VASISTHA continued:

In this connection I shall narrate a legend to you, O Rāma, to which please lend your ear.

There once lived a mendicant who was devoted to meditation. His mind, having been purified by such meditation, came to possess the power to materialise its thoughts.

One day, being tired of continous meditation, yet having his mind fully concentrated, he thought of doing something. He fancied birth as one who was illiterate and of a non-brāhmaṇa family. Instantly, he had become, as it were, a tribesman: there arose in him the feeling 'I am Jīvata'. This dream-being roamed for some time in the city also built of dream-objects. One day he got drunk and slept. He dreamt that he was a brāhmana endowed with knowledge of the scriptures. While he was living a righteous life, one day this brā hmaṇa dreamt that he was a powerful king. He dreamt that he was a mighty emperor of unequalled glory. One day he indulged in royal pleasures and after that slept and dreamt of a celestial nymph.

Similarly, this nymph one day dreamt that she was a deer. And this deer dreamt that it was a creeper. Surely, even animals behold dreams, for such is the nature of the mind which can recollect what has been seen and what has been heard. The deer became a creeper. The inner intelligence in the creeper saw in its own heart a bee. It became a bee—and the bee began to drink the nectar in the flowers on the creeper. It became attached to the nectar in one of those flowers, surely for its own destruction!

At night an elephant approached this creeper and plucked it, along with the bee, and crushed it in its mouth. However, the bee, having seen the elephant, contemplated the elephant and became an elephant. The elephant was captured by a king. One day it saw a hive of bees and on account of the memory of its own past birth it became a bee. It began to drink the nectar of the flowers in wild creepers. It became a creeper. The creeper was destroyed by an elephant, but because the creeper had seen swans in the nearby lake, it became a swan.

One day this swan was roaming in the company of many other swans. While the mendicant was meditating upon this swan, he was overcome by death. His consciousness therefore became embodied in the swan.

VASIṢṬHA continued: VI.1:63

That swan once beheld lord Rudra and in his heart there arose the conviction 'I am Rudra'. Instantly it abandoned its body as swan and became Rudra. And that Rudra dwelt in the abode of Rudra. However, since Rudra was endowed with true knowledge, he remembered all that had taken place!

RUDRA recollected thus:

Behold! How mysterious is this Māyā which deludes all the worlds: though it is unreal it appears to be real. First of all, in that indefinite consciousness which was myself there arose the mind with objective consciousness, though yet cosmic and omniscient. Then accidentally I happened to be the jīva which felt attracted to and charmed by the finest part of the cosmic elements. Therefore during a certain creation-cycle I became the mendicant who remained totally unagitated. He was able to overcome all distractions and remain immersed in the practice of contemplation.

However, every subsequent action is more powerful than a previous act. The mendicant considered himself Jīvaṭa and so did he become. After that he bethought he was a brāhmaṇa. Surely the more powerful thought-form overwhelms the weaker one. Then in course of time and on account of persistent contemplation, he became a king: surely, water imbibed by the plant becomes its fruit! Associated with royal pleasures are nymphs; contemplating them, the king became a nymph. Purely on account of infatuation this nymph became a deer. The deer became a creeper which was obsessed with the idea that it would be pierced and a hole would be made. Contemplating the bee, it became a bee which then pierced a hole in the creeper. The bee became an elephant.

I am Rudra who has been a Rudra during the past one hundred creation-cycles, and I roam this world-appearance which is nothing more than a psychological delusion. In one creation-cycle I was Jīvaṭa, in another I was the brāhmaṇa, in another I was the king and in yet another I was the swan. Thus have I been revolving in this wheel known as the mind and the body.

It is aeons since I slipped from that supreme self or infinite consciousness. Soon after that fall I was that mendicant who was still endowed with knowledge of the truth. Then after passing through very many incarnations, through the grace of Rudra whom I happened to behold, I have become Rudra. When the jīva by coincidence comes into contact with an enlightened person, then its impure vāsanās (tendencies) turn away. This happens to that person who constantly longs for such contact with an enlightened person. Such constant longing (or abhyāsa) itself materialises and becomes an accomplished fact.

RUDRA continued to recollect thus:

Surely it is because of one's inner conviction 'This body is my self' that this unreal perception expands. If one were to enquire into its true nature, one would find that nothing remained! Enough of even such enquiry, which leads to nothing. This world is an optical illusion like the blueness of the sky. It is ignorance. Enough of even this effort to purify that ignorance! If this world-appearance which is unreal continues to appear, let it: it can do no harm. I shall retrace the chain of imaginary transformations and restore their underlying unity.

VASIṢṬHA continued:

Thus having resolved, Rudra went to where the body of the mendicant lay. He awakened it and inspired it to remember all that had taken place. The mendicant saw Rudra as his own self and also recollected all that had happened.

Then both of them went to where Jīvaṭa lived in the same infinite consciousness. They revived his body. The three were indeed one. These three who were wonderstruck at this mystery, then proceeded to the place of the brāhmaṇa who was asleep embraced by his wife. They awakened his consciousness. Then they went to where the king was asleep in his royal bedchamber surrounded by nymphs. They awakened his intelligence, too. He too was amazed at the realisation of the truth. Thus they went to where the swan lived—the swan that became Rudra.

They roamed the world of the one hundred Rudras of the past. They realised that it was all one infinite consciousness in which all these diverse illusory events had apparently taken place. The one form had become many, as it were. These one hundred Rudras pervaded the entire universe and were omnipresent.

On account of the fact that the jīva is surrounded on all sides by the world that arises from it, the unawakened jīvas do not see one another, do not understand one another. Just as all waves are of the same substance and are therefore one, the awakened jīvas realise their oneness and thus understand one another. Each jīva has its own illusory world-appearance. However, even as one finds empty space wherever one digs the ground, when this world-appearance of the jīvas is enquired into it invariably leads to the same infinite consciousness.

Differentiated consciousness is bondage: liberation is its absence. Whatever pleases you, affirm that and be firm in that. There is no difference between the two, for awareness is the same in both. Who will bemoan the loss of what exists only in ignorance? That which is gained by 'being still', that exists already and has therefore already been 'gained'!

VASIṢṬHA continued: VI.1:64

All of them attained awakening of their spiritual consciousness along with lord Rudra. Realising that they were part of Rudra, they were happy. Rudra saw the play of Māyā as it arose and he inspired the others to play their roles in it once again, commanding them to return to him after such seemingly independent existence and assuring them that at the end of the world-cycle they would reach the supreme state. Rudra then vanished from sight, and Jīvaṭa and the others returned to their own respective abodes.

RĀMA asked:

Were Jīvaṭa and the others not mere dream-objects (imaginary entities) of the mendicant? How could they become real entities?

VASIṢṬHA replied:

Abandon the notion that imagination is something real! When thus the illusoriness of illusion is abandoned, what exists exists in the infinite consciousness. What is seen in dream and what is imagined to be real, they appear as such at all times, even as to a traveller the temporal and spatial experiences are real relative to the different places. In the heart of that infinite consciousness everything exists and one experiences what one sees in it.

The dream-like nature of thought-form is realised only by the intense practice of yoga, not otherwise. It is by such practice that lord Śiva and others perceive everything everywhere. That which is in front of you and at the same time apprehended by your mind, is not realised if there is misapprehension in such perception or in such existence. Only when such misapprehension does not exist can that object be known and realised. Whatever one wishes is obtained only when one's inner being is wholly and solely devoted to it. He who is thus totally devoted to what is in front of him knows it perfectly; he who is totally devoted to an imaginary object knows it perfectly. If such one-pointed devotion is not there, then he destroys that object (is not aware of it). It was thus (by such one-pointed devotion) that the mendicant became Rudra and all the rest of it. Each of them had his own world: hence, until the Rudra-consciousness was awakened in them, they were unaware of one another. It was in fact by the will of Rudra that they were thus veiled, that they became of different forms and nature.

It is by one-pointed contemplation of 'May I become a celestial' or 'May I become a learned man' and as the fruit of such contemplation that one is enabled to become one or many or an ignoramus or a man of knowledge. It is possible by concentration and meditation to become a divinity or a human being and function accordingly.

VI.1:64, 65 VASIṢṬHA continued:

The infinite consciousness which is the true self of all is endowed with omnipotence, but the jīva (which is essentially non-different from the self) is endowed with one faculty (appropriate to its notion). Hence, depending upon the nature of the jīva it enjoys endless powers or limited powers. The infinite consciousness is free from expansion and contraction: it is the jīva that gets what it seeks. The yogis who have acquired various faculties exist and manifest such faculties here and also elsewhere. However, since they are enjoyed here and there and in different places, such experiences appear to be many and varied—even as the famous Kārtavīrya generated fear in the hearts of many, though he remained at home! (A modern example is the radio: without leaving the studio, the speaker or singer enters countless drawing rooms. S.V.)

Similarly, lord Viṣṇu, without leaving his abode, incarnates as a human being on earth. Similarly, Indra (who presides over sacred rites), without leaving his heavenly abode, is present in a thousand places where such rites are performed. In response to the call of the devotees, lord Viṣṇu who is one becomes thousands and appears before the devotees. Even so, Jīvaṭa and the others who were but the creatures of the mendicant's imagination or wish and who were animated by Rudra-consciousness went to their various abodes and functioned as if independently. They played their different roles for some time and then returned to the abode of Rudra.

All this was nothing but a momentary delusion which arose in the consciousness of the mendicant, though it was seen as if it were independent of the mendicant. Even so the birth and death of countless beings takes place in the one infinite consciousness, as it were. They imagine diversity in this world-appearance and then they seek unity in the self. At the time of their death they imagine another state of existence within themselves which appears to them as if outside! Until the realisation of liberation, the embodied being undergoes unfathomable sorrow. I told you the story to illustrate this truth. This is the fate not only of the mendicant but of all beings. That being who forgets his inseparability from the supreme self imagines his own notions to be independent and utterly real and substantial. From one such dream he goes on to another dream until he abandons the false notion 'I am the body'.

RĀMA asked:

O what a wonderful story! Lord, you said that all things that are conceived to be real are real and experienced as real. Pray, tell me, does this mendicant also exist somewhere?

VASIṢṬHA replied:

I shall contemplate this question and reply later. (The assembly rose for their noon prayers, at this stage.)

VASIṢṬHA continued: VI.1:66

O king, O Rāma! With the help of my eye of wisdom, I searched for the mendicant. I entered into deep meditation wishing to see that mendicant. I searched for him in this universe, but could not find him. How does one's imagination appear outside also as if real?

Then I proceeded north to the land of the Jīnas. On top of an anthill there exists a vihara (shrine? or Bihar) inhabited by people. There, in his own cottage, was a mendicant (bhikṣu) known as Dīrgha-dṛśa whose head was yellow in colour. He was in deep meditation. Even his attendants did not enter his cottage, afraid to disturb his meditation. It was the twenty-first day of such meditation. It was destined to be his last day.

Though from one point of view, he had been in meditation for only twenty-one days, from another point of view thousands of years had passed. For, such was the notion that arose in his mind. I knew that such a mendicant had lived in another epoch; and even in this epoch he is the second such mendicant. However, other than these two, I could not see a third mendicant. With all the wits at my disposal and all the faculties I could command, I entered into the very heart of this creation, looking for the third mendicant.

At last I found him, but he was not in this universe. He was in another universe which, however, was almost exactly like this universe, though created by another Brahmā. Even so have there been (and there will be in the future) countless beings. In this very assembly there are sages and holy brāhmaṇas who will thus entertain notions of other beings who will thereupon appear to be. Such is the nature of Māyā.

Some of these beings will be of natures similar to the one that imagines them. Others will be quite dissimilar. Yet others will partly resemble them. Thus is the great Māyā which baffles even great men. But it does not exist nor does it function here—for it is only delusion that causes all these to appear and disappear! Else, where is a short period of twenty-one days and where is a whole epoch? It is frightening even to think of the play of the mind.

All this is but appearance which unfolds like the lotus in the morning and reveals diversity like a full-blown lotus. All this arises in the infinite consciousness which is pure; yet the appearance appears to be tainted by impurity. Each thing appears as if fragmented and at the end of that fragmented existence it undergoes other strange fragmentation; all this is relatively real, not totally unreal. All of them manifest in the All—the cause is in the cause!

VI.1:67 DAŚARATHA said:

O sage, tell me where that mendicant (bhikṣu) is meditating and I shall at once despatch my soldiers to wake him up from his meditation and bring him here.

VASIṢṬHA replied:

O king, that mendicant's body has already become lifeless and it cannot be revived. His jīva has attained enlightenment and liberation: it cannot be subjected to the experience of this world-appearance any more. His own attendants stand outside his cottage waiting to open the door at the end of one month as instructed by him. They will find that by that time he has abandoned his body and will then install someone else in his place.

This Māyā (or world-appearance or delusion) is of the nature of limited and limiting qualities and attributes. It is said to be impossible to cross it by ignorance, but by the knowledge of truth it is easily crossed over.

It is wrong perception that sees a bracelet in gold. The mere appearance becomes the cause for such wrong perception. This Māyā (unreal appearance) is but a figure of speech, the appearance has the same relation to the supreme self that a wave has to the ocean. When one sees this truth, the appearance ceases to be a delusion. It is on account of ignorance that this long-dream world-appearance appears to be real: thus does the jīva come into being. But when the truth is realised, it is seen that all this is the self.

Whatever be the notion that one entertains, it is the self alone that appears as that notion. This universe is the result of the notions thus entertained by countless such individuals. The original notion entertained by Brahmā has come to be experienced by the jīva as a solid reality. But when one attains the purity of consciousness similar to that of Brahmā, one sees all this as a long dream.

It is the notion of the object that becomes the mind and thus slips from infinite consciousness. It then undergoes varied experiences. But is this mind independent of the supreme self, is not the supreme self the mind, too? The jīva, the body and all the rest of it are but reflections or appearances of the supreme self! All these movements, etc., happen in the one infinite consciousness which is for ever infinite and consciousness, naught else: movements, etc., are imaginary expressions. There is neither motion nor non-motion, neither one nor many—what is is as it is. Diversity arises in the unawakened state and it vanishes when one commences one's enquiry. The enquirer exists but without any doubt, which indeed is the supreme state. Peace is known as the world; peace alone IS as this world-appearance. Ignorance is unreal: there is neither the seer, the seen nor the sight! The mind imagines a defect in the moon; it is not there as defect. The infinite consciousness has consciousness alone as its 'body' or manifestation or appearance.

VASIṢṬHA continued: VI.1:68

O Rāma, remain for ever, firmly established in that state of utter freedom from movement of thought, resorting to the silence of deep sleep.

RĀMA said:

Sir, I have heard of silence of speech, silence of the eyes and other senses and I have also heard of the rigid silence of extreme asceticism. But what is this silence of deep sleep?

VASIṢṬHA replied:

Rāma, there are two types of muni (a sage who observes mouna or silence). One is the rigid ascetic and the other the liberated sage. The former forcibly restrains his senses and engages himself in dry (devoid of wisdom) kriyās (activities) with fanaticism. The liberated sage, on the other hand, knows what is what (the truth as truth and the unreal as unreal), he is endowed with self-knowledge and yet he behaves as any ordinary person here. What is regarded as silence or mouna is based on the nature and the behaviour of these munis.

Four types of silence have been described: (1) silence of speech, (2) silence of the senses (eyes, etc.), (3) violent restraint, as also (4) the silence of deep sleep. There is another known as silence of the mind. However, that is possible only in one who is dead or one who practises the rigid mouna (kāṣṭha mauna) or the silence of deep sleep (suṣupti mauna). Of these the first three involve elements of the rigid mouna. It is the fourth that is really conducive to liberation. Hence, even at the risk of incurring the displeasure of those who resort to the first three types of mouna, I say that there is nothing in those three which is desirable.

The silence of deep sleep is conducive to liberation. In it the prāṇa or life-force is neither restrained nor promoted, the senses are neither fed nor starved, the perception of diversity is neither expressed nor suppressed, the mind is neither mind nor non-mind. There is no division and hence no effort at abolishing it; it is called the silence of deep sleep and one who is established in it may or may not meditate. There is knowledge of what IS as it is and there is freedom from doubt. It is utter emptiness. It is supportless. It is of the nature of supreme peace of which it can neither be said that it is real nor that it is unreal. That state in which one knows "There is no 'I', nor another, no mind nor anything derived from the mind", in which one knows "'I' is but an idea in this universe, and it is really pure existence" —that is known as the silence of deep sleep. In that pure existence which is infinite consciousness, where is 'I' or 'another'?

VI.1:69 RĀMA asked:

How did the one hundred Rudras come into being, O sage?

VASIṢṬHA replied:

The mendicant (bhikṣu) dreamt all the one hundred Rudras. Whatever they whose minds are pure and unobscured by impurities, imagine or will-into-being, that alone they experience as being real. Whatever thought-form thus arises in the one infinite consciousness appears to be so.

RĀMA asked again:

Why is it, O sage, that lord Śiva chose to appear as one unclad, inhabiting the cremation ground, garlanded with human skulls, smeared with ashes and as one who is easily overcome by lust?

VASIṢṬHA replied:

The conduct of the gods, the perfected beings and the liberated sages is not determined by rules and codes of conduct—these are invented by ignorant people. Yet, since the mind of the ignorant is heavily conditioned, if they are not governed by such rules of conduct, there will then arise disorder in which the big fish will eat the small fish. The man of wisdom, on the other hand, does not drown himself in what is desirable and what is undesirable because he has his senses naturally in control and because he is awake and alert. He lives and works without intending to do so, without reacting to events on a causal basis, his actions being pure and spontaneous (as the cocoanut falling without any causal relation with the alighting of the crow on it); or he may not do anything at all!

Thus have even the members of the trinity (Brahmā, Viṣṇu and Śiva) engaged themselves in incarnation. In the case of the enlightened ones, their actions are beyond praise and reproach, beyond acceptance and rejection, for they have no notion of 'This is mine' and 'This is other'. Their actions are pure like the heat of fire.

I did not wish to elaborate on the other form of mouna, known as the silence of the disembodied, for you are still embodied. However,

I shall briefly describe it now. They who are fully awakened and who are constantly engaged in samādhi and who are thoroughly enlightened are known as sāṃkhya-yogis. They who have reached the state of bodiless consciousness through prāṇāyāma, etc., are known as yoga-yogis. Indeed, the two are essentially the same. The cause of this world-appearance and bondage is indeed the mind. Both these paths lead to the cessation of the mind. Hence, by the devoted and dedicated practice of either the cessation of the movement of prāṇa or the cessation of thought, liberation is attained. This is the essence of all scriptures dealing with liberation.

RĀMA asked:

O sage, if the cessation of the movement of prāṇa is liberation, then death is liberation! And all people attain liberation at death!

VASIṢṬHA replied:

O Rāma, when prāṇa is about to leave the body it already makes contact with those elements with which the next one is to be fashioned. These elements are indeed the crystallisation of the vāsanās (psychological conditioning, memory-store, past impressions and predisposition) of the jīva, the reason why the jīva clings to those elements. When the prāṇa leaves the body it takes with it all the vāsanās of the jīva.

Not indeed until these vāsanās have been destroyed will the mind become no-mind. The mind does not abandon the life-force till self-knowledge arises. By self-knowledge the vāsanās are destroyed and thus the mind, too; it is then that the prāṇa does not move. That indeed is the supreme peace. It is by self-knowledge that the unreality of the concepts concerning worldly objects is realised. This puts an end to vāsanās and to the link between the mind and the life-force. Vāsanās constitute mind. Mind is the aggregate of the vāsanās and naught else; if the latter cease, that itself is the supreme state. Knowledge is the knowledge of the reality. Vicāra or enquiry itself is knowledge.

Total dedication to one thing, restraint of prāṇa and the cessation of the mind—if one of these three is perfected, one attains the supreme state. The life-force and the mind are closely related like a flower and its fragrance, or sesame seed and oil. Hence, if the movement of thought in the mind ceases, the movement of prāṇa ceases, too. If the total mind is one-pointedly devoted to a single truth, the movement of mind and therefore of life-force ceases. The best method is by enquiring into the nature of the self which is infinite. Your mind will be completely absorbed. Then both the mind and the enquiry will cease. Remain firmly established in what remains after that.

When the mind does not crave for pleasure it is absorbed into the self, along with the life-force. Ignorance is non-existence: self-knowledge is the supreme state! Mind alone is ignorance when it appears to be a reality; the realisation of its non-existence is the supreme state. If the mind remains absorbed even for a quarter of an hour it undergoes a complete change, for it tastes the supreme state of self-knowledge and will not abandon it. Nay, even if the mind has tasted it for a second, it does not return to this-worldly state. The very seeds of samsāra (world-appearance or cycle of birth and death) are fried. With them, ignorance is dispelled and the vāsanās are utterly pacified; one who has reached this is rooted in satva (truth). He beholds the inner light and rests in supreme peace.

The Story of the Vampire

VI.1:70, 71 VASIṢṬHA continued:

That is known as mokṣa or liberation when ignorance ceases through self-enquiry, when the jīva becomes no-jīva instantly and when the mind becomes no-mind. Since the egosense, etc., are but like water in the mirage, they cease when the light of enquiry is directed to them. In this connection, O Rāma, listen to the following inspiring and enlightening questions asked by a vampire.

There lives a vampire in the Vindhya forests. Once it entered a certain territory, desirous of appeasing its hunger. However, it would not kill anyone even when it was hungry, unless the victim deserved such treatment. Finding no such person in the forest, it entered a city and met the king.

The VAMPIRE said to the king:

O king, I shall not kill you and eat you unless you deserve it. You are the ruler and you fulfil the wishes of the needy. Pray, fulfil my desire. I shall ask you a few questions. Give me the correct answers to them.

What is that sun the particles of whose rays are these universes? In what mighty wind does this mighty space manifest? One goes from one dream to another dream ad infinitum, yet one does not abandon the self, though constantly abandoning the dream-reality. What is the self? The stem of a banana tree, when it is opened, reveals layer after layer until you reach the pith. What is that subtle essence when this world-appearance is similarly enquired into? Of which atom are the universes themselves minuter atoms? In what formless 'rock' are the three worlds hidden (like an unsculpted figure in a rock)? Answer these questions. If you do not you certainly deserve to be eaten by me!

The KING answered:

O vampire! This universe was once enveloped by a series of coverings, even as a fruit is enveloped by its skin. There was a branch on which there were thousands of such fruits. There was a tree with thousands of such branches, a forest with thousands of such trees, a hill with thousands of such forests, a country with thousands of such hills, a continent with thousands of such countries, a sphere with thousands of such continents, an ocean with thousands of such spheres, a being with thousands of such oceans within him and a supreme person who wears thousands of such beings as a garland. There is a sun in whose rays thousands of such supreme persons are found: that sun illumines all. That sun is the sun of consciousness, O vampire! In that light of that sun, these universes are but minutest atomic particles. It is because of the light of that sun that all these other things enumerated appear to be real.

The KING said: VI.1:72, 73

In the supreme self shine as dust-particles substances (concepts or relative realities) known as time, space and motion which are conscious (movement in and of consciousness) and pure intelligence.

The self or Brahman though appearing to migrate from one dream-world to another does not in fact abandon its own essential nature, nor is it ever ignorant of itself.

Even as when the stem of a banana is peeled, every layer as it is peeled off reveals another similar layer, when this world-appearance is enquired into it is seen as none other than Brahman. This Brahman is referred to positively as the truth, Brahman, etc., and since it is beyond description it is also negatively indicated as emptiness and indescribable, etc. Whatever is experienced as real is the reality. Though its particular form is put together by the experience, it is naught but pure consciousness—even as the banana stem is nothing but banana stem and every layer of it is of identical nature.

The self is considered to be of atomic nature because it is extremely subtle and intangible; yet since the self alone is, it is the infinite and it is the very root of the entire existence. It is formless though it appears in all forms.

This world-appearance is but the flesh in which the truth which is pure consciousness is clothed.

VASIṢṬHA continued:

Having heard this answer from the lips of the king, the vampire became silent and deeply contemplative. It forgot its great hunger and entered into profound meditation.

Thus have I told you, O Rāma, the tale of the vampire which illustrates the truth concerning the subtle infinite consciousness.

The universe is but an envelope or a veil of this consciousness; and it is rent asunder by a diligent enquiry into its real nature. It is in fact as real as the 'body' of the vampire!

Rāma, expand the mind with the mind. Remain at peace within yourself, seeing the one infinite being in all. Like the king Bhagīratha you will achieve the impossible if you are able to remain firm in your knowledge of the truth and if you engage yourself in appropriate action in a life characterised by effortless experiencing of the natural course of events.

The Story of Bhagīratha

VI.1:74 At Rāma's request, VASIṢṬHA narrated the following story:

Once upon a time there was a king named Bhagīratha who was devoted to dharma. He gave liberal gifts to the pious and holy ones and he was terror to the evil-doers. He worked tirelessly to eradicate the very causes of poverty. When he was in the company of the holy ones his heart melted in devotion.

Bhagīratha brought the holy river Gaṅgā from the heavens down to the earth. In this he had to encounter great difficulties and propitiate the gods Brahmā and Śiva and also the sage Jahnu. In all this he suffered frequent frustrations and disappointments.

He, too, was endowed with discrimination and dispassion even at an early age, O Rāma. One day while remaining alone he reflected thus: "This worldly life is really essenceless and stupid. Day and night chase each other. People repeat the same meaningless actions again and again. I regard only that as proper action which leads to the attainment beyond which there is nothing to be gained; the rest is repeated foul excretion (as in cholera)." He approached his guru Tritala and prayed, "Lord, how can one put an end to this sorrow and to old age, death and delusion which contribute to repeated birth here?"

TRITALA said:

Sorrow ceases, all the bondages are rent asunder and doubts are dispelled when one is fully established in the equanimity of the self for a long time, when the perception of division has ceased and when there is the experience of fullness through the knowledge of that which is to be known. What is to be known? It is the self which is pure and which is of the nature of pure consciousness which is omnipresent and eternal.

BHAGĪRATHA asked:

I know that the self alone is real and the body, etc., are not real. But how is it that it is not perfectly clear to me?

TRITALA said:

Such intellectual knowledge is not knowledge! Unattachment to wife, son and house, equanimity in pleasure and pain, love of solitude, being firmly established in self-knowledge—this is knowledge, all else is ignorance! Only when the egosense is thinned out does this self-knowledge arise.

BHAGĪRATHA asked:

Since this egosense is firmly established in this body, how can it be uprooted?

TRITALA replied:

By self-effort and by resolutely turning away from the pursuit of pleasure. And by the resolute breaking down of the prison-house of shame (false dignity), etc. If you abandon all this and remain firm, the egosense will vanish and you will realise that you are the supreme being!

VASIṢṬHA continued: VI.1:75, 76

Having heard the precepts of the preceptor, Bhagīratha decided to perform a religious rite as a prelude to total renunciation of the world. In three days he had given away everything to the priests and to his own relatives, whether they were endowed with good nature or not. His own kingdom he handed over to his enemies living across the borders. Clad in a small piece of loin-cloth, he left the kingdom and roamed in countries and forests where he was totally unknown.

Very soon, he had attained the state of supreme peace within himself. Accidentally and unknowingly Bhagīratha entered his own previous kingdom and solicited alms from the citizens there. They recognised him, worshipped him and prayed that he should be their king. But he accepted from them nothing but food. They bewailed, "This is king Bhagīratha, what a sad plight, what an unfortunate turn of events!" After a few days he left the kingdom again.

Bhagīratha once again met his preceptor and the two of them roamed the country all the time engaged in spiritual dialogue: "Why do we still carry the burden of this physical body? On the other hand, why should it be discarded? Let it be as long as it will be!" They were devoid of sorrow and of rejoicing, nor could they be said to adhere to the middle path. Even if the gods and sages offered them wealth and psychic powers, they spurned them as blades of dry grass.

In a certain kingdom the king had died without an heir and the ministers were in search of a suitable ruler. Bhagīratha, clad in a loin-cloth, happened to be in that kingdom. The ministers decided that he was the person fit to ascend the throne, and surrounded him. Bhagīratha mounted the royal elephant. Soon he was crowned king.

While he was ruling that kingdom, the people of his previous kingdom approached him once again and prayed that he should rule that kingdom also. Bhagīratha accepted. Thus he became the emperor of the whole world. Remaining at peace within himself, with his mind silenced, free from desires and jealousy, he engaged himself in doing appropriate action in circumstances as they arose.

Once he heard that the only way to propitiate the souls of his departed ancestors was to offer libation with the waters of the Gaṅgā. In order to bring the heavenly Gaṅgā down to earth, he repaired to the forest to perform austerities, having entrusted the empire to his ministers. There he propitiated the gods and the sages and achieved the most difficult task of bringing the Gaṅgā down to earth so that all the people for all time to come might offer libations to their ancestors with the waters of the holy Gaṅgā. It is only from that time that this sacred Gaṅgā which adorned the crown of lord Śiva's head began to flow on the earth.

The Story of Śikhidhvaja and Cūḍālā

VI.1:77 VASIṢṬHA continued:

Even so, Rāma, remain in a state of equanimity like king Bhagīratha. And, like Śikhidhvaja, having renounced everything, remain unmoved. I shall narrate to you the story of Śikhidhvaja. Pray, listen. Once there were two lovers who were re-born in a later age on account of their divine love for each other.

RĀMA asked:

O sage, how is it possible that the couple who lived together as husband and wife in one age is born again to be husband and wife in a later age?

VASIṢṬHA replied:

Such is the subtle nature of the world order, O Rāma. Some things appear in abundance and once again they manifest in abundance. Others are born now, having never been before; and having been now they are not born again. Others which have been before reappear in the same form now. It is like the waves on the ocean: there are similar ones and there are dissimilar ones.

In the Mālva kingdom there was a king named Śikhidhvaja. He was endowed with every kind of royal excellence. He was righteous and noble, courageous and courteous. He lost his father very early in life. Though young, he was able to assert his sovereignty and he ruled the kingdom assisted by his able ministers.

The spring season set in. There was romance in the air. The young king began to dream of a partner. Day and night his heart longed for the beloved. The clever and wise ministers divined the state of their king's heart. They went to the Saurāṣṭra kingdom and sought the hand of a princess for their king. Soon, the king Śikhidhvaja married Cūḍālā.

Śikhidhvaja and Cūḍālā were so greatly devoted to each other that they were one jīva in two bodies. They shared many common interests and they played together in the pleasure-gardens. Even as the sun sends down his rays to make the lotus unfold, the king showered his beloved with his love and tried to please her in every way.

They shared their knowledge and their wisdom with each other so that both of them became highly learned in all branches of knowledge. Each dwelt in all radiance in the other's heart. In fact, it appeared as if the lord Viṣṇu and his consort had come down on earth in order to accomplish a special mission!

VASIṢṬHA continued: VI.1:78

Thus Śikhidhvaja and Cūḍālā enjoyed themselves for a number of years without a dull moment. No one can arrest the passage of time. Life appears and disappears like a juggler's trick. Pleasure, when pursued, flies beyond reach even as an arrow which has left the bow. Sorrow preys upon the mind even as vultures prey upon a carcass. "What is there in this world having attained which the mind is never again subjected to sorrow?" Reflecting thus, the royal couple turned their attention to the study of spiritual texts.

They came to the conclusion that self-knowledge alone can enable one to overcome sorrow. They devoted themselves to self-knowledge with their heart and soul. They resorted to the company of sages of self-knowledge and adored them. They engaged themselves constantly in discussing self-knowledge and in promoting self-knowledge in each other.

Having thus constantly contemplated the means of self-knowledge, the queen began to reflect thus:

"Now I see myself and enquire 'Who am I?' How could ignorance of self, and delusion arise? The physical body is surely inert and it is certainly not the self. It is experienced only on account of the movement of thought in the mind. The organs of action are but parts of the body and hence they too are inert, being parts of the body which is inert. The sense-organs are inert, too, for they depend upon the mind for their functioning. I consider even the mind to be inert. The mind thinks and entertains notions, but it is prompted to do so by the intellect which is the determining agent. Even this intellect (buddhi) is surely inert for it is directed by the egosense. Even this egosense is inert, for it is conjured up by the jīva, just as a ghost is conjured up by the ignorant child. The jīva is but pure consciousness clothed, as it were, by the life-force and it dwells in the heart.

"Lo and behold! I have realised that it is the self which is pure consciousness that dwells as the jīva because the consciousness becomes aware of itself as its own object. This object is insentient and unreal; and because the self identifies itself with this object it apparently clothes itself with insentience, having apparently (but not in truth) abandoned its essential nature as consciousness. For, such is the nature of consciousness: whatever it conceives itself to be, whether real or imaginary, that it becomes, apparently having abandoned its own nature. Thus, though the self is pure consciousness, it imagines itself to be insentient and unreal on account of its perception of objects."

Contemplating thus for a considerable time, Cūḍālā became enlightened.

VASIṢṬHA continued:

Delighted by this self-discovery, the queen exclaimed: "At last I have attained that which is to be attained (known). Now there is no loss. Even the mind and the senses are but the reflections of consciousness, though they are unreal independent of consciousness. This supreme consciousness alone exists. It is the supreme truth, untainted by any impurity, for ever in a state of perfect equilibrium and devoid of egosense. Once this truth is realised, it shines constantly without setting.

"It is this consciousness that is known by various names—Brahman, supreme self, etc. In it there is no division into subject-object and their relation (knowledge). Consciousness becomes conscious of its own consciousness; it cannot be realised otherwise (as an object of consciousness). It is this consciousness alone that is manifest as the mind, intellect and the senses. This world-appearance, too, is but consciousness apart from which nothing is. Consciousness does not undergo any change: the only apparent change is the illusory appearance, which is illusory and therefore not real! In an imaginary ocean, imaginary waves arise. The mind-stuff itself is the ocean and the waves are of the mind-stuff, too. Even so the world-appearance arises in consciousness and is therefore non-different from it.

"I am pure consciousness, devoid of egosense and all-pervading. There is neither birth nor death for this consciousness. It is not subject to destruction, for it is like space. It cannot be cut or burnt. It is pure light of consciousness, without defect.

"I am free from all delusion. I am at peace. All these gods, demons and numerous beings are essentially unmade, for they are non-different from the consciousness. The appearance is illusory, even as soldiers made of clay are clay, not soldiers.

"The seer (subject) and the seen (object) are in reality the one pure consciousness. How has this delusion which gives rise to concepts like 'This is oneness' and 'There is duality' come into being? In whom does that delusion exist? Whose is it? I rest in nirvāṇa (liberation or enlightenment), without the least mental agitation, having realised that all that is (whether sentient or insentient) is pure consciousness. There is no 'this' nor 'I' nor 'the other'; there is no being nor non-being. All this is peace." Having thus realised, Cūḍālā rested in supreme peace.

VASIṢṬHA continued: VI.1:79

Day by day, the queen grew more and more introverted, rejoicing more and more in the bliss of the self. She was utterly free from craving and from attachment. Without abandoning anything and without seeking anything, she was natural in her behaviour and spontaneous in her actions. All her doubts were at rest. She had crossed the ocean of becoming. She rested in an incomparable state of peace.

Thus within a very short time she had reached the realisation that this world-appearance will also disappear in the same way in which it came into being! She shone radiant in the light of self-knowledge.

Seeing her thus radiant and peaceful, Śikhidhvaja asked her: "You appear to have regained your youthfulness and you shine with an extraordinary radiance, my beloved. You are not distracted by anything at all, and you have no craving. Yet, you are full of bliss. Tell me: is it that you have quaffed the nectar of the gods? Surely, you have attained something which is extremely difficult to attain?"

CŪḌĀLĀ replied:

I have abandoned this emptiness which has assumed some sort of a form. I remain rooted in that which is truth, not in the appearance. Hence I am radiant. I have abandoned all these and I have resorted to something other than these, which is both real and unreal. Hence I am radiant. That is something and that is also not-something. I know that as it is. Hence I am radiant. I delight in the non-enjoyment of pleasures as if I have enjoyed them. I give way neither to joy nor to anger. Hence I am radiant. I experience the greatest joy in remaining established in the reality that shines in my heart. I am not distracted by the royal pleasures. Hence I am radiant. Even when I am in the pleasure-gardens, I remain firmly established in the self, neither in the enjoyment of pleasure nor in shyness, etc. Hence I am radiant.

I am the ruler of the universe. I am not the finite being. I delight in the self. Hence I am radiant. This I am, I am not, in truth I am nor am I; I am the all, I am naught. Hence I am radiant. I seek not pleasure nor wealth nor poverty nor any other form of existence. I am happy with whatever is obtained without effort. Hence I am radiant. I sport with attenuated states of attraction and repulsion, with the insights gained through the scriptures. Hence I am radiant. Whatever I see with these eyes and experience with these senses, whatever I behold through my mind—I see nothing but the one truth which is seen clearly by me within myself.

VI.1:80 Unable to understand the queen's words, ŚIKHIDHVAJA laughed at them and said:

You are childish and ignorant, my dear, and surely you are prattling! Having abandoned something for nothing, having abandoned real substances and attained the state of nothingness—how does one shine resplendent? Even as an angry man rejects a bed, if one abandons pleasures boasting, "I delight in unenjoyed pleasures", it is not conducive to delight! When one abandons everything (pleasures, etc.) and thinks he delights in emptiness, that does not make any sense. Nor does it make any sense if one thinks he is happy after having renounced clothes, food, bed, etc. 'I am not the body', 'Nor am I anything else', 'Nothing is everything'—what else are these statements but sheer prattle? 'I do not see what I see' and 'I see something else'—these too are nothing but prattle.

Never mind: enjoy the pleasures that are afforded to you. I shall continue to sport with you; enjoy yourself.

VASIṢṬHA continued:

Having said this, the king went away from the inner apartments. Cūḍālā thought, "It is a pity that the king is unable to understand" and she continued to go about her work. Thus they continued to live for a considerable time. Though Cūḍālā had no desires, a wish arose in her to move about in space. In order to acquire this power, she sought solitude and there exercised the vital air which has an upward tendency.

There are three types of attainable goals in this world, O Rāma: desirable, detestable and ignorable. What is desirable is sought with great effort; what is detestable is abandoned; between these two is that towards which one is indifferent. Normally, one regards that as desirable which promotes happiness, its opposite is considered undesirable and one is indifferent to those which bring neither happiness or unhappiness. However, in the case of the enlightened ones these categories do not exist. For they look upon everything as a mere play and hence they are utterly indifferent to everything seen or unseen.

I shall now describe to you the method of gaining what is attainable (siddhi or psychic powers) towards which the sage of self-knowledge is indifferent, which the deluded person considers desirable and which one who is intent on the cultivation of self-knowledge is keen to avoid.

VASIṢṬHA continued:

All achievements are dependent upon four factors: time, place, action and means. Among these action or effort holds the key because, surely, all endeavours towards the achievement are based on action or effort.

Some perverse practices also prevail and they are said to make achievements possible. Especially in the hands of immature practicants they are conducive to great harm. To this category belong the magic pill or unguent or wand, as also the use of gems, drugs, self-mortification and magic formulae. The belief that the mere dwelling in holy places like Śrīśaila or Meru enables one to attain spiritual perfection is also defective.

Hence, in the context of the story of Śikhidhvaja I shall describe the technique of prāṇāyāma or the exercise of the life-force and the achievements it brings about. Kindly listen.

In preparation, one should abandon all habits and tendencies that are unrelated to what one wishes to achieve. One should learn to close the apertures in the body and also learn the practice of the different postures. The diet should be pure. One should contemplate the meaning of holy scriptures. Right conduct and the company of holy ones are essential. Having renounced everything, one should sit comfortably. If then one practises prāṇāyāma for some time without allowing anger, greed, etc., to rise within oneself, the life-force comes under one's perfect control.

Right from sovereignty over the earth to total liberation—everything is dependent upon the movement of the life-force. Hence all such achievements are possible through the practice of prāṇāyāma.

Deep within the body, there is a nāḍī known as the āntraveṣṭikā. It rests in the vitals and it is the source of a hundred other nāḍīs. It exists in all beings—gods, demons and humans, animals and birds, worms and fish. It is coiled at its source. It is in contact with all the avenues in the body, from the waist right up to the crown of the head.

Within this nāḍī dwells the supreme power. It is known as kuṇḍalinī, because it is coiled in appearance. It is the supreme power in all beings and it is the prime mover of all power. When the prāṇā or life-force which is in the heart reaches the abode of the kuṇḍalinī, there arises within oneself an awareness of the elements of nature. It is when the kuṇḍalinī unfolds and begins to move that there is awareness within oneself.

All the other nāḍīs (radiating flow of energy) are tied to the kuṇḍalinī, as it were. Hence the kuṇḍalinī is the very seed of consciousness and understanding or knowledge.

RĀMA asked:

Is not the infinite consciousness forever indivisible? If so how does this kuṇḍalinī arise and manifest itself, thus revealing this consciousness?

VASIṢṬHA continued:

Indeed, there is the infinite consciousness alone everywhere at all times. However, it manifests as the elements here and there. The sun shines on everything, but it is reflected in a special way when its rays fall on a mirror. Similarly, the same infinite consciousness appears to be 'lost' in some, clearly manifest in some, at the height of its glory in yet others.

Even as space is (empty) space everywhere, consciousness is consciousness and naught else, whatever the appearance may be. It does not undergo any change. This consciousness itself is the five root-elements. You behold with your consciousness the same consciousness which is the five root-elements, as if you were seeing another within yourself, even as with one lamp you see a hundred lamps.

On account of a slight movement of thought, the same reality which is consciousness seems to become the fivefold elements and thence the body. In the same way, the same consciousness becomes worms and other creatures, metals and minerals, earth and what is on it, water and other elements. Thus the whole world is nothing but the movement of energy in consciousness which appears as the fivefold elements. Somewhere this energy is sentient and elsewhere it appears as insentient, even as water when exposed to cool wind hardens and becomes solid. Thus is nature formed, and all things conform to nature.

However, all this is but a play of words, a figure of speech. What else is heat and cold, ice and fire? Again, these distinctions arise on account of conditioning and thought-patterns. The wise man therefore enquires into the nature of such conditioning, whether it is latent or patent, good or evil. Such is fruitful quest; vain argumentation is like boxing with space.

Latent conditioning produces insentient beings; patent conditioning gives rise to gods, humans, etc. In some there is dense conditioning conducive to ignorance; in others there is attenuated conditioning conducive to liberation. Conditioning alone is responsible for the diversity in creatures.

For this cosmic tree known as creation, the first thought-form is the seed, with the various spheres for various parts of the tree and the past, present and future as the fruits. The fivefold elements of which the tree is formed arise of their own accord and cease of their own accord. Of their own accord they diversify and in due course they become unified and tranquil.

VASIṢṬHA continued: VI.1:81

Kuṇḍalinī functions in the body composed of the fivefold elements, in the form of the life-force. It is this same kuṇḍalinī which is known variously as conditioning or limitation, as the mind, jīva, movement of thought, intellect (or the determining faculty) and egosense, for it is the supreme life-force in the body. As the apāna it constantly flows downward, as samāna it dwells in the solar plexus and as udāna the same life-force rises up. On account of these forces, there is balance in the system. If, however, the downward pull is excessive and the downward force is not arrested by appropriate effort, death ensues. Similarly, if the upward pull is excessive and it is not arrested by appropriate effort, death ensues. If the movement of the life-force is governed in such a way that it neither goes up nor down, there is an unceasing state of equilibrium and all diseases are overcome. Otherwise, if there is malfunction of ordinary (secondary) nāḍīs one is subject to minor ailments and if the principal nāḍīs are involved there is serious ailment.

RĀMA asked:

What are vyādhis (illnesses) and what are ādhis (psychic disorders) and what are the degenerative conditions of the body? Pray, enlighten me on these.

VASIṢṬHA continued:

Ādhi and vyādhi are sources of sorrow. Their avoidance is happiness; their cessation is liberation. Sometimes they arise together, sometimes they cause each other and sometimes they follow each other. Physical malady is known as vyādhi, and psychic disturbance caused by psychological conditioning (neuroses) is known as ādhi. Both these are rooted in ignorance and wickedness. They end when self-knowledge or knowledge of truth is attained.

Ignorance gives rise to absence of self-control and one is constantly assailed by likes and dislikes and by thoughts like 'I have gained this, I have yet to gain that'. All this intensifies delusion; all these give rise to psychic disturbances.

Physical ailments are caused by ignorance and its concomitant total absence of mental restraint which leads to improper eating and living habits. Other causes are untimely and irregular activities, unhealthy habits, evil company, wicked thoughts. They are also caused by the weakening of the nāḍīs or by their being cluttered or clogged up, thus preventing the free flow of life-force. Lastly, they are caused by unhealthy environment. All these are of course ultimately determined by the fruits of past actions performed either in the near or in the distant past.

VASIṢṬHA continued:

All these psychic disturbances and physical ailments arise from the fivefold elements. I shall now tell you how they cease. Physical ailments are twofold: ordinary and serious. The former arise from day-to-day causes and the latter are congenital. The former are corrected by day-to-day remedial measures and by adopting the proper mental attitude. But the latter (serious) ailments, as also the psychic disturbances, do not cease until self-knowledge is attained: the snake seen in the rope dies only when the rope is again seen as rope. Self-knowledge ends all physical and psychic disturbances. However, physical ailments that are not psychosomatic may be dealt with by medication, prayers and by right action, as also by baths. All these have been described in medical treatises.

RĀMA asked:

Pray, tell me how does physical ailment arise from psychic disturbance and how can it be dealt with by means other than medical.

VASIṢṬHA continued:

When there is mental confusion, one does not perceive one's path clearly. Unable to see the path in front of oneself, one takes a wrong path. The life-forces are agitated by this confusion and they flow haphazardly along the nāḍīs. As a result, some nāḍīs are depleted of energy and others are clogged.

Then there arises disturbance in the metabolism, indigestion, excessive appetite as also improper functioning of the digestive system. Food eaten turns into poison. The natural movement of food in and through the body is arrested. This gives rise to various physical ailments.

Thus psychic disturbance leads to physical ailments. Just as myrobalan is capable of making the bowels move, even so certain mantras like ya, ra, la, va, can also remedy these psychosomatic disorders. Other measures are pure and auspicious actions, service of holy men, etc. By these the mind becomes pure and there is great joy in the heart. The life-forces flow along the nāḍīs as they should. Digestion becomes normal, diseases cease.

By the practice of pūraka or inhalation, if the kuṇḍalinī at the base of the spine is 'filled' and made to rest in a state of equilibrium, the body remains firm. When through the retention of the breath all the nāḍīs are warmed up, the kuṇḍalinī rises up like a stick and its energies flood all the nāḍīs of the body. On account of this the nāḍīs are purified and made light. Then the yogi is able to travel in space.

When the kuṇḍalinī arises through the brahma-nāḍī and reaches the spot known as dvādaśānta (twelve finger-breadths from the crown of the head) during the recaka or exhalation, if the kuṇḍalinī can be held there for an hour, the yogi sees the gods and perfected beings who travel in space.

RĀMA asked:

How is it possible for these mortal eyes to behold the celestials?

VASIṢṬHA said:

Indeed, no mortal can behold the celestials with these mortal eyes. But through the eyes of pure intelligence the celestials are seen, as in a dream. The celestials are able to fulfil one's desires. Vision of celestials is nondifferent from dream, in fact, the only difference being that the effect of the vision is lasting. Again, if one is able to hold the life-force in the dvāsaśānta (twelve finger-breadths from the body) for a considerable time after exhalation, the life-force is able to enter other bodies. This power is inherent in the life-force; though by nature unsteady, it can be steadied. Since the ignorance which envelops everything is insubstantial, such exceptions are often seen in the movement of energy in this world. Surely, all this is indeed Brahman; the diversity and diverse functions are mere figures of speech.

RĀMA asked:

In order to enter into minute spaces (nāḍīs) and then in order to fill the inner space with the life-force, one's body has to be made both atomic and solid at the same time! How is this made?

VASIṢṬHA said:

When wood and the saw come together, wood is split. But when two pieces of wood come together, there is fire! All this is part of nature.

*In this physical body, two forces come together in the abdomen. Together they form a hollow stick. In it rests the kuṇḍalinī. This kuṇḍalinī stands midway between heaven and earth and is ever vibrant with life-force. Dwelling in the heart it experiences all. It keeps all the psychic centres in a state of constant vibration or motion. It digests or devours everything. It makes the psychic centres tremble by the movement of prāṇa. It sustains the fire in the body till all the essences have been exhausted.

By nature it is cool, but because of it the body becomes warm. It is spread throughout the body, though it dwells in the heart where it is contemplated by the yogi. It is of the nature of jñāna (knowledge) and

(* The 'it' in this paragraph may refer to the gastric fire, life-force or even the kuṇḍalinī. Vasiṣṭha is surely not terribly keen on making and sustaining such distinctions!!)

in its light a distant object is seen as if near. Whatever is cool is the moon, the self; from this moon arises fire. The body is made of this moon and this fire. In fact, the entire world is made of these two, the cool moon and the warm fire. Or, you may consider that this world is the creation of knowledge and ignorance, the real and the unreal. In which case, consciousness, light and knowledge are considered the sun or the fire, and inertness, darkness and ignorance are considered as the moon.

VASIṢṬHA continued:

Fire and the moon exist in a mutual causal relationship (in the body). In a way, theirs is the relationship of seed and tree, one giving birth to the other; in a way, it is like light and darkness in which one destroys the other. (One who questions all this, saying "Since there is no desire-motivation, such causality and such activity are illogical", should be quickly dismissed. For such activity is obvious and is the experience of all.)

The (fire) prāṇa drinks the nectarine coolness at the mouth of the cool moon, filling the entire space within the body. (It is the yogi's theory that nectar flows from the palate, which is consumed by the gastric fire in the solar plexus—thus the cool moon is the cause of the burning fire—and he prescribes the viparītakaraṇī to prevent this loss of nectar. S.V.) Fire dies and becomes the moon, even as day ends and night arrives.

At the junction of the fire and the moon, at the junction of light and darkness, of night and day, there is the revelation of the truth which eludes the understanding of even wise men.

Even as a day consists of day and night, the jīva is characterised by consciousness and inertia. Fire and the sun symbolise consciousness and the moon symbolises darkness or inertia. Even as when the sun is seen in the sky, darkness vanishes on earth, when the light of consciousness is seen, the darkness of ignorance and the cycle of becoming come to an end. And, if the moon (the darkness of ignorance or inertia) is seen for what it is, consciousness is realised as the only truth. It is the light of consciousness that reveals the inert body. Consciousness, being non-moving and non-dual, is not grasped. However it can be realised through its own reflection, the body.

Consciousness, when it becomes aware of itself, gains the world. When such objectification is abandoned, there is liberation. Prāṇa is heat (fire), apāna is the cool moon, and the two exist like light and shade in the same body. The light of consciousness and the moon of description together bring about experience. The phenomena called the sun and the moon, which had existed from the beginning of world-creation, also exist in the body.

O Rāma, remain in that state where the sun has absorbed the moon into itself. Remain in that state in which the moon has merged with the sun in the heart. Remain in that state where there is the realisation that the moon is but the reflection of the sun. Know the junction of the sun and the moon within yourself. The external phenomena are utterly useless.

VASIṢṬHA continued: VI.1:82

Now I shall describe to you how the yogis made their bodies atomic, as also enormous.

There is a spark of fire that burns just above the heart-lotus. This fire is quickly augmented, but since it is of the nature of consciousness, it arises as the light of knowledge. When it thus grows in magnitude in a moment, it is able to dissolve the entire body; even the water-element in the body is evaporated by its heat. Then, having abandoned the two bodies (the physical and the subtle), it is able to go where it likes. The kuṇḍalinī-power rises up like smoke from fire and is merged in the space, as it were. Holding fast the mind, buddhi and the egosense, this kuṇḍalinī shines radiantly as a particle of dust. This spark or this particle is then able to enter into anything whatsoever. Then this kuṇḍalinī releases the water and the earth elements that had previously been absorbed into itself and the body resumes its original shape. Thus, the jīva is able to become as small as an atom and as big as a mountain.

I have thus described to you the yogic method, and shall now deal with the wisdom-approach.

There is but one consciousness which is pure, invisible, the subtlest of the subtle, tranquil, which is neither the world nor its activities. It is aware of itself: hence this jīva-hood arises. This jīva perceives this unreal body as real. But when the jīva perceives it in the light of self-knowledge, this delusion vanishes. And the body also becomes utterly tranquil. Then the jīva does not perceive the body. The confusion of the body with the self is the greatest delusion, which the light of the sun cannot dispel.

When the body is considered real, it becomes a real body. When it is perceived with the knowledge that it is unreal, it is merged in space. Whatever notion is firmly held concerning the body, that it becomes.

Another method is the practice of exhalation whereby the jīva is raised from the abode of the kuṇḍalinī and made to abandon this body, which then becomes inert like a log of wood. Then the jīva can enter into any other body, moving or non-moving, and undergo the desired experience. After thus having acquired the experience, it can re-enter the previous body or any other body at its will and pleasure.

Or, it may remain as the all-pervading consciousness without entering into any particular body.

VI.1:83 VASIṢṬHA continued:

Thus, the Queen Cuḍālā came to be endowed with all the pyschic powers (like the ability to make oneself atomic and enormous). She traversed the sky and entered into the deepest oceans and roamed the earth, without ever leaving the company of her husband. She entered into every type of substance—wood, rock, mountain, grass, sky and water, without any hindrance. She moved with the celestials and with the liberated sages and conversed with them.

Though she made every endeavor to enlighten her husband also, he was not only unresponsive but he laughed at her foolishness. He remained ignorant. She felt it unwise to exhibit her psychic powers before him.

RĀMA asked:

If even such a great siddha-yogini as Cūḍālā could not bring about the spiritual awakening and the enlightenment of king Śikhidhvaja, how does one attain enlightenment at all?

VASIṢṬHA said:

The instruction of a disciple by a preceptor is but a tradition: the cause of enlightenment is but the purity of the disciple's consciousness. Not by hearing nor by righteous acts is self-knowledge attained. Only the self knows the self, only the snake knows its feet! Yet, . . .

The Story of the Philosopher's Stone

There was a wealthy villager in the Vindhya hills. Once when he was walking in the forest he lost a copper-coin (one cent). He was a miser and so he began to search for it in the thick bush. All the time he was calculating, "With that one cent I shall do some business, it will become four cents and then eight cents and so on". For three days he searched, unmindful of the taunts of spectators. At the end of those three days, he suddenly found a precious stone! (It was a philosopher's stone.) Taking it with him, he returned home and lived happily.

What was the cause of this miser's finding the philosopher's stone? Surely, his miserliness and his searching the bush for the lost cent! Even so, in the case of the preceptor's instructions, the disciple looks for something but obtains something else! Brahman is beyond the mind and the senses; it cannot be known through someone else's instruction. Yet, without the instruction of the preceptor it is not known either! The miser would not have found the precious stone if he had not searched the bush for his one cent! Hence the instruction of the preceptor is considered the cause of self-knowledge, and yet it is not the cause! Look at this mystery of Māyā, O Rāma: one seeks something and obtains something else!

VASIṢṬHA continued: VI.1:84

Devoid of self-knowledge, the king Śikhidhvaja became blinded by delusion. He was sunk in grief which nothing in the world could assuage. Soon he began to seek solitude, like you, O Rāma, doing just those royal duties which his ministers made him do. He gave plenty in charity. He performed various austerities. But there was no change in the delusion and in the sorrow. After considerable deliberation, one day

ŚIKHIDHVAJA said to the queen:

My dear, I have enjoyed sovereignty for a long time and I have enjoyed all the royal pleasures. Neither pleasure nor pain, neither prosperity nor adversity is able to disturb the mind of the ascetic. Hence I wish to go to the forest and become an ascetic. The beloved forest which resembles you in every respect (here he gives a romantic description of the forest, comparing it to the limbs of the queen) will delight my heart even as you do. So give me leave to go, for a good housewife does not obstruct her husband's wishes.

CŪḌĀLĀ replied:

Lord, that action alone shines as appropriate which is done at the appropriate time: flowers are appropriate to spring and fruits to the winter. Forest-life is appropriate to old age, not for people of your age. At your age the household life is appropriate. When we grow old, both of us shall leave this household life and go to the forest! Moreover, your subjects will grieve over your untimely departure from the kingdom.

ŚIKHIDHVAJA said:

My dear, do not place obstacles on my path. Know that I have already left for the forest! You are but a child and it is not proper that you should go to the forest, too, and lead the hard ascetic life. Hence, remain here and rule the kingdom.

VASISTHA continued:

That night, while the queen was still asleep, the king left the palace on the pretext of patrolling the city. He rode a whole day and reached a dense forest on the Mandara mountain. It was far, far from habitation and there were signs that the place had been inhabited previously by holy brāhmanas. There he built a cottage for himself and equipped it with whatever he considered necessary for the ascetic life—like a stick made of bamboo, eating utensil (plate), water-vessel, a tray for flowers, a kamaṇḍalu, a rosary, a garment to protect him from the cold, a deer-skin. There he commenced his ascetic life. The first part of the day he spent in meditation and japa (repetition of the holy mantra). The second part of the day he spent in gathering flowers, and this was followed by bath and worship of the deity. Thereafter, he took a frugal meal consisting of fruits and roots. The rest of the time he spent in japa or the repetition of the mantra. Thus he spent a long time in that cottage without ever thinking of his kingdom, etc.

VI.1:85 VASIṢṬHA continued:

Cūḍālā awoke with a fright when she discovered that her husband had left the palace. She felt unhappy and decided that her place was by her husband's side. Quickly she also got out of the palace through a small window and flew in the sky, looking for her husband. Soon she found him wandering in the forest. But, before alighting near him, she considered future events through her psychic vision. She saw everything as it was destined to happen, to the smallest detail. Bowing to the inevitable, she returned to the palace by the same aerial route she had taken.

Cūḍālā announced that the king had left the palace on an important mission. From then on, she herself conducted the affairs of the state. For eighteen years she dwelt in the palace and he in the forest, without their seeing each other. He had begun to show signs of old age.

At that time, Cūḍālā 'saw' that her husband's mind had ripened considerably and that it was time for her to help him attain enlightenment. Having thus determined, she left the palace at night and flew to where he was. She beheld the celestials and the perfected sages in the heavens. She flew through clouds, inhaling the heavenly perfume and looking forward with great eagerness to her reunion with her husband. She was excited and her mind was agitated. Becoming aware of this mental state, she said to herself: "Ah, surely as long as there is life in the body, one's nature does not cease to be active. Even my mind is agitated so much! Or, perhaps, O mind, you are seeking your own consort. On the other hand my husband has surely forgotten all about his kingdom and me, after all these years of asceticism. It that case it is futile on your part, O mind, to get excited at the prospect of meeting him once again. . . . I shall restore equilibrium to the heart of my husband in such a way that he will return to the kingdom, where we shall dwell together happily for a long time. That delight which is had in a state of utter equilibrium is superior to all other happiness."

Thinking thus, Cūḍālā reached the Mandara mountain. Still remaining in the sky, she saw her husband as if he were another person, for the king who was always clothed in royal robes now appeared as an emaciated ascetic. Cūḍālā was depressed at this heart-breaking sight of her husband clad in coarse garment, with matted locks, quiet and lonely, with his colour darkened considerably as if he had had a bath in a river of ink. For a moment she thought: "Alas, the fruit of foolishness! For only the foolish reach such a condition as the king has reached. Surely, it is on account of his own delusion that he has thus secluded himself in this hermitage. Here and now, I shall enable him to attain enlightenment. I shall approach him in a disguise."

VASIṢṬHA continued:

Afraid that Śikhidhvaja might once again spurn her teaching, considering that she was an ignorant girl, Cūḍālā transformed herself into a young brāhmaṇa ascetic and descended right in front of her husband. Śikhidhvaja saw the young ascetic and was delighted. The two vied with each other in spiritual radiance. The young ascetic was in fact incomparably radiant, so that Śikhidhvaja took him to be a celestial. He worshipped the ascetic appropriately. Cūḍālā appreciatively accepted the worship and remarked: "I have travelled around the world but never have I been worshipped with such devotion! I admire your tranquility and your austerity. You have chosen to tread the razor's edge in as much as you have abandoned your kingdom and resorted to the forest-life."

Śikhidhvaja replied: "Surely, you know everything, O son of the gods! By your very look you are showering nectar upon me. I have a lovely wife who is just now ruling my kingdom; you resemble her in some ways. And the flowers I have offered you in worship—may they be blessed. One's life attains its fruition by the worship of the guest who arrives unsolicited; the worship of such a guest is superior even to the worship of the gods. Pray, tell me who you are and to what I owe this blessing of your visit to me?"

THE BRĀHMAṆA (CŪḌĀLĀ) said:

There is a holy sage in this universe known as Nārada. Once he was engaged in meditation in a cave on the bank of the holy river Gaṅgā. At the end of his meditation, he heard the sound of bracelets apparently belonging to some people engaged in water-sports. Out of curiosity he looked in that direction and saw a few of the foremost celestial nymphs sporting in water, naked. They were indescribably beautiful. His heart experienced pleasure and his mind momentarily lost its equilibrium, overcome by lust.

ŚIKHIDHVAJA asked:

Holy one, though he was a sage of great learning and a liberated one at that, though he was free from desire and from attachment and though his consciousness was as limitless as the sky, how was it that he was overcome by lust?

THE BRĀHMANA (CŪḌĀLĀ) said:

O royal sage, all beings in the three worlds, including the gods in heaven, have a body that is subject to the dual forces. Whether one is ignorant or one is wise, as long as one is embodied the body is subject to happiness and unhappiness, pleasure and pain. By enjoying satisfying objects, one experiences pleasure, and by deprivation (hunger, etc.) one experiences pain. Such is nature.

THE BRĀHMAṆA (CŪḌĀLĀ) continued:

If the self which is the reality and which is pure is forgotten even for a moment, the object of experience attains expansion. If there is unbroken awareness, this does not happen. Even as darkness and light have come to be firmly associated with night and day, the experience of pleasure and pain has confirmed the existence of the body in the case of the ignorant. In the wise, however, even if such an experience is reflected in consciousness, it does not produce an impression. As in the case of a crystal, the wise man is influenced only by the object when it is actually and physically present nearby. But the ignorant person is so heavily influenced that he broods on the object even in its absence. Such are their characteristics: thinned out vulnerability is liberation, whereas dense colouring of the mind is bondage.

(In response to Śikhidhvaja's question: "How do pleasure and pain arise even in the absence of the concerned object?" the brāhmaṇa said:) The cause is the impression received by the heart through the body, the eyes, etc. Later this expands by itself. When the heart is agitated, the memory agitates the jīva in its kuṇḍalinī-abode. The nāḍīs which branch out throughout the body are affected. Pleasure-experiences and pain-experiences affect the nāḍīs differently. The nāḍīs expand and blossom, as it were, in pleasure, not in pain.

When the jīva does not thus enter into the agitated nāḍīs, it is liberated. Bondage is none other than subjection of the jīva to pleasure and pain: when such subjection does not exist there is liberation. The jīva gets agitated at the very 'sight' of pleasure and pain. However, if through self-knowledge it realises that pain and pleasure do not exist in truth, then it regains its equilibrium. Or, if it realises that these do not exist in itself nor does it (the jīva) exist in them, it realises total freedom. If it realises that all this is nothing but the one infinite consciousness, then again it attains equilibrium. Like a lamp without fuel, it does not get agitated again, for the jīva itself is then realised as a non-entity and it is reabsorbed in the consciousness of which it is but the first thought-emanation.

(Asked by Śikhidhvaja to elaborate on how the pleasure-experience leads to the loss of energy, the brāhmaṇa said:) As I said, the jīva agitates the life-force. The movement of the life-force extracts the vital energy from the entire body. This energy then descends as the seminal energy which is discharged naturally.

(Asked what is nature, the brāhmaṇa said:) Originally, Brahman alone existed as Brahman. In it innumerable substances appeared like ripples on the surface of the ocean. This is known as nature. It is not causally related to Brahman, but it happened like a cocoanut accidentally falling when a crow happened to alight on it. In that nature are found diverse creatures endowed with diverse characteristics.

THE BRĀHMAṆA (CŪḌĀLĀ) continued: VI.1:86, 87

It is by such nature of the self that this universe is born. It is sustained by self-limitation or conditioning on account of alternating order and disorder. When such self-limitation and such conflict between order and disorder cease, the beings will not be born again.

(Continuing the story of Nārada, the brāhmaṇa said:) Soon, Nārada regained his self-control. He gathered the seed which had been spilt, in a pot made of crystal. He then filled the pot with milk produced by his thought-force. In due course, that pot gave birth to an infant which was perfect in every respect. Nārada christened the baby and in course of time imparted the highest wisdom to it. The young boy was a peer to his father.

Later, Nārada took the boy to Brahmā the creator, the father of Nārada. Brahmā conferred upon the boy (whose name was Kuṃbha) the blessing of the highest wisdom. It is that boy, that Kuṃbha, that grandson of Brahmā, who is standing before you. I roam the world playfully, for I have nothing to gain from anyone. When I come into this world, my feet do not touch the earth.

(As Vasiṣṭha said this, the seventeenth day came to an end.)

ŚIKHIDHVAJA said:

It is truly by the fruition of the good deeds done in many past incarnations that I have obtained your company today and am able to drink the nectar of your wisdom! Nothing in the world gives that peace which the company of the holy ones bestows on man.

THE BRĀHMAṆA (CŪḌĀLĀ) said:

I have told you my life-story. Pray, now tell me who you are and what you are doing here. How long have you been here? Tell me everything truthfully, for recluses do not speak anything but the truth.

ŚIKHIDHVAJA replied:

O son of the gods, you know everything as it is. What else shall I tell you? I dwell in this forest on account of my fear of this saṃsāra (world-cycle or the cycle of birth and death). Though you know all this, I shall briefly relate my story to you. I am king Śikhidhvaja. I have abandoned my kingdom. I dread this saṃsāra in which one repeatedly and alternately experiences pleasure and pain, birth and death. However, though I have wandered everywhere and though I perform intense austerities, I have not found peace and tranquility. My mind is not at rest. I do not indulge in activities nor do I seek to gain anything, I am alone here and unattached to anything; yet I am dry and devoid of fulfilment. I have practised all the kriyās (yogic methods) uninterruptedly. But I only progress from sorrow to greater sorrow; and even nectar turns into poison for me.

THE BRĀHMANA (CŪDĀLĀ) said:

I once asked my grandfather, "Which is superior, kriyā (action, the practice of a technique) or jñāna (self-knowledge)?" And, he said to me:

"Indeed, jñāna is supreme for through jñāna one realises the one which alone is. On the other hand, kriyā has been described in colourful terms, as a pastime. If one does not have jñāna then one clings to kriyā: if one does not have good clothes to wear, he clings to the sack.

"The ignorant are trapped by the fruits of their actions on account of their conditioning (vāsanā). When the latter is given up, action becomes no-action, whether it is conventionally regarded as good or evil. In the absence of self-limitation or volition, actions do not bear fruit. Actions by themselves do not generate reaction or 'fruit'; it is the vāsanā or the volition that makes action bear fruit. Just as the frightened boy thinks of a ghost and sees a ghost, the ignorant man entertains the notion of sorrow and suffers sorrow.

"Neither the vāsanā (self-limitation or conditioning) nor the egosense is a real entity! They arise because of foolishness. When this foolishness is abandoned, there is the realisation that all this is Brahman and there is no self-limitation. When there is vāsanā, there is mind; when the vāsanā ceases in the mind, there is self-knowledge. One who has attained self-knowledge is not born."

Thus, even the gods, Brahmā and others, have declared that self-knowledge alone is supreme. Why then do you remain ignorant? Why do you think, "This is the kamandalu" and "This is a stick" and remain immersed in ignorance? Why do you not enquire "Who am I?", "How has this world arisen?" and "How does all this cease?"? Why do you not reach the state of the enlightened by enquiring into the nature of bondage and liberation? Why are you wasting your life in these futile austerities and other kriyās? It is by resorting to the company of holy ones, by serving them and enquiring of them, that you will attain self-knowledge.

ŚIKHIDHVAJA said:

Aha, I have truly been awakened by you, O sage. I am freed of foolishness. You are my guru; I am your disciple. Pray instruct me in what you know, knowing which one does not grieve.

THE BRĀHMAṆA (CŪḌĀLĀ) replied:

O royal sage, I shall instruct you if you are in a receptive mood and cherish my words. If one playfully instructs another merely in answer to a query, when the latter does not intend to receive, cherish and assimilate the teaching, it becomes fruitless. (After receiving such an assurance from Śikhidhvaja, Cūḍālā said:) Listen attentively: I shall narrate to you a story which resembles yours.

The Story of Cintāmaṇi

THE BRĀHMAṆA (CŪḌĀLĀ) said: VI.1:88

There was a man in whom there was the almost impossible combination of wealth and wisdom. He was endowed with all excellences, he was clever in his dealings, he achieved all his ambitions, but he was unaware of the self. He began to engage himself in austerities with the desire of acquiring the celestial jewel known as cintāmaṇi (the philosopher's stone which is supposed to be capable of fulfilling all the desires of its possessor). His effort was intense. So, within a very short period of time, this jewel appeared before him. Indeed, what is impossible for one who strives his utmost! One who applies himself to the task he has undertaken, unmindful of the effort and the difficulties, reaches the desired end even if he is poor.

This man saw the jewel in front of him, within his easy reach. But he was unable to reach any certainty concerning it. He began to muse with a mind confused by prolonged striving and suffering: "Is this the cintāmani? Or is it not? Shall I touch it or not? Perhaps, it will disappear if I touch it? Surely, it cannot be obtained within so short a period of time! The scriptures say that it can only be obtained after a whole lifetime of striving. Surely, because I am a poverty-stricken, greedy man, I am merely hallucinating the existence of this jewel before me. How could I be so lucky as to get it so soon? There may be some great ones who might obtain this jewel within a short time, but I am an ordinary person with just a little austerity to my credit. How is it possible for me to get this so soon?"

Thus confused in his mind, he did not make any effort to take the jewel. He was not destined to get it. One gets only what he deserves, when he deserves it. Even if the celestial jewel stands in front of him, the fool ignores it! The jewel, thus ignored, disappeared. Psychic attainments (siddhis) bestow everything on one whom they seek: after having destroyed his wisdom they go away. And the man engaged himself further in austerities for the attainment of the cintāmaṇi. The industrious do not abandon their undertaking. After some time, he saw a glass-piece thrown playfully in front of him by the celestials. He thought it was the cintāmaṇi. Thus deluded he greedily picked it up. Confident that he could get whatever he sought with its help, he gave up all his wealth, family, etc., and went away to a forest. On account of his foolishness he suffered there. Great calamities, old age and death are nothing in comparison to the suffering caused by foolishness. In fact, foolishness adorns the head of all sufferings and calamities!

The Story of the Foolish Elephant

VI.1:89 THE BRĀHMAṆA (CŪḌĀLĀ) continued:

Listen, O king, to another story which also resembles yours. In the Vindhya forests there was an elephant which was extremely strong and equipped with strong and powerful tusks. The rider of this elephant had, however, imprisoned it in a cage. By this and the repeated use by the rider of weapons like the goad, the elephant was subjected to great pain.

While the rider was away the elephant struggled to free itself from the cage. This effort went on for three whole days. Eventually it shattered the cage. Just at this time, the rider saw what the elephant had done. While the elephant was making good its escape, the rider climbed up a tree from which he planned to throw himself on its back and thus subdue it once again. However, he missed the elephant's head as he fell and landed right in front of it. The elephant saw its enemy (the rider) fallen in front of it: yet it was overcome by pity and therefore did not harm him. Such compassion is seen even in beasts. The elephant went away.

The rider got up, not seriously injured. The evil-doer's body does not break down easily! Their evil deeds seem to strengthen their body. The rider, however, was unhappy at the loss of the elephant. He continued to search the forest for the lost elephant. After a very long time, he saw the elephant standing in a thick forest. He gathered other elephant tamers and with their help dug a huge pit and covered it with foliage, eager to recapture that elephant.

Within the next few days, that mighty elephant fell into that pit.

Thus recaptured and bound by the wicked rider, the elephant still stands there!

The elephant had neglected to kill its enemy though he had fallen right in front of it, and hence it had to undergo fresh suffering. One who does not, on account of his foolishness, act appropriately when the opportunity offers itself and thus remove all the obstacles, invites sorrow. By the false satisfaction 'I am free' the elephant fell into bondage again: foolishness invites sorrow. Foolishness is bondage, O holy one! One who is bound thinks he is free in his foolishness. Though all that exists in all the three worlds is but the self, to one who is firmly established in foolishness, all that is but the expansion of foolishness.

ŚIKHIDHVAJA said: VI.1:90

Holy one, explain the significance of these stories!

THE BRĀHMAṆA (CŪḌĀLĀ) said:

The wealthy learned man who went in search of the celestial jewel is you, O king! You have knowledge of the scriptures, yet you are not at rest within yourself as a stone rests in water. Cintāmaṇi is the total renunciation of everything, which puts an end to all sorrow. By pure total renunciation everything is gained. What is the celestial jewel in comparison? In as much as you were able to abandon the empire, etc., you have experienced such total renunciation.

After renouncing everything, you have come to this hermitage. However, one thing still remains to be renounced—your egosense. If the heart abandons the mind (the movement of thought), there is realisation of the absolute: but you are overcome by the thought of the renunciation which your renunciation has created in you. Hence, this is not the bliss that arises from total renunciation. One who has abandoned everything is not agitated by worry: if wind can sway the branches of a tree, it cannot be called immovable.

Such worries (or movements of thought) alone are known as mind. Thought (notion, concept) is another name for the same thing. If thoughts still operate, how can the mind be considered to have been renounced? When the mind is agitated by thoughts (worries, etc.) the three worlds appear to it instantly. As long as thoughts are still there, how can there be pure and total renunciation? Hence, when such thoughts arise in your heart, your renunciation leaves your heart (like the cintāmaṇi leaving the man). Because you did not recognise the spirit of renunciation and cherish it, it left you—taking with it freedom from thoughts and worries.

When thus you were abandoned by the jewel (spirit of total renunciation), you picked up the glass-piece (austerities and all the rest of it). You began to cherish it on account of your delusion. You have replaced the unconditioned and unattached infinite consciousness with the futile performance of austerities which has a beginning and an end, alas, for your own sorrow. One who abandons infinite joy which is easily attained and engages himself in the acquisition of the impossible, is surely a pig-headed fool and suicidal. You fell into the trap of this forest-life and did not strive to sustain the spirit of total renunciation. You abandoned the bondage to kingdom and all the rest of it, but you have become bound again by what is known as the ascetic life. Now you are even more worried than before by cold, heat, wind, etc., and hence more firmly bound. Foolishly thinking, "I have obtained the cintāmaṇi", you have really gained not even a piece of crystal!

This is the meaning of the first parable.

VI.1:91 THE BRĀHMAṆA (CŪḌĀLĀ) continued:

Now listen to the significance of the second parable.

What was described as the elephant in the Vindhya hills, that you are on this earth. The two powerful tusks are viveka (discrimination, wisdom) and vairāgya (dispassion) which you possess. The rider who inflicted pain on the elephant is ignorance which caused you sorrow. Though powerful, the elephant was overcome by the rider: though excellent in every way, you are overcome by this ignorance or foolishness.

The elephant's cage is the cage of desires in which you are imprisoned. The only difference is that the iron cage decays in course of time but the cage of desire grows stronger with time. Even as the elephant broke out of its cage, you abandoned your kingdom and came here. However, psychological abandonment is not as easy as breaking out of a material cage.

Even as the rider was alerted by the escape, the ignorance and the foolishness in you tremble when the spirit of renunciation manifests in you. When the wise man abandons the pursuit of pleasure, ignorance flees from him. When you went to the forest, you had seriously wounded this ignorance, but you had failed to destroy it by the abandonment of the mind or movement of energy in consciousness, even as the elephant failed to kill the rider. Therefore, this ignorance has arisen once again and, remembering the way in which you overpowered the previous desires, it has trapped you in the pit known as asceticism.

If you had destroyed this ignorance once and for all when you renounced your kingdom, you would not have been trapped by this asceticism.

You are the king of the elephants, endowed with the powerful tusk of viveka or wisdom. However, alas, in this dense forest you have been trapped by the rider known as ignorance, and you lie imprisoned in the blind well, known as asceticism.

O king, why did you not listen to the wise words of your wife, Cūḍālā, who is indeed a knower of the truth? She is the foremost among the knowers of the self and there is no contradiction between her words and her deeds. Whatever she says is true and is worth putting into practice. However, even if you did not in the past listen to her words and assimilate them, why did you not abandon everything in total renunciation?

ŚIKHIDHVAJA said: VI.1:92

I have renounced the kingdom, the palace, the country and my wife, too. How is it then that you think that I have not renounced everything?

THE BRĀHMAṆA (CŪḌĀLĀ) replied:

Wealth, wife, palace, kingdom, the earth and the royal umbrella and your relatives are not yours, O king: renouncing them does not constitute total renunciation! There is something else which seems to be yours and which you have not renounced, and that is the best part of renunciation. Renounce that totally and without any residue and attain freedom from sorrow.

ŚIKHIDHVAJA said:

If the kingdom and all that was in it are not mine, then I abandon this forest and all that is in it. (So saying, Śikhidhvaja mentally renounced the forest, etc.)

(On being told by the brāhmaṇa, "All these things are not yours, hence there is no meaning in renouncing them", Śikhidhvaja said:) Surely, this hermitage is everything for me right now, it is mine. I shall abandon that, too. (Thus resolved, Śikhidhvaja cleansed his heart of the very idea that the hermitage was his:) Surely, now I have completely renounced everything!

THE BRĀHMAṆA (CŪḌĀLĀ) repeated:

Surely, all these too are not yours. How then do you renounce them? There is something which you have not renounced and that is the best part of it. By renouncing that, attain freedom from sorrow.

ŚIKHIDHVAJA said:

If these, too, are not mine, then I shall abandon my staff, the deerskin, etc., and my cottage, too.

VASIṢṬHA said:

So saying, he sprang up from his seat. While the brāhmaṇa was passively looking on, Śikhidhvaja collected whatever there was in the cottage and made a bonfire of it. He threw away his rosary: "I am freed from the delusion that the repetition of a mantra is holy and so I have no need for you". He reduced the deer-skin to ashes. He gave away his water-pot (kamaṇḍalu) to a brāhmaṇa (or threw it into the fire).

He said to himself, "Whatever is to be renounced must be renounced all at once and for ever, otherwise it expands once again and is gathered once again. Hence, I shall once and for all burn everything up."

Thus having resolved, Śikhidhvaja, who had decided to give up all activities sacred and secular, collected all those articles that he had used till then and burnt them all up.

VI.1:93 VASIṢṬHA continued:

Then, Śikhidhvaja set fire to the cottage which he had built unnecessarily, guided by his own previous (false) notions. After that, systematically he burnt whatever there was and whatever was left. He burnt or threw away everything, including his own clothes. Frightened by this bonfire even the animals ran away from that place.

ŚIKHIDHVAJA then said to the brāhmaṇa:

Awakened by you, O son of the gods, I have abandoned all the notions I had entertained for such a long time. I am now established in pure and and blissful knowledge. From whatever proves to be the cause of bondage the mind turns away and rests in equilibrium. I have renounced everything. I am free from all bondage. I am at peace. I am blissful. I am victorious. The space is my dress; space is my abode and I am like space. Is there anything beyond this supreme renunciation, O son of the gods?

THE BRĀHMAṆA (CŪḌĀLĀ) replied:

You have not renounced everything, O king: hence, do not act as if you are enjoying the bliss of supreme renunciation! You have something, as it were, which you have not renounced, that is the best part of renunciation. When that is also utterly abandoned without leaving a residue, then you will attain the supreme state, free from sorrow.

After some thought, ŚIKHIDHVAJA said:

There is only one more thing left, O son of the gods: and that is this body which is the abode of the deadly snakes known as the senses, and which is composed of blood, flesh, etc. I shall now abandon that too and destroy it, and thus achieve total renunciation.

As he was about to execute his resolve, THE BRĀHMAṆA said:

O king, why do you vainly endeavour to destroy this innocent body? Abandon this anger which is characteristic of the bull that sets out to destroy a calf! This ascetic body is inert and dumb. You have nothing to do with it. Therefore, do not attempt to destroy it. The body remains what it is, inert and dumb. It is motivated and made to function by some other power or energy. The body is not responsible for the experience of pleasure and pain. Further, destroying the body does not mean total renunciation. On the other hand, you are throwing away something which is an aid to such renunciation! If you are able to renounce that which functions through this body and which agitates this body, then you have truly abandoned all sin and evil and then you will have become a supreme renouncer. If that is renounced, everything (including the body) is renounced. Otherwise, the sin and evil, even if they remain submerged temporarily, will arise again.

THE BRĀHMAṆA (CŪḌĀLĀ) said:

That alone is total renunciation which is the renunciation of that which is all, which is the sole cause of all these and in which all these abide.

ŚIKHIDHVAJA prayed:

Holy sir, please tell me what that is which should be renounced.

THE BRĀHMAṆA (CŪDĀLĀ) said:

O noble one! It is the mind (which also goes by the names 'jīva', 'prāṇa', etc.) or the citta, which is neither inert nor non-inert and is in a state of confusion which is the 'all'. It is this citta (mind) which is confusion, it is the human being, it is the world, it is all. It is the seed for the kingdom, for the body, wife and all the rest of it. When this seed is abandoned there it total renunciation of all that is in the present and even in the future!

All these—good and evil, kingdom and forest—cause distress in the heart of one who is endowed with the citta, and great joy in one who is mindless. Just as the tree is agitated by the wind, this body is agitated by the mind. The diverse experiences of beings (old age, death, birth and so on) and also the firmness of the holy sages—all these are verily the modifications of the mind. It is this mind alone which is referred to variously as buddhi, the cosmos, egosense, prāṇa, etc. Hence, its abandonment alone is total renunciation. Once it is abandoned, the truth is experienced at once. All notions of unity and diversity come to an end; there is peace.

On the other hand, by renouncing what you consider not-yours, you are creating a division within yourself. If one renounces everything, then everything exists within the void of the one infinite consciousness. When one rests in that state of total renunciation like the lamp without fuel, he shines with supreme brilliance like a lamp with fuel. Even after renouncing the kingdom etc., you exist. Similarly, even after the mind has been renounced, that infinite consciousness will exist. Even when all these have been burnt, you have not undergone any change; even when you have totally abandoned the mind, there will be no change. One who has totally renounced everything is not afflicted by fear of old age, death and such other events in life. That alone is supreme bliss. All else is terrible sorrow. OM! Thus assimilate this truth and do what you wish to do. In that total renunciation does the highest wisdom or self-knowledge exist: the utter emptiness of a pot is where precious jewels are stored. It is by such total renunciation that the Śākya Muni (Buddha) reached that state beyond doubt in which he was firmly established. Hence, O king, having abandoned everything, remain in that form and in that state in which you find yourself. Abandon even the notion of "I have renounced all" and remain in a state of supreme peace.

VI.1:94 ŚIKHIDHVAJA said:

Pray, tell me the exact nature of this citta (mind) and also how to abandon it so that it does not arise again and again.

KUṂBHA (THE BRĀHMAṆA—CŪḌĀLĀ) replied:

Vāsanā (memory, subtle impressions of the past, conditioning) is the nature of this citta (mind). In fact they are synonyms. Its abandonment or renunciation is easy, easily accomplished, more delightful than even the sovereignty over a kingdom, and more beautiful than a flower. It is certainly very difficult for a foolish person to renounce the mind, even as it is difficult for a simpleton to rule the kingdom.

The utter destruction or extinction of the mind is the extinction of saṃsāra (the creation-cycle). It is also known as the abandonment of the mind. Therefore, uproot this tree whose seed is the 'I'-idea, with all its branches, fruits and leaves, and rest in the space in the heart.

What is known as 'I' arises in the absence of the knowledge of the mind (self-knowledge); this 'I' is the seed of the tree known as mind. It grows in the field of the supreme self which is also pervaded by the illusory power known as Māyā. Thus, a division is created in that field and experience arises. With this, the determining faculty known as the buddhi arises. Of course it has no distinct form, as it is but the expanded form of the seed. Its nature is conceptualisation or notional; and it is also known as the mind, jīva and void.

The trunk of this tree is the body. The movement of energy within it that results in its growth is the effect of psychological conditioning. Its branches are long and they reach out to great distances; they are the finite sense-experiences which are characterised by being and non-being. Its fruits are good and evil (pleasure and pain, happiness and unhappiness).

This is a vicious tree. Endeavour every moment to cut down its branches and to uproot it. Its branches, too, are of the nature of conditioning, of concepts and of percepts. They (the branches) are endowed with the fruits of all these. If you remain unattached to them, unconcerned about them and without identifying yourself with them, through the strength of your intelligence (consciousness) these vāsanās are greatly weakened. You will then be able to uproot the tree altogether. The destruction of the branches is secondary; the primary thing is to uproot it.

How is the tree to be uprooted? By engaging oneself in the enquiry into the nature of the self—"Who am I?" This enquiry is the fire in which the very seed and the very roots of the tree known as citta (mind) are burnt completely.

ŚIKHIDHVAJA said:

I know that I am pure consciousness. How this impurity (ignorance) arose in it, I do not know. I am distressed because I am unable to get rid of this impurity which is not-self and unreal.

KUMBHA asked:

Tell me if that impurity (ignorance), on account of which you are an ignorant man bound to this saṃsāra, is real or unreal?

ŚIKHIDHVAJA replied:

That impurity is also the egosense and the seed for this big tree known as citta (mind). I do not know how to get rid of it. It returns to me even when it is renounced by me!

KUṂBHA said:

The effect arising from a real cause is self-evident at all times everywhere. Where the cause is not real, the effect is surely as unreal as the second moon seen in diplopia. The sprout of saṃsāra has arisen from the seed of egosense. Enquire into its cause and tell me now.

ŚIKHIDHVAJA replied:

O sage, I see that experience is the cause of egosense. But, tell me how to get rid of it.

KUṂBHA asked again:

Ah, you are able to find the causes of effects! Tell me then the cause of such experience. I shall then tell you how to get rid of the cause. When consciousness is both the experiencing and the experience, and when there was no cause for the experience as the object to arise, how did the effect (experience) arise?

ŚIKHIDHVAJA replied:

Surely on account of the objective reality, such as the body? I am unable to see how such objective reality is seen as false.

KUMBHA said:

If experience rests on the reality of objects like the body, then if the body, etc., are proved to be unreal, on what will experience rest? When the cause is absent or unreal, the effect is non-existent and the experience of such an effect is delusion. What, then, is the cause of objects like the body?

ŚIKHIDHVAJA asked:

The second moon is surely not unreal because it has a cause which is eye-disease. The barren woman's son is never seen—and that is unreal. Why, is not the father the cause for the existence of the body?

KUṂBHA replied:

But, then, that father is unreal: that which is born of unreality is unreal, too. If one says that the first Creator is the original cause of all subsequent bodies, in fact even that is not true! The Creator himself is non-different from the reality; hence his appearance as other than the reality (this creation, etc.) is delusion. The realisation of this truth enables one to get rid of the ignorance and egosense.

VI.1:95 ŚIKHIDHVAJA asked:

If all this—from the Creator to the pillar—is unreal, how has this real sorrow come into being?

KUṂBHA replied:

This delusion of the world-existence attains expansion by its repeated affirmation: when water is frozen into a block it serves as a seat! Only when ignorance is dispelled does one realise the truth; only then does the original state manifest itself. When the perception of diversity is attenuated, then this samsāra ceases to be experienced and you shine in your own original glory.

Thus, you are the supreme primordial being. This body, this form, etc., have come into being on account of ignorance and misunderstanding. All these notions of a creator and of a creation of diverse beings have not been proved to be real. When the cause is unproven how can one take the effect to be real?

All these diverse creatures are but appearances, like water in the mirage. Such a deceptive appearance ceases on being enquired into.

ŚIKHIDHVAJA asked:

Why can it not be said that the supreme self or the infinite consciousness (Brahman) is the cause whose effect is the Creator?

KUṂBHA replied:

Brahman or the supreme self is one without a second, without a cause and without an effect, for it has no reason (motivation or need) to do anything, to create anything. It is therefore not the doer, neither is there any action, instrument nor seed for such activity. Hence it is not the cause for this creation or the Creator.

Hence, there is no such thing as creation. You are therefore neither the doer of actions nor the enjoyer of experiences. You are the all, ever at peace, unborn and perfect. Since there is no cause (reason for creation), there is no effect known as the world; the world-appearance is but delusion.

When thus the objectivity of the world is seen to be unreal, what is experience and of what? When there is no experience, there is no experiencer (the egosense). Thus, you are pure and liberated. Bondage and liberation are mere words.

ŚIKHIDHVAJA said:

Lord, by the wise and well-reasoned words which you have uttered I have been fully awakened. I realise that, since there is no cause, Brahman is not the doer of anything nor the creator of anything. Hence, there is no mind nor an egosense. Such being the case, I am pure, I am awakened. I salute my self, there is naught which is the object of my consciousness.

VASIṢṬHA continued: VI.1:96

Thus awakened spiritually, Śikhidhvaja entered into deep meditation from which he was playfully awakened by Kuṃbha, who said: "O king, you have been duly awakened and enlightened. What has to be done now has to be done, regardless of whether this world-vision ceases or does not cease. Once the light of the self has been seen, you are instantly freed from the undesirable and from mental modifications and you remain as one liberated while still living."

Śikhidhvaja who was now radiant with self-knowledge asked the brahmaṇa Kuṃbha 'for further understanding': "When the reality is one indivisible, infinite consciousness, how could this apparent division of the seer, the seen and sight arise in it?"

KUṂBHA replied:

Well asked, O king. This is all that remains for you to know. Whatever there is in this universe will cease to be at the end of this world-cycle, leaving only the essence which is neither light nor darkness. That is pure consciousness which is supreme peace and infinite. It is beyond logic and intellectual comprehension. It is known as Brahman or nirvāṇa. It is smaller than the smallest, larger than the biggest and the best among the excellent. In relation to it, what now appears to be is but an atomic particle!

That which shines as the I-consciousness and which is the universal self is what exists as this universe. There is indeed no real distinction between that universal self and the universe, as there is no distinction between air and its movement. One may say that between the waves and the ocean there is a causal relationship in terms of time and space: but in the universal self or infinite consciousness there is no such relationship and hence the universe is without a cause. In that infinite consciousness this universe floats as a particle of dust. In it the word 'world' comes to be endowed with substantiality or reality.

That (infinite consciousness) alone is the essence here. It pervades all. It is one. It is consciousness. It holds everything together. Yet, one cannot say it is one because of the total absence of divisibility or duality. Hence, it is sufficient to know that the self alone is the truth and not let the notion of duality arise. That alone is everywhere at all times in all the diverse forms. It is not seen (not experienced through the senses and the mind) nor is it an object to be attained. Hence, it is neither the cause nor the effect. It is extremely subtle. It is pure experiencing (neither the experiencer nor the experience). Though it is thus described, it is beyond description. Hence one cannot say it is nor that it is not. How then can it be the cause of this creation?

KUṂBHA said:

That which has no seed (cause) and which is indescribable is therefore not the cause of another—naught is born of that. Hence, the self is neither the doer nor the action nor the instrument. It is the truth. It is the eternal absolute consciousness. It is self-knowledge. There is no creation in the supreme Brahman. One may theoretically establish the arising and the existence of a wave in the ocean on the basis of time (of its arising) and space (in which it seems to exist as a wave). But, who has tried to establish even such a relationship between Brahman and the creation? For, in Brahman time and space do not exist. Thus, the world has no basis at all.

ŚIKHIDHVAJA said:

Surely, one can rationalise the existence of waves in the ocean. But I do not understand how it is that the world and the egosense are uncaused.

KUṂBHA said:

Now you have correctly understood the truth, O king! That is because there is in fact no reality which corresponds to the words 'world' and 'egosense'. Just as emptiness (or the notion of distance) exists, non-different from space, even so this world-appearance exists in the supreme being or infinite consciousness—whether in the same form or with another form.

When thus the reality of this world is well understood, then it is realised as the supreme self (Śiva). When rightly understood, even poison turns into nectar. When it is not thus rightly understood, it becomes evil (aŚivam), the world of sorrow. For whatever this consciousness realises itself to be, that it becomes. It is because of a confusion in the self that this consciousness sees itself as embodied and as the world.

It is that supreme self alone that shines here as the supreme being (Śivam). Hence, the very questions concerning the world and the egosense are inappropriate. Surely questions are appropriate only concerning those substances that are real, not with regard to those whose existence is unproved. The world and the egosense have no existence independent of the supreme self. Since there is no reason for their existence, the truth is that it is the supreme self alone that exists. It is the energy of Brahman (Māyā) that has created this illusion by the combination of the five elements. But consciousness remains consciousness and is realised by consciousness; diversity is perceived by the notion of diversity. The infinite raises infinity within itself, the infinite creates infinity, infinite is born of infinity and infinity remains infinite. Consciousness shines as consciousness.

KUṂBHA said: VI.1:97

In the case of gold, it may be said that at a certain time and at a certain place it gave rise to an ornament. But from the self (which is absolute peace) nothing is created and nothing ever returns to it. Brahman rests in itself. Hence, it is neither the seed nor the cause for the creation of the world which is a matter of mere experience. Apart from this experience nothing exists which could be referred to as the world or the egosense. Therefore, the infinite consciousness alone exists.

ŚIKHIDHVAJA said:

I realise, O sage, that in the Lord there is no world nor the egosense. But how do the world and the egosense shine as if they exist?

KUṂBHA replied:

Indeed, it is the infinite which, beginningless and endless, exists as pure experiencing consciousness. That alone is this expanded universe which is its body, as it were. There is no other substance known as the intellect, nor is there an outside nor void. The essence of existence is pure experiencing which is therefore the essence of consciousness. Just as liquidity exists inseparable from water, consciousness and unconsciousness exist together. There is no rationale for such existence, for what is is as it is.

Since there is neither a contradiction nor a division in consciousness it is self-evident.

If the infinite consciousness is the cause of something else, then how can it be regarded as indescribable and incomparable? Hence, Brahman is not a cause or a seed. What then shall we regard as the effect? It is therefore inappropriate to associate the creation with

Brahman and to associate the inert with the infinite consciousness. If there appears to be a world or egosense, these are but empty words meant to entertain.

Consciousness is not destroyed. However, if such destruction can be comprehended, the consciousness that comprehends it is free from destruction and creation. If such destruction can be comprehended, it is surely the trick of consciousness. Hence consciousness alone exists, neither one nor many! Enough of this discussion.

When thus there is no material existence, thinking does not exist either. There is neither a world nor the egosense. Remain well established in peace and tranquility, free from mental conditioning, whether you are embodied or disembodied. When the reality of Brahman is realised, there is no room for worry and anxiety.

VI.1:98 ŚIKHIDHVAJA said:

Holy one, pray instruct me in such a way that it will be perfectly clear to me that the mind is non-existent.

KUṂBHA said:

O king, indeed there is not and there has never been an entity known as the mind. That which shines here and is known as the mind is indeed the infinite Brahman (consciousness). It is ignorance of its true nature that gives rise to the notion of a mind and the world and all the rest of it. When even these are insubstantial notions, how can 'I', 'you', etc. be considered real? Thus, there is no such thing as the 'world', and whatever appears to be is uncreated. All this is indeed Brahman. How can that be known and by whom?

Even in the beginning of the present world-cycle this world was not created. It was described as creation by me only for your comprehension. In the total absence of any causative factors, all these could not have been created at all. Therefore, whatever there is is Brahman and naught else. It is not even logical to say that the Lord who is nameless and formless created this world! It is not true. When thus the creation of this world is seen to be false, then surely the mind that entertains the notion of such a creation is false, too.

Mind is but a bundle of such notions which limit the truth. But, then, division implies divisibility. When the infinite consciousness is incapable of division, there is no divisibility and hence there is no division. How can mind, the divider, be real? Whatever appears to be here is perceived in Brahman, by Brahman, and such perception is, by courtesy, known as the mind! It is the infinite consciousness alone that is spread out as the universe. Why then call it the universe? In this plane or dimension of infinite consciousness whatever slight appearance there seems to be is but the reflection of consciousness in itself: hence there is neither a mind nor the world. Only in ignorance is all this seen as 'the world'. Hence the mind is unreal.

Only creation is negated by this, not what *is*. The reality that is seen as this world is beginningless and uncreated. Hence, the scriptural declarations and one's own experiences concerning the appearance and the disappearance of substances here cannot be considered invalid, except by an ignoramus. One who denies the validity of such declarations and experiences is fit to be shunned. The transcendental reality is eternal; the world is not unreal (only the limiting adjunct, the mind, is false). Therefore, all this is the indivisible, illimitable, nameless and formless infinite consciousness. It is the self-reflection of Brahman which is of infinite forms that appears to be the universe with its creation-dissolution cycle. It is this Brahman itself which knows itself for a moment as this universe and appears to be such. There is no mind.

ŚIKHIDHVAJA said: VI.1:99

My delusion is gone. Wisdom has been gained by your grace. I remain free from all doubts. I know what there is to be known. The ocean of illusion has been crossed. I am at peace, without the notion of 'I' but as pure knowledge.

KUṂBHA said:

When the world does not exist as such, where is 'I' or 'you'? Hence, remaining at peace within yourself, engage yourself in non-volitional actions as are appropriate from moment to moment. All this is but Brahman which is peace; 'I' and 'the world' are words without substance. When the insubstantiality of such expressions is realised, then what was seen as the world is realised as Brahman.

The creator Brahmā is but an idea or notion. Even so is 'self' or 'I'. In their right or wrong comprehension lies liberation or bondage! The notion 'I am' gives rise to bondage and self-destruction. The realisation 'I am (is) not' leads to freedom and purity. Bondage and liberation are but notions. That which is aware of these notions is the infinite consciousness which alone is. The notion 'I am' is the source of all distress. The absence of such a feeling is perfection. Realise 'I am not that egosense' and rest in pure awareness.

When such pure awareness arises, all notions subside. There is perfection. In the pure awareness, perfection or the Lord, there is neither causality nor the resultant creation or objects. In the absence of objects, there is no experience nor its concomitant egosense. When the egosense is non-existent, where is saṃsāra (the cycle of birth and death)? When thus saṃsāra does not exist, the supreme being alone remains. In it the universe exists as carvings in uncarved stone. He who thus sees the universe, without the intervention of the mind and therefore without the notion of a universe, he alone sees the truth. Such a vision is known as nirvāṇa.

Even as the ocean alone exists when the word 'wave' is deprived of its meaning, Brahman alone exists when the word 'creation' is seen as meaningless. This creation is Brahman; Brahman alone is aware of this creation. When the word-meaning of 'creation' is dropped, the true meaning of 'creation' is seen as the eternal Brahman. When one enquires into the word 'Brahman', the ALL is comprehended. When one similarly enquires into the word 'creation', Brahman is comprehended. However, that consciousness which is the basis and the substratum for all such notions and their awareness is known by the word 'Brahman'. When this truth is clearly realised and when the duality of knowledge and known is discarded, what remains is supreme peace which is indescribable and inexpressible.

VI.1:100 ŚIKHIDHVAJA said:

If the supreme being is real and the world is real, then I assume that the supreme being is the cause and the world the effect!

KUṂBHA replied:

Only if there is causality can the effect be assumed. But, where there is no causality, how can the effect arise from it? There is no causal relationship between Brahman and the universe: whatever there is here is Brahman. When there is no seed even, then how is something born? When Brahman is nameless and formless, there is surely no causality (seed) in it. Hence, Brahman is non-doer in whom causality does not exist. Therefore, there is no effect which can be called the world.

Brahman alone thou art and Brahman alone exists. When that Brahman is comprehended by unwisdom, it is experienced as this universe. This universe is, as it were, the body of Brahman. When that infinite consciousness considers itself as other than it really is, that is said to be self-destruction or self-experience. That self-destruction is the mind. Its very nature is the destruction (veiling) of self-knowledge. Even if such self-destruction is momentary, it is known as the mind that lasts for a world-cycle.

Such a notional existence ceases only by the dawn of right knowledge and the cessation of all notions. Since the notional existence is unreal it ceases naturally when the truth is realised. When the world exists only as a word but not as a real independent substance, how then can it be accepted as a real existence? Its independent existence is like water in the mirage. How can that be real? The confused state in which this unreality appears to be real is known as the mind. Non-comprehension of the truth is ignorance or the mind; right comprehension is self-knowledge or self-realisation.

Even as the realisation 'This is not water' brings about the realisation of the mirage as mirage, the realisation that 'This is not pure consciousness but kinetic consciousness which is known as the mind' brings about its destruction.

When thus the non-existence of the mind is realised, it is seen that the egosense, etc., do not exist. One alone exists—the infinite consciousness. All notions cease. The falsity which arose as the mind ceases when notions cease. I am not, nor is there another, nor do you nor do these exist; there is neither mind nor senses. One alone is—the pure consciousness. Nothing in the three worlds is ever born or dies. The infinite consciousness alone exists. There is neither unity nor diversity, neither confusion nor delusion. Nothing perishes and nothing flourishes. Everything (even the energy that manifests as desire and desirelessness) is your own self.

KUṂBHA (CŪḌĀLĀ) said: VI.1:101

I hope that you have been inwardly awakened spiritually, and that you know what there is to be known and see what there is to be seen.

ŚIKHIDHVAJA replied:

Indeed, Lord, by your grace I have seen the supreme state. How was it that it eluded my understanding so far?

KUṂBHA said:

Only when the mind is utterly quiet, when one has completely abandoned all desire for pleasure and when the senses have also been rid of their colouring or covering, are the words of the preceptor rightly comprehended. (The previous efforts were not wasted, for) The various efforts made so far have attained fruition today and the impurities in the bodies have dropped away. When thus one is freed from psychological conditioning and the impurities have been removed or purified, the words of the guru enter directly into the innermost core of one's being just as an arrow enters the stalk of the lotus. You have attained that state of purity and therefore you have been enlightened by my discourse and your ignorance has been dispelled.

By our satsaṅga (holy company) your karmas (actions and their residual impressions) have been destroyed. Till this very forenoon you were filled with the false notions of 'I' and 'mine' on account of ignorance. Now that on account of the light of my words the mind has been abandoned from your heart, you have been awakened fully, for ignorance lasts only so long as the mind functions in your heart. Now you are enlightened, liberated. Remain established in the infinite consciousness, freed from sorrow, from striving and from all attachment.

ŚIKHIDHVAJA said:

Lord, is there a mind even for the liberated person? How does he live and function here without a mind?

KUṂBHA replied:

Truly, there is no mind in the liberated ones. What is the mind? The psychological conditioning or limitation which is dense and which leads to rebirth is known as mind: this is absent in the liberated sages. The liberated sages live with the help of the mind which is free from conditioning and which does not cause rebirth. It is not mind at all but pure light (satva). The liberated ones live and function here established in this satva, not in the mind. The ignorant and inert mind is mind; the enlightened mind is known as satva. The ignorant live in their mind, the enlightened ones live in satva.

VI.1:101, 102 KUṂBHA continued:

You have attained to the state of satva (the unconditioned mind) on account of your supreme renunciation. The conditioned mind has been totally renounced, of this I am convinced. Your mind has become like pure infinite space. You have reached the state of complete equilibrium which is the state of perfection. This is the total renunciation in which everything is abandoned without residue.

What sort of happiness (destruction of sorrow) does one gain through austerities? Supreme and unending happiness is attained only through utter equanimity. What sort of happiness is that which is gained in heaven? He who has not attained self-knowledge tries to snatch a little pleasure through the performance of some rituals. One who does not have gold clings to copper!

O royal sage, you could easily have become wise with the help of Cūḍālā. Why did you have to indulge in this useless and meaningless austerity? It has a beginning and an end, and in the middle there is an appearance of happiness. However, your austerity has in a way led to this spiritual awakening. Now remain rooted in wisdom.

It is in the infinite consciousness that all these realities and even the unreal notions arise and into it they dissolve. Even ideas like 'This is to be done' and 'This is not to be done' are droplets of this infinite consciousness. Abandon even these and rest in the unconditioned. All these (austerity, etc.) are indirect methods. Why should one not adopt the direct method of self-knowledge?

That which has been described as satva should be renounced by the satva itself—that is, by total freedom from it or by non-attachment to it. Whatever sorrow arises in the three worlds, O king, arises only from mental craving. If you are established in that state of equanimity which treats of both movement and non-movement of thought as non-different, you will rest in the eternal.

There is only one infinite consciousness. That Brahman which is pure consciousness is itself known as satva. The ignorant see it as the world. Movement (agitation) as also non-movement in that infinite consciousness are only notions in the mind of the spectator: the totality of the infinite consciousness is all these but devoid of such notions. Its reality is beyond words!

VASIṢṬHA continued:

Having said this, Kuṃbha vanished from sight even while the king was about to offer flowers in adoration. Reflecting over the words of Kuṃbha, Śikhidhvaja entered into deep meditation, completely free from all desires and cravings and firmly established in the unconditioned state.

VASIṢṬHA continued: VI.1:103

While Śikhidhvaja was thus engaged in deep meditation utterly free from the least mental modification or movement in consciousness, Cūḍālā abandoned her disguise, returned to the palace and in her own female form conducted the affairs of the state. She returned to where Śikhidhvaja was after three days and was delighted to see that he was still absorbed in meditation. She thought, "I should make him return to world-consciousness; why should he abandon the body now? Let him rule the kingdom for some time and then both of us can simultaneously abandon the body. Surely, the instructions I have given him will not be lost. I shall keep him alert and awake through the practice of yoga."

She roared like a lion again and again. Still he did not open his eyes. She pushed the body down. Yet he remained immersed in the self. She thought, "Alas, he is completely absorbed in the self. How shall I bring him back to body-consciousness? On the other hand, why should I do so? Let him reach the disembodied state and I shall also abandon this body now!"

While she was getting ready to abandon her body, she again thought, "Before I abandon my body, let me see if there is the seed of mind (vāsanā) somewhere in his body. If there is, he can be awakened and then both of us can live as liberated beings. If there is not and if he has attained final liberation, I shall also abandon this body." She examined his body and found that the seed of individuality was still present in him.

RĀMA asked:

Lord, when the body of the sage lies like a log of wood, how can one know that there is still a trace of satva (purified mind) in him?

VASIṢṬHA said:

In his heart, unseen and subtle, there is the trace of satva which is the cause for the revival of body-consciousness. It is like the flower and the fruit which are potentially present in the seed. In the case of the sage whose mind is totally free from the movement of thought, who is devoid of the least notion of duality or unity, whose consciousness is utterly firm and steady like a mountain—his body is in a state of perfect equilibrium and does not show signs of pain or pleasure; it does not rise or fall (live or die) but remains in perfect harmony with nature. It is only as long as there are notions of duality or unity that the body undergoes changes as the mind does. It is the movement of thought that appears as this world. Because of that the mind experiences pleasure, anger and delusion which thus remain irrepressible. But when the mind is firmly established in equanimity, such disturbances do not arise in one. He is like pure space.

VASIṢṬHA continued:

When the satva is in a state of total equilibrium, then no physical or psychological defects are experienced. It is not possible to abandon satva, it reaches its end in course of time. When there is neither the mind nor even the satva in the body, then, like snow melting in the heat, the body dissolves in the elements. Śikhidhvaja's body was free from the mind (movement of thought) but was endowed with a trace of satva. Therefore it did not thus dissolve into the elements. Noticing this, Cūḍālā decided, "I shall enter into the pure intelligence which is omnipresent and endeavour to awaken body-consciousness in him. If I do not do so, he will surely awaken after some time. But, why should I remain alone till then?"

Cūḍālā thereupon left her body and entered into the pure mind (satva) of Śikhidhvaja. She agitated that pure mind and quickly re-entered her own body which she instantly transformed into that of the young ascetic Kuṃbha. Kuṃbha began to sing the Sāma Vedic hymns gently. Listening to this, the king returned to body-consciousness. He saw Kuṃbha once again in front of him. He was happy. He said to Kuṃbha: "Luckily, we have once again arisen in your consciousness, O Lord! And you have come here again merely to shower your blessings on me!"

KUṂBHA said:

Since the time I left you and went away, my mind (heart) has been here with you. There is no desire to go to heaven but only to be near you. I do not have a relative, friend, trustworthy person or disciple like you in this world.

ŚIKHIDHVAJA replied:

I consider myself supremely blessed that, though you are perfectly enlightened and unattached, you wish to be with me. Pray, do stay with me here in this forest!

KUṂBHA asked:

Tell me: did you rest in the supreme state for a while? Have you abandoned notions like 'This is different', 'This is unhappiness', etc.? Has your craving for pleasure ceased?

ŚIKHIDHVAJA replied:

By your grace, I have reached the other shore of this saṃsāra (world-appearance). I have gained what there is to be gained. There is naught but the self—neither the known nor what is yet to be known (unknown), neither attainment nor what is renounced and what should be renounced, neither an entity nor the other nor even satva (a pure mind). Like the limitless space, I remain in the unconditioned state.

VASIṢṬHA continued: VI.1:104

After spending an hour at that place, the king and Kuṃbha went into the forest where they roamed freely for eight days. Kuṃbha suggested that they should go to another forest and the king consented. They observed the normal rules of life and performed appropriate religious rites to propitiate ancestors and the gods. False notions like 'This is our home' and 'This is not' did not arise in their hearts. Sometimes they were clad in gorgeous robes, at others in rags. Sometimes they were anointed with sandal-paste, at others with ashes. After a few days, the king also shone with the same radiance as Kuṃbha.

Seeing the radiance of the king, Kuṃbha (Cūḍālā) began to think: "Here is my husband who is noble and strong. The forest is delightful. We are in a state in which fatigue is unknown. How then does desire for pleasure not arise in the heart? The liberated sage welcomes and experiences whatever comes to him unsought; if he is caught up in conformity (rigidity) it gives rise to foolishness (ignorance). She whose passions are not aroused in the proximity of her noble and strong husband when they dwell surrounded by a garden of flowers, is as good as dead! What does the knower of the truth or the sage of self-knowledge gain by abandoning what is obtained without effort? I should make it possible for my husband to enjoy conjugal pleasures with me." Having thus decided, Kuṃbha said to Śikhidhvaja: "Today is an auspicious day when I should be in heaven to see my father. Give me leave to go and I shall return this evening."

The two friends exchanged flowers. Kuṃbha left. Soon Cūḍālā abandoned the disguise, went to the palace and discharged the royal duties. She returned to where Śikhidhvaja was, again in the disguise of Kuṃbha. Noticing a change in Kuṃbha's facial expression, the king asked: "O son of the gods, why do you look so unhappy? Holy ones do not allow any external influence to disturb their equilibrium."

KUṂBHA said:

They who, though remaining established in equilibrium, do not let their organs function naturally as long as the body is alive, are obstinate and stubborn people. As long as there is sesame there is oil; as long as there is the body there are the different moods also. He who rebels against the states that the body is naturally subject to cuts space to pieces with a sword. The equilibrium of yoga is for the mind not for the organs of action and their states. As long as the body lasts, one should let the organs of action perform their proper function, though the intellect and the senses remain in a state of equanimity. Such is the law of nature to which even the gods are subject.

VI.1:105 KUṂBHA continued:

Now, O king, please listen to what misfortune has befallen me. For, if one confides his unhappiness to a friend, it is greatly ameliorated even as the heavy and dark cloud becomes light by shedding rain. The mind also becomes clear and peaceful when a friend listens to one's fate, even as water becomes clear when a piece of alum is dropped into it.

After I left you I went to heaven and performed my duties there. As evening approached, I left heaven to return to you. In space en route I saw the sage Durvāsa flying in haste to be in time for his evening prayers. He was clad, as it were, in the dark clouds and adorned with lightning. This made him look like a woman rushing to meet her lover. I saluted him and said so, in fun. Enraged at my impudence, he cursed me: "For this insolence, you will become a woman every night." I am grieved at the very thought that every night I shall become a woman. It is indeed a tragedy that the sons of god who are easily overcome by lust thus suffer the consequences of insulting holy sages. However, why should I grieve, for this does not affect my self.

ŚIKHIDHVAJA said:

What is the use of grief, O son of the gods? Let come what may, for the self is not affected by the fate of the body. Whatever be the joy or sorrow that is allotted to one affects the body, not the indweller. If even you yield to grief, what about the ignorant people! Or, perhaps, while narrating an unfortunate incident you are merely using appropriate words and expressions!!

VASIṢṬHA continued:

Thus they consoled each other for they were inseparable friends now. The sun had set and the darkness of the night was creeping on earth. They performed their evening prayers. Soon, Kuṃbha's body began to show a creeping change. Fighting back his tears and in a choked voice, he said to Śikhidhvaja: "Alas, see, I feel as if my body is melting away and that it is pouring down on earth. My chest is sprouting breasts. My skeletal structure undergoes changes appropriate to a woman. Look, dress and ornaments appropriate to a woman spring from the body itself. O what shall I do, how shall I hide my shame, for I have truly become a woman!"

Śikhidhvaja replied: "Holy one, you know what there is to be known. Do not grieve over the inevitable. One's fate affects only the body, not the embodied one." Kuṃbha also agreed: "You are right. I do not now feel any sorrow. Who can defy the world order or nature?"

Thus conversing, they went to bed (slept in the same bed). Thus Cūḍālā lived with her husband, as a young male ascetic during the day and as a woman at night.

VASIṢṬHA continued: VI.1:106

After a few days of such companionship, Kuṃbha (Cūḍālā in disguise) said to Śikhidhvaja: "O king, listen to my submission. For some time now I have been a woman by night. I wish to fulfil the role of a woman at night. I feel that I should live as the wife of a worthy husband. In the three worlds there is none who is as dear to me as you are. Hence, I wish to marry you and enjoy conjugal pleasures with you. This is natural, pleasant and possible. What fault is there in it? We have given up both desire and rejection and we have total equal vision. Hence, let us do what is natural, without desire and aversion."

Śikhidhvaja replied: "O friend, I do not see either good or evil in doing this. Therefore, O wise one, do what you wish to do. Because the mind rests in perfect equilibrium, I see only the self everywhere. Hence do what you wish to do."

Kuṃbha replied: "If that is how you feel, O king, then today itself is the most auspicious day. The celestial bodies shall witness our wedding."

Both of them then gathered all the articles necessary for the wedding rite. They bathed each other with holy water in preparation for the sacred rite. They offered worship to the ancestors and gods.

By this time, the night-time had arrived. Kuṃbha became transformed into a lovely woman. 'He' said to the king: "O dear friend, now I am a woman. My name is Madanikā. I salute you. I am your wife." Śikhidhvaja then adorned Madanikā with garlands, flowers and jewels. Admiring her beauty, the king said: "O Madanikā, you are radiant like goddess Lakṣmī. May we be blessed to live together like the sun and the shadow, Lakṣmī and Nārāyaṇa, Śiva and Pārvatī. May we be blessed with all auspiciousness."

The couple themselves tended the sacred fire and performed the nuptial rite, in strict accord with the injunctions of the scriptures. The altar had been decorated with flowery creepers and with precious and semi-precious stones. Its four corners were decorated with cocoanuts and there were also pots full of holy water of the Gaṅgā. In the centre was the sacred fire. They went round this fire and offered the prescribed oblations into it with the appropriate sacred hymns. Even while doing so the king frequently held Madanikā's hand thus revealing his fondness for her and his joy on that occasion. They then circumambulated the sacred fire thrice, performing what is known as the Lājā Homa. Then they retired to the nuptial chamber (a cave specially prepared for the occasion). The moon was showering cool rays. The nuptial bed was made of fragrant flowers. They ascended this bed and consummated their wedding.

VI.1:107 VASIṢṬHA continued:

As the sun rose, Madanikā became Kuṃbha. Thus, this pair lived as friends during the day and as husband and wife during the night. While Śikhidhvaja was asleep one night, Kuṃbha (Cūḍālā in disguise) slipped away to the palace and discharged the royal duties there and quickly returned to the king's bedside.

For a month they lived in the caves of the Mahendra mountain. They then roamed in different forests and migrated from one mountainside to another. For some time they lived in the garden of the gods known as the Pārijāta forest on the southern slopes of the Maināka mountain. They also roamed the Kuru territory and the Kosala territory.

After they had enjoyed themselves in this manner for a number of months, Cūḍālā (disguised as Kuṃbha) thought: "I should test the maturity of the king by placing before him the pleasures and the delights of heaven. If he is unaffected by them, surely he will never again seek pleasure."

Having thus decided, Cūḍālā created by her magic powers the illusion in which Śikhidhvaja saw the chief of the gods (Indra) accompanied by the celestials standing right in front of him. Unruffled by their sudden appearance, the king offered them due worship. Then he asked Indra: "Pray, tell me: what have I done to deserve this, that you have taken all this trouble to come here today?"

Indra replied: "Holy one, we have all come here drawn irresistibly to your presence. We have heard your glories sung in heaven. Come, come to heaven: having heard of your greatness the celestials long to see you. Pray, accept these celestial insignia which will enable you to traverse the space even as the perfected sages do. Surely, O sage, liberated beings like you do not spurn happiness that seeks them unsought. May your visit purify the heaven." Śikhidhvaja said: "I know the conditions that prevail in heaven, O Indra! But to me heaven is everywhere and also nowhere. I am happy wherever I am because I desire nothing. However, I am unable to go to the kind of heaven which you describe and which is limited to one place! Hence I am unable to fulfil your command." "But," said Indra, "I think it is proper that liberated sages should suffer to experience the pleasures allotted to them." Śikhidhvaja remained silent. Indra was getting ready to leave. Śikhidhvaja said, "I shall not come now for now is not the time."

Having blessed the king and Kuṃbha, Indra and all his retinue disappeared.

VASIṢṬHA continued: VI.1:108

After withdrawing that magical display, Cūḍālā said to herself: "Luckily, the king is not attracted by temptations of pleasure. Even when Indra visited him and invited him to heaven, the king remained unaffected and pure like space. I shall now subject him to another test to see if he is swayed by the twin forces of attraction and repulsion."

That very night, Cūḍālā created by her magic powers a delightful pleasure garden and an extraordinarily beautiful bed in it. She created a young man, physically more attractive than even Śikhidhvaja. There on that bed she appeared to be seated with her lover in close embrace.

Śikhidhvaja had concluded his evening prayers and he looked for his wife Madanikā. After some search, he discovered the secret hiding place of this couple. He saw them completely immersed in their love-play. Her hair encircled him. With her hands she held his face. Their mouths were joined to each other in a fervent kiss. They were obviously very excited with passionate love for each other. With every movement of their limbs they expressed their extreme love for each other. On their faces danced the delight of their hearts. The chest of one was beating against the chest of the other. They were utterly oblivious of their surroundings.

Śikhidhvaja saw all this but was unmoved. He did not wish to disturb them and so turned to go. But his presence had been noticed by the couple. He said to them, "Pray, let me not disturb your happiness."

After a time, Madanikā came out of the garden and met Śikhidhvaja feeling ashamed of her own conduct. But the king said: "My dear, why did you come away so soon? Surely all beings live in order to enjoy happiness. And it is difficult to find in this world a couple who are in such harmony. I am not agitated on this account for I know very well what people like very much in this world. Kuṃbha and I are great friends, Madanikā is but the fruit of Durvāsa's curse!"

Madanikā pleaded: "Such is the nature of women, O lord! They are wavering in their loyalty. They are eight times as passionate as men. They are weak and so cannot resist lust in the presence of a desirable person. Hence, please forgive me and do not be angry." Śikhidhvaja replied: "I am not at all angry with you, my dear. But it is appropriate that I should henceforth treat you as a good friend and not as my wife." Cūḍālā was delighted with the king's attitude which conclusively proved that he had gone beyond lust and anger. She instantly shed her previous form as Madanikā and resumed her original form as Cūḍālā.

VI.1:109 ŚIKHIDHVAJA said:

Who are you, O lovely lady, and how did you come here? How long have you been here? You look very much like my wife!

CŪḌĀLĀ replied:

Indeed, I am Cūḍālā. I myself assumed the form of Kuṃbha and others in order to awaken your spirit. I myself also assumed the form of this small illusory world with all this garden, etc., which you saw just now. From the very day you unwisely abandoned your kingdom and came here to perform austerities, I have been endeavouring to bring about your spiritual awakening. It is I, assuming the form of Kuṃbha, who instructed you. The forms you perceived, of Kuṃbha and others, were not real. And now you have been fully awakened and you know all that there is to know.

VASIṢṬHA continued:

Śikhidhvaja entered into deep meditation and inwardly saw all that had happened from the time he left the palace. He was delighted and his affection for his wife increased greatly. Coming back to body-consciousness he embraced Cūḍālā with such fervour that is impossible to describe. Their hearts overflowing with love for each other they remained for some time as if in a superconscious state.

ŚIKHIDHVAJA then said to Cūḍālā:

Oh how sweet is the affection of a dear wife which is sweeter than nectar! To what discomfort and pain you have subjected yourself for my sake! The way in which you have redeemed me from this dreadful ocean of ignorance has no comparison whatsoever. Tradition has given us several great women who have been exemplary wives, but they are nothing compared to you. You excel them all in all the virtues and noble qualities. You have struggled hard and brought about my enlightenment. How shall I recompense you for this? Indeed, loving wives thus strive to liberate their husbands from this ocean of saṃsāra. In this they achieve what even the scriptures, guru and mantra are unable to achieve, on account of their love for their husbands. The wife is everything to her husband—friend, brother, well-wisher, servant, guru, companion, wealth, happiness, scripture, abode (vessel), slave. Hence, such a wife should at all times and in all ways be adored and worshipped.

My dear Cūḍālā, you are indeed the supreme among women in this world. Come, embrace me again.

VASIṢṬHA said:

Having said so, Śikhidhvaja again fondly and fervently embraced Cūḍālā.

CŪḌĀLĀ said:

Lord, when I saw that you were performing meaningless austerities, my heart was greatly pained. I relieved myself of that pain by coming here and striving to awaken you. It was indeed for my own joy and delight. I do not deserve any praise for that!

ŚIKHIDHVAJA replied:

From now on may all the wives fulfil their own selfish ends by awakening their husbands' spirit, as you have done!

CŪḌĀLĀ said:

I do not see in you now the petty cravings, thoughts and feelings that tormented you years ago. Pray, tell me, what are you now, in what are you established and what do you see.

ŚIKHIDHVAJA replied:

My dear, I rest in that which you, within me, bring about. I have no attachment. I am like the infinite, indivisible space. I am peace. I have attained that state which is difficult even for the gods like Viṣṇu and Śiva to reach. I am free from confusion and delusion. I experience neither sorrow nor joy. I cannot say "This is" or "The other is". I am freed of all coverings and I enjoy a state of inner well-being. What I am that I am—it is difficult to put into words! You are my guru, my dear: I salute you. By your grace, my beloved, I have crossed this ocean of saṃsāra; I shall not once again fall into error.

CŪḌĀLĀ asked:

In that case, what do you wish to do now?

ŚIKHIDHVAJA answered:

I know no prohibitions nor injunctions. Whatever you do, that I shall know as appropriate. Do what you think appropriate and I shall follow you.

CŪḌĀLĀ said:

Lord, we are now established in the state of liberated ones. To us both desire and its opposite are the same. Of what use is the discipline of prāṇa or the practice of infinite consciousness? Hence, we should be what we are in the beginning, in the middle and in the end and abandon the one thing that remains after this. We are the king and the queen in the beginning, in the middle and in the end. The one thing to be abandoned is delusion! Hence, let us return to the kingdom and provide it with a wise ruler.

ŚIKHIDHVAJA asked:

Then, why should we not accept Indra's invitation to heaven?

CŪḌĀLĀ replied:

O king, I do not desire pleasure nor the glamour of a kingdom. I remain in whatever condition I am placed by my very nature. When the thought 'This is pleasure' is confronted by the thought 'This is not', they both perish. I remain in that peace that survives this.

The two liberated ones then spent the night in conjugal delight.

The Story of Kaca

VI.1:110 VASIṢṬHA continued:

At daybreak the couple arose and performed their morning duties. Cūḍālā materialised by her thought-power a golden vessel containing the sacred waters of the seven oceans. With these waters, she bathed the king and crowned him emperor. She said: "May you be endowed with the lustre of the eight divine protectors of the universe."

In his turn, the king re-established Cūḍālā as his queen. He suggested to her that she should create an army by her thought-power. She did so.

Headed by the royal couple mounted on the most stately elephant, the entire army marched towards their kingdom. On the way, Śikhidhvaja pointed out to Cūḍālā the various places associated with his ascetic life. They soon reached the outskirts of their city where they were given a rousing welcome by the citizens.

Assisted by Cūḍālā, Śikhidhvaja ruled the kingdom for a period of ten thousand years, after which he attained nirvāṇa (liberation, like a lamp without oil) from which there is no rebirth. After enjoying the pleasures of the world because he was the foremost among kings, after having lived for a very long time, he attained the supreme state because in him there was but a little residue of satva. Even so, O Rāma, engage yourself in spontaneous and natural activity, without grief. Arise. Enjoy the pleasures of the world and also final liberation.

Thus have I told you, O Rāma, the story of Śikhidhvaja. Pursuing this path, you will never grieve. Rule as Śikhidhvaja ruled. You will enjoy the pleasures of this world and attain final liberation, too. Even so did Kaca who was the son of Bṛhaspati, the preceptor of the gods.

RĀMA asked:

Lord, please tell me how Kaca, the son of Bṛhaspati, attained enlightenment.

VASIṢṬHA said:

Like Śikhidhvaja, Kaca also attained enlightenment. One day, while he was still young, he was eager to attain liberation from saṃsāra. He went to his father Bṛhaspati, and asked: "Lord, you know everything. Please tell me how can one free oneself from this cage known as saṃsāra."

BṚHASPATI said: VI.1:111

Liberation from this prison-house known as saṃsāra is possible only by total renunciation, my son!

VASIṢṬHA continued:

Hearing this, Kaca went away to the forest, having renounced everything. Bṛhaspati was unaffected by this turn of events. Wise ones remain unaffected by union and separation. After eight years of seclusion and austerity, Kaca happened to meet his father once again and asked him: "Father, I have performed austerities for eight years after renouncing everything; how is it I have not attained the state of supreme peace?"

Bṛhaspati merely repeated his previous commandment, "Renounce everything," and went away. Taking it as a hint, Kaca discarded even the bark with which he covered his body. Thus he continued his austerities for three years. Again he sought the presence of his father and after worshipping him, asked: "Father, I have renounced even the stick and clothes, etc. I have still not gained self-knowledge!"

Bṛhaspati thereupon said: "By 'total' is meant only the mind, for mind is the all. Renunciation of the mind is total renunciation." Having said so, Bṛhaspati vanished from sight. Kaca looked within in an effort to find the mind in order that it might be renounced. However much he searched, he could not find what could be called the mind! Unable to find the mind, he began to think: "The physical substances like the body cannot be regarded as mind. Why, then, do I vainly punish the innocent body? I shall go back to my father and shall enquire into the whereabouts of the terrible enemy known as the mind. Knowing it, I shall renounce it."

Having thus resolved, Kaca sought his father's presence and asked, "Please tell me what the mind is so that I may renounce it." Bṛhaspati replied: "They who know the mind say that the mind is the 'I'. The egosense that arises within you is the mind." "But, that is difficult, if not impossible," said Kaca. Bṛhaspati responded: "On the other hand, it is easier than crushing a flower which is in your hand, easier than closing your eyes! For that which appears to be because of ignorance perishes at the dawn of knowledge. In truth there is no egosense. It seems to exist on account of ignorance and delusion. Where is this egosense, how did it arise, what is it? In all beings at all times there is but the one pure consciousness! Hence, this egosense is but a word. Give it up, my son, and give up self-limitation or psychological conditioning. You are the unconditioned, never conditioned by time, space, etc."

The Story of the Deluded Man

VI.1:112, 113 VASIṢṬHA continued:

Thus instructed in the highest wisdom, Kaca became enlightened. He remained free from egosense and possessiveness. Live like him, O Rāma. The egosense is unreal. Do not trust it and do not abandon it. How can the unreal be grasped or renounced? When the egosense is itself unreal, what are birth and death? You are that subtle and pure consciousness which is indivisible, free from ideation but which encompasses all beings. It is only in the state of ignorance that the world is seen as an illusory appearance; in the vision of the enlightened, all this is seen as Brahman. Abandon the concepts of unity and diversity and remain blissful. Do not behave like the deluded man, and suffer!

RĀMA said:

I derive supreme bliss from your nectarine words. I am now established in the transcendental state. Yet, there is no satiety. Though I am satisfied, again I ask you, for no one will be satisfied with nectar. Who is the deluded man you referred to?

VASIṢṬHA said:

Listen to this humorous story of the deluded man, O Rāma. There is a man who was fashioned by the machinery of delusion. He was born in a desert and grew up in the desert. There arose a deluded notion in him: "I am born of space, I am space, the space is mine. I should therefore protect that space." Having thus decided, he built a house to protect space. Seeing the space safely enclosed in the house he was happy. But in course of time, the house crumbled. He wept aloud, "O my space! Where have you gone? Alas it is lost."

Then he dug a well and felt that the space in it was protected. It, too, was lost in time. One after the other, he built a pot, a pit and also a small grove with four sal trees. Each of them perished after a short time, leaving the deluded man unhappy.

Listen to the meaning of this story, O Rāma. The man fashioned by delusion is the egosense. It arises as motion arises in wind. Its reality is Brahman. Not knowing this, the egosense looks upon space around it as itself and its possession. Thus it identifies itself with the body, etc., which it desires to protect. The body, etc., exist and perish after some time. On account of this delusion, the egosense grieves repeatedly, thinking that the self is dead and lost. When the pot, etc., are lost, the space remains unaffected. Even so, when the bodies are lost, the self remains unaffected. The self is pure consciousness, subtler than even space, O Rāma. It is never destroyed. It is unborn. It does not perish. And it is the infinite Brahman alone that shines as this world-appearance. Knowing this, be happy for ever.

VASIṢṬHA continued: VI.1:114

From the supreme Brahman, the mind first arose with its faculty of thinking and imagination. And this mind remains as such in that Brahman, even as fragrance in a flower, as waves in the ocean and as rays of light in the sun. Brahman, which is extremely subtle and invisible, was forgotten, as it were, and thus arose the wrong notion of the real existence of the world-appearance.

If one thinks that the light rays are different and distinct from the sun, to him the light rays have a distinct reality. If one thinks that a bracelet made of gold is a bracelet, to him it is indeed a bracelet and not gold.

But if one realises that the light rays are non-different from the sun, his understanding is said to be unmodified (nirvikalpa). If one realises that the waves are non-different from the ocean, his understanding is said to be unmodified (nirvikalpa). If one realises that the bracelet is non-different from gold, his understanding is said to be unmodified (nirvikalpa).

He who sees the display of sparks does not realise that it is but fire. His mind experiences joy and sorrow as these sparks fly up and scatter on the ground. If he sees that the sparks are but fire and non-different from it, he sees only fire and his understanding is said to be unmodified (nirvikalpa).

He who is thus established in the nirvikalpa is indeed a great one. His understanding does not diminish. He has attained whatever is worth attaining. His heart does not get enmeshed in the objects. Hence, O Rāma, abandon this perception of diversity or objectification and remain established in consciousness.

Whatever the self contemplates is materialised on account of the inherent power in the consciousness. That materialised thought then shines as if independent! Thus, whatever the mind (which is endowed with the faculty of thought) contemplates materialises instantly. This is the origin of diversity. Hence, this world-appearance is neither real nor unreal. Even as sentient beings create and experience diverse objects in their own day-dreams, this world-appearance is the day-dream of Brahman. When it is realised as Brahman, then the world-appearance is dissolved; for from the absolute point of view this world is non-existent. Brahman remains as Brahman and it does not create something which was not already in existence!

O Rāma, whatever you do, know that it is nothing but pure consciousness. Brahman alone is manifest here as all this, for naught else exists. There is no scope for 'this' and the 'other'. Therefore, abandon even the concepts of liberation and bondage. Remain in the pure, egoless state engaging yourself in natural activity.

The Story of Bhṛṅgīśa

VI.1:115 VASIṢṬHA continued:

Give up all your doubts. Resort to moral courage. Be a supreme doer of actions, supreme enjoyer of delight and supreme renouncer of all! Such a triple discipline was taught in days of yore by lord Śiva to Bhṛṅgīśa by which the latter attained total freedom. Bhṛṅgīśa was a man of ordinary or traditional self-knowledge. He approached lord Śiva and asked: "Lord, I am deluded by this world-appearance. Pray, tell me the attitude equipped with which I shall be freed from this delusion."

LORD ŚIVA replied:

Give up all your doubts. Resort to moral courage. Be a mahābhokttā (great enjoyer of delight), mahākartā (great doer of actions) and mahātyāgī (perfect renouncer).

He is a mahākartā (great doer of actions) who is freed of doubts and performs appropriate actions in natural situations whether they be regarded as dharma (right) or adharma (wrong), without being swayed by likes and dislikes, by success and failure, without egosense or jealousy, remaining with his mind in a state of silence and purity. He is unattached to anything but remains as a witness of everything, without selfish desires or motives, without excitement or exultation but with a mind at peace, without sorrow or grief, indifferent to action and inaction, whose very nature is peace and equilibrium or equanimity which is sustained in all situations (in the birth, existence or annihilation of all things).

He is a mahābhokttā (great enjoyer) who does not hate anything nor long for anything but enjoys all natural experiences, who does not cling to nor renounce anything even while engaged in actions, who does not experience though experiencing, who witnesses the world-play unaffected by it. His heart is not affected by pleasure and pain that arise in the course of life and the changes that cause confusion, and he regards with delight old age and death, sovereignty and poverty and even great calamities and fortunes. His very nature is non-violent and virtuous, and he enjoys what is sweet and what is bitter with equal relish, without making an arbitrary distinction 'This is enjoyable' and 'This is not'.

He is a mahātyāgī (great renouncer) who has banished from his mind concepts like dharma and adharma, pain and pleasure, birth and death, all desires, all doubts, all convictions, who sees the falsity in the experience of pain by his body, mind, etc., who has realised 'I have no body, no birth, no right and no wrong', who has completely abandoned from his heart the notion of world-appearance.

VASIṢṬHA continued:

Thus did lord Śiva instruct Bhṛṅgīśa who then became enlightened. Adopt this attitude, O Rāma, and transcend sorrow.

RĀMA asked: VI.1:116, 117

Lord, you know all the truths. When the egosense is dissolved in the mind, by what signs does one recognise the nature of satva?

VASIṢṬHA said:

Such a mind, O Rāma, is untouched by sins like greed and delusion even under the worst of provocation. Virtues like delight (in the prosperity of others) do not leave the person whose egosense has been dissolved. The knots of mental conditioning and tendencies are cut asunder. Anger is greatly attenuated and delusion becomes ineffective. Desire becomes powerless. Greed flees. The senses function on an even keel, neither getting excited nor depressed. Even if pleasure and pain are reflected on his face, they do not agitate the mind which regards them all as insignificant. The heart rests in equanimity.

The enlightened man who is endowed with all these virtues effortlessly and naturally wears the body. Being and non-being (like prosperity and adversity) when they follow each other creating diverse and even great contradictions, do not generate joy and sorrow in the holy ones.

Woe unto him who does not tread this path to self-knowledge which is within reach if he directs his intelligence properly. The means for crossing this ocean of saṃsāra (world-appearance or the cycle of birth and death) and for the attainment of supreme peace are enquiry into the nature of the self (Who am I?) and of the world (What is this world?) and of the truth (What is truth?).

Your own ancestor, Ikṣvāku, even while he was ruling his kingdom, reflected within himself one day: "What may be the origin of this world which is full of diverse sufferings—old age, death, pain and pleasure and delusion?" He could not arrive at an answer. So, after having duly worshipped his father Manu, the son of Brahmā, he asked him: "Lord, your own will prompts me to place a problem before you. What is the origin of this world? How can I be free from this saṃsāra?"

Manu replied: "What you see here does not exist, my son, none of it! Nor is there anything which is unseen and which is beyond the mind and the senses. There is but the self which is eternal and infinite. What is seen as the universe is but a reflection in that self. On account of the energy inherent in the cosmic consciousness that reflection is seen here as the cosmos and elsewhere as living beings. That is what you call the world. There is neither bondage nor liberation. The one infinite consciousness alone exists, neither one nor many! Abandon all thought of bondage and liberation and rest in peace."

VI.1:118, 119, 120 MANU continued:

It is when pure consciousness gives rise to concepts and notions within itself that it assumes an individuality (jīva). Such individuals wander in this saṃsāra (world-appearance). In an eclipse what was unseen earlier is seen: even so it is possible to perceive through the individual's experiences the pure experiencing which is the infinite consciousness. But this self-knowledge is not gained by study of scriptures or with the help of a guru; it can only be gained by the self for itself.

Regard your body and senses as instruments for experiencing, not as self. The notion 'I am the body' is bondage; the seeker should avoid it. 'I am no-thing but pure consciousness'—such understanding when it is sustained is conducive to liberation. It is only when one does not realise the self which is free from old age, death, etc., that one wails aloud, "Alas, I am dead or I am helpless". It is by such thoughts that ignorance is fortified. Free your mind from such impure thoughts and notions. Rest in the self free from such notions. Though engaged in diverse activities remain established in a state of perfect equilibrium and rule this kingdom in peace and joy.

The Lord sports in this world-appearance and then withdraws it into himself. The power or energy that creates and brings about bondage is also the power or the energy that dissolves creation and liberates. Just as the tree pervades all its parts and leaves, this infinite consciousness pervades the entire universe. Alas, the ignorant person does not realise it though it is in every cell of his being. He who sees that the self alone is all enjoys bliss.

One should gain this understanding through study of scriptures and company of holy ones. This is the first step. Reflection or enquiry is the second. Non-attachment or psychological freedom is the third.

The fourth is snapping of the bonds of vāsanās (conditioning and tendencies). The bliss that is derived from pure awareness is the fifth; in it the liberated sage lives as if in half-sleep. Self-knowledge is the sixth in which the sage is immersed in a mass of bliss and lives as if in deep sleep. The seventh state which is known as turīya (the transcendental) is itself liberation; in it there is perfect equanimity and purity. Beyond this (still the seventh state) is the turīyātīta which is beyond description. The first three states are 'waking' states. The fourth is the dream state. The fifth is the deep sleep state because it is full of bliss. The sixth is the turīya or the non-dual consciousness. The seventh is indescribable. One who has reached this is established in pure being devoid of subject-object division. He is not eager to die nor to live. He is one with all. He is free from individuation.*

MANU continued: VI.1:120, 121, 122

The liberated sage may be one who has formally renounced the world or he may live a householder's life. But knowing 'I do nothing' he grieves not. Knowing that 'I am untouched and my mind is uncoloured and freed from all conditioning, I am pure and infinite consciousness' he grieves not. Freed from notions of 'I' and 'the other' the enlightened one does not grieve. Wherever he is and in whatever society, he knows that all that is is as it is and does not grieve. He knows that all the directions are filled with the radiance of the self, which is eternal. It is indeed on account of ignorant self-limitation that one experiences joy and sorrow in alternating circumstances. When such ignorant self-limitation is either weakened or destroyed, there is neither excitement nor grief. That action which proceeds from such weakened vāsanā or conditioning is non-action whose seeds do not germinate! He performs his actions merely with the limbs of the body, but with his mind and heart at rest in supreme peace.

All other faculties that one acquires perish when not repeatedly used. But this self-knowledge, once acquired, grows day by day.

Individuality (jīvahood) exists only as long as desire for pleasure lasts. Even this desire is born of ignorance! When self-knowledge arises, desire drops away and with it the self abandons the notion of individuality and realises its infinite nature. They who entertain such notions as 'This is mine' and 'I am this' fall into the pit of ignorance; they who have abandoned such notions with their heart and mind ascend higher and higher. Behold the self-luminous self which pervades everything. The very moment that this omnipresence

---

*NOTE: There seems to be some confusion in this paragraph. However, it is clarified in chapter 126 of this section.

of consciousness is realised, one crosses the ocean of saṃsāra.

Know that whatever is done by Brahmā, Viṣṇu, etc., is done by you. Whatever is seen at any time, all that is the self or the infinite consciousness. You are that infinite consciousness. With what can that be compared? You are neither the void nor non-void, neither consciousness nor unconsciousness, neither the self nor another! Rest in this knowledge. There is neither a place called liberation nor another! When the egosense dies, ignorance perishes and that is known as liberation.

He who has attained this self-knowledge goes beyond the caste system and the regulations concerning the orders of life and the scriptural injunctions and prohibitions, even as the lion breaks out of its cage. His actions are not motivated and are non-volitional: hence he is not tainted by their merit. He is beyond praise and censure; he does not worship nor receive worship. He is not agitated by others; he does not agitate others. He alone is fit to be worshipped, glorified and saluted. Not by rites and rituals but by the worship of such sages alone does one attain wisdom.

The Story of Ikṣvāku

VI.1:123, 124 VASIṢṬHA continued:

Thus instructed by Manu, Ikṣvāku attained enlightenment. Adopt such an attitude, O Rāma.

RĀMA asked:

If such be the nature of the enlightened person, what is so extraordinary and wonderful in it?

VASIṢṬHA continued:

On the other hand, what is so extraordinary and wonderful about the attainment of psychic powers like the ability to fly in the air? The nature of the ignorant is the absence of equanimity. The characteristic of the enlightened one is purity of mind and absence of craving. The enlightened one is not characterised by characteristics. He is devoid of confusion and delusion. Saṃsāra has come to an end. And lust, anger, grief, delusion, greed and such disastrous qualities are greatly weakened in him.

The Lord assumes individuality (jīva). The elements arise in the cosmos without any reason whatsoever. The individual which emanated from the Lord experiences the elements (objects) as if they were created by him. Thus do all jīvas arise and function for no obvious reason. But from then on, their own individual actions become the causes for their subsequent experience of pleasure and pain. The limitation of one's own understanding is the cause for the individual's actions.

One's limited understanding and one's own notions are the cause of bondage, and liberation is their absence. Hence abandon all notions (saṅkalpa). If you are attracted by anything here, you are bound; if you are not attracted at all you are free. Whatever you do and whatever you enjoy, you do not really do, nor do you enjoy. Know this and be free.

All these notions exist in the mind. Subdue the mind by the mind. Purify the mind by the mind. Destroy the mind by the mind. Expert washermen wash dirt with dirt. A thorn is removed by another thorn. Poison antidotes poison. The jīva has three forms, the dense, the subtle and the supreme. The physical body is the dense form. The mind with its notions and limitations is the subtle body. Abandon these two and resort to the supreme which is the reality—pure, unmodified consciousness. This is the cosmic being. Remain established in it, having firmly rejected the former two.

RĀMA asked: VI.1:124, 125

Pray, describe the state of turīya which runs through the waking, dream and deep sleep states without being recognised.

VASIṢṬHA continued:

That pure and equanimous state which is devoid of egosense and non-egosense, of the real and the unreal, and which is free is known as turīya (the fourth state). It is the state of the liberated sage. It is the unbroken witness consciousness. It is different from the waking and the dreaming states which are characterised by movement of thought; it is different from the deep sleep state which is characterised by inertia and ignorance. When the egosense is abandoned, there arises the state of perfect equilibrium in which the turīya manifests itself.

I shall narrate a parable, hearing which you will become enlightened even if you are already enlightened! In a certain forest there was a great sage. Seeing this extraordinary sage, a hunter approached him and asked him: "O sage, a deer which had been wounded by my arrow came this way. Tell me which way it went." The sage replied: "We are holy men who dwell in the forest and our nature is peace. We are devoid of egosense. The egosense and the mind which make the activities of the senses possible have come to a rest. I do not know what are known as waking, dream, and deep sleep. I remain established in the turīya. In it there is no object to be seen!" The hunter could not grasp the meaning of the sage's words. He went his way.

Hence, I tell you, O Rāma, there is naught but the turīya. The turīya is unmodified consciousness and that alone exists. Waking, dream and sleep are states of the mind. When they cease, the mind dies. Satva alone remains—which the yogis aspire to reach.

This is the conclusion of all scriptures: there is no avidyā (ignorance) and no Māyā (illusion) in reality; Brahman alone exists. Some call it the void, others pure consciousness, others the Lord; and they argue among themselves. Abandon all these notions. Rest in nirvāṇa without movement of thought, with the mind greatly 'weakened' and the intelligence at peace; rest in the self as if you are deaf, dumb and blind. Inwardly abandon everything; externally engage yourself in appropriate action. The existence of the mind alone is happiness, the existence of the mind alone is unhappiness. By remaining unaware of the mind let all these cease. Remain unaffected by what is attractive and what is unattractive; by just this much of self-effort, this saṃsāra is overcome! By remaining unaware of pleasure and pain and of even that which lies between the two, you rise above sorrow. Just by this little self-effort you attain the infinite.

VI.1:126 RĀMA asked:

How does one tread the seven states of yoga and what are the characteristics of these seven states?

VASIṢṬHA continued:

Man is either world-accepting (pravṛtta) or world-negating (nivṛtta). The former questions, "What is all this liberation? For me this saṃsāra and life in it are better" and engages himself in the performance of his worldly duties. After very many births he gains wisdom. He realises that the activities of the world are a meaningless repetition and does not wish to waste his life in them. He thinks, "What is the meaning of all this? Let me retire from them." He is considered nivṛtta.

"How shall I cultivate dispassion and thus cross this ocean of saṃsāra?" thus he enquires constantly. Day by day this thought itself generates dispassion in him and there arise peace and joy in his heart. He is disinterested in the activities of the marketplace but engages himself in meritorious activities. He is afraid to sin. His speech is appropriate to the occasion, soft, truthful and sweet. He has set his foot on the first yoga-bhūmikā (state of yoga). He is devoted to the service of holy ones. He gathers scriptures whenever and wherever he finds them and studies them. His constant quest is the crossing of the ocean of saṃsāra. He alone is a seeker. Others are selfish.

He then enters the second state of yoga known as vicāra, enquiry. He eagerly resorts to the company of holy ones who are well versed in the scriptures and in spiritual practices. He knows what is to be done and what is not to be done. He abandons evils like vanity, jealousy, delusion and greed. From the preceptors he learns all the secrets of yoga.*

Easily thereafter he graduates to the third state of yoga known as asaṃsaṅga, non-attachment or freedom. He roams the forests in seclusion and strives to quieten the mind. Adherence to the scriptures and to virtuous conduct bestows upon him the faculty of seeing the truth. This non-attachment or freedom is of two types, the ordinary and the superior. One who practises the first type of freedom feels, "I am neither the doer, nor the enjoyer, neither do I afflict others nor am I afflicted by others. All this happens on account of past karma under the aegis of god. I do nothing whether there is pain or pleasure, good fortune or calamity. All these, as also meeting and parting, psychic distress and physical illness, are brought about by time alone." Thus thinking, he investigates the truth. He is practising ordinary non-attachment or freedom.

VASIṢṬHA continued:

By the diligent practice of this yogic method, by resorting to the company of the holy ones and the avoidance of evil company, the truth is clearly revealed. When thus one realises the supreme which is the only essence or truth beyond this ocean of saṃsāra, he realises "I am not the doer but god alone is the doer; not even in the past did I do anything." He abandons vain and meaningless words and remains inwardly and mentally silent. This is superior non-attachment or freedom. He has abandoned all dependency, above and below, within and without, tangible and intangible, sentient and insentient. He shines like supportless and limitless space itself. This is superior freedom. In it he enjoys peace and contentment, virtue and purity, wisdom and self-enquiry.

The first stage of yoga presents itself to one by accidental coincidence, as it were, after one has led a pure life full of virtuous deeds. One who sets his foot on it should cherish it and protect it with great zeal, diligence and effort. Thus he should proceed to the next state, enquiry. By diligently practising enquiry he should ascend to the third state, freedom.

RĀMA asked:

How is it possible for an ignorant person born in a wicked family and who does not enjoy the company of holy ones to cross this ocean of saṃsāra? Also, if one dies while yet in the first or the

---

* NOTE: Of course, vicāra means 'direct observation or looking into'.

second or the third state of yoga, what happens to him?

VASIṢṬHA said:

After very many lives, the ignorant man is awakened by accidental coincidence. Till then he experiences this saṃsāra. When dispassion arises in his heart, then saṃsāra recedes. Even an imperfect practice of this yoga destroys the effects of past sins. If one leaves the body during the practice, he ascends to heaven and is then born in circumstances favourable to the pursuit of his practice. Very soon he ascends the ladder of yoga again.

These three states are known as 'waking state' because in them there is division in consciousness. However, the practitioner becomes an adorable person (ārya). Seeing him, the ignorant are inspired. He who engages himself in righteous actions and avoids evil is adorable (ārya). This adorable holiness is in a seed state in the first state of yoga, it sprouts in the second and attains fruition in the third. One who dies after thus having gained the status of an adorable one (ārya) and who has obviously cultivated noble thoughts, enjoys the delights of heaven for a long time and then he is born as a yogi. By the diligent practice of the first three states of yoga, ignorance is destroyed and the light of wisdom arises in one's heart.

VASIṢṬHA continued:

In the fourth state of yoga, the yogis behold the one in all with a mind that is free from division. Division has ceased and unity is steady, and therefore they behold the world as if it were a dream.

In the fifth state, only the undivided reality remains. Hence it is likened to deep sleep. He who has reached this state, though he is engaged in diverse external activities, rests in himself.

After thus proceeding from one state to another, he reaches the sixth which is the turīya. In this he realises, "I am neither real nor unreal, nor even egoless. I am beyond duality and unity. All doubts are at rest." He remains like a painting of a lamp (hence, though he has not reached nirvāṇa—lamp without fuel—he is like a lamp without fuel as the lamp is only a painted figure). He is void within, void without, void like an empty vessel; at the same time he is full within and full without, like a full vessel immersed in the sea.

They who reach the seventh state are known as "the disembodied liberated beings". Their state is not for words to describe. Yet, they have been described variously.

They who practice these seven states do not come to grief. But there is a terrible elephant roaming in a forest working havoc. If that elephant is killed, then man attains success in all these seven states, not otherwise. Desire is that elephant. It roams in the forest known as the body. It is maddened by sensuousness. It is restless with conditioning and tendencies (vāsanā). This elephant destroys everybody in this world. It is known by different names—desire, vāsanā (tendency or mental conditioning), mind, thought, feeling, attachment, etc. It should be slain by the weapon known as courage or determination born of the realisation of oneness.

Only as long as one believes in objective existence does desire arise! This alone is saṃsāra: the feeling 'This is'. Its cessation is liberation (mokṣa). This is the essence of jñāna or wisdom. Recognition of 'objects' gives rise to desire. Non-recognition of objects ends desire. When desire ends, the jīva drops its self-limitation. The great man therefore abandons all thoughts concerning what has been experienced and what has not been experienced. I declare with uplifted arms that the thought-free, notion-less state is the best. It is infinitely superior to the sovereignty of the world. Non-thinking is known as yoga. Remaining in that state, perform appropriate actions or do nothing! As long as thoughts of 'I' and 'mine' persist, sorrow does not cease. When such thoughts cease, sorrow ceases. Knowing this, do as you please.*

VĀLMĪKI said to Bharadvāja: VI.1:127

Having heard this quintessence of the highest wisdom and having been overwhelmed by śakti-pāta, Rāma remained immersed in the ocean of bliss for a while. He had ceased to ask questions, request answers and endeavour to understand them. He had become established in the highest state of self-knowledge.

BHARADVĀJA asked:

O preceptor! It is indeed a delight to hear that thus Rāma attained the supreme state. But how is it possible for us who are foolish and ignorant and who are of sinful disposition to attain that state which is difficult even for gods like Brahmā to reach?

VĀLMĪKI said:

I have narrated to you in full the dialogue between Rāma and Vasiṣṭha. Consider it well. For that is also my instruction to you.

There is no division in consciousness which can be called the world. Rid yourself of the notion of division by the practice of the secrets revealed to you. Both waking and sleep states are parts of this creation. Enlightenment is characterised by the pure inner light. This creation emerges from nothing, it dissolves in nothing, its

---

*NOTE: For the words 'thinking' and 'non-thinking' in this paragraph, the text uses the words 'samvedanam' and 'asamvedanam' which imply much more than mere thinking. Cognition, comprehension, feeling, experience and knowledge are also implied by 'samvedanam'.

very nature is void, it does not exist. On account of beginningless and false self-limitation this creation appears to exist, creating countless confusions. You are deluded because you do not recollect repeatedly and frequently the truth concerning the infinite consciousness, but you partake of the poison of self-limitation and the consequent psychological conditioning.

This delusion continues till you reach the feet of the enlightened sages and gain the right knowledge from them. Dear one, that which did not exist in the beginning and will not exist in the end does not exist even now. This world-appearance is like a dream. The sole reality in which it appears and disappears is the infinite consciousness. In the ocean of saṃsāra or ignorance there arises the notion of 'I', on account of the beginningless potential of self-limitation. Thereupon, the movement of thought generates other notions like 'mineness', 'attraction' and 'repulsion', etc. Once these notions strike root in one's consciousness, one inevitably falls a prey to endless calamities and sorrow.

Dive deep into the inner peace, not into the sea of diversity. Who lives, who is dead, who has come—why do you get lost in such false notions? When the one self alone is the reality, where is room for 'another'? The theory that Brahman appears as the world (just as rope appears as snake) is meant only for the entertainment of the childish and ignorant. The enlightened ones rest for ever in the truth which does not even appear to be different.

VĀLMĪKI continued:

Ignorant people who dislike seclusion are sunk in sorrow and occasionally they may smile. The knowers of the truth on the other hand are happy and smiling at all times. The truth or the self is subtle and hence it appears to be veiled by ignorance. But even if you believe in the atomic substantiality of the world, the self does not go away. Why then do you grieve? The unreal (ignorance, etc.) does not come into being at any time, nor does the reality or the self ever cease to be.

However, on account of various reasons, confusion arises. In order to overcome this, worship the Lord who is the preceptor of the whole universe. Your evil karmas have not fallen away from you; but they have become the noose with which you are bound. Till your mind becomes no-mind (satva), adopt the adoration of name and form. After that you will be established in the contemplation of the absolute. Then behold, even for an instant, the inner self with the self, in the inner light.

The supreme is attained by one who through self-effort and right actions has earned the grace of the Lord. Past habits and tendencies are very strong. Hence mere self-effort is inadequate. Even the gods are unable to defy the inevitable (fate). Everyone is subject to this world order (niyati) which is beyond thought and expression.

But the spiritual hero should firmly believe that even after several incarnations, enlightenment is certain. By evil actions one is bound to this saṃsāra and by right actions one is liberated! By the present right action the effects of past evil actions are weakened. If you surrender all your actions to Brahman, you will never again whirl on this wheel of saṃsāra.

Behold, ignorant people in this world are made to play different roles in this world by the director, Time! Time creates, preserves and destroys. Why do you become agitated by the loss of wealth, etc., and why do you yourself begin to dance? Be still and witness this cosmic dance! They who are devoted to the gods, to the holy brāhmaṇas and to the guru, and who adhere to the tenets of the scriptures, earn the grace of the supreme Lord.

BHARADVĀJA said:

Lord, I have known all that there is to be known. I know that there is no greater friend than dispassion (vairāgya) and no greater enemy than saṃsāra. I wish to hear from you the very essence of the teachings of the holy sage Vasiṣṭha.

VĀLMĪKI replied:

O Bharadvāja, listen to what I am going to say. By merely listening to it you will never again drown in this saṃsāra.

VĀLMĪKI continued: VI.1:128

One should be at peace within with the mind under control, having abandoned forbidden and selfish actions and also pleasures which arise from sense-contacts. One should endow oneself with faith. He should then sit on a soft seat in a comfortable posture conducive to equilibrium. He should then restrain the activities of the mind and the senses. He should then repeat OM till the mind gains perfect peace.

Then do prāṇāyāma for the purification of the mind, etc. Gently and gradually withdraw the senses from their contact with the external objects. Investigate that method by which you know the source of the body, the senses, the mind, and the buddhi (intelligence) and let them return to their source. First rest in the cosmic manifest being (virāṭ). After this rest in the unmanifest and then in the supreme cause of all.

This is how all these factors return to their source. The physical body (the flesh, etc.) is earthy, so returns to the earth. Blood, etc., are liquid and they return to water-element. The fire (heat) and the light in the body belong to the fire-element, they return to it.

The air is offered to the cosmic air. Space merges in space.

Similarly, the senses return to their source: the sense of hearing to space, the sense of touch to air, the sense of sight to the sun, the sense of taste to water. The life-breath is returned to air, the power of speech to fire, the hands to Indra, the power of locomotion to Viṣṇu, the reproductive organ to Kaśyapa, the excretory organ to Mitra, the mind to the moon and the buddhi to Brahman—for these are the deities presiding over the respective organs which were not created by oneself (the 'I'). Thus having returned them all to their source, see yourself as the cosmic being (virāṭ). The Lord who as hermaphrodite (consciousness-energy) dwells in the heart of the universe is its support.

In this universe earth, water, fire, air and space are each of them twice the magnitude of the preceding one. Dissolve the earth in water, water in fire, fire in air and air in space. Space should be merged in the cosmic space which is the cause for all. Remaining there for an instant in his subtle body, the yogi should feel that 'I am the self of all', having abandoned all self-limitation. That in which this universe rests and which is devoid of name and form is known as prakṛti (nature) by some, as Māyā (illusion) by others and as sub-atom by others. It is also known as avidyā (ignorance). All of them are confused by polemics. In this, all things exist in their unmanifest state, without any relationship among them. They arise from it and exist as such during the world-cycle. Ether, air, fire, water and earth: this is the order of creation. Dissolution takes place in the reverse order. By the abandonment of the three states (waking, dream and sleep) the turīya is attained. In meditation even the subtle body is merged in the supreme.

BHARADVĀJA said:

Lord, I am now free from the subtle body and I am swimming in the ocean of bliss. I am the indivisible self which is the supreme self and which itself possesses the two powers of consciousness and unconsciousness. Just as fire thrown into fire becomes indistinguishably fire, just as straw, etc., which are thrown into the sea become salt, this insentient world when it is offered into the infinite consciousness becomes one with it. Just as a salt doll thrown into the sea abandons its name and form and becomes one with the ocean, just as water mixes with water and ghee mixes with ghee, even so I have entered into this infinite consciousness.

'I am that supreme Brahman which is eternal, omnipresent, pure, peaceful, indivisible and free from motion, which is devoid of gathering and scattering but whose thoughts materialise, which is free from merit and demerit, which is the source of this universe, and which is the supreme light, one without a second'. Thus should one contemplate. Thus does the mind cease to be agitated. When the movement of the mind has ceased the self shines by its own light. In that light all sorrow comes to an end and there is the bliss which the self experiences in itself. There is direct awareness of the truth, 'There is none but the self'.

VĀLMĪKI said:

Dear friend, if you wish that this delusion known as saṃsāra should come to an end, then give up all actions and become a lover of Brahman.

BHARADVĀJA said:

O guru, your enlightening discourse has completely awakened me, my intelligence is pure and the world-appearance does not stretch out in front of me. I wish to know what the men of self-knowledge do. Do they have any duties or none at all?

VĀLMĪKI said:

They who desire liberation should engage themselves only in such actions which are free from defects and desist from selfish and sinful actions. When the qualities of the mind are abandoned, it takes on the qualities of the infinite. The jīva is liberated when one contemplates, 'I am that which is beyond the body, mind and senses', when one is free from notions of 'I am the doer' and 'I am the enjoyer' as also from notions of pain and pleasure, when one realises that all beings are in the self and the self is in all beings, when one abandons the waking, dream and deep sleep states and remains in the transcendental consciousness. That is the state of bliss which is infinite consciousness. Immerse yourself in that ocean of nectar which is full of peace; do not drown in diversity.

Thus have I narrated to you the discourse of the sage Vasiṣṭha. Steady your mind by practice. Tread the path of wisdom and of yoga. You will realise everything.

VĀLMĪKI continued:

Seeing that Rāma had become totally absorbed in the self, Viśvāmitra said to the sage Vasiṣṭha: "O son of the Creator, O holy one, you are indeed great. You have proved that you are the guru by this śakti-pāta (direct transmission of spiritual energy). He is a guru who is able to give rise to god-consciousness in the disciple by a look, by a touch, by verbal communication or by grace. However, the intelligence of the disciple is awakened when the disciple has rid himself of threefold impurities and thereby acquired a keen intellect. But, O sage, please bring Rāma back to body-consciousness for he has still many things to do for the welfare of the three worlds and of myself."

All the assembled sages and others bowed to Rāma. Then Vasiṣṭha said to Viśvāmitra: "Pray, tell them who Rāma is in truth." Viśvāmitra said to them: "Rāma is the supreme personality of godhead. He is the creator, protector and redeemer. He is the Lord and the friend of all. He is manifest variously, sometimes as a fully enlightened being, sometimes as if ignorant. In truth, he is the god of gods and all the gods are but his part-manifestations. Blessed is this king Daśaratha whose son is lord Rāma himself. Blessed is Rāvaṇa whose head will fall at the hands of Rāma. O sage Vasiṣṭha, kindly bring him back to body-consciousness."

Vasiṣṭha said to Rāma: "O Rāma, this is not the time to rest! Get up and bring joy to the world. When people are still in bondage, it is not proper for the yogi to merge in the self." Rāma remained oblivious of these words. Vasiṣṭha thereupon entered the heart of Rāma through the latter's suṣumnā-nāḍī. There was movement of prāṇa in Rāma and the mind began to function. The jīva which is of the form of inner light shed its lustre on all the nāḍīs of the body. Rāma slightly opened his eyes and beheld Vasiṣṭha in front of him. Rāma said to Vasiṣṭha: "There is nothing I should do or should not do. However, your words should always be honoured." Saying so, Rāma placed his head at the sage's feet and then proclaimed: "Listen all of you! There is nothing superior to self-knowledge, nothing superior to the guru."

All the assembled sages and celestials showered flowers on Rāma and blessed him. They departed from the assembly.

Thus have I told you the story of Rāma, O Bharadvāja. By the practice of this yoga, attain supreme bliss. He who constantly listens to this dialogue between Rāma and Vasiṣṭha is liberated, whatever be the circumstances of his life, and attains knowledge of Brahman.

VI.2:1 RĀMA asked:

When one abandons action and the will to perform actions, the body falls away. How then it is possible for a living being to live in such a state?

VASIṢṬHA replied:

The abandonment of mental conditioning and notions is appropriate only to the living creature, not to one that is dead. What is kalpanā (notion or mental activity)? It is only the egosense. When that is realised to be void there is abandonment of the egosense. The notion created within oneself by the external object is known as kalpanā. When that notion takes on the characteristic of void or space, there is the abandonment of the notion. Memory is kalpanā. Hence the wise say that non-remembering is the best. Memory encompasses that which has been experienced as well as that which has not been experienced. Abandon 'remembering' what has been experienced and what has not been experienced and remain established in the self, like a baby who is half-awake.

Even as the potter's wheel keeps revolving on account of past momentum, continue to live and act here without entertaining any notions, without the operation of the mind which has now been transformed into pure satva. I declare with uplifted arms: "The abandonment of notions is the supreme good." Why do people not listen? How powerful is delusion! Under its influence one who holds the precious gem of vicāra (self-enquiry) on his palm does not abandon his delusion. This alone is one's supreme good: the non-perception of objects and the non-arising of notions. This should be experienced.

If you rest peacefully in your own self, you will know that in comparison even the state of an emperor is like a blade of grass. When one has made up his mind to go to a certain place, his feet function without any mental activity. Function like those feet, and perform action here. Act here after abandoning desire for reward or the fruits of actions, without the motivation of pleasure or profit. Then the objects of the senses will be devoid of attraction but will be what they are. Even when sensation of pleasure arises on contact with the objects let it lead you inward to the self. Do not long for the fruits of action; do not be inactive either. Or, be devoted to both or neither, as it might happen. For, it is the will to do or not to do that binds, and its absence is liberation. There is in fact neither a must nor a must-not: all this is pure being. Let your intelligence not recognise any of these. Remain forever what you are in truth. The awareness of 'I' and 'mine' is the root of sorrow; its cessation is emancipation. Do what appeals to you.

VASIṢṬHA continued: VI.2:2

Just as an army fashioned with clay is nothing but clay figurines, the entire universe is pure self and non-dual. Since this non-dual self alone exists, what is object and by whom is it perceived? Apart from that supreme self there is nothing which can be referred to as 'I' or as 'mine'.

RĀMA said:

If that is so, Lord, why should evil action be abandoned and why should one be devoted to good action?

VASIṢṬHA said:

But, first tell me, O Rāma, what is action. How does action arise, what is its root and how is that root to be destroyed?

RĀMA said:

Surely, Lord, that which has to be destroyed must be completely uprooted and its very roots destroyed. As long as the body lasts, there is action. It is rooted in this saṃsāra, world-appearance. In that body, actions spring from the limbs (organs of action). Vāsanā or mental habit is the seed for the organs of action. This mental habit functioning through the senses is capable of comprehending that which is at a great distance. These senses themselves are rooted in the mind, the mind is rooted in the jīva which is conditioned consciousness, and this in turn is rooted in the unconditioned which is therefore the root of all. Brahman is the root of this unconditioned and Brahman has no roots. Thus all actions are based on consciousness which objectifies itself and thus generates actions. If this does not happen, that itself is the supreme state.

VASIṢṬHA said:

In that case, O Rāma, what is to be done and what is to be abandoned? The mind continues to exist as long as the body continues to live, whether the embodied person is enlightened or ignorant. How can one abandon what is known as the jīvahood (individuality)? But one should abandon that wrong notion of 'I do' and be engaged in the performance of appropriate action. On the awakening of the inner intelligence the world-perception ceases and there arises psychological freedom or non-attachment. That is known as emancipation. When the objective or conditioned perception is abandoned, there is peace which is known as Brahman. Perception or awareness of objects is known as action which expands into this saṃsāra or world-appearance; cessation of such awareness is known as emancipation. Therefore, O Rāma, abandonment of action is inappropriate as long as the body lives. Such abandonment gives action a value; that which is valued cannot be abandoned.

VI.2:3 RĀMA asked:

Since that which is cannot cease to be and since what is not cannot exist, how can awareness (experience) be made non-awareness or non-experience?

VASIṢṬHA replied:

It is true that that which is ceases not and that which is not does not exist. Experience and non-experience are also that simple and easy of accomplishment. For the word 'experience' and what is indicated by it are born of falsehood or delusion. Hence, they give rise to sorrow. Abandon this awareness of 'experience' and remain established in the awareness of the highest wisdom. The latter is nirvāṇa.

Good and evil actions cease when it is realised that they do not exist in reality. Hence, one should enquire into the root of action till that root is destroyed. For just as everything that springs from the earth is non-different from the earth, even so all that arises out of consciousness is non-different from consciousness. Liquidity is non-different from liquid; in the same way, in Brahman there is no division even between the mind and consciousness. The activity known as awareness arises without a cause in that consciousness; hence it is as good as non-existent, being non-different from consciousness.

Action is rooted in the body which is rooted in the egosense. If the apprehension of the egosense is abandoned, it ceases. Thus is the root of action destroyed. They in whom action has thus ceased are eager neither to renounce nor to possess. They remain established in what is and their actions are spontaneous; in fact, they do nothing. As objects borne down by a flood move non-volitionally, they work merely with their organs of action. When the mind abandons its conditioning, the objects lose their temptation.

Such an understanding or awakening of intelligence alone is the abandonment of action. What is the use of 'doing' or of 'desisting'? It is the cessation of the awareness of action and of experience, the giving up of conditioning and thus the attainment of peace and the state of equilibrium that is known by the expression 'abandonment of action'. When non-abandonment (or false abandonment) is mistaken for abandonment, the deluded ones who are like ignorant animals are possessed by the goblin of abandonment of activity. For they who have rightly understood the truth concerning abandonment of action have nothing whatsoever to do with activity nor with inactivity. They enjoy supreme peace whether they live in their house or in a forest. To the peaceful a house is like a forest and to the restless even a forest is like a crowded city. To one who is at peace, the entire world is a peaceful forest. To one who is restless with a thousand thoughts, it is an ocean of sorrow.

VASIṢṬHA continued: VI.2:4

O Rāma, when the egosense is quieted the world-appearance vanishes. There is then spontaneous abandonment of objective perception, even as a lamp without fuel goes out. Renunciation is not of activity. True renunciation is based on understanding. When the lamp of understanding is not fed with the fuel of the egosense and possessiveness, what remains is self-knowledge. One who has not thus abandoned the egosense and mine-ness knows neither renunciation nor wisdom nor peace. One can easily give up the notion of I-ness by replacing it with the understanding 'The egosense is not', without any hindrance. Where is the need to doubt this?

All these notions like 'I am this' and 'I am not this' are not independent of consciousness. Consciousness is like space, a void. How can delusion exist in it? Hence, there is neither delusion nor the deluded, neither confusion nor the confused. All these seem to arise because one does not clearly perceive the truth. See this. Remain at peace in silence. This is nirvāṇa.

The very thing with which you entertain the notion of egosense enables you in the twinkling of an eye to realise the non-existence of the egosense. Then you will go beyond this ocean of saṃsāra. He attains the highest state who is able thus to conquer his own nature. He is a hero. He who is able to overcome the six enemies (lust, anger, greed, etc.) is a great man; others are donkeys in human garb. He who is able to overcome the notions that arise in the mind is a man (puruṣa). He is a man of wisdom.

As and when the perception of an object arises within you, meet it with the understanding 'I am not this'. Such ignorant perception will immediately cease. In fact, there is nothing to be known in all this: there is need only to get rid of confusion or deluded understanding. If this delusion is not repeatedly revived, it ceases to be. Whatever notion arises in you, even as movement arises in wind, realise that 'I am not this' and thus deprive it of support.

He who has not gained a victory over greed, shame, vanity and delusion derives no benefit by reading this scripture: it is a useless waste of time.

The egosense arises in the self just as movement arises in wind. Hence it is non-different from the self. The egosense seems to shine on account of the self which is the reality or the substratum. The self does not arise at any time nor does it set. There is nothing other than the self. Hence how can one say that it is or that it is not? The supreme self is in the supreme self, the infinite in the infinite, the peace in peace. That is all there is—neither 'I' nor 'the world' nor 'the mind'.

VI.2:4, 5 VASIṢṬHA continued:

Nirvāṇa (emancipation) is nirvāṇa. In peace there is peace. In the divine there is divinity. Nirvāṇa (emancipation) is also anirvāṇa (non-emancipation) associated with space, and also not so associated. When the right understanding concerning the unreality of the egosense arises, there is no difficulty in enduring attacks with weapons or illness, etc. For when the seed for the world-appearance (which is the egosense) has been destroyed the world-appearance goes with it. Even as the mirror gets misted by moisture, the self is veiled by the unreal egosense. This egosense gives rise to all the rest of this world-appearance. When it goes, then the self shines by its own light, even as the sun shines when the veiling cloud is blown away. Just as an object thrown into the ocean dissolves in the ocean, the egosense which enters the self is dissolved in it.

As long as the egosense lasts, the same Brahman or the infinite consciousness shines as the diverse objects with different names. When the egosense is quieted, then Brahman shines as the pure infinite consciousness. The egosense is the seed for this universe. When that is fried, there is no sense in words like 'world', 'bondage' or 'egosense'. When the pot is broken only the clay remains: when the egosense goes, diversity is dissolved. Just as the objects of the world are perceived when the sun rises, the diversity of world-appearance arises with the rising of the egosense. O Rāma, I do not see any alternative to self-knowledge which is the realisation of the unreality of the egosense. Nothing else can ensure your true welfare. Hence, first abandon the individualised egosense and behold your self as the entire universe. Then realise that the entire universe is the self or Brahman and naught else. Be free from all agitation caused by world-notions.

He who has not conquered this egosense does not reach the supreme state. However, if his heart is pure then instruction concerning spiritual understanding is able to penetrate it like a drop of oil on clean cloth. In this connection I shall narrate to you an ancient legend. Long, long ago I questioned Bhuśuṇḍa: "Whom do you regard as ignorant and deluded in this world?"

BHUŚUṆḌA replied:

There was a celestial who lived on a hill-top. He was ignorant and devoted to sense-pleasure, but he had adopted such a righteous life-style as would ensure a very long life. After a very long time, the understanding arose in him that he should attain that state in which there was no birth nor death. Having thus made up his mind, he came to me. Having duly worshipped me, the celestial asked me: "These senses, O Lord, are constantly agitated with craving for gratification and they are the source of endless pain and suffering. I have realised this and hence I take refuge in your feet."

THE CELESTIAL continued: VI.2:6

Please tell me of that which is limitless and which is free from growth and decay and which is pure and beginningless and endless. For up to this time I have been asleep, as it were, and now by the grace of the self I have been awakened. Kindly save me from this terrible fire of delusion.

Beings are born and they die after being worn out here: all this is neither for dharma nor for emancipation. There does not seem to be an end to this wandering in delusion. The pleasure-centres in this world only intensify this delusion and are ever changing. I do not delight in them. I have seen and enjoyed all the pleasures of the heaven. The desire for such enjoyment has been reduced to ashes by the fire of discrimination now. I clearly understand the havoc caused by the senses of sight, hearing, smelling, tasting and touch. What shall I do with these repetitive enjoyments? Even after a thousand years of their enjoyment, no one is really satisfied. Even if one enjoys the sovereignty of the world with all the pleasures that come with it, what is so extraordinary about it? For all these are subject to destruction and death. Pray, tell me, what there is to gain from which I shall attain eternal satisfaction.

I have now clearly understood the poisonous nature of these sense-experiences which only intensify my suffering here. He alone is the real hero in this world who is determined to give battle to this formidable army known as one's senses. This army is commanded by the egosense. It is endowed with horses known as sense-experiences. It has completely encircled the city known as this body. Even the holy ones have to battle with these senses. Only they who come out victorious in this are truly great; the others are fleshy automatons (machines).

There is no remedy for the disease known as sense-craving other than the firm abandonment of desire for pleasure: no medicines, no pilgrimage, no mantras are of any use. I have been waylaid by these senses as robbers waylay a lone traveller in a dense forest. These senses are filthy and they lead to great misfortune. They generate greed. They are difficult to overcome. They bring about rebirth. They are the enemies of the men of wisdom and the friends of the foolish. They are resorted to by the fallen ones and they are shunned by the noble men. They roam about freely in the darkness of ignorance like goblins. They are empty and valueless and like dry bamboo, fit only to be burnt.

Lord, you are the sole refuge of the supplicant. You are his redeemer. Pray, save me from this terrible ocean of saṃsāra by your enlightening admonitions. Devotion to sages like you in this world is the surest destroyer of sorrow.

VI.2:7, 8 BHUŚUṆḌA replied:

You are indeed blessed, O celestial, that you are spiritually awake and you wish to uplift yourself. Your intelligence is fully awakened. Hence I feel that you will understand my instruction effortlessly. Please listen to what I am about to say. What I say is born of long experience.

What appears to us as 'I' and 'the other' is in truth not your self. For when you look for these you cannot see them. The conviction that neither 'I' nor 'you' nor 'the world' exists is conducive to happiness, not to sorrow. The origin of ignorance cannot be determined. Even after considerable enquiry we are unable to determine whether the world-appearance arises from ignorance, or ignorance is born of the world-appearance. The two are in fact two aspects of the same thing. Whatever exists is the one infinite consciousness or Brahman; the world-appearance is like a mirage, of which it can be said 'It is' and 'It is not'.

The seed for this world-appearance is the egosense, for this tree of world-appearance grows from the egosense. The senses and their objects, the various forms of conditioning, heaven and earth with its mountains, oceans, etc., the divisions of time and all the names and forms are different parts of this tree of world-appearance.

When that seed is burnt it gives rise to nothing. How is this seed burnt? When you enquire into the nature of the egosense, you realise that it is not to be seen. This is knowledge. By this fire of knowledge is the egosense burnt. By entertaining the notion of egosense, it appears to be and to give rise to the world-appearance. When this false notion is abandoned, the egosense disappears and self-knowledge arises.

In the very beginning of this world-appearance the egosense did not exist as a reality. Then how can we believe in the existence of the egosense, in the reality of 'I' and 'you' and in duality or non-duality? They who seriously and earnestly strive to realise the truth, after having duly received it from the lips of a preceptor and having studied it in the scriptures, easily attain this self-knowledge.

What appears to be the world is the expansion of one's own notions or thoughts (saṅkalpa). It is based on consciousness. It is an optical illusion which has consciousness for its substratum. Hence, it is regarded as both real and unreal. In the bracelet, gold is the truth and bracelet is but an idea or notion. Thus, both the appearance and disappearance of this world-illusion are but the modifications of the idea. He who has realised this is disinterested in the delights of this world or heaven: this is his last incarnation.

BHUŚUṆḌA continued: VI.2:9, 10

O celestial, give up thinking of the objects of this world-appearance as being the manifestation of the infinite consciousness. Remain in the pure self. Inertia arises in consciousness because of its own manifestation, though such inertia seems to be dissimilar to consciousness. Just as the same wind that fans the fire can also put it out, the same consciousness promotes consciousness as well as inertia. Hence, let your consciousness or your awakened intelligence realise that the egosense ('I') is not, and then be what you are. Then your consciousness merges in consciousness absolute, without giving rise to the object of consciousness: that is Brahman which is incomparable.

The whole universe is filled with this infinite and undivided consciousness. Realise this and do as you please. It is only when the eyes are blinded by ignorance that one perceives the world of diversity. But in truth all these diverse objects are as real as a tree seen in space by one with defective vision.

This inert universe is non-different from the infinite consciousness, even as fire reflected in water is non-different from it. Even so there is no real distinction between knowledge and ignorance. Since Brahman is endowed with infinite potencies, inertia or unconsciousness manifests in consciousness. This inertia exists as a potentiality in Brahman even as future waves and ripples exist on the calm surface of water. Water has no motivation to throw up ripples. Nor does Brahman have any motive in 'creating' the world. Hence, it is right to say that, in the absence of a valid cause, creation has not taken place. It is but an appearance like the mirage. Brahman alone exists. Brahman is peace and uncreated; nor does Brahman create anything.

O celestial, you are that Brahman which is homogeneous and undivided and indivisible, like space. You are a knower. Whether you know something or do not, remain free from doubt. When you realise that you are the unborn, infinite consciousness, then all ignorance and foolishness cease and this world-appearance ceases. Wherever the supreme Brahman exists (and it is infinite and exists everywhere) there arises this world-appearance. In a blade of grass, wood, water and in all things in the universe the same Brahman, the infinite consciousness, exists. The nature of Brahman is indescribable and indefinable. In it there is no other and hence it is incomparable. Hence, it is inappropriate even to talk of the nature of Brahman. That which is experienced when this egosense ceases is the same Brahman which is attained by one in whom the egosense prevails when that one enquires into the nature of the egosense. It thereupon dissolves in consciousness.

VI.2:11, 12 BHUŚUṆḌA continued:

He in whom the contact of sharp weapons and the contact of a naked woman produce the same experience—he is established in the supreme state. One should diligently engage oneself in spiritual practice until one reaches the state in which one's contact with the objects provokes the same reaction that it would if one were asleep. The knower of the self is totally unaffected by mental illness or psychological distress.

Just as poison, when swallowed by one, produces physical ailment without losing its identity as poison, the self becomes the jīva without abandoning its nature as the self or undivided consciousness. Even so, consciousness takes on the nature of unconsciousness or inertia.

Something seems to have arisen in Brahman though it is in fact non-different from Brahman. Poison, without ceasing to be poison, becomes poisonous in the body. In the same way the self is neither born nor does it die—and from another point of view it comes into being and dies.

Only when one's intelligence does not get drowned in objective perception is one able to cross this ocean of saṃsāra as if it were the footprint of a calf—it is not achieved with the help of god or by other means. In the self which is omnipresent and which dwells in all, how can the mind or the egosense arise at all? There is neither good nor evil anywhere to anyone at any time, there is neither pleasure nor pain, neither adversity nor prosperity. No one is the doer and no one is the enjoyer of anything.

To say that the egosense has arisen in the self is like saying that space (distance) has been brought into being in space. The egosense is but a delusion, and unreal. In space there is only spatiality; even so, consciousness alone exists in consciousness. That which is called the egosense ('I')—I am neither that nor not that. This consciousness exists like a mountain within every atom because it is extremely subtle. This extremely subtle consciousness entertains notions of 'I' and 'this' and these notions appear to exist as the respective substances. Even as a whirlpool, etc., are but notional forms of water, the egosense and space, etc., are notions that arise in consciousness. The cessation of such notions is known as cosmic dissolution. Thus all these worlds, etc., come into being and cease to be as notions and nothing more. Consciousness does not undergo any change in all these. In consciousness there is no experience of pleasure or pain, nor does a notion arise in it as 'This I am'. Consciousness does not entertain qualities like courage, pleasure, prosperity, fear, memory, fame or resplendence. They are not perceived in the self any more than the feet of a snake are perceived in darkness.

BHUŚUṆḌA continued:

There is a shower of nectar from Brahman and this is considered creation. However, since time and space do not exist in reality, such creation is unreal and what appears to be is non-different from the Lord. Just as it is water that appears as a whirlpool and just as smoke seen from a distance has the appearance of a cloud, even so when consciousness becomes aware of itself, thus giving rise to a notion (which is inert), between the two (consciousness and notion) there arises the third factor which is known as creation. This creation is but an appearance, like a plantain tree reflected in a pillar or crystal. But when rightly investigated this notion of reality in the unreal appearance vanishes.

This world-appearance is like an empire painted on a canvas. Just as the canvas is made attractive by the use of different colours, this world-appearance seems to be attractive with diverse sense-experiences. This appearance is dependent upon the seer, the ego-sense, which itself is unreal. Hence, it is non-different from the supreme self, even as liquidity is inseparable from water.

The light of consciousness is the self. It is when the notion of 'I' arises in it that this creation comes into being. Other than this notion, there is neither a creation nor a creator. Motion being the inherent nature of water, there is no flow of water in relation to itself (it is as it is—flowing water). Even so, consciousness is vast and stable like space and is therefore not aware of a space within itself. When the same water is seen at a different time and place, the notion of motion arises. Even so, the awareness that arises in consciousness in conjunction with the notions of time and space gives rise to the notion of creation. (Though in fact, since time and space are unreal, such creation is impossible and the comparison of consciousness with water is inadequate.) Know that all that you experience in the name of mind, egosense, intellect, etc., is nothing but ignorance. This ignorance vanishes through self-effort. Half of this ignorance is dispelled by the company of the holy ones, one-fourth of it is destroyed by the study of scriptures and the other one-fourth by self-effort.

(In response to Rāma's question,) VASIṢṬHA explained:

One should resort to the company of the wise and in their company one should examine the truth concerning this creation. One should diligently search for the holy one and adore him. For the very moment such a holy one is found, half the ignorance ceases in his company. Another one-fourth is dispelled by the study of scripture and the last part by self-effort. The company of the holy one puts an end to craving for pleasure; and when it is firmly rejected by self-effort, ignorance ceases. All these may happen together or one after the other.

VI.2:13 BHUŚUṆḌA continued:

A mansion visualised in space does not need the support of real pillars. Even so, the imaginary or illusory world-appearance does not depend upon real time and space. Time, space and world-appearance are all but notional. This world-appearance is extremely subtle and it is built merely by mental activity or the movement of thought: it is like scent in the air. However, unlike such scent in the air this world-appearance is experienced only by the mind that conceives it, whereas scent can be experienced by others also. Just as one's dream is experienced only by the dreamer, this creation is experienced only by the one in whose mind it arises.

In this connnection there is an ancient legend which tells how Indra, the king of the gods, hid himself within the bowels of a subatomic particle.

Somewhere at some time some kind of an imaginary wish-fulfulling tree existed. On one of its branches there appeared a fruit which is this universe. This fruit was unique and completely different from all other fruits. Like worms within this fruit dwelt all types of beings—gods, demons, etc. It contained the earth as well as the heaven and the netherworlds. It was enormous in size because it was a manifestation of the infinite consciousness and it was attractive because it contained in itself the infinite potentialities of diverse experiences. It was radiant with intelligence and in its core was the egosense. In it were all kinds of beings—from the dullest and the ignorant to the one that was closest to enlightenment.

Indra, the king of the gods, was also in that fruit. Once when the lord Viṣṇu and others had retired, this Indra was assailed by powerful demons. Pursued by these demons, Indra ran in the ten directions. He was eventually overcome by the demons. When the attention of the demons was distracted for a moment, Indra, taking advantage of the situation, assumed a subtle and minute form (by abandoning the notion that he was huge and by entertaining the notion that he was subtle and minute) and entered into a subatomic particle.

In it he found rest and peace. He forgot the war with the demons. In it he visualised a palace for himself, then a city, then a whole nation with other cities and forests, and then he saw in it the whole world—an entire universe with heaven and hell. He thought that he was Indra, the king of that heaven. To him was born a son whom he named Kunda. After some time this Indra abandoned his body and attained nirvāṇa, like a lamp without fuel.

Kunda became Indra and ruled the three worlds. He too was blessed with a son equal in valour and radiance. Thus his progeny multiplied and even today one of his descendants rules the heaven. Thus, in that subatomic particle there are many such kings ruling their own kingdoms.

BHUŚUṆḌA continued: VI.2:14

In that family was born one who became the ruler of heaven, but who was determined to put an end to the cycle of birth and death. He gained wisdom from the instructions of the preceptor of the gods (Bṛhaspati). He engaged himself in the performance of appropriate actions in situations which arose without his seeking. Thus he performed religious rites and even fought with the demons.

In his mind there arose a wish: "I should perceive the reality concerning Brahman the absolute." He entered into deep meditation. He was at peace within himself, remaining in seclusion. There he saw the supreme self or Brahman, omnipotent, all-pervasive all, who is everything, everywhere at all times, to whom all feet and hands belong; that Brahman whose eyes and heads and faces are everything; free from the senses yet the very essence of all the senses; totally free (unattached) though upholding everything; simultaneously free from and endowed with all the qualities; within and without all creatures (moving and non-moving); that Brahman who is far and near yet unknown because of its extreme subtlety. He is the sun and the moon and the earth-element everywhere, the reality in the mountain and ocean—the very essence of all. That Brahman is of the nature of this creation and world, yet the emancipated self, the primordial consciousness. Though he is the all, he is yet devoid of all these things.

He (Indra) saw Brahman in the pot, cloth, tree, monkey, man, sky, mountain, water, fire and air, manifesting differently and functioning variously. He realised that that is the reality in this world-appearance. Thus contemplating Brahman with his own pure and purified consciousness, this Indra became immersed in meditation. Realising that Brahman was the celestial sovereignty in Indra, he ruled the universe.

Just as this Indra ruled the whole universe while remaining within the subatomic particle, even so there have been countless Indras and universes. As long as one experiences the perceived object as something real and substantial, this world-appearance continues to flow. This māyā (world-appearance) will continue to flow with ever-changing appearance until the truth is realised, and only then will māyā cease to operate. Wherever this māyā functions in whatever manner, remember it is only because of the existence of the egosense. Immediately the truth concerning the egosense is investigated and understood, this māyā vanishes. For the reality or the infinite consciousness is totally free from the subject-object division, from the least trace of gross substantiality; it is pure void, with the infinite, unconditioned consciousness alone as its reality.

VI.2:15, 16 BHUŚUṆḌA continued:

Just as the whole universe came into being in the very heart of the subatom on account of Indra entertaining the notion of such a creation, wherever the egosense arises, there the world manifests itself. The egosense is the first cause of this world-illusion which is comparable to the blueness of the sky.

This tree of world-appearance grows in space on the hill known as Brahman on account of the latent tendencies or notions. Its seed is the egosense. The stars are its flowers. The rivers are its veins.

The mountains are its leaves. The very essence of notions and limitations is its fruits. This world is but the expansion of the notion of its existence.

This world-appearance is like the vast expanse of water. The worlds appear in this ocean like ripples and waves. It expands on account of delusion which obstructs self-knowledge and therefore emancipation. It seems to be attractive and beautiful on account of the constantly changing panorama of beings coming into existence and perishing in it.

O celestial, this creation can also be compared to the movement of wind. Egosense is the wind and its movement is the world. Just as such movement is non-different from the wind, as scent is inseparable from the flower, even so this egosense is inseparable from the world. The world exists in the very meaning of 'egosense'; and the egosense exists in the very meaning of the word 'world'. They are thus interdependent. If one is able to remove the egosense by means of one's awakened intelligence, he cleanses from his consciousness the impurity known as world-appearance.

O celestial, in fact, there is no such thing as egosense. It has somehow mysteriously arisen without any cause and without substantiality. Brahman alone pervades everything. The egosense is false. Since the egosense itself is false, surely the world which appears to be real to the egosense is unreal, too. What is unreal is unreal: what remains is eternal and peace. You are that.

When I said this to the celestial he entered into deep meditation. He attained the supreme state. (VASIṢṬHA said to Rāma: "If the teaching falls on a qualified heart, it expands in that intelligence. It does not stay in the unqualified heart. From the egosense arises the notion 'This is mine' and this expands into the world-appearance.")

Thus, O sage, in this manner sometimes even an ignorant person becomes immortal like this celestial. Immortality is attained only by the knowledge of the reality. There is no other means.

VASIṢṬHA continued: O Rāma, after this I returned to the place where the other sages had gathered in a conference. Thus have I narrated to you the story of the celestial's easy emancipation. Since I heard this from the lips of Bhuśuṇḍa eleven world-cycles have passed.

VASIṢṬHA continued: VI.2:17, 18

This mighty tree known as creation which yields the sweet and bitter fruits of happiness and unhappiness (or good and evil) ceases the moment the egosense is known to be false. He who knows the egosense to be false and who thereby gains the state of perfect equanimity never again comes to grief. When self-knowledge dispels the ignorant notion of the egosense, the egosense which till then was believed to be a solid reality disappears and one does not know where it goes. Neither does one know where the prime mover of the body, which had also been assumed to be a solid reality, goes. The leaf (body) draws to itself the moisture (egosense) from the earth, but the sun (self-knowledge in which the egosense is seen to be false) evaporates it and turns it into subtle water-vapour (Brahman). In the absence of the self-knowledge, however, the seed of egosense expands into a mighty tree in the twinkling of an eye, for in the seed is hidden the entire tree with all its innumerable branches, leaves, flowers and fruits. The men of wisdom perceive that the entire creation is hidden in the egosense.

Even death does not put an end to all this. When the notion of reality is transferred from one substance to another that is known as death. Behold right in front of you now countless creations of countless beings which exist within those beings. There is mind within prāṇa or life-force, and the world exists in the mind. At the time of death, this prāṇa leaves the body and enters into space. It is wafted here and there by the cosmic air. Behold these prāṇas (jīvas) with all their notions (worlds) hidden within them filling the entire space. I see them here in front of me with my inner eye of intelligence.

The air in the entire space is filled with the prāṇas of the departed ones. Mind exists in those prāṇas. And the world exists within the mind like oil in seeds. Just as the life-force (prāṇa) is wafted in the wind in space, all these worlds are wafted in the mind, like the scent of flowers is wafted by air. These are seen only by the eye of intelligence, not by these physical eyes, O Rāma. These worlds exist everywhere at all times. They are subtler than even space for they are of the nature of the essence of notions. Hence in fact they are not wafted nor moved from one place to another. But to each jīva (which is composed of the prāṇa, mind and notion combined) the notion it entertains of the world of its own creation is real, for that jīva firmly believes in the substantiality of that creation. When the objects on the bank of a fast-flowing river are seen reflected in the water, these objects appear to be agitated, too, though in fact they are not. Even so, these worlds within the jīvas may be said to be in motion or unmoving. But in the self which is infinite consciousness there is no such movement at all, even as when a pot is moved from one place to another, the space that is in it does not move from one place to another. So, this world only appears to be on account of the deluded belief in its existence: in reality it is Brahman only and it is neither created nor destroyed.

VASIṢṬHA continued:

Even if it is considered that this world arises in cosmic space it is not experienced as such by those who dwell in it. The passengers in a boat move with it; but one who is seated in the boat does not see another moving. Just as an efficient artist creates the illusion of distance in his painting or carving, even so within a subatomic particle the mind entertains the notions of immeasurable distance. Again, there is perversion of experience in regard to the smallness or largeness of objects. Similarly, there is the unreal experience of this world and what is known as the other-world, though all these are false. Out of all this arise false notions, such as 'This is desirable' and 'This is undesirable'.

A sentient being experiences the existence of his own limbs within himself by means of his own inner intelligence; even so, the jīva (the cosmic being in this case) perceives the existence of the world of diversity within itself. The infinite consciousness is unborn and divided like space; all these worlds are its limbs, as it were. A sentient ball of iron may visualise within itself the potential existence of a knife and a needle, etc. Even so, the jīva sees or experiences within itself the existence of the three worlds though this is no more than a delusion or false perception. Even in the insentient seed there is the potential tree with all its numerous branches, leaves, flowers and fruits—though not as such diverse objects. Even so, all these worlds exist in Brahman—though not as such, but in an undifferentiated state. In a mirror (whether you regard it as sentient or insentient) the city is reflected (though you may also truthfully say that there is no such reflection in the mirror) and it is seen and also not seen; such is the relationship between the three worlds and Brahman. What is known as the world is nothing but time, space, motion and substantiality, and all these are non-different from the egosense on account of their mutual interdependence.

What is seen here as the world is but the supreme self which appears as the world without undergoing any change in its own true nature. It appears to be that which one conceives it to be at a particular time and place. All these apparent appearances arise in the mind as notions; mind itself is nothing but consciousness. Hence, the appearances arise in the mind as notions; mind itself is nothing but consciousness. Hence, the appearance is false and not real. Concepts or notions (saṅkalpa), latent conditioning (vāsanā) and a living being (jīva) are non-different from the infinite consciousness; even if they are experienced, they are still unreal except as the one reality which is the infinite consciousness. Therefore, when the unreal notion is done away with, there is emancipation or mokṣa. However, one cannot truly say that these worlds are wafted in air here and there, for all these are but false notions with the infinite consciousness as their substratum and sole reality.

VI.2:19 RĀMA asked:

O sage, kindly tell me the form, the nature, the location of the jīva and its relation to the supreme self.

VASIṢṬHA replied:

O Rāma, it is the infinite consciousness that is known as the jīva when it becomes aware of itself as the object on account of the notion it entertains of itself. It is also known as cit or pure consciousness. This jīva is neither a subatomic particle, nor is it gross and physical, nor void nor anything else. The omnipresent pure consciousness is known as jīva when it experiences its own being. It is more minute than an atom and larger than the largest. It is all and it is pure consciousness. That is known as the jīva by the wise. Whatever object is experienced here is but its own reflection so experienced by it. Whatever it thinks of from moment to moment, that it experiences then and there. Such experiencing is the very nature of the jīva, even as motion is the nature of wind. When such experiencing ceases, the jīva becomes Brahman.

On account of its nature as consciousness, when the jīva entertains the notion of egosense, it builds time, space, motion and substance and functions in and through the body. It then perceives all these unrealities within itself as if they were real, even as a person dreams of his own death. Forgetting its true nature, it then identifies itself with its own false notions. It assumes an accidental relationship with the five senses and experiences their function as if such experience were its own. It shines as the puruṣa (indwelling presence) and virāṭ (cosmic person), endowed with these five faculties. This is still the subtle and mental being and this is the first emanation from the supreme being.

This person arises of his own accord, grows, decays, expands and contracts, then ceases to be. He is of the nature of mind (notion or thought) and being subtle is known as the puryaṣṭaka (the eightfold city). This subtle being is small and large, manifest and unmanifest, and pervades everything inside and out. His limbs are eight—the five senses and mind for the sixth, the egosense and being-cum-non-being. All the vedas have been sung by him. By him have the modes or rules of conduct been laid down. All these prevail even today.

His head is the highest of all, his feet are the netherworld, space is his belly, all the worlds his side, water his blood, the mountains and the earth are his flesh, the rivers are his blood vessels, the directions are his arms, the stars are his hairs, the cosmic winds his prāṇa, his life-spark is the lunar sphere and his mind is the aggregate of all notions. His self is the supreme self.

From this cosmic person or jīva other jīvas arise and are distributed throughout the three worlds. Brahmā, Viṣṇu, Rudra and others are its mental creations. The manifestations of its thought-forms are the gods and the demons and the celestials. The jīva arose from consciousness and that is its location. Thousands of such virāṭ have arisen and will arise in the future.

VASIṢṬHA continued: VI.2:20, 21

The cosmic person is himself of the nature of a notion (or concept, thought, etc.). Whatever notion is entertained by him appears to be embodied in the five elements in the cosmic space. Hence, O Rāma, whatever appears to have been created is regarded by the wise as the expansion of notions. The cosmic person is the original cause for all this world-appearance; the effect is of the same nature as the cause.

However, all this takes place in consciousness, not in unconsciousness. All these diverse creatures (from a worm to the god Rudra) have arisen from the original notion, just as a mighty tree grows out of a small seed. Though the universe has thus expanded from a minute subatom, the expansion or evolution is rooted in intelligence, not inertia. Just as the cosmic person has come to be manifest as this cosmos, even so have all things come into being, right down to the minutest atom.

But in truth there is nothing large nor minute. Whatever notion arises in the self is experienced as if it were real. The mind arises in the lunar element, and the moon is created by the mind. In the same way, one jīva gives rise to other jīvas. The wise consider jīva to be the essence in the sperm. In it is hidden the bliss of the self which it experiences as if independent of itself. There arises in it its identification with the five elements for no apparent reason. Yet the jīva continues to be jīva, not really limited by these elements; it is inside and outside these elements and their composition known as the body. But veiled by its identification with the elements it does not see its true nature, even as a man born blind does not see his way. Emancipation or mokṣa is the destruction of this ignorance and the realisation of the independence of the jīva from these elements and the egosense.

O Rāma, one should strive to be a jñānī (man of wisdom or direct experience) and not a jñānabandhu, a pseudo-jñānī. Who is a pseudo-jñānī? He who studies the scripture for pleasure or profit like a sculptor studying art, and who does not live up to the teaching, is a pseudo-jñānī. His scriptural knowledge is not reflected in his daily life. He is more interested in applying scriptural knowledge to promote his physical welfare and sensual happiness. Hence, I regard an ignorant man as superior to the pseudo-jñānī.

Jñāna or wisdom is self-knowledge; other forms of knowledge are but its pale reflections. One should work in this world as much as is needed to earn an honest living. One should live (eat) in order to sustain the life-force. One should sustain one's life-force only for the sake of acquiring knowledge. One should enquire into and know that which frees him from sorrow.

VI.2:22 VASIṢṬHA continued:

He is a jñānī who is unaware of (or oblivious of) the consequences of actions, because he is established in self-knowledge and ignores both the individualised mind and its objects. He is a jñānī whose psychological conditioning has been utterly removed. His intelligence is free from perversion. His knowledge is such as does not lead to rebirth. He engages himself in the simple acts of eating and dressing and in such spontaneous and appropriate actions which are free from desire and mental activity. He is known as a paṇḍita.

The diverse creatures have no purpose for coming into being or for their continued existence. They are not real entities though they appear to be so. The causal relationship is brought in later on in order to rationalise this unreal creation. Is there a purpose for the appearance of a mirage? They who try to find the reason for the appearance of these optical illusions are trying to ride on the shoulders of the grandson of the barren woman's son. The only cause for these optical illusions or illusory appearances is non-perception, for they disappear when looked into. When rightly investigated and perceived, they are found to be the supreme self; but when they are perceived through the mind, the conditioned jīva arises. This jīva when correctly investigated and looked into, is in fact the supreme self. When it is grasped by the mind, then it appears to be the jīva subject to all sorts of change, birth, decay, etc. They who have the direct experience of the cosmic being do not perceive the diversity, even when their eyes behold the world. In their mind, even while it functions, there is no disorderly movement of thought or movement in different directions; their mind is therefore no-mind in which there is non-movement of thought. Their behaviour is non-volitional like a dry leaf in wind.

The ignorant fool who is bound to psychological conditioning extols scripturally-enjoined action because he is not spiritually awakened. His senses prey upon their objects. The wise one, however, restrains the senses and remains centred in the self. There is no formless gold nor Brahman totally devoid of manifestation. However, emancipation is the removal of the concept of creation or manifestation. At the conclusion of this cosmic world-cycle there is, during the period of dissolution, one utter darkness covering the entire creation; even so, in the eyes of the wise ones the whole universe is enveloped by the one reality of Brahman. The ocean is one homogeneous unit in spite of diversity and motion within itself; there is but one Brahman which includes all this diversity and motion. There is the world within the egosense and egosense within this creation; the two are inseparable. The jīva sees this creation within itself, without any cause or motivation. The bracelet is gold; when the bracelet is not seen as bracelet, it ceases and gold alone is. Thus, the seers of truth do not live though living, do not die though dying, do not exist though existing. Their actions are non-volitional functions of the body.

VASIṢṬHA continued:

In every body the jīva exists like a snowflake, apparently heavy and large in heavy and large beings, and light and subtle in small beings. The 'I' enters into the triangle in its own conception; and because it is aware of itself, it believes itself to be a body, though this is unreal and only appears to be real. In that triangle which is the sheath of karma, the jīva which is of the very essence of the sperm exists in that body just as fragrance exists in a flower. Even as the sun's rays spread throughout the earth, this jīva which is in the sperm and which has entered the triangle spreads itself throughout the body.

Though this jīva is everywhere inside and outside, yet it has a special identification with this vital energy (sperm) which is therefore considered its special abode. Thus it exists in the very heart of beings; whatever it conceives of while thus existing in the beings is the very experience it experiences. But until it abandons all movement of thought in consciousness and until it becomes of no-mind, it does not attain peace and it does not cease to entertain the false notion of 'I am this'. Hence, O Rāma, though you may still continue to entertain thoughts and feelings, if the I-ness or egosense ceases in you, you will remain like the space and there will be peace.

There are sages of self-knowledge who live and function in this world as if they were sculptured images. Their organs of action function here, though the world does not produce the least disturbance in their consciousness. He who lives like space here (which is unaffected by the activity that goes on within it) is freed of all bondage and is liberated.

He who does not abandon his confirmed conviction in the existence of diversity is not abandoned by sorrow. He who is happy with whatever dress is put on him, with whatever food he is fed and with whatever resting place is offered to him shines like an emperor. Though he appears to live a conditioned life, he is really unconditioned for inwardly he is free and void. Though appearing to be active, he does not strive but functions like one in deep sleep. There is really no difference between the ignorant and the wise (the knower of the truth) except that the latter is free from the conditioned mind. What appears as the world to the conditioned mind is seen by the unconditioned as Brahman.

Whatever appears to be here exists, perishes and comes into being again; but you are that, O Rāma, that has neither birth nor death. Once self-knowledge has arisen in you this world-appearance is powerless to make any impression in you, even as a burnt seed does not give rise to a plant. Such a one rests in the self whether he is active or inactive. Only he in whom the craving for pleasure has utterly ceased experiences supreme peace, not one who has gained peace of mind by other means.

VI.2:23 VASIṢṬHA continued:

O Rāma, devoid of desire or mental colouring and free from mental conditioning, arise and proceed towards the supreme state, even as Maṅki did.

Your forbear Aja had invited me to a religious ceremony. As I descended from the air to attend this ceremony, I entered a dense forest which was dusty and hot. Whilst I was trying to go through that forest, I heard a wayfarer wail: "Alas, just as this sun burns everything, the company of the wicked is productive only of sorrow and sin. Let me go to that village yonder and find some relief from fatigue."

As he was thus about to enter the next village, I said to him: "Welcome, O wanderer, who has not found the right path! You cannot find eternal satisfaction in this place inhabited by the ignorant any more that you can quench your thirst by drinking salty water, which will only worsen your thirst. The ignorant wander aimlessly and take to the wrong paths. They do not engage themselves in self-enquiry nor do they disengage themselves from wicked action. They function like machines here. It is better to be a snake in a dark cave; it is better to be a worm in a rock; it is better to be a lame deer in a desert (mirage) than to remain in the company of ignorant people. Their company gives rise to momentary pleasure but is destructive of self. It is poisonous."

On my saying so, he said to me: "Lord, who are you? You are radiant like an emperor though you do not have anything. Have you quaffed nectar? You are devoid of everything and yet you are perfectly full. What is this form of yours, O sage, which seems to be nothing and yet everything, transcendental though seeming to rest on the earth? You are free from all desire and hope and yet you appear to entertain desire and hope. In your consciousness different concepts or notions arise in accordance with your own wish, and this entire universe rests in you like a seed in a fruit. I am a pilgrim, by name Maṅki. I have wandered far and I desire to return to my own abode. But I do not have the energy needed to return home. Lord, the great ones cultivate friendship at first sight. I feel that I am unable to overcome this world-illusion; pray, enlighten me."

I replied to him: "O pilgrim, I am Vasiṣṭha. Do not fear. You have indeed reached the door to emancipation. You have sought the company of Man (who is characterised by self-enquiry) and therefore you have almost reached the other shore of this world-appearance. Hence, in your mind dispassion has arisen and there is peace. When the veils that hide the truth are removed, the truth shines by itself. Pray, tell me what you wish to know. How do you propose to destroy this world-illusion?"

MAṄKI said: VI.2:24

Lord, I have searched in the ten directions for one who could remove my doubts, but till now I have not found such a person. Today by your company I have obtained the highest blessing that falls to the lot of the most fortunate among beings.

In this world all things come into being and perish and therefore there is repeated experience of sorrow. All the pleasures of the world inevitably end in sorrow. I therefore consider that sorrow is preferable to pleasure which leads to sorrow. Being subjected to the repeated experience of pleasure and pain, my mind is filled with perverse notions and it does not reflect the inner light of awakened intelligence. Tied to the latent tendencies born of such an ignorant life, the mind only leads me to sinful existence and activity. Thus have I wasted my days. This craving for pleasure never attains fulfilment, never finds satisfaction and, though all its aspirations end in failure, it (the craving) itself does not come to an end. In autumn the leaves dry up and fall away, but the desire for pleasure does not —nor does the anxiety that arises in the heart and which subjects me to terrible calamities. Even he who is endowed with many blessings and who enjoys prosperity is reduced to a miserable state of existence: such prosperity is often seen to be a bait to trap the unwary one in the pit of sorrow.

Since my heart is thus tainted with sinful tendencies and restlessness, the wise ones, seeing that I am only interested in sense-gratification, take no notice of me. In spite of all this, my mind still pursues its destructive course since it has not been overcome by death. The darkness of my ignorance in which the egosense thrives has not yet been dispelled by the moonlight of the study of scriptures and company of enlightened beings. The elephant of ignorance in me has not yet met with the lion of knowledge. The grass of my karma has not encountered the fire of its destruction. The sun of self-enquiry has not risen in me to dispel the darkness of mental conditioning.

O sage, that which I intellectually understand to be nothing still appears to me to be a real entity or substance. My senses are eating me away. Even the knowledge of the scriptures seems to form one more veil instead of helping me destroy the existing veils.

Thus, I am besieged by ignorance and confusion. Lord, tell me what is truly good for me.

VI.2:25 VASIṢṬHA replied:

Experience, thinking (entertaining notions, etc.), mental conditioning and imagination are meaningless and are productive only of psychological distress. All the sorrows and misfortunes of life are rooted in, and rest in, sense-experience and thinking. This path of life or saṃsāra is twisted and tortuous to the one who is ruled by psychological conditioning or latent tendencies. In the case of the awakened one, however, this saṃsāra ceases along with the cessation of his mental conditioning.

There is nothing other than pure consciousness even as there is nothing but pure void in space. That there is something known as experiencer other than this pure consciousness is ignorance whose expansion is this saṃsāra (world-appearance). That which arises in the absence of observation disappears when the light of observation is directed towards it. Even so, this fictitious experiencing-self, which is but the reflection of the true self, vanishes when its true nature is examined.

The division created by objective consciousness ceases when the knowledge of the indivisibility of consciousness arises. Pots do not exist independently of clay for pots are but modifications of clay. Objects are of consciousness; they are not different from consciousness as 'objects of consciousness'. That which is known through knowledge is non-different from that knowledge; the unknown is not known! Consciousness is the common factor in the subject, the predicate (knowing) and the object: hence there is nothing other than knowledge or consciousness. If it were otherwise there could be no comprehension (i.e., of two totally different substances). Hence even wood and stone are of the essential nature of consciousness, otherwise they could not be apprehended. Whatever there is in this world is pure consciousness. Though the objects (like wood and wax) may appear to be different, they are non-different from the observer's viewpoint since it is the same observer that observes both of them, and the observer is consciousness.

The egosense that perceives the diversity is the creator of the division. The egosense is bondage and its cessation is liberation. It is so simple. Where is the difficulty? The division 'has arisen' just as the vision of two moons arises in diplopia. In that case, how can it be said to have 'arisen'? It is false. Consciousness and inertness cannot be related to each other. Consciousness cannot become unconsciousness. It is consciousness alone which somehow thinks it is inert, and then the limitation bounces down into the conception of materiality, like a rock from a hill-top.

VASIṢṬHA continued: VI.2:26

When one thus falls into this illusion of world-appearance, he is at once preyed upon by countless other illusions which arise in the original illusion, just like insects arise after the rain. The mind is like a forest in spring. It is so dense with very many notions and concepts, that dense darkness prevails in it. On account of self-limitation or ignorance, people undergo countless experiences of pleasure and pain in this world.

There is no difference between the sage and the moon: both of them radiate joy. They are peaceful, cool and tranquil, full of immortalising nectar, and they enable one to see. There is no difference between the ignorant and the child: they are motivated in their lives by whims and fancies, they do not reflect what was nor what will be, and they are devoid of right conduct.

No one, from the Creator down to the smallest insect, can attain supreme peace unless he acquires perfect control of the mind. By the mere investigation of the nature of bondage, it ceases to bind, even as the obstacles on the path do not hinder one who examines them carefully. Ghosts do not haunt one who is careful and who is awake. If you close your eyes the vision of the external world is blotted out: if you remove the notion of the world from your consciousness, pure consciousness alone exists. This pure consciousness alone exists even now; the world is an unreal appearance brought about by just a little agitation in it. It is the creation of the cosmic mind, as it were. This cosmic mind merely entertains the notion of such a creation for it does not have the material substances needed for material creation! The world is a painting on the Brahman-canvas without colours and without instruments. How then can it be said that this world has really been created—by whom, how, when and where?!

The notion 'I am happy' experiences happiness and the notion 'I am unhappy' experiences unhappiness. All these notions are but pure consciousness. As notions they are false. Since the self or the infinite consciousness is unlimited and unconditioned, there is no agitation or movement it it. There are no desires, no attachment (dependence) and therefore no restlessness or movement in the self. Dependence alone is bondage; non-dependence is freedom or emancipation. He who rests in what is indicated by the 'All', 'Infinite' or 'Fullness', does not desire anything. When the physical body is as unreal as the body seen in a dream, what will the wise man desire for its sake?

In the spiritually awakened and enlightened state the sage rests in the self; all his desires reach their fulfilment. O Rāma, Maṅki heard all this and entered into deep contemplation, having abandoned his delusion. He lived performing spontaneous and appropriate actions (pravāhapatitaṃ kāryaṃ: inevitable action, lit.: the action of one fallen in a stream.)

VI.2:27, 28 VASIṢṬHA continued:

In the self is unity and diversity, yet not unity or diversity as opposed to each other. How can one assert diversity in it? The one self exists—subtle and omnipresent like space. It is undivided by the birth and death of bodies. 'I am the body' is delusion, not truth. You are the pure self or undivided consciousness. The subject (observer), the object (observed) and the predicate (observation) are but the modifications of the mind. The truth or the self is undivided by this division and hence it is beyond contemplation (dhyāna). All this is one indivisible Brahman and there is no such thing as the world. How can illusion arise or exist at all? The deluded feeling that there is a world (either as a reality or as an illusion) has been dispelled by my instruction: there is no reason now for you to suffer bondage. In prosperity and adversity, be free and live without egosense and desire.

RĀMA said:

I wish to hear from you once again the truth concerning karma or what is known as the divine will (fate).

VASIṢṬHA replied:

Divine will (fate—daivam) and karma are but concepts; the truth is that they are movements in consciousness. When there is such movement, the world-appearance arises; when the movement ceases, the world-appearance also ceases. There is not the least distinction between the movement and consciousness. There is not the least distinction between a person and his karma (action). A creature is known by its characteristic action and such action reveals the character of the creature: they are inseparable. Hence, the words or concepts 'divine' (daiva), 'action' (karma) and 'person' (nara) are but expressions which denote movement in consciousness.

This movement in consciousness, along with the self-limitation in consciousness, serves as the seed for everything, but there is no cause or seed for the movement in consciousness. There is no distinction between the seed and the sprout: therefore all this (body, etc.) is but movement in consciousness. This movement is obviously omnipotent and hence is able to manifest the gods and the demons and other creatures, mobile and immobile, sentient and insentient. They who assert that a person and his actions (karma) are different and distinct are animals in human semblance: salutation to them.

The seed which sprouts as the world is the self-limitation or conditioning in consciousness. Burn that seed by non-attachment or freedom. Non-volitional action (non-action in action) is known as non-attachment or freedom. Or, the uprooting of conditioning (vāsanā) is known as non-attachment or freedom. Attain this freedom by any means. That means by which you are able to destroy the seed of vāsanā is the best. In this nothing but self-effort is of any avail.

VASIṢṬHA continued: VI.2:29

O Rāma, regard all actions everywhere as pure consciousness and live with your vision introverted. In sorrow and in calamity, in dire distress and in pain, remain free from sorrow within yourself, but behave as if in sorrow in accordance with propriety and in accordance with local etiquette, even shedding tears and wailing and seemingly experiencing pleasure and pain. While enjoying the company of your wife and participating in festivals, etc., manifest delight as if you were subject to mental conditioning. Engage yourself in funeral rites and even in war as one with limited understanding and ignorant. Acquire wealth and destroy your enemies as ignorant people of limited understanding do. Be compassionate towards the suffering. Adore the holy ones. Rejoice in happiness. Grieve in sorrow. Be a hero among heroes. With your gaze turned inward, swimming in the bliss of the self and with your heart and mind at peace, what you do you do not do.

When you thus rest in the self, even the sharpest weapon cannot cut you (the self-knowledge). This self-knowledge is not cut by weapons nor burnt by fire, neither wetted by rain nor dried by wind. Cling to the pillar of self-knowledge, knowing the self to be free from old age and death. Thus rooted in self-knowledge though active externally, you will not once again fall into the error of self-limitation, vāsanā. Lead an active life though remaining inwardly as if in the deep sleep state.

Abandon all notion of division. Rest in self-knowledge with your awareness extending just a little outside. Thus, you are utterly at rest as if in deep sleep within yourself, whether you are active externally or not so active, whether you hold on to something or abandon something. You will then be totally free from all disharmony since you realise the non-distinction between the waking and the deep sleep states. Thus, by the practice of self-awareness which is beginningless and endless, you will gradually reach that supreme state of consciousness in which there is no duality and which is beyond all materiality. In it there is neither unity nor diversity but supreme peace.

RĀMA asked:

If such be the truth concerning the egosense, O sage, how do you appear here being called Vasiṣṭha? (When Rāma said this, Vasiṣṭha became totally silent. The members of the assembly were concerned. Seeing this, Rāma asked again:) Why are you silent, O sage? There is nothing in the whole world which a holy sage is unable to answer.

VASIṢṬHA replied:

I was silent not because I could not answer but because silence is the only answer to your question.

VASIṢṬHA continued:

There are two types of questioners: the enlightened and the ignorant. One should answer the ignorant from the point of view of the ignorant and the wise from the point of view of the wise. Till now you were ignorant and hence you deserved only intellectual answers. Now you know the truth and you rest in the supreme state, hence intellectual and logical answers will no longer do for you. O Rāma, all verbal statements (whether they are verbose or brief, whether their purport is subtle or transcendental) are all limited by logic, by duality and division.

Such tainted answers are not worthy of you, my dear one: and words are incapable of forming a pure and untainted statement. To one such as you, one should transmit the purest truth; and the purest truth is expressed only by complete silence. That silence which is free from rational enquiry and mental activity is the supreme state; hence, that alone was the appropriate answer to a question by a wise one like you. Again, all expression is the expression of the nature of one who expresses it. I am firmly established in the pure non-dual and indivisible consciousness which is the supreme state. How can I subject myself to the imperfection of expressing the inexpressible? Hence I did not attempt to reduce the infinite to words which spring from mental activity.

RĀMA said:

I realise that all expressions are tainted with duality and limitation. Making due allowance for this, tell me who you are.

VASIṢṬHA replied:

I am the pure space-like consciousness devoid of objective experience and beyond all mental activity or thought. I am the pure and infinite consciousness. Even so are you. The whole world is that, too. Everything is the pure, indivisible consciousness. I am pure consciousness and nothing but that. Since there is nothing apart from that, I do not know how to describe that. It is when one endeavours to give expression to one's self that the egosense and all the rest of it arise, even if one's attempt is to attain total freedom. They call it the supreme state in which one though alive behaves as if he were dead.

It is absurd for the egosense to seek this emancipation, for it can never comprehend the truth. The infinite consciousness surely stands in no need of realising the infinite consciousness! Either way, it is like the born-blind endeavouring to see a painting. That is nirvāṇa (emancipation or freedom) in which one stands firm like a rock whether or not there is agitation or movement in consciousness. He sees no 'other'. He is free from all desires and cravings. In him there is no 'I', 'you' or the 'other'. It is alone (all + one).

VASIṢṬHA continued:

The awareness of the infinite consciousness of itself is the mind. This itself is saṃsāra and bondage which lead to psychic distress. When the infinite consciousness remains itself as if unaware of itself, that is mokṣa or liberation. Mind, intellect, etc., are but modifications of pure consciousness, for they are mere words. In fact the pure undivided consciousness alone exists. When pure consciousness alone exists, pervading everything inside and out, how does the notion of division arise, and where?

Is there a difference between pure consciousness and utter void? Even if there is, it is impossible to put it into words. I am the pure (space of) consciousness, if the notion of self-limitation (mental conditioning) ceases. However since such limitation is but a notion, it cannot limit the infinite. When this understanding arises in one, though there is self-awareness, even that ceases for there is no division between the observer and the observed. It is as if void is the ultimate truth!

Ignorance points to the hidden wisdom. Wisdom then destroys that ignorance and eventually that, too, comes to rest. That is the supreme state. The wise muni (one who is inwardly silent) becomes a mānava (Man) by self-knowledge. (Or, man becomes muni.) Being ignorant, the ignorant become animals and trees. 'I am Brahman' and 'This is the world' are deluded notions. They are not seen on enquiry or investigation. When light goes in search of darkness, darkness vanishes. The peaceful man of right understanding possesses all the senses, but since he is not swayed by false notions, he does not subject himself to their experiences. He lives as if in deep sleep.

All dreams end in deep sleep, similarly deep sleep ends in samādhi; all the objects of perception merge in knowledge and everything is then seen as the one self. One who sees that all these objects are experienced only in the conditioned state of the mind realises instantly that the self is unconditioned. Since in the unconditioned there is neither doership nor enjoyership, there is in reality no sorrow and no pleasure, no virtue, no sin, no loss to anyone. All this is pure void. Even the notion of egosense and mine-ness is void. All appearance is illusion and it does not exist in us. One who sees this engages himself in non-volitional action or remains in complete silence (kāṣṭha mauna or the silence of a log of wood). He is Brahman. For the attainment of supreme peace the embodied being has no other means.

VI.2:30 VASIṢṬHA continued:

The notion of 'I' is utter ignorance; it blocks the path to nirvāṇa or liberation. Yet the foolish man endeavours with the help of this darkness of ignorance to find the light of truth! The investigation of the egosense reveals its limitation and conditioned nature or its total absence. It is found only in the ignorant and not in the knower of truth. The knower of truth, on the other hand, exists in the embodied or disembodied state without the least anxiety or sorrow, having totally abandoned the notion of the ego. There is no fear of destruction in the battle painted on a canvas: even so when the knower of truth is established in inner equanimity, activity does not affect him. In the case of the liberated sage even the manifestations of conditioned behaviour are apparent, not real. As in the case of the mantle of a gas-lamp, which retains its form and shape though it has really been burnt to ashes, the liberated sage's personality is no-personality, his mind is no-mind and his conditioning is truly unconditioned. It is Brahman and naught else. He who rests in total peace within though apparently engaged in diverse activities externally is a liberated one.

The elephants and chariots which float in the sky are but the cloud-formations which are cloud. The worlds that seem to exist are similarly nothing but the supreme self or Brahman. The cause of sorrow is therefore the acceptance of the unreal as the real, which arises from misunderstanding or deluded understanding of the real. The truth is that on account of the egosense the ignorant person experiences the existence of the world within it, though in reality he is the infinite consciousness. Just as a firebrand when it is whirled around creates illusory forms in space, whereas the only reality is the single spark of fire at the end of the stick, even so all these diverse forms are but the apparent appearance of the one indivisible Brahman or infinite consciousness. Let all this (the beginning and the end, the rising and the falling, space and time) exist as it pleases. One should rest in the inner peace.

The inert water is able to sustain the ship that carries a load across the water and thus overcome the obstacle created by itself (the water); even so, this inert world itself enables a man to cross this apparent world-appearance. That which is created by thought can also be destroyed by thought. Hence, attain fearlessness by realising that there is neither 'I' nor 'the other'. For nothing called 'I' is discovered when one investigates the body, mind, etc. Abandon the pursuit of pleasure, engage yourself in enquiry and be devoted to self-effort.

VASIṢṬHA continued: VI.2:31

The infinite consciousness reflects itself as the infinite and unconditioned consciousness in all, and that alone is truly experienced in all. But when the notion of an object arises and when that notion is confirmed by repetition, this consciousness manifests as the object —like the dream-objects—which, though within oneself, appear in that dream to be objects. When a dream-object perishes nothing is lost: when 'the world' or 'the I' is lost, nothing is lost. There is no sense even in condemning this world and the egosense. Who will extol or condemn an hallucination? Investigation alone is appropriate here. What remains is the truth. Remain firmly established in it.

This world-appearance is but a notion and it is utterly dispelled by enquiry. What remains then is Brahman. To accept the reality of this world-appearance is like trusting the words of the barren women's son. The individual personality is vāsanā or mental conditioning which disappears on investigation. However, in a state of ignorance, when one fails to observe it, this world-appearance arises.

The body is the result of the permutation and combination of the five elements and is inert. Even the mind, the intellect and the egosense are also of the same elements. When one is able to abandon the inert materiality of the mind, the intellect and the egosense, one attains the pure unconditioned being. This is liberation.

The 'object' arises in the 'subject' but has no independent existence. Hence, even 'the conditioned state or being' is but a notion: it is not real. Therefore, it vanishes when enquired into. It is best to reject the notion and stop it from arising again by never thinking of it again. There is neither the subject (seer) nor an experiencer, neither the real nor the unreal. There is the supreme peace alone. One who is established in this peace is free from likes and dislikes though engaged in activity. Or he may not engage himself in activity. When the mind is freed of all notions that limit the unconditioned consciousness, how does the sage act in a dualistic way? Free from love, hate and fear, he exists as the immutable self firmly established in the supreme peace.

The notion of 'object' which arises in the 'subject' is then experienced by the latter as different from it. In fact, the two (like the dreamer and the wakeful person) are indistinguishably one, like milk that is kept in two cups. The supreme self is free from all notions. Notions give rise to objects and when the notions are abandoned the objects cease to be.

VI.2:32 VASIṢṬHA continued:

When there is movement in the infinite consciousness, the notions of 'I' and 'the world' arise. These in themselves are harmless if one realises that in fact they are non-different from the self or the infinite consciousness. But, when they are considered real in themselves and the world is perceived as real then there is great misfortune.

Even this movement in the unconditioned is not a real entity. If it is unreal, how much more unreal are the notions that arise on account of such movement! It is as true as the dancing of the barren woman's son. Such movement arises in ignorance; it is ignorance. In the light of right understanding it ceases.

In the same way, the egosense arises when its existence is conceived. When that concept is rejected, the egosense ceases to be. This is known as dhyāna (meditation) and samādhi (superconscious state). It is the unconditioned consciousness. Pray, do not fall into the net of duality and non-duality, etc. All such controversy and polemics only lead to sorrow and despair. When one pursues the unreal or impermanent, there is sorrow. When the conditioning of consciousness drops away there is no sorrow, even as in sleep there is no sorrow. The consciousness that abandons conditioning realises its unconditioned nature. That is liberation.

With the help of my instructions if you realise that the 'I' does not exist, then your understanding is firm and unshakable. The world and the 'I' exist only as notions, not as fact nor as reality. They cease to be when one enquires "Who am I?" and "How has this world arisen?" The realisation of the non-existence of the 'I' is nirvāṇa or liberation. The light of this realisation dispels the darkness of ignorance. Therefore, one should enquire till the end of one's life: "Who am I?", "How did this world arise?", "What is jīva or the individual personality?" and "What is life?" as instructed by the knowers of the truth. When you betake yourself to the company of the knowers of truth, the light of their self-knowledge dispels the darkness of ignorance and its retinue, including the egosense. Hence, keep their company.

Resort to these knowers of truth in privacy, not in public. For when different people express different points of view, your understanding may be stunted or perverted. The wise man should approach the knower of truth in privacy, learn the truth and contemplate that truth. This contemplation dispels the cloud of concepts and notions which cast a shadow on consciousness.

VASIṢṬHA continued: VI.2:33

When one has attained wisdom through self-effort and with the help of the company of the holy ones, this world-appearance does not expand in his consciousness. Notions arise in one's consciousness and, when a counter-notion is raised, the former undergo radical mutation. The total abandonment of all notions or ideas is liberation and such an abandonment is possible when the pursuit of pleasure is abandoned. Notions and ideas gradually cease to arise and to expand in one who resolutely refrains from associating words with meanings, in his own mind—whether these words are uttered by others or they arise in one's own mind.

The abandonment of egosense is the cessation of ignorance; this and nothing else is liberation. Whether this world exists or does not exist, its apprehension or recognition by the mind leads to sorrow; its non-recognition is bliss. For all embodied beings there are two forms of disease: the first relates to this world and the second relates to the other world. For illnesses which are related to life in this world, ignorant people try to find a remedy before their lives come to an end. But there are no such remedies for the problems connected with the life beyond. One cannot hope to remedy them in the other world, for such remedies do not exist in the other world. If one is unable to find a remedy for the dreadful disease known as ignorance here in this world, one can surely not find a remedy after leaving this world. Therefore, do not waste your time in trying to find futile remedies for the problems connected with your life in this world. By self-knowledge rid yourself of the problems connected with the life hereafter. There is no time to lose, for life is ebbing away all the time.

If you do not uplift yourself from the mire of pleasure, you cannot find any other remedy. The fool who revels in pleasure invites sorrow and misfortune. Just as the strength of manhood manifests in the energy of childhood, the fullness of perfection (nirvāṇa) begins with the effectiveness of self-discipline or the abandonment of the pursuit of pleasure. The life stream of the knower of truth flows in harmony, while the life stream of the ignorant is full of whirlpools.

Universes arise in the infinite consciousness like bubbles on the surface of the ocean. But they are non-different from the unconditioned existence. Brahman is beyond all description and does not even have a 'nature' which can be conceived of; hence, it is unwise to suggest that the manifestation of the universes is its nature! Creation, world, movement of consciousness, etc., are mere words without substance. When such ideas are abandoned, the 'world' and the 'I' cease to be and consciousness alone exists, pure and immutable. This unconditioned consciousness alone is, naught else is—not even the nature of diverse objects here. All such notions (concerning the nature of diverse objects) are the offshoots of delusion.

VI.2:34 VASIṢṬHA continued:

That which is annihilated by happiness or unhappiness in life is so annihilated; but that which is not annihilated is not annihilated. This is the essence of the scriptural teachings. One who has desires undergoes pleasant and unpleasant experiences. If one wishes to get rid of the disease of such experiences, the only thing to do is to get rid of the desires.

There is no delusion in the supreme self that the 'I' and 'the world' exist. Who has invented these expressions and superimposed them on the pure void which is supreme peace? There is neither an 'I', nor the 'world' nor even 'Brahman'. All these are words. The only reality is supreme peace. Since this is the all, there is no division in it nor a doer nor an experiencer. For the sake of instruction, definitions are coined. That is the only truth that the self and the self alone is. But, just as the dream-experiences of two people sleeping side by side are not the same and one does not know what the other is dreaming about, one's understanding and inner experience are personal and unique.

Surely, it is consciousness as the self that is aware of everything in the universe. Hence, I am that consciousness; I, the world and all things in it are non-different from it. It is the one self that appears as the many, but because of ignorance and because of the extreme subtlety of the self, this is not seen as such. It is the self that sees this universe within itself as if the universe had a form, though in fact it has no form. All distinctions like sentient, insentient, etc., though they are not real are intended only for the instruction of seekers.

The notion 'I' arises in Brahman accidentally (like the crow alighting on the cocoanut tree and the cocoanut falling down without causal relationship). In truth, I am Brahman, the world is Brahman, there is neither a beginning nor a ceasing. Hence, where is the reason to rejoice or to grieve? Because the Lord is omnipotent some things appear to be sentient and others insentient. But there are no such divisions in Brahman. This creation appears to be a limb of the Lord and there appears to be a causal relationship, but this is not true, for in Brahman there does not exist anything which can be referred to as its nature.

Dualistic experience is bondage and liberation is its abandonment.

If such experience is abandoned, all divisions between the seer (subject) and the seen (object), the observer and the observed cease. Movement in consciousness is considered creation; and when that movement is seen to be false and non-existent, there is nirvāṇa. Brahman is unconditioned and unmodified. The entire universe is absolute Brahman, without any division whatsoever.

VASIṢṬHA continued: VI.2:35

The infinite consciousness, O Rāma, is everywhere and hence it seems to go from one part of the universe to another in the twinkling of an eye. Whatever be the activity you are engaged in, remain established in the unconditioned self. The characteristic of ignorance is that it is not found on enquiry or investigation; if it can be seen or observed, then it will become knowledge. When, thus, ignorance does not exist, then surely there is no division in consciousness.

Brahman alone exists as if it were the world, the one as if divided, the pure as if impure, the full as if void, the void as if full, movement as if stable and vice versa, the unmodified as if modified, the tranquil as if restless, the reality as if non-existent, consciousness as if inert, the self as if the object, the not-self as if the self, the eternal as if perishable, the unknowable as if knowable, the obvious as if shrouded in darkness—and though it is all existence, it is difficult to see it.

The infinite is unconditioned and therefore it does not seem to exist anywhere in particular. In it there is no division as doer, action, instrument and cause. It exists as all everywhere at all times. It is invisible but ever in front of you. There is no distinction in it between consciousness and inertia. I am and I am even the notion 'I am not'; if there is another, that too I am.

All these universes appear to be in the infinite consciousness, though no such appearance or division is possible in it. It is as if this consciousness wished to see itself and thus became its own mirror in which it reflected itself without any such intention. Thus the pure being becomes its own inert reflection—the universe. The infinite consciousness itself is known as the world.

All the substances or material creatures arise in it; they shine in it and they are absorbed into it. The whole world is a painting and this consciousness itself is the pure and colourless paint with which the world has been painted. The objects seem to be subject to creation and destruction, but consciousness is eternal and unconditioned. Though thousands of worlds appear to arise in this consciousness, it remains at peace, for in it there is no intention to create, even as a mirror remains unaffected by the many reflections seen in it. This infinite consciousness is the unintentional and non-volitional (non) cause of the appearance of the world now and of the world to come.

When it opens its eyes the worlds arise and when it closes its eyes the worlds disappear.

VI.2:36 VASIṢṬHA continued:

Just as a child's hallucination is not experienced by me but is real for the child, there is no creation in my consciousness. Since the forms, the vision and the intelligence which comprehends them are pure consciousness, only that exists, not the universe. I do not perceive the egosense, etc., but I realise the existence of the pure consciousness or absolute peace. Know that even these words of mine are pure consciousness and that this dialogue exists in the plane of your own consciousness.

That is known as the supreme state in which no desire arises. The sage who is free from desire functions here as if he were made of wood. He experiences pure void within and pure void without; to him the world is like an empty reed. He who is not enamoured of this world and whose heart delights in the cosmic being alone, is at peace and he has overcome this ocean of saṃsāra. Having overcome desire and abandoned latent tendencies or mental conditioning, speak what is to be spoken, touch what is to be touched, taste diverse flavours, see diverse scenes, and smell diverse scents.

It is only by thus understanding the essencelessness of the objects of experience that one becomes free from the disease of desire. The arising of desire is sorrow and the cessation of desire is supreme joy; there is no sorrow and no joy comparable to them even in hell and in heaven. The mind is desire and the cessation of desire is mokṣa (liberation): this is the essence of all scriptures. If this desire cannot be overcome by self-effort, then surely it is powerful and no other remedy is of any use! If you cannot overcome desire completely, then deal with it step by step. The wayfarer does not despair at the sight of the long road ahead but takes one step at a time. Desire alone is saṃsāra or the world-appearance which is an extension or projection of one's desire; its non-cognition is liberation. Hence, one should diligently strive to overcome desire; all else is vain. Why does one vainly study the scriptures and hear the instructions of the preceptors? There is no samādhi without the cessation of desire! If one finds that it is impossible to overcome desire by his own wisdom, then of what use is the study of scriptures or the instruction of the preceptor? Once this restlessness caused by desire is restrained, then very little effort is needed to attain self-knowledge. Hence, let everyone strive by every means to overcome desire which is the seed for birth, old age and death. With the arising of desire, bondage arises; and with the cessation of desire, bondage ceases. Let, therefore, the seed of desire be burnt in one's own heart by the fire of peace, equanimity and self-control.

VASIṢṬHA continued: VI.2:37

Yoga is getting rid of the poison of desire. I have already dealt with it and I shall tell you again so that it may be very clear.

Even if you desire to have something, there is nothing other than the self. What would you desire? Consciousness is subtle like space and indivisible; that itself is this world. How do you desire and what? There are no objects which can be desired. We do not see, either, if there is a distinction and relationship between gain (of an object) and its possessor. How is an unreal substance gained? Who has obtained a black moon? When thus the nature of the gain and its possessor is clearly understood, we do not know where they disappear!

When the distinction between the seer, sight and the scene is also seen to be non-existent, the egosense, etc., are merged in the self or consciousness. In nirvāṇa or liberation there is no seer, nor sight nor scene; when the latter exist there is no nirvāṇa. The illusory appearance of objects is of no practical use: a shell that looks like silver has no cash-value. When you affirm the reality of the illusory appearance, you invite unhappiness; when its unreality is realised there is great happiness.

There is not even a cause-and-effect relationship between any two things here, because the one infinite consciousness alone is real. 'Cause' and 'effect' are words which indicate nothing. What is the cause of the liquidity of water or movement of air? There is no sorrow, no happiness, since the whole world is the Lord. There is nothing other than the unconditioned consciousness. How then can desire arise?

RĀMA asked:

If all that is is Brahman or the infinite consciousness, then surely desire is also that! Where is the justification for injunctions and prohibitions?

VASIṢṬHA replied:

Once the truth is realised, then desire is Brahman and nothing else. But, O Rāma, as and when self-knowledge or the knowledge of the truth arises, at that very moment desire ceases, even as darkness vanishes at the very moment the sun rises. When the sun of self-knowledge arises, the sense of duality ceases along with vāsanā or mental conditioning. How can desire exist in that state? In the man of self-knowledge there is neither an aversion to objects, nor attraction nor desire for them; the absence of taste for them is natural.

VASIṢṬHA continued:

If the man of self-knowledge entertains any desire at all, it is accidental and causeless or it is at the request of others. Such desire is Brahman. However, this much is certain: a desire does not arise in the wise man. Injunctions and prohibitions do not apply to the man of self-knowledge. Who will wish to give what instruction to one in whom all desires have ceased? In fact, these are the signs by which one recognises the knower of truth: in him desire has been greatly weakened and he is devoted to the happiness and joy of all.

When the objects are understood to be essenceless and there is no taste for pleasure, desire does not arise—and that is liberation. When the enlightened person goes beyond the notions of unity and duality, he treats desire and non-desire as equal and divine. He is free from agitation and rests in the Lord in peace. He is not interested in doing anything nor is there anything for him to gain by refraining from doing something. Nothing matters any more: desire or non-desire, truth or falsehood, self or another, life or death. In such a person no desire arises; and if a desire does arise, it is Brahman.

He to whom there is neither joy nor sorrow, who rests in peace and who is inwardly unagitated, he is enlightened. He is able to transform even sorrow into joy. When one is firmly established in the realisation of the truth, then space rests in space, peace in peace, auspiciousness in auspiciousness, void in void, the world in Brahman. The false egosense vanishes.

If the world appears to be, it is surely like the city which appears in the imagination of someone else. It is an illusory appearance. The egosense is unreal though it appears to be real. This world-appearance is neither real nor unreal: it is indescribable. Hence, though it is true that the knower of truth is not affected by desire or by non-desire, I think it is preferable that even in his case the desire does not arise. For the mind is movement in consciousness as it becomes aware of itself; that itself is saṃsāra and also desire. To be free from it is liberation. Knowing it thus, let desire be abandoned.

In truth, however, whether there is desire or no desire, whether there is creation or cosmic dissolution, there is no loss of anything to anyone here. Desire and non-desire, truth and falsehood, existence and non-existence, happiness and sorrow—all these are but notions which arise in space but which do not give rise to anything. But he is regarded as a candidate for liberation in whom desire is weakened day after day. No other remedy in the world can remove the dreadful pain caused in the heart by desire.

VASIṢṬHA continued:

No remedy other than self-knowledge or the knowledge of the truth is effective in getting rid of desire: it is vain to deal with it with the help of remedies which are themselves based on falsehood (like the egosense, etc.).

Consciousness appears to become inert matter on account of the egosense. Thus arise the mind and the body. Yet, because it is consciousness, it experiences itself (though now as the body) without abandoning its reality as consciousness. Hence, this creation (of the world, the body, etc.) is neither true nor false.

The earth is void, the mountains are void, the solid substances are void, the worlds are void, movement is void and even the experience of this creation is void. Hence, this world-appearance does not arise nor cease. In this ocean of infinite consciousness, worlds are like waves and ripples, non-different though appearing to be different, arising without any reason or cause whatsoever and yet not arising in truth nor ever ceasing to be. In the infinite consciousness it is impossible for an object other than itself to arise at all.

The yogis or the perfected beings can make the whole world a void and also convert the void into the world in the twinkling of an eye, with the help of the magic potion known as consciousness. There are countless such worlds created by these siddhas (perfected beings) in space, countless creations, all of which are but pure, infinite consciousness. Enlightened yogis even travel from one such creation to another.

All such creation is non-different from consciousness, like fragrance and flower, yet they appear to be different. Their appearance in the infinite consciousness is illusory. Since they are apprehended by the notions that arise in every observer, they are experienced in accordance with those notions. In the yogis these notions are greatly weakened and, therefore, they see the truth and their statements are close to truth. In the case of the others, their declarations are coloured by their own notions or mental conditioning.

O Rāma, time sets the worlds in motion and in them the fictitious 'I', 'you', 'they', 'there' and 'thus'. All this is one pure infinite consciousness which is supreme peace, uncreated and undecaying. This is the Lord, the self. How and in whom do desire and all the rest of it arise?

VASIṢṬHA continued: VI.2:38

Consciousness sees in itself its own self as if it were its own object. Though creation is regarded as twofold—the creation by Brahmā and the creation by one's mind—they are essentially the same because both of them spring from the self or infinite consciousness. It is the awareness inherent in consciousness that makes this notion of creation appear to be outside of consciousness. Hence, we see no difference between subjective idealism and absolute idealism.

All these diverse objects arise in the infinite consciousness, exist in it and are non-different from it. It is because of this truth that experience of these diverse objects arises. Since both the subject and the object of experience are consciousness, the object merges in the subject like water with water. Thereby experience arises. Otherwise, if this were not so there could be no experience, as between two pieces of wood. In the object there exist the various elements (earth, water, etc.). In the subject there exist life-force, mind, jīva, etc. But these are not pure consciousness. They are the apparent appearances that arise in consciousness. Hence, they are in fact unreal. Since the unreal can have no existence, it is clear that the reality or the infinite consciousness or Brahman alone exists.

When the dream-objects of the person sleeping next to you come to an end on account of the dreamer waking up, you do not lose anything. To the one who has risen above the egosense, the whole universe appears to be worth less than a blade of grass. Such a person is not tempted by anything in the three worlds and to him the status of even the gods is worth less than that of a piece of hair. Unto him duality or diversity is unreal and false.

When thus the whole universe is void in the eyes of the wise man, how does desire arise in his heart? To him even life and death are non-different. On examination, even the body, etc., are seen to be unreal and false. When even the mind has ceased with the cessation of notions concerning the body and the world, the self or the infinite consciousness alone remains.

The egosense seems to arise only in the absence of such investigation into the nature of truth; when one enquires into it, the egosense ceases and there is pure, infinite consciousness. The mind is freed from objectification. Daily life is transmuted into divine life. Whatever you do, whatever you enjoy—all that becomes divine. Desireless and free from delusion, remain established in self-knowledge. Since there are no other motivations, let the scriptures guide your conduct.

VI.2:39 VASIṢṬHA continued:

He in whom the veil of ignorance has been rent asunder and in whom there is no desire shines with the light of pure intelligence. All his doubts are at rest and he illumines all around him. He who comes into contact with him who is free from doubt and who is independent (free from all dependence), is also purified and illumined.

The notion of the reality of the objects of this world arises only in ignorance. If it is realised that the objects are unreal, how does desire for them arise? Even 'creation' and 'liberation' are words without meaning. But this world is consciousness; if that were not so, neither 'I' nor 'that' could be comprehended.

Real peace is attained when one does not apprehend egosense and all the rest of its retinue, including sorrow. In deep sleep there are no dreams; and the state of deep sleep is not experienced during dreams. Even so, the apprehension of egosense, sorrow (born of the notion of world-appearance) and peace (born of nirvāṇa) do not exist at the same time. All these are but notions: in truth, there is neither creation nor nirvāṇa, neither sleep nor dreams. When all these are rejected there is real peace.

Confusion or delusion is unreal and the unreal does not exist. That which is not found on investigation does not exist. What is realised on investigation is one's true nature which alone exists and there is no diversity in it. When one moves away from one's real nature there is great sorrow; when one rests in the self there is great peace and self-control.

The elements (the senses, mind, etc.) act only with the help of their own other counterparts (light, space, etc.). The self or the infinite consciousness does not do anything and is not involved in activities. They who consider this world real do not have self-knowledge and to them we are 'unreal'. In me there is pure awareness of the one cosmic consciousness and even the activities of the world appear non-different from it—just as movement is non-different from the wind. In their mind my body seems to be real; but to my illumined intelligence their physical existence is unreal, as it is to a sleeping person. My relationship with them is also Brahman which exists in Brahman. Whatever be their vision, let it be so; that is all right with me. Since all this is pervaded by Brahman, I do not exist as 'I'. Even these words apparently arise, for your sake. In the heart of such a knower of truth, there is neither desire for pleasure nor desire for liberation. Neither liberation, nor wealth, etc., is of any use to him who is established in the realisation that 'I am not, nor is the world'.

VASIṢṬHA continued: VI.2:40, 41

O Rāma, that is called the self (svarūpaṃ) which knows external forms and internal psychological states. When the not-self is weakened and self-nature expands, in the light that then arises the world is realised as a mere experience. When one is fully established in the self, then this world-appearance ceases like a dream during deep sleep.

Knowing that pleasures are dreaded diseases, that relatives are bondage, and wealth (artha) is the source of unhappiness (anartha), one should rest in the self. The not-self is saṃsāra and resting in the self is supreme good. Hence, one should be oneself, as the void of consciousness. I am not the self, nor the objects, nor the world-appearance; I am Brahman, the supreme peace into which I have entered. You alone are aware of the 'you'; I see only the supreme peace. The Brahman-consciousness does not know the creation-consciousness and vice versa, even as the dreamer does not know the sleep state and one asleep does not experience the dream-state. The enlightened person sees both Brahman and the world as the waking and the dreaming states. Hence, he knows all these as they are.

As surely as it is a certainty that where there is sunlight there is illumination, where there is experience of the essencelessness of the worldly objects, there occurs spiritual awakening. The only reality here is that the supreme essence of cosmic consciousness dances in every atom of existence. Who can measure the immeasurable or count the infinite? This delightful cosmic dance that you see in front of you, O Rāma, is but the play of the infinite consciousness. The sleeping person when he is not in deep sleep becomes the field for the play of dreams; in the same manner, the self when it is not in self-knowledge appears to become the seed for this world-appearance. Contemplate the self and live in the waking state as if fast asleep, free from psychological distress.

When one is spiritually awakened and when one lives with his wakeful state resembling deep sleep, the state in which he is, is known as svabhāva (self-nature) and this state leads one to liberation. One who is established in Brahman and who does not see a distinction between Brahman and the 'world', lives in this world, too, without creating a division between subject, object and predicate and therefore without a sense of doership. In his eyes everything appears as it is and there is neither unity nor diversity.

An imaginary city is imagination, not a city. This world-appearance is appearance, not the world. The reality is infinite consciousness or Brahman.

VI.2:42 VASIṢṬHA continued:

The world-appearance arises in ignorance and wisdom puts an end to it. But all this is meaningless to the reality itself, which neither arises nor ceases. That reality is the indivisible, infinite consciousness, apart from which nothing is. That seems to undergo polarisation within itself, thus becoming aware of itself as its own object; this seems to create a division and partial knowledge which is

---

NOTE: Cidākāśa is said to be the 'void of consciousness' because it is devoid of the egosense.

ignorance. Such awareness is inherent in consciousness but it is non-different from consciousness.

The distinction between the world and its Lord is verbal and false. In the indivisible, infinite consciousness no such distinction is meaningful. On account of the illusory notions of time and space, somewhere at some time gold appears to have become a bracelet; even so does the notion of a creation arise in consciousness. When thus even duality is non-existent, investigation into the causal relationship between the Creator and this creation becomes meaningless.

When what exists is realised as it is (i.e., as the indivisible consciousness), the world-appearance ceases. Remain firmly established like a rock in the realisation of this truth, while functioning as an intelligent being here. Worship the self which is the supreme Lord with all your natural actions and experiences, including your wisdom. Worshipped with these articles, the self instantly bestows upon you the boon of spiritual unfoldment; in comparison, the worship of gods like Rudra and Viṣṇu is worthless. The self which is the Lord immediately confers mokṣa or final liberation when worshipped with enquiry into the nature of the self, with self-control and satsaṅga (company of the wise).

Perception of the reality is the best form of worship. When the Lord exists as the self, only a fool worships others. Worship of the gods, pilgrimage, austerity, etc., are said to confer their blessings if they are performed with wisdom or viveka. Surely, it is this wisdom that is vital in all these. Is it not sufficient then to worship the self with viveka itself? With this wisdom get rid of body-consciousness and along with it shame, fear, despair, pleasure and pain. Wisdom reveals consciousness as the self, but in the absence of objects like body, etc., this consciousness enters into supreme peace which is indescribable. To describe it is to destroy it. And to rest content with the knowledge gained from the scriptures, considering oneself to be enlightened, is like the vain imagination of the born-blind. When the unreality of the objects is understood and it is realised that consciousness is not the object of knowledge, then there is enlightenment which is beyond description.

VASIṢṬHA continued: VI.2:43

The characteristic of one who is free from the fever of ignorance and whose heart is calm and cool on account of self-knowledge, is that he is not tempted by pleasure. Enough of all this talk about knowledge and wisdom which are words and the notions indicated by those words, without a corresponding truth. Nirvāṇa or liberation is the non-experience of egosense. Let this truth be clearly understood.

Just as the man who is awake does not derive any pleasure from the objects he saw during his dream, we do not derive any pleasure from the objects of this world-appearance. Just as vampires and goblins arise in a dark forest, all these fourteen worlds arise in the darkness of ignorance and delusion. When the truth is investigated, the goblin is seen not to exist; and when the truth concerning these fourteen worlds is investigated, they are seen to be pure consciousness. The objects surely do not exist independently and hence they are unreal; they are pervaded by the consciousness which is the subject. But, then, since there is no object in relation to which consciousness can be considered the subject, the latter too can be said to be non-existent as the subject. Something which cannot be described exists.

Remain as the pure consciousness. Drink the essence of self-knowledge. Rest free from all doubts in the garden of nirvāṇa or liberation. Why do you, O men, roam this forest of saṃsāra which is devoid of any essence? O deluded people, do not run after this mirage known as hope and desire for happiness in this world. Pleasures are pain in disguise. Why do you not see that they are the sources of your own destruction? Do not be deluded by this illusory world-appearance. Behold this delusion and enquire into it. You will then rest in your own self which is beginningless and endless.

The ignorant regard this saṃsāra as real. In reality it does not exist at all. What does exist after this appearance is rejected, is in fact the truth. But it has no name! Like a lion, break away from this cage of ignorance and rise above everything. To abandon the notions of 'I' and 'mine' is liberation; nothing else is liberation. Liberation is peace. Liberation is extinction of all conditioning. Liberation is freedom from every kind of physical, psychological and psychic distress.

This world is not seen by the ignorant and by the wise in the same light. To one who has attained self-knowledge this world does not appear as saṃsāra but as the one infinite and indivisible consciousness. The man of self-knowledge is awake to that which is non-existent to the ignorant. That which is real to the latter is non-existent to the enlightened.

VASIṢṬHA continued:

The knower of truth experiences the world just as the man born blind 'sees' the world in his dreams and sees nothing in deep sleep. His heart and mind are cool with the extinction of the fire of desire. Since the mind of the knower of truth is freed from attraction, it is in a state of perfect equilibrium even when he is not 'practising meditation', even as the waters of a pool remain undisturbed when there are no outlets.

The object is (externalised) mental activity, and mental activity is the impression formed in intelligence by the object. Just as the same water flows in different streams with different names till it reaches the ocean, the same consciousness is both the diverse objects and the corresponding mental action. The object and the mind are thus non-different. When either is not, both of them cease. Both of them are essenceless. Therefore when they cease there is peace. The knower of truth abandons them, though by this he loses nothing, for 'object' and 'mind' are but words without corresponding entities. What is IS the infinite consciousness.

To the man of self-knowledge what the ignorant man thinks real (time, space, matter, etc.) are non-existent. Just as in the eyes of a brave man there is no goblin, in the eyes of the wise man there is no world. But to the ignorant man even the knower of truth is ignorant.

O Rāma, do not get involved in notions of matter and mind for they are false. Rest in your own self. It is consciousness alone which assumes these apparent 'forms', like the seed which grows into the diverse parts of the tree. When these objects are dropped, what remains (consciousness) is indescribable, for to call it 'consciousness' is to limit it.

Matter and mind are identical; and both are false. You are deluded by this false appearance. Self-knowledge will dispel this delusion. Both self-knowledge and the cessation of world-appearance are the characteristics of wisdom (bodham or awakening). The egosense, which arises in the absence of the extinction of desire, is conducive to sorrow.

Right from the roots, the entire tree with all its branches, leaves, flowers and fruits is but one and the same tree. In the same way, consciousness alone is all, indivisible and unmodified. Just as ghee by its very nature hardens like stone (when frozen), consciousness 'freezes' into matter. However, in the infinite and unmodified or unconditioned consciousness such modification is impossible: the conditioning is but a false notion. Therefore, it melts away in the heart of one who has self-knowledge and who is free from delusion and egosense.

VASIṢṬHA continued: VI.2:44

I shall now describe the tree known as samādhāna (equanimity) which grows in the forest known as the heart of the wise.

Its seed is a turning away from 'the world', whether this is caused naturally or otherwise by the experience of sorrow. Mind is a field.

It is ploughed by right action, it is watered day and night by right feeling, it is nourished by the practice of prāṇāyāma. On this field known as the mind the seed known as samādhi (turning away from the world) falls of its own accord when one is alone in the forest known as wisdom. The wise man should endeavour constantly to keep this seed of meditation watered and nourished by intelligent methods.

One should seek the company of the wise who are one's own real well-wishers and who are pure and friendly. Then one should water the seed of samādhi or meditation by means of hearing, reflecting on and contemplating the scriptures which bring about total inner emptiness and which are full of wisdom, pure and cool like nectar. Being aware of the precious seed of meditation or samādhi that has fallen in the field of one's mind, the wise man should carefully cherish and nourish it by means of austerities, charity, etc.

When this seed begins to sprout, it should be further protected by peace and contentment. At the same time, one should guard it against the birds of desire, attachment to family, pride, greed, etc., with the help of contentment. With the broom of right and loving action the dirt of rājasic restlessness must be swept away, whereas the darkness of tāmasic ignorance must be driven away by the light of right understanding.

The lightning known as pride of wealth and the thunderstorm known as pursuit of pleasure strike the field and devastate it. These should be prevented with the trident of magnanimity, compassion, japa, austerity, self-control and contemplation of the significance of the praṇava (OM).

If it is thus protected, this seed grows into wisdom. With it the entire field of the mind shines beautifully. The sprout grows two leaves. One is known as study of scriptures and the other is satsaṅga (company of the men of wisdom). Soon it will grow the bark known as contentment with the sap known as dispassion or uncolouredness of mind. Fed by the rain of scriptural wisdom, it will soon grow into a tree. Then it is not easily swayed even if it is shaken by the monkeys known as rāga-dveṣa (attraction and aversion). Then there arise in it the branches known as pure knowledge which reach out far and wide. Clarity of vision, truthfulness, courage, unclouded understanding, equanimity, peace, friendliness, compassion, fame, etc., are its other branches that arise when one is fully established in dhyāna or meditation.

VASIṢṬHA continued:

The tree of meditation casts a cool shade in which all desires and cravings come to an end and all the burning distress ceases.

Meditation expands the shade of self-control which promotes steadiness of the mind.

A deer known as the mind, which had been wandering in the wilderness of countless concepts, notions and prejudices and which somehow finds the right path, takes shelter under this tree. This deer is pursued by its many enemies who covet its hide or covering. It hides itself in thorny bushes known as the body in an attempt to save itself. All this effort wears out its energies. Running hither and thither in the forest of saṃsāra, harassed by the winds known as vāsanā or latent tendencies and scorched by the heat of egosense, the deer is afflicted by interminable distress.

This deer is not easily satisfied with what it gets. Its cravings multiply and it continues to go out far in search of satisfaction of those cravings. It gets attached to the many pleasure-centres known as wife, children, etc., and it wears itself out in looking after them. It is caught in the net of wealth, etc., and it struggles to free itself. In this struggle it falls down again and again and injures itself. Borne down by the current of craving, it is carried far away. It is haunted and hunted by innumerable ailments. It is also trapped by the different sense-experiences. It is bewildered by its alternate rise to the heavenly regions and its fall into the hell. It is crushed and wounded by the stones and rocks known as mental modifications and evil qualities. To remedy all these, it conjures up by its own intellect various codes of conduct, which prove ineffectual. It has no knowledge of the self or the infinite consciousness.

This deer known as the mind is made insensible by the poisonous exhalation of the snake known as worldly pleasure and craving for such pleasure. It is burnt by the fire of anger. It is dried up by worries and anxieties. It is pursued by the tiger known as poverty. It falls into the pit of attachment. Its heart is broken by the frustration of its own pride.

At some stage, this deer turns away from all this and seeks the refuge of some tree already described (the tree of meditation) and there it shines brightly. Supreme peace or bliss is not attained in any other condition but the unconditioned state of consciousness, and this is attained only in the shade of the tree known as samādhi or meditation.

VASIṢṬHA continued: VI.2:45

Thus having obtained rest, the deer (mind) delights itself there and does not seek to go elsewhere. After some time, the tree known as meditation or samādhi begins to yield its fruit, which is the revelation of the supreme self. The mind-deer beholds that fruit above itself on the tree of meditation. Thereupon it abandons all other pursuits and climbs that tree to taste its fruits. Having ascended that tree, the mind-deer abandons the worldly thought-patterns and it does not contemplate the baser life again. Even as the snake abandons its slough, this mind-deer abandons its previous habits so that it might ascend the tree of meditation. Whenever memory of its own past arises, it laughs aloud, "How was it that I remained such a fool till now!" Having discarded greed, etc., it rests on that tree like an emperor.

Day by day, its cravings decrease. It does not avoid what it gets unsought nor does it long for what it does not obtain effortlessly. It surrounds itself with the knowledge of the scriptures that deal with the infinite consciousness or the unconditioned being. It perceives inwardly its own past states of ignorance and laughs. It sees its own wife and children, etc., and laughs at them, as if they were either relatives in a previous life-span or people seen in a dream. All the activities that are based on attachment and aversion, fear and vanity, pride and delusion, appear to it as if they were all play-acting. Looking at the momentary experiences in this world, it laughs derisively, knowing that they are like the experiences of a madman.

Being established in that extraordinary state, it (the mind-deer) does not entertain any worry or anxiety concerning wife, children, etc. It beholds with an enlightened vision that which alone is (the reality) in that which alone is (the infinite). With its vision fully concentrated, it ascends the tree of samādhi. It rejoices even in what it previously considered misfortunes. It engages itself in the necessary activities as if it had just been awakened for doing just that work, after which it returns to the state of meditation. But naturally it seeks to be in the state of samādhi all the time. It is totally free from egosense; though, because it is also breathing like others, it appears to be alive to the egosense. Even in the case of such pleasures that seek it unsought, it entertains no zest; its heart naturally turns away from all pleasure. It is full. It is asleep to worldly activities and pursuits. Who knows in what state it exists! It draws closer and closer to the supreme fruit of mokṣa or liberation. Lastly, it abandons even the buddhi or intellect and enters into the unconditioned consciousness.

VASIṢṬHA continued:

That is known as the attainment of the highest in which one abandons the notions of the existence of objects and in which one rests in one's own pure self. When all divisions are given up, the indivisible alone remains. It is pure, one, beginningless and endless. This is known as Brahman. One who has given up desires for wealth, wife and worldly objects rests in the supreme self. When even the division between the mind and the infinite consciousness drops away, then all division melts into nothingness. After this, one exists in the supreme being even as the unsculpted image exists in the marble slab.

The ignorant person cannot meditate: nor is it desirable for him to do so. The enlightened person is already established in the self! He is an enlightened person who is totally disinterested in the objects of perception, but this is not possible for an ignorant person. When the awareness of the object is seen as the pure consciousness which is eternal, it is known as samādhāna, the state of equanimity. When the subject and the object merge, the mind is said to be in the state of samādhāna. Resting in the self implies the disinterestedness of the self in the objects. On the other hand, ignorance is the movement of the self towards the objects. Surely such movement takes place only in the ignorant: no one who has tasted nectar is interested in bitter things. Hence, in the case of the wise, meditation becomes natural and effortless. When there is no craving, the self is never abandoned. Or, when the mind expands to include the entire universe, again, the self is not abandoned. This much is certain: until one attains self-knowledge, there is need to strive for samādhi. He who is established in samādhi is Brahman in human form. Salutations to him.

When there is disinterestedness in the objects, not even the gods can disturb one's meditation. Hence, one should cultivate firm meditation (vajra-dhyānam). The means to this are (1) scriptures, (2) company of holy ones and (3) meditation. Ignorance is not dispelled by half-knowledge, even as there is no relief from cold when one sits near a painting of fire. The ignorant sees the world as a physical reality, the wise as consciousness. To the wise there is neither egosense nor the world. His vision of the world is indescribably wonderful. To the ignorant the world is one of dry wood and stone. One who is enlightened sees the world as one self; the ignorant does not see it as the one self. The ignorant engages himself in endless arguments. The enlightened is friendly with all. Turīya or samādhi is the natural state which is what exists in and through the wakeful, dream and sleep states. Conditioning alone is the mind, which ceases when enquired into.

VASIṢṬHA continued: VI.2:46

When the fruit of the supreme truth has been gained and it has become liberation, even awareness becomes non-existent, as it were, since the mind is absorbed in the supreme truth. The deerness of the deer-mind vanishes, like a lamp without fuel. The supreme truth alone remains. The mind which has attained the fruit of meditation, which is self-knowledge, is firm like a thunderbolt (vajra). The characteristic motion or restlessness of the mind goes away, who knows where. Illumination alone remains as pure consciousness without disturbance or division.

In that state, there is effortless dropping away of all desires, and effortless meditation alone remains. Unless and until Brahman is realised, one cannot rest in the self; until then meditation is impossible merely by thinking about the self, etc. When the supreme truth is realised, the mind goes away, who knows where; and who knows how vāsanā or mental conditioning, karma, as also joy and despair disappear. The yogi is then seen to be in a state of continuous and unbroken meditation, firmly established in adamantine meditation or samādhi (vajra-samādhāna), like a mountain.

When the yogi is disinterested in pleasure, when his senses are utterly peaceful and controlled, when he rests delighted in the self, when all his mental modifications have ceased—what else is there to be done in the name of samādhi? When the yogi is unaware of the world as an object of observation, on account of the absence of mental conditioning, he cannot help remaining in vajra-samādhi (adamantine meditation), as if compelled by some other power. The mind is not distracted from it. When the mind is at peace because it is disinterested in worldly objects (having known the truth) that is samādhi, not else. Firm rejection of pleasure is meditation; when it reaches fruition it is vajra-sāra (adamantine). Since this is also the state of perfect knowledge, it is known as nirvāṇa or the blissful state.

If there is craving for pleasure, what is the use of something called meditation? If such craving does not exist, what is the use of something called meditation? When there is perfect knowledge and at the same time disinterestedness in pleasure, unconditioned consciousness (nirvikalpa samādhi) follows naturally and effortlessly. He who is not swayed by craving for pleasure is known as perfectly enlightened (saṃbuddha). Such perfect enlightenment arises from complete turning away from the pursuit of pleasure. He who rests in the self does not experience craving at all. Desire for pleasure-experience only arises when there is movement away from the self. At the conclusion of the study of scripture, japa, etc., one enters into samādhi; after the practice of samādhi, one should study, do japa, etc. O Rāma, rest in the state of nirvāṇa at all times.

VI.2:47 VASIṢṬHA continued:

When one is knocked about by the troubles and tribulations of earthly existence and is 'tired of all this', he seeks refuge from all this. I shall describe to you the progressive stages by which such a person reaches rest and peace. Either on account of an immediate cause or without one, he turns away from worldly pursuits (the pursuits of pleasure and wealth) and seeks the shelter of the company of a wise person. He avoids bad company from a very great distance.

The blessings that flow from the company of holy men are incomparable to any other blessings. The holy man's nature is cool and peaceful; his behaviour and actions are pure. Therefore his company promotes peace and goodness in everyone who seeks it. In his company one loses fear. Sinfulness comes to an end and one grows in purity. Even the love and affection that the gods and the angels possess are nothing compared to the limitless love that flows from the holy ones.

When one engages oneself in the performance of right action, his intelligence rests in peace and reflects the truth like a perfect mirror. It is then that the meaning of the scriptural declarations becomes abundantly clear. The wise man radiates wisdom and goodness. Then seeking to free himself from the cage of ignorance, he flies away from pleasure towards the unconditioned bliss.

It is a great misfortune to pursue pleasures. Although the wise man rejects them, they create some uneasiness in his heart. He is supremely happy, therefore, when he does not find himself in pleasurable situations. The sages or yogis and perfected ones approach such a wise man. But the wise man does not value even the gifts of psychic powers or knowledge that they bestow upon him. He seeks the company of enlightened beings. In their company he dives into the truths of the scriptures. It is the characteristic of these enlightened ones to raise others to their own level.

The wise person gradually abandons all selfish actions and the endeavour to gain wealth or pleasure. He gives everything away in self-sacrificing charity. O Rāma, remember that even hell is not so painful as the suffering caused by selfish activity. Wealth is the source of endless misfortune, prosperity is perpetual adversity, enjoyment of pleasure is enduring disease. All these are misunderstood by the perverse intellect. In this world contentment alone is the best medicine, the best tonic and the greatest good fortune. The contented heart is ready for enlightenment. First turn away from worldliness, then resort to satsaṅga, enquire into the truth of the scriptures and cultivate disinterestedness in pleasure and you will attain the supreme truth.

VASIṢṬHA continued: VI.2:48

When the mind is established in dispassion and in holy company, and when through the study of the scriptures there is disinterestedness in the pursuit of pleasure, one does not long for wealth and treats even the wealth that one has as dry dung. He treats his relatives and friends as co-pilgrims and serves them appropriately at the proper times. He is not attached to seclusion, gardens, holy places or his own home, to fun and frolic with friends or scriptural discussions, and he does not spend too much time in any of these.

He rests in the supreme state. The supreme state is that which is. Diversion in it is created by ignorance and this ignorance is false and non-existent! He who is firmly established in the self and who is undisturbed like a sculpted figure, is not swayed by sense-objects. 'I' and 'the world', time and space, knowledge or void—these, though they may continue to be, are not experienced by the knower of truth. One should salute that sun in human form whose personality is devoid of rajas (restless action or impurity), who has transcended even satva or purity and in whom the darkness of ignorance has no place at all. The state of one who has transcended all division and whose mind has become no-mind is beyond description. Adored by him day and night, the Lord bestows upon him the supreme state of nirvāṇa.

The Lord is neither far nor inaccessible. One's own illumined self is the Lord. From him are all things and to him they return. All things here worship and adore him at all times in their own diverse ways. By thus being adored in diverse forms by someone, birth after birth, the self is pleased. Thus pleased, the self sends a messenger for one's inner awakening and enlightenment.

The messenger thus sent by the self is viveka or wisdom. It dwells in the cave of one's heart. It is this wisdom that brings about the gradual awakening of one who is conditioned by ignorance. The one that is thus awakened is the inner self, that is the supreme self whose 'name' is OM. He is the omnipresent being. The universe is his body, as it were. All heads, eyes, hands, etc., belong to him. He is pleased with japa, charity, ritual worship, study, and such practices. When this self awakens with the help of wisdom or viveka, there is an inner unfoldment, the mind vanishes and the jīva disappears, too. In this terrible ocean of saṃsāra, wisdom (viveka) alone is the boat which enables one to cross it.

The self is highly pleased with the diverse (do as you please) forms of worship one adopted before. It bestows on one the pure messenger known as viveka (wisdom). By means of holy company, study of scriptural truth and illumination it brings the jīva closer to the pure, primordial state of oneness.

VI.2:49 VASIṢṬHA continued:

When this viveka or wisdom is strengthened and confirmed and when the impurity of conditioning is washed away, the holy one shines with an extraordinary radiance. Both the inner notion and the external perception of the world cease for him. But, then, since all these were born of ignorance which is false, nothing real ceases to be. The world is but an appearance: it is neither not-self nor is it gross and physical. These elements are unreal; neither the world nor the void is real. Brahman alone is spread out and Brahman alone shines.

The world is not material; the void is not seen. The mind has come to naught. What remains is the truth, indescribable but not non-being. The intellect is baffled by conflicting statements, but when the truth is investigated by proper methods, it is realised. He whose intelligence is awakened is known as the knower of truth. He is established in non-dual consciousness and he does not perceive the world as 'the world'.

The world-appearance arises only when the infinite consciousness sees itself as an object: it were better that this did not happen. But once this has arisen, it is externalised and materialised. The awareness of the matter is the mind and the mind binds itself to the body. But all these are but notions and verbal descriptions and these distinctions are notional and imaginary. The self which is consciousness does not ever become an object or material. When one is established in self-knowledge even 'consciousness' and 'unconsciousness' become meaningless words.

The material body arises from the subtle mental body, on account of persistent thinking. Hence matter is unreal. By constantly thinking "I am confused, I am mad" one becomes mad; by realising "I am not mad" one regains his mental balance. When the dream is realised as dream one is not fooled by it. Just as the subtle body becomes a gross material body by persistent thinking, the process can be reversed by right knowledge. One should lead by persistent right contemplation, even the subtle body to its real state as the jīva and then to Brahman.

Unless and until both these (matter and mind, the gross and the subtle) are realised to be the one infinite consciousness, the wise seeker should endeavour to purify them and to investigate their real nature. He who is established in self-knowledge is unshaken by the worst calamities—even if there were a shower of fire and brimstone, or the earth disintegrated and vanished into thin air or the great flood swallowed everything. One who is endowed with supreme dispassion enjoys the adamantine samādhi (vajra samādhi). The inner peace that ensues from such dispassion is incomparable to that which arises from austerities, etc.

VASIṢṬHA continued: VI.2:50

All these diverse beings seen in the ten directions belong to one or the other of the following categories: some are in the dream-wakeful state; others are in a notional-wakeful state; some are in a pure wakeful state; others are in a long wakeful state; some are in a gross wakeful state; others are in the state of wakeful-dream; yet others are in a decreasing wakeful state.

O Rāma, in a certain previous world-cycle, in a certain corner of creation, some beings remained in a state of deep sleep, though alive. The dreams that they dream are what appears as this universe. They are in what is known as the dream-wakeful state. We are all their dream-objects. On account of the fact that theirs is a very long dream, it appears to be a real and wakeful state to us. And the dreamers continue to be the jīvas in all this. Because the omnipresent is omniscient consciousness, everything exists everywhere. Therefore, we exist as the dream-objects of the dreams of those original dreamers.

In this dream-world if one rejects delusion, one is liberated; or, in accordance with one's idea of oneself, one considers oneself to be another body. The world-appearance that arises by such a notion is experienced by them.

In a certain previous world-cycle at some place, some beings lived in the wakeful state entertaining different notions which gave rise to diverse creatures. These are in the notional-wakeful state. Because of the perseverance of the notions that gave rise to them they are firmly established in it. Even when the notions cease, they continue to exist on account of their own past notions.

They who arose in the beginning in the expanded consciousness of Brahmā, when there was neither sleep nor dream, are known as those who exist in the pure wakeful state. They themselves, when they continue to exist in subsequent embodiments, are in the long or continued wakeful state. When they are in a dense state of consciousness which is unconsciousness they are said to be in a gross wakeful state.

After listening to the scriptural expositions, they who look upon the wakeful state as dream are in the state of wakeful-dream. When they are fully awakened and when they rest in the supreme state, their perception of the world in the waking state decreases in grossness and they who are in such a decreasing wakeful state reach the turīya or the fourth state of consciousness.

These are the seven states in which diverse beings exist. In fact, even as the seven oceans are but one mass of water, all these are but one ocean of consciousness.

VI.2:51 RĀMA asked:

Lord, how does the pure wakeful state arise and how do beings exist in such a state without any cause or motivation whatsoever?

VASIṢṬHA replied:

O Rāma, without a cause no effect is produced. Therefore, the pure wakeful state does not happen nor does all the rest of this apparent creation come into being at all. Nothing is created and nothing perishes: all these descriptions are incidental to instruction.

RĀMA asked again:

Who is it that creates the bodies, the mind, etc., and who deludes all these beings with bondage known as friendship, likes, etc.?

VASIṢṬHA replied:

O Rāma, no one creates these bodies at any time and no one deludes beings at any time. Consciousness is beginningless and eternal, and it alone exists as all these diverse beings. Nothing is outside of this consciousness, though it appears to be outside itself. This appearance, too, arises within itself, like a sprout from a seed. This universe exists within consciousness even as a figure exists in a marble slab. This consciousness which is everywhere, within and without, spreads itself as the world-appearance on account of time and space, just like the fragrance of a flower spreads out. 'This' itself is 'the other world'. Let there be an end to the mental conditioning that creates the other world. When the notion of the other world has been given up, from where do such notions arise?

The self alone is real, devoid of the concepts of time, space and such other notions; the self is not a void. This truth is realised only by those who are established in the supreme state, not by those who rest in the egosense. To one who has realised the truth, the fourteen worlds are his own limbs. In his vision, the division between dream-state and wakeful state ceases to exist. When this world-appearance is seen to be pure consciousness, it becomes similar to a dream. Just as all that is thrown into the fire becomes one (ash), all the states and the world-appearance are reduced to oneness by the fire of wisdom.

Consciousness alone appears as this gross universe. When this is realised, the belief in the existence of matter ceases. With it ceases desire to possess such matter. Then one remains in one's own inner peace. When the self is realised as neither the world nor the void, everything remains as it truly is. The sage of self-realisation has crossed this saṃsāra and has reached the end of all karma.

VASIṢṬHA continued: VI.2:52

The notion of the existence of the world arises in the ignorant just as the awareness of its various limbs may arise in the 'mind' of a tree! This illusory apprehension of the objective world, which goes by the name 'avidyā' or 'ignorance' does not in fact exist: it is as real as water in the mirage (sound without substance). However, just for the sake of clear understanding, take this ignorance as real and listen! Then you will yourself understand that it does not exist in fact.

Whatever appears to be here perishes at the end of the world-cycle. No one can avert this total destruction. Brahman alone exists then. This realisation is not like drug-induced experience: we know with certainty that the body is like a dream-object and that consciousness alone is real. This world-appearance perishes again and again. What has perished and how does it come into being again and again? If it is said that all these objects remained hidden in space, then one has to admit that they were not destroyed even in the cosmic dissolution.

There is similarity between cause and effect. Since there is no cause for this world-appearance, it is not an effect. One alone is. The numerous branches, leaves, flowers and fruits of a tree are but the expansion of the single seed. There is no need to invent a causal relationship. The seed alone is the reality. When the truth is investigated, we realise that the one consciousness alone remains as the truth.

At the end of the world-cycle, all these objects of perception cease to be. The one self which is consciousness alone remains, and this is indescribable, being beyond thought and description. Only the sage of self-knowledge experiences this: others merely read these words. For it is neither time nor mind, neither being nor non-being, neither consciousness nor unconsciousness. I have thus described it negatively because the scriptures have done so. In my vision, it is pure and supreme peace. In this there are infinite potentialities like figures in an uncut marble. Thus the supreme self is at the same time diverse and non-diverse. It is when you do not have direct self-knowledge that there arises in you doubt concerning this.

The perception of diversity is due to the division that arises in the self. However, the self is devoid of any division into time, space, etc. The self is the very substratum and undivided reality of time, space, etc., just as the ocean is of the waves. Hence, the reality is undivided and divided, it is and it is not. The uncut images in the marble may be carved out of it, but it is not possible to carve the world out of the infinite consciousness. Hence, divided though undivided, it merely appears to be different from the totality though really non-different from it.

VI.2:53, 54 VASIṢṬHA continued:

The reality is the infinite, undivided consciousness which, not being an object of observation, is unknowable. Brahmā, Viṣṇu, Rudra, etc., are names which have by repeated use come to be regarded as real. Creation, not having a cause or a reason, is non-existent. But one cannot assert that there is non-existence or that there is something.

When one's mind rests in perfect tranquility, what it is is the reality. In that reality this world appears to be. The world-appearance does not arise out of nothing! Hence, one has to conclude that Brahman alone is, even in the form of this creation. Creation is but a word, a name. The reality is Brahman. 'I', 'you' and 'the world' are names that exist in Brahman as Brahman.

The ocean, the mountain, the clouds, earth, etc., are all the unborn and uncreated. This universe exists in Brahman as the Great Silence (kāṣṭha mauna—silence of a log of wood). The seer exists in the scene as seeing, on account of his own essential nature. The doer exists as the deed, since there is no reason for him to do anything. In it there is neither a knower nor a doer, neither inertness nor experiencer, neither void nor substance. Life and death, truth and falsity, good and evil—all these are of one substance, like waves in the ocean. The division between the seer (subject) and the scene (object) is fanciful.

However much one may try, the cause for this creation is not found: that which shines without reason or cause is surely non-existent except as an illusion. It exists as itself and it shines because it is it, without creator-creation relationship.

RĀMA asked:

One sees that the whole tree is hidden in the banyan seed. Why should we not accept that even so is the world hidden in Brahman?

VASIṢṬHA replied:

Where such a seed exists and where co-operating causes exist too, there is the possibility of a creation. When all the elements are dissolved during cosmic dissolution, where is the seed-form and where are the co-operating causes? When the infinite, indivisible consciousness alone is the truth, there is no scope for the existence even of the subatomic particle, much less the seed for this creation. Whatever is the supreme being, that itself is this universe. The one infinite consciousness conceives of itself as the false in the false and as pure consciousness in pure consciousness. Just as space (distance) exists in space, all this exists in Brahman.

VASIṢṬHA continued: VI.2:55

Since right in the very beginning there was neither a cause nor a motivation for creation to arise, there is neither being nor non-being, neither gross matter nor subtle mind, neither moving objects nor immobile objects. Consciousness is without form and cannot create this world of name and form, since cause and effect are identical and only that which has form can create or change into some other form. The self remains the self all the time, fancying within the undivided consciousness all these diverse objects. Whatever that consciousness experiences as if within itself, that and that alone is 'called' the world or this creation.

Before all this happened (that is, when one realises that all this is unreal and non-existent), know that the one Brahman alone existed, utterly peaceful and homogeneous. Infinite consciousness is infinite consciousness, water is water: and since this 'creation' is conjured up by consciousness, it appears to be so created. Just as the world one dreams of is an illusory appearance in one's consciousness, even so in the wakeful state this world appears in consciousness, as consciousness.

In the original creation, the dream of the undivided consciousness is known as the wakeful state (the world which is experienced in the wakeful state). The dream that rises in the consciousness of the beings that arise in that ignorance, is known as the dream state. This fanciful dream has 'materialised' into this world order by constant repetition. The river is but the movement of water; creation is the fancy of the infinite consciousness.

It is not right to consider that 'death' is a state of bliss on account of the total destruction of the self. It is a state of void (like space). This vision of saṃsāra will arise again. If there is fear on account of evil actions, the consequences are the same here or 'there'. Hence, there is no vital distinction between life and death. Knowing this one attains peace of mind. When thus perception of division ceases, the vision of oneness arises. This is known as liberation. Whether this creation is or is not, there is then both a total understanding of the absence of objects and the experience of the indivisibility of the infinite. When thus the object and therefore the subject is unrealised, then there is great peace. In the supreme self, of course, there is neither bondage nor liberation.

One who thus realises the truth attains nirvāṇa. This very world-appearance, which is but the slight movement in consciousness, is also realised as nirvāṇa by him. He realises that this creation is not diversity but is pure Brahman only.

VI.2:56 VASIṢṬHA continued:

The pure void exists everywhere in every way at all times in this space which is consciousness. Consciousness exists here and there in the form of this creation; there is no unconsciousness anywhere because all this is but pure consciousness. Even that which appears to be matter is but pure consciousness. In this connection, O Rāma, listen to the following story of the rock which was seen by myself.

Once upon a time, I desired to renounce all the activities of the world, having clearly understood whatever there was to know. I wished to meditate in total seclusion without ceasing and without interruption. Resorting to a secluded spot, I contemplated as follows:

The entire world is devoid of any worth or value. Nothing in this world is capable of giving me the least happiness. What am I seeing and who am I? In order to find the right answers, I must go away to that place which is beyond the reach of even the demons and the gods and there meditate in total seclusion without fear of distraction.

Where shall I find such a spot? The forests are full of the noise of flowing water and of roaming lions. Just as the city full of people is distracting, the ocean is also full of various sources of distraction. Even the caves are not free from distraction; they resound with the movement of wind and they are full of creepers, etc. The lakes are often the sporting grounds for people as well as the celestials and are therefore full of distractions. Having thus examined all the spots on earth, I decided to go away into the outerspace. But even there I found distractions caused by the clouds, by the celestials and the demons, by the celestial bodies and the departed souls.

Having abandoned all these, I went to a lonely spot far, far away where even the natural elements could not reach. In that empty place I fancied the existence of a hermitage. In my own mind I made it inaccessible to any being. I sat in the lotus posture. I made my mind tranquil. I resolved that I would sit in samādhi for a hundred years. In accordance with the rule that one sees what one contemplates for a long time, my fanciful wishes materialised and were spread out in front of me. These one hundred years passed as if in the twinkling of an eye, because when one's mind is perfectly concentrated the passage of time is not noticed.

When this period came to an end, my mind began to expand and spread out. All the goblins of 'I' and 'you' reached me slowly with the help of the life-forces which began to move in me. Immediately desire entered my heart; I do not know from where it came and how it came into me.

RĀMA asked: VI.2:57

O sage, how is it that even in the case of a person who is established in nirvāṇa, the egosense could thus arise?

VASIṢṬHA replied:

Whether one is a knower of the truth or ignorant of it, without the egosense the body cannot exist. That which needs to be sustained cannot exist without a support. But there is a vital difference which I shall presently explain to you.

The little boy known as ignorance has created this goblin known as egosense which seems to exist within oneself unperceived. This ignorance is a non-entity, too, because it is not seen to exist when investigated; darkness does not exist when it is seen with the help of a lamp. When one looks for this goblin known as ignorance it does not exist. But in the absence of such investigation when it is taken for granted and when one is under its influence, it expands and gets established. This world is created by that ignorance which is real only to the ignorant; it is not real. That (infinite consciousness or Brahman) which is beyond the mind and the senses cannot be the seed nor the cause for the coming into being of that which is the object of the mind and the senses. When there is no seed, how can there be a sprout?

In this infinite consciousness it is a mere fancy that appears to be the created universe. This consciousness alone is known as Īśvara or god and also as this creation. It is like one's own dream-creation which is everybody's daily experience. Because the dreamer is a conscious being, the dream-objects appear to have an intelligence and a mind of their own; even so this non-creation known as the universe seems to possess independent existence and intelligence as if it had been created. There is no creation as such: the one Brahman exists as Brahman. Whatever notion arises in this Brahman is experienced by Brahman as if it were an object of experience. That Brahman itself fancies that all this is 'creation'. But then the experiencer, experiencing and experience are one and indivisible: even so Brahman, the notion of creation and creation are only Brahman. Such being the case, how can egosense or the false notion of 'I' arise?

Thus have I told how to lay this ghost of egosense which vanishes on being rightly understood. The egosense has thus been clearly understood by me. Hence, even though the egosense seems to arise in me, it is inoperative, like a painting of fire. Thus have I abandoned the egosense. I exist in space as if outside it, in creation as if out of it. I do not belong to the egosense nor does it belong to me or exist in me. I am not nor is there another in my vision; all is and nothing is.

VI.2:58, 59 VASIṢṬHA continued:

In the story of the rock that I am going to narrate to you, O Rāma, it will become clear that within the core of the rock there are thousands of creations. In this physical space, too, there are similarly countless creations. In fact, in every element or object there are countless creatures. But all these exist only in the indivisible infinite consciousness, not as real substances or entites. Nothing has ever been created right from the beginning. Brahman alone exists in Brahman, as space, air, fire, water, earth, mountains, etc. There is no division or duality between Brahman and creation, which are but two words without meaning. Even unity and duality are words without meaning. That which creates these notions of unity and diversity also creates the notions of Brahman and creation. When these notions have ceased, there is great inner peace even if one is engaged in activity. Everything is nirvāṇa. The perceived creation is like the sky (void though appearing to have a form and colour). Behold the entire universe composed of you, I, mountains, gods and demons, etc., as you would behold the creations and the happenings of a dream.

The World Within the Rock

After having remained in samādhi for one hundred years, I returned to body-consciousness and heard a sigh. I listened to it and tried to guess what it might be. I was far, far in the outerspace so how could any person or even a bee exist so near me there? Moreover, I could not see any one. I decided to investigate it further. I decided to enter into samādhi again. I silenced the mind and the senses. I merged in the infinite consciousness. I saw reflected in that consciousness the image of countless universes. I was able to go anywhere and to see everything. I saw countless creations though they did not know of one another's existence. Some were coming into being, others were perishing, all of them had different shielding atmospheres (from five to thirty-six atmospheres). There were different elements in each, they were inhabited by different types of beings in different stages of evolution with different natures and cultures, some had other universes within them, in some there were creatures you would not believe possible to exist, in some there was apparent natural order and in others there was utter disorder, in some there was no light and hence no time-sense. All these are but the fruits of the one indivisible infinite consciousness. How and when they arose it is impossible to say; but this much is certain—they are the creations of ignorance. In this creation there are gods and demons numerous as mosquitoes. Whether one regards these universes as the creations of the supreme Creator or as false notions, it is certain that they are in fact the infinite consciousness, non-different and not independent of it. They rest like inert realities in the descriptions found in the scriptures. Thus did I behold all these infinite creations.

VASIṢṬHA continued: VI.2:60

Eventually, my attention was directed to the source of the sound. I saw a woman who was radiant and who illumined all the directions of space. She was highly cultured. She approached me gently and said in a sweet voice: "O sage, you have truly conquered the evils like lust, anger and greed. Your mind is totally free and unattached. Hence I salute you from all sides." Now that I knew the source of the sound, I decided to move on, considering that I had nothing to do with this woman.

Then I saw many universes and their diversity aroused my curiosity. I wanted to roam more and more to see the magnitude of creation. After some time I abandoned that idea knowing that it was delusion and remained established in the infinite consciousness. Instantly, all this perception of diversity vanished from my sight. There was the pure consciousness, nothing else. This is the truth: all else is imagination, notion, delusion or illusory perception.

Because the entire creation is enveloped by this ignorance or delusion, the inhabitants of one creation or one universe or one world do not even know of the existence of others. These diverse worlds are unaware of the notions or creations of others, even as people sleeping in the same room are unaware of the battle cries uttered by one another in their dreams. In these universes I saw thousands of Brahmās, Viṣṇus and Rudras. All these are in consciousness, all these are consciousness and consciousness alone is all this: hence as consciousness I saw all this.

Rāma, when you look at something and say, "It is such and such", consciousness shines there as such and such, though in truth this consciousness alone exists as itself and no such name and form exist there. This space or plane of consciousness alone exists everywhere at all times: and that itself is called the world. The perception of objects here (which we call knowledge of that object) is the only ignorance or delusion. I saw that the truth, on the other hand, is that the space or plane of consciousness alone exists. With the enlightened intelligence I also experienced the final truth concerning all this—that all this is pure, indivisible, infinite consciousness. On account of the persistence of the perception of diversity, I saw in it countless Vasiṣṭhas, countless ages and world-cycles and many ages in which Rāma flourished. When there is perception of diversity all these arise; when there is realisation of the truth, all these are seen to be pure, indivisible, infinite consciousness. In the infinite, of course, there are no name and no form which could be referred to as 'This is the world or creation'. Brahman alone exists as Brahman.

VI.2:60, 61 VASIṢṬHA continued:

Brahman is one and all these are appearances which the light of Brahman makes manifest without intending to do so. On account of this there arises great diversity of experience. For instance, in some universes moonlight is hot and sunlight cool, there is sight in darkness and blindness in daylight, good is destructive and evil constructive, poison promotes health and nectar kills, in accordance with the notions that arises in consciousness. In some universes there are no woman and therefore no sexuality and in others people have pitiless hearts. In some universes people do not possess one or more of the senses. In some, only one or two of the elements exist, though they, too, are inhabited by living creatures adapted to suit local conditions.

All these arise as consciousness in consciousness through consciousness; and this is known as the mind.

RĀMA asked:

Since everything attains liberation at the end of a world-cycle, during the cosmic dissolution, how does the notion of the next creation arise?

VASIṢṬHA replied:

O Rāma, Brahman is an indescribable mass of cosmic consciousness. The creation is its very heart and therefore non-different from it. It is apprehended as creation mysteriously, not really. Since its creation is false, how can one say that it perishes at some time? Even cosmic dissolution, etc., are the limbs of Brahman, as it were. Such divisions appear only in ignorance. Therefore, nothing perishes at any time, nor does anything come into being. The supreme truth or consciousness is indestructible by weapons, fire, wind and water. It is not realised by those who do not know it. The universe which is the heart of this truth is also like it; it is neither born nor does it die. Experience of its existence and non-existence arises with the rising and cessation of the appropriate notion. Hence, even words like 'world-cycle', 'cosmic dissolution', etc., are sound without substance. The ghost exists or disappears only in the heart of one who thinks of it. What are seen as birth, death, pain, pleasure, form and formlessness are all limbs of the one being. There is no division among them, even as there is no division in the several parts of the one tree. When this truth is not realised, then the apparent divisions seem to arise. In Brahman there is neither knowledge nor ignorance; it is beyond bondage and liberation. Realising this is liberation.

RĀMA asked: VI.2:62

Did you see all this from one spot where you were or did you roam about in space?

VASIṢṬHA replied:

I had attained infinite consciousness then. In it there is no coming or going. I did not remain in one spot nor did I roam about. I witnessed all this within the self which had assumed the form of what I witnessed. Just as you see your body from head to foot with even closed eyes, thus I saw everything with the eye that is consciousness.

This is like the dream: whatever is experienced in the dream is pure space (dimension) of consciousness. Even now, on account of enlightenment, I behold all this. I am now one with all the enlightened beings; I know them all as my own self, without the division of subject, object and observation, since the one consciousness alone exists indivisibly.

In answer to the question concerning the lady, VASIṢṬHA said: She, too, with a space-body stood with me in space. I had not noticed her earlier. Though she was endowed with a space-body, she was able to communicate with me (who also had a space-body) in a cultured voice and diction, even as in dream one speaks to another. What sort of certainty do you have to assert the existence of the inner senses? We had bodies similar to them. This is true in my case, yours, hers and everything else. Just as one experiences warfare in one's dream, even so do people experience the events in this creation as if they were real. However, all illustrations are inadequate and truth is beyond words. If one were to ask, "How do you see a dream?" the answer would be "As you see it". All this is for your understanding: The truth is that this universe as well as all that you see in your dream is but Brahman.

There is no essential difference between the dream state and this visible creation. That experience which immediately precedes the waking state is known as a dream; that experience or knowledge which arose in the beginning of this world-creation is known as the waking state. The experience of the existence of the world is a long dream, or it is a void. It is pure consciousness because it is established in the eternal reality. You are the witness or observer of your own dream; even so the infinite consciousness is the observer of the long dream known as creation. Even as the observer and the observed are consciousness, that which is in the middle (the observation) is also pure, indivisible and unmodified Brahman. Such being the case, how can this creation be considered solid and substantial or material? Even the dream of embodied (with form) beings like you is immaterial. How can the long dream of infinite consciousness which has no form come to have form? Hence, it is uncreated Brahman alone.

VI.2:63 RĀMA asked:

O sage, how could that formless woman utter words?

VASIṢṬHA replied:

Of course, they who are endowed with a space-body cannot utter audible sounds. If that were possible then your dream conversation could be heard by another sleeping near you. Hence, it is clear that what is seen in a dream is an illusion based on pure consciousness alone. What is experienced as the waking life is not entirely different from the dream-experience. It is but the play of consciousness: the notions that arise in that consciousness appear to be clothed in solid reality.

The seeds of past experience are in consciousness and they sprout new experiences which are sometimes identical with past experience and sometimes somewhat different. The worlds that thus sprout from those seeds are not aware of one another. During the course of life in this dream-world the demons are killed by the gods, and the demons remain in their dream-state. Not being enlightened, they do not attain liberation. Not being insentient, they do not become insentient but retain awareness. Hence they live in a space-body in a dream-world. Even so is the case with the so-called human beings. Their world, their life and their mentality are like ours, and vice versa. We exist as their dream-objects. Their own compatriots, though they are also dream-objects, are considered to be real entities by them. In the same way, the objects that appear in every one of my dreams are real to me.

Because of the very nature of the infinite consciousness, these dream-creations seem to exist in the waking state, too. Their reality is of course the sole reality, Brahman. Everything exists everywhere at all times as the indivisible, pure consciousness, but it is nothing and nothing is therefore destroyed.

In the eternal space (dimension) of infinite consciousness, in the infinite play of the infinite, there are infinite minds and infinite worlds in them. In every one of them there are continents and mountains, villages and cities with houses inhabited by people who have their own time-scale and life span. When these jīvas reach the end of the life span, if they are not enlightened they continue to exist in infinite space, creating their own dream-worlds. Within them are other people within whom are minds; within those minds are worlds in which there are more people, ad infinitum.

This illusory appearance has no beginning and no end; it is Brahman and Brahman alone. O Rāma, in all these diverse objects there is nothing but pure consciousness. Consciousness alone is this universe. Then how is it possible to say that there are worlds which seem to exist in the minds of the ignorant?

Asked by Vasiṣṭha who she was, the CELESTIAL replied: VI.2:64

O sage, in this vast universe, in a corner, you have the world in which you live. Beyond the boundaries of this universe are mountains known as the Lokāloka mountains. That region has every form of climatic and elemental permutation and combination. (The description in the text is elaborate and interesting. S.V.) Somewhere in it only humans dwell, elsewhere gods dwell; in it there are goblins as also very long-lived beings. In it there are self-luminous places and others of utter darkness, fertile fields and deserts, densely populated places and uninhabited areas.

I dwell within a solid rock which lies on the north-eastern slopes of that mountain-range. I am bound by destiny to live within the heart of this rock. I have thus lived in it for countless aeons. My husband, too, is destined to live here. Till today we have not been able to attain liberation on account of our intense desire (kāma) and on account of our intense attachment for each other. Similar is the fate of our relatives.

My husband who is thus in bondage is a brāhmaṇa by birth. He is ancient. He does not move from his seat though he has been sitting there for countless centuries. He is a celibate from birth (brahmacārī), educated and lazy. He lives in seclusion as he is not moved by craving for pleasure. Being his wife I lead a miserable life, yet I cannot live without him even for a single moment.

I shall tell you how I became his wife. When he was young he was partially awakened inwardly. He desired to have as his wife one who would help him in his spiritual quest. I was born of that wish, a mental creature to be his mental wife. As such I grew up to be a young woman. I began to delight in hearing good music and enjoying myself in different ways.

I support not only my husband but all the three worlds which exist in him. Though I had come of age and my body was bursting with signs of beauty and youth, my husband remained in the state of deep sleep over long periods of time or he was engaged in religious activities. He did not consummate our marriage, though I crave for such consummation all the time. I am burning with desire. My attendants do their best to alleviate my suffering, but all such efforts only add to my anguish. Burning with desire I shed tears constantly. O sage, there are lovely flowers and cool snow all around here; but because I am burnt by the fire of desire, I experience them as useless ashes. Lying in the bed decked with flowers and garlands which are meant to enhance my delight, I experience a dryness and an emptiness and my youth is being wasted.

VI.2:65 The CELESTIAL continued:

After a considerable time, the same attachment and affection I had for my husband became non-attachment and dispassion. My husband had grown old, he was interested only in seclusion and was devoid of all attachment and taste for sensual pleasures; he was ever silent. Of what use is life itself to me? I consider child-widowhood, even death or disease or even the worst calamity preferable to a husband whose nature is not after one's own heart. Indeed, the greatest blessing and the fruition of the life of a woman are that she obtains a young husband who enjoys life and whose conduct and behaviour are sweet and agreeable.

A woman whose husband does not enjoy life is frustrated. The uncultivated intellect is destructive. Wealth which falls into the hands of wicked people is misfortune. When one's shame has been extinguished by a prostitute there is great harm. She is a woman who follows the husband. That is wealth which seeks the good people. That alone is intelligence which is sweet and not limited, noble and endowed with equal vision.

If the husband and wife are fond of each other, then neither diseases of the body nor those of the mind, neither calamities nor natural disasters, afflict their minds. To the woman whose husband is of bad character or who does not have a husband, the pleasure-gardens of the world are burning sands. A woman can abandon everything in this world for one reason or another, but she cannot abandon her husband.

You yourself see, O sage, what unhappiness I have endured all these years. But now I have cultivated dispassion. Now I have only one desire: to be instructed by you so that I may attain nirvāṇa. Death is preferable to life to one whose desires are frustrated here and whose heart is agitated and who is slowly proceeding towards death. My husband, too, is desirous of attaining nirvāṇa. He is endeavouring to control the mind by the mind. Lord, awaken self-knowledge in both of us with your words of the highest wisdom.

Because my husband had no interest in me, I developed dispassion. The mental conditioning became weak and I practised yoga which conferred on me control over space, so that I can move in space. Thereupon I practised such concentration as would bring about my meeting with the perfected ones. All these have borne fruit.

When I flew away from my own world, I saw a rock on the Lokāloka mountains which I had not seen before. We had no desire to see this before. My husband and I now desire to attain self-knowledge. I beg of you to grant this boon, for holy men do not decline such a request. I have seen many perfected ones, but none like you. I take refuge at your feet; do not abandon me.

When asked by Vasiṣṭha how she lived in the rock, the CELESTIAL said: VI.2:66, 67

O sage, that world of ours within that rock is just like your world out here! In our world, too, there are heaven and hell, gods and demons, the sun and the moon, the firmament and the stars, the mobile and the immobile creatures, hills and oceans and the particles of dust that are known as living beings. Come, why don't you bless that rock with a visit: sages are always interested in wonders. (This earth is also a pebble in the vast space!—S.V.)

VASIṢṬHA continued:

Accompanied by her I coursed the space and reached the Lokāloka and saw the rock. I saw it was but a rock and there was no world in it. I questioned her: where is your world with all its gods and demons, mountains and oceans, the world which you described so graphically?

The CELESTIAL replied:

Truly, O sage, I now see that what I previously saw in the rock is only in me. It was by repeatedly projecting that vision and experiencing it in the rock that I thought that I saw it: now that I do not so experience it, that vision has gone. In you the sense of duality had ceased long ago: hence you do not entertain any false notions. Even in me the long-standing illusion has been dispelled by right perception: hence I do not see that world clearly. The present realisation of the truth being stronger than the past illusory notion, the latter has become dim.

O sage, this is the only path to salvation: one should be totally devoted to the one desirable cause, one should be instructed in the right effort for its attainment and one should again and again engage oneself in such right action. By the right effort (abhyāsa) ignorance is dispelled and the ignorant become enlightened. It is by right effort that even bitter things are relished. It is by repeated practice that a stranger becomes a friend, and when a close relative is separated from oneself it is through the absence of such repeated contemplation that the relationship is lost. It is by repetition that the subtle body becomes the physical body. By persistent effort, the impossible becomes possible. False relationships have been forged by persistent effort; they should also be resolutely abandoned by persistent effort till the end of one's life. By persistent effort one brings the desired object close to himself. Such effort enables him to attain it without obstacle.

Persistent and repeated effort is known as abhyāsa. That alone is the greatest goal of man (puruṣārtha) and there is no other path. Only by persistent and determined self-effort and by one's own direct experience is perfection attained, not by any other means. It is by such abhyāsa that one becomes utterly fearless everywhere in the world.

The description in chapter 66 of the world-within-the-rock is elaborate and highly interesting.

VASIṢṬHA continued: VI.2:68

When the celestial said thus, I sat in the lotus-posture and entered into samādhi or deep contemplation. I abandoned all material and physical concepts and held on to the vision of the pure consciousness. I had become the infinite consciousness, as it were, and had attained cosmic vision which is of the greatest purity.

On account of this realisation of the truth, the delusion concerning the material or physical ceased in me. In its place there was the great consciousness which neither rises nor sets. There was awareness in which I saw neither space nor the rock but I was aware of only the infinite. Whatever was seen before was but the one self and now I realised the self alone was all that was seen and experienced. What appeared to be the rock before was nothing but the (space of) infinite consciousness (cidākāśa).

Man is but the dream-object of another and he dreams he is a man. However, in course of time even they who are victims of the worst form of delusion are enlightened (awakened) because there is nothing but the truth or Brahman, which is eternal. Therefore that which I saw earlier as the rock I knew not to be a mass of pure consciousness. There is no such thing as earth or matter.

The self of the elements or beings is the body of Brahman. That concept alone is now seen as a notion or imagination. The cosmic subtle body appears to be, on account of the rising of this notion. The first-arising notion or thought is the body of the jīva. That ignorant thought (viz., the I-thought) now thinks that the mind is an obvious reality. For no reason or purpose at all, these notions that the mind is an obvious reality (pratyakṣa) arise; consciousness thus becomes other than itself. What is called obvious reality now (the body, etc.) is an obvious unreality. Paradoxically, the obvious is unreal and the unreal becomes obvious. Such is the mysterious power of illusion.

The subtle body is the first among these obvious truths. The truth is omnipresent and matter is but illusion, even though it may be experienced—just as 'the braceletness' of gold is an illusory appearance of gold, though people may point to it and proclaim that it is a bracelet. The subtle cosmic body (ātivāhika) is not material. It is on account of non-understanding that the jīva falls under the sway of this illusion: what foolishness! The material or physical body is not found on enquiry; and the subtle body exists unchanged even in the two worlds (the here and the hereafter).

VASIṢṬHA continued:

The gross physical body exists in the ātivāhika or the subtle body even as water exists in a mirage. On account of the erroneous perception of the body, this physical body comes to be accepted as an entity—even as a piece of wood is taken to be a man. How mysterious and how powerful is illusion that it makes the unreal appear real and the real appear unreal! This illusion exists only because of the non-understanding of the truth.

The activity and the behaviour of beings in this world are governed mainly by the vision of the yogis, and to a small degree by the perception of the mind. Hence, these two may be accepted as true. But, he who abandons the former and clings to the reality of matter endeavours to quench his thirst with the water of the mirage.

Momentary pleasure is pain. Real delight is unmodified, beginningless and endless. Hence, investigate the truth with the help of direct experience; behold the primordial truth by direct experience. One who abandons this experience and runs after illusory 'realities' is a fool.

The subtle immaterial body alone is real; in it the perception of the material or physical body is unreal and illusory. How can the latter be experienced as real when it is only notional and has never been created? When you know that what is obviously seen is illusory and unreal, what else can be accepted as real? How can that be accepted as real, which is established by what is unreal?

When such is the case of the first and foremost proof (pratyakṣa or direct experience), what value can be placed in inference?

Hence, the existence of the objective universe said to have been proved by these methods (direct sense-experience, inference and scientific investigation) is false and unreal. Duality or diversity is false: the one mass of infinite consciousness alone is real. Just as an object seen in a dream is unreal, even so what was seen by us as a rock is unreal; it is pure consciousness only. Realise that this mountain, this space, the world and the 'I' are all but the one infinite, indivisible consciousness.

One who is enlightened (awakened) realises this, not the unenlightened. It is because of the false feeling 'I am not enlightened' that this ignorance of the reality has come to be firmly established. He who abandons the realisation of the direct experience of the Lord who is of the nature of the indivisible, infinite consciousness and clings to other forms of experience, is surely foolish. What have we to do with such people?

VI.2:69 VASIṢṬHA continued:

Then that celestial entered into the world within the rock. I too went with her. There she went to where the Creator of that world was seated and sat in front of him. She then said to me: "O sage, this is my husband. He created me in order to have me as his wife.

However, he did not consummate that marriage. Now he and I are both aged. I have attained dispassion. He is not distracted from his meditation. Pray, enlighten both of us concerning the root-cause of this saṃsāra so that we may be liberated from it." Having said this, she 'awakened' her husband, the Creator, to ordinary consciousness and said to him: "Lord, behold the sage who has arrived at our abode. He is our guest. He is the son of the creator of another world. It is our duty as householders to honour and worship our guests."

The Creator of the other world (of the rock) opened his eyes. He became aware of his own 'limbs'. These limbs were in fact different 'created' beings who arose in that awareness. At once there appeared before him different types of beings—gods, demons, humans, etc. He saw me and also his wife seated in front of him. He welcomed me and bade me be seated on a bejewelled seat. I returned the salute and sat on the seat. There was celestial music and also singing of hymns. We all appropriately greeted one another.

Then I asked the second Brahmā: "Lord, this celestial brought me here and she said to me that I should instruct both of you in a way that you may both be enlightened. Is that right and appropriate? For you yourself are the Lord of all creatures and the master of the highest wisdom; she is not overcome by desire. How is it that you created her to be your wife; and if that is a fact, how is it that you ignored her and did not consummate the marriage?"

THE CREATOR IN THE ROCK replied:

O sage, listen and I shall tell you everything as it happened. There is only one consciousness which is unborn and tranquil. There arose in it a little movement, a vibration or a ripple. That is what I am. I am of the essential nature of pure space. I rest in the self. Since I arose without any cause or material, I am known as self-born. I have not been created at all and I do not see anything. What is seen here as you and I and what is seen as this dialogue between us are like two waves colliding in the ocean and making a sound. We are like the waves of the ocean, non-different from the ocean of infinite consciousness. We are but notions that spontaneously arise in it. This lady here who appears to be different from it has never been created, has not come into being at all: she is but a notion, a concept, a thought-wave or psychological conditioning. This body is made of the trace of egosense which existed in me and she is but the presiding deity, as it were, of this egosense. She is, therefore, neither my wife nor was she created as one.

THE OTHER WORLD'S BRAHMĀ continued: VI.2:70

Now I wish to enter into the plane or space of infinite consciousness; hence, I have manifested this dissolution which signals the cosmic dissolution. Hence, there is this dispassion in us. When I abandon the cosmic mind and merge in the infinite consciousness the destruction of all vāsanās (notions, etc.) is certain. Hence, this woman (who is the embodied vāsanā) has become dispassionate and follows me.

Now the world-cycle comes to an end and with it the end of the gods. This is also the moment of cosmic dissolution. It is the end of my own conditioning (vāsanā) and the utter transmutation of the body into space. Therefore, this vāsanā is about to perish. The desire for liberation arises in the vāsanā for no apparent reason; that is how vāsanā finds its own destruction. She had undertaken the practice of meditation, etc., but could not realise the self. She then saw the world in which you (the enlightened sage) lived.

At that time, she even saw the corner-stone of this my creation. This corner-stone of creation can only be perceived when the mind is ready to abandon perception of diversity, not while it is bound to such perception. There are countless worlds within worlds within all these objects and elements at all times, as if in this rock. Its appearance as 'the world' is of course an illusion, for it is pure consciousness. This illusory vision of 'the world' vanishes for one who has understood its true nature; but it continues to exist in the eyes of others.

By the previous practice of concentration, meditation, etc., she (the vāsanā) had gained dispassion; then in order to gain self-knowledge, she sought you.

Thus it is the power of the infinite consciousness alone that exists here as the impassable illusory power or Māyā. This power is beginningless, endless and imperishable. Time, space, matter, motion, mind, intellect, etc., are but parts of the consciousness like parts of the rock. The infinite consciousness alone exists as the rock of consciousness; its limbs are the worlds. This mass of consciousness thinks of itself as the world. Though it is beginningless and endless, it thinks it has a beginning and an end. Thus it seems to become. This mass of consciousness is formless yet it assumes the form of a rock. There are no rivers here. There is no revolving wheel nor matter undergoing change and transformation. All these are but appearances in the space or plane of infinite consciousness (cidambaram). Just as in the cosmic space there appears to exist the space called house and another called a pot (though surely space is indivisible and the existence of the space within the house does not diminish the total space), all these 'worlds' seem to exist in the infinite which is indivisible and which does not undergo any diminution thereby.

VI.2:71 VASIṢṬHA continued:

Having said this, the Creator (of the world-in-the-rock) entered into the deep and final state of meditation. He uttered OM and contemplated on the last phase of its intonation. His mind was utterly calm. He remained as if he were a painted picture. Vāsanā (the embodiment of the psychological conditioning in the form of the lady) also followed the Creator and entered into deep meditation. She attained the form of space. I too entered into deep meditation and witnessed all these, having become the omnipresent, infinite consciousness.

As the notions in the cosmic mind of the Creator began to die down, at that very moment itself the earth with its mountains, continents and oceans began to disappear. The grass and the trees ceased to be. The earth is one of the limbs of the cosmic person, the Creator. Hence, when the cosmic person withdrew his awareness from it, the earth ceased to be, even as in a state of paralysis when our awareness of a limb is withdrawn, it withers away and disintegrates.

The earth was hit at the same time by numerous natural catastrophes. The evil-doers were burnt by fire and they headed for hell. The earth had lost all its charm and its fruitfulness. The women had become immoral and men had lost their self-respect. A dense duststorm arose veiling the sun. The people were distressed by the pairs of opposites which in their foolishness they subjected themselves to. On account of floods and famine, wars and pestilence, humanity had been decimated. On account of numerous sufferings, people had become uncivilised and uncultured. Because of the suddenness with which all these terrible things happened, the noble people of the earth perished and there was hue and cry everywhere. There was scarcity of water and people began to dig deep wells. There was indiscriminate mixing between men and women and the social order broke down. Everyone lived by trade. Women lived (earned their living) by exhibiting the beauty of their hair. Kings followed the dictum 'might is right'. There was unrighteousness everywhere. The leaders were devoted to intoxicating drinks. They harassed and tortured the learned and the saintly men. People resorted to other ways of living or other faiths than that which was natural to them. The learned men became subject to violence and aggressiveness. Temples were looted. Even the holy ones abandoned the performance of the religious rites on account of laziness.

The cities had been burnt down by the fire that showered from the skies. Seasons became erratic. Thus had the earth-element reached its destruction, since the Creator had merged himself in the infinite consciousness.

VASIṢṬHA continued:

Once the earth-element had thus been absorbed in the infinite consciousness and had transcended its limitation, the water-element turned towards its own dissolution. When the water got agitated, it exceeded its own natural bounds and the oceans transgressed their bounds, overflowing in all directions. Making dreadful sounds, the waves lashed at the forests and began to destroy them. These mighty waves mingled with the clouds in the space and it became one mass of water. All the mountains were submerged under water. The aquatic creatures were in panic and ran helter-skelter in an attempt to escape from the calamity. When the waves destroyed the mountain caves, lions ran out of them, destroyed other creatures and were eventually themselves destroyed. The tumult raised by all this reached even the region of the sun.

It appeared as if the oceans had invaded the regions of the gods themselves and had occupied them. On account of the destruction of the forests and mountains caused by the power of the tidal waves, it looked as if the whole space were a big forest of trees and mountains. The great mountains were being dissolved in the waters of the ocean. At one stage it looked as though the mountains were laughing with their teeth bared, because, washed by the tidal waters, the precious and semi-precious stones that remained underground had become exposed on the mountain sides.

It looked as though even the celestial bodies were affected by this. The earth-mountains fell on some of them, making a loud noise. Even the fires of cosmic destruction appeared to be afraid of being put out by these tidal waves. At one stage there was terrible warfare between the earth-elephants and sea-elephants! The single ocean shone with a supernatural radiance at that time when so many earthly objects were getting drowned in it.

Then it looked as if the space itself were falling into the waters of cosmic dissolution. The firmament with all its light and its precious jewels fell into the flood.

Flames of fire spread out in all directions, consuming all that existed in space. Since the Creator had withdrawn his realisation of the world, the demons and others were let loose to cause what havoc they pleased. All the gods (Indra, etc., who are the deities presiding over the natural elements to maintain order among them) had been overpowered by the demons. There was chaos. Even the abodes of Śiva, etc., were shaken and disturbed. The stars and planets collided with one another and there was cosmic destruction.

VI.2:72 VASIṢṬHA continued:

When the creator Brahmā withdrew his prāṇa (the life-forces) the air which moves in space abandoned its natural function of motion in space. What else can sustain the elements and other beings?

When thus the force that held all the heavenly bodies had been withdrawn, the stars began to fall away from their orbits like flowers from trees. The satellites that were coursing the outer space also disintegrated on account of the time-space continuum being withdrawn when the life-forces were withdrawn. Even the path of the siddhas or the perfected ones was obliterated. Like bits of cottonwool, these siddhas began to fall in space. Even Indra (the chief of the gods) and his heaven began to fall and disintegrate.

RĀMA asked:

Consciousness is pure and the cosmic person is but a notion. How does this cosmic person or Brahmā come to acquire limbs like earth, heaven and the netherworld?

VASIṢṬHA continued:

In the beginning, O Rāma, there was but pure consciousness which could not be said to be either existence or non-existence. Within itself it became aware of itself as its object of awareness. Without abandoning its position as the subject it seems also to become the object. That is the jīva from which the mind, etc., arise. However, all these are non-different from pure consciousness.

When the mind which is also pure consciousness thinks 'I am space', it experiences space, though such space is non-existent. The self or pure consciousness is void and immaterial. As long as there is the notion of the physical universe, consciousness experiences it as if it were real; when it so wills it, it winds up this creation which then comes to an end.

Vāsanā or psychological conditioning, which gives rise to notions and to experiences of all kinds, ceases to be when the vision of the truth or the understanding of the reality arises. There is egolessness and therefore oneness: liberation or mokṣa alone remains after that.

This is the nature of Brahmā. This is how the world exists as the body of Brahmā, the cosmic person. The notion that arises in that cosmic person appears to be this universe. It is pure void; in fact, there is no such thing as the world nor what can be regarded as 'you' or 'I'. In pure and indivisible consciousness what is the world, how and by whom is it created and with what materials or co-operating causes? It appears but it is no more than an illusory appearance. It is neither one with the infinite consciousness nor different from it. There is neither unity nor diversity. Infinite, indivisible consciousness alone is the reality. Hence, live free from all conditioning, acting spontaneously and appropriately in each situation.

RĀMA said: VI.2:73

Lord, I have clearly understood whatever you have been telling me so far, but there is no satiety in your discourse. It is like immortalising nectar. Hence, describe the experience of creation again.

VASIṢṬHA continued:

During what is known as the cosmic dissolution, whatever appears to exist now is dissolved. What remains is the eternal. It is beyond description. In comparison with a mustard seed, the Meru-mountain is immense; so in comparison with that eternal infinite consciousness the space is like a mustard seed. In comparison with the greatest among mountains, a subatomic particle is minute: even so are the comparative dimensions of this world universe and that eternal infinite consciousness. During the cosmic dissolution when all world-appearance has ceased, the eternal infinite consciousness remains aware of every subatomic particle that exists in the cosmic space. It sees them (though they are unreal) as if in a dream; then it imagines itself to be 'Brahman'. It even conceives of itself as the infinite consciousness. Considering itself as the atomic particle of consciousness, it exists as the subject, apparently seeing the atomic particle which becomes the object. This is like a man seeing himself in a dream. Thus, consciousness apparently polarises itself into the subject and the object without ever abandoning its own indivisibility.

At that moment the following principles arise spontaneously: time, space, action, matter, the seer (subject), sight and the scene (object). However, the forces that restrain or obstruct these do not arise. Where the consciousness-particles shine, space manifests there; when this happens there is time; and the way in which it happens becomes action; whatever is experienced as existing becomes matter; the experiencer becomes the subject; the experiencing or the seeing of this matter is the sight; and that which is responsible for this seeing or experiencing becomes the object. Thus do all these apparently come into being, though they are all false. Space alone appears in space without any particular order of sequence or principle.

Similarly, that material in which this consciousness shines is known as the body; that by which it sees is known as the eye. Even so with regard to the other senses, etc. That state in which this consciousness shines without name and form is known as the tanmātra (pure element) which is of the nature of space or void alone. This radiance of the atomic particle of consciousness itself becomes gross and comes to be known as the body; then there arise the five senses in it. That which is aware of all this is known as buddhi or intelligence. With thinking arises mind in which the egosense is rooted.

VASIṢṬHA continued:

As the particle of consciousness moves in space, it does 'there' what it did 'here' earlier. Thus sequence of time arises, as well as spatial distinctions like 'above', 'below' and the directions. Though it is of the nature of space or void, it seems to become time, space, action, matter and awareness of the meaning of words, etc. Thus the ātivāhika (subtle) body comes into being. This itself by continued awareness of itself seems to condense into the material body.

Consciousness becomes embodied though it is truly like space, incapable of being contained. In it there arise the ideas of 'head' and of 'feet', and it sees these as existing organs. Even so with the other limbs of the physical body. The same consciousness considers itself to be being and non-being, taking and rejecting, order and all the rest of it. It sees these notions as if they were real. Even so does it become Brahmā the creator; even so does it attain (to the state) of Hari or Viṣṇu; even so does it attain (or seemingly become) Rudra or Śiva; even so does it seemingly become a worm. In truth, however, it has not become any of these; it is as it is, pure void in void, consciousness in consciousness.

That is the seed of all bodies in the three worlds. It is the seed of even the saṃsāra (world-illusion) which bars the gate to liberation. It is the cause of all and it is the leader of time and action. It is the first person who, though unborn, seems to be born. It does not have a material or physical body; hence it cannot be caught. Just as a man who is fighting with a lion in a dream shouts in that dream, though in truth he is silent and asleep, the infinite consciousness which entertains all these notions is at peace and silent within itself. The universe which extends to millions of miles in all directions exists in the minutest subatomic particle and the three worlds exist within one strand of hair (in comparison to the infinite consciousness).

Even Brahmā the creator, though he presides over the universe which is unimaginably vast and which is his body, exists in an atom; in fact, he does not occupy any space at all, just like the mountains seen in a dream. The cosmic person has been called svayambhū Brahmā (the self-born creator) also as virāṭ (cosmic person); but in truth, O Rāma, he is but pure consciousness. Because this consciousness becomes aware of motion, it experiences such motion or life-force. This is the prāṇa and the apāna whose whirling motion comes to be known as wind in the universe, which is the very heart of the universe. The exudations, as it were, of this prāṇa are known as vāta or wind, pitta or heat and śleṣma or moisture (the three humours of the body) and their cosmic counterparts—wind, sun and the moon.

VASIṢṬHA continued: VI.2:74

The cosmic person (virāṭ) has two bodies: the superior body is pure consciousness which is without beginning, end or 'middle', and the other body is this world. Hence, he is able to view the world (like an egg) from outside it (as a hen does). He divided the egg into two: the upper part he called the sky or the heaven and the lower part he called the earth. The upper part is known as the head of the virāṭ, the lower part is his feet and the middle (atmosphere) is his back or buttocks. The upper part, because it is so far away, is seen as the blue and empty sky.

The firmament is the palate of the virāṭ, and the stars are drops of blood. The 'particles of air' that course the body are gods, demons and humans. The germs and viruses in the body are the ghosts and goblins. The holes in the body are other worlds. His loins are the oceans. The nāḍis are rivers and the continent known as jambūdvīpa is his heart. The empty space is his stomach. The mountains are his liver and spleen. The clouds are his flesh. The sun and the moon are his eyes. The world of Brahmā is his face. Soma is his energy. The snow-bound mountains are his phlegm, the subterranean fire is his bile, the winds are his prāṇa and apāna. All the trees and the snakes are his hairs.

Since he is himself the cosmic mind, he has no mind. Since the infinite self alone apparently becomes the experience which is but pure consciousness, there is no experiencer apart from it. In the same way, since he is the experiencer in all the senses, there are no indriyas or senses in him. Therefore, the distinctions among the senses are but notions. The concept that indriyas (senses) stand in relation to the mind as the limbs to the body, is erroneous: there is no such distinction—even the body and the limbs are one unit.

Whatever actions take place in this world originate in him. On account of him the world is seen to be real; if he ceases to be, the world ceases to be. The world (creation), Brahmā the creator and virāṭ (the cosmic person) are figures of speech: they are but notions that arise in the pure, infinite consciousness.

RĀMA asked:

When this cosmic person is a mere notion, how does he exist in that body?

VASIṢṬHA replied:

In exactly the same way as you exist in your heart when you are in meditation. Just as the jīva exists in the bodies of all beings and just as a reflection exists in the mirror, this cosmic person exists in his own cosmic body. Though he appears to have all these limbs, etc., there is no division in him and he exists as a rock exists, whole and undivided, pure, infinite consciousness.

VI.2:75 VASIṢṬHA continued:

When Brahmā the creator was thus meditating, I looked around. I saw a sun rising in every direction. While I was looking at this extraordinary phenomenon, a sun arose right from the bowels of the earth, like a subterranean fire. There were eleven in all, with three more satellite-suns like the three eyes of lord Śiva, which together formed the twelfth sun. It was getting too hot there. So, I left that place and went away to a far-off place. The entire firmament was ablaze with the light of these suns. There was 'kat kat' and 'cat cat' sound everywhere.

Living beings were everywhere being scorched by the heat. Even the aquatic creatures were not exempt. The destruction was colossal and complete. Mountains fell on burning cities, grinding them into a paste. At that time people were weeping and wailing aloud. Others (yogis) who were able to make their life-force depart through the crown of their head, attained immortality. The earth was scorched by the fire that arose from above and below.

The entire world with all the beings in it was set ablaze by the fire that emanated from the eyes of Rudra. There was the sound 'bhum bhum bhum' everywhere and it looked as if the demonesses were playing by throwing streams of fire at one another. Meteors began to fall on the mountain-tops and began to 'dance' the dance of death and destruction. The fire that arose in the earth seemed to link the earth with the heaven or the entire universe. Even the Sumeru mountain which was made of solid gold began to melt. The snow-bound mountain (Himālaya) melted away. Only the Malaya mountain remained unharmed. Like the heart of a noble man who, even in his own suffering seeks to promote the happiness of others, that mountain stood spreading joy and peace—just as sandalwood gives of its fragrance even to one who burns it.

Only two objects remained unaffected: space being all-pervading could not be destroyed and gold being pure could not be destroyed. Hence, I believe that only satva (purity) is good and desirable, not rajas (activity or impurity) and tamas (inertia, stupidity).

When thus everything else had been destroyed, not even the ashes were seen. Even as when ignorance and its consequences are destroyed by the fire of the sage's wisdom, only the absolute purity remains without even the 'ashes' of past ignorance. For some time these fires could not reach Kailāsa, the abode of lord Rudra, but then he turned his fiery gaze on it and it began to burn.

Nothing was left. Future generations could only wonder, "Perhaps there was a world, a universe, a creation before".

VASIṢṬHA continued: VI.2:76

Then there arose the terrible winds of dissolution which blew so violently that the mountains and the oceans became exceedingly agitated and lost their natural behaviour and even the netherworld seemed to fall into something far below it. The entire creation became dried and essenceless.

After this there arose like an irate demon an enormous cloud which produced dreadful noise. It was like the sound that was made when Brahmā the creator broke the golden egg which gave rise to the created universe. The sound struck terror in everyone's heart because of the added sound of the disintegrating worlds and the oceans. It filled the entire created universe and united the earth with the heaven and the netherworld. It was unmistakably the sound of cosmic dissolution.

I heard that sound of the cloud. I wondered, "How could this cloud co-exist with the fires of cosmic dissolution?" I looked in all directions. I saw all round me showers of adamant and thunderbolt. In a moment I experienced the sensation of something cold above and something very hot and burning below. The cloud was so high above that it could neither be seen, nor could the fire reach it.

After consuming the worlds the fires had become pure sparks and shone with an extraordinary radiance. When the cloud of dissolution descended it appeared to be made of the most brilliant lightning. The waters of the seven oceans equalled only a very small part of a corner of that cloud. It appeared as though these very oceans had risen into the sky. The twelve suns were whirlpools in that cloud and the aquatic creatures were the lightning flashes that moved in it.

The rains came. Every drop of that rain was like a thunderbolt. These raindrops filled the entire space. They fell with such force that they destroyed whatever was left of the universe. The whole sky was one mass of water. The rain put out the fires and reached the earth-plane.

The waters of this extraordinary and supernatural rain mixed with the fires that were still burning. The two could not defeat or conquer each other, and hence they were ill-matched enemies (because their equal prowess made the conflict interminable and inconclusive). They were of great strength and power. Therefore, their collision was extremely fearsome to witness.

VI.2:77 VASIṢṬHA continued:

At that time, the entire space was clothed in the ashes of destruction. These ashes were churned by terrible winds. Falling rain was making more dreadful noise everywhere, which sounded like the victory cries of the demons of dissolution. The winds were carrying away the burnt remains of the cities of Indra (the god of heaven) and other deities.

Thus the three elements—water, fire and wind, were completely out of control, alignment or harmony; and it looked as though they were fighting with each other. The tumult and the sound of this chaos were deafening. The torrential rain put out the fires, producing the sound 'cham cham cham'. The mighty rivers that flowed down the mountains carried away other mountains, continents and cities. The planets and stars in the heavens were also falling out of their orbits. The great tidal waves were everywhere breaking down mountains and the wind was blowing these mountains away.

There was utter darkness everywhere as the rays of the sun were veiled by the rain and the clouds, which were of dark blue colour. The very support of the earth had completely disintegrated and therefore the mountains were disintegrating, too. The tidal waves were picking up these mountains and were hurling them at the clouds. It appeared as if the three worlds were weeping and wailing aloud.

The gods and the demons were all subject to these dreadful calamities, and yet they were still flying at one another's throats in interminable enmity.

Only the vital air or prāṇa which presides over the disintegration of material or physical bodies sustained these disintegrating objects and wafted them here and there. At that same time the entire space was filled with flying cities, demons, fire, serpents and suns, which looked like so many flies and mosquitoes.

Even the deities presiding over the different directions were approaching destruction and there was confusion in those directions. The dust of destroyed creation was everywhere. The entire universe was filled with the debris of 'temples' made of different precious stones and metals of different colours. It was difficult to see the universe.

Devoid of the veil of creation, that (truth or god) which remains after the total destruction of what is known as creation, alone existed. Once again there was fullness, the fullness that becomes apparent when the diverse creatures are destroyed, the fullness that was there all the time. By this time, of course, the cosmic fires of destruction had been completely put out by the torrential rains from the cosmic clouds.

VASIṢṬHA continued: VI.2:78, 79

There was no space. There were no directions. There was neither 'below' nor 'above'. There were neither elements nor a creation. There was but one limitless ocean.

Meanwhile, I saw Brahmaloka as the sun beholds the earth at sunrise. There Brahmā the creator was seated in samādhi or meditation as if he were an unshakable mountain, surrounded by the pradhāna or the first principles, the gods and the sages, the celestials and the siddhas who were also seated in the meditation-posture deeply engrossed in meditation, as if they were without life. The twelve suns also arrived there and entered into meditation.

After a brief period, I saw Brahmā and the others as one sees one's dream-objects on waking up. I saw them as so many manifestations of mental conditioning, not as the materialisation of the dream-objects.

I then realised that all these gods, etc., were also pure void. Without leaving that place they had vanished from sight. I realised that they too had attained nirvāṇa after having abandoned name and form, like Brahmā the creator. When the vāsanā or self-limiting conditioning had ceased in them they had become invisible. This body is but pure void, it seems to exist on account of the vāsanā or mental conditioning. When the latter ceases, the body ceases to be seen or experienced, just as the dream-object is not experienced on waking up. Even so neither the subtle (ātivāhika) body nor the gross (ādhibhautika) body is seen even in the waking state when the mental conditioning ceases. The example of the dream-state is given here because that is something everybody experiences. He who rejects his own experience is fit to be shunned from a great distance; who can wake up a man who pretends to sleep?

If it is argued that when the body which causes dream ceases to be, dream ceases, then in the absence of the body there is no life in the otherworld. Then surely there is no creation! If it is said that the world has never been what it is not, then it does not exist even now. If it is said that consciousness is an exudation of the body, etc., then the teachings of the scriptures become utterly useless. If you decide against their authority, why have any authority at all? If you accept that delusion exists as long as the body exists, then delusion becomes a reality. If consciousness arises in the body accidentally, why should not that consciousness realise its infinite nature?

Anyhow, whatever consciousness becomes aware of within itself, it experiences (whether one calls it real or unreal). Therefore, in the first instance, the self-nature knows itself as consciousness on account of its own inherent movement. Then on account of mental conditioning (vāsanā) it experiences deluded perception. Conditioned awareness is bondage; when there is no awareness of conditioning (or conditioned awareness) there is nirvāṇa.

VI.2:80 VASIṢṬHA continued:

When thus all the gods and also the twelve suns had become one with Brahmā, these suns began to burn away even the world of the Creator, as they had done with the earth. After burning the world of the Creator and entering into deep meditation like Brahmā, they entered into nirvāṇa like a lamp without fuel. Everything was then enveloped in dense darkness.

Meanwhile, I saw there a fearsome form. He was like embodied dissolution of the universe, like embodied darkness. However, he shone by his own radiance. He had five faces, ten arms and three eyes. He had a trident in his hand. He was moving in the space of his own being. He was dark like the rain-bearing cloud. It was as if he rose out of the cosmic ocean and as if he himself were the embodiment of that cosmic ocean. He looked like a winged mountain. From his trident and three eyes I thought "This is Rudra" and I bowed to him from a great distance.

RĀMA asked:

Who is this Rudra and what are his five faces, ten hands, etc.?

VASIṢṬHA continued:

O Rāma, he is known as Rudra and he is the egosense. He is devoted to the disturbance of the equilibrium. His form is pure space or void. He is of the form of space and therefore his colour is like that of space. Since he is pure, indivisible (like space) consciousness, he is known as the space-self (ākāśa-ātmā). Since he is the self of all and is omnipresent, he is known as the great self or the supreme self. The five senses (of knowledge) are his faces. The five organs of action and their five fields are his ten arms.

Only when the infinite consciousness becomes aware of itself does this form become manifest. Again, this form as the Rudra is but a small particle, as it were, of the infinite consciousness and hence does not exist as such in reality. The form is but an illusory perception.

He exists as the unfoldment or movement in cidākāśa (infinite consciousness) and as air in both the space in creation and in living beings (as the life-breath). In course of time, when all his movements come to an end, he attains supreme equilibrium. The three guṇas (satva, rajas and tamas), the three periods of time (past, present and future), the three inner instruments (citta, buddhi and ahaṃkāra), the three aspects of AUM and the three vedas are the three eyes of Rudra. The trident implies that he holds the three worlds in his hands. Since he is attained by satva or goodness and his very existence is for the good of all, he is known as Śiva. He then attains to the state of supreme peace and is therefore known as Kṛṣṇa. He himself creates (as kalpanā, imagination) the whole universe, and he drinks the one ocean of cosmic being and attains to that supreme peace.

VASIṢṬHA continued:

I then saw that this Rudra began to drink the cosmic ocean with the speed of the life-force or prāṇa. The waters of the cosmic ocean entered into his mouth in which a great fire was burning fiercely. That Rudra or egosense exists as the fire in the bowels of the ocean (or earth) and then at the end of the world-cycle he drinks the ocean. Indeed, this egosense is the all at all times.

At that time there were only four things in that pure and limitless space: (1) the black-coloured Rudra who stood without any support and without any motion, (2) the earth which was rather muddy and which was the abode of all the worlds, from the netherworld to the heaven, (3) the upper part of the creation, which being far, far away was beyond sight and (4) among all these, everywhere, there was the pure Brahman or the infinite consciousness pervading the different parts of the creation. Nothing else existed.

RĀMA asked:

What is the abode of Brahmā the creator, what are its veils and how does it exist?

VASIṢṬHA replied:

The abode of Brahmā (the centre of the earth-plane) is enveloped by water which is ten times the extent of the earth-plane. Even so the region of fire is ten times the extent of the water-plane. The region of air beyond it is ten times the extent of the fire-plane. Lastly, the space-plane is ten times the extent of the air-plane. Beyond that is the limitless space of Brahma-ākāśa.

RĀMA asked:

O sage, who holds this creation from above and from below?

VASIṢṬHA continued:

The earth, etc., are held in their position by the great body of the brahma-aṇḍa (the golden egg or the cosmic person).

RĀMA asked again:

O Lord, tell me by whom is the brahma-aṇḍa sustained.

VASIṢṬHA replied:

O Rāma, it is not supported by anyone at all, whether you regard it as falling or not-falling. For this universe has no form, no body, no materiality, though it seems to have a form. What exactly do we mean by 'it falls' and by 'holding it'? Whatever be the notion in the infinite consciousness, it remains in that manner. This creation is but the dream-city of the infinite consciousness. When it is thought of as 'falling' it seems to fall all the time; when it is thought of as existing in space, it stands and moves in space; when it is thought of as unmoving, it remains motionless. When it is thought to have been destroyed, it appears to have been destroyed.

VI.2:81 VASIṢṬHA continued:

Then I saw that Rudra began to dance in space, as if he were intoxicated. It was as if the waters of the cosmic dissolution had assumed a form and were dancing in that form. Lo and behold! Even as I was watching the dance of Rudra, I saw a shadow behind him. How could shadow exist without sun, I asked myself. As I was reflecting over this phenomenon, that shadow (female) stepped in front of Rudra, and she was also dancing.

She had three eyes. She was of dark colour. She was thin. But she was huge. Her mouth emitted fire. She looked like the dark night or the limitless space embodied as a female. Her arms extended to the farthest reach of space. She was so thin that her nerves were visible and it appeared that since she was thin and tall someone had bound her with those nerves so that she might not collapse. She wore a garland made of the heads of gods, suns and demons. She wore earrings of snakes.

Now she had one arm, a moment later she had many arms and a moment later she hurled her arms on the dance-floor. Now she had one mouth, a moment later she had many mouths and a moment later still she had no mouth at all. Now she had one foot, a moment later she had many feet and a moment later still she was without feet. I concluded from all this that she was Kālarātri (the Night of Death). Holy men call her Kālī or Bhagavatī.

She had three eyes which were pits of fire. She had high cheek bones and a chin. She had a necklace of stars strung on air. With her mighty arms, which had sparkling and radiant nails, she filled the directions. Her breathing was so powerful that the biggest mountains could be blown away by it.

Her body seemed to swell enormously when she was dancing. While I was witnessing this dance, she playfully strung the mountains into a garland for herself. The three worlds became mirrors in the three (upper, middle and lower) parts of her body. Cities, forests, mountains, etc., became so many flowers for the garland she wore around her body (neck).

In her limbs were cities and towns, the seasons, the three worlds, the months and the day and night. Dharma and adharma became her earrings. Vedas were her breasts filled with the milk of the highest knowledge. She held many different weapons in her hands. The fourteen types of beings, like the gods and all the rest of them, were hairs on her body. All these beings with their cities and villages were dancing with her, delighted at the thought of being born again. The entire universe was in constant motion because she was dancing: from another point of view, of course, they were firmly established (in her).

The whole universe was reflected on her body as if in a mirror.

Even as I was looking they appeared, disappeared and reappeared.

VASIṢṬHA continued:

What was that dance? The stellar firmament was revolving, the mountains were revolving and the gods and the demons were also revolving like mosquitoes. The revolving firmament looked like her flowing garment. It was delightful to watch the very big trees (the kalpa tree) which were but hairs on her body revolve while she danced. They were ascending and descending between heaven and earth, as it were.

The sun and the moon, the day and the night were reflected on her fingernails, as it were, when she danced. The big mountains like the Himālayas, the Meru, etc., were also dancing with delight. It looked as though another cosmic dissolution was about to take place.

The goddess wore the sacred thread made of three strands, which were all kinds of prosperity, perfect knowledge and sacrifice.

Though it appeared that everything was revolving, nothing really happened. The air that flowed in and out of her nostrils was making great sounds "ghum ghum". On account of the movement of the countless arms of the goddess, the air in the entire space was being churned. By merely watching all this, even my eyes (and mind, too) began to get fatigued and confused. When the mirrors on her body were agitated by the dancing, then the mountains began to fall, the gods and celestials began to fall and their palaces to collapse.

In her body all the immovable objects became movable. Still more astonishing, oceans danced on mountain peaks and the mountain was dancing in empty space. The space danced beneath the earth-plane, and continents with flowering gardens and cities were dancing in the orb of the sun. All these were floating around like straw within the mirror of the goddess, as it were. Fish were swimming in the mirage, and cities were seen in space, which also seemed to hold mountains. The sky and the clouds of cosmic dissolution were resting on the mountains which had fallen.

In the body of Kālarātri were found night and day, creation and dissolution, purity and impurity. Though all the gods, etc., were tumbled by her dance, they were apparently steady because of the steadiness of the infinite consciousness. In her consciousness there was natural knowledge. By her dance she created and dissolved the universes moment after moment, just as a small boy shifts his attention from moment to moment. Now she is near, now she is far, now she is infinitesimal and now she is cosmic. Such is the manifestation of her cosmic creative power. She dances, holding the horns of the buffalo which is the vehicle of the god of death, to the accompaniment of sounds like 'dimbam dimbam paca paca jhamya'. She wears a garland of skulls and on her head is a peacock feather. She bows to Rudra, the god of dissolution. May he protect you.

RĀMA asked: VI.2:82

Lord, when everything had been destroyed, how does she dance and with whom? And how could she have all those garlands and all the rest of it?

VASIṢṬHA replied:

O Rāma, this was neither a male nor a female, nor did they dance. They were not of any such nature nor did they have any such form. Only the eternal, infinite consciousness which is the first cause and the cause of all causes existed—as infinite, as peace and as pervading everything by its mere appearance. The Lord (Śivam) is that. The Lord himself took on the appearance or form of Bhairava when the entire universe had ceased to exist; but in fact he was as formless as the infinite space. It is not appropriate even to assume that the infinite consciousness, which had become manifest in all its glory on account of its inherent nature, would suddenly be without it: just as gold cannot be without any form whatsoever.

How can consciousness remain without being conscious? Can you see gold without any form? How can anything remain without expressing its nature? How can sugar cane lose its sweetness? If it has lost its sweetness it is no longer sugar cane, and its juice is not sweet.

When consciousness loses consciousness, it is no longer consciousness. Everything has to be what it is and it is impossible to have it any other way. Hence, that infinite consciousness is pure existence at all times and it does not undergo any diminution. It shines by its own light, it has no beginning nor middle nor end and it is omnipotent. That itself at the end of a world-cycle appears as the space and the earth-plane, etc., and seems to undergo natural calamities and wholesale destruction; though there is no reality in all these.

Birth, death, Māyā, delusion, blindness, non-substantiality, substantiality, wisdom, bondage, liberation, good and evil, knowledge and ignorance, embodied and disembodied states, a moment and eternity, unsteadiness and firmness, you and I and the other, truth and falsehood, cleverness and foolishness, notions concerning time, space, action and matter, form, sight and related thought, action springing from the intellect and the senses, and all the five elements by which everything is pervaded—all these are pure consciousness which, without abandoning its nature, appears to be all these (just as space seems to be cut up though it is really not so cut up). This infinite consciousness alone is known as lord Śiva, Hari, Brahmā, the moon and the sun, Indra and Varuṇa, Yama, Kubera and fire. He who is enlightened, however, sees not the diversity, but the one infinite consciousness.

VI.2:83 VASIṢṬHA continued:

The cosmic form that I described to you as lord Śiva was pure consciousness; that itself was Rudra the dancer. There was no such form nor was there formlessness. In the mass of consciousness, all this was felt to have been experienced. I saw only that space (plane) which was supreme peace; and I experienced it in the form which I described. No one else saw it that way.

What was described as the end of a world-cycle, as Rudra and as Bhairavi—all that was but an illusory appearance; they were experienced in those forms only by me. The mass of consciousness alone exists. When it is perceived as a certain form (Bhairava), it is seen in that form and it seems to assume such a form. The comprehension of a word and its meaning (object) is not possible without consciousness. It is because of persistent use of such comprehension that you begin to feel that the object denoted by the expression is absolutely real. There was neither a Bhairavi nor a Bhairava (Kālarātri and Rudra) nor even the cosmic dissolution; all these were illusory appearances. The only reality is the infinite consciousness. Thus I have described to you the significance of the form and the formlessness of Rudra. I shall now explain to you the significance of the dance.

Consciousness is never without some movement within itself. Without this movement it might become 'unreal'. Thus consciousness appeared to be Rudra on account of this movement within itself. Movement is the very nature of consciousness and therefore inseparable from it. This movement of consciousness within itself is what was experienced as the dance of the lord Rudra. That movement was but pure movement. It was experienced by me as the dance of the Lord on account of my own psychological conditioning. Thus, the dance of the Lord was the movement within pure consciousness.

RĀMA asked:

When all that is unreal is dissolved during the cosmic dissolution, how does consciousness become aware, and of what?

VASIṢṬHA continued:

Of course, consciousness does not become aware of another. What is said to be the object of observation here is only a reference to the very nature of that consciousness. Just as in a dream, the cities, etc., are all within the consciousness of the dreamer, consciousness becomes aware of its own movement within itself right from the moment this movement arises. Thus arise in it notions of a moment, an age, a world-cycle, etc., as also notions of 'I' and 'you', etc. Thus, there is neither a duality, nor a unity, nor a void, neither consciousness (as the subject), nor unconsciousness. There is pure silence, or not even that. The infinite consciousness alone exists.

VASIṢṬHA continued: VI.2:84

The plane (space) of consciousness itself is known as Bhairava or Śiva. Inseparable and non-different from him is his dynamic energy which is of the nature of the mind. Air is seen (experienced) in its motion; fire is known by its heat; the pure consciousness is pure and tranquil and it is known as Śiva. This Śiva is beyond description. It is the dynamic energy of the Lord which executes all his wishes, as it were, and makes the wishes appear as visions. This energy or power or Māyā is consciousness. 'She' is a living force and therefore she is called the jīva. Since this creation-manifestation is natural to the infinite consciousness, she is known as prakṛti or nature. Since she is the cause of all things being seen and experienced, she is known as kriyā or action.

Since she manifests great anger towards evil she is known as caṇḍikā. Since she is of the colour of the blue-lotus, she is known as utpalā. She is known as jayā because she is always victorious. She is known as siddhā because perfection rests in her. Jayā is also known as jayantī, as also vijayā, all of which signify victory. Since she is unconquerable she is known as parājitā. She is known as durgā since her form or real nature is beyond our grasp. She is known as umā because she is the very essence of the sacred monosyllable OM. She is called gāyatrī because her names are sung by all and also sāvitrī because she is the creatrix of all. She is the expansion of one's vision of all things and hence she is known as sarasvatī. Since she is of white (yellow or red) colour she is known as gaurī. Since she exists as a ray of light in one who sleeps, and in one who has been awakened by the contemplation of the subtle inner vibrations produced by the sound of OM, she is known as indukalā (ray of the moon).

Since she and Śiva have space as their real form, their bodies have a blue colour. Space is their flesh, bones, everything. They exist in space as space. Her dance with different gestures, etc., symbolises the creation, decay and death of all beings. She is conceived of as having limbs because she creates the worlds by the movement of her energy. This kālī invests all things with their characteristics by the power inherent in her own limbs, as it were. But one cannot by any means apprehend her limbs nor can her real nature be described. Just as a motion within space is experienced by us as air, even so the dynamic energy of consciousness is experienced by the action or motion that takes place in that consciousness. However, motion or action cannot be regarded as the quality of consciousness because it has no qualities nor characteristics: consciousness is pure and utterly tranquil, beyond all description. The notion of motion in consciousness is ignorance.

VASIṢṬHA continued:

When this dynamic energy of consciousness rests at each place as it is (without becoming something else), that itself is known as Śiva the Lord. That is, the thing in itself is the Lord. The following are the limbs of this dynamic energy of consciousness which have been created as notions in her: all these created worlds, the earth with all the continents and oceans, the forests and the mountains, the scriptures, the different forms of sacred rites, wars in which various forms of weapons are used and all the fourteen worlds.

RĀMA said:

O sage, are these things which are said to be the limbs in the body of this dynamic energy real or false?

VASIṢṬHA replied:

O Rāma, all these are indeed real, for they have all been brought about by the operation of this dynamic energy of consciousness, and they are all experienced by consciousness. Just as the mirror reflects a real object that exists outside, this consciousness reflects within itself that which is within itself—hence, it is real. Even the imaginary city or the illusory appearance of the city arises only in consciousness, whether the appearance arises because of persistent contemplation or because of the purity of consciousness. This creation is real whether it is regarded as a reflection or a dream-object or a fancy, because it is based on the truth which is the self—this is my opinion. If you object: "But these fanciful creations are of no practical use to me," consider of what use are they who have gone to a distant country. They are of use to the inhabitants of the village to which they have gone. Even so with everything.

Whatever there is here which exists and functions here is real to the self and not to another who does not perceive it and is unaware of it. Therefore, all these creations and creatures that exist within the field of the energy of consciousness are true to the perceiving self and are unreal to the non-perceiver. All the notions and the dreams that exist in the present, past or the future are all real, because the self which is the self of all is real. They are all experienced by those who have reached the appropriate state of consciousness, just as he who goes to a distant land sees the sights there. However, motion of the energy of consciousness does not alter the truth, even as a dreamer transported to another place without his sleep being disturbed does not have his dream interrupted. When it is realised that the perception of the three worlds is but an unreal fancy, there is no question of its interruption or otherwise.

VASIṢṬHA continued: VI.2:85

An imaginary city is imagination, not city. Even so the creation is but the notion that arises in the energy of the infinite consciousness. Or, the notion that so arises is the creation.

Kālarātri is to the Lord what movement is to air. Just as in empty space, air moves as if it has form, she moves in the infinite consciousness executing the will or the wish of the Lord, as it were. When there is no such movement of the energy, then the Lord alone exists.

While she continues to dance in this fashion in space, then by accidental coincidence (the crow and the cocoanut) she comes into contact with the Lord. The moment this contact is made, she is weakened and made thin and transparent. She abandons her cosmic form and becomes a mountain, then she becomes a small town and then a beautiful tree. Then she becomes like space and lastly she becomes of the form of the Lord himself, like the river entering the ocean. Then the Lord shines as one without a second.

RĀMA asked:

But, holy sir, tell me why the divine mother thus becomes tranquil?

VASIṢṬHA replied:

O Rāma, it is the dynamic energy of consciousness that is known as prakṛti, jaganmāyā, etc. She is unperverted. That which is superior to this energy is consciousness itself which is the very self of consciousness, supreme peace. This dynamic energy functions and moves as long as there is the momentum of the Lord's wish. In a way, she dances as long as she does not see the Lord.

Since consciousness and energy are inseparably one, the energy comes into contact with (becomes aware of) the Lord and becomes the Lord himself. When the prakṛti touches the Lord she abandons the prakṛti-hood (the state of being movement). She merges in the Lord even as the river merges in the ocean. The movement of energy is but the result of a notion arising in consciousness and the energy naturally returns to consciousness, just as the shadow may be said to enter a person when the shadow ceases to be. A holy man may live in the company of thieves till he discovers the truth; afterwards he does not relish such company. Consciousness revels in duality till it sees its own self. The energy of consciousness dances until it beholds the glory of nirvāṇa. When it beholds consciousness, it becomes pure consciousness.

One roams this saṃsāra with its birth and death only till one beholds the supreme. Having seen it, he is immediately immersed in the supreme. Who will again abandon that which frees him from all sorrow?

VI.2:86 VASIṢṬHA continued:

I shall now tell you, O Rāma, how lord Rudra, who was standing in the cosmic space with an apparent form, cast it off and attained total tranquility.

That Rudra stood observing the division in consciousness known as the creation. In a moment he 'swallowed the division' as it were. Then Rudra stood alone, one with the space as if he himself were space. In a few minutes, he became as light as cloud and his size was fast shrinking. I saw through my own divine vision that he had become smaller than an atom. In a moment he had become invisible. He had become supreme peace. He had become one with the absolute Brahman or pure consciousness.

Thus, O Rāma, I saw within that rock the creation, sustenance and the dissolution of the universe. I was amazed at all this illusory perception. Again I looked at the rock and I saw all sorts of creations and creatures in it, like the limbs of Kālarātri. All this is seen only with the eyes of awakened intelligence or by the divine eye which sees everything everywhere at all times as everything is. If one sees the rock with the physical eyes as if it lies at a distance, only the rock is seen, but no creation, etc.

After all this, I turned my inner eye to another part of the same rock. Once again I saw a whole creation come into being and all the rest of it. In every part of that rock I saw a whole creation. Even so I saw innumerable creations in the very many rocks that I found on that hill.

In some of these creations the Brahmā had just begun his work of creation, in others the gods were springing from the mind of the Creator, some were populated by human beings, in some there were no gods and in some no demons, in some the satyayuga (golden age) reigned and in others the kaliyuga (iron age), in some the people had conquered old age and death, in some the people were all enlightened because they encountered no obstruction to their righteousness. Thus I saw the state of the universe in the past, present and future. In some I saw dense darkness and ignorance, in some I saw Rāma fighting Rāvaṇa and in some Rāvaṇa abducting Sītā. Some were ruled by the gods and some by demons.

RĀMA asked:

Lord, tell me, did I exist as Rāma before this incarnation?

VASIṢṬHA replied:

You and I have been born here again and again, O Rāma. Of course from the point of view of the absolute reality, neither you nor I nor this world has ever come into being. All these are like ripples on the surface of water. Their particular appearance and disappearance are due to illusory perception and deluded understanding.

VASIṢṬHA continued: VI.2:87

After thus contemplating the infinite consciousness for some time I suddenly realised that all this creation was within myself, my own body, just as the tree is in the seed. When one closes his eyes to sleep, he enters into an inner world created by his inner vision; when sleep comes to an end, one wakes up and his vision enters the world of the waking state. In the same way creation is experienced by one's entering into it within his own heart.

Having seen the appearance of this creation in pure space, I entered into other parts of myself eager to see other aspects of creation. When thus the light of my inner intelligence was directed to that 'space', there arose in it an experience of that space. O Rāma, when you enter into the consciousness of your own self, whether in sleep or in the waking state, you know that it is equally a mass of consciousness. To begin with there is only this pure space or emptiness. In it there arises the notion 'I am'. The condensation of that is known as buddhi or intellect and the condensation of that is known as the mind. That knows or experiences the pure element of sound and also the other elements, the tanmātras. From these experiences arise the various senses.

Some say that there is some order in this creation, others declare that there is no such order. However, it is not possible to alter the nature and characteristics of created objects which have acquired those characteristics through the appropriate notion that arose in the infinite consciousness in the beginning.

As I was thus observing creation, I had become atomic. I realised myself as a ray of light. Contemplating that alone, I had become gross. In this grossness there were the potentialities of sense-experiences. . . . I began to see. The organs through which I saw became the eyes, that which I saw became the scene (object), the fruit of this experience was sight, 'when' I saw all this became time (duration), the manner in which I saw became the method or order, 'wherever' I saw became space. By conviction these became the order of creation.

When thus consciousness 'opened its eyes', as it were, or became aware of its own inherent potentialities, the tanmātras (pure elements) arose, and then all the senses which are in fact and in truth pure void or space came into being.

Even so, I thought "Let me hear something." From this sound arose, as also the organ of hearing. Then there arose the sense of touch, the sense of taste and the sense of smell, etc. Even though all these seem to have arisen in me, in fact nothing has ever happened.

VASIṢṬHA continued:

When thus the five elements and the five senses came into being, their corresponding knowledge and experience arose in me irresistibly. They were without 'form' (substantiality) and they were illusory. When I thus stood contemplating these notions and experiences, that state of my being is known by people like you as I-ness or egosense. When this notion of egosense becomes more gross, it is known as buddhi or intellect; when that becomes gross, it is known as the mind. Thus, though I am pure consciousness, I seem to have acquired a subtle body (ātivāhika) and an antaḥkaraṇa (inner instrument consisting of mind, intellect, etc.).

I am subtler and more empty than even the air. Hence, I do not obstruct the coming into being of anything. But since I continue to be in this notional existence for a considerable period of time, you imagine that I have a body. It is on account of this notion existing in you that I produce this sound known as speech. You hear it even as a sleeping person hears sounds in his dream. The first sound that a child utters is OM and hence OM has come to be regarded as the foremost among sounds. After that, whatever I have been saying as if in dream, appears to you to be my speech.

I am the absolute Brahman. I am self-contained, the creator of this creation and the preceptor of all. I have created all this through my own thoughts and notions. Thus do I exist, but I am unborn. I have seen the universe, beyond that I have seen nothing. But all this that I have seen is but pure void. All this is but pure experiencing. Nothing (the earth, etc.) exists nor has anything ever come into being. Nothing exists outside. Everything is in consciousness; everything is consciousness. There is no world in Brahman but Brahman sees or experiences a world. This perception is not a fact or reality but just a notion.

This truth cannot be seen by physical eyes which can only see material objects. When you see with your subtle (ātivāhika) eyes you will behold the creation as it is, as the truth, as pure Brahman-nirvāṇa.

When I experienced space, I knew what earth was. I became earth. In that earth I experienced the existence of countless universes, without ever abandoning the awareness that I am the infinite consciousness. I saw the most amazing earthly phenomena and events within that earth (within me). In fact, I experienced even the farmer ploughing 'me' (the earth), and I experienced the burning heat of the sun and the cool flow of rainwater. I became the fearful space in which the Lokāloka mountains (the boundaries of the world) exist and I experienced the actions and the movements of countless beings.

Countless beings of different types—gods, demons, humans, animals and worms—filled me. I was filled with mountains, forests, etc., which exist on earth.

VASIṢṬHA continued: VI.2:88, 89

While I remained in the earth-consciousness I experienced the experiences of the earth, with all its rivers, etc. Here I experienced the weeping and wailing of those who had lost their dear and near ones, here I experienced the joy of dancing girls; there were the cries of the hungry, the joy of the affluent, drought and earth-quake, war and destruction, beautiful birds and lakes, suffering worms, flourishing forests, meditating sages. O Rāma, in this earth-body of mine all these took place.

RĀMA asked: When you were thus engaged in the contemplation of the earth (pārthiva-dhāraṇā), was that earth real or only mental?

VASIṢṬHA replied:

Truly, this was mental and I had myself become the earth; equally truly, this was not mental nor did I actually become the earth. Apart from the mind, there is no earth. Whether you consider something as real or as unreal it is but mental action. I am but the pure infinite consciousness; that notion which arises in it is known as saṅkalpa or thought or imagination. That notion is the mind, it is the earth, it is the world, it is the creator; this world appears in space on account of that notion, just as a fancied city exists in the sky.

What I experienced as the earth was but a simple notion and therefore mental. It is pervaded by the mind; on account of the persistent contemplation (dhāraṇā) it remains as if it is the earth. The earth-plane is mental; it is the notion that arises in consciousness and it is otherwise void. When this notion remains constant for some time, it apparently abandons its mental state and it seems to become this solid, material, hard and firm earth.

From this point of view the earth does not exist. But it has come to be regarded as solid material existence from the beginning of creation. Just as the dream-object is nothing but the consciousness of the dreamer, this world-appearance is nothing but pure consciousness. The notion that arises in consciousness is pure consciousness and nothing else. Hence, there is no notion as such, neither a self nor a world. When it is thus seen, the world does not exist; when it is not observed carefully, it seems to come into being.

Just as a crystal reflects colours without intending to do so, the infinite consciousness reflects in it the entire universe. Hence the world is neither mental nor material. It is pure consciousness alone that appears as this earth. It is the false notion entertained by countless beings in the three worlds that has attained relative or existential reality known as the earth. 'I am all this and all that is within all this.' With this realisation I saw everything.

VI.2:90 VASIṢṬHA continued:

Thus in my heart I experienced the earth-plane. Whatever was seen and experienced was there, in my heart; but it looked as though it were different from me, in a subject-object relationship. That was because there is the universe everywhere, there is Brahman everywhere and there is a void everywhere. The earth-plane exists everywhere (it is of course nothing in truth); but it is pure consciousness. Like a dream-city it has never been truly created in fact.

There is neither a diversity nor a non-diversity. There is neither being nor non-being. There is no 'I'. How can one say that there is something? Though this creation is experienced, it does not exist in truth; or, if it is said to exist, it is Brahman alone that exists. When it is like a dream-city how can one affirm or deny its existence?

Just as I experienced the earth-plane by the earth-contemplation (pṛthvī-dhāraṇā), I also experienced the water-plane by the water-dhāraṇā. By contemplation of water, I became water; though not-inert I became inert. I dwelt in the bowels of the ocean for a long long time making the appropriate sounds. I dwelt in the body of plants and creepers and made my own channels within them. I entered into the mouths of living beings and mingled with the vital organs in their bodies. I flowed restlessly along river beds and I took rest at the dams en route. Rising as vapour I entered into the heavens as cloud. There I rested for some time with my friend the lightning.

I dwelt in all beings as the water-element, even as the infinite consciousness dwells in all beings. Coming into contact with the taste-buds in the tongue, I experienced different tastes; surely that experience is pure knowledge. The taste was not experienced by me nor by the body nor by any other. The experience happened within as the object of experiencing—and as such it is false.

When the flowers blossomed I descended upon them as dew and tasted whatever sweetness was left in them after the bees had had their share. I dwelt in the fourteen classes of beings as awareness of taste—consciousness, though appearing to be unconsciousness. Assuming the form of droplets of water or spray, I enjoyed riding on wind and travelling from one place to another. Thus in that state as water I had varied and interesting experiences. I saw hundreds of worlds come into being and vanish. Whether this world has form or no form, it is pure consciousness and immaterial void. O Rāma, you are nothing, but you are not non-existent. You are pure and supreme consciousness.

VASIṢṬHA continued: VI.2:91

Then I became the fire-element through the contemplation of that element (teja-dhāraṇā). Fire or light is predominantly satva and therefore it is always luminous and it dispels darkness even as a king makes thieves flee his presence. I realised the misery of darkness which destroys all good qualities because I became the light in which everything is seen. Light bestows form on everything even as a father bestows form on his offspring. In the netherworld light shines at a minimum level and there is greater darkness. In heaven there is light alone—and always. Light is the sun that makes the lotus of action blossom.

I became the good colour (suvarṇa) in gold, etc., I became vitality and valour in men, in jewels I sparkled as their fire, in rainclouds I became the light of the lightning, in passionate women I became the twinkle in their eyes, I became the strength of the lion. I was myself the hatred of the demons in the gods and the hatred of the gods in the demons. I became the vital essence of all beings. I experienced being the sun, the moon, the stars, precious stones, fire (including the fire of cosmic destruction), lightning, lamp. When I became fire, the burning cinders became my teeth, the smoke my hair and fuel was my food. In the blacksmith's workshop I became the fire that made the iron red-hot, and when it was beaten I flew out as sparks.

RĀMA asked:

O sage, when you had thus become the fire-element, were you happy or unhappy?

VASIṢṬHA replied:

Just as when a person sleeps he becomes temporarily insentient though he is a sentient being, consciousness becomes an inert object. When it thinks of itself as the elements (earth, etc.,) it thinks of itself as being inert. In fact, however, there is no such division of consciousness into subject and object.

Hence, whatever I experienced in the states of earth, water and fire, I experienced only as Brahman. If I had in fact become inert, how could I experience what it is to be earth, etc.? The sentient person thinks "I am asleep" and he appears to be insentient. If one wakes up to the truth concerning oneself, then the materiality of the body vanishes. With the subtle (ātivāhika) body he is then able to enter anything anywhere. This subtle body is nothing but pure intelligence. When one enters another state with this intelligence out of his own wish, then obviously one does not experience unhappiness or sorrow.

Just as the world seen and experienced in a dream is enveloped by the darkness of ignorance and is therefore unreal, even so are the other elements that one experiences. When one touches a river of sparks which he fancies in his own mind, he does not experience pain. Such was the case with my elemental experiences.

VI.2:92 VASIṢṬHA continued:

Then I became the air-element by vāyu-dhāraṇā (contemplation of oneself as wind). I taught the grass, leaves, creepers and straw the art of dancing. Wafting cool breeze, I became the dear friend of young ladies. At the same time I was dreaded for my heat wave, hurricane and tornadoes. In pleasure-gardens I carried sweet scent; in hell I carried sparks of fire. My motion was so fast that people considered mind and wind to be brothers. I flowed with the waters of the holy Gaṅgā and it would have been tiresome but I was happy that we were able to relieve the tiresomeness and fatigue of others. I assisted space by carrying sound-waves; and there I came to be known as the dear friend of space. I dwelt in the vital organs of all beings. I knew the secrets of fire and I was also known as the friend of the fire. I was operating the body-machine of all embodied (living) beings by being their life-breath. Hence, I became their friend and their enemy at the same time.

Though I stood in front of all, I could not be perceived by any. During the cosmic dissolution I could lift huge mountains and hurl them as I pleased. As air, I performed six functions: gathering into a mass, drying up, upholding or supporting, vibrating or causing motion, conveying scent, and cooling. I was dedicated to the tasks of building and destroying bodies.

Being the element air, I perceived within each molecule of air a whole universe. In each of those universes I again saw all the elements, etc., as in this universe. They were not real existences; they were but notions that arise in the cosmic void or space.

In those worlds, too, there were the gods and the planets, mountains and oceans, and the illusory notions of birth, old age and death. I roamed all those realms to my heart's content. Countless types of beings like the celestials and the sages rested on my body like so many flies and mosquitoes. By my leave they obtained their various forms and colours. They derived immense pleasure when I touched them, but they could not see me.

Though the netherworlds were my feet, the earth my abdomen and the heavens my head, even then I did not abandon my subatomic nature. I was spread in all directions everywhere at all times and I did everything. I was the self of all. I was all. Yet I was pure void. I experienced being something and being nothing, the formless state as also form, while retaining awareness of all this as well as being unaware of these. There are countless such universes as the one that I experienced. Just as a man dreams that he dreams countless objects,

I experienced universes within every atom and universes within the atoms of those universes. I myself became all these universes; and though I was the self of all and I pervaded all these, I did not so envelop all these. These are but words, even as are 'There is heat in fire' (heat in fire—denotes but one fact though three words are used).

The Story of the Sage from Outer Space

VASIṢṬHA continued: VI.2:93

After all this, I re-entered my cottage or hermitage in outer space. I looked for my physical body. It was not there. But, I found an aged sage sitting in that hermitage. He was in deep meditation. He was seated in the lotus-posture. His face was radiant and beautiful on account of the peace and bliss that filled him. His lotus-like hands had been placed in front of his navel, and they shone with an extraordinary brilliance. His eyes were closed and he was obviously beyond body-consciousness. Not seeing my own body but observing the sage sitting in meditation I began to think as follows:

Surely, this is a great and perfected sage. Like me, he must have arrived here seeking total seclusion. Since he sought seclusion he must have seen this hermitage in space. Perhaps he expected me to return and seeing that I had not returned for a long time, he must have thrown that body out and himself occupied the hermitage. Let me return to my own realm.

When I thus reflected and when my desire to stay in that hermitage ceased, that hermitage disappeared and with it even that sage disappeared. When one's thoughts (notions or concepts) cease, that which those thoughts brought into being also ceases. When my wish for the hermitage ceased, it disappeared. Like a spacecraft that hermitage fell. The sage fell. And I too descended along with him on to the earth-plane. The sage landed in the same state and posture in which he was in that hermitage. This was because, through the union of prāṇa and apāna, he had overcome the force of gravity. He did not even wake up from his meditation. His body was strong as a rock and light as cotton.

In order to bring him back to normal body-consciousness, I assumed the form of a big cloud which rained and thundered. Then he regained body-consciousness. I enquired of him: "Where are you, O sage? What are you doing? Who are you? Though you fell from such height, you are oblivious of it; how is that?"

After contemplating the past for a few moments, the SAGE said: "I have now recognised you, O holy one; I salute you. Kindly pardon me for not having saluted you earlier. It is indeed the nature of sages to be forgiving. O sage, I have wandered in the realms of the gods for a considerable time. I am tired of this saṃsāra. When all this is pure consciousness, what is it that we call pleasure? Hence I reside in space, free from mental distractions and attraction. None of these sense-experiences is real, independent of consciousness. Objects of pleasure are sources of poison, sexual delights are delusion, sweetness robs the enjoyer of sweetness: he who is overcome by them is surely destroyed. This life is short. It is full of distractions. By sheer accident sometimes one gets a little happiness here. Nothing is permanent or stable here. Like a pot on the potter's wheel, this body revolves endlessly in this life. There are powerful thieves (sense-objects) everywhere. Hence, I should be vigilant."

THE SAGE continued:

'This has happened today', 'This is mine' and 'This is his'—occupied with such thoughts people do not realise the passing of time. We have eaten and drunk a lot, we have roamed a lot, and we have experienced pain and pleasure. What is left to be done? How shall we gain supreme peace? All trees are wood, all beings are flesh, all earth is clay, everything is tainted by pain and impermanence. In what shall I repose confidence?

Who is my protector here? Neither wealth nor friends nor relatives nor acquaintances (or pleasures): all these are themselves victims of time. Whom shall I trust, when I realise that everyone is bound to die today or tomorrow?

Even the religious rites which are governed by injunctions and prohibitions make a man fall into this saṃsāra, even as water flows from a higher place to a lower one. They bewilder and confuse a person. The unreal, by persistent apprehension, seems to be real; hence since essentially the unreal is unreal, it is unreal though it may appear to be real. But people are deluded and they run after the objects of sense-pleasure even as a river runs down fast to reach self-destruction in the ocean. The ignorant mind rushes towards sense-enjoyment like an arrow released from a bow and it is not interested in goodness.

Pleasure is dreadful pain, prosperity is adversity, sensual enjoyment is the worst disease and pursuit of pleasure is disgusting. Adversity is a great blessing. Happiness is followed by unhappiness. Life ends in death. Aha, the power of Māyā! Sensual pleasure is worse than the most poisonous snake: the former kills instantly, by the merest contact. Since wealth, etc., cause delusion they are worse than poison. It is true that pleasure is enjoyable and affluence is beautiful, but life is fleeting and hence they are rendered meaningless.

Pleasure and wealth are pleasing on the surface but the end is unhappiness and sorrow.

With the advancing of age the hairs turn grey and the teeth and everything else (the faculties and vitality, etc.) decrease; only craving does not decrease. There is a similarity between childhood and youth—both pass away quickly. Life ebbs away like a flowing river, and the past can never be recovered.

After a long time I have attained egolessness. I am not interested in heavenly pleasures. Like you, O sage, I too longed to resort to a secluded place. Hence I saw that hermitage in space. I did not realise that it was your hermitage and that you would one day return to it. I did not pay attention to it. Only now I know this. Only when one's attention is directed to these facts does one perceive them with one's inner eye of intelligence, then one knows the past, present and future—not until then. Such is the nature of the mind even to the gods.

VASIṢṬHA continued: VI.2:94

I said to the sage: "Having heard your story, I think that you should continue to live in that hermitage in outer space. Get up and let us live in the world of the perfected beings (siddhas). It is good for each one to live in his own environment which does not cause mental distraction."

Both of us rose into space. We saluted each other and took leave of each other. He went where he thought fit and I parted from him and went my own way.

RĀMA asked: Lord, as your body had disintegrated on this earth, with what sort of body did you roam the world of the siddhas?

VASIṢṬHA replied:

When I went to the city of Indra, the king of the gods, I had a spatial body and therefore nobody there recognised me. I could not be touched or held by anyone. I was like a thought, devoid of matter but endowed with a form made of pure wish (saṅkalpa). This is comparable to the dream-experience in which dream bodies are produced of non-material substance. One who considers this impossible ignores the experience of dream and one who thus ignores the obvious experience is fit to be ignored. I was able to see others, especially those endowed with a material body, but they could not see me.

RĀMA asked again: But, then, how was it possible for that sage to see you?

VASIṢṬHA replied:

O Rāma, people like us have the power to materialise and realise our wish. Nothing ever happens to us that we do not so wish. Only people who are drowned in worldly activities forget in a moment the fact that they have a subtle (ātivāhika) body. When I decided "May this sage see me", then that sage saw me. People in whom the perception of division has been deep-rooted do not have the power to realise their wish; when one like the sage has weakened the perception of division it is possible for him to realise his wish. Even among siddhas or perfected ones he who has more psychic transparency is able to succeed in his efforts.

To return to the story, I roamed the celestial regions like a ghost.

RĀMA asked: Lord, do ghosts exist? What do they look like and what do they do?

VASIṢṬHA replied:

O Rāma, ghosts do exist in this world. I shall now tell you what they are and what they do. Surely, he who does not deal with a subject when requested to do so is not a worthy teacher.

VASIṢṬHA continued:

Some ghosts (piśāca) have an ethereal body though endowed with hands and feet and they see people like you. Others have fearful shadowy forms; they overwhelm the bodies of human beings and influence their minds. Some of them kill or harm people. Some are like fog or mist and others have dream-like bodies. Some of them have bodies made of air alone. Some have bodies which are no more than the delusion of the perceiver. They cannot be grasped; nor can they grasp others. They experience heat and cold, pleasure and pain. But they cannot eat, drink or take anything. They have desire, hate, fear, anger, greed and delusion. They are charmed and brought under control by mantras, drugs, penance, charity, courage and righteousness. They are seen and also grasped if one rests on satva. Also, this can happen by the use of magical symbols (maṇḍalas) and formulas (mantras) and by worship performed by someone at some time and somewhere.

Some ghosts are of a divine nature and appear to be gods. Some are like humans and others like serpents. Some are like dogs and jackals and live in villages and forests, or in blind wells, roadsides and other impure places. I shall now tell you about their origin.

In the one infinite consciousness there arises a notion which becomes the jīva and then by becoming more and more dense it becomes the egosense, or mind (which is later called Brahmā the creator). All these and the whole world arise and exist in a notion: hence they are unreal. It is experienced as real, just as one feels that one's notion is something real. In that sense all these gods and other creatures are real. In truth, however, there is neither a field here, nor a seed nor a farmer nor the tree (known as creation or the world).

However, in that notion of the field of creation there exist all these beings. The resplendent ones among them are the gods; the half-baked ones are humans; they in whom there is a thick veil of impurity are the worms and such creatures; they who are devoid of any fruitfulness, who are empty and bodiless (aśarīra), are known as ghosts or piṣācas. The differentiation is due not to the whim or fancy of the creator Brahmā but to their own choice. They became whatever they wished to become. However, in fact, they are all but consciousness appearing to be subtle (ātivāhika) bodies. It is on account of persistent self-deception that they seem to have physical or material forms.

The ghosts, too, exist in their own forms doing what they have to do according to their own nature and experiencing various experiences. They see and communicate with one another as if in a dream. Some of them do not communicate, like the dream-objects in a person's dream. Like the ghosts, there are also the goblins and disembodied beings. The ghosts create their own circle of darkness of ignorance which even the sun's rays cannot penetrate. They thrive in the darkness of ignorance, the light of knowledge is their enemy.

VASIṢṬHA continued: VI.2:95

As I said, I was roaming the heaven like a ghost. No one could see me. Though they were under my control, they could not control me. One day I thought, "I can realise my wish; may I be seen henceforth by these gods." Immediately my wish became real. They saw me.

The gods had different notions concerning my appearances in their midst. They who did not know my identity thought that I had risen from the earth: they called me Pārthiva (Earth) Vasiṣṭha. Some thought I had descended through the rays of the sun and I became known as Taijasa (Light) Vasiṣṭha. They who thought I wafted in with the wind called me Vāta (Air) Vasiṣṭha. They who thought that I had risen from the waters called me Vāri (Water) Vasiṣṭha.

In due course of time I came to have a physical or material body. To me there was no difference between the subtle and the physical bodies: they were both pure consciousness in reality. Even here I appear to function in and through this body because of this discourse. A jīvanmukta (a sage liberated while living) is indeed Brahman and he has an ethereal body; even so one who is a bodiless sage is also Brahman. There is no notion in me other than of Brahman. Hence even when I am engaged in diverse activities this realisation of Brahman does not cease. Just as to a dreamer the unborn and bodiless dream-object is real, even so this world is real and material to me. Even so do all these creations and worlds shine as if real and material, but they have never been created.

Because of the recurrent feeling of the ethereal Vasiṣṭha that arises in the minds of all of you and also in me, I appear to be seated here. In truth, however, all this is pure void and all these are only notions that arise in the mind of the Creator. Notions like 'I' and 'you' have become firmly established in your consciousness because you have not cared to investigate them. If they are investigated and their true nature is understood they vanish very soon. When the truth is realised all these scenes of so-called creations vanish, even as a mirage ceases to be seen as water when its true nature is understood.

In fact, by a mere study of this Mahārāmāyaṇa (Yoga Vāsiṣṭha) the reality is realised; there is no difficulty in it whatsoever. But he who is not interested in liberation is a worm, not human. One should carefully investigate the bliss of liberation and the sorrow inevitable to ignorance. By the study of the Mahārāmāyaṇa one attains to supreme peace. Liberation confers 'inner coolness' (peace) on the mind; bondage promotes psychological distress (psychological scorching fire). Even after realising this, one does not strive for liberation. How foolish are the people! Such people are overcome by desire for sense-gratification. But even they can cultivate a desire for liberation by a study of this scripture.

(The assembly dispersed: end of seventeenth day.)

VI.2:96 VASIṢṬHA continued:

I have narrated the story of the rock which enables you to realise the truth quite clearly. Nothing exists anywhere at any time; Brahman alone exists as a mass of Brahman without any division whatsoever. Brahman is a mass of consciousness. It does not undergo any change. The cosmic being is but a dream-object in that consciousness, whether that being is subtle or gross. Hence, there is neither a Brahmā the creator nor the creation, nothing but the indivisible consciousness. The diversity perceived in a dream does not create a diversity in the dreamer; even so the notion of a creation does not create a division in consciousness. Consciousness alone is, no creation; the dream-mountain is the dreamer not a mountain. The infinite consciousness (cidākāśa) is I, it is the three worlds, it is the puruṣa (cosmic being) and it is you.

Minus this cidākāśa, the body is a corpse. This infinite consciousness cannot be cut nor burnt and hence it never ceases. Therefore, no one ever dies nor is anyone born. Consciousness is the person; if it is said that that person dies and therefore consciousness dies, it is like saying that when a son dies, his father dies too. If consciousness dies, then everything dies and the world becomes empty. O Rāma, this consciousness is not dead till now anywhere in anyone;

nor has this creation stood as a void; hence it is clear that the innermost being of everyone which is pure consciousness is unchanging. When this is realised, where is birth and death?

When one realises "I am pure consciousness," he is unconcerned with life or death, pleasure or pain. Fie on that wretch in whom this realisation has not arisen (or has ceased). One who realises "I am pure experiencing or consciousness" is unaffected by any calamity. He is not affected by mental distress or psychological illness. When one feels "I am the body," he forfeits strength and wisdom; he who realises "I am pure consciousness" gains them. The latter is not subjected to greed, delusion or vanity. Alas, how foolish are they who wail "We shall die" when thinking of the death of the body. When one rests in the knowledge "I am consciousness" he feels a blow from the most powerful weapon as if it were the touch of a flower.

If consciousness can die, then people die all the time. Please tell me how is it that you have not died already? Nothing dies. Consciousness alone entertains the twin notions 'I am alive' and 'I am dead'. Consciousness sees or becomes aware of saṃsāra (the world-appearance) and consciousness becomes aware of liberation. It becomes aware of pleasure and pain without abandoning its true nature. In a state of self-ignorance it gets involved in delusion; in a state of self-knowledge it frees itself from delusion. But, consciousness itself never rises and it never sets. There is no such thing as the reality and there is nothing called ignorance or falsehood. Whatever is conceived of by one, that exists in that manner.

VASIṢṬHA continued: VI.2:97

Since the world is the dream of the supreme self and since everything is pervaded by Brahman, it is experienced as Brahman. The world-appearance or illusion is perceived; the supreme consciousness remains unseen. Hence, the illusion may be regarded as the real imagination of the self. From another point of view, this world-appearance is an illusion though the reality of infinite consciousness remains incomprehensible. Hence, there arises the notion of a complete void or śūnya; this, too, is real. The infinite consciousness (or the supreme person that arises in it) is not involved in activity; the world springs from the unmanifest cause (nature). This view is also tenable since it is experienced as such. Others hold that Brahman appears to be the world in a state of ignorance (just as a rope appears as a snake in darkness). This, too, is based on direct experience and hence real. The theory that the entire universe is the conglomeration of atoms is also acceptable; by proper investigation this knowledge or understanding has been arrived at.

There are some who say that the world is what one sees it to be and that this principle applies to 'the other world', too, and that therefore this world is neither real nor unreal but the reality is purely subjective. There are others who declare that the external world alone is real and there is no other reality. They also express the truth in as much as they do not reach whatever may be beyond the experience of their own and others' senses. They are also right who declare that everything is changing all the time, for the power that thus engineers constant change is omnipotent. The belief that the jīva dwells in the body, like a sparrow imprisoned in a pot, and at death flies away from it to another realm and also a similar belief held by foreigners are also acceptable since they are accepted in their own countries and communities. Saintly men look upon all with equal vision; they who know the reality know that it is the self of all.

There are those who assert that nature manifests itself naturally, without an intelligent creator, for one sees that in nature there are many undesired and unintelligent happenings (like natural calamities) —such a view is also reasonable. On the other hand, they who assert the existence of the one universal doer of everything are also right; their mind is saturated with this universal power. They who say that this world exists as also 'the other world' are right, too. In their eyes, pilgrimage, rituals, etc., are meaningful. The notion that everything is void or śūnya is right for it is the result of much investigation. The infinite consciousness is like the purest crystal: it reflects whatever notion one holds. The knowers of the truth have realised that this infinite consciousness is neither a void nor a non-void; it is omnipotent but not that which is seen or known. Hence, whatever be one's conviction, if one adheres to that conviction one surely reaches the same goal (attains the same fruit) as long as he does not toy with these notions or realisations in a childish manner. One should investigate the truth in the company of the knowers of the truth and then one should stand firm in one's own realisation without being distracted or deflected.

VASIṢṬHA continued:

There are wise people here and there, who are wise in terms of the knowledge of the scriptures as also in terms of their conduct. One should seek their company. There may be many who talk a lot about the scriptures, but he among them who promotes the joy and delight of all and whose conduct is unimpeachable is the best among them. All people at all times seek their own good as if under compulsion, just as water flows downwards. One should understand this and resort to the company of the wise.

RĀMA asked:

This world rests like a creeper on the tree of the supreme being.

In it who are the ones who see the ultimate truth after having duly investigated the past and the future?

VASIṢṬHA replied:

In every community there are a number of wise men by whose light (or grace) there is light in this world. All the people run up and down like dry blades of grass floating on this ocean of saṃsāra. Forgetful of the self, the dwellers in heaven are burnt in the fire of pleasure. The deluded demons are destroyed by their enemies, the gods, and hurled into a pit (hell) by Nārāyaṇa. The celestial artistes (gandharvas) do not even inhale a bit of the scent (gandha) of wisdom. They are lost in the enjoyment of their own music, etc. The celestials known as vidyādharas do not respect sages; being the supporters (ādhāra) of learning (vidyā) they are full of vanity. The demi-gods known as yakṣas consider themselves immortals and they display their dexterity before aged and infirm people. The demons known as rākṣasas live in delusion. The ghosts (piśācas) are forever interested in harassing people. The dwellers of the netherworld known as the nāgas are inert and unintelligent. The demons known as asuras are more like worms which dwell in holes in the ground. How can they acquire any wisdom at all?

Even human beings are narrow-minded and petty minded, interested in the trivia of life. They spend most of their time in the pursuit of evil desires. They do not come into contact with anything that is good or wise at all. They are tempted away from the path of order and wisdom by their own vanities and desires. The class of people known as yoginī (NOTE: the practitioners of 'black' arts) are fallen into the pit of drinking and eating like uncultured people.

But there are some liberated beings among the gods (Viṣṇu, Brahmā, Rudra, etc.), among the leaders (like Kaśyapa, Nārada, Sanatkumāra), among demons (Hiraṇyākṣa, Bali, Prahlāda, etc.), among rākṣasas (like Vibhīṣaṇa, Prahasta, Indrajit), among nāgas (Takṣaka, etc.), and other liberated ones in other planes. Even among human beings there are liberated ones, but they are extremely rare. There are millions of beings; but a liberated one is rare.

VASIṢṬHA continued: VI.2:98

The enemies of holiness, which are greed, delusion, etc., are greatly weakened in the case of the wise men who are full of dispassion and who rest in the supreme state. They do not give way to exhilaration or to anger; they do not get involved in anything or take anything. They neither agitate people nor are they agitated by them. They are neither atheists nor are they confined to a traditional belief. They do not engage themselves in torturous practices even if they are ordained by the scriptures. Their actions and behaviour are full of common-sense and sweetness, soft (gentle) and affectionate.

They gladden the hearts of all. They point out the wise path and instantly and spontaneously they decide what is best. They engage themselves in all kinds of activity externally; but inwardly they are cool and tranquil. They love investigating the meanings of the scriptures. They know who is who (who is a mature person and who is immature). They know what to accept and what to reject. Their actions are appropriate to the occasion.

They avoid forbidden actions. They enjoy good company. They worship with the flowers of wisdom everyone who seeks their company and their teaching. They rob the people of their sorrow and grief. They are kind and gentle; but when the rulers of the earth become unrighteous and oppressive, they shake them up even as an earthquake shakes a mountain. They encourage people in distress and enhance the joy of the happy one. They restrain the ignorant and foolish behaviour of people.

When one is afflicted by calamities and mental confusion, trials and tribulations, the saints alone are one's refuge. Recognising them by the characteristics given above one should resort to them for peace. This ocean of saṃsāra is impassable except with the help of the saints. One should not become passive, fatalistically accepting whatever happens. If all the qualities described are not found in one person, if even one of these qualities is present, one should resort to such a holy man, ignoring all the other defects that may be found in him. One should learn to recognise the good in others as well as the defects; and then one should strive to resort to the company of the good and the wise. Even if a good person has some defect, one should serve him, avoiding major evil tendencies. If one does not overcome evil tendencies, even a good man becomes wicked. This is what I have observed. It is indeed a great misfortune and a calamity to the entire society when a good man turns wicked on account of circumstances.

Hence, one should abandon all other activity and be devoted to the saintly ones. There is no obstacle to this. This alone is capable of bestowing on one the best of both the worlds. One should never be far away from the saints, for by their very proximity the saints promote goodness everywhere.

VI.2:99 RĀMA asked:

We human beings have diverse means of overcoming sorrow. What about the worms and flies, as also the trees?

VASIṢṬHA said:

All beings rest in consciousness as is appropriate to their nature.

They, too, have their own cravings and desires. In our case there are minor obstructions to the fulfilment of our desires and in their case the difficulties are enormous. Just as the cosmic person (virāṭ) strives, even so do worms and flies: a little boy flourishes a clenched fist—marvellous is vanity! Birds are born and die in empty space. Even an ant has to eat and look after the family needs. The little fly flitting across a room is equal in dignity to the vulture Garuḍa flying aloft. Notions like 'I am this' 'This is mine' are common to both human beings and worms, with all the lofty implications of such notions.

Even as we strive to gain means of livelihood the worms strive for it. They, too, love life. A slave takes little interest in the new country; even so do the cows and other animals not take interest in their 'owner's' house. They too have pleasure and pain, but they are free from a sense of 'mine' and 'thine'. Even a seed and a young sprout experience some pain (or awareness) when bitten by a worm, even as a sleeping man experiences the annoyance of a flea. Both Indra (the king of gods) and a worm experience the same attraction, aversion, fear, desire for food and sex, pain and pleasure and the distress caused by birth and death. The only difference exists in understanding the meaning of words and the nature of the elements and the anticipation of the future events.

Trees which are asleep, as it were, and also the immovable objects like rocks, etc., exist in the unbroken experience of infinite consciousness. In them there is no notion of division. All this is but pure, infinite consciousness which thinks it is asleep in the rocks, etc., as it was in the previous creation. Hence, you remain as you are and I remain as I am. There is no pleasure or pain in the supreme self or consciousness. Ignorance alone is the cause for all delusion. But when the ignorance is dispelled by understanding, then what is seen is no-thing. When the truth concerning this world-dream is understood, it ceases. What then is desirable here and what is fit to be gained? When the wave subsides, water is not destroyed. When the body is destroyed, the consciousness remains unchanged.

Only an ignorant person persists in his notion concerning the world and he experiences it as if real. The right understanding of this truth opens the door to self-knowledge. Just as an object is reflected in a mirror, so does this world appear in Brahman. Though the reflection seems to be in the mirror, it is not there: even so, though the world appears to be, it is not there. It seems to produce an effect though it itself is unreal, even as there is discharge of energy when one dreams of having sex. However, only an ignorant man knows why he considers the world to be real!

VI.2:100 RĀMA asked:

There are others, O sage, who hold that since death is inevitable one should live happily as long as one lives, and that once the body is reduced to ashes, there is nothing which survives. What is their way out of the sorrow inherent in saṃsāra?

VASIṢṬHA replied:

Whatever the inner intelligence firmly believes in, that alone is experienced by it, as if it is obvious. Consciousness is universal and indivisible: that is one and that alone is diverse. Nothing else existed before the concept of creation arose; hence, nothing else is really true. They are surely ignorant who do not see the reality that is expounded in the scripture. For us they are as good as dead. They who have realised that all this is pure consciousness (Brahman), do not need our instruction either.

Whatever arises as real in the 'body' of consciousness is experienced as real; everyone is made of that, whether there is a real physical body or not. If it is contended that (sense-)experience alone is consciousness, then one is bound to suffer, for as long as one lives there are bound to be contradictory experiences. On the other hand, if one realises that this world is but a notion that arises in consciousness, the division or the contradiction ceases and therefore there is no contradictory experience either. Even as floating dust-particles do not affect space, pleasure and pain do not touch one who is established in the realisation of the one indivisible, infinite consciousness.

We do not apprehend a body or a personality or even a jīva: all this is pure consciousness and whatever notion arises in it is experienced as such. Whether it is real or unreal, it is that which experiences the existence of the body. Whether consciousness is regarded as real or unreal, the person is that alone; what that consciousness considers real is surely real (or, consciousness is real as the person or self). (That is, even the materialist does not deny the existence of the person and hence he cannot deny the existence of consciousness.) This doctrine confirms the teaching of all scriptures.

When this understanding is clouded, perverse doctrines arise; when that misunderstanding is removed, it yields the highest fruit. But even when it is not rightly understood, it does not cease to be. If it is said that even after self-knowledge this right understanding can once again be clouded, then there is no hope of getting rid of sorrow. If consciousness is realised as real, it is resorted to by the wise. If it is considered unreal, then one becomes inert like a rock. It is when this infinite consciousness 'sleeps', as it were, that the experience of objects arises and this world comes into being. Thus, he who considers this world and the sense-experience alone as real, is inert and 'asleep'.

RĀMA asked:

There are they, O sage, who think that this limitless universe exists on all sides. They do not see that it is a mass of consciousness. They see it as it is ordinarily seen; but they do not see that it is changing and is moving towards destruction. In the case of such persons, what method is there to overcome mental distress?

VASIṢṬHA replied:

Before answering that question, one should pose another. Does that person feel that matter is indestructible as matter and that the body is immortal? Then, where is sorrow? But, if this body is made of its various parts, then surely it will perish.

If one knows that the self is pure consciousness (and not the physical body) then when he dies there is no saṃsāra (world-appearance) in his consciousness. If one's understanding is not thus purified by right understanding or wisdom, it does not remain without the support of saṃsāra. If, however, he thinks that there is no such thing as consciousness, then he experiences a state which is inertness. One may think that the experiences in the embodied state alone are real. Being firmly established in this conviction, he thinks that death is the final end to sorrow. But this is only because of imperfect experience. They who believe in the non-existence of consciousness become inert substances when the body is abandoned and thus they sink into the impenetrable darkness of ignorance. They, on the other hand, who believe that the world exists as a relative reality (as in a dream), continue to experience this world-illusion.

Whether one considers this world to be a permanent reality or a changing phenomenon, there is the experience of pain and pleasure all the same. They who think that the world is a changing but purely material substance (devoid of consciousness) are childish. Have nothing to do with them. They who realise that bodies exist in consciousness are wise; salutations to them. They who think that there is intelligence in the body are ignorant.

It is pure consciousness, with the jīva as its body, that keeps going up and down in this cosmic space. Whatever that jīva contemplates within itself, that it experiences. Just as clouds make different patterns in the sky and just as waves arise on the surface of the ocean, even so do these worlds appear in the infinite consciousness. The dream-city is only the dreamer's mind; it did not even need the co-operating causes (like the building materials) to build it. Even so is the universe; it is pure consciousness and nothing else. They who realise this are free from delusion, from attachment (dependency) and from mental distress, while continuing to perform appropriate actions spontaneously in situations which the stream of life bears along.

VI.2:101 VASIṢṬHA continued:

Everyone is pure consciousness alone. What else can there be except this consciousness? When consciousness alone exists, what is there to gain and what to reject? When there is no other, rāga (attraction or affection) and dveṣa (rejection or aversion) become meaningless.

Consciousness alone is human beings, god, nāga (inhabitants of the netherworld), mountains and moving objects. I am pure consciousness and so are you. We shall die some time or the other, but consciousness does not perish. Consciousness does not have an object for it to become aware of: hence all talk of unity and diversity is meaningless.

Even the materialists (they who believe in the reality of the physical world) allude to this consciousness only because they do not deny the self, the intelligence or consciousness that makes them think and say what they say. This consciousness is called Brahman by some, jñānaṃ (self-knowledge), śūnya (void), the power of delusion, puruṣa (the self), cidākāśa (space or plane of consciousness), Śiva, self (ātman), etc., by others. All these descriptions are consciousness because it is consciousness alone that considers itself thus (i.e., the intelligence in each one of these people who holds a different view).

May my limbs be pulverised or may they become as powerful as the Meru-mountain. What is lost and what is gained (increased) when it is realised that I am pure consciousness? My grandfather and others are dead, but consciousness is not dead. Consciousness is unborn and undying. It is like space. How can sky die? Just as the world is unseen (is destroyed) by the darkness of the night and just as the world is seen (created) again at dawn, even so is birth and death. One should therefore regard death as a joyful event, for one goes from one body to another: only fools grieve on such joyful occasions. Or, if you think that one is not born again in another body, even then there is no cause for grief, for then death puts an end to the disease of birth and death. Hence, the wise man does not grieve or rejoice in life or in death. If one who is conscious of his own evil-doings fears death, even that is meaningless, since such a person suffers here as well as in the other world. Hence, why do you wail, "Oh, I die, I die, I die" instead of exclaiming in joy, "I shall be, I shall be, I shall be." Even these are meaningless words when you realise that the infinite consciousness alone exists. Space exists in space. What is the meaning of words like 'birth' and 'death'? Knowing that you are pure consciousness, eat, drink and live without the sense of 'I' and 'mine'. You are like the sky. How can desires arise in you? The wise man enjoys what is pure if it comes to him unsought, borne down by the river of life. If there are impurities borne down by the river of life or by circumstances, the wise man is unconcerned about them, as in deep sleep.

RĀMA asked: VI.2:102

When one has realised the supreme truth, what does he become?

VASIṢṬHA replied:

To such a one even the rocks become friends and the trees in the forest are relatives; even when he lives in the middle of a forest the very animals become his kith and kin. A kingdom appears to be void in his eyes, calamities become great good fortune; even when he lives in a kingdom, he rejoices in (celebrates) his misfortunes. Disharmony becomes harmony, sorrow is great joy, and even when engaged in intense activity he experiences deep silence. He sees utter non-action in action. Awake he is in deep sleep; alive he is as good as dead. He does everything but nothing. He enjoys without tasting the pleasure. He is a very dear friend of all. He is free from pity for others, but full of compassion. Free from craving, he appears to want. He is only interested in the proper performance of his actions.

He appears to be happy and unhappy in the respective situation. He does not abandon what is natural and plays his appropriate role in this drama of life. He sympathises with the sorrowful and rejoices with the happy ones, without being tainted at heart.

RĀMA asked:

But some clever though ignorant people can also pretend to be in that state (observing celibacy like a horse, without the right spirit). How does one distinguish the true from the false?

VASIṢṬHA replied:

Whether it is true or false, such a nature is praiseworthy. The truly wise ones live as if they had various desires and they laugh with the fools, though they themselves are wise. No one knows their inner peace and illumined state. Only wise ones know other wise men. The true men of wisdom do not expose their wisdom nor parade it to win the admiration of the masses. The latter are distractions in the eyes of the wise. 'I wish everyone to know how good I am so that they may worship me'—such thoughts arise in the mind of the vain man, not of the wise one.

Powers like levitation, etc., are gained by mantras, drugs, etc., even by the ignorant people. He who is prepared to make the necessary effort can gain these, whether he is enlightened or not. It is the ego that makes the effort and gains the powers. These powers intensify the vāsanās or mental conditioning. But the enlightened is not interested in any of these. He regards the world as a blade of grass. The enlightened one lives a non-volitional life engaging himself spontaneously in appropriate action. Even the celestial pleasure-gardens do not make one as happy as the wisdom of the enlightened man. The latter sees, when his own body is subjected to heat and cold, etc., as if all these happened to someone else. He lives for the sake of others, with a heart full of compassion for all beings. He may live in a cave, in a hermitage or a house, or he may be wandering constantly. He may be a teacher or a student. He may have psychic powers or he may be forever in samādhi.

VI.2:103 VASIṢṬHA continued:

The infinite consciousness alone shines as this world-appearance. How can it perish? There is no possibility for the existence of another other than consciousness. When the body perishes, consciousness does not perish. If it is said that consciousness ceases when the body perishes, then it is a matter for rejoicing as there is cessation of saṃsāra and sorrow! If it is said that consciousness exists as long as the body exists, how is it that the dead body is not conscious? All these arguments are not valid. The infinite consciousness alone is real and whatever it wishes to experience it does experience as existence because there is no obstruction to the realisation of its notions. The world has never been created: what is IS the infinite consciousness.

This consciousness itself wishes to experience its infinite potencies. It knows itself when it is aware of itself, and it is ignorant of itself when it is unaware of itself. Therefore, even knowledge and ignorance are pure consciousness and there is no such division, in truth. Hence, one should engage oneself seriously in the realisation of the self; self-knowledge bestows on one the best of both worlds.

Abandon every kind of mental agitation and devote every moment of your life to the study and investigation of this scripture. One surely gains that for which one strives; if one neglects it he loses it. The mind flows along the course of wisdom or of ignorance, in whichever direction you make it flow. Except through this scripture, one cannot gain what is good, now or at any time. Therefore, for perfect realisation of the supreme truth, one should fervently investigate this scripture alone. This scripture does more good to you than your father and mother and all your friends put together.

The dreadful illness known as saṃsāra or bondage to worldly existence is not cured by any remedy other than self-knowledge. It is a great pity that you waste your time and await the hour of death. Foolish people who run after wealth and fame pawn their very lives in gaining and preserving them. Why do they not spend their life and their time in the investigation of the scripture and the attainment of immortality? It is through self-knowledge that one can destroy misfortunes and calamities by their very roots.

It is for your good that I cry aloud day and night and declare the truth. Listen to this and realise the self by the self. If you do not rid yourself now of this dire illness, what will you do after death? There is no scripture like this to help you in attaining self-knowledge. Let it shine like a lamp, let it awaken and instruct you like a father and let it bring you joy like a wife. In this scripture there is nothing new; but the truth has been presented in a pleasant fashion with a number of stories. It is the truth that is proclaimed in this scripture, that is important; not the one who has declared the truth or composed the scripture.

VASIṢṬHA continued:

One should not associate with another who derides and belittles this scripture either through ignorance or through delusion. I know what I am and I know who you all are. I am but your own consciousness, seated here in order to instruct you: I am neither human, nor celestial nor divine. I am here as the fruit of your merit. In fact, I am neither this nor the other.

One should find here in this world the appropriate remedy for the illness known as saṃsāra (world-illusion). Unless one cultivates a disinterest in the objective and material existence of this world, the belief or the notion of its existence cannot be weakened. There is no others means to rid the self of its impurity of self-limitation. The only way is to weaken the vāsanā (self-limitation or conditioning or the notion that the world exists). If the object does exist then such a notion of its existence is natural: but it does not, though it seems to be, in the absence of the light of enquiry.

The apparent world-existence has no real cause; how can the effect of an unreality be other than unreal? How can a non-material (spiritual) cause bring about a material effect? How can matter arise in pure consciousness any more that a shadow exist in the sun? It is not correct to say that the world is a pure and accidental combination of atoms: they are inert substances. The world-creation is not the action of ignorance but, on the other hand, if it is the action of intelligence, why will an intelligent being indulge in such futile action, like a madman? Hence, it is clear that the world is an appearance, and not existence. We appear to exist in pure void, like objects in a dream. The world is but pure consciousness and there is no difference between the two; the one is expressed in two ways like 'air' and 'motion in space'. The infinite consciousness plus the appearance is known as the world; the world minus its form (appearance) is the infinite consciousness (appearance is illusory and illusion does not exist). Just as consciousness creates dreams in a dreamer, it creates the world in the waking state; the two are constituted of the same substance. Where then is the reality of the body even of Brahmā the creator? It arose as the first dream-object in consciousness.

Brahman alone exists, not even the cosmic person. But all these are experienced, as if they were real, over a long period of time. Yet, what is unreal is unreal, even if it has been experienced for a long period of time, and by all. From the creator Brahmā right down to the pillar, all appearance of materiality is unreal like objects seen in a dream. These objects appear to have a form even as the objects seen in a dream seem to have a form during the dream. Therefore, tell me what is material existence and what are the objects of this world-appearance? Where are they? What are they? What is unity? What is diversity? What am I? What are notions concerning the objects of existence? What are notions and vāsanās or self-limitation or psychological conditioning which perpetuate the notion of world-existence? Where are they? They are not! Realise this and rest in a state of nirvāṇa.

VI.2:104, 105 VASIṢṬHA continued:

The subtle sound-vibration constitutes space and the subtle touch-vibration constitutues air. Their friction causes heat or the fire-element. When the fire subsides there is water. When all these get together earth arises from it. But all these are a play of simple vibrations which are formless. How does form arise? After reflecting on this for a considerable time one comes to the understanding that it is consciousness that gives rise to form. Why not understand this truth right in the beginning? Neither the gross elements nor the forms exist in truth: they arise as they arise in a dream. As forms arise in dreams, so do they arise in the waking state, too. If this is realised, there is liberation. Whether the body continues to exist or ceases to exist, there is no sorrow.

Neither in the waking state nor in dream is there a real world. Consciousness experiences itself as such and that experience is known as the world. Just as the world seen in a dream is 'nothing' even so the world seen in the waking state is 'nothing'. Just as one man's dream-experiences are unknown to the person sleeping next to him, one man's experiences in this world are unknown to another.

In dream, the barren woman seems to have a son: in the waking state the impossible seems to have happened. The unreal appears to be real. Something which has not really been experienced appears to be a real experience, even as one experiences one's own funeral in a dream. When one dreams of falling into a pit, his bed becomes that pit. In blinding light one sees nothing (it is like darkness).

In dream, the dreamer dies, abandoning his dream-relatives. But, then he wakes up, freed from that dream-life and death. Even so, after experiencing joy and sorrow here for a long time, one dies. The dreamer wakes to experience another dream known as the world. Even so, after experiencing this world, he goes on to yet another. While dreaming, the dreamer does not realise that a previous dream was unreal (dream). Even so, one does not remember the past life but considers the present life alone to be real. The dreamer is said to 'wake up' when his sleep comes to an end; even so, the person who lives in this world and dies, wakes up elsewhere. The distinction between dream and waking is, therefore, purely arbitrary and academic. Both of them are based on the sole reality of the infinite consciousness.

All the moving and unmoving things are but pure consciousness. When an illusory notion of division arises in it, consciousness comes to be known as the world. A pot is but clay; in the absence of clay there is no pot. All objects are pure consciousness and if consciousness is not, nothing is seen. Water is liquid; minus its liquidity it is not water (what is dehydrated water?). Even so is consciousness. Everything here is pure consciousness; minus pure consciousness nothing is.

VASIṢṬHA continued: VI.2:106

The same thing has been given two names for the sake of convenience: the two (waking and dreaming) are the same, like two cups of water. That which is common to them, which is their common substratum, is pure consciousness.

The attitude or the nature of a tree which draws nourishment through its roots and exists is pure consciousness. Similarly, when one's desires have turned away and when the mind is at perfect peace, then there is pure consciousness. In the case of a healthy man, when his mind is free from objective notions, and sleep has not yet come, there is pure consciousness. That nature which exists in grass and creepers growing in their proper seasons without the feeling of mine-ness, is pure consciousness. The nature of one who is free from percepts and concepts but is not dead, and whose being is clear and pure like the winter sky, is pure consciousness. The pure being of wood and rock which are as they were created, as also the mind of pure beings, is pure consciousness. That is pure consciousness (cid-ākāśa) in which all things exist, from which they emerge, which is everything, and which is all in all.

When sleep has ceased, the world-appearance rises; when that ceases there is pure consciousness (cidaṃbaraṃ). That 'nothing' which remains after everything has been negated as 'not this, not this' is pure consciousness (cidaṃbaraṃ). The entire universe is but pure consciousness, as it was and as it is. Even when there is perception of forms and apprehension of notions and concepts, that consciousness alone exists.

Knowing this, be free from conditioning even while perceiving the objects of the senses, just as a man who sleeps is yet inwardly 'awake'. Remaining inwardly silent like a rock, talk, walk, drink and take. This world has not been created at all, for it has no cause; no effect arises without a cause. Hence consciousness remains as consciousness, without change. When its experience of its own inherent potentialities is continued, it appears as this world. Thus, this objective world has not been created at all, does not exist and will not come into being; it will not perish either, for how can non-existence perish? What appears to be is the reflection of consciousness within itself. However, since there is no duality, there is neither a reflection nor an appearance. Who knows whether 'what is' is real or unreal?! Who knows why and how a man dreams or what the dreams are, except that they are his own consciousness? The Creator and all things are but pure consciousness. When this is realised, it is known as Brahman; when it is not realised, it is known as illusion, Māyā, ignorance and the world. It is that consciousness alone that knows itself as 'I am mountain', 'I am Rudra', 'I am the ocean' and 'I am the cosmic person' just as a person while dreaming thinks that all these exist in his dream. All external objects are reflected in the mirror of one's consciousness which when enquired into is seen immediately. When thus investigated, their true nature as pure consciousness is realised.

The Story of Vipaścit

VI.2:107, 108 VASIṢṬHA continued:

The whole universe is pure consciousness, but as an object it is inert appearance. Hence, though alive, everything is as if dead; even so I and you are as if dead though live. Abandoning the world-idea in the world and the I-you-idea in ourselves, engage yourself in appropriate action. Why? Why does this world-appearance arise at all? There is no reason, even as in the play of a young child there is no reason or motivation. Hence, one should not waste one's lifetime in useless pursuit of knowledge concerning matter and mind: if one seeks gold one does not clean the sky!

Listen to the following story: In this universe, in this continent known as Jaṃbūdvīpa, there was a famous city by name Tatam which was ruled by a king known as Vipaścit (lit: learned, wise). His glory was indescribable. Even the court poets had exhausted all their talents without exhausting a description of his virtues. But they loved and enjoyed his company. He was fond of them and gave them lavish gifts every day. He was devoted to the brāhmaṇas (priests) and also to the fire which he devoutly worshipped every day.

He had four ministers who were zealously guarding his kingdom at its four boundaries. On account of their wisdom and valour, the king was victorious and unassailable. One day, he was visited by a wise man from the east. He had harsh and unpleasant words for the king.

He said: "O king, you have bound yourself hand and foot to this earth. Now listen to what I have to say and decide what to do. Your minister who was guarding the eastern side of your city is dead. The one guarding the south endeavoured to cover the eastern side, too, but he was overcome by the enemy. He, too, is dead. When the minister guarding the west rushed to the southern side, he was intercepted by the enemy and killed."

As he was saying this, another man rushed into the court and announced that the minister guarding the north was at the palace gate. The king alerted his army and asked that the minister be brought in. The minister entered and saluted the king. He was weak and his breathing was laboured. He had been overpowered by the enemy on account of his weakness. He said to the king: "Lord, all the other three ministers have gone to the world of death to win that realm for you. Only you have the power to quell the enemy."

In the meantime, yet another man entered the royal presence and reported: "Lord, the city has been completely surrounded by the enemy. Their weapons are seen everywhere. They are extremely powerful like demons. Their armour shines with the light equal to your own glory. Their armies are in excellent array. They are angry and their battle cries are fierce. The lord of that army sent me to convey this news to you. Now do what is appropriate."

After having conveyed this message, that man went away. Everyone in the king's army got ready for the battle with their arms and weapons uplifted.

VASIṢṬHA continued: VI.2:109, 110

In the meantime, all the ministers had assembled around the king. They counselled him thus: "Lord, we have duly considered the situation concerning our enemy. We have come to the conclusion that the three peaceful courses of dealing with the enemy are inappropriate in this case and that only the fourth—punishment or violence—is adequate. In fact, we have not shown friendship or alliance with these enemies at any time before; hence it is of no use now. Enemies who come under the following classification are not amenable to peaceful negotiation: sinners, barbarians, foreigners, they who are firmly united among themselves, as well as they who know our weakness very well. Therefore let there be no delay. Order general mobilisation and preparation for a full-scale war."

The king issued the necessary orders and sent the ministers to the battlefield saying that he would soon join them after his customary worship of the sacred fire. He then had his bath and approached the sacred fire for worship. He prayed: "Lord, I have effortlessly overcome all my enemies so far and ruled this far-flung empire exercising my sovereignty over many islands and continents. I held sway over many peoples, including demons. But now perhaps I have grown old. Therefore, these my enemies have thought it fit to invade my territory. Lord, just as till now I have made different oblations to this sacred fire, today I shall offer my own head as oblation. I pray that out of this fire, four powerful beings may emerge like the four arms of lord Nārāyaṇa."

So saying, the king cut off his head with the greatest ease and the next instant his body fell into the fire along with the severed head. Out of that fire the king re-emerged as four radiant warriors of extraordinary radiance and vitality and equipped with the very best of weapons of every description. It was obvious that they could not be overcome by any warlike device that the enemy might adopt, whether it be missiles or mantras, drugs, etc.

The enemy forces were advancing at the same time. There was a terrible battle. The sky was covered with smoke and also with missiles. Swords gleamed, revolvers emitted fire continuously; it was terrible to look at. There was a river of blood in which even elephants were borne down. Here and there two missiles collided in the sky which was illumined by the light emitted by them. In the mind and the heart of every warrior there was only one thought, "I should kill the enemy or be killed by him". The war was also bringing out the good and noble qualities in the people which were dormant till then. On the other hand, there was also extremely cruel behaviour. Here and there warriors killed even refugees and looted whatever they could.

The people who were not directly involved in the war, the non-combatants, fled the place. The battlefield was filled with warriors to whom the distinction between life and death had vanished.

VI.2:111, 112 VASIṢṬHA continued:

The king in his four forms proceeded in the four directions on the battlefield. He saw that his army was much weaker than the enemy's well-prepared and well-equipped army. He contemplated, "The sage

Agastya drank the ocean; I should become another Agastya now and dry up this ocean of the enemy forces". He thought of the wind-missile which instantly reached him. He once again saluted and offered a prayer on behalf of his subjects and directed the missile at the enemy forces. Instantly there were rivers of missiles and weapons everywhere. The gale that blew resembled the winds of cosmic dissolution. Surely enough, by the power of the missile, the enemy forces were reduced to nothing very soon. The wind-missile also caused torrential rains, gale-force winds and dense dark clouds.

The different units of the enemy army fled in different directions. The Cedi-army (from the land of pearls and snakes) fled in a southerly direction. The Pārsis perished in the forest known as Vañjula. The Darada soldiers hid themselves in caves. The Daśārṇa warriors who went into the nearby forests were killed by the lions there. The warriors from Śaka territory could not bear the missiles made of iron and they ran trembling in fear. The forces of Tuṅgaṇa (whose colour was golden) were robbed by robbers of their clothes, and then they were eaten up by demons.

The survivors in the enemy army hid themselves in the mountain known as Sahya-adri and rested for a period of seven days. Their wounds were attended to by the celestials (vidhyādhara-women) who were from the territory known as Gāndhāra. The warriors from Hūṇa, Cīna and Kirāṭa had suffered dreadful disfigurement from the missiles of the king Vipaścit. Even the trees were frightened of the king's power and stood still for a very long time even after the war.

The air force of Vidūra territory was caught up in the winds and crashed into the lakes. The infantry could not even run on account of the blinding rain that fell. The Hūṇas who fled to the north were caught up in the quicksands and perished. The Śakas who fled to the east were caught and imprisoned by the king for one day and then released.

The soldiers from the Mandra territory climbed up the Mahendra mountain to seek a refuge. They literally dragged themselves up little by little and then fell near the hermitage of sages who served them with food, drink, etc. They climbed the hill for the purpose of avoiding death on the battlefield and of begging for food; but they got from the cave of the gods two things (immediate safety and the company of sages which ensures permanent peace). Good follows evil sometimes, by accidental coincidence (the crow and the cocoanut.) The Daśārṇa soldiers accidentally ate poison and died. The Haihaya soldiers accidentally ate a healing herb which turned them into celestials with ability to fly in the air.

VI.2:113, 114, 115 VASIṢṬHA continued:

Thus pursuing their fleeing enemies the four kings (which were Vipaścit) had traversed a long, long distance. Impelled by the indwelling consciousness which is omnipotent they had embarked on a campaign for the conquest of the world, known as digvijaya. For a considerable distance they were accompanied by their own forces. As they were marching without rest or respite, these forces and their equipment, as also the forces of the enemy which they pursued, weakened and perished. The missiles that kings had had also ceased to be effective, just as fire is quenched after burning all its fuel.

The four kings going in the four different directions were met by huge oceans. The remaining missiles that they had fell into mud created by the terrible rain that fell, and they disintegrated. The four brothers beheld that limitless ocean with great wonder. (N.B.: There follows a highly poetic description of the ocean.)

The kings' ministers who had followed them on this expedition pointed out to the kings the various beautiful sights—the forests, the trees, the oceans, the mountains, the clouds and also the hill tribes. (N.B. Again, there is a poetic description of all these in the text. There is also a 'reverse'—comparison . . .) Just as Brahman, though one, appears to be divided into diversity and, though infinite, appears to have created this finite and perishable world, even so this ocean, though one, appears to be divided into several oceans, and it appears to be both eternal and the transient waves.

The ministers pointed to more oceans and said: "Lord, here on this ocean, lord Nārāyaṇa rests. Here in the other ocean his enemies the demons lie hidden. In that other ocean, mountains lie hidden. Beneath this ocean there is the cosmic fire of unimaginable heat, along with the clouds of cosmic dissolution. How wonderful it is that this ocean is so vast, so firmly established and able to support so much of burden. Look at the moon. As it rises on the eastern horizon, it spreads its soft light everywhere and thus brings auspiciousness to all, ridding all of their fear of darkness and night. But even this moon is tainted with dark spots. When such is the case with these celestial bodies, what can we call an untainted object in this world, what shall we call good and excellent in this world, which time or fate will not tarnish in the twinkling of an eye? Surely, there is no such thing on earth."

VI.2:116 THE MINISTERS AND OTHERS said:

Behold, O king, the rulers of the boundaries of the earth engaged in battle. The celestial nymphs are driving the space vehicles carrying away those noble ones who are slain in battle. This is considered as the best of all fruits of living: that one should live a life of prosperity, health and wealth, which does not incur the displeasure of society, and should engage oneself in righteous warfare for the sake of others. He who kills another when the latter comes to fight with him, without transgressing the moral code that applies to warfare, he is a hero and he goes to heaven.

Behold the sky, O king, where the mighty gods and demons appear in the form of stars, which is also the field for the movement of mighty planets and stars like the sun and the moon. Fools regard it as empty void even now. In spite of the movement of all these stars and planets, in spite of the battle between gods (light) and demons (darkness), this space is not polluted or tainted or altered in any way.

O space! Though you bear the sun on your lap, and even lord Nārāyaṇa and all his divine retinue, yet you have not abandoned the darkness that resides in you. This is indeed a great mystery. Yet, we consider the space wise and enlightened as it is unaffected by the defects and shortcomings of the worlds which abide in it (the space).

O space! During the day you are bright. At dawn and dusk you are crimson. At night you are dark. You are devoid of materiality. You do not hold or bear the burden of any substance. Hence you are regarded as Māyā. No one, not even the learned and the wise, can truly understand you and your function. O space, he who owns nothing achieves everything. You are pure void within yourself and yet you cause everything to grow and to be exalted.

In space there are no cities or villages, no forests or parks, no trees or shade, yet the sun courses through space every day. Truly, the noble ones do their duty without fail, however difficult and irksome it may be.

Though apparently doing nothing, space regulates the growth of plants and trees by preventing them from excessive growth. That in which infinite universes are born and into which they dissolve—how can that space be considered devoid of everything? There is something wrong with the scholars.

THE MINISTERS AND OTHERS continued: VI.2:117-121

(The next few chapters are also full of highly poetic and artistic descriptions of natural phenomena, the flora and the fauna, with interesting spiritual parallels, from which the following two are but samples.—S.V.)

O lord, behold the crane. How diligent and efficient it is in capturing and consuming the fish. Wicked people see in the natural behaviour of the crane the justification for their own vicious doctrine that even so one should destroy others for the attainment of one's own selfish ends.

Look at the peacock. It quenches its thirst from the purest rain-water. It does not drink of the polluted waters of the drains and the canals. However, it continuously remembers the clouds and the rain that falls from them and derives satisfaction. When one's heart is fixed in devotion to the holy ones, even unpleasant experiences become pleasant.

O king, behold that young couple talking to each other and refreshing themselves over there. The young man, smitten with love for his beloved, met her just now after a very long separation. This is what he said to her:

"Beloved, listen to what happened to me one day during our separation. I looked at the cloud and prayed to the cloud to convey a message to you. I was so greatly overcome by longing for you that I fainted. My breathing stopped. My memory failed. My body became cold and rigid like a log of wood. Who can ever describe adequately the unhappiness caused by separation from a beloved one?

"Travellers who witnessed this thought I was dead and made preparations for the cremation of the destitute body. I was taken to the crematorium. They laid me on the pyre and set it alight. In a few moments I experienced all kinds of strange feelings and sensations and visions. I felt that I was falling into a hole in the ground. I was protected by the armour of your love and of contemplation of your form. I enjoyed your company in my own heart. I remember even now the smallest detail of the amorous dalliance in which we self-forgetfully enjoyed each other. In the meantime I saw flames around me." Hearing this, the girl swooned but the lover revived her and continued the narrative:

"At once I shouted 'Fire, fire' and woke up from the swoon. The people around the funeral pyre thought that I had returned from the dead and they were thrilled. They sang and danced. We all returned home."

VASIṢṬHA continued:

After listening to all this, the fourfold Vipaścit worshipped the fire. The fire-god appeared to them. They prayed to him: "We wish to behold the universe composed of the five elements in its totality. Grant that we may do so and that we may not die till we have seen all—as much as possible with the physical body and beyond that through the mind." The fire-god granted this boon and vanished.

VI.2:124 RĀMA asked:

Lord, how was it that though the fourfold Vipaścit was but one person with a single consciousness, the four of them entertained different desires?

VASIṢṬHA replied:

Though consciousness is one, non-dual and omnipresent, it seems to become diverse like the mind of the sleeping (dreaming) person.

Even as the mirror reflects diverse objects within itself because it is pure, even so consciousness, being absolutely pure, reflects everything within itself. Though mirrors may be made of the same metal, they reflect diverse objects in one another ad infinitum. Similarly, consciousness reflects within itself whatever is placed before it.

Thus the diverse appears to be one, but it is both diverse and non-diverse (one); because it is neither diverse nor non-diverse, it is both diverse and one. Therefore, whatever appeared before each of the four Vipaścits reflected in his consciousness and was experienced by him. Yogis can perform actions everywhere and experience all things in all the three periods of time, though apparently remaining in one place. Water which is one and all-pervasive does several things at the same time and seems to undergo diverse experiences. The one Viṣṇu with his four arms or four bodies perform diverse functions in protecting the world. A being (animal) with many arms holds something with two arms and with the others kills that thing. It was in that manner that the kings Vipaścit engaged themselves in diverse activities.

They diversely slept on the grassy beds on earth. They lived and enjoyed themselves in different continents. They sported in different forests. They roamed the deserts. They dwelt on the peaks of mountains and in the bowels of the oceans. They sometimes hid themselves in mountain-caves. They sported on the oceans and in the wind, on the waves as well as on the seashore and in the cities.

The Vipaścit who went east slept for seven years on the slopes of the sunrise mountain on the continent known as Śāka, for he had been charmed by the celestials there; having drunk of the water that was in the rock, he had become like stone. The Vipaścit who went west to the sunset mountain on the same continent fell a victim to the charms of a nymph who enjoyed him for a whole month. The Vipaścit who went east remained incognito in the turmeric forest for some time. On account of the charm of a celestial, he lived as a lion for ten days. Overpowered by a goblin, he lived as a frog for ten years. The Vipaścit who went north dwelt for a hundred years in a blind well in the Nīlagiri (blue mountain) in the Śāka continent. The one who went west learnt the method of becoming a celestial and lived as a celestial (vidyādhara) for fourteen years.

VASIṢṬHA continued: VI.2:125

When the king that went east was under the spell of the water he had drunk, it was the one that went west who rescued him. When the king that went west became a rock, it was the one that went south who rescued him by the use of beef, etc. When the king that went west had been transformed into a bull by a female goblin who had the form of a cow, it was the one that went south who rescued him again. When the king that went south was turned into a celestial, he was rescued by another celestial at the intercession of the one who went west. When the king who went east was turned into a lion, it was the one who went west that rescued him.

RĀMA asked:

But how do these yogis perform such varied actions in the three periods of time? Pray tell me this.

VASIṢṬHA continued:

Whatever be the explanation that the unenlightened people may give for this, let them: but listen to the enlightened explanation.

In the vision of the knowers of the truth, there is nothing other than the pure and infinite consciousness, and the objective universe is completely and totally non-existent. There is neither a creation nor its opposite. He who rests for ever in this pure and infinite consciousness is the omnipresent and omnipotent Lord; he is the all and he is the self of all at all times. Tell me, who can restrain him, how, where and when. The omnipresent shines as and when he likes, for he is the self of all. What is not present in the self of all? Hence, he shines how, when and where he likes, whether it is the past or the future or the present and whether it is the gross or subtle field in which such action takes place. Without ever abandoning his reality as pure consciousness, he functions at a distance and near, creating an epoch or the twinkling of an eye. All this is in the self but the appearance is Māyā (illusory); he is unborn and uncreated and has not been restrained or inhibited. What IS is as it is. Whatever IS is a mass of consciousness; and that itself is the three worlds. It is the self of the world, it is the form of the world which has arisen on account of the polarisation of consciousness into the subject and the object. Who has created this seer of all, the subject of all—how and when?

Nothing is impossible for this consciousness. The consciousness of Vipaścit had become awakened but it had not attained the supreme state. Hence, though it is one it manifests as the all everywhere. In a state in which there is both awakening and non-awakening, all these things are possible; when the supreme truth has not been attained, such materialisation is possible. It is when there is such partial awakening that one enjoys psychic powers. Thus, the four Vipaścits experienced the states that the others had.

RĀMA asked:

If Vipaścit was an enlightened person, how could he consider himself a lion, etc.?

VASIṢṬHA replied:

My description of these kings as awakened or enlightened was only a figure of speech: in fact Vipaścit was not enlightened. The four Vipaścits were neither enlightened nor were they ignorant: they were swinging in-between. In such people the signs of enlightenment or liberation are seen, as also the signs of ignorance and bondage. They are half-awakened. Whatever Vipaścit had attained had been attained through contemplation, not because he had reached the supreme state. All these siddhis or psychic powers are had by such contemplation.

In those who have reached the supreme state, there is no ignorance or delusion. How can they have a deluded vision and how can they see falsehood? The yogis who practise contemplation and who attain various psychic powers through grace or boons are subject to ignorance which is noticed in them. Hence, they contemplate not the truth but something which is other than the real.

There is something more. Even in the case of those liberated sages who are still alive, there is comprehension of materiality while they are engaged in day-to-day activity. Mokṣa or liberation is also a state of the mind. The natural function of the body adheres to it and does not cease. One who is freed from ignorance, or the mind, is never again bound by the mind; even as once the fruit has fallen from the tree, no amount of effort can connect it to the tree. The body functions as is natural to it even in the case of the liberated person; but the consciousness in that person is stable and is not affected by the states of the physical body.

The powers gained through contemplation, etc., can be seen by others; but the state of liberation that one attains cannot be seen by others, even as the taste of honey is capable of being tasted only by oneself. When one who has experienced the state of bondage and also pain and pleasure is liberated from all these, he is said to be liberated. He is considered a liberated person whose inner consciousness is cool and peaceful; he is in bondage whose mind and heart are disturbed and distracted. Bondage and liberation are not noticed in physical functions.

Whether his body is cut into a thousand pieces or he is crowned an emperor, the liberated one is liberated even if he apparently weeps and laughs. Within himself he is neither elated nor depressed. He experiences neither happiness nor unhappiness, even while receiving all these experiences. He is not dead even when he is dead, he does not weep though he weeps, he does not laugh though he laughs— such is a liberated one. He is free from attraction or attachment, though he is attracted and attached. He gets angry though he is not angry; he is not deluded though he is deluded.

VASIṢṬHA continued:

The notions 'This is happiness' and 'This is unhappiness' do not arise in the liberated ones. When they have realised the truth that there is neither 'the world' nor 'the self' and that the one is the all, 'happiness' and 'unhappiness' are seen as meaningless words. Their grief is superficial, for they are free from sorrow.

It is said that lord Śiva plucked off one of the five heads of lord Brahmā. The latter was surely capable of growing one more to replace it. But he did not, for he knew "When all this creation is illusory, what shall I do with one more head?". He had nothing to gain from doing something or from refraining from doing something. Whatever happens, let it happen even so; why should it be otherwise?

Lord Śiva has his consort in one half of his body, though he has the power to burn up even the god of love. He has the power to abandon all attachment or affection, but he behaves as if he is attached to his consort. He has nothing to gain by remaining so attached nor does he gain anything by non-attachment. Let it be as it is.

Even so lord Viṣṇu engages himself in various activities and inspires others to engage themselves in such activities, too; he 'dies' and he kills others; he is born and he grows—though all the time he is totally free from all this. He could easily refrain from all this but what is to be gained from such restraint? Let all these be as they are. Such is the attitude of one who is established in the realisation of the infinite consciousness.

Even so do the sun, the moon and the fire perform their natural functions, though they are all liberated beings (jīvanmukta). The preceptors of the gods (Bṛhaspati) and of the demons (Śukra) are also jīvanmuktas, though they play the roles of the leaders of opposing forces, fighting each other like ignorant men. King Janaka is also a liberated royal sage; yet, he engages himself in dreadful wars. There were also several royal sages who engaged themselves in royal duties while inwardly remaining free from bondage. While discharging his worldly duties, the enlightened person behaves in the same way as the ignorant person. The distinction between bondage and liberation lies in the state of one's consciousness, which is conditioned in bondage and unconditioned in liberation. Even several demons had attained liberation—like Bali, Prahlāda, Namuci, Vṛtra, Andhaka, Mura, etc. The enlightened consciousness is unaffected by the rising and setting of likes and dislikes, mental action and supramental consciousness. When one is firmly established in the infinite and unconditioned consciousness, even these distinctions vanish. The diversity which people experience in this creation is but an appearance, like the colours of a rainbow.

The world appears to be in relation to the infinite consciousness just as spatiality (void or distance) appears to be in relation to space.

VASIṢṬHA continued: VI.2:126

Now, listen to what happened to the four Vipaścits. One of them was killed by an elephant. The second was taken away by some celestials (yakṣas) who dropped him into blazing fire, and he perished. The third one was taken up to heaven by the celestials known as vidyādhara; there, that Vipaścit did not bow to the king (Indra), who cursed him and reduced him to ashes. The fourth was killed by a crocodile.

Remaining in their subtle bodies, these four saw their own previous history in their own minds, where they had created subtle impressions. In the space of their own consciousness they saw the whole universe with all its oceans and mountains, towns and cities, the sun and the moon, the stars and the clouds. They even saw their own bodies as before. Endowed with the subtle (ātivāhika) bodies, they saw in the space before them their own physical bodies. On account of their past-life impressions or memories, they saw themselves as being clothed in physical bodies in order to witness the magnitude of the world. In order to see the actual extent of the earth, they roamed other realms.

The western Vipaścit crossed seven continents and seven seas and had the good fortune to meet lord Viṣṇu. From him Vipaścit received the highest wisdom, and remained immersed in samādhi for five years. After that he abandoned the physical body and attained nirvāṇa.

The oriental Vipaścit remained close to the rays of the moon and contemplated the moon constantly; hence he attained the realm of the moon.

The southern Vipaścit destroyed all his enemies and even now he rules the country because he did not lose his memory or his convictions.

The northern Vipaścit was eaten by a crocodile in whose body he lived for a thousand and one years. When that crocodile died, he emerged from its body as another crocodile. Then he crossed oceans and ice-packs of unimaginable distance and reached the lake of the gods known as Suvarṇa. There he died. Because he died in that realm of the gods, this Vipaścit became a god, even as a piece of wood lying in the midst of coals of fire instantly becomes fire.

This last Vipaścit reached the boundaries of the earth-plane known as the Lokāloka mountains which he remembered from his past-birth experiences. These mountains are several thousand miles in height; one side is illumined, whereas the other is not. From there he saw the earth, etc., as if they were distant stars. Then he went to that side of these mountains which was forever shrouded in darkness. Beyond that is the great void in which there is no earth, no beings and nothing mobile or immobile. In it even the potentiality of creation does not exist.

VI.2:127 RĀMA asked:

Lord, pray tell me: how does this earth exist, how does the stellar sphere revolve and how do the Lokāloka mountains exist.

VASIṢṬHA replied:

Just as a little child imagines a plaything in the empty space and thinks it is there, the notion of the existence of this earth arises in the infinite consciousness. He whose vision is defective sees little balls of 'hair' in space, where no such balls exist. Even so, such notions as 'the existence of the earth' arose in the infinite consciousness at the moment which has come to be known as creation. A city which exists in the mind of the day-dreamer needs no support (with the imagination as its sole support); even so, this world is supported only by the experiencing of the infinite consciousness.

Whatever appears in the consciousness and however it appears to be and for whatever duration, it seems to exist in that consciousness in that manner for that duration, on account of the inherent power in consciousness. Therefore, just as in the eyes of one with eye-defect the 'ball of hair' does float in space, this earth, etc., does exist in consciousness. If consciousness had 'seen' water flowing up and fire burning down in the very beginning, such would have been the nature of these elements even now. But it is because that consciousness 'saw' the earth as falling in space that it seems to fall even now and consciousness correspondingly seems to 'rise' in relation to the earth. Thus duality or diverse motion arises.

The Lokāloka mountains are the boundary of the earth-plane. Beyond that is the great spatial pit filled with total darkness, though something exists in it here and there. Because the stellar sphere is at a considerable distance, there seems to be some light somewhere and some darkness elsewhere. These stars are at a very great distance from the Lokāloka mountains. The entire stellar sphere, with the exception of the pole star, constantly revolves around its own axis. But all this is non-different from the notion that arises in pure consciousness.

Beyond the worlds or the earth-plane whose boundaries are the Lokāloka mountains, the stellar sphere appears something like the skin of a fruit. However, all this is but the firm notion that arises in the infinite consciousness; it should not be taken that these worlds exist as reality.

Beyond even this stellar sphere, there is another sphere twice its size; that, too, is illumined in part and is sunk in darkness elsewhere. All this is enclosed in two skull-caps, as it were: one is above and the other is below and between them is space. This universe, which is a cosmic circle, is illumined by the sun and stars. What is 'above' and what is 'below' in all this? Rising, falling, moving or remaining steady —all these are notions that arise in consciousness. None of these exist in truth.

VASIṢṬHA continued: VI.2:128

The description of the universe I have given you is the fruit of direct experience, not inferential guesswork. Besides this there are other universes of which I have not told you. For of what use is investigation into the nature of the world and others, which are but of the nature of a dream; wise men do not waste their time talking about useless things.

The northernmost extremity is the Meru mountain; and the southernmost extremity is the Lokāloka mountain-range. The inhabitants of the various planes of consciousness and the different worlds experience the materialisation of those worlds, not others.

I told you of the skull-caps of the universe. Beyond them the whole universe is enveloped by water which is tenfold in extent. Beyond that there is another envelope, this time of fire, which is tenfold the previous one. Beyond that is the wind-envelope and then the plane of space, which are each ten times the extent of the previous one.

Beyond even that is the infinite space; this is neither illumined nor is it dark. It is full of pure consciousness. It is beginningless, middleless and endless. In that, countless millions of universes arise again and again at different points, and again and again they are dissolved in it. There is no being in this infinite space to entertain a notion of these universes, but they exist in whatever form and manner they exist.

Now listen to the story of the king Vipaścit who was on top of the Lokāloka mountains. After he died, he saw his body being eaten by a huge vulture. In his consciousness the notion of another physical body did not arise, nor did he reach enlightenment. Hence, he wished to engage himself in further activity. For pure mental activity, a physical body is unnecessary. In the case of illusion, dream, day-dreaming and hallucination, the mind creates its own field, which is known as the subtle body (ātivāhika). Only when that is forgotten or abandoned does the physical body arise. When one realises the unreality of the physical body through proper investigation, then once again the subtle (ātivāhika) body arises.

Hence, investigate the nature of the ātivāhika body till the knowledge that the infinite consciousness alone is the truth, arises. The realisation 'Where is duality, where is hate or affection? All this is pure Śiva, beginningless and endless' is enlightenment.

Vipaścit was still in the subtle body, unenlightened. He was enveloped by darkness as if in a foetus. He then experienced the earth-plane, water-plane, fire-plane and space-plane. Then he began to investigate the nature of his own subtle body and wondered: "What sustains me who am pure consciousness?" He entered the infinite space of Brahmā and saw everything there. But not having investigated the illusory nature of ignorance he rests in it even now, though in fact there is no ignorance and Brahman alone exists.

VI.2:129 VASIṢṬHA continued:

Another of the Vipaścits also attained the same state after wandering from continent to continent for a long time and after reaching the infinite space of Brahmā in which he saw millions of universes. There he exists even now. Yet another of the Vipaścits fell a victim to his own mental conditioning and, after renouncing his body, became a deer and lives on a mountain.

RĀMA asked:

Lord, when the vāsanā (mental conditioning) of the king Vipaścit was but one, how did it become diverse, producing diverse results in the four Vipaścits?

VASIṢṬHA replied:

The vāsanā of beings becomes either dense or light by repeated exercise and repetition of its effects. It is also subject to the influence of time, place and activity. If it becomes 'light', it undergoes change into something else; if it is deep-rooted it does not change. On the one hand are the time, place and activity (repetition of the habit born of the vāsanā); on the other is the vāsanā (mental conditioning) itself. The two (circumstances and vāsanā) act upon each other. Whichever be the stronger wins instantly. Thus the four Vipaścits were drawn in different directions, though they had the same vāsanā to start with; two of them were caught in the net of ignorance, one was liberated and the other became a deer.

Even now the two who were caught up in the net of ignorance have been unable to find a way out. Ignorance is also infinite in a manner of speaking, because it has no real existence. However, if one develops the inner light and begins to examine it in that light this ignorance vanishes in the twinkling of an eye.

The Vipaścit who went from one country to another, from one world to another, saw an illusory creation. He saw an illusory world which in fact was Brahman only. He somehow came into contact with a holy man. With his help, Vipaścit realised the truth concerning the illusory perception of the world and instantly realised the infinite consciousness or Brahman. At that very instant his ignorance (as also his body) ceased to be.

Thus have I told you, O Rāma, the story of Vipaścit. This ignorance, too, is infinite even as Brahman is infinite, because the ignorance has no independent existence apart from Brahman. It is the infinite consciousness alone that sees countless universes and worlds here and there, now and then. When this truth is not realised, it is known as ignorance; when this truth is realised, the very same consciousness is known as Brahman. There is no division between the two, for the division is unreal ignorance which in reality is Brahman. The division seems to arise in consciousness and is, therefore, non-different from consciousness. Thus Brahman alone is the world-appearance; and the division is consciousness.

RĀMA asked:

How was it that the Vipaścit could not reach the skull-cap of the universe which Brahmā the creator had created?

VASIṢṬHA replied:

At the very moment he came into being, Brahmā the creator pushed space apart with his two arms. That which was above was pushed far, far above and that which was below went far, far below. All the created elements rest in it, being supported by these two extremities. That which is between these two extremities is known as space, which appears to be limitless and of a blue-colour. Water and such other elements do not taint this space; in fact they are not in it (for space is independent of them and exists where one thinks water, air, etc., exist). These elements are but the notions that arise in others.

Vipaścit took that path in order to examine the extent of ignorance, and he began to investigate the stellar sphere. Brahman is infinite; and therefore ignorance of Brahman is also infinite. Ignorance exists when Brahman is not realised; and when Brahman is realised ignorance is seen not to exist. However far Vipaścit went, he was still wandering in the realm of this ignorance.

Of the others, one attained liberation, another became a deer and another is also wandering in ignorance. The two who thus wander in distant worlds are not seen in our consciousness. But the one that became a deer is within the field of our understanding. That world in which that Vipaścit lives as the deer (after having wandered in distant worlds) is this very world which is in one distant corner of the infinite space of consciousness.

RĀMA asked:

Lord, Vipaścit lived in this world itself and went away from here. How is it that he has become a deer in this world?

VASIṢṬHA replied:

Even as one who is endowed with limbs knows them, even so I know everything which may exist in Brahman, as Brahman is my own self. The past does not know the future and vice versa; but consciousness which is not divided by time is aware of all this. In that consciousness everything is 'here', though to ordinary perception something may be far away. Thus I see the world in which Vipaścit wandered and how he became a deer in this very world. In fact I know where that deer is right now, O Rāma. It is the deer that was presented to you as a gift by the king of the Trigartha.

VASIṢṬHA said:

When the sage Vasiṣṭha said this, Rāma and the assembled sages and others were wonderstruck. Rāma despatched a few boys to go and fetch the deer. Seeing it, the assembly was amazed and everyone exclaimed: "Truly, Māyā (illusion) is limitless and infinite."

VI.2:130 RĀMA asked:

O sage, how, by whom and by what means will this deer be freed from its unfortunate state of existence?

VASIṢṬHA replied:

The way out of this misfortune is that which was its original cause. Any other path is not the right one and it will not be productive of happiness, welfare or fruition. The king Vipaścit adored the fire; and by entering into the fire this deer will regain its former state, just as gold regains its lustre by being purified in the fire. Behold, I shall make this deer enter into the fire.

VĀLMĪKI said:

So saying, the sage Vasiṣṭha sipped water from his sacred water-pot and created a fire in the middle of the hall, without any fuel. It burned brightly without any sparks and without any smoke. The people in the assembly moved away from the centre of the hall. The deer was delighted to see that fire. It began to frisk about in delight. Vasiṣṭha was in a deep state of contemplation and blessed the deer that it should be freed from its past sinful tendencies. He further prayed to the fire-god: "Remembering his previous existence, O fire, please restore to this deer his old form as the king Vipaścit."

The moment the sage uttered these words, the deer rushed with great joy into the fire. It rested for a few minutes in the fire while everyone was looking; gradually its form changed into that of a human being. He was radiant and handsome. As soon as he arose in the fire, the fire vanished from sight. All the assembled sages with one voice exclaimed "Ah, what radiance (bhā) does this person possess! He shines (bhāsa) like the sun. Surely, he shall become famous as Bhāsa." Hence, he came to be known as Bhāsa.

Bhāsa realised in a moment, by deep contemplation, all that had happened in his previous incarnations.

In the meantime, the excitement and the conversation in the assembly had subsided and there was silence once again. Bhāsa arose and proceeded towards the sage Vasiṣṭha and bowed to him. The sage, in turn, blessed him saying, "May the ignorance under which you have been labouring for so long leave you". Then Bhāsa saluted Rāma and hailed him.

After this, the king Daśaratha welcomed Bhāsa: "Welcome, O king. Be seated here. You have wandered far and wide and for a very long time in this saṃsāra. Now rest here." Bhāsa took his seat among the sages in the assembly. King Daśaratha continued: "Alas, like a tethered elephant, this king Vipaścit had to undergo countless trials and tribulations. What a great calamity follows imperfect vision of the reality and the perverse understanding of the truth. Though essentially unreal and non-existent, it is amazing what power this illusion has, that it can seemingly create such diverse worlds in the infinite consciousness, and such varied experiences."

VIŚVĀMITRA said: VI.2:131

Even so, O king, there are very many people who wander in this saṃsāra because they have not gained the best knowledge or enlightenment. There is a king who has wandered in this saṃsāra for the past one million and seven hundred thousand years. These ignorant people are interested in investigating the nature of worldly objects; and they continually flow in this saṃsāra without ever turning away from it.

This creation exists in the infinite space as a mere notion in the mind of the creator Brahmā. Just as little ants move here and there on the surface of a ball, people move about on the surface of this earth. In space there is no 'below' and there is no 'above'. The direction in which an object falls is known as 'below', and the direction in which birds rise to fly is called 'above'.

In this world there is a place known as Vaṭadhānā. In that kingdom there were three princes. They resolved to go to the very limits of this world to investigate all that it contains. For some time they examined the objects of the earth, and then they examined the objects in the oceans. They took birth after birth and continued to pursue their goal of gaining a complete knowledge of this earth. They could not go to the 'ends' of the earth, because, like ants moving on a ball, they were only going from one part of the earth to another all the time. They are thus wandering on the earth even today.

Thus, there is no end to the illusion in this saṃsāra. Since this illusion arises as a notion in the infinite consciousness, it also seems to be infinite. The essence (reality or substance) of the notion is the supreme Brahman and vice versa. They are both pure consciousness and there is no difference or division in consciousness, just as there is no distinction between space and emptiness. The currents and whirlpools that appear on the surface of water are only water. Since there can be nothing other than consciousness, how can there be something other than consciousness? The infinite consciousness alone shines of its own accord as this world without even intending to do so. Wherever the infinite consciousness wishes to appear in whatever form, it does so and experiences its own nature in that form for as long as it pleases.

Within the smallest atom of the infinite consciousness exists the potentiality of all experiences, just as there are stones and rocks within the mountain. All these experiences exist, constantly experiencing their own particular modes of experience everywhere. In reality, of course, they do not exist as experiences but only as infinite consciousness. These manifold experiences are collectively known as the world, which is the shining appearance of Brahman. But it indeed is a great wonder, that this infinite consciousness, without ever abandoning its reality, thinks of itelf "I am a jīva". Now, O king Bhāsa, tell us of your past experiences.

BHĀSA said:

I saw many things and I wandered a lot without experiencing fatigue. I experienced many things in many different ways. All this I remember. I experienced many pleasures and much sorrow in many bodies over a long period of time and in distant places in this limitless space. I attained various bodies on account of boons and curses, and in those embodiments I saw countless objects and scenes. I was also determined to see and experience everything. This was the original boon that I obtained from the fire-god. Therefore, even though I had different bodies on different planes, I still pursued the original intention of gaining a thorough knowledge of this world.

For a thousand years I lived as a tree. I had to endure many sufferings during that period. My mind was totally centred within myself, and without mental activity I produced flowers and fruits. For a hundred years I was a deer on the mount Meru. I had a golden colour. I lived on grass and I loved music. I was very small and therefore non-violent. For fifty years I was a śarabha (an eight-footed animal more powerful than the lion). After that I became a vidyādhara-celestial. Then I became the son of the swan which is the vehicle of the creator Brahmā. I lived as a swan for fifteen hundred years. For a hundred years I listened to the divine music of the celestial attendants of lord Nārāyaṇa (Viṣṇu). Then I became a jackal and lived in a forest. A huge elephant ravaged the brush in which I lived. While I was dying on account of this, I saw that elephant killed by a lion. After this, I became a nymph in another world and lived alone for half an epoch, on account of the curse of a sage. After this, I lived for a hundred years as a valmīka-bird. When our nest was destroyed along with the tree on which we lived, I lost my partner and then lived the rest of my life alone in a far-off place. Then I became an ascetic, having gained a certain amount of dispassion.

I saw many amazing things. I saw a world which was made entirely of water. Elsewhere I saw a woman in whose body the three worlds were reflected as in a mirror. When I asked her who she was, she replied: "I am pure consciousness and all the worlds are my limbs. Even as I create such bewilderment in you, even so are all things. Till you see everything with the same bewilderment and wonder, you cannot know their real nature. All the worlds are one's own limbs. I hear them all as one hears sounds and expressions during one's dream." I saw countless beings emerge in her and then dissolve in her, too. Elsewhere I saw an unusual form of cloud which produced a dreadful sound of clashing missiles and which rained weapons on the earth. I saw another wonder: the whole earth was covered in darkness and whole villages were flying away to a distant world. I saw your village in another world. Elsewhere I saw that all beings were of the same nature. Elsewhere I saw a world without a sun, moon and stars, and there was no darkness: all its inhabitants were radiant and illumined. . . . There is no world I have not seen, nothing I have not experienced.

BHĀSA continued: VI.2:132

Once I was asleep with a celestial nymph in a garden. Suddenly I woke up to find myself floating downstream like a blade of grass. Surprised, I asked the nymph: "What is this?" She explained to me: "There is a moonstone mountain nearby. When the moon rises, the springs that issue from that mountain swell and there is a sudden flood. In the supreme delight I experienced in your company I forgot to warn you of this."

Having said this, the nymph took me with her and flew into space without any difficulty. For a period of seven years from then I lived with her on the top of the mount Mandara.

After this I roamed other worlds in which the people were self-luminous. I saw a world in which there were no directions like east and west, no days and nights, no scriptures and no polemics, no distinctions between gods and demons. Then I became a celestial, by name Amarasoma, and lived for fourteen years as an ascetic.

Endowed with the boon granted to me by the fire-god, I moved in space with extraordinary speed. Somewhere I fell into a great ocean and somewhere I experienced the sensation of falling through space. Moving about in space was my only occupation. I became fatigued and I slept for a considerable time.

While asleep, I entered into the world of dreams. There again I experienced various worlds and various objects and there was great restlessness in me. Whatever my eyes saw, I was there in a moment. From there I saw something else and there I was again in an instant, regardless of the distance.

Thus wandering from one world to another with great speed, I spent many years. But I had not seen the end of the manifestation of ignorance known as 'the objective universe': for it was an illusion which had somehow got itself firmly rooted in my heart, just as the fear of a ghost gets hold of the heart of a child. However well I realise "This is not real', 'This is not real' after intense enquiry, the feeling 'This is' does not cease. From moment to moment, new experiences of pleasure and pain arise and cease, like the flowing stream of a river.

I also remember a great mountain peak which shone by its own light though there was neither the sun nor the moon there. It was so beautiful that it charmed the heart of those sages who love to live in solitude.

VI.2:133 VIPAŚCIT (BHĀSA) continued:

I shall now relate to you another great wonder which I saw in another world. There is a shining world in the great space, which is beyond your reach. That world is as different from this as the dream-world is different from the world of the waking-state experience. While I was roaming that world in order to find the extent of the objective universe, I noticed a gigantic shadow enveloping the whole of that earth. As I lifted my eyes to the sky in order to find out what that cause of that shadow might be, I saw an enormous thing looking like a person falling in space and descending upon the world I was in. It even hid the sun so effectively that the world was totally enveloped in darkness.

It fell on the earth, even as I was thus gazing at it with awe and wonder. I felt that my end was near and overcome by fear I quickly entered into fire. I had worshipped the fire-god in very many incarnations; hence, the fire-god reassured me with the words "Do not be afraid". I, too, prayed to the fire-god for his protection. The fire-god commanded me to ascend his own vehicle and said, "Let us both go to the world of fire". The fire-god then made a small hole in that huge body that had fallen on the earth and both of us escaped into the outer space.

It was only from there that we could realise the colossal nature of that body which had fallen on the earth. By its fall it had agitated all the oceans and destroyed all the cities, towns and forests. It had stopped the flow of the rivers. There was weeping and wailing everywhere. The earth itself was groaning under its weight. Gale-force winds and torrential rains reminded one of the cosmic dissolution. The peaks of the Himālayas had descended into the netherworld. The sun fell on the earth. The entire earth had been shattered. The celestials who were coursing the heavens saw this enormous body and thought that it was another newly-created earth or another half of the universe or perhaps a portion of space which had fallen from its place!

But when I saw it with great attention, I saw that it was made of flesh and that the entire earth could not even cover a limb in that body. Having seen this, I turned to my tutelary deity, the fire-god, and asked him "Lord, what is this?"

The fire-god replied: "Child, wait till the disturbances caused by the fall of this corpse subside. I shall then tell you all about it."

Then the space around the earth was filled with sages, siddhas and celestials, the manes and the gods, all of whom had etheric bodies. They bowed their heads and offered a prayer to the divine mother Kālarātri: "May the divine mother who is endowed with a black body, who consumes the entire universe, who holds the head of Brahmā at the tip of her sword and who wears the garland of the heads of the demons and who is yet absolutely pure, protect us."

VIPAŚCIT (BHĀSA) continued: VI.2:134

In response to the prayers of the sages and the siddhas, the divine mother appeared in the sky. She was 'dry' and bloodless. She was accompanied by countless goblins and other spirits. She was several thousand miles tall. She was established in the supreme being. She was seated on the corpse.

The gods said to her: "O divine mother, this is our offering to you. We pray that you may consume it quickly, along with your attendant hosts." As soon as the gods said this, the divine mother began sucking the life-blood of the dead body with the help of her own prāṇa-śakti (life-force). As this blood flowed into her mouth, her own lean body filled with blood and her belly became distended. She began to dance. The gods, seated on the Lokāloka mountains (the boundaries of the earth-plane), witnessed this dance. The goblins began to eat the corpse. The state of the world at that time was indeed pitiable.

The mountains of the earth had disappeared. The firmament appeared to be dressed in a red cloth. As the mother danced swirling her divine weapons in all directions, whatever remained of the towns and cities of the earth was destroyed; only their memory remained. The whole world was populated now only by the goblins and the hosts that formed the retinue of the divine mother. Seeing all this utter destruction, the gods seated on the Lokāloka mountains were distressed.

RĀMA asked Vasiṣṭha:

When it was said that the corpse covered the whole earth-plane, how is it that the Lokāloka mountains were still visible?

VASIṢṬHA said:

Those mountains were visible over the shoulders of the corpse. The distressed gods reflected thus: "Alas, alas, where has the earth gone, where have the oceans gone, what happened to the people and to the mountains? Where has the Malaya mountain gone with all its sandalwood forests and various fragrant flower-gardens? Alas, the pure white snow of the Himālaya mountains appears to be muddy now. Alas, the ocean of milk (the abode of lord Viṣṇu), the wish-fulfilling tree, all other oceans (those full of curd, wine or honey) and the mountains full of cocoanut palms have vanished. Alas, the Krauñca continent with its own beautiful mountain, the Puṣkara continent (in which the swan which is the vehicle of Brahmā the creator lived in a lake full of lotuses and in whose mountain-caves the celestials used to enjoy themselves), the Gomedha continent surrounded by fresh-water ocean and the Śāka continent whose very remembrance is auspicious, have all been destroyed. All the gardens and forests have vanished. Where will the people who are tired and fatigued take rest now? When shall we again taste the sweetness of sugar and the little figurines made of sugar, since all the sugar cane fields have been destroyed? Alas, the Jaṃbūdvīpa which was the support of all other continents has also been destroyed. Alas, where has the good earth disappeared?"

The Story of the Hunter and the Deer

VI.2:135, 136 VASIṢṬHA (or BHĀSA) continued:

The gods continued to say thus among themselves: "The goblins have now eaten the flesh and drunk the blood of this corpse; hence one can see the earth again. The very bones of that body form the new mountains." As the gods were saying so, the satisfied goblins began to dance in space. The gods saw that there was some blood left on the earth; they filled the oceans with it and willed that it should become liquor. The goblins drank of this liquor and continued to dance: even now they do so. This earth was made out of the flesh (meda) of the corpse and hence it is known as 'medinī' (earth). Thus the earth and its inhabitants were brought again into being. The Creator created a new mankind.

(BHĀSA said:) Then I asked the fire-god: Who was this person before he died? The FIRE-GOD narrated to me the following story:

Listen, there is infinite space which is full of pure consciousness. In it are countless worlds floating like so many atoms. In that there arose a cosmic person endowed with self-awareness. That person experiences his own light as you see an object in a dream. From those experiences arise the various senses and their respective organs which together form the body. These senses perceive their own respective objects which become the world.

In that world there arose a person named Asura (demon). He was proud of his might. Once he destroyed the hermitage of a sage who cursed him thus: "You have done this because you are proud of your gigantic body. You will die and become a mosquito." The fire of that curse burnt Asura to ashes. He became a disembodied personality, just like the mind of an unconscious person. It became one with the physical space. It then became united with the wind in that space. This wind is the life-force (prāṇa). The Asura now awoke as a living being and acquired energy, water, etc. Once again endowed with the five elements (the tanmātras) and a particle of the infinite consciousness, he began to vibrate as an individual. There arose in him self-awareness, just as a seed sprouts in favourable conditions. In that self-awareness lay the sage's curse and therefore the notion of a mosquito. Therefore he became a mosquito.

(In answer to Rāma's question, Vasiṣṭha said: "Right from Brahmā down to the blade of grass all beings are subject to two forms of birth: the first is Brahmā's creation and the other is illusory creation. The creation that arises spontaneously in the mind of the Creator which he had not experienced before is the creation of Brahmā, not 'birth through the womb'. That which arises on account of latent delusion is the illusory birth, born of subject-object relationship.")

The mosquito dwelt happily on a blade of grass with its partner. This grass was eaten by a deer. Because he died looking at the deer, he became a deer. The deer was killed by a hunter: hence the deer was born as a hunter in the next birth. While the hunter was roaming the forest, he had the good fortune to meet a holy sage who awakened him: "Why do you engage yourself in this cruel life of a hunter? Abandon this sinful life and seek to attain nirvāṇa."

THE HUNTER asked: VI.2:137

If that is so, O sage, tell me how can one overcome sorrow without engaging oneself in 'hard' or 'soft' practices.

THE SAGE replied:

Abandon the bow and the arrows this very moment. Remain here resorting to a life of silence free from sorrow.

VASIṢṬHA continued:

The hunter did so without hesitation. In a matter of days he entered into the wisdom of the scriptures, just as a flower enters a man's body as its fragrance. One day he asked the sage: "How is it, O sage, that dream which takes place within, appears to be outside?"

THE SAGE replied:

This question arose in my mind, too, in the very beginning. In order to find an answer to this question, I practised concentration. I sat in the lotus-posture and remained as pure consciousness. I gathered all the rays of the mind which were dissipated over a thousand things and focused them on my own heart. Along with the life-force I 'exhaled' the mind outside the body. That prāṇa entered into a living being which appeared in front of me. That being 'inhaled' that prāṇa and received it in its own heart.

Then I entered into the very heart of that being. Bound by my own intellect, I followed it into that being. I saw that the inside of that person was full of countless channels, as if they were all outside. It was also filled with various organs and viscera like the liver, spleen, etc., just as a house is full of furniture. It was warm inside. The cool breeze that flowed into that body from outside kept it alive and conscious. The channels bore the essence of food. It was very dark inside, like hell. The flow of the life-force along these channels gave ample indications of the physical disturbances that followed the irregular flow of the life-force. In a channel which resembled the lotus stalk, there flowed a radiant and fiery force making a distant noise of a wind flowing through a narrow tube. It was filled with all sorts of objects. It was bound together by the movement of air. It was pleasant in places and agitated in others. It appeared as if the celestial musicians were singing somewhere below the tongue-area and elsewhere it was as if there were fine music.

I entered the heart of that being. In that heart I attained the principle of light. In it are the three worlds reflected. It is the light of the three worlds. It is the very essence of all things. The jīva is there in it. The jīva pervades the entire body, but this 'ojas' (inner light) is its special seat. It is protected on all sides by the life-force. I entered it, as water permeates an earthen pot. Remaining there, I saw the entire universe, as if I were seeing it from my own 'ojas'.

THE SAGE continued:

In that dream-world, too, there were the sun, the mountains and the oceans, as also the gods and the demons and human beings; there were the cities and the forests, the time-scales and the directions. That dream-vision appeared to be permanent; it was as if it arose after the termination of my sleep. I asked myself: "How is it that I see this dream though I am not asleep?" After considerable enquiry I realised: "This surely is the divine form of the truth concerning consciousness. Whatever that consciousness manifests in itself is known as the world." Wherever this seed of consciousness sees its own form, as it were, there and then it sees the world, without ever abandoning its own reality as the infinite consciousness.

I have realised now that this world which is said to be the dream-object is the perception of this infinite consciousness. The manifestation (shining) of this consciousness is called the waking-world and also the dream-world. It is one consciousness; there is no division in it. Dream is dream in relation to the waking state, but a dream is waking state in relation to the dream itself. Dream is non-different from the waking state; waking state itself is twofold.

A person is but consciousness. Even if a hundred bodies perish, consciousness does not perish. Consciousness is like space, but it exists as if it is the body. The infinite appears to be divided into infinite objects, with and without form. This is because countless particles of experiences shine within the infinite consciousness. When the jīva turns away from the experiencing of the external world and towards the inner world in the heart, then dream arises. When the jīva has externalised consciousness, there is the waking state. When the same jīva turns its gaze upon itself, dream arises. The jīva itself is spread out as the space, the earth, the wind, the mountains and the oceans, whether they are seen outside or inside. When this truth is realised, one is freed from vāsanā or mental conditioning.

I then asked myself, "What is sleep?" I began to investigate sleep. When one thinks, "What have I got to do with these objects of the world? Let me rest in utter peace for some time", sleep arises. Just as in the same body there are sentient and also insentient (like nails, hair) parts, sleep is characterised by both sentience and insentience. 'Let me rest in peace'—when this one notion prevails in the mind, there is sleep. This can arise even in the waking state.

Then I began to investigate the state of turīya (the fourth one). If one is established in turīya, the world-appearance ceases on account of perfect illumination. Then the world exists as it is; nothing ceases to be. It is because of the existence of this turīya that waking, dream and sleep exist as they do. The realisation that 'The world has not been created at all since there is no cause for it to arise', and that 'It is Brahman alone that shines as this world', is turīya.

VI.2:138 THE SAGE continued:

Then I desired to become one with the consciousness of that being. When I left that being's 'ojas' in order to enter into the consciousness, my own senses were immediately awakened. However, I restrained them at once and entered into the consciousness. As I entered that consciousness, I experienced two worlds at the same time. Everything appeared double. However, since the two perceiving intelligences were similar, the duality appeared to be similar and mixed well, like water and milk.

In a moment, I drew into myself the consciousness of that other being with the help of consciousness. At once the 'two worlds' merged into one even as for one who is suffering from diplopia, the perception of two moons gives way to the perception of a single moon when he is cured. I had not abandoned my own wisdom, but my own thought-form had greatly weakened and taken on the thought-form of the other being. Hence, I began to experience the world as he did.

After some time, he retired to sleep. He collected the rays of his mind. Even as a tortoise draws its limbs into itself, his senses were drawn into his heart along with their functions. His sense-organs became as if they were dead, or as if they were but painted images. I was within him and I followed the course of his mind and entered into his heart. For a moment I enjoyed the happiness of sleep, having abandoned the experience of external objects and having entered into the 'ojas'. All the channels within him were dense and congested on account of fatigue; and on account of food, drink, etc., the life-breath flowed slowly through the nostrils. The life-force turns upon its own source within the heart and relieves the mind of materiality (or, makes the mind unimportant), because naturally it is its own object. The self is its own object now and there is no other externalising activity. Hence, it shines in itself as itself.

RĀMA asked:

The mind is able to think only on account of the life-force, and it has no existence in itself. Then, what is it in itself?

VASIṢṬHA replied:

Though the body is experienced to be real, it does not exist in truth. Mind is as real as the mountain seen in a dream. Since no 'object' has ever been created on account of the absence of any cause, the mind (citta) does not exist. All this is Brahman and since Brahman is everything, this world exists as it is. Even the body, the mind, etc., are Brahman only: but how the knowers of truth see this is not for us to describe.

The one indivisible, infinite consciousness perceived itself as its own object and that is said to be the mind. When there arose the notion of motion, that notion manifested as prāṇa or life-force. Prāṇa gives rise to the experience through the senses, and thus arises the world.

VASIṢṬHA continued: VI.2:139

The mind (citta) is the creator of the world with all that is real, unreal or mixed which is in it. Prāṇa (life-force) was brought into being by the mind with the idea: 'Prāṇa is my movement and I shall not be without prāṇa or life-force. Hence it shall be my goal. Even if I am without prāṇa for some time, I shall immediately be with prāṇa again.' The moment this prāṇa gets united with the mind, it sees the illusory world. Because of the firm notion 'I shall never again be without the life-force and the body', it does not regain its true nature as pure consciousness.

It experiences sorrow, since it swings from one extreme to the other on account of doubt. This sorrow cannot cease except when the self-knowledge arises. Nothing other than self-knowledge can remove the wrong notion 'I am this'. Self-knowledge does not arise except through the investigation of the means for liberation. Hence, by every means one should investigate the means for liberation.

The mind constantly entertains the notion that 'The life-force is my own life,' and therefore the mind rests in prāṇa. When the body is in a state of well-being, the mind functions well, but when the body does not enjoy a state of well-being, the mind does not see anything other than the physical disturbance. When the prāṇa (life-force) is busily engaged in its own vigorous movement, then it is absorbed in its own movement and is unable to exert in self-knowledge.

Thus, the relationship between the mind and the prāṇa is that of a rider and the vehicle. Such was the notion entertained by the infinite consciousness right in the beginning; and therefore this relationship prevails even today. One who is not enlightened is unable to transcend it. The ignorant person continues to entertain unshakable notions concerning time, space, matter, mind, prāṇa and body. When the mind and the prāṇa function in harmony, the person engages himself in various activities. When there is disturbance there is disharmony. When both are at rest, there is sleep. When the nāḍīs (channels of energy) are clogged by food, etc., and there is inertia, the movement of prāṇa becomes dull and there is sleep. Again, even when the nāḍīs are not clogged by food, etc., but when there is weakness or fatigue, the prāṇa is unable to move properly and one sleeps. When the nāḍīs themselves become soft and weak for whatever reason, when they are loaded with all sorts of impurities and when the prāṇa is thus engaged in some extraordinary activity, then, too, sleep arises.

THE SAGE said:

When darkness fell, then the person into whose heart I had entered fell into deep sleep. I too enjoyed this deep sleep. Then, when the food he had eaten had been digested and when the nāḍīs were clear, the life-force began to move vigorously and sleep weakened.

THE SAGE continued:

When thus sleep had been weakened, I saw the world with its sun, etc., as if it arose in the heart. I saw all this where I was. But this world was being overwhelmed by the flood of cosmic dissolution. I saw myself seated with my bride in a house. The flood was carrying us all away, with the whole house, etc., floating as if to try to fight the flood and stay alive. Soon the house in which I was seated, which was being carried down by the flood, broke into pieces. I jumped into the water. I had abandoned the family and friends, being solely interested in the preservation of my life. Sometimes I went down under and sometimes I rose to the surface. When I obtained a foothold on a rock and tried to rest a while, a huge wave came and knocked me into the flood again. There was not a single form of suffering that I did not experience during this period and I was subjected to every type of painful experience.

In the meantime, because I was in a state of utter despair—though quite conscious—I recollected a previous life-time experience in a state of samādhi. Then I was an ascetic. I had entered another person, eager to witness the dream-state. I knew that I was perceiving an illusion. At the same time, I also perceived the present experience: though I was being carried away by the flood, I experienced joy.

While observing the flood and the destruction caused by it, I reflected thus: "What cannot fate do? Even the three-eyed god is being crushed by this flood. In this flood all the gods and the demons are being whirled around. These mountainous waves rise right up to the seat of Brahmā the creator. These waves look like elephants, they are as powerful as lions and they seem to float in the sky like clouds. Even the protectors of this earth along with their palaces and vehicles, fall into this flood and get drowned. The gods and the demons float in this flood together and hold on to one another. Because of the falling cities and the floating palaces, the waters of the flood appear to be solid walls. Even the sun has been overcome by this flood and the sun is being led into the netherworld. Only the knowers of the truth (the sages of self-knowledge) experience no sorrow at all: they see their bodies being borne down the stream but without the false notion 'I am that body'. Helpless women are drowning. In this flood of cosmic dissolution where all are being chewed by death, who can save whom? The entire universe now seems only to be an infinite ocean. Where are all the gods headed by Indra?"

THE HUNTER asked: VI.2:140

Do such hallucinations arise even in such great ones like you, O sage? Does not the practice of meditation put an end to them?

THE SAGE replied:

Everything ceases at the end of a world-cycle. Some things come to an end gradually while others end abruptly. Again, what has to happen will happen inevitably. Moreover, with the advent of adversity, strength, intelligence and vitality (radiance) are all adversely affected everywhere at all times even in the case of the great ones. Lastly, what I described so far was but a dream. What is impossible or irreconcilable with a dream?

Yet, it is important that I should narrate this dream-experience to you. Now I shall tell you the truth.

While I was thus witnessing this great flood of cosmic dissolution, I came upon the peak of a mountain. I got on top of it. The very next instant the entire scene changed. I do not even know how the flood-waters disappeared. The whole earth was a mass of mud in which the gods like Indra and animals like elephants were all sunk neck-deep. Soon I was overcome by fatigue and sleep.

After this, though I remained in my own 'ojas', I still carried the psychological conditioning of the previous experience. After thus experiencing a sort of double-consciousness, when I awoke, I saw the mountain-peak in the other person's heart. On the second day I saw the sunrise there. After this arose all other objects of the world.

I tried to forget everything else and to engage myself in my usual activity in that world. I said to myself, "I am sixteen years of age, these are my parents, etc." Then I saw a village and in it a hermitage. I began to live in that hermitage which became real to me; the memory of the previous experience began to fade. I considered the body to be my only hope. Wisdom was far from me. Vāsanā or mental conditioning was the very essence of my being and I was devoted to wealth. I observed all my social and religious duties. I knew what to do and what not to do.

One day a sage came to me as my guest. I entertained him well. At night he told me a story. He described the limitless universe in detail and concluded by saying that all that was the infinite consciousness. My own intelligence was awakened. At once I remembered all the past, how I entered into another's body, etc. I thought that the other person was the cosmic person and tried to get out of it. I entered into that person's prāṇa. Becoming one with it I came out. Then I saw immediately in front of me my own body seated in the lotus-posture, in a hermitage, attended to by disciples. According to these disciples only an hour had passed after I entered into samādhi. The person into whose heart I had entered was another traveller who was asleep. I did not tell all this to anyone, but quickly re-entered the heart of the sleeping person. In his heart the cosmic dissolution had been completed. And the village in which I lived with my relatives had disappeared. Everything was ablaze with the fire of dissolution. I practised the wind-contemplation and roamed in it.

VI.2:141, 142 THE SAGE continued:

Though I was surrounded by that terrible fire there, I was not unhappy at all. When you know while dreaming that it is dream only, you are freed from even fire. While I was investigating the nature of the fire, unaffected by it because I knew the truth that it was dream, a dreadful heat-wave arose. In that gale everything began to fly around and to get totally burnt. It was like the dance of destruction.

I began to wonder: After all, all this is only a dream dreamt by me while I am living in someone else's heart. Why should I not get out of all this, instead of witnessing this suffering?

THE HUNTER asked:

You had entered that person's heart in order to know what dream was. Why did you decide to pull out? Did you find out the truth?

THE SAGE replied:

To begin with, the creation has no cause for coming into being. Hence, neither the word 'creation' nor the object 'creation' are real. They do not exist. But this ignorance or unreality is also a notion which arises in consciousness or reality, and in consciousness or reality what exists (as 'creation') is obvious. I can only tell you the truth from the point of view of one in whom ignorance and foolishness have ceased: what is true from the point of view of the ignorant and the foolish, I do not know. The truth is: all this is pure consciousness which pervades everything.

Where is body, where is the heart, what is dream, where are water and flood, etc., where is awakening and the cessation of such awakening, where is birth and where is death? There is only pure consciousness. In the presence of this consciousness even the smallest and the subtlest of space appears macrocosmic. Spontaneously this consciousness 'thinks' for a moment and the notion of the world arises, though it is still pure space. Just as in dream, only consciousness puts on various guises and there are no cities, etc., the world is pure consciousness only. For us there is no appearance, nothing unreal or real, no space: but there is only one formless, beginningless, endless, non-dual infinite consciousness. Dream arises without any cause and there is only the pure consciousness of the perceiver (without an independent object). Here, too, there is no cause and therefore there is neither a subject nor an object; what exists is the pure consciousness or whatever it is, but it is pure experiencing which is non-dual and beyond description.

Time is both existence and destruction; the seed is itself all that emerges out of it right up to the flowers and the fruits. Even so Brahman is all this. Consciousness always shines pure. Just as during dreaming the dream has the quality of wakefulness, even so wakefulness is also of the nature of dream only. When all mental activity ceases, you are that which is.

THE HUNTER asked:

Lord, who are affected by past karma and who are not?

THE SAGE replied:

They who come into being at the very commencement of creation—like Brahmā the creator—have no birth and no karma. To them there is no notion of duality, no saṃsāra and no notions: their consciousness is pure. Surely, at the very beginning of creation no one has any karma, for before that only the infinite and absolute Brahman existed. Therefore at the beginning of creation it was Brahman who manifested as the creation. Just as Brahmā the creator and the others manifested at the beginning of creation, even so did countless jīvas manifest then. But they who consider themselves other than Brahman consider themselves ignorant and perceive duality. In their case birth and karma arise of their own accord, because these beings lean on the unreality. But in the case of those who do not thus consider themselves different from Brahman (like Brahmā, Viṣṇu, Śiva, etc.) they are unaffected by karma.

The infinite consciousness is absolutely pure. Brahman rests in himself. However, in it there arises just a little notion of the jīva. Where this notion of jīva arises, there ignorance arises: that itself is considered as creation by the same consciousness. Of its own accord, consciousness awakens itself to its own true nature and realises that it is, and has always been, Brahman.

Water itself takes on the appearance of a whirlpool: Brahman itself takes on the appearance of this creation. This creation is manifest Brahman; it is neither a dream nor a waking state reality. In that case, what is karma, to whom is it and of how many types is it? In truth, there is no karma, no ignorance, no creation: all these notions arise only because of one's own experience.

Brahman alone shines as creation, individual selves, karma, birth and such other notions. Because it is the Lord, it experiences these notions as if they were true. In the beginning of creation, the jīva is not subject to any karma; after this, however, it gets involved in karma, on account of the notions it entertains. What is the body or personality of a whirlpool and what is its karma? It is water, and even so is everything Brahman.

The persons seen in a dream have no past karma. Even so, the jīvas that arose in the beginning of creation have no karma because they are pure consciousness. It is only when one becomes firmly rooted in the notion of this world-appearance as the reality, that the notion of karma arises. Then the jīvas roam here bound by their karma. If it is realised that this creation itself is no-creation and that Brahman alone exists, then where is karma, whose is karma and who belongs to that karma? Karma exists only in ignorance; the moment right knowledge arises, karma ceases to bind.

VI.2:143 THE SAGE continued:

The paṇḍita (one who has self-knowledge) is like the sun which makes the lotus of all dharma, karma and knowledge blossom. Compared to the wisdom of the sage of self-knowledge, even the status of the king of the gods is like a worthless straw. When self-knowledge arises, the illusory notion of a world-existence vanishes and the realisation of Brahman as the only truth arises; just as when light dispels darkness, the garland which had been mistaken for a snake shines as a garland.

The people seen in a dream do not have parents: this world-dream has no cause. The dream-people had no previous karma to cause their present birth. The apparently real people in this dream-world do not have a previous karma either. Even as the jīva perceives and experiences dreams here, even so it fancies and experiences, as if real, a previous existence and karma, in accordance with its own mental conditioning (vāsanā).

In the beginning of creation and at the end of the existence of the body, the jīva experiences a dream-like state. Whatever it experiences seems to be—and that is both real and unreal. In a dream there is contact with 'other' objects though no such exist. Even so, the perception of the other objects in the waking state is possible, though they are unreal. 'Waking' and 'dreaming' are two words used to denote the movement in consciousness which brings about awareness. That awareness or experience which arises in the beginning of creation (sargādi) and at the end of the life-span of the body (dehānta), that awareness or experience continues to exist till it ceases to be (or till liberation is attained) and that is known as creation.

There is no distinction between consciousness and awareness of objects seen either in the waking state or in a dream, just as there is no distinction between wind and movement. Brahman alone appears to rise and to perish or to die and to experience objects: but it is pure consciousness alone, which does not undergo any change and which is for ever at peace and pure. Whatever that infinite consciousness or cosmic person becomes aware of within itself, becomes both cause and effect. This creation is in the heart of that infinite consciousness, even as the dream is in your heart, both as the cause and effect.

In whatever manner it appeared in the beginning, that has continued to be its natural order, time, space, etc. Whatever characteristic the creation acquired then has continued to exist since then. First there arises a notion or a feeling or a concept in the consciousness and then follows what is known as creation: but all this is but the amazing work of consciousness. The immeasurable space appears to have a blue colour; the immeasurable consciousness appears to exist as this creation.

THE HUNTER asked:

After leaving this body, how does one get another body for the purpose of experiencing pleasure and pain: what is the causal factor and what are the co-operating causes?

THE SAGE replied:

Dharma (virtue), adharma (sin), vāsanā (latent tendency or mental conditioning), the active self and jīva—all these are synonyms which are notions with no corresponding reality. Consciousness entertains these notions in the space (or the plane) of consciousness. The self experiences the body-notion because it is pure consciousness, totally independent of the body. Though the body-notion is unreal it is experienced as if it were real, just like the dream-object. To the dead person, the 'other world' shines as a notion in his own consciousness. Because he sees this for some time, it is assumed to be real.

If it is contended that someone else gives birth to the dead person, how does the latter remember the past in the present incarnation? The dead one is not born again: but he experiences the notion 'I am here in this manner' etc., on account of his own mental conditioning, within his own consciousness. When this experience is sustained for some time and it takes deep root, it takes on the quality of reality. The self which is but pure space (void) sees a dream in that space (void) itself; it remembers that dream again and again and thereby arise rebirth and another world. It then believes that world and that birth to be real and begins to function in that world as that jīva.

In this way, there are millions upon millions of worlds; when their truth is clearly understood, they are but pure consciousness or Brahman, otherwise they appear to be the world-creation. They are nothing and they belong to none. They have never been really created. Each jīva experiences each one of those worlds as 'This is the world'. It is this mutual relationship that confers reality upon this illusion: when their truth is realised, they are known to be the uncreated reality. What is real to the sage is impenetrable illusion to the ignorant. What is unreal to the sage is the most obvious truth to the ignorant.

Whatever the infinite consciousness experiences, that appears to be, then and there: hence those experiences are real in relation to the particular experiencer. But, then, since all these (the experiencer and the experiences) are pure consciousness, there is nothing to be spoken of as 'the other' or as duality. In the infinite consciousness when the notion 'This is this' arises, it shines as 'This is this': but when it is seen as 'This is this', then of course it becomes unreal! If it is the experience of consciousness, then it is non-different from consciousness; only in the non-existent state of ignorance is the experience experienced independently. Thus self-knowledge has no object to be known. When the knowledge is the known, then the self knows itself.

THE SAGE continued:

However carefully we look and investigate, we do not see anything other than the reality. What the ignorant and the foolish see, we do not know. In the enlightened vision of the sage all this is the pure, indivisible consciousness; that itself appears to be countless separate objects (both sentient and insentient) in the eyes of the ignorant. The one pure consciousness appears as the diverse dream-objects in a dream. All these millions of objects which appear in the dream become one again in deep sleep. Similarly, when this dream-world appears in the infinite consciousness that itself is called creation; when this itself enters into the equivalent of the deep sleep state, it is known as the cosmic dissolution. This is pure commonsense.

The one indivisible consciousness becomes both the diverse objects and also the infinite individuals; it itself becomes both the void and also the matter—just like in dream. All this diversity is just experiencing. It is pure. It shines in the manner in which it is conceived of. It cannot be removed. This consciousness alone becomes fire, etc., in the beginning of creation, for the purpose of constituting this dream-world. It is pure experiencing alone that shines as the earth, etc., though in truth it is nothing but space or void which shines as the created world. This awareness or experiencing appears to be impossible to overcome at times and at times it seems to be capable of being put to an end; in fact it is not possible to put an end to it, because pure experiencing remains even after all the other things have been put to an end. It is like your going from the east to the west. Now you know the east and now you know the west—but the experience of knowing remains the same. Whatever you think of intently for a considerable time, that you experience: or you rest in peace, and experience that peace. You go from the east to the west and know these. Another does not go but stays in one place and still knows these. The infinite consciousness, being non-moving, remains the same whether it is thus experienced or thought of. Both experiences arise and both experiences cease. When the wish arises in one 'I shall go from the south to the north', both these arise in the non-moving consciousness; but when such a wish does not arise, the directions 'north' and 'south' do not exist. When the consciousness thinks, "May I become a city in the sky" or "May I become an animal on earth," these two come into being; when that notion is not there they cease. To others the world is something else.

Whether the body is mortal or immortal, the truth is that this saṃsāra and the jīva are like dream. Even among the foreigners there are accounts of people recalling events in their past-lives. Surely, they did not 'die'. Thus, the infinite consciousness which alone appears as all this is undying, unchanging and eternal. The unmoving consciousness remains, appearing to be whatever notion arises in it here and there. What is truth and what is false? So, let one experience bodies, actions, sorrow or pleasure as and when they arise: or let them all go. There is no meaning in all this. Let it be 'this' way or 'that' way, let it be or not be: give up this delusion and remain enlightened.

THE SAGE continued: VI.2:144

All that exists and all that does not exist are like dream-experiences. Such being the truth, what is bondage and who is liberated? The cloud-formations in the sky throw up ever-changing forms and patterns. Even so is the world-appearance ever changing. It seems to be stable and unchanging on account of ignorance. In this infinite space there are countless worlds even as we have our own world: one man's world is not experienced by another person. The measure and the experience of frogs living in a well, lake and ocean are different from one another. They do not share one another's knowledge. People sleeping in one house have different dreams in which they experience life in different worlds, as it were: even so, the people have different worlds in the same space, while some may not have. All this is but the mysterious and efficient work of the infinite consciousness.

Consciousness has the faculty of holding on to something; a notion so held is known as saṃskāra. But when it is realised that the notion is only reflected in consciousness, it is seen that there is no saṃskāra independent of consciousness. In dream there is no previous memory but only the experience of the objects that are experienced for the time being. One may even experience in a dream one's own death as also objects that appear like those seen before.

This creation was but a mirror-reflection in the indivisible consciousness in the beginning and hence it was non-different from that consciousness. Brahman (the infinite consciousness) alone shines as this world, which is not something new. The cause alone is the effect. The cause was there before the effect and will remain even after the effect ceases to be. Because the cause 'acts efficiently' (saṃyak karoti) in bringing about the effect, it itself is known as saṃskāra.

That which existed before the arising of the dream but which shines as that which was seen before, that is known as saṃskāra. There is no other external factor known as saṃskāra (popularly translated into 'latent impressions of past experiences and actions'). Things seen and unseen exist in the consciousness which shines in its own light and experiences all those things as if already seen. In dream the saṃskāras created in the waking state arise; but in the waking state itself they are created anew. But they who know the truth declare that they were in fact created in a state that appeared to be the waking state but which in fact is not. Just as movement arises in air spontaneously, even so notions arise in consciousness: where is the need for saṃskāra to create them? When the experience of a thousand things arises in consciousness, it is known as creation; and when the experience of the thousand things ceases in consciousness, that is known as the cosmic dissolution. Thus the pure consciousness (cidākāśa) brings into being this diversity with all its names and forms, without ever abandoning is indivisibility, just as you create a world in your dream.

THE SAGE continued:

The perception or the experience of 'the world' exists within the atomic particle of infinite consciousness. Just as the reflection in a mirror is only mirror, however, it is non-different from the infinite consciousness. This infinite consciousness is beginningless and endless; that itself is called creation. Wherever this consciousness shines, there this creation exists, non-different from it even as a body is non-different from its limbs. You and I are consciousness, the entire world is consciousness: by this realisation the creation is seen as an integral part of consciousness and therefore uncreated. Hence, I am that atomic particle of consciousness and as such I am infinite and omnipresent. Therefore, wherever I am, I see everything from there itself. I am a particle of consciousness but I am one with the infinite consciousness on account of the realisation of this truth, even as water is the same as water.

Therefore, by entering into the 'ojas' I experienced the three worlds. All this happened within it and within it I saw the three worlds—not outside. Whether it is called dream or waking, inside or outside, all this is within the infinite consciousness.

THE HUNTER asked:

If this creation is causeless how does it come into being? If it has a cause, what is the cause of the dream-creation?

THE SAGE replied:

In the beginning, creation had no cause whatsoever. Since the objects of this creation had no cause whatsoever, conflicting diversity of objects opposed to one another does not arise. The one absolute Brahman alone shines as all this and is denoted by words like 'creation', etc. Thus, this causeless creation is Brahman but it appears to be part of that which has no parts, to be diverse in the indivisible, to have a form in the formless. Because it is pure consciousness it appears to assume various forms like the mobile and the immobile objects. And as the gods and the sages it creates and sustains a world order with all the injunctions and prohibitions. Existence, non-existence, the gross and the subtle, etc., do not in any way affect the omnipresent consciousness.

However, from there on effects do not arise without a cause. The world order and its lord (Brahman) act on one another just like one arm restrains the other, though both belong to the same person.

Thus, this creation arises without desire and without psychological causation. The world order (niyati) exists within Brahman; Brahman does not exist without niyati. Thus, this creation has a cause, but only in relation to the one whose creation it is and as long as that creation lasts in relation to him. The ignorant think that Brahman shines or appears as this creation without a cause; and it is again the ignorant that are caught up in this cause-and-effect tangle or deluded notion that causality is inviolably real. The creation takes place as a coincidence—the ripe cocoanut falls accidentally just when a crow alights on it. Then niyati determines 'This is this' and 'That is that'.

THE SAGE continued: VI.2:145

The jīva knows and experiences the external world with the externalised senses and the inner dream-world with the inner senses. When the senses are engaged in the experience of the external world, then the field of internal notions is vague and unclear. But when the senses are turned within, then the jīva experiences the world within himself with the greatest clarity. There is no contradiction in this world-appearance whatsoever at any time; it is as one sees it is. Therefore, when the eyes are extroverted the jīva experiences the world as if it were outside in the infinite consciousness. The aggregate of the sense of hearing, touch (skin), sight (eyes), smell (nose), taste (tongue) and desire is known as the jīva, which is of the nature of pure consciousness endowed with life-force. This jīva exists therefore in everything everywhere as everything and hence he experiences everything everywhere.

When the jīva (the 'ojas' or the vital essence) is filled with 'phlegm' (śleṣma or kapha, one of the three humours that constitute the vital essence of the body), he sees its effects there and then. He 'sees' himself rising from the ocean of milk; he sees the moon floating in the sky; he sees lakes and lotuses, gardens and flowers, rejoicing and festivals in which women sing and dance, feasts with a lot of food and drink, rivers flowing into the ocean, huge palaces painted white, fields covered with fresh snow, parks with deer resting in them, and mountain ranges.

When the jīva is filled with 'bile' (pitta, which is another humour) he experiences its effects there and then. He 'sees' flames which are beautiful and which produce sweating of the nerves and which throw up black smoke which darkens the sky, suns which are dazzling in their brilliance and scorching in their heat, oceans and mist rising from them, impassable forests, mirages with swans swimming in them; he sees himself running along the road in fear and covered with hot dust, he sees the earth scorched dry and hot. Wherever the eyes see, they see everything on fire, even the clouds rain fire, and because of this pervasive fire, everything looks brilliant.

When the jīva is filled with 'wind' (vāta which is another humour) he experiences the following effects. He sees the world as if it is new, he sees himself and even rocks and mountains flying, everything revolves and rotates, flying angels and celestials, the earth and all that is in it quakes; he sees himself as having fallen into a blind well or into a dreadful calamity or as standing perilously on top of a tree of great height or a mountain peak.

THE SAGE continued:

When the jīva is filled with vāta, pitta and śleṣma (wind, bile and phlegm), he comes under the influence of the wind and experiences distress. He sees a shower of mountains and of rocks, he hears dreadful sounds with which trees revolve in the bowels of the earth. Whole forests whirl around with all the animals in the forests. All the trees are on fire and there is the sound of burning issuing from all the caves. He sees the collision of mountains. He sees the oceans rising to fill the entire sky and carrying away whole forests and even clouds, lifting them up to the region of Brahmā the creator. The whole sky seems to be clear and clean because of all this friction and rubbing within it. The three worlds appear to be filled with the battle cries of soldiers and warriors.

When thus the jīva is agitated and distressed by all this dreadful vision, he becomes unconscious. Like a worm which lies buried in the earth, like a frog hidden in a rock, like a foetus in the womb, like the seed within the fruit, like the unborn sprout in a seed, like an atom in a molecule, like an uncut figure in a rock, he rests within himself, undisturbed by the movement of prāṇa because in his resting place there are no 'holes' or outlets. He enters into deep sleep, which is like resting inside a rock or inside a blind well.

When mental effort makes a hole in that resting place, then he knows the world of dreams, having been made aware of it by the movement of the life-force or prāṇa. When this life-force falls from one nāḍī (nerve-channel) on to another, there is a vision of a shower of mountains. If there is too much of such movement caused by vāta, pitta, and śleṣma then there is a lot of such experiences; if it is less, the experience is less.

Whatever the jīva experiences within (in dream, etc.) on account of the vāta, pitta, and śleṣma, that he experiences outside, too, and in that field his own organs of action function appropriately. When agitated or disturbed inside and outside, he (the jīva) experiences a little disturbance if the disturbance of the vāta, pitta and kapha (śleṣma) is slight, and he experiences equanimity if they are in a state of balance or equilibrium. The jīva experiences all these outside when the three humours are agitated or disturbed: burning, drowning, moving in air, resting on rocks and mountains, hell, rising and falling from the sky, hallucinations like drowning in a playground, sunshine at midnight, perversion of intelligence in which one's own appear to be strangers and enemies appear like friends. With closed eyes these are all seen within oneself and with open eyes these are seen outside: but all these delusions are brought about by the disturbed equilibrium of the three humours. When they are in a state of equilibrium, the jīva residing within them sees the whole world as it is, as it really IS, non-different from Brahman.

THE SAGE continued: VI.2:146

While I was within the 'ojas' of that other person, there arose symptoms of the cosmic dissolution. Mountains began to rain from the sky. I saw it while I was sitting within the 'ojas' of the other person: in fact, it was particles of food that were coursing in the channels of his body that created this illusion of mountains being showered from the dark sky, and this darkness was the darkness of his own deep sleep. I also entered into deep sleep. After some time, I experienced the dawn of awakening consciousness.

As I was waking up from sleep, I experienced the dream state. Within the same 'ojas' I saw a mighty ocean which appeared to be like me. Whatever appeared in that 'ojas', which was the field of experience, I saw without any distortion or perversion because my consciousness was non-moving and steady. Consciousness is spread all round and in it this world-appearance arises; this world-appearance issues from the deep sleep state even as a baby is born of the mother.

THE HUNTER asked:

You say that the world-appearance issues from the deep sleep: pray tell me what one experiences in deep sleep.

THE SAGE continued:

'Is born', 'appears', 'arises as the world', and such other dualistic expressions are but mere words, utterly meaningless. I shall tell you what 'is born' (jāta) means. The essence of that expression is 'to come into being' and that 'being' alludes to the eternally existent reality. Even so the word 'creation' (sarga) also has the same connotation and it refers to 'existence'. (N.B. The structure of the words 'jāyate' and 'sarga' are examined here in accordance with sanskrit grammar. 'Jani' is equated to 'prādurbhāva' and the vital part of the latter is 'bhūḥ' which refers to 'being'.)

To us who are enlightened there is no creation, no death or cessation; all is for ever unborn and peaceful. Brahman is pure existence. The world is pure existence, too. Whom do injunctions and prohibitions affect? The illusory power known as Māyā alone is the subject of discussion and argumentation—'it is' and 'it is not'. Therefore, such disputation is extended by ignorant people to Brahman or the infinite consciousness.

To those who know the truth or the supreme state, the states of waking, dream and sleep do not exist at all. Whatever is is as it is. The dream-world as also the world which one sees in his own imagination is not real, even though they are experienced to be so for the time being. Even so, in the beginning of this world-creation, it did not exist or come into being. When thus the world is realised as pure consciousness, then it is not an object of perception; therefore there is no subject or observer either, there is no experience or experiencer.

VI.2:147 THE SAGE continued:

When I had emerged from deep sleep, this world arose in my dream as from an ocean, as a statue emerges from a stone, as flowers emerge from the tree, as memory emerges from the mind, as waves emerge from the ocean. It was as if they dropped from the sky, as if they arose from the earth, as if they arose in the heart, as if they were food grains that sprang from the earth, as if the curtain that hid them had been lifted, as if they emerged from a temple. From where did the world arrive? One does not know. It is surely the figure fashioned in the stone called the infinite consciousness. It is an imaginary city made of walls which are pure space or void. It is the trick of the juggler known as ignorance. Though it seems to be a firm reality, it is essentially devoid of space and time. Though it seems to be diverse, yet it is non-dual, diverse and nothing at the same time. Surely, it can only be compared to a castle in the air: for it is seen and experienced even in the waking state.

Though it has never been created, it exists as if it had been created. It is pure consciousness. It seems to be endowed with time, space, matter, activity, creation and destruction. It has gods, demons, human beings and various other forms of creatures. In it are the rivers, mountains, forests, the sky and the stars.

I saw this 'field of observation'. At the same time I saw there the house I had seen before, along with all my relatives' buildings, and everything as they were before. All these had been dragged into the field of observation by the latent vāsanā or psychological tendency. On account of the vāsanā, I immediately engaged myself in greeting and embracing my relatives etc., having temporarily lost the knowledge that it was illusory.

Just as a mirror reflects whatever object is placed in front of it, even so, consciousness takes on the form of whatever is presented to it. However, one who has realised that everything is the pure, infinite consciousness is not affected by the apparent duality. He remains free, alone and unaffected. One who never loses the knowledge of oneness is not troubled by this goblin known as perception of difference or division. They in whom this knowledge has arisen, due to the company of the holy ones and the study of this scripture, do not lose it again. At that time, however, my own understanding had not become clear and firm; hence even I was swayed by the notions of relationship. But now nothing in the world can shake my understanding nor cloud my realisation. Your mind, too, is not steady now, O hunter, because you have not had satsaṅga, company of the holy ones.

THE HUNTER said:

True indeed, O sage. It is as you say. Therefore, even though I have listened to your illuminating words, there is still some doubt in me, "Can all this really be true?" Alas, what a great tragedy! Even when this ignorance seems to be obvious, it is hard to abandon it.

VI.2:148 THE HUNTER asked:

I have a great doubt, O sage: how can the dream-objects be regarded both as real and unreal?

THE SAGE replied:

In a dream there is the appearance of time, space, action and materiality. This appearance arises because of the notion that arises in consciousness, by sheer coincidence. Therefore, that appearance shines as reality in the dream. In the case of hallucinations produced with the help of precious stones (magic wand?), mantras and drugs, they are sometimes real and at others totally illusory. But when one experiences real substantiality in a dream, it is only due to coincidence. Whenever a firm notion arises in consciousness, it materialises in that manner because consciousness is endowed with such power to materialise. If this materialisation can be altered by another force, how can we affirm that the notion that arises in consciousness is firm?

There is no materiality either inside or outside, except the materialisation of the 'wish' or the notion of the infinite consciousness. When the notion 'This is dream' arises, that dream becomes real; but if there is the notion of doubt, the dream also takes on the characteristic of the doubt and becomes unreal. It is possible that simultaneously with the dreaming the dreamer may undergo experiences unrelated to the dream; but he attributes them to the dream itself. Thus, by sheer coincidence, the world-appearance which arises in consciousness undergoes some change sooner or later.

This notion of creation arises in consciousness in the very beginning and it materialises; this materialisation is pure consciousness. Barring this, all else is both real and unreal, orderly and disorderly. Therefore, in the eyes of the ignorant dreams appear to be true sometimes and untrue sometimes, but in the eyes of the enlightened they are neither real nor unreal. The world-appearance is an appearance that arises in consciousness: the very word 'appearance' rules out any positive investigation concerning it.

After dream, one sleeps; and after the waking state, one sleeps. Hence, waking and dream are non-different. The inert 'object' of consciousness alone is regarded as waking, dream and sleep states —words which have no real meaning. In this long-dream, there is neither order nor disorder. Whatever arises in dream, that alone is—like the movement that arises in air: in the absence of definite causation, order is irrelevant. Even so is the entire creation devoid of definite causation; whatever an object appears to be, that it is— and this is the world order. Dreams are sometimes real and sometimes unreal: hence it is not subject to a fixed principle or order. It is pure coincidence. The vision that arises on account of magic, mantra or drugs also exists in the waking state. Hence, that which is not conditioned by the waking, dream and deep sleep states, the unconditioned pure consciousness alone is real.

THE SAGE continued: VI.2:149

When I saw, while still in the heart of the other person, my own relatives, etc., I forgot momentarily that they were the products of my own notions and I lived with them for a period of sixteen years. Then one day a great ascetic came to my house. I served him well and with devotion. I took this opportunity of asking him the following question: "In this world people are said to experience the good and evil results of their own good and evil actions. Is this true in all cases?"

The ascetic looked surprised at this question.

THE ASCETIC replied:

Pray tell me what it is in you that distinguishes good from evil. Who are you, where are you, who am I, what is this world? All this is but a dream. I am your dream-object and you are my dream-object. The object has no form in truth. But when consciousness considers this to have this form, it takes on that form. The notion that 'All this has a cause' gives rise to a causal relationship; the notion that 'There is no cause' sees no causality.

All of us are in the heart of a macrocosmic being who is regarded as such by all of us. Even so, there will be other macrocosmic beings for others. This macrocosmic being is the cause for the experiences of pleasure and pain and for the diverse types of actions. When the 'ojas' of this macrocosmic being is disturbed, it is agitated and that effect is experienced by all of us who are in his heart. We are affected by natural calamities which cease when his heart regains equanimity. Therefore, this macrocosmic being is the reality of this particular creation. By coincidence, when some people engage themselves in evil actions the resultant unhappiness befalls all.

Consciousness bestows reward on one when the actions arise from one's own personal notion ("I do this"); when the consciousness is freed from such a notion, such action is not followed by its fruits. Whatever notion arises wherever and of whatever magnitude, that bears fruits, whether there was a corresponding cause or not. As in a dream, the effect of an action is not governed by a definite cause. At times the dream-experience has a cause; and at other times it has no cause. It is simply accidental coincidence. The waking state experience seems to have a definite causality: but that notion itself is a dream. For all this is mere appearance of the infinite consciousness.

What is the cause of ignorance, of creation, of the creation of Brahmā the creator; what is the original cause for air, fire, water or space; why do people die and get into a subtle body? These have no cause at all: all these have happened like this from the beginning. After some time, these notions or appearances have attained materiality. Whatever notions arose in the consciousness originally, have remained as such till now. However, the consciousness can alter this by a fresh effort in the present.

VI.2:150 THE SAGE continued:

Thus instructed by the ascetic I was instantly enlightened. I could not leave him. At my request he lived with me. That very ascetic is sitting right next to you.

THE HUNTER was surprised and he said:

It is wonderful and strange, O sage, that that which was considered dream appears to have materialised in the waking state. How is it that this holy man who appeared in your dream has become a reality even in the waking state?

THE SAGE continued:

Do not be in a hurry. I shall explain everything to you. When I had heard the admonitions of this holy man, I began to reflect: "Alas, on account of my desire for sense-pleasure and for the objects of pleasure, I have slipped away from my path, though I have been a wise man. Or, the notion 'This am I' is illusory and unreal: yet it is able to give rise to a thousand strange happenings. Or, even if I consider all this to be unreal and that 'I am not', yet all this IS. What must I do now? I see the seed of division in me: I shall instantly renounce that. Let this illusion or ignorance remain: it is a vain appearance, what can it do? I have now given up delusion. Even the sage who instructed me is but an illusion. I am the infinite and absolute Brahman and so is he; the relative form is but a passing cloud."

Having arrived at this knowledge, I said to the ascetic: "O sage, I am going, in order to see my own body as well as the body which I had begun to investigate." When he heard this, he began to smile: "Where are those bodies? They have gone far, far away. If, however, you wish to verify this for yourself, please go." I requested him, "Please stay here till I return." After this I ascended an aerial vehicle and flew for a very long time. Yet, I could not find an exit from the heart of the person where I was. I was dejected. I realised that I was bound to that house. I returned there and asked the ascetic: "Pray, tell me what is all this. The body into which I had entered and that which was mine—where are they? How is it that I could not find an exit?"

The ascetic replied: "Surely you will know everything if you see it with your inner vision. You are not this little personality; you are the macrocosmic person himself. Once you desired to enter into the heart of a being in order to experience a dream. That into which you entered is this creation. While you continued to dream in that body, a great fire arose and it began to consume the forest in the body into which you had entered. That fire had destroyed your body as well as the body of the person into whose heart you had entered."

(In answer to the Hunter's question, the sage replied: "The cause of the fire is but the movement of thought in consciousness, just as the cause for the appearance of the world is the movement of thought in the infinite consciousness, and the movement of thought in the consciousness of Brahmā the creator.")

THE ASCETIC continued: VI.2:151, 152

When thus the two bodies had been destroyed by the great fire, while both of you were asleep, you continued to vibrate as just consciousness. Since the body belongs to the 'ojas' and the two bodies had been destroyed with the 'ojas', you could not find an exit. Not finding the two bodies you exist in this 'world'. Thus, your dream has materialised into the waking state reality. All of us here are your own dream-objects. Similarly, you are our dream-objects. That in which all this happens is the pure consciousness (cidākāśa) which exists everywhere at all times. You were a dream-object before; but since you assumed that this is the world of the waking state, you became a householder with a family and relations, etc. Thus have I told you all that has happened.

THE SAGE said:

If this is the nature of dream, I consider all this real.

THE ASCETIC replied:

If the real can come into being, then it is possible to consider something else as real, too. When the reality of the former itself is doubtful, how can one affirm the reality of the latter? On the other hand, even the original creation is like a dream. It is but an illusory appearance. Though devoid of earth, and all the rest of it, it appears to have earth, etc., O teacher of the hunter! The original dream-like creation of the world and also the dream that we experience now are both unreal. The present dream has the objects seen already as its material; the dream-like creation appears in the space as if it had been seen before. Why do you hesitantly say, as if in doubt: "I think the dream is real"? When you experience this world as if it were real, how does a doubt concerning its real nature arise?

THE SAGE said (to the Hunter):

I interrupted the ascetic's speech and asked him: "How and why did you refer to me as the teacher of the hunter?"

THE ASCETIC replied:

Listen, I shall tell you what is going to happen in the future. I am an ascetic with long-standing asceticism. You are a righteous person. Therefore, when you listen to this truth, you will be happy. You and I will continue to remain here. I shall not leave you.

After some years, there will arise a great famine here. In that all your relatives will perish. The vicious kings will then wage war with one another and destroy all the rest. We shall however know no sorrow since we are knowers of the truth and since we are unattached to (free from) all. We shall continue to live here at the foot of a tree. In course of time a nice forest will grow here. That forest will resemble the pleasure-gardens that abound in heaven itself.

VI.2:153, 154 THE SAGE continued:

The ascetic said: "Both of us will be engaged in austerities there in that forest for a considerable time. To that place will come one day a hunter in pursuit of game. You will enlighten him with your talks and stories. He, too, shall renounce the world and engage himself in austerities in the same forest. He will question you concerning dreams, in his quest for self-knowledge. You will discourse upon self-knowledge. Thus you will become his guru; hence I called you the guru of the hunter. I have told you all about myself and you and what is going to happen to you in the future."

I was astonished to hear all this. The ascetic continued to stay in the same house and I devoutly worshipped him and served him. I remain here like a mountain, undergoing varied experiences. I do not desire death nor do I wish to live. I am what I am, free from mental agitation.

Then I began to enquire into the nature of the objective world: what is the cause of this world, what is it, and who is aware of it? Surely the one infinite consciousness alone exists. The firmament, earth, air, space, mountains, rivers and the directions are all but the same indivisible (space-like) consciousness. They exist as notions in that consciousness. As such, there is no division or contradiction in it. These are not mountains, nor is this the earth nor space. This is not 'I' either. All these are mere appearances that arise in pure consciousness.

What is the cause for the appearance of this body, as nothing can arise without a cause? If it is said that it is delusion, then what is the cause for this delusion? Who is it that sees this delusion and who thinks about it? He in whose heart I lived as the experiencer, and I together have been reduced to ashes. Therefore I exist in pure consciousness which is devoid of action, the doer and the instruments. What exists is not even the appearance of the infinite consciousness, but it is pure consciousness. How can it become an appearance? Who is the seer of this appearance?

Thus, I continue to live in this objective world without any mental agitation, without support or dependence and without vanity. I do what has to be done at the appropriate moment, but I do nothing. What happens happens. The sky, the earth, wind, etc., are but one self; all the elements are the body of consciousness. I am at peace, free from injunctions and prohibitions, without even the division between inside and outside. As I have been living like this you approached me, by coincidence. Thus have I told you all about dreams, about us and about this creation. Knowing this, be at peace. Nirvāṇa will arise by itself, or nothing may happen.

THE HUNTER said:

In that case, we shall all become unreal!

THE SAGE continued:

True, all these beings are real to one another. To the extent they perceive one another they experience one another. You have heard all this, but you do not rest in the truth. Only by constant practice does this truth become fully established.

THE FIRE-GOD said: VI.2:155

Having heard the sage's instructions, the hunter remained seated like a painted image there in that forest itself. However, since he had not engaged himself in the persistent practice of the teachings, his heart was not fully established in the supreme state. Instead he was being tossed about as on the crest of waves or on a revolving mechanism. He felt helpless as if he were being attacked by a crocodile and unable to defend himself. He was full of doubts. He constantly was asking himself, "Is this nirvāṇa?" or "May be this is not nirvāṇa and something else is nirvāṇa." He thought, "Because this world-appearance has arisen in ignorance, the sage's teachings are not firmly rooted in my heart. Hence, I should get away from it. Attaining a subtle body through the performance of austerities, I should go far, far away to where even space does not exist." Thus he proved that he was still utterly ignorant and that the teaching of the sage had been utterly useless, because it had not been assimilated and it had not become active.

He abandoned hunting. Accompanied by the sage, he began to practice intense penance. He continued to practice austerities for many thousands of years, having adopted the mode of living appropriate to ascetics. One day, he again asked the sage the following question: "How shall I ever rest in the self?"

THE SAGE replied:

The wisdom that I imparted to you has remained weak in your heart like a dull fire which lies dormant in an old tree-trunk. It has not been able to burn and destroy ignorance. You are not established in the Lord because you have not assimilated the teaching and it has not become active; when you thus assimilate the teaching and it becomes active, surely you will be established in the Lord. I shall describe to you the future events. Listen.

You have no doubt set out to attain self-knowledge, but you have not found your foothold on sound wisdom. Hence you are swinging like a pendulum. You wish to get out of this world-appearance and with this end in view you wish to know its extent. In order to ascertain this, you are engaged in penance. You will continue to perform such penance for several world-cycles. Then the Lord will appear before you, pleased with your penance. You will then ask him to confer upon you the following boon:

"Lord, I understand that this whole universe arises in ignorance. In it I cannot experience the pure and transparent knowledge of the self. Where is the end to this world-appearance and what is beyond this? In order to find the answer to this question, I beg of you to grant me the following boon:

"Ordain that I shall die only when I wish to. May my body be free from all ailments. May I be endowed with the speed of Garuḍa. May I be able to course in space without hindrance. May my body grow a mile an hour, so that soon I will grow larger than the world. Thus will I realise the extent of this creation."

The Lord will grant the boon and vanish from sight.

THE SAGE continued:

After the departure of the Lord, you will continue your penance. Your body would have been reduced to a skeleton by this time; but now it will acquire a radiance on account of the boon. You will bow down to me and soon your body will become divine. It will 'fly around' faster than Garuḍa, progressively expanding and including the celestial bodies within it. In that expanding body you will see the countless universes as so many waves in the ocean. Just as in the beginning all these universes arose in the infinite consciousness, even so at that time these universes will come within the sphere of your vision. You will then realise that just as all this is unreal and diverse in the vision of the ignorant, they are real and indivisible to the enlightened.

Thus seeing the alternate arising and subsiding of these countless universes, you will spend a long, long time. You will then be filled with admiration for this infinite intelligence. You will become aware of your own body and say to yourself: "What is this wretched body which is huge and heavy? It has become of incomparable dimensions since with it I have filled the entire space. What shall I do after this—I myself do not know. It seems to me that this ignorance (and the world-appearance) is immeasurable. It cannot be measured at all without a direct knowledge of Brahman. I shall discard this body, for nothing can be attained with it. This body of mine is huge and supportless but it is not possible for me to have the company of enlightened sages with its help."

Having thus decided, you will abandon your body. Your jīva endowed with just the life-force (prāṇa) will become even subtler than air. Abandoned by the jīva, the body will fall (reduced in size) crushing the earth, etc., by its sheer size and weight. The goddess known as 'Dryness' will consume that body and thus purify the earth. Thus have I told you what the future holds for you.

THE HUNTER asked:

Lord, terrible is the sorrow that has to be endured by me for no real gain at all. Is there a means by which this fate can be averted?

THE SAGE replied:

That which is inevitable cannot be averted by anyone at any time. It is not altered by any amount of effort. The right arm is the right arm and left arm is the left arm; no one can alter that fact. The head and the feet cannot be exchanged for one another. Whatever is is. Even the science of astrology can only foretell what is to come, but it cannot avert what is bound inevitably to happen. However, the sages of self-knowledge live in this world as if in deep sleep. They experience the result of past actions without allowing the inner consciousness ever to become perverted, even if the body is to be burnt. They overcome all karmas.

THE HUNTER asked: Lord, tell me what will happen to me VI.2:156
after that.

THE SAGE replied:

Your jīva will then behold the entire world as you see the world in your dream. It will then regard itself as the king. It will think, "I am the king named Sindhu who is respected widely. My father having retired to the forest I became king when I was only eight years of age. Beyond the borders of my kingdom there is another ruled over by a mighty king Vidūratha who is hard to conquer. . . . Till now I have ruled this kingdom for over a hundred years, enjoying all the royal pleasures. Alas, now my kingdom is invaded by the king Vidūratha." On account of this thought, there will ensue a fierce battle between you and the king Vidūratha. You will kill Vidūratha. You will then become the king of the whole world. Surrounded by the ministers you will engage yourself in the following dialogue:

The MINISTER will say to you: It is a wonder, O king, that you have been able to conquer this king Vidūratha. YOU will respond: I am indeed wealthy and powerful; why then do you regard it as a wonder that I was able to conquer Vidūratha?

The MINISTER will say: He has a wife named Līlā who had, by her austerity and devotion, propitiated goddess Sarasvatī who had adopted Līlā as her daughter and fulfilled all her prayers; it would not have been difficult for her to destroy you. YOU will say: If that is the case,it was certainly a great wonder that I was able to vanquish Vidūratha. Tell me, why did not Vidūratha seek to defeat me with the help of the goddess?

The MINISTER will say: He had prayed for liberation from bondage to saṃsāra and therefore he had actually sought to be killed by you. YOU will say: If such is the case, why should I not worship the goddess and pray for liberation?

The MINISTER will say: She is the wisdom that shines in the hearts of all. Since she is the essence (rasa) of intelligence in all, she is known as Sarasvatī. She bestows immediately on all whatever is prayed for, for she is the self of all. Hence one experiences the fruition of one's own prayers. You have not asked for liberation; you have only prayed for the destruction of enemies.

YOU will say: Why have I not prayed for liberation? You say that she dwells in my own heart; why has she not inspired me to pray for liberation? The MINISTER will say: It is because in your heart there was the impure habit of wishing for the destruction of enemies. Therefore, you did not pray for liberation but you did pray for the destruction of enemies. Whatever be the citta (mind, heart), that a being is, and this is the experience of even a child. Whatever one knows in his own heart and whatever one experiences again and again in his heart, so that it becomes a habit, materialises whether it be good or not good.

VI.2:157 THE SAGE continued:

YOU will say: What did I do in the past birth that I was subjected to such an evil habit of thought? The MINISTER will reply: I shall reveal the secret to you. There is something which exists without beginning and without end, as 'I' and 'you', etc., but which is known as Brahman. That Brahman became its own object of awareness and therefore it became the jīva and then the mind. This subtle psychological or ethereal body condensed into physical body. It is but the mind which has no form, but which exists as if it has a form (the body). The mind alone is this world; there is no distinction between the two. Satva (the purest form of mind) alone arose in Brahman originally; and it has now become extremely dense and dull (tāmasa-tāmasa).

YOU will say: What is this tāmasa-tāmasa and how did it arise in the supreme state? The MINISTER will say: Living beings here have various limbs, even so the subtle self or consciousness has, so to say, the subtle ethereal body as its limb. That itself thinks of itself as the gross body with the physical elements like earth. That itself functions with the help of its own notions in this world-appearance which arises in the same consciousness as in a dream. You yourself entertain in your own ethereal body the notion, 'This is the densest darkness' and thus that notion is born. All these diversities exist in Brahman, though it is absolutely pure.

The first notion that arises in Brahman when it becomes a jīva, as it were, is experienced by the buddhi (intelligence) as perfect purity (sātvika-sātvika). When it enters into the stream of life and if it is endowed with all the noble qualities, it is known as mere sātvika birth. The birth which arises in the stream of life and which is subjected to diverse pleasures, but directed towards liberation, is called rājasa-rājasa. When the birth arises in the stream of life and when it is devoid of noble qualities, it is known as simple rājasa. When the being has been in the stream of life for a very long time and has just turned towards liberation, it is known as tāmasa-tāmasa. But the ordinary birth which is one in the sequence of several oriented towards liberation is known as simple tāmasa.

In this manner there are very many classifications of births. You were born in the tāmasa-tāmasa class. You have had many births and so have I. I know them, you do not. Wandering in all these you have wasted a lot of time. Because you were so conditioned you found it difficult to free yourself.

YOU will say: How can I overcome the effect of such past life? The MINISTER will say: There is nothing that one who strives without agitation cannot achieve. Yesterday's evil action is transformed into good action by today's noble deeds. Therefore, strive to be good and do good now. One strives to attain what one wishes to attain; and surely one shall attain it.

Being thus advised by the minister, the king Sindhu will at once renounce the kingdom and resort to a forest. He will take refuge at the feet of the holy ones. By their very association he will gain the highest wisdom and will be liberated.

THE FIRE-GOD continued: VI.2:158, 159

The hunter heard all this from the sage and was filled with wonder. The hunter and the sage continued to perform austerities. A little later, the sage attained nirvāṇa and he abandoned his body. After a very long time, Brahmā the creator appeared before the hunter to grant him boons. The hunter was unable to avert the natural force of his own mental conditioning though he remembered the sage's prophecy. Therefore, he asked for the very boons that he had been conditioned to request.

As a result of the boon, the hunter's body began to expand to cosmic proportions. When in spite of all this he discovered that he could not find the limits of ignorance, he became both astonished and agitated. By the mystic process of giving up prāṇa, he abandoned the body which thereupon fell in space. He himself remained in space and began to consider himself the king Sindhu.

The body appeared above a certain world-appearance in this universe and it had the shape of a ball of hair. It looked big enough to cover the whole of the earth.

O Vipaścit, thus have I described to you the identity of that body. That world-appearance on which the body fell appears to us as the world. It was after consuming the blood of that body that the dried up body of the goddess began to be filled and she came to be known as Caṇḍikā. The flesh of that corpse became the earth-element. In course of time, the world acquired its present nature as the earth. Once again, the earth was endowed with living beings and forests, villages and cities.

The earth is once again firm and substantial. O good man, go where you wish to go. I have been invited to the kingdom of heaven by Indra, the chief of the gods, who wishes to perform a sacred rite with my help. I shall go there.

BHĀSA (VIPAŚCIT) said:

Having said this, the fire-god vanished from sight. With all the psychological conditioning in my mind, I went my way to do what I had to do.

Once again, I saw in the infinite space countless worlds and universes. Some of them were like umbrellas, some were like animals, some were full of trees, others were full of rocks. But I had not arrived at the end of ignorance, at the limits of ignorance; hence I was depressed and dejected. Thereupon, I decided to engage myself in penance. Seeing this, Indra said to me: "O Vipaścit, in space you and I have bodies of deer. On account of the deluded notion of a heaven which was in me before, I am wandering in heaven." Hearing this, I said to Indra: "O king of heaven, I am tired of this saṃsāra. Kindly release me from this saṃsāra quickly."

INDRA said to Vipaścit:

Your consciousness is moving in the deer-species. Hence, I see that birth as a deer is inevitable. As a deer you will reach that great assembly where you will be awakened after listening to your own story. When you enter into the fire of wisdom, you will gain a human form and also spiritual unfoldment in your heart. Then you will abandon your ignorance and regain utter peace like wind devoid of movement.

VIPAŚCIT (BHĀSA) continued:

When Indra said so, the awareness arose in me: 'I am a deer.' From that time I have been roaming the forests as a deer. Once when a hunter pursued me, I began to run. But he overpowered me and took me home. He kept me there for a few days and then he brought me to you to be your pet. Thus have I told you my story, O Rāma, which clearly illustrates the illusory nature of this saṃsāra. Limitless is this ignorance with countless branches in all directions; it cannot come to an end by any means other than self-knowledge.

RĀMA asked:

How was it possible for you to be seen by others when your form arose in your saṅkalpa?

VIPAŚCIT (BHĀSA) continued:

Once while Indra was passing through the sky, full of vanity at having successfully completed a sacred rite, he kicked the body of the sage Durvāsa who was in meditation. The sage cursed him: "O Indra, that earth to which you are going will soon be reduced to nothing. Because you kicked me thinking I was dead, you will soon go to that very earth and live as a deer as long as Vipaścit lives there as a deer." Therefore, we became deer which could be seen by others. Of course, an object that arises in one's own mind is as unreal as an object that arises in another's. Again, since Brahman the infinite consciousness is all this and is capable of doing all this, what is impossible in it and for it? On the basis of its omnipotence, it is possible for two imaginary objects to become aware of one another or to be unaware of one another. Where there is shadow, there is also light and the shadow arises because of the light. In the infinite consciousness there is limitless ignorance; hence anything is possible in it. Strange and wonderful is this Māyā which is perplexing and which gives rise to delusion in the mind and in which thesis and antithesis exist together without conflict or contradiction. Such is the truth concerning Brahman that experiences this ignorance within itself, both as something which has had a beginning and as something which has had no beginning at all.

If the three worlds are not just the materialisation of the notions that arise in the infinite consciousness, how is it possible for that consciousness to re-create the three worlds after the periodic cosmic dissolution? Hence, it is clear that this creation is nothing more than movement in the infinite consciousness and the consequent arising of the appearance latent in it.

VIPAŚCIT (BHĀSA) continued:

The wise ones know that everything is immediately understood aright from the point of view of pure wisdom; there is no other way. This world-appearance is the result of the infinite consciousness entertaining the notion 'I am ignorant'. (Thus even ignorance arises only because of the infinite consciousness.)

No one dies here nor is anyone born: these two notions arise in consciousness and it appears as though death and birth are real. If there is death as the final end in fact and in truth, then it is indeed a most welcome and happy event! But, if one who dies is capable of being seen again, then surely he was alive all the time. Thus, there is no death, and by the same token there is no birth either. The two events appear to be real because of the movement in consciousness; they are otherwise unreal. If they are thought of as real, they are real; if they are known to be unreal, they are unreal. This means thought alone is real. Tell me if there is any life at all devoid of consciousness. In that pure consciousness there is no sorrow or death: then, who experiences sorrow and who dies? What a whirlpool is to water, the body is to the supreme truth. The appearance is pervaded by the reality, and the appearance is but an appearance, without a substantiality of its own. There is no division, distinction or contradiction between the two. Yet, the infinite consciousness appears to be this creation full of contradictions—this indeed is a great wonder.

Realise that this world-appearance with all its contradictions is nothing more than appearance which is non-existent. That infinite and indivisible consciousness alone exists as one thing here and as another thing there; therefore, there is neither diversity nor even unity. There is no contradiction nor is there a non-contradiction. They who know the truth realise that it is neither real nor unreal: hence, they realise the truth as utter silence. What is seen here as the objective universe is in truth the supreme Brahman. That Brahman alone entertains various notions which are manifest here as these diverse objects; but in that which entertains these notions there is no division and therefore such division is not real.

Every inch of space is filled with the creations of 'dead' jīvas. Such worlds are countless. They are unseen. They exist all together, without any contradiction or conflict among them. They do not see one another. All these objects of perception are but pure space. Consciousness alone is the perceiver or observer of all and consciousness perceives these objects in space as one sees an object in dream. Though this consciousness may be fully awake and enlightened, its object continues to appear to be, even as darkness continues till dawn. But whether the world-appearance is real or unreal, when the truth is realised there is great peace. Even as ripples and spray arise on the surface of the ocean, seem to exist for a moment and then get merged in the ocean the next minute, this world appears in Brahman and ceases to be the next moment, for Brahman alone is real.

VĀLMĪKI said: VI.2:160

The king Daśaratha made adequate provision for the maintenance of Vipaścit (Bhāsa). At that time, another day came to an end. The next day the members of the assembly gathered again and

THE SAGE continued:

Surely, that which is seen here is not ignorance. That is why Vipaścit could not find its limits or its extent. It remains ignorance only as long as it is not rightly understood. When its reality is seen, it is realised that there was never ever any 'water in the mirage'. You have yourself seen all this with your own eyes and heard it from the lips of this Vipaścit (or Bhāsa). He, too, will be enlightened like all of you when he listens to our discourse.

When Brahman holds on to the awareness of ignorance, this ignorance seems to be real. On account of this delusion, the unreal appears to be real. When it is realised that this ignorance is Brahman, then it is realised to be non-different from Brahman and that division disappears.

This ignorance gives rise to the most fascinating objects, though it itself is nothing. One who sets out to investigate the extent of dreams soon discovers that they have no limit; one who investigates the extent of the world-appearance arising in this ignorance soon discovers that it has none either. The objects which have materialised on account of notions that arise in consciousness and which are abandoned by the perceiver of those notions who thereupon goes on to entertain other notions, exist in space as the worlds of the siddhas, unaware of one another's existence. These worlds are of diverse natures and they are inhabited by diverse creatures. However, since there is nothing other than Brahman, all these are also full of Brahman only. Right in the beginning of creation, there was no cause and hence there was no creation at all. The infinite consciousness conceives of infinite notions and these materialise where those notions arise. What is so strange about this? Even now, you and all the others are the appearances created by the existence of intense notions which are endowed with the extraordinary force of concentration.

He who considers two things (like this world and heaven) to be real, obtains both these. Some siddhas consider hell to be real too and it appears to be real. That which is firmly believed to exist is experienced by that person physically, for the body is only mind.

The jīva abandons a particular state when it leaves one body and then there itself entertains the notion of another state. If the notion is good, it experiences a good world and if it is evil, it experiences an evil world. If it thinks of the world of the siddhas, it experiences it; if its thoughts are impure, it experiences hell then and there.

In hell, the jīva experiences diverse sufferings and calamities—like being pierced by arrows, having the chest hammered by rocks, embracing a red-hot pillar, being burnt alive, eating each other's bodies in hunger, swimming in rivers of blood and pus, feeling 'That evil action has led to this evil experience'.

VI.2:161 RĀMA asked:

In the story that we just heard we saw how the sage and the hunter passed through diverse experiences. Is it the very nature of things that determines such experiences or is there another reason for it?

VASIṢṬHA replied:

Such whirlpools of appearances keep occurring of their own accord in the ocean of infinite consciousness all the time. One set of whirlpool-like appearances remains steady till another arises and supersedes it. Some of these appearances seem to be permanent because they are long-standing and others are temporary: but just as movement, however slight, is inevitable to air, even so this appearance exists always in the infinite consciousness. The enlightened ones call it pure consciousness; the ignorant call it the world. It is neither real nor unreal: what should one call it? This universe is movement of awareness in the infinite consciousness, or the Lord. Hence, both hope and hopelessness are irrelevant to it. O wise men, be what you are.

The infinite consciousness itself regards the movement that arose within it as the world: where is earth (and such other elements) in it? It is the light of the infinite consciousness which shines, there is no other light. Brahman alone rests forever in Brahman and this self-awareness is known as ignorance! The entire space is filled with the fullness of consciousness and that is known as creation. In it there is no contradiction or duality.

When that infinite consciousness alone exists, what is there to come to an end? Just as the world experienced in a dream does not exist, this world does not exist as a material entity, though it is seen. Just as it is one's own consciousness only that shines as the dream, it is the same consciousness that shines as the objective world in the waking state. Hence, there is no difference between the dream and the waking state. One who wakes up from a dream thinks, "It is like this and not like that which I saw in the dream"; after death, too, one thinks "It is like this and not like that which I saw before death".

The dream may be brief and the life may be long, but the experience of the moment is the same in both. Just as in one lifetime one experiences hundreds of dreams, till one attains nirvāṇa one experiences hundreds of waking states. Just as some people remember their dreams, some people also remember their past experiences.

When thus there is no difference between the two, what is known as the world and what is ignorance? When ignorance does not exist, what is bondage? Pray, do not bind one who is ever free! There does not exist 'another' except the one pure, formless consciousness. Even when this world-appearance arises in that consciousness, it does not get bound to it; and therefore there is no liberation either. There is no ignorance in consciousness; there is no notion in pure consciousness. Space alone is space. That which is 'aware' even in deep sleep, that alone is aware in dreams as well as in the waking state: that is pure consciousness. It is that consciousness alone that is responsible even for the awareness of diversity. Creation itself is the supreme Brahman, both the unity and the diversity.

VASIṢṬHA continued: VI.2:162

This world exists with all its objects as the very meaning of materialisation of the infinite consciousness: hence even the form, its seeing and the thought concerning it are all the same pure consciousness and nothing else. The diversity of dream-objects is a dream, not diversity. Even so, the diversity that is seen during the waking state in the infinite space is the infinite space (consciousness) and there is no diversity. It is the indivisible consciousness that has the appearance of diversity.

This reality of consciousness is experienced differently by the wise and by the ignorant. Hence, this creation is said to be both unreal and real. Since their viewpoints are diametrically opposite, it becomes impossible for one to see what the other sees, and they cannot make one another understand what they see. Creation is what one sees and is aware of, and this is within oneself. When this inner experience is lasting, the creation is said to be lasting and when it is changing, the creation is said to be changing, too.

In dream, the objects are really immaterial and subtle, yet they are seen to be substantial. Even so, the objects in this creation are truly subtle and unseen, yet they appear to be solid and perceptible. This is true even of the body: it is a delusion and non-existent as such, but like a ghost it is conjured up as a reality. Even psychological or physical conditioning is an appearance, like the sound that is heard when the wind blows (which is heard, though it is not there at all).

Whatever is seen here or thought of to exist, all that is pure consciousness alone. There has never been a reason why something else should have come into being. Hence, realise "I am at peace, I am like the infinite space;" abandon the notion that you are the jīva. If one cannot thus redeem oneself, there are no other means: for one is one's own friend and one is one's own enemy. Strive to liberate yourself while you are yet young with the help of pure and right understanding, or buddhi. Do it now. What will you do when you are old and senile? Old age itself is a burden; you cannot carry anything more. Both childhood and old age are useless; youth alone is the right time, if you are a wise one, to live wisely. Having come into this saṃsāra where life is so impermanent, one should, through association with holy scriptures and holy men, endeavour to uplift oneself.

When the truth is realised, this objective universe ceases to bother you even if it continues to be seen and even if it is full of restlessness.

VI.2:163 RĀMA asked:

Ignorance does not cease without the full control of the senses: pray tell me, how does one control the senses?

VASIṢṬHA said:

I shall now describe to you how one gains control over the senses easily by one's own effort. The self (or the personality) is indeed pure consciousness only: on account of its self-awareness, it comes to be known as the jīva. Whatever that jīva thinks, it becomes that instantly. Hence, the attempt to gain control over the self or the senses should be directed to that self-awareness. The mind (citta) is the commander-in-chief and the senses are the armed forces. Hence, control of the mind is control (or victory) over the senses. If one's feet are covered with leather shoes, the entire world is covered with leather!

When one's awareness is raised to one's heart and firmly set in the pure consciousness, the mind naturally and effortlessly becomes tranquil. It does not become tranquil by other means like austerities, pilgrimage and rituals. When thus the awareness of the self becomes aware of the experience, then the experience does not leave an impression or memory on consciousness and is immediately 'forgotten', as it were. Even an attempt to do this takes one closer to the supreme state of self-knowledge.

Be firmly rooted in the contented state in which you know only that to be yours which is obtained in the course of the due performance of your own appropriate action. He is a man of self-conquest who rests in peace and contentment performing whatever has to be performed and avoiding what should be avoided. His mind is at rest who enjoys observing or watching himself and is disinterested in external events and observations. When one's awareness is thus firmly held within oneself, the mind abandons its usual restlessness and flows towards wisdom. The wise man attains victory over the senses and does not drown in the waves of vāsanās or mental conditioning. He sees the world as it is. Then the illusion of saṃsāra or world-appearance ceases and with it all sorrow comes to an end.

When one realises that it is the pure consciousness alone (which is beyond thought and which therefore never becomes the object of perception or experience) which appears as this world, what is bondage and what is liberation? Dehydrated water does not flow; uncaused experience does not create a psychological division. Experience is like space which puts on the different forms of 'I' and 'you', etc., and which seems to create a diversity where none can arise. That which fills this space is pure consciousness, beside which nothing exists.

VASIṢṬHA continued:

When there is direct experience of the truth that 'I am neither the doer nor the action nor the instrument, but I am the pure consciousness, and the world is indefinable', then it is known that there is self-awareness. The world appears to be what it is not: hence the self-knowledge that reveals the world is the supreme truth.

In the case of a being with several limbs, it is one being with several limbs; even so Brahman is one being with countless limbs known as jīva, etc. The object is but an appearance; consciousness is infinite peace which exists forever unmodified. It is useless to investigate these as if they are different. In the infinite there are infinite notions; the latter are called 'ignorance'; there is no other ignorance here.

The jīva alternately passes from the waking to the dreaming and from the dreaming to the waking states; but he is constant whether he is awake or asleep. The two states of deep sleep and turīya (the fourth state) are the reality underlying both the waking and the dream states; the two latter are identical and in fact it is the turīya that knows all the others. To the enlightened, the waking, the dreaming and the deep sleep states are only the turīya, for in the turīya there is no ignorance. Therefore, though there appears to be a diversity in it, it is non-dual. It is only the childish and ignorant people who talk of duality and non-duality; the enlightened ones laugh at all this. However, without such discussion based on duality and non-duality it is not possible to clean one's consciousness of ignorance. It is only in that spirit that I have dealt with all this, as your dear friend.

The wise ones do constantly talk about this truth, thus enlightening one another. When they thus contemplate this truth constantly, they gain enlightenment (buddhi-yoga) by which they attain the highest state. (NOTE: These two verses also resemble the Gita, but with the significant alteration in the second which makes it seem that when the student is ready, enlightenment happens. S.V.)

The supreme state is not attained without effort. Thus, in order to help you get a clear grasp of the truth I have explained it repeatedly, using different illustrations. If even an ignorant person tastes this truth thus expounded again and again, he will attain enlightenment. He is surely a fool who thinks "I know this and I have nothing more to know" after once reading this. The knowledge that is gained by a study of this scripture is not gained by the study of any other scripture. This scripture bestows on you both efficiency in action and perfection in wisdom.

VI.2:164, 165 VASIṢṬHA continued:

In the infinite consciousness (which may be compared to the orb of the sun) there are countless particles of light, called jīvas. When one says, "They are in it", they are considered its parts, but in fact it has no such parts. The many abandons its diversity when it attains enlightenment. However, when it (the many) is described as the one, it has not become something other than it was before. It is the same in all conditions and states. It is the content of the consciousness or awareness of the sage of wisdom. That alone is; nothing else has ever existed. It is with the help of that consciousness alone that the ignorant apprehend the object of their own ignorance. We do not know the 'I' or the 'you' or even the object that the ignorant perceive in their ignorance. The feelings 'I am enlightened' and 'He is ignorant' and 'This is the truth' do not arise in the enlightened. This that is known as the creation has never been created nor has it ever come into being. This world is Brahman which is as it is here. Therefore, there do not exist any ignorant people or beings here. There is only the infinite space in which such notions as 'This is Brahmā the creator', etc., float around.

The consciousness that exists in the waking state enters the dream state and becomes dream. The dream-consciousness being awake in the dream attains the status of wakefulness in dream. The dream state enters the waking state; and the waking state abandons the dream and wakes up. When the waking state enters into the dream state, the dreamer wakes up, as it were. The dreamer regards the waking state as a dream; to him the consciousness of the dream is the real waking state. Surely, to the dreamer the true waking state is the dream, not the other waking state.

In relation to the waking state, the dream seems to be short-lived. Even so the dreamer regards the waking state to be brief. There is no difference whatsoever between the two, and neither of them is real. When awareness ceases, both waking and dreaming cease. There is void. The living person does not experience 'the other world' either in dream or in waking, not till the consciousness of death arises. Just as dreams arise in consciousness and create the three worlds, even so the world appears in the waking state. Just as the dream-creation is pure void, even so the world of the waking state is void except for the infinite consciousness in which alone the appearance arises. The world is the illusion that appears in consciousness on account of its inherent power. Consciousness alone shines as the water, earth, space and walls. There is nothing in it which can be grasped or held.

VASIṢṬHA continued: VI.2:166

The self or the infinite consciousness is the most obvious truth, which does not stand in need of and is independent of the words like 'self' or 'knowledge'. Right from the beginning of the original creation, this infinite consciousness alone exists, with this notion of creation. Wise men and scholars have declared that self-knowledge is devoid of notions and of knowledge of material objects. But all this is the self alone. No knowledge (category) called non-knowledge has ever been known here. Knowledge and non-knowledge (ignorance) are two concepts which do not have corresponding realities. What is there to know or not to know? Knowledge of what is, knowledge that this is this, and knowledge that it is unreal—all these arise in consciousness. Knowledge of the self, knowledge of the unreal, absence of knowledge, knowledge that the truth is other than the appearance —all these are but the play of the infinite consciousness and they are the manifestations or expansions of self-knowledge.

The fact of self-knowledge exists even when the term 'self-knowledge' has been discarded. Self-knowledge alone is. Let me illustrate it. There is a mighty rock which is vast and whose sides are the blue sky. It has no joints because it has no divisions. It is absolutely solid and undivided. It is imperishable. It is incomparable and unique. Its origin is unknown. Its content is non-material but solid. Within it are countless impressions or images, known to itself as the jīva. It is sentient and insentient.

No one is able to break it. However, in it are these impressions known as gods, demons and humans, with forms and without forms. I have seen these impressions that exist within the rock. If you wish, you can also see them.

RĀMA asked: If that rock was indivisible, how could you see inside it?

VASIṢṬHA said:

Indeed no one can break it. But since I am within that rock

as an impression in it, I am able to see all the rest.

It is the supreme reality or the self that I have thus described to you. We are integral parts of that indivisible, infinite consciousness. This space, wind and other elements, all these actions and activities, all these conditionings and the time-sense—all these are limbs of that being. Earth, water, fire, air, space, mind, buddhi and the ego-sense are limbs of that supreme self. What else is there other than this infinite consciousness? The objects of this world are but pure awareness or experiencing which is a mass of pure consciousness.

VI.2:167 VASIṢṬHA continued:

Self-knowledge, non-knowledge or knowledge of the unreal, etc., are words and viewpoints. They are totally unreal in the eyes of the knower of truth. All these arise in the pure consciousness which is clearly seen in me. 'This is the self' and 'This is knowledge'—these are surely false notions that arise within, but they are not real. Abandon the words but remain established in the experience of the truth they indicate.

Though countless activities go on within it, it is utterly silent and tranquil. Though it is described in countless superlatives, it remains undisturbed. Though it is constantly in motion, it remains stable like a rock. Though it is the very substance in the five elements, it is unaffected by them like space. Though it is the abode of all objects, it remains pure consciousness. Though it is seen, like a dream-city, it remains unseen consciousness.

RĀMA said:

Just as memory is at the root of the perception in both the waking and the dream states, it is memory alone that gives rise to the feeling that the external objects are real.

VASIṢṬHA continued:

The appearance of diverse objects in the universe arises in the infinite consciousness when it becomes aware of itself—coincidentally (like a ripe cocoanut falling when a crow alights on it). Whenever and wherever this consciousness contemplates itself in whatever manner, then and there it appears so, without any cause. The notions 'This is waking', 'This is dream', 'This is sleep' and 'This is turīya' arise in consciousness because they are consciousness. In fact there is neither dream nor waking state nor sleep nor turīya nor something beyond: everything is pure tranquility and silence. Or, one may say that all this is waking at all times, or dream or deep sleep or turīya. Or we do not know what it is, for everything is experienced to be what it is thought of.

Its manifestation and unmanifestation—knowledge or ignorance—are two inherent states—like the movement or non-movement of air.

Therefore, there is no distinction in the states of waking, etc., nor is there anything known as memory or desire. All these are limited vision. When it is only inner experience that shines as external object, where is objectivity or memory? Memory can arise only from experience and experience is possible only if the object is real. The notional appearance of the infinite consciousness becomes later known as the earth, etc. Let this consciousness shine as it will: it is neither real nor unreal, neither something nor nothing. That itself dwells in the heart as the notion of an object which is conceived to be outside. What is 'inside' or 'outside'? Consider it OM and rest in peace.

VASIṢṬHA continued: VI.2:168

Just as a tree brings forth diverse beautiful branches without mental activity or volition (intention), even so the unborn and uncreated infinite consciousness gives rise to diverse and colourful world-appearance (creation). It is like space giving rise to space. Just as the ocean gives rise to whirlpools without mental activity or intention, even so, without intending to do so, consciousness gives rise to every kind of experience, because it is the lord of all. To those very experiences the same consciousness gives various 'names' like 'mind', 'buddhi', 'egosense', etc. Again without mental activity and intention, the infinite consciousness has given rise within itself to the notion of an object with all the sequence of buddhi, etc. Even the world order (niyati), which includes the fundamental characteristic of the objects, arises in the infinite consciousness without any intention or mental activity whatsoever.

Moreover, it is all one: the tree includes the trunk, the branches, the leaves and the flowers—the distinction being verbal. Even so the infinite consciousness includes everything, the distinction being verbal. If you still ask, "Why then is this futile experience of the objects?", it is good to remind yourself that all this is but a long dream. Who will resort to the non-existent or the hidden thing? Just as we have formed in our mind an image 'This is a tree', in the infinite consciousness there exist images of space, etc. Just as space (distance) is indistinguishably one with space and movement with air, even so the buddhi (intelligence) etc., are with the supreme being or the infinite consciousness. This creation is non-different from the infinite consciousness.

This creation appears right from the beginning in the infinite consciousness as if in a dream. This appearance, moreover, has no cause. How then can it be other than the infinite consciousness? It is analogous to the dream which is a daily universal experience: hence one should investigate it. What is the essence or the reality in the dream except the pure intelligence or consciousness which creates it and in which it exists?

This creation does not arise as a 'memory' in the infinite consciousness. It arises in the consciousness without any reason or cause whatsoever (it is a coincidence like the ripe cocoanut falling when a crow alights on it); dreaming, conceptualisation, etc., follow later. Once this creation has arisen without any cause in the infinite consciousness, its 'existence' follows later. Therefore, even though this creation seems to have been created, it has not been created; when thus it has not been created at all, surely it does not exist.

In the pure space of the infinite consciousness these countless world-appearances exist. They come into being and they dissolve, though they are all essentially void (śūnya) in their nature. They react upon one another and thus create this world-appearance though they are essentially void (śūnya). This creation is void, and the void grows and the void alone ceases to be (void because it is devoid of the notion of a 'self').

VASIṢṬHA continued:

Creation of the universe and its dissolution are only deluded notions that arise in consciousness; when the notion of creation remains sustained for a long time, it is taken to be real. The objective appearance of the universe appears spontaneously in the cosmic being, just as a dream arises after a period of deep sleep. Consciousness alone shines as this universe which therefore is its body. After this, consciousness itself gives rise within itself to the notions of memory and psychological categories, earth and the other elements.

RĀMA asked:

Lord, memories are the impressions that are left on the buddhi. If such impressions, and therefore memories, are absent, how can anything come into being, or even notions arise?

VASIṢṬHA replied:

I shall presently dispel your doubt, O Rāma, and establish non-duality. This world-appearance is like a figure that has not been carved out of the tree. Only when a figure is actually carved out of the tree, does it become a figure: but since the infinite consciousness is non-dual, such a thing does not happen. In the inert and insentient wood the figure does not emerge until it is actually carved. But, since consciousness is full of consciousness, the world-appearance shines within itself. In fact, consciousness never ceases to be consciousness, nor is the world carved out of it: yet it shines as this world.

In the beginning of creation, consciousness, being full of potential notions, manifests them. Since those notions are also endowed with consciousness, they appear to be real, as in a dream. Within the space of the heart itself, consciousness gives rise to various notions: 'This is the notion of Brahman; this itself is the notion of pure consciousness.' 'This is the notion of jīva', and 'This is the egosense, buddhi, mind, time and space'. 'I am so and so.' 'This is activity.' 'These are the elements.' 'These are the senses.' 'This is the subtle (puryaṣṭaka) body and that is the gross physical body.' 'I am Brahmā the creator, I am Śiva, I am Viṣṇu, I am the sun.' 'This is inside and that is outside.' 'This is creation and this is world'. . . . Such notions arise in consciousness itself. There are neither physical or material substances, nor memory, nor duality.

Without cause this world-appearance arises in consciousness. It is experienced by the consciousness within itself. It is consciousness which considers itself the world and experiences the world. There is therefore no memory, or dream or time, etc. involved in this. This which is a mass of consciousness within appears to be the world outside; however, there is neither an outside nor an inside, nothing whatsoever except the supreme reality. Therefore, just as the infinite Brahman is real, in the same way this observed objective universe is also real.

VASIṢṬHA continued: VI.2:169

He to whom joy is no joy and sorrow is no sorrow, is a liberated one. He whose heart is not agitated even while being engaged in pleasure is a liberated one. He is a liberated one who rejoices in pure consciousness itself, as well as in the objective world.

RĀMA asked:

If the liberated one does not find pleasure in pleasure and sorrow in sorrow, then surely he is insentient and insensitive.

VASIṢṬHA continued:

Because his awareness is totally absorbed in consciousness, he does not experience pleasure unless he makes an effort to do so. He is said to rest in consciousness. His doubts have been dissolved and his contact with all the objects of the world is flavoured by wisdom. The world has lost its 'taste' for him, though he is still active in it, doing what needs to be done from moment to moment.

On account of the fact that the liberated ones thus rest in the self or consciousness, they appear to be asleep though they are engaged in activity. In fact, they are not insentient nor insensitive. They are considered to be 'asleep' because they treat this world-appearance as if it were a long dream, not because they are insentient. They rest in that truth or supreme peace which is utterly dark as night to the ignorant: therefore they are considered to be asleep, but they are not insentient. Since they are disinterested in the world of the ignorant, they are considered to be asleep in the world. They rejoice in the self at all times; hence they are not insentient. They have risen above sorrow.

Having roamed this saṃsāra and experienced all kinds of pleasure and pain, the jīva has the good fortune to come into contact with a holy man and cross this ocean of saṃsāra. He sleeps in great peace even without a bed. Though he is engaged in intense activity here, he enjoys the peace of deep sleep. This is a great wonder. This 'sleep' cannot be disturbed by anything. He is truly intoxicated who does not see 'the world' even though his eyes are wide open. He enjoys the bliss of deep sleep. He has dispelled the notion of the world from his heart and he has reached fullness. He has quaffed nectar and he is at peace. His delight is independent of pleasure. He has turned away from greed. He knows that in every atom there is a universe. He is engaged in diverse and intense activity, though he does nothing. He is aware that this world-appearance has the same reality as a dream, thus he has entered into the peace and the bliss of deep sleep. His consciousness is more expansive than even space. By a supreme self-effort, he has realised self-knowledge and he lives as if he were seeing a long dream in pure space. He is fully awake and enlightened, though he appears to be asleep; he enjoys the greatest delight, though he appears to be asleep. He has reached the highest state.

VI.2:170 RĀMA asked:

Lord, who is the wise man's friend, with whom does he enjoy, what is his enjoyment or delight and in what manner does he enjoy those pleasures?

VASIṢṬHA replied:

The wise man's friend, O Rāma, is his own action which arises spontaneously in him and in which there is no division or conflict. Like a father, it encourages him and provides him with enthusiasm. Like a wife, it checks him, restrains him and guides him. It does not abandon him even in the worst calamities. It is free from doubt. It promotes the spirit of renunciation. Because it turns anger and hate upon themselves, it is like quaffing nectar. It is his friend and helper even in the densest forest of troubles and difficulties. It is the treasure chest which contains the precious gems of faith. It saves him from evil and like a father, it is ever intent on protecting him.

It (one's own action) brings him every type of delight. In all kinds of situations and conditions, it promotes the health of his body. It reveals to him 'This is to be done' and 'This is not to be done'. It is intent on bringing desirable objects and experiences and warding off undesirable objects and experiences. It causes the speech to be soft and pleasant and it causes one's behaviour also to be soft and sweet, helpful, adorable, free from selfish desires or passions and conducive to the supreme attainment of self-knowledge. It is devoted to the protection of the good and the community as a whole. It prevents illnesses of the body and the mind. It promotes the happiness of learned men by engaging in healthy discussions with them. In the case of equals, there is just a semblance of duality. Whatever may be one's station in life, it (one's own action) is devoted to self-sacrifice, charity, austerity and pilgrimage. It establishes a healthy relation with the son, wife, brāhmaṇas, servants and relatives by means of the sharing of food and drink. The wise man by his very nature enjoys the company of such a bosom-friend, along with the latter's consort. That friend is known as one's own action.

This friend (one's own action) has sons who are known as bathing (purity of body), charity, austerity and meditation. They, too, promote the welfare and happiness of all beings. The spirit of happiness (or a happy spirit) is its wife who showers happiness on all naturally and effortlessly. Her name is samatā (equanimity or evenness of mind). She encourages her husband (natural action) in the performance of righteous or appropriate action.

She has another constant companion known as maitrī (friendliness).

The wise man who enjoys the company of this best of all friends with its wife and other companions has no need to rejoice when he is in joy or pleasure or grieve when in unpleasant situations. He does not hate nor become angered. Wherever and in whatever condition he is, he enjoys the state of nirvāṇa, though he is constantly engaged in the activities of the world. He is silent in useless arguments, he is deaf to useless talk, he is a corpse in relation to unrighteous actions, he is very much alive in righteous actions, he is brilliant in exposing what is auspicious and in a moment he reveals the greatest truth.

All this is natural to the wise man. He does not have to strive to acquire these qualities.

VASIṢṬHA continued: VI.2:171

It is the infinite consciousness alone that shines as the world here. In reality, however, it is neither world, nor void nor even consciousness. Only this much can be said: that which is called world is not that. Because it is subtler than even space, it appears to be other than what it is.

Between 'this' and 'that' is the body of consciousness and that body is experienced as an object of perception. However, such a creation has no cause and hence there was no reason for it to arise. How then can it be said to exist now? Therefore, there is no justification to assume the existence of the external universe—not even an atom of it. If something is seen as the external universe here, surely that is the infinite consciousness in fact. Just as the same person who is fast asleep goes on to dream without abandoning his sleep, even so this consciousness which is pure and indivisible gives rise within itself to the notion of the objective universe, without ever abandoning its own essential nature as consciousness. Therefore there is no materiality known as earth, etc., but, whether one feels that what one sees are forms or not forms, the final truth is that all this is the one infinite Brahman which alone shines as all these. Just as the dream-mountain is realised as pure void when the dreamer wakes up, even so are all these forms realised to be non-existent when one is enlightened.

This world is the indivisible and supreme Brahman to those who are enlightened. Though we are highly intelligent, we do not know what non-enlightenment (ignorance) is. Between 'this' and 'that' is the mass of consciousness which is the essential nature of all beings. That is the supreme state of the self. Between 'this' and 'that' is that infinite space which is the mass of consciousness in which everything is firmly established. Whatever is that mass of consciousness, that alone is all this—real and unreal at the same time. Form, perception and also the corresponding concepts that arise in the mind are all pure consciousness, even as whirlpools are in the ocean. Between 'this' and 'that' is the infinite consciousness; when that is realised without any modification or subtraction whatsoever, it is seen that it alone is and that there is no world. Then even attraction and aversion, existence and non-existence become its own limbs, without in any way affecting the true nature of the consciousness. Between the two 'ends' is the pure consciousness; the 'ends' are but concepts and do not exist independent of the reality which is the middle—that is the essential nature of the infinite self or consciousness. For that consciousness which exists between 'this' and 'that' another name is 'world'.

Right from the very beginning, the creation has not come into being at all. To say that this world exists as such is pure fiction. It is a pity and it is a tragedy that people say that this world exists (though it does not) and that the supreme Brahman does not exist (though it alone exists).

VASIṢṬHA continued:

Where shall I go for that which is not Brahman or the infinite consciousness? Alas, the world is a strange place where people regard the unreal world (the object of perception) to be real. Yet they do reach the same Brahman. The radiance of a precious gem is not its creation nor is it independent of the gem: even so, the world-appearance is non-different from the self which is pure consciousness. The sun shines in that supreme state of consciousness; the sun is non-different from that self. However, neither the sun nor the moon can illumine or reveal the self. It is because of the inherent power of that consciousness that the sun and the moon themselves shine and thus illumine and reveal the objects of perception.

That consciousness is with form and it is without form—all these are words and meaningless concepts. Particles of light that constitute the rays of the sun are the rays of the sun, non-different from it. So it is right to say that they shine and also to say that they do not shine. Even so, it is right to say that the sun and the moon shine; and it is also right to say that they do not. Since the sun and all the other luminous bodies shine because of the infinite consciousness, how can it be said that they do not shine or it does not shine?

That supreme state is beyond all concepts, even those of 'mass of consciousness' and 'void'; it is devoid of everything but it is also full of everything. Hence, the earth, etc., do exist; on the other hand, nothing exists in it. Though there are infinite jīvas in it, yet they do not exist as jīvas independent of the consciousness. 'Something', 'nothing', etc., are concepts which are far from the reality or the infinite consciousness.

The pure consciousness, which is non-dual, eternal and all-pervading, exists and is known as 'world'. When merely the objectivity of all this is removed, what remains of the world of diversity is the truth. It is that consciousness itself which is manifest as the infinite experiences. The waking state of consciousness stands in exactly the same relation to the turīya (transcendental) state as the dream state stands in relation to the deep sleep state. To the enlightened person, however, all these states are but one turīya state of consciousness.

Theories concerning creation or the transformation of the self or consciousness into matter are expressions used by teachers while instructing students; there is not an iota of truth in all this. When one realises the dream as a dream, then there is joy, but if this is not realised then there is unhappiness when one dreams of an unhappy event. The enlightened sage lives in a state of realisation of the truth even while he engages himself in diverse activities. In diversity he experiences unity; he rejoices even in unpleasant situations. Though he lives in the world he is really not in it. What more does an enlightened person have to gain? Just as ice is ever cool, the sage lives a natural life, doing what is natural to him, without aspiring for or abandoning anything. The characteristic of the ignorant man is that he strives to be other than what he is.

VASIṢṬHA continued: VI.2:172

The Creator is only the mind, devoid of any trace of materiality.

Hence, he has no body or the senses or vāsanā or mental conditioning. Since he had attained liberation at the end of the previous world-cycle, there is no memory in him. When there is no memory at all, there is no cause for embodiment. Even if such memory were possible in the Creator, even that would be devoid of matter, like a dream-city. However, this is said for the sake of argument: memory is impossible in the liberated ones.

RĀMA asked:

Lord, tell me why is there no memory in them and how the guṇas (the building blocks of creation) arise in the absence of memory.

VASIṢṬHA replied:

Memory arises only in relation to the objective universe, thus providing the cause-and-effect sequence. When such an object of perception itself is non-existent, how and where does memory arise or exist? When the truth is that all this is indeed Brahman or the infinite consciousness, there is no room for memory.

The contemplation of objects that arises in living beings is considered smṛti (remembrance). Of course such objects are non-existent. How can smṛti exist then? However, since the infinite consciousness is the reality in all beings, such contemplation of objects is, in a manner of speaking, inherent in consciousness—hence I referred to smṛti. However, it is only from the point of view of the common ignorant men. Enough of it. The natural movement that arises in consciousness is also known as smṛti. When that movement occurs repeatedly it is seen externally as matter. Whatever the consciousness experiences by its own nature, that is said to be smṛti. All these experiences arise in the infinite consciousness of their own accord, as the very limbs of consciousness, without any causal connection (just as a ripe cocoanut falls coincidentally when a crow happens to alight on it). They are called memory. This is true of all happenings, even when there appears to be coincidental cause.

Why should we investigate memory which is thus accidental, when we realise that the objects of perception to which it is related themselves are non-existent? They exist only in the eyes of the ignorant. I am not expounding the means of liberation for the benefit of such ignorant people. It is only meant for those who have been awakened but who have some doubts concerning it. One should never associate with ignorant people who cannot recognise the truth. When a thing is experienced by the consciousness even just a little and when that experience is repeated, a mental impression (saṃskāra) is created. Thus is the world-appearance created. However, all this is pervaded by the infinite consciousness. There is neither a form nor memory related to it. When duality itself is non-existent, then surely there is no bondage.

RĀMA asked: VI.2:173

How does the omnipresent consciousness identify itself with the body? How does consciousness identify itself with rocks and wood?

VASIṢṬHA replied:

Even as the embodied being identifies itself with the hand, so the infinite consciousness identifies itself with the body. In the same way as the body identifies itself with the nails and the hair, the omnipresent self identifies itself with rocks and wood, etc. Just as it is pure consciousness alone that becomes rocks and wood in a dream, these notions arose in the infinite consciousness right in the beginning of creation. Just as in an individual's body there are sentient and insentient parts, even so in the cosmic body of the infinite consciousness there are apparently sentient and insentient objects, whereas in truth there are no such forms. When all this is clearly seen they cease to appear, just as a dream vanishes the moment the dreamer awakes. All this is pure consciousness; there is neither a seer nor an object of perception.

Thousands of world-cycles may arise and cease in the infinite consciousness, yet they are non-different from the infinite consciousness, even as waves are non-different from the ocean. 'I am not a wave, I am the ocean'—when thus the truth is realised, the wave-ness ceases. The world-appearance is like the wave in relation to Brahman which is the ocean. The existence and the non-existence of this world-appearance are the two ways in which the energy inherent in Brahman manifests.

The experience that arises in consciousness, as in a dream, is known as mind, Brahmā the creator, the grandfather of all creation. This being is nameless, formless and immutable. In that, the notions of 'I' and 'you', etc., arise. Even they are non-different from the Creator. The pure consciousness in which all these notions arise is the great-grandfather of all creatures. Just as the waves which rise and fall on the ocean are only the ocean and non-different from it, all these creations and dissolutions are non-different from the infinite consciousness.

The movement of energy that occurs in the infinite consciousness is known as the cosmic person who is endowed with a magnetic field and gravitational force. This creation arises in him like a dream. Creation is a dream. The waking state is a dream. Even though this creation or world-appearance is apparently seen and experienced, it is in reality the realisation of the notions that arise in us, and they alone exist as the cosmic personality. Consciousness itself experiences the notions that arise in it again and again. It is that cosmic person who is pervaded and permeated by consciousness that appears as all the dream-objects. Just as an actor who dreams that he is acting sees himself acting on a stage entertaining an audience, this consciousness becomes aware of its own experience of this world-appearance.

VI.2:174 VASIṢṬHA continued:

It is consciousness alone that shines as this universe right in the very beginning of creation. Therefore, the three worlds are non-different from Brahman. Brahman is like the ocean; in it the creations are like the waves and experiencing is the water. Even after this (creation), there is pure unconditioned bliss. Where are duality, non-duality or anything else? Both deep sleep and dreaming are alternating states that arise during sleep; even so, appearance and disappearance of this creation are alternating events in the infinite consciousness.

When the wise one realises that this world is like a dream-city, his hopes are not centered in it. The day-dreamer dreams of a great diversity of visions and hopes. Though there seems to be some reality in such day-dreams, they are in fact non-existent. If, however, you are looking for some other explanation for this world-appearance, why do you not accept the possibility of delusion or delirious notions and hallucination?

The practice of contemplation in which the mind is restrained from undergoing any modification is as good as supreme inertia; on the other hand, when such modifications exist in the mind, it is the seat of diversity or saṃsāra. By such contemplation a state of equanimity is not attained. If it is claimed that liberation is attained when the mind is forcibly restrained from all modifications, then why is it not attained in sleep? Therefore, only when it is realised that there is no creation at all, does real self-knowledge arise which leads to liberation. Such liberation is unending, infinite and unconditioned—truly nirvikalpa samādhāna (samādhi). In it one remains firmly rooted in self-knowledge, without the least agitation. It is also known as eternal sleep, turīya, nirvāṇa and mokṣa.

Dhyāna or contemplation or meditation is perfect awakening or enlightenment. The realisation that the objective universe does not exist is perfect awakening. It does not resemble a state of inertia, nor deep sleep, nor nirvikalpa samādhi nor savikalpa samādhi, nor is it an unreal imaginary state. In it the universe exists as it is but it is dissolved at the same time. In it there are no concepts of unity, diversity, their mixture and their non-existence. In it there is supreme peace.

That perfect awakening is attained by a careful investigation of this scripture constantly, day and night, not by pilgrimage nor by charity, not by acquiring knowledge nor by the practice of meditation or yoga, not by austerity (penance) nor by religious rites. By none of these methods does illusion come to an end. They only lead to heaven and such other rewards, not to liberation. Delusion ends only when self-knowledge arises in one who has carefully studied and investigated this scripture.

VASIṢṬHA continued: VI.2:175

In the beginning neither this world nor the other world came into being in the infinite consciousness. An unreal, imaginary experience arose in consciousness, just like the experience of embracing a woman in a dream. Only the dreamer exists in the dream; only the infinite consciousness exists in the unreal experience. What appears to be the world thus arises in that consciousness which is ever pure. How can impurity arise in the pure consciousness? This experience is also pure. That itself is the dream-city or the dream-creation. That is the world, for in the very beginning of creation there was no earth, etc. It was the movement of energy in the infinite consciousness that subsequently created earth and the physical elements, mind and other psychological categories, which were nothing but notions in consciousness. This movement of energy is like the inherent motion in air which takes place without mental activity or intention.

Consciousness appears in consciousness as its own body or materialisation. The mind itself appears to be the objects of perception, just as in dream. There is no other cause possible. Hence, there is no duality and there is no division in consciousness. The supreme Brahman is free from all forms; that itself when it appears to have a form is this world-appearance. This exists eternally. Just as diversity arises in the one during a dream, this world-appearance of diversity seems to arise in the one infinite Brahman.

The mind itself is Brahmā the creator. It is in the very heart of this creation and it alone does everything and destroys everything. When one thoroughly investigates all this it is clearly seen that the pure consciousness alone exists and nothing else. It is beyond description. At the end of the investigation utter silence alone remains. Though engaged in all activities, it remains unaffected like space, as if it were dumb. The enlightened one, therefore, attains a knowledge of the infinite and remains utterly silent. He is the best among men.

Brahmā the creator brings about this world-appearance without intending to do so. The infinite consciousness with its 'eyes closed' is itself; and with its 'eyes opened' it is the world. But the infinite consciousness remains itself in both these states. Hence, it is both 'is' and 'is-not', real and unreal. These two states constantly alternate; one is never without the other. Therefore, know the truth as it is, as supreme peace, and know that it is unborn and undying space. Know, too, that the world-appearance is like it, though it is sometimes unlike it. The objective universe has never arisen, nor does it cease, though it is apparently experienced now. It is a mysterious product of the energy or the power of the infinite consciousness.

Whatever is experienced whenever and wherever, that seems to exist then and there, whether it is real or unreal. No other reason is appropriate.

VASIṢṬHA continued:

Whatever one constantly contemplates, whatever constantly occupies one's mind and to whatever one is devoted with all his life, that he knows to be real and obvious. When the mind is saturated with consciousness of Brahman it becomes that; whatever the mind loves most it becomes that. When one's mind rests in the supreme reality or the infinite consciousness, then one engages himself in righteous activity without being interested in the activity itself for its own sake.

When this objective universe itself does not exist or when one cannot affirm or deny its existence, it is not possible to determine who is the doer of actions and the enjoyer of experiences. What is commonly known as Brahmā the creator or buddhi the awakened intelligence, etc., is itself the infinite consciousness which is absolutely pure. The peace in the sky is pure void. The appearance of duality in all these is illusory and non-existent. Therefore, diversity is a meaningless concept. Just as one enters into the dream state after the deep sleep state, the same infinite consciousness moves to the creation state from the state of absolute quiescence; in it there is no duality or unity. The infinite consciousness perceives this creation within the space of its own consciousness.

Just as there is no definite sequence or order or causal connection in dreams, in this world-appearance there is no definite causal connection or sequence, though it appears to have one. There is no division in dream; nor is there a division in the objects of perception. It is the same Brahman or infinite consciousness that appears in front of you as this universe or creation. In dream there is no recognition of the objects seen in the dream nor is there saṃskāra (mental impression) nor even memory, because the dreamer does not think, 'I have seen this before'. Similarly, in the waking state, too, when these three considerations are removed, there is the infinite consciousness alone which the ignorant man identifies with memory.

Affirmations and negations, injunctions and prohibitions seem to exist in the supreme being, though they do not exist in it. When a man is dizzy he feels that the world is going around him, though the dizziness is in him. Even when one knows this and knows that the objective universe is delusion or illusion, it does not disappear except through persistent practice. Hence, this illusion ceases only through the devout study of this scripture—there is no other way. It is by self-knowledge or enlightenment that these three (the mind, the objects of perception and the body) will reach a quiescent state of equanimity, not otherwise. For these three arise from ignorance. By a mere study of this scripture that ignorance is dispelled. The beauty in this scripture is that its student is not abandoned to his despair; if something is not clear in the first instance, a further study of the scripture makes it clear. This scripture dispels delusion and enables you to realise that the ordinary life itself is the supreme state.

Therefore, one should study at least a small part of this scripture daily. If, however, one thinks it is not authoritative because it is of human origin, one can resort to the study of any other scripture dealing with self-knowledge and final liberation. But one should not waste one's lifetime.

RĀMA asked: VI.2:176

When thus there are countless universes arising and dissolving in the infinite consciousness, why do you teach me of their nature?

VASIṢṬHA replied:

It was in that way that you have gained the understanding that the world is a long dream. You have gained knowledge of the relationship between a word and its meaning or the object it denotes. Hence, all this discussion of the world-appearance and imaginary creation has not been in vain. That illustration best serves its purpose of bringing home a spiritual truth which enables one to understand the word and its corresponding concept; and only that becomes a living truth to guide one in one's daily living. When, having known all that there is to be known, you attain knowledge of the three periods of time (past, present and future), you will see all this to be true.

In every atom of this existence there are countless universes—who has the power even to count them? In this connection I recall a story which my father Brahmā the creator once narrated to me. I shall presently narrate it to you—pray listen. I asked my father Brahmā, "What is this world-appearance and where does it exist?"

BRAHMĀ said:

All this that appears as this universe, O sage, is nothing but the infinite consciousness, Brahman. The wise know this to be pure satva (the unconditioned intelligence) which is infinite; and the ignorant see it as the material universe. I shall illustrate this truth with the following narrative concerning this Brahmāṇḍa (the cosmic egg).

In this limitless space there is the infinite self which is non-different from that space. That self perceived itself within itself as a jīva, a conditioned and living entity. Without at any time abandoning its own essential nature as the infinite space, it considered itself as 'I am' or the egosense, though still with space for its body. This 'I am' expanded into 'I am buddhi or the intellect'. It then saw itself as the buddhi which determines what is 'this' and what is 'that', but which follows the basic illusion of conditioned perception. After this, that itself entertained the notion 'I am mind' and became involved in notions or diverse and perverse thinking. That mind thereupon conceived the notion of the existence of the five senses which, though they are formless, appear to be gross and material, like mountains seen in a dream. The mind assumed that it had a body composed of the three worlds with a variety of creatures with all sorts of relationships which were assumed to exist between them, all these subject to time.

Thus it saw everything as one sees diverse objects in a mirror. What it saw was enchanting and colourful. In every subatomic particle there exist such universes. Ignorance thinks of all this as ignorance and as limitless creation; but, when it is realised as Brahman it itself becomes the pure Brahman. Even if all this is actually seen, nothing is seen because all this is but a dream. Who is the perceiver here, what is perceived, how can there be duality in the infinite being?

VI.2:177 RĀMA asked:

The world-appearance arises in the infinite consciousness without any cause at all. That being so, why do not such uncaused events continue to happen even now?

VASIṢṬHA replied:

Whatever notion one entertains, one perceives that to be true. In Brahman both causation and causelessness exist, since Brahman is omnipotent. Even so in the case of a living being, the intelligent body has also inert hair and nails. If something other than Brahman is experienced, then surely there is perverse causation which is responsible for that. But, when only the one infinite consciousness shines everywhere, in that what is the cause and what is the result?

RĀMA asked:

In the case of the ignorant, however, there is causal sequence. What is uncaused in him and how does it exist?

VASIṢṬHA replied:

To the enlightened one, there is none who is ignorant. Why should we waste our time discussing what is non-existent?

There are some things which are caused and there are others which do not have a cause. It depends upon one's point of view; what one regards as valid that alone he accepts as valid. This creation has no cause at all. The belief that the world was created by god, etc., is a play of words. There is nothing that illustrates this truth as the experience of dream does.

If the creation as a dream is not clearly understood, there is great delusion. If it is rightly understood, delusion vanishes. Speculative reasoning advanced in connection with this creation is ignorance and foolishness. Is fire the 'cause' of the heat which is natural to it? The constituents of the body are in fact formless, ethereal substances; hence the physical body has no real cause. Also, what can be the cause of the body which experiences the non-existent universe?

All this is natural to nature (whatever it may be) even if a cause may be assumed. Even the word 'nature' that is used here is a figure of speech. Therefore, all these objects and their assumed causes are but delusions that arise in the mind of the ignorant. The wise ones know that all effects proceed from causes. When one dreams of being robbed and when one knows that it was but a dream, there is no sorrow: even so, when the truth is realised life is freed from sorrow.

The truth certainly is that this universe has never been created, as creation had no cause in the first place. It came into being and it exists as a dream-object exists in the infinite consciousness. It is Brahman alone and it shines in Brahman. Just as both sleep and dream are aspects of one sleep, even so this creation and dissolution of the universe are two aspects of the one indivisible, infinite consciousness.

RĀMA said: VI.2:178

Lord, there are substances in this world which are divisible and which are indivisible. The divisible ones collide with one another and the indivisible ones do not so collide with one another. For instance, one sees the moon and in a manner of speaking the eyesight strikes the moon without dividing it or touching it. . . . I am asking this question from the point of view of the unawakened person. Who is it that governs the inhalation and the exhalation of the life-breath in the body? The body is solid and it offers resistance; what is that force which is subtle and which has no resistance in itself yet which is able to move the body? If that which is subtle and non-resistant can act on the solid and resistant substance, then why can one not move a mountain by the power of thought alone?

VASIṢṬHA said:

The life-breath enters the body and leaves it during inhalation and exhalation when the subtle nerve-force which rests in the heart expands and contracts like the bellows of the blacksmith.

RĀMA said:

In the case of the bellows of the blacksmith, it is the blacksmith who operates them. What is it that makes the nāḍī in the heart thus expand and contract?

VASIṢṬHA said:

Just as the blacksmith makes the bellows expand and contract in this world, there is an inner consciousness which makes all the inner organs function in the body. It is on account of this that everyone lives and functions in this world.

RĀMA asked again:

But, the body and all its constituents are solid; how does the subtle consciousness move them? For there is no contact between the solid and the subtle.

VASIṢṬHA said:

Listen to this teaching which uproots the whole tree of doubt. There is nothing solid and resistant in this world. All things everywhere are for ever subtle and non-resistant. All this is pure consciousness, which experiences these apparent solid substances as one experiences dream-objects. Earth, water, wind, space, the mountains and the oceans, etc., are all subtle consciousness only. Even so are the mind and all the rest of the inner instruments. In this connection I shall narrate to you an ancient legend. I have already narrated the same story to you in another context. Listening to it, you will realise that all that you see here is pure consciousness and nothing else.

VASIṢṬHA continued:

There once lived a brāhmaṇa named Indu. He had ten sons. In course of time, Indu passed away and his wife too followed him to the other world. The sons performed the funeral. They were not interested in the affairs of the world. They began to consider what might be the best form of contemplation that would enable them to live like gods.

In pursuit of their aspiration, they went away to the forest and they engaged themselves in intense contemplation and penance. They remained like statues or painted pictures. Their bodies withered away and what remained was consumed by carnivores. They were immersed in contemplation, 'I am Brahmā the creator', 'I am the world' and 'I am the entire creation'. Now that the minds of these ten were devoid of embodiment but were saturated with such contemplation, those very minds became what they contemplated. Thus it is their thought that exists as this creation.

This universe is pure consciousness. Even the earth, the mountains, etc., are pure consciousness. What else is it? Just as the minds of the sons of Indu manifested here as the universe, even so the notion of the universe or creation that arises in Brahmā the creator itself appears as this creation. Hence, all these elements, the earth and the mountains are all nothing but pure consciousness.

The potter known as consciousness, with the help of the wheel of his own body (consciousness) and of clay which is also his own body, fashions this creation. If all these creatures and substances are not consciousness, what else are they? This creation stands in the same relation to consciousness as radiance to a jewel. All this is indeed Brahman: this is certain and indisputable.

As and when this truth is clearly seen, immediately there is an end to sorrow. If this truth is not seen, then sorrow becomes firmly and solidly established. The wicked and the ignorant do not see this truth. In their eyes this saṃsāra is a solid reality and they do not perceive this truth at all. There are no forms. There is no existence nor non-existence, no birth and no death. There is nothing known as reality, nor something which can be called unreal. The supreme which is absolute peace perceives this creation within itself—it is not independent of Brahman the infinite consciousness, so why create the false notion of an independent manifestation? In its unliberated form it has thousands of eyes and other limbs; in its liberated state it is all, peace, tranquility—enough of such descriptions.

VASIṢṬHA continued: VI.2:179

All the three worlds are but pure consciousness; they are the unconditioned mind (satva). The elements and the creatures which the ignorant visualise in these worlds do not exist at all. Such being the truth, where is a solid body, etc.? Whatever is perceived here is truly non-solid and extremely subtle consciousness. Consciousness alone exists in consciousness; peace rests in peace; space exists in space, wisdom alone exists in wisdom.

Where is the body and where are the limbs, where are the internal organs and the skeleton? Know that this body is pure consciousness which is like space—subtle though it looks solid. The arms are consciousness, so are the head and all the senses. All these are subtle and there is nothing which is solid. This world seems to arise in the infinite space or Brahman, like a dream. Because of the very nature of the infinite consciousness, it seems to exist as this creation. Therefore, it is both caused and uncaused. Of course, without a cause there is no effect. Whatever one constructs in one's own consciousness is also seen by oneself. Just as in dream all things appear everywhere in every manner, even so in the waking state the world appears in all manner everywhere.

One becomes many, just as the sons of Indu became the universe by the power of their contemplation. The many become one, just as devotees of lord Viṣṇu become one with him. Rivers are many, the ocean is one. Time is one, though the seasons and the years may be called by different names. This body is also pure consciousness and it exists in consciousness like a dream-object. Like a dream-object again it is formless, though its form seems to be obviously experienced as a reality.

The one sleep is regarded as dream-experience at one time and as deep, dreamless sleep at another: but sleep is one and indivisible. Even so, consciousness is one, whether in it there is awareness of objects or not. Therefore what is experienced as the world is nothing but pure consciousness. The seer (experiencer) the object (experience) and the act of seeing (experiencing) are all the one consciousness which is truly indivisible. The appearance of the world in this consciousness, as something other than consciousness, is an illusion: it ceases when its truth is realised, even as when the truth of a nightmare is realised it ceases to haunt one. It is the infinite potencies of the one infinite consciousness that appear here as the infinite objects of creation.

The Story of Kundadanta

VI.2:180 RĀMA said:

Lord, once when I was in my teacher's house, someone came in. He was extremely radiant. He had come from the court of the king of Videha. He saluted the assembled holy ones; we students also greeted him appropriately. When he had settled down in his seat and had rested a little, I asked him: "Holy one, you seem to be fatigued from a long journey. Where do you come from?"

THE BRĀHMAṆA replied:

Yes, you are right: I am seeking for something and I am fatigued on account of intense exertion to attain it. I shall tell you why I am here. I am a brāhmaṇa from the country of Videha. I am known as Kundadanta. I became disinterested in the affairs of the world and I sought the company of holy men and ascetics. On the Śrī mountain I lived for a considerable time practicing penance.

On that mountain one day I saw a strange sight. An ascetic dangled from the branch of a tree with his feet tied to the branch. I saluted him and drew near to him. I thought, "This ascetic is surely alive, for his body responds to the changes in the climatic conditions." I stayed there for a few days and served him and won his confidence. One day I asked him: "With what aim are you engaged in this penance?" The ascetic replied: "Embodied beings have many interesting goals in life." I persisted in my question.

THE ASCETIC said:

I was born in the city of Mathurā and was brought up there. I had acquired knowledge of the scriptures. I heard "The king enjoys all kinds of pleasures". I was inspired by that goal. I decided to become the emperor of the entire world. Hence, I came here and have been engaged in this penance for the past twelve years. I have answered your question. You had better go your way. I shall continue my penance.

THE BRĀHMAṆA continued:

I requested him to accept my service as long as he carried on his penance. The moment I said this, he closed his eyes and became as if dead. For six months from that day I remained in that place and served him. One day there appeared on that scene a being as radiant as the sun. I offered him due worship, and the ascetic worshipped him mentally. That radiant being said to the ascetic: "O ascetic, let this asceticism cease and I shall grant you the boon of your choice. You will become the emperor of the whole earth and rule for seven thousand years, remaining in this very body of yours." After bestowing this boon, the radiant being vanished from sight. When he had gone, I said to the ascetic: "Now that you have obtained the boon of your choice, terminate this penance and return to your normal duties." He accepted. I snapped the rope with which his feet were bound to the tree. Both of us then went to Mathurā.

THE BRĀHMAṆA KUNDADANTA continued: VI.2:181

En route to Mathurā we spent some time in a village known as Rodha and two days in a city known as Salim. On the third day we reached a forest. There the ascetic abandoned the popular route and said to me: "Let us go to the Gaurī Āśramaṃ which is near here. There my seven brothers live. We are eight brothers. Though we were born as separate individuals, we were all united in the one consciousness and we all had the same goal which we determined to reach. On account of that, they too are engaged in the performance of penance. I came here along with them and in the beginning I saw this forest in which there was the Gaurī Āśramaṃ. Come, let us go to the Āśramaṃ which purifies one of all sins. The minds and the hearts of even scholars and knowers of the truth are filled with eagerness to visit holy men: surely, we should consider it a great blessing to have the opportunity of visiting this hermitage."

When we approached the area of the Āśramaṃ, we saw only barren ground as if a deluge had washed the hermitage away. There was not a tree, no hermitage, no human being, no sage—nothing.

Both of us simultaneously exclaimed: "Alas, what has happened to this place?" Then we roamed that area and saw a solitary tree. When we approached this tree, we saw seated under it an aged ascetic who was deeply engrossed in samādhi. We sat near him and waited for a considerable time. But he did not get up from his meditation. I then went near him and shouted at the top of my voice, "O sage, get up from meditation". When I said this, the sage opened his eyes and uttered these words in a voice resembling the roaring of a lion: "Holy ones, who are you? What happened to the Gauri Āśramaṃ that stood here? Or who has brought me to this desolate place? What epoch is the present?" We were puzzled. I said to him, "Surely, O sage, you know everything. Therefore, only you can answer your own questions. Why do you not see all that has happened through your own yogic vision?"

When I said this, the sage once again went into deep meditation and through his inner psychic vision, he learned everything that had happened.

The sage remained silent for a while and then said to us: "Holy ones! Listen to this wondrous narration."

THE SAGE said:

You see this tree here. Because of my presence here, it blossomed profusely. For some unknown reason, the goddess of learning and speech dwelt here for ten years, being adored by all the different seasons of the year. This place became a dense forest and it became known a Gauri-vana (Gauri-forest). In this forest even the goddesses and the women folk of the siddhas or the perfected ones played. Even the gods came here to pay their homage at the feet of the goddess.

VI.2:182 THE SAGE continued:

After spending a period of ten years there, Gauri returned to her place on the left side of lord Śiva. On account of her touch this tree never grew old. After some time the forest became an ordinary forest which the people of the area made use of. At that time I was the king of Mālava. I renounced the kingdom and came here to practice penance. I entered into deep meditation here. After some time, all of you eight brothers also came here. After spending some time here, you went away to Śrī mountain, another went to Krauñca mountain, another to Kāśī and yet another to the Himālaya. The remaining four continued their penance here. All of them wanted to be rulers of the whole earth. They all obtained appropriate boons from the gods. After enjoying the fruits of their penance all of them returned home except you. I did not leave this place. The people held me and this tree in great esteem. I have been here for a long time. All this I have seen by my yogic vision. Now, you, too, return home and rejoin your family.

(In reply to Kundadanta's question: "The earth is one, how can eight people rule it at the same time?" the sage said:) This is not the only puzzling feature, there are others! In fact, all these eight brothers will rule the earth within their own house, after they give up their physical bodies. They will also have their (eight) wives remain constantly with them as stars. . . . For, these wives of theirs were sunk in inconsolable grief when their husbands left their home for doing penance; women cannot bear separation from their husbands. These women also performed intense penance. Goddess Pārvati was pleased with them and asked them to choose a boon. They said, "Just as you love your lord, we love our husbands: pray grant that they shall be immortal." But the goddess pointed out that that was contrary to natural order and asked them to choose another boon. They asked, "Even when our husbands die and cast off their bodies, may they not leave the home even for a moment." The goddess granted the boon and also granted that their husbands would rule the earth. Soon after this, the seven brothers returned home. Today the eighth will return too.

There is yet another wonder in this story. When all the eight boys had gone away to the forest to perform penance, the grieving parents, accompanied by the wives of the eight brothers, set out on a pilgrimage. On the way they came across a short-statured, reddish coloured and ash-besmeared ascetic, who was on the road to the holy place known as Kalāpagrāma. They did not respect him but treated him with suspicion. The ascetic, who was Durvāsa, was annoyed and cursed them: "You will pay the price for your haughtiness. Though your sons and your daughters-in-law will earn boons from the gods, those boons will produce contrary results." They realised their error and rushed forward to beg the ascetic's pardon. But before they could reach him, he vanished from sight.

KUNDADANTA said: VI.2:183

O sage, the earth is one; how can there be seven rulers of the earth simultaneously? One who does not leave his own house, how does he become the emperor of the earth? When a person has earned both blessings (boons) and curses which contradict each other, what is his fate?

THE SAGE said to the ascetic:

You will see how all these are made possible!

You will soon return home and be reunited with the family. In due course of time, you will all die. Your bodies will all be cremated by your relations. All of you will remain separately in the space of consciousness for a brief while, as if in deep sleep. In the meantime, all your karmas (the boons and the curses) will gather around you. The boons will assume their own forms and the curses will assume their forms, too. The boons will have a pleasant countenance and lotus-like palms, four arms and a mace. The curses will be fierce-looking, dark, two armed, three eyed and will hold a trident.

The boons will say to the curses: "Go away, you curses: our time has arrived and you cannot transgress it." The curses will say to the boons: "Go away, you boons: it is our time and no one can transgress it."

The boons will say: "You have been made by the sage, but we have been created by the sun." But the curses will reply: "You have indeed been created by the sun, but we are born of a part of lord Rudra himself who is superior even to the devas or gods; the sage is a part or limb of lord Rudra." Saying this, the curses will lift up their trident ready to strike.

The boons will thereupon say, "O curses, consider what evil flows from our quarrel here. Abandon your aggressive attitude and let us decide what is the best course of action. We have eventually to go to Brahmā the creator for a decision. Why not go there now?" The curses will agree: surely, even a fool agrees to wise counsel. They will all go to Brahmā and inform him of the dispute. Brahmā will say to them: "Whichever of you has truth within will win the dispute. Therefore, look within and see what the inner contents are."

The curses thereupon will say, "We are defeated, O Lord, for there is nothing worthy in us. All of us, O Lord, both the boons and the curses, are in fact pure consciousness; and we do not even possess a body."

THE SAGE continued:

The curses will further say: "The consciousness which grants the boon through the giver of the boon considers in the receiver of the boon 'I have received the boon.' The same consciousness experiences suitable embodiment and the fruits of the boons. Therefore, the granting of the boon by those who grant the boons and the receiving of the boon by those who sought the boons are firmly grounded in their consciousness and therefore form part of their essence. Hence they are invincible to us. The pure conquer the impure at all times. Only if the boons and the curses are of equal force, do they yield mixed results like milk mixed with water. These results are experienced by the person as if in a dream. Lord, give us leave to go." The curses will withdraw.

Another situation will arise. Here the very boon that the jīvas of the brothers would not leave the house, turns into a curse and challenges the boon that they would rule the whole earth. The former will appeal to Brahmā the creator for a ruling. Brahmā will say: "Though the two boons seem to be conflicting on the surface, indeed both them have already been fulfilled. For the eight brothers exist within their own house, yet they also exist as the rulers of the whole world since their physical bodies have been shed."

All the boons will now question Brahmā: "We have heard that there is only one earth. How is it possible for all the eight brothers to rule the earth and yet remain in their own house?" Brahmā will say: "Your world and our world are all pure void and they exist within a subatomic particle, as a dream-object is experienced within oneself. What is then so astonishing about the eight brothers experiencing the existence of several worlds in their own house?

"Immediately after death, this world is realised exactly as it is—as a dense void—within one's own mind. Even in an atom the entire earth shines, not to speak of the house. Whatever is is the infinite consciousness; there is naught known as the earth." When Brahma says this the boons will bow to him, and, having abandoned their false notion of a physical existence, will resume their subtle existence.

Then and there the eight brothers, unknown to one another, will become the rulers of the earth. One will rule from Ujjaini. Another will rule over Śākadvīpa. Another will rule over Kuśadvīpa. Another will rule over Sālmālidvīpa, sporting in water with celestials. Another will rule Krauñcadvīpa and another Gomedadvīpa, and the last will rule Puṣkaradvīpa. Thus both the boons will duly be fulfilled.

KUNDADANTA asked: VI.2:184

How can eight earths exist in one house?

THE SAGE replied:

The infinite consciousness, being omnipresent, shines everywhere in every way. The self perceives the worlds within itself.

KUNDADANTA asked again:

In one Lord, who is the infinite consciousness, how does diversity exist as if real?

THE SAGE said:

There is only one infinite consciousness which is supreme peace; there is no diversity at all, though such diversity may be experienced. The diversity that appears to exist is apparent and false, like dreams and deep sleep. Though there seems to be movement, there is no movement; mountains are not mountains. Even as in a dream, the nature of the self alone exists as all this. But even that nature does not exist, and hence diverse objects do not exist either. Whatever was fancied by the infinite consciousness in the beginning, that alone exists as it was. Even that fancy is not real: the infinite consciousness exists as it always exists.

In flowers, leaves, fruits, pillars, trees and in everything as everything and everywhere, the supreme being alone exists as 'the other'. The two expressions, viz., 'the supreme being' and 'the universe' are synonymous. When, through the study of the scriptures dealing with self-knowledge, this truth is realised, there is liberation. The content or the reality of notions and thoughts is Brahman or the infinite consciousness, and that itself is the content or the reality of the world-appearance, too. Hence, the world is Brahman. Descriptions and that which is beyond description, injunctions and prohibitions, existence and non-existence, silence and non-silence, jīva and the self—all this is Brahman; the reality alone appears to be the unreal appearance. When all this is Brahman alone, what is activity and what is renunciation and all the rest of it? In one sleep there arise both sleep and a thousand dreams; even so in the one indivisible consciousness countless appearances arise. All these are essentially pure consciousness which is extremely subtle. They are really invisible though they appear to be visible. The whole universe (including Rudra, Viṣṇu and Brahmā) is like a dream.

In that single ocean of consciousness, this diversity with all its joys and sorrows arises. Just as one with defective vision sees strange objects in space, even so the ignorant perceive the world. The notion that arises in Brahmā the creator (known as the world order) brings about all these and sustains them.

VI.2:184, 185 KUNDADANTA said:

Memory arises when a past experience is revived in one's consciousness. In the beginning of creation, whose memory expands as this creation?

THE SAGE replied:

Everything is seen and experienced even though all this had not been seen or experienced before—even as one may dream of one's own death. The very notion 'This I have seen before' when repeatedly entertained becomes a memory. In the space of one's own consciousness the imaginary object appears: it cannot be said that it is real or unreal. It is only by the grace (or the power) of consciousness that even dreams and the like are experienced: how then is it impossible for this pure consciousness to bring about the world-appearance as if it were revived memory? Just as at the end of deep sleep one dreams, even so in the infinite consciousness the three worlds appear. That which is called the world is pure void. What is, and in what it is and from what it is, that which is all, exists everywhere at all times.

Now, arise and do what has to be done. I shall resume my

contemplation; for without such contemplation there is possibility of contact with sorrow.

KUNDADANTA said:

Having said thus, the sage immediately closed his eyes and entered into deep contemplation. His life-breath and his mind had ceased to move and therefore he sat there like a painted picture. We tried to speak to him, but he did not even hear us. We were sorry to lose him. However, we moved away from there and slowly reached the house.

In course of time all the seven brothers passed away. Only my friend, the eighth brother, lived. Later, he too passed away. I was overcome by grief. Therefore, once again I went to that sage at the foot of the Kadamba tree. I waited upon him. After three months he opened his eyes. In answer to my prayer, he said to me: "I am devoted to contemplation or samādhi. I cannot stay away from it even for a moment. The truth does not become clear in you until it is heard again and again and meditated upon again and again. I shall therefore tell you what to do. Go to Ayodhyā. There is a king there known as Daśaratha. His son is Rāma. His guru Vasiṣṭha is discoursing upon the means to liberation. Listen to this. By that means you will attain supreme peace." Having said this, he once again entered into samādhi. I then came to this place to be with you.

RĀMA said:

That Kundadanta is sitting next to me and has devoutly heard this discourse on the means to liberation. Today he is free from all doubts.

VASIṢṬHA asked Kundadanta: VI.2:185, 186

Tell us what you have learnt during the course of this discourse.

KUNDADANTA replied:

Conquest of the mind alone is the destruction of all doubts. I have knowledge in which there is no contradiction. All my doubts are at rest. I am firmly established in the supreme state. I have learnt this from you: the infinite self or consciousness alone exists in the infinite space as this world. Everything exists in everything as everything everywhere for ever. The whole universe exists in a mustard seed; but when the reality is known the universe does not exist in a mustard seed. The universe exists in a house; but the house itself is pure void. It is Brahman or the infinite consciousness alone that appears as all this and is experienced as all this.

VASIṢṬHA continued:

It is wonderful that this great man has attained enlightenment. He has realised perfectly that the whole universe is Brahman.

It is only through delusion that Brahman is seen as the world. But that delusion also is Brahman which is supreme and infinite peace. Whatever is, wherever, whenever and in whatever manner, that is there and then and in that manner. Whatever the infinite consciousness considers itself to be, that it appears to be. The entire universe (brahmāṇḍa) exists in an atom of the infinite consciousness; hence an atom itself is the universe. The infinite consciousness is indivisible. When this is realised there is cessation of the bondage of birth, etc., and what is liberation. Be as you are, free from distress.

You are the object of perception; you are the seer. You are consciousness and you are inertia. You are something and you are nothing. Because Brahman rests in itself. There are no two things known as Brahman and the objective universe: they are one like space and void. An intelligent, conscious man appears to be an insentient and inert person while he sleeps; even so does the infinite consciousness appear to be the insentient objects in this creation. The infinite consciousness later becomes the sentient objects, just as the sleeping man begins to dream. This continues till the person attains liberation and realises that this world-appearance has been a long dream. It is on account of the infinite consciousness's inherent awareness that it considers itself an insentient and immobile being; and it is on account of the same awareness that elsewhere it considers itself sentient and mobile. Just as the same person has sentient and apparently insentient limbs, all the sentient and insentient objects of this creation put together form the body of the infinite consciousness.

VASIṢṬHA continued:

In the very beginning of creation, whatever dream-like appearance arose in the infinite consciousness has remained as this creation till now. However, consciousness is indivisible and extremely subtle and therefore in it there is no diversity, even now. Creation, existence and dissolution are non-existent in the vision of the enlightened ones like us. Though the infinite consciousness is indivisible, it experiences within itself the two states of bondage and liberation: the dream-like experience of diversity is known as bondage and the sleep-like state is liberation. It is the infinite consciousness alone which sees 'This is creation', 'This is dissolution', 'This is waking' and 'This is dreaming'. If the infinite consciousness is compared to the homogeneous deep sleep state, that part of it which is comparable to a dream is known as the mind. It is this mind that, as the jīva, sees itself as god, demon, etc., and also liberates all beings from such diversity. When this is realised the homogeneity of dreamless sleep state is reached: that is considered liberation by those who aspire for liberation.

The mind alone is all this: man, god, demon, trees and mountains, goblins, birds and worms. It alone becomes the infinite diversity that is seen here—from Brahmā the creator to the pillar. It is the mind that sees the space above. The mind is the dynamic and aggressive form of the infinite consciousness. Thus, when the notion of the universe arises in the infinite consciousness, we think that it is the mind that brought about all this. The mind alone is jīva. It is without beginning and without end. It is like space which seems to occupy pots and jars without being limited by them. It takes on and abandons bodies. But when it realises its own true nature, the deluded notion of physical embodiment ceases.

The mind is like the smallest particle of an atom. The mind is the personality or the jīva. Hence, the world or this creation exists in the person or the jīva. Whatever objects are perceived in this world are the mind only, even as the dream-objects are the mind only; again, the person or the jīva is also nothing other than the mind. Therefore, it is clear that the world-appearance and the self are non-different.

All these substances that are seen in this universe are in fact pure consciousness: apart from consciousness, what is seen is like a dream—just a notion or an idea, like the braceletness of gold.

Such a notion of creation, when it arises in the infinite consciousness, is known as the universe. This phenomenon has been variously described as saṅkalpa (thought or idea), etc.

VASIṢṬHA continued:

In course of time, by the constant practice of vicāra or enquiry and of equanimity, or by being endowed with purity at birth, perfect knowledge arises in the wise man who sees the reality in everything. Then his buddhi or awakened intelligence regains its nature as pure consciousness, devoid of duality. The infinite consciousness is devoid of body and is unhidden by veils: its only body is its faculty of awareness and its ability to illumine all things. It is through these that consciousness perceives everything that it considers to exist as a result of the notions that arise in it. This entire universe is an idea that arises in the infinite consciousness. Even so the self is also able to give rise to different notions within itself and experience the materialisation of these notions. Thus boons and curses are also realised as notions that arise in the consciousness, but they are non-different from it. But if the veil of ignorance has not been removed and if one still entertains notions of duality or diversity, the boons granted by such a one are ineffective.

RĀMA asked:

How does an unenlightened but righteous person confer boons?

VASIṢṬHA continued:

Whatever Brahmā the creator ordained in the beginning of this creation prevails even now. Brahmā is non-different from Brahman the infinite consciousness. That Brahmā brought into being through his own thought-force the standard of righteousness, charity, austerity, good qualities, the vedas and other scriptures and the five great elements. He also ordained that the utterances (boons, etc.) of the ascetics and the knowers of the vedas should come true. It was Brahmā who also ordained the nature of all substances here. Just as we become our own dream-objects while dreaming, consciousness though it is real and conscious becomes even the unreal world-appearance with all its sentient and insentient objects. The unreal world-appearance itself is later regarded as real on account of constantly repeated affirmation and conviction of its reality. When one indulges in daydreaming he can even see stone images dance as if they were real: even so this world-appearance which appears in Brahman is thought to be real.

The seer and the seen are non-different; consciousness is conscious of itself as consciousness. Therefore, it sees whatever it wishes to see. I am the infinite Brahman who is the cosmic person whose body is the world: hence the world and Brahman are non-different. Just as a conscious being may sometimes be in an unconscious state, even so the supreme being or the infinite consciousness itself exists as the apparently inert world. In dream there is 'light', in deep sleep there is darkness, though both these are in sleep: even so both light and darkness seem to exist in the one infinite consciousness.

VI.2:187 RĀMA said:

In this world-appearance with all its bewildering diversity, how does the cosmic order (niyati) function? How is it that the sun of all the celestial bodies is so hot and who ordained that the days be long some times and short at other times?

VASIṢṬHA replied:

The cosmic order arises and exists in the supreme being or the infinite consciousness by sheer coincidence (as the ripe cocoanut falls when a crow coincidentally alights on it). The manner in which it is is known as the universe. Because of the infinity and the omnipotence of consciousness, this cosmic order is seen to be endowed with intelligence. What thus exists is known as the cosmic order, niyati.

A momentary movement in consciousness is understood by it as 'This is creation'; when there is a momentary movement of energy in consciousness, it knows it as 'This is an epoch'. Similar movement of energy in consciousness alone is known as time, action, space, substance, etc. Even form, sight and the thought concerning these are but movement of energy which arises of its own accord in consciousness which is formless. Whatever arises in this manner is known as the character of the respective substance: this has come to be known as the cosmic order.

Essentially, a moment and an epoch are similar movements of energy in the infinite consciousness. They both arise naturally in consciousness and are therefore regarded as nature or the cosmic order. In this manner, in the one consciousness countless substances arise with their own characteristics. Thus, for instance, the earth is endowed with solidity and firmness and is able to support living beings—that is its characteristic in the cosmic order. Even so, it is the same in the case of the five elements, etc., including the sun. Their characteristics arise in the infinite consciousness as a corresponding movement of energy, and they come to be known as the cosmic order. The stellar sphere revolves like a wheel, again on account of the movement of energy that arises in consciousness. In that, some are brilliant and some less brilliant and some do not shine at all. Diverse are the characteristics of these diverse objects in this world-appearance. In reality, however, these have not really been created as objects. It is the infinite consciousness alone that appears as all these. The manner in which they appear to exist as long as they do exist is known as nature or the cosmic order, niyati.

VASIṢṬHA continued:

Within the infinite space is the root-element of sound hidden, like a sprout in a seed. From this, foolish people have spun theories concerning a material creation for the entertainment of other fools. Nothing ever comes into being nor does anything cease to be; what is exists firmly established in the supreme peace like the center of a rock. Just as in the case of one who has limbs and organs, there is constant renewal of the cells (atoms) constituting those organs endlessly, even so there is no end to the existence of universes in the supreme being.

The infinite consciousness becomes aware of a part of its own being and thus awareness arises in it. This is followed by the notion of relationship, the word and its corresponding object. Since this awareness is endowed with the faculty to observe and examine what it observes, it is recognised as consciousness.

Out of this mass of consciousness arise jīva and all the rest of it. However, at this stage it is still not individualised, for want of ignorance. But when ignorance arises in it, then it is turned towards saṃsāra. It is filled with the unborn elements. At this stage, the egosense or individualisation arises along with the sense of time. This is the vital factor in the existence of the world.

It is the consciousness itself that thus becomes individualised.

In it arises the notion of the root-element of space. With it also appear its relationship, the word (its name) and the meaning (the object). From this arise later all the other elements and the fourteen worlds.

The consciousness then entertains the notion of motion. This motion is air, with its corresponding action as the sense of touch and the life of all beings. Similarly, the light that shines in consciousness is the root-element of form which bestows form on all beings. The experience of seeing is light, the experience of touch is the sense of touch, the experience of hearing is the sense of hearing. Even so the root-elements responsible for taste and smell arise. Though unreal as independent substances they appear to be real as in a dream. All these later compound with one another and create gross forms, etc. They are but the materialisation of notions or ideas that arise in the infinite consciousness, not real entities.

That by which form is seen is known as eye, that by which sound is heard is known as ear, that by which touch is experienced is known as skin, that by which taste is experienced is known as the tongue, that by which smell is experienced is known as nose (or their corresponding inner sense, rather than the organ). On account of spatial and temporal limitations, the jīva gets involved in the cosmic order and is unable to experience everything.

VI.2:188 VASIṢṬHA continued:

The expression 'in the beginning', used as if there were such a beginning of such a creation of even a notion, is meant only for the purpose of instruction: it is not true. The notion which arises in consciousness, but which is non-different from consciousness itself, is known as jīva when it is outgoing to perceive the 'object'.

This notion or concept has several names and descriptions. Because through it consciousness becomes a living entity, it is known as jīva. Because it is conscious of the object, it is known as consciousness (cit). Because it designates all things as 'This is this', it is known as buddhi (designating intelligence). Because it thinks of concepts and percepts, it is known as the mind (manas). Because it considers itself 'I am', it is known as egosense (ahaṃkāra). Because it is rich in consciousness, it is known as citta (psyche). Because it forms a network of firm notions, it is known as the puryaṣṭaka. Because it arises in the beginning of creation, it is known as prakṛti (nature). Because it is not known (i.e., it ceases) when one attains enlightenment, it is known as ignorance (avidyā). All these descriptions are based on the existence of the subtle (ātivāhika) body. Though this illusory world-appearance has thus been described, it does not exist.

The ātivāhika body is but a subtle void. It does not arise and therefore has no need to cease. Yet, in the field known as the infinite consciousness, countless universes will continue to appear. The subtle mental body reflects the universe as a mirror reflects an object placed in front of it.

At the end of the period following the cosmic dissolution the supreme being thinks of the subtle (ātivāhika) body which arises in the infinite consciousness. This subtle body thinks of itself as Brahmā, Virāṭ, Viṣṇu, etc. Whatever the subtle body identifies itself with, that it appears to be. Though all these diverse entities seem to have been created, it is only an optical illusion. For nothing is ever created. Everything is but pure void which pervades all. The beginningless Brahman alone exists. However, on account of the fact that this cosmic subtle body entertains the notion that it experiences this diversity, such diversity seems to be uncontradicted truth.

In this ātivāhika (subtle) body there arise the thoughts or concepts of physical bodies and their component parts, concepts of birth, activity, etc., concepts of time, space, sequence, etc., as also concepts of old age, death, virtue and defect, knowledge, etc. Having conjured up these concepts, the subtle body itself experiences the objective universe composed of the five elements as if it existed in reality. But all this is surely illusory, like dream-objects and dream-experiences.

VASIṢṬHA continued: VI.2:189

The cosmic subtle (ātivāhika) body that arose as the creator Brahmā by sheer coincidence (just as a ripe cocoanut falls when a crow alights on it) continues to exist on account of the inherent nature of consciousness. It itself is the universe. The seer, the seen and the act of seeing are all unreal. Or if they are all considered real, even then they are all Brahman, and Brahman alone is real.

The cosmic subtle body arises of its own accord and that itself becomes a solid substance by being constantly thought of as such, even as a dream may appear to be real when it is prolonged. Thus, even materiality or substantiality arises of its own accord from the subtle (ātivāhika) body. 'I am this', 'I am that'—thus the notions that arise in that body appear as mountains and the various directions, but all this is mere delusion, appearance or optical illusion. When the ātivāhika body is thought of as material or physical substance by the creator Brahmā, such materiality arises.

Consciousness considers itself as Brahmā the creator; it considers, 'This is body' and 'This is the support for the body' and thus creates a relationship between the body and the support which thereafter becomes a bondage. When there is the notion of reality in unreal phenomena, there is bondage. When many such notions arise, then diversity is brought into being.

That person then utters sounds, makes gestures and indicates whatever he wishes to convey. He sings the mantras of the veda after uttering OM. Soon he engages himself in diverse activities with the help of all these. He is of the nature of the mind and whatever he thinks, that he experiences. It cannot be difficult for one to see his own nature and that which has arisen in him on account of his own nature. However, when he thus perceived the notion of the world within himself, soon it became a solid reality. Though this physical and material universe is but a long dream or magic product, it shines as if it is true in the subtle body or Brahmā the creator.

Hence, it is clear that the physical or material universe does not exist at any time anywhere. The subtle body itself appears to be the solid body on account of the notion of such solidity arising in it repeatedly. Its very source is unreal. The sole reality in all this is Brahman. There is naught here but Brahman.

VI.2:190 VASIṢṬHA continued: When knowledge becomes the object of knowing, it is known as bondage. Liberation is when knowledge ceases to be such an object of knowing.

RĀMA asked: How does the firm conviction that knowledge is the object of knowing come to an end?

VASIṢṬHA said: When there is full awakening, the dullness of intelligence comes to an end. Then liberation which is formless, peaceful and real comes into being.

RĀMA said: What is that perfect awakening which is perfect knowledge and by which a living being here is freed from bondage?

VASIṢṬHA said: Knowledge does not have an object to know. Knowledge is independent and eternal; it is beyond description and definition. When this truth is directly realised there is perfect knowledge.

RĀMA said: What is the division that arises between knowledge and the object of knowing? In what sense do we use the word 'knowledge'?

VASIṢṬHA said: Full awakening or enlightenment is jñāna or knowledge. Its contemplation is the means to such awakening. There is in reality no division between knowledge and the object of knowing.

RĀMA said: If that is so, how has this deluded vision of knowledge and the object of knowing arisen in the first place and become firmly rooted?

VASIṢṬHA said: It is on account of the deluded belief that there is something other than knowledge, something outside of itself, that the division has arisen. In fact, there is nothing either inside or outside.

RĀMA said: All this that seems to be obvious—I, you, etc., and all these elements and the diverse beings that we surely experience—how can it be accepted that they do not exist?

VASIṢṬHA said: The cosmic person or virāṭ and the cosmos, etc., did not in fact come into being at the very beginning of creation. Hence, there has never been an 'object of seeing' at any time whatsoever.

RĀMA asked: This world was, is and will be, and it is experienced every day. How can it be said that it was never created?

VASIṢṬHA replied: This world-appearance is unreal even as the following are unreal, though they appear to be real: the dream-objects, water in the mirage, the second moon when one is suffering from diplopia and castles in the air.

RĀMA asked: How can it be said that 'I', 'you', etc., did not arise at all even in the very beginning of creation?

VASIṢṬHA replied: An effect arises from a cause, not otherwise. During the state of cosmic dissolution preceding the assumed creation, there is supreme peace in which there is no cause for the creation of a universe.

RĀMA said: Even during the state of cosmic dissolution, surely the unborn and eternal being remains. Why can it not be regarded as the cause for this creation?

VASIṢṬHA replied: Whatever is in the cause that alone is found in the effect. Something which is unreal does not arise in the real. A piece of cloth is not produced with the help of a pot.

RĀMA said: Perhaps this whole creation exists in a subtle state in Brahman the infinite consciousness during the cosmic dissolution and perhaps that alone manifests itself during the next creation.

VASIṢṬHA replied: Who has experienced the truth of that assumption and so why repose faith in such a speculation?

RĀMA said: Surely the knowers of the truth have experienced in that state that there is pure and infinite consciousness. Of course space was non-existent then. The 'real' and material world can obviously not spring from void.

VASIṢṬHA said: If that is so, then surely the three worlds are nothing but pure consciousness. To one whose body is of pure consciousness there is neither birth nor death.

RĀMA asked: Then, pray, tell me how has this world-illusion arisen at all?

VASIṢṬHA replied: In the absence of cause and effect, there is neither being nor non-being. How does this 'object of perception' arise then? It does not: the self itself thinks of itself and experiences itself as the object of perception. All this is but consciousness and naught else.

RĀMA asked: The inert 'object of perception' thinks! The Lord who is the seer of all becomes the object. How is all this possible? Is it possible for wood to burn fire?

VASIṢṬHA replied: The seer does not become the object of perception because the latter does not exist. The seer alone is all this—the one mass of consciousness.

RĀMA asked: The infinite consciousness becomes aware of consciousness as its object within itself and thus does this world-appearance come into being. How does the object arise?

VASIṢṬHA replied: For want of a cause, the object does not arise at all. Therefore, consciousness is ever free and ever indescribable and indefinable.

RĀMA asked: If that is so, how do the egosense and such other categories arise? How does one experience the world?

VASIṢṬHA replied: For want of a cause, none of these things ever arises. Where is the object of perception? All the so-called created objects are but illusions of perception.

RĀMA asked: In this pure consciousness, which is free from movement and therefore free from the awareness of an object, how does illusion arise?

VASIṢṬHA replied: O Rāma, for want of a cause, there is no illusion either. All this (I, you and all the rest of it) is the one infinite peace.

RĀMA asked: Lord, I am bewildered and I do not know what to ask now. I am totally awakened or enlightened: what shall I ask now?

VASIṢṬHA replied: In the absence of a cause for any of this, do not enquire into the cause ('why'). Then you will easily rest in the supreme, indescribable reality.

RĀMA said: I accept that for want of a cause there has never been a creation. But to whom does this confusion concerning knowledge and its object arise?

VASIṢṬHA replied: For want of a cause and also because the one infinite peace alone exists, there is no illusion either. You do not rest in that peace because you have not repeatedly contemplated this truth.

RĀMA asked: How does contemplation arise and what is non-contemplation? Again, we are caught in the same trap.

VASIṢṬHA replied: In fact there is no illusion in the infinite. However, because consciousness is infinite and indiminishable, the concept of repeated contemplation of this truth arises in it.

RĀMA asked: If all this is the one infinite peace, what is the meaning of the words 'teacher' and 'student' and how does this duality arise?

VASIṢṬHA replied: The 'teacher' and the 'student' are all Brahman existing in Brahman. To the enlightened there is neither bondage nor liberation.

RĀMA asked: If the diversity of time, space, matter, energy and all the rest of it do not exist, then how has the concept of the oneness of this diversity come into being?

VASIṢṬHA replied: The diversity of time, space, matter, energy (action) and experiencing exist only in non-existent ignorance. There is no concept independent of this.

RĀMA asked: If the duality of 'teacher' and 'student' is false, then what is awakening or enlightenment?

VASIṢṬHA replied: By awakening, awakening is attained; and the concept of 'awakening' is clearly understood. Of course, all this is comprehensible only to people like you, not to us.

RĀMA asked: When thus enlightenment itself is related to the egosense, then it itself becomes other than enlightenment. How can such division exist in the pure, indivisible consciousness?

VASIṢṬHA replied: The light of the enlightened itself is self-awareness. The apparent division or duality is like the wind and its movement.

RĀMA said: If that is the truth, then is it not possible to accept the existence of diversity (the knower, the knowledge and the object of knowledge) on the basis of the analogy that the ocean and the waves are non-different?

VASIṢṬHA replied: If that is accepted, then there is no defect in division, though the truth is that the reality is one indivisible consciousness.

RĀMA said: Lord, in whom does egosense arise and who experiences this world-appearance or illusion?

VASIṢṬHA replied: The conviction in the reality of the object of experience alone is bondage. It is enough to know that the object does not exist. Since consciousness is all, there is neither bondage nor liberation.

RĀMA said: A lamp illumines objects which are seen. Even so, consciousness illumines the objects outside which are real?

VASIṢṬHA replied: The external world has no cause for its creation. An effect does not arise without a cause. Hence it is illusory perception.

RĀMA said: Whether it is considered real or unreal, a nightmare causes sorrow while it lasts. Even so is the world-appearance. By what means can we overcome it?

VASIṢṬHA replied: Just as the nightmare and the sorrow caused by it cease when one wakes up, the sorrow caused by the perception of the world-illusion ceases when one wakes up from that illusion and consequently refrains from acquiring and clinging to the objects of the world.

RĀMA asked: How does one attain the object of one's happiness? Also, how does the solidity of the objects of this world-dream come to an end?

VASIṢṬHA replied: By examining the 'before' and the 'after' the solidity of substances ceases. By the contemplation of the truth that it is even so in dream, the belief in the grossness of these substances ceases.

RĀMA asked: When such belief has weakened, what does one see? How does this world-illusion cease in his vision?

VASIṢṬHA replied: In his vision the unreal world-appearance has the character of a castle in the air or a painting which has been washed by rain—his mind is free from vāsanā or psychological conditioning.

RĀMA asked: What happens to him after that?

VASIṢṬHA replied: The world-appearance which exists as a mere notion fades away. Soon he is totally free from limitations and conditioning.

RĀMA asked: Surely this conditioning has gained deep roots on account of being revived in very many life-times: how does it cease?

VASIṢṬHA replied: By the realisation of the truth that all objects and substances exist in the self or the infinite consciousness as perverted notions, his hold on those substances (and vice versa) comes to an end. The wheel of saṃsāra stops by and by.

RĀMA asked: What happens then and how does he attain peace?

VASIṢṬHA replied: When thus the illusion of solidity of the objects has ceased and even the effort at restraining that illusion has ceased, all reliance on the world comes to an end.

RĀMA asked: When this world-appearance exists as an idea in a child's mind, why does its cessation not cause sorrow?

VASIṢṬHA replied: How does sorrow arise when an imaginary object is lost? Hence, as long as there are thoughts, notions, concepts and percepts in the mind, one should be engaged in enquiry into their nature.

RĀMA asked: What is the mind (cittam), how does one enquire into its nature and what is the fruit of such enquiry?

VASIṢṬHA replied: Consciousness becoming aware of itself as an object is known as cittam (mind). Enquiry is what you are doing now. By this, mental conditioning comes to an end.

RĀMA asked: How is it possible for this cittam to be unconditioned so that nirvāṇa may be attained?

VASIṢṬHA replied: Surely an object or mental conditioning is not a reality. Hence, the cittam too is not a real entity.

RĀMA said: But we do experience its existence!

VASIṢṬHA replied: The world is not what it appears in the eyes of the ignorant: what is real in the eyes of the enlightened is indescribable.

RĀMA said: What is the vision of the ignorant? And why is it indescribable in the eyes of the enlightened?

VASIṢṬHA replied: The ignorant perceive the world as having a beginning and an end. The enlightened do not see it at all for it has not been created at all and hence does not exist.

RĀMA said: But how is it that we experience its existence?

VASIṢṬHA replied: It is experienced as an object is experienced in a dream when it does not exist in truth.

RĀMA asked: But, then, it is because of the previous experience in the waking state that the dream-object is experienced.

VASIṢṬHA said: Are these two experiences related to the same object?

RĀMA replied: On account of the impressions created in the mind by the waking state, only such experiences appear in dream.

VASIṢṬHA said: In that case, why is it that the house that was destroyed in sleep is seen to exist the next morning?

RĀMA said: Of course, the waking state reality is not real during dream. What appears then is consciousness (Brahman). But how does that which had not been before come into being?

VASIṢṬHA replied: It is pure consciousness that shines at all times as if all this had been experienced before, whether or not this is the case.

RĀMA asked: Lord, how is this illusion got rid of?

VASIṢṬHA replied: Enquire, "How can this saṃsāra appear to exist, when it has no cause to come into being?"

RĀMA said: The mind (cittam) is the support for the dream-objects and hence they are mind only. Even so is the world.

VASIṢṬHA said: The mind is non-different from the mass of pure consciousness. There is naught else.

RĀMA said: Just as the body is not different from the limbs it is composed of, even so the universe is non-different from Brahman.

VASIṢṬHA said: Hence, the world has not been created at all. It is the eternal Brahman.

RĀMA said: I realise that the illusion of the creation and dissolution of the world is a pure coincidence, accompanied by illusory notions of 'I am doer' and 'I experience'.

VI.2:191 RĀMA said:

Lord, this world is filled with the supreme reality at all times and in all ways: hence it does not arise nor does it cease. The world-appearance is an illusion; but whether it is regarded as an illusion or not, it is in reality Brahman only.

VASIṢṬHA said:

Brahman shines in itself as itself coincidentally (just as a ripe cocoanut falls when a crow happens to alight on it) and that is known, by itself and in itself, as this creation.

RĀMA said:

Lord, tell me, how does the light of the infinite consciousness shine before the creation commences and after the creation has been dissolved, and how does it shine with a division?

VASIṢṬHA said:

Behold the light of consciousness within yourself by your self. Light is experienced only in relation to another. Since in the beginning there was no such division or duality, let this light be experienced within yourself. This light itself is the seer, sight and the seen (object), just like the dream-experience. That light of consciousness itself shines in the beginning of creation as that creation. The one consciousness shines as the three (the subject, the object and the experience), and in the beginning of creation it appears to be creation. Such is its very nature that it shines as it shines.

Such is the experience also of dreams and daydreams or hallucinations: the light of consciousness thus shines in these also. What shines as the world in space, without beginning and without end, is this light of consciousness. The emanation of its light shines as these universes.

This light of consciousness shines naturally in us, the enlightened ones, without the division of the subject and the object. In the beginning of creation, however, there was no subject and there was no object: somehow this ignorant division has arisen like the false appearance of a man in a tree trunk. On account of this perception of division in the beginning, such a division has continued to be experienced. But since there is no cause for such a division, it is clear that even now only the light of consciousness shines as all this.

There is neither a waking state, nor a dream state nor even a deep sleep state. Throughout it is only Brahman that shines from the very beginning of creation. That Brahman considers this universe as its own body; what is known as the world is non-different from Brahman.

VI.2:192 RĀMA said:

Alas, for a long time we have roamed this infinite space, without knowing the reality, and deluded. This illusion of world-appearance vanishes when one is awakened and enlightened. Then one realises that it has never been, it is not and it will never be. All this is pure consciousness and supreme peace; it exists as the infinite.

All this is indeed the supreme consciousness which appeared to us to be saṃsāra because we had not rightly understood its nature. It is the supreme being itself that appears as the object of such statements as 'This is different', 'It shines like this', 'These are worlds' and 'These are mountains'.

In the beginning of creation, at the commencement of one's life in the other world, and at the beginning of a dream or of a reverie, it is consciousness alone that arises as its own object: how could there be another? When there is the notion, 'I am in heaven or I am in hell', one experiences that as a fact.

There is no seer, no object, no creation, no world and not even consciousness; no waking, nor dreaming, nor sleep. What seems to be is also unreal. If one enquires, "How has this illusory perception of unreality come into being", such an enquiry is inappropriate: an illusion is not a reality. Illusion does not arise in consciousness which is incorruptible. Hence what appears to be illusion is also consciousness.

Illusory perception arises on account of non-understanding, like one's own death in a dream; when one enquires into the nature of the reality, the illusion vanishes. It is like the fear of ghosts that exists in the mind of a young boy: it becomes deep-rooted when there is no enquiry, but on enquiry it ceases.

Hence, the question, 'How has the unreal come into being' is improper; there is meaning only in enquiry concerning the reality, not the unreal. That which is not realised when enquired into is unreal; and if it is experienced to be real, such experience is delusion. When a certain thing is not to be found after intense and protracted enquiry, it is surely unreal like the barren woman's son.

But, then, the unreal does not exist at all at any time. Therefore, all this is pervaded and permeated by the mass of consciousness without any veils. What shines as the world is but the supreme being; and the supreme being alone exists in the supreme being. There is no light and there is no darkness. The supreme being alone exists as whatever exists.

RĀMA said: VI.2:193-194

That reality which is beginningless and endless and which even the gods and the sages do not know, that reality alone shines: what is 'world' and what is 'object'? Enough of this confusing argumentation concerning unity and diversity. That which was in the beginning, that peace is unchanging. Just as there is space (distance) in space, there is this creation in Brahman, the infinite consciousness. When this realisation arises in the jīva, this goblin known as saṃsāra is set at rest, though it may still appear to be. When the sun of ignorance sets, then the heat of sorrow ceases and the daylight known as conviction in the reality of saṃsāra comes to an end. Freed from ignorance, the knower of the truth engages himself in all kinds of activity as part of this pattern of birth, death and old age, etc., and continues to be, though in truth he is not.

There is no ignorance here, no delusion, no sorrow nor pleasure. Knowledge and ignorance, pleasure and pain are all Brahman alone. In the light of knowledge it is realised as Brahman; in the absence of knowledge, there is nothing which can be designated as non-Brahman. I am enlightened and all my perverse thoughts have been set at rest. I am at peace and equanimous. I am that, and I see this world as pure void. Prior to enlightenment Brahman was, but as self-ignorance; now the same Brahman is as self-knowledge. As knowledge or as ignorance, as known or as unknown, Brahman alone is at all times, just as the sky is one though it is void, it is undivided and it is blue.

I am nirvāṇa. I am free from doubt. I am free. I am blissful. I am as I am as the infinite. I am the all at all times or I am nothing and at peace. I am the one reality and I am not. Wonderful is this supreme peace. What is to be gained has been gained. The perception of the objects has been abandoned. True enlightenment has dawned and it shall never set again.

The enlightened intelligence experiences whatever there is as it is. Countless universes arise and disappear in the infinite consciousness all the time. Some are seen by some and others are not. Who can count their number? The distinction between the organs and the organism is arbitrary and verbal: even so is that between Brahman and the universe. The former alone is; the latter is not. When this is realised, there is cessation of cravings and supreme peace which is nirvāṇa.

This enlightenment is not brought about by buddhi or intellect. Nor is it attained by the suppression of the intellect. Enlightenment is not aware of itself for it is not an object of awareness.

RĀMA continued:

The awakening or the enlightenment happens by itself, just like the sun's brilliance at noon. All cravings and desires come to an end in the awakened person; therefore nirvāṇa arises in him without his desiring it. He is forever engaged in meditation, he is always established in his own real nature: therefore he does not seek anything or reject anything. Like a lamp in whose light all actions take place and in which the lamp itself is not interested, he lives and acts but is free from volition.

The infinite consciousness alone is: it is manifest as creation and it is otherwise known as Brahmā. He who sees this is at peace. All objects in this universe are in fact non-different from this infinite consciousness. Beyond this, the knowers of truth rest in the infinite consciousness alone: but that is indescribable and indefinable. Even expressions like 'That alone is' are inadequate and misleading.

This saṃsāra is full of sorrow; nirvāṇa is absolute coolness. The latter alone is the reality; the former is not. Like the uncarved figures that exist in a piece of wood, this saṃsāra exists in the infinite consciousness—which is indivisible but experienced diversely by diverse beings, each of whom carves out of it, as it were, what he desires—whether it is pleasure or liberation. However, all these are in essence the reality itself, even as the carved figures are in essence non-different from the wood. The life or death of relatives seen in a dream has no effect on oneself after awakening from sleep; even so the enlightened ones are unaffected by the world-appearance.

When all this is seen as the one infinite consciousness, there is no room for delusion. There is cessation of craving. Cessation of craving intensifies awakening or enlightenment; and the latter intensifies the cessation of craving. The hall-mark of enlightenment is this cessation of craving. When the latter is absent, there is no enlightenment but scholasticity which is in fact ignorance or viciousness. If these two do not promote each other, then they are obviously unreal and absent. The perfect cessation of craving born of the perfect enlightenment, itself is known as liberation. When this is attained, one does not grieve even though continuing to live.

For one who rests in his own self and rejoices in the self, in whom cravings have ceased and egosense is absent, life becomes non-volitional and there is perfect purity. One in millions, however, is able to reach this unconditioned state of pure being.

VASIṢṬHA said: VI.2:195

Bravo, O Rāma, you have attained enlightenment. Your words have the power of enlightenment. The unreality which seems to exist here disappears when it is not conceived or thought of. This supreme peace is nirvāṇa and this is the supreme truth. That state in which the enlightened one exists as if he lives in the very center of a rock, whether he is alone and at rest or engaged in diverse activities—that is the state of purity and that is liberation. We live in that state, O Rāma, though we are constantly engaged in diverse activity. You, too, rest in that state and carry on your work.

Now, O Rāma, please tell me how you realise that this world, though it seems to be so real, is non-existent.

RĀMA replied:

This world has not been created even at the very beginning. How then can be it considered to exist now? It has no cause: how can an effect be without a cause? Change implies the cessation of one state and the arising of the subsequent state. This is impossible in the changeless reality. If this world is an illusory appearance that is imagined to exist in Brahman, then it is only an illusion. In a dream a moment is experienced as a lifetime: even so, in this world-appearance time is experienced along with the sun and the moon on which time is based.

In the infinite consciousness, there is this notion of creation with all its corollaries—time, space, etc. This non-entity appears to function and that, too, is false. The accidental arising of this notion appears to persist and become deep-rooted.

Or, it has to be considered real. How can the false ever even appear to exist? Or perhaps there is no such thing as the real and nothing as unreal. Whatever is, is. That which is is clear as the sky, full as the center of a rock, silent and peaceful as the stone, and infinite. Such is the creation. For this creation exists in the pure, infinite consciousness which is the reality of all thoughts and concepts which together form the subtle body, as it were, of the infinite consciousness. The pure experiencing or awareness that arises in that 'body' is known as this creation. Thus this creation itself is Brahman.

In the supreme being itself does the 'other' (creation) exist; the latter belongs to the former and is non-different from it. It is therefore supreme peace itself. There is neither a creation nor movement nor activity. When dream is realised as dream, the false notion vanishes. Awareness drops its object (the world) and rests in the infinite consciousness.

VASIṢṬHA asked:

Why should we not assume that just as the seed is the cause for the sprout, Brahman is the cause for the creation?

RĀMA replied:

The sprout in the seed is not seen as sprout, but only as seed. Hence it is only seed. In the same way, if this world exists in Brahman, it is only Brahman and not the world; and Brahman undergoes no change. Since Brahman is unchanging and formless, it is impossible to accept that it gives rise to the world which is changing and which is endowed with form. To say that this creation exists in the indivisible Brahman just as a gem lies in the box, is meaningless prattle. The theory that the supreme Brahman is the support for the universe which has a form is also unacceptable: for that which has a form must perish. The concept that this world is but the dream-object that has thus materialised is unacceptable, for the dream-objects are those which have been experienced by oneself. However, the waking and the dream realities belong to two different planes: for the person whose death was dreamed of is seen on waking up from dream. Thus the world has not been created even as a dream-object; but just as the dream-object is only consciousness, even so all that is seen as the world is only the infinite consciousness.

There is naught known as 'real', 'unreal', 'experiencer' nor 'experience', nor are these experienced. Whatever is is indescribable. In the infinite consciousness all distinctions between 'being' and 'non-being' vanish. Brahman exists as Brahman in Brahman, just as space exists as space in space. This that is known as creation is the indivisible Brahman only. Just as the seed that has been sown begins to sprout, the movement in Brahman becomes capable of being described. All beings in the universe appear to me to be enlightened. To those who consider it real, this world appears to be real; to those who are endowed with self-knowledge it is a false appearance. In fact it is Brahman only.

In the vision of the knowers of the reality all that exists (both the sentient and the insentient, the mobile and the immobile) is pure void. I am void, you are void, the universe is pure void. I salute the best of all beings, who is like the limitless space, with the knowledge that is like the limitless space and which is free from subject-object (knower and knowable) relationship. You have transcended all the states described in the scriptures and you remain established in the supreme non-dual consciousness.

This supreme truth is established only in total silence, not by logic, discussion and argumentation.

RĀMA said: VI.2:196, 197

Thus, O sage, it is clear that self-knowledge is beyond the reach of the jugglery of words. How is it attained by the conflicting statements of scriptures? If it is not so attained what is the use of these scriptures? Pray tell me whether self-knowledge follows the instruction of the preceptor and the study of scriptures.

VASIṢṬHA said:

It is true, O Rāma, that the study of the scriptures is not the cause for the attainment of self-knowledge. Scriptures are composed of diverse expressions; the supreme being is indescribable. However, I shall explain to you how the study of scriptures has come to be associated with self-knowledge.

The people of a certain village had been subjected to continued misfortune. They were starving and dying. Oppressed by poverty and misery, they began to consider ways and means of earning their livelihood. They decided that they would go into a nearby forest, gather firewood, sell it and earn a living.

Thus they earned their living from day to day. In that forest they found also precious stones, which lay sometimes hidden and sometimes in the open. Of the people who went to the forest for firewood, some found these precious stones, others had excellent sandalwood, others found fruits, and yet others were unfortunate even there, and found only useless firewood. Of them, they who obtained the precious stones were free from poverty and sorrow immediately.

As they were thus engaged in gathering firewood and making a living, one day they found the philosopher's stone (which fulfils everyone's wishes). They obtained with its help all that they needed and desired, and lived happily for ever after. They were looking for firewood, but they eventually obtained the most precious philosopher's stone.

The villagers in this parable are the people of the earth. Their poverty is the worst of all poverty, that is ignorance which is the cause of all sorrow. The forest in the parable is the spiritual preceptor and the scripture. They went to the forest for the fulfilment of their needs; people resort to the preceptor and the scripture for the fulfilment of their needs. However, in course of time, by the practice of the precepts of the preceptor and the scripture, they attain something more precious. They who went to the forest to gather firewood got the philosopher's stone. People who resort to the scriptures for the fulfilment of their desires attain the supreme truth.

VASIṢṬHA continued:

Some people are impelled by curiosity or by doubt ('What can the study of the scriptures do?') to study the scriptures; others seek to find the key to prosperity and pleasure in them; yet others study the scriptures motivated by other considerations—and just as the villagers who went to the forest to gather firewood obtained the philosopher's stone, they who study the scriptures for various reasons obtain the supreme truth. In all this the people are guided by the conduct of the saintly ones who are devoted to the welfare of humanity. The people see that these saints do not use the scriptures for other than the highest spiritual gain, though they do study the scriptures. Inspired by them, people study the scriptures.

Just as some of the villagers obtained sandalwood, etc., in the forest, even so, among those who study scriptures some attain pleasure, others wealth and yet others guidance in right conduct. Only these three are expounded in the scriptures; the attainment of the realization of Brahman is beyond description and, therefore it is not found in the teachings of the scriptures.

Not by the study of the scriptures, nor by hearing the instructions of a preceptor, nor by charity nor even by the worship of god is the direct realisation of the supreme truth attained. Because that is beyond all these. However, I shall tell you how these, though not the actual means, have come to be regarded as the means to self-realisation. By the practice of the precepts of the scriptures, the mind becomes pure and transparent; then without even wishing for it one sees the supreme truth. The scripture promotes the sātvika part of ignorance, which is purity of mind. This purity destroys the tāmasic (dull) part of ignorance.

By its very appearance in the sky the sun is reflected in the ocean, without either of them desiring this. Even so by the simple coming together of the scripture and the seeker, the truth is reflected in the latter. A child with muddy hands picks up more mud and rubs the hands together and washes them; the hands are clean now. Even so the scripture purifies the mind and the clean mind reflects the truth.

There is light everywhere in the sky, but it is only when light meets with an obstruction that it is able to illumine: even so when the scripture (or the guru) meets the seeker there is illumination. Hence, the supreme truth is realised when one contemplates the real meaning of the scriptures with the aid of the words of the preceptor, satsaṅga (holy company), self-discipline and control of the mind.

VASIṢṬHA continued: VI.2:198

Once again I shall tell you something, O Rāma, to which please lend your ear. By repeatedly listening to the truth even an ignorant person is awakened.

To begin with I expounded the sthiti prakaraṇaṃ in which the truth concerning the creation of this universe was revealed. After that I expounded in the upaśānti prakaraṇaṃ the means by which this world-illusion might be dispelled. After thus getting rid of this world-illusion, one should live here free from all mental agitation and distress.

One should live in this world fully established in the state of equanimity which confers all blessings and which bestows the highest consolation, which is the greatest wealth and which enhances one's good fortune. Equanimity enables purity to grow. All other noble virtues follow this one. None of the blessings and wealth in the world is comparable to equanimity. It puts an end to all sorrow. Rare are those souls who are established in equanimity, to whom all are friends.

To one who is established in equanimity, sorrow is happiness and death is new life. Who can measure the greatness of one who is free from exultation and depression, who does what has to be done when and how it is to be done, and who sees what is to be seen, as it is. Friends and relations, enemies and kings have the greatest trust in one who thus lives a natural life. In the course of such natural living, even if he should become angry, it does not hurt anyone. The people applaud whatever he does and whatever he eats, even if he overpowers another or reprimands another—for he is established in equanimity. They applaud whatever he does now or whatever he did long ago, whether good or not so good.

They who are established in equanimity do not experience despair, whether they are subjected to happiness or to great unhappiness.

(There follow brief references to some great men who gladly sacrificed themselves for the good of others, and who were totally unaffected by the worst calamities: the king Śibi, the king whose wife was insulted in his presence, Yudhiṣṭhira, the king of Trigarta, the king Janaka, the king of Sālva, Sauvīra, Kandapa, the demon of Kadamba forest, Jaḍa Bharata, the noble hunter, the sage Kapardana. Two factors are important: (1) these exemplars of equanimity come from different walks of life and (2) historically, many of them came after the period of Rāma.)

All of them had attained equanimity and therefore they came to be adored even by the gods, though they were kings as well as ordinary men. Hence, one should attain equanimity in all conditions of life, pleasant and unpleasant, in honour and dishonour.

VI.2:199 RĀMA asked:

When these sages are constantly immersed in the bliss of self-knowledge, why do they not abandon all activities?

VASIṢṬHA replied:

They have abandoned all notions of 'This is desirable' and 'This is undesirable'. In their case, therefore, both the abandonment of action and the performance of action are meaningless. Therefore, they do what has to be done how it has to be done.

Rāma, as long as there is life, so long the body lives and moves and functions. Let this continue—why should one desire otherwise? When somehow something has to be done at all times, why not do what is right? Whatever one does with a pure and clear mind which rests in equanimity, is right and appropriate, never defective. Among us, O Rāma, there are many who are involved in defective action but they are wise and clear-sighted.

There are some liberated ones who live the householder's life but without attachment. There are some who are royal sages like you who perform their royal duties without attachment and without agitation. There are some who perform the scriptural duties and rites. There are some who are devoted to god and meditation and to their own duties. There are some who have abandoned everything inwardly but who live as if they were ignorant, engaged in all kinds of activities. There are some who dwell in dense forests totally immersed in meditation. There are some who dwell in holy places. There are some who roam in distant foreign lands in order to overcome completely all likes and dislikes. Some are constantly wandering from place to place.

Some have abandoned their natural duties and others are devoted to them. Some behave like wise men and others behave like mad men. Some are human, some are gods and others are demons.

In this world there are the fully enlightened ones, unenlightened ones and semi-enlightened ones who abandon right actions, too, and are thus neither here nor there. The forest-life is not essential for liberation, nor living in one's own country nor an ascetic life, nor the abandonment of activity. Liberation is attained by one whose very nature is totally free and unattached. He whose mind is free and unattached does not get involved once again in this saṃsāra. O Rāma, you are the supreme state. Remain what you are, free from likes and dislikes, established in the supreme truth. In that Brahman there are no impurities, changes, veils, cravings or aversions. There is nothing more to say.

VĀLMĪKI said: VI.2:200

Having concluded his discourse on nirvāṇa, the sage Vasiṣṭha remained silent. All the members of the assembly were deeply immersed in the highest (nirvikalpa) samādhi or contemplation. The very heavens resounded with the cheers of the assembled sages and perfected ones. The celestials sounded their drums and other instruments. There was a shower of flowers.

The SIDDHAS (perfected ones) said:

From the beginning of this epoch we have given and heard numerous discourses on the means to liberation, but none like this. Even animals and children will attain enlightenment by listening to the sage's words.

THE KING DAŚARATHA said:

Lord, there is nothing in the world with which you could be appropriately worshipped. However, listen to my prayer and be not offended. I adore you and worship you with myself, my family and the merits that I have acquired and all the good works I have performed here and in the other world. All these are thine, Lord. It is for you to command us.

VASIṢṬHA said:

We are satisfied with salutations, O king. And that is enough for me. You alone know how to rule the world.

RĀMA said:

Lord, what shall I offer you? I fall at your feet.

After him, his brothers saluted the sage. Then the kings and the others who had come from great distance to listen to the sage offered flowers of worship. Vasiṣṭha was literally covered with flowers.

When all this had been completed, VASIṢṬHA said:

O sages, pray tell me if there were any defects or shortcomings or perverse teaching during the discourse.

The ASSEMBLED SAGES replied:

In your discourse, O Lord, there was not a single inappropriate note. It was characterised uniformly by the highest truth. You have instantly dispelled the veil of sin that had covered our minds and hearts. Our heart-lotus has fully unfolded. We salute you; you are our guru.

So saying, all of them with one voice exclaimed: "Salutations to you." Again they showered flowers on him. The assembled sages then glorified the king Daśaratha who had convened that assembly. They glorified Rāma. They saluted Rāma and his three brothers. They glorified the sages Vasiṣṭha and Viśvāmitra. For it is only due to the grace of all of them that they were able to listen to the supreme discourse of Vasiṣṭha which instantly dispels delusion.

Thus all of them worshipped and glorified the sage Vasiṣṭha again and again.

VI.2:201, 202 Then, VASIṢṬHA asked Rāma:

O Rāma, what else do you want to hear from me? How do you perceive the world-appearance now? What is your inner experience?

RĀMA replied:

By your grace, I have attained supreme purity; all the impurities have cleared away. All my misunderstandings and delusions have been dispelled. My bondage has been cut. My intelligence is pure like a crystal. My mind does not crave for more instruction.

I have nothing to do with anything—neither instructions nor any objects, neither relatives nor scriptures, nor even renunciation. I behold the world as the pure, infinite, indivisible consciousness. The world is otherwise a void which disappears the moment the illusion vanishes.

I shall do whatever you wish that I should do and I shall live doing whatever I have to do or wish to do, without exultation or depression, for my delusion has been dispelled. Whether this creation becomes something else or whether the winds of cosmic dissolution blow or whether this country be prosperous, I am established in self-knowledge. I am at peace. My vision is clear. It is difficult for my real state to be seen and understood. I am free from hopes and desires. I shall live and rule like the other kings, whether they are enlightened or ignorant, but without mental agitation and endowed with equal vision. As long as this body lasts I shall rule this kingdom, endowed with a pure vision and freed from all doubts concerning the nature of this saṃsāra, just as a child engages itself in play.

VASIṢṬHA said:

Bravo, O Rāma, you have truly reached the supreme state, beyond joy and sorrow, and you have transcended all that is found in this world and in the next. You will now fulfil the wishes of the sage Viśvāmitra and rule the kingdom.

After the assembly once again cheered, RĀMA said:

Lord, just as fire purifies gold, you have purified our hearts. They who considered their body as the all now see the entire universe as the self.

I have attained the plenum of existence. I am free from all doubts. I am full of bliss which is eternal and undiluted. I rejoice in my own heart which has been purified by the nectarine words of supreme wisdom. By your grace I have attained the state in which the whole world itself appears to be the eternal, immortal and infinite reality.

VASIṢṬHA said to Rāma: VI.2:203, 204

O Rāma, you have heard all that is worth hearing and you know all that is worth knowing. What I have said to you and what you have studied in the scripture, now bring into harmony with your own direct experience.

However, once again I declare the supreme truth to you. The mirror shines with greater clarity the more it is cleaned and polished. All the objects here are the measure of one's own experience or awareness. All sounds are like the sound produced by running water. All that is seen here is the illusory appearance of the infinite consciousness. This world has arisen like a dream. What is known as the waking state reality is a dream; it is non-different from the consciousness which is the sole reality. Hence, the world is truly without form.

Tell me, O Rāma, how do the earth and all the rest of it appear in this dream-city? By whom has all this been fashioned, what is their real nature and what is their function?

RĀMA said:

The self or the infinite consciousness alone is the reality of all this—the earth, the mountains, etc.—and the self is like space, formless and supportless. All these have not been created at all. This notion that arises in consciousness is known as the mind and it is the mind alone that exists as all this.

Time, space, and all the rest of it, are the appearance of the consciousness. Even so are the mountains nothing but consciousness. All the elements are consciousness, too. It is consciousness alone that is the essence of the characteristic of the elements like solidity of the earth, fluidity of water, etc. In fact, however, the earth and the other elements do not exist: the infinite consciousness alone exists. It is because of the liquidity of water that the one ocean is able to give rise to waves and currents; it is because of the infinite potentiality of consciousness that it is similarly able to appear to be diverse. When the notion of solidity and hardness arises in it, it becomes a mountain: even so with all the other objects. Consciousness itself does not undergo any change in all this. The notions of 'I', 'you', etc., arise in it without any reason or cause, and they are non-different from consciousness.

The mind, buddhi, egosense, the five elements and all this world-appearance exist in the infinite consciousness, non-different from it. Nothing has been created, nothing is lost.

VI.2:205 RĀMA asked:

When, thus it is the infinite consciousness that is all this and the world is but a dream, how does this consciousness appear to be embodied in the wakeful dream state?

VASIṢṬHA said:

Whatever is seen either in a dream or in the waking state, has space alone as support. It is born of space and it is of the nature of space (void). This space is not other than the supreme, infinite consciousness. Nothing, not even this body, has ever been created and hence nothing exists. The infinite consciousness experiences the existence of all this as if in a dream. This experience exists in consciousness as if it is the solid creation. The diversity that arises in consciousness on account of the limitlessness of its potentiality appears to give rise to diversity of creatures.

RĀMA asked:

You described that there were countless creations. You said that they were inhabited by diverse beings with very different natures and functions. Pray tell me, among all of them, how this creation exists.

VASIṢṬHA replied:

While expounding whatever has not been experienced before, nor seen nor even heard of before, the teacher resorts to appropriate illustrations with the aid of which the truth is grasped and inferred. However, you know the nature of this universe.

The one infinite Brahman alone exists, without beginning and end, without form and without change. In the infinite space which is permeated by Brahman, this universe exists non-different from Brahman. The universe, too, is beginningless and endless. This universe is what the infinite consciousness considers it to be within itself, whatever it experiences within itself: and the infinite consciousness itself considers that experience to be the universe, hence it is illusory, like the dream-object of one who is dreaming.

The mountains are not hard nor are waters fluid. Whatever the infinite consciousness considers itself to be and wherever, that appears to be so there. A mountain arises in a dream and exists in nothing and as nothing: even so is this universe, for it is the dream of the infinite consciousness. Brahman alone exists as Brahman at all times; nothing is created nor is anything destroyed. There is no diversity in Brahman, nor is there non-diversity in it. All concepts like unity, diversity, truth, falsehood, etc., are irrelevant to it.

VASIṢṬHA said: VI.2:206

That which appears to be without any cause, that is not: therefore that (the reality) which is alone is.

I shall narrate to you an interesting question I was once asked, for your clear understanding. There is an island known as Kuśadvīpa. On it was a city named Ilāvatī. It was ruled by king Prajñapti. Once I happened to meet him. After offering me due worship, he asked me the following question:

"After the entire visible universe had been dissolved, what were the reason and the cause for the creation of the universe? What is this universe? Some part of it is always veiled by darkness, somewhere it is inhabited by worms. How did these elements that constitute the world arise, and how were the mind, buddhi, etc., created? Who is the creator of all this and who perceives it? Who is its support?

"There is obviously no final dissolution of the universe. Whatever every living being becomes aware of, that alone it experiences. What then is indestructible and what is real? When a person dies here and his body is cremated, who creates a body for him in hell to undergo the necessary experiences there? Surely not virtue (dharma) or vice (adharma), for they are themselves subtle and formless. To say that 'the other world' does not exist seems to be equally fallacious, for it contradicts the statements of the scriptures.

"It is absurd to suggest that one who is formless can undergo experiences like punishment. Tell me also how substances undergo change here. What is the use of scriptures that deal with injunctions and prohibitions? What is meant by the scriptural declaration that the unreal alone existed at first and that it became real later on? If Brahmā the creator springs from void, why does that void not create very many creators everywhere? How have the herbs, etc., acquired their characteristics and their nature? In a holy place at the same time two people live, one's friend and one's enemy. The friend prays for one's long life and the enemy prays for one's death: whose prayer will be fulfilled? If thousands of people wished, "May I be a moon in the sky", why can there not be thousands of moons shining at the same time? If thousands of men meditate and pray that they may all attain a particular woman as their wife, and if at the same time she meditates and prays that she might remain a virgin, what is the result?

"How are the fruits of funeral and subsequent rites experienced by the departed ones in the absence of embodiment?"

VI.2:207 VASIṢṬHA said:

O king, listen: I shall answer your questions in such a way that all your doubts are at rest.

All things in this world are for ever unreal, but they are also real because of the consciousness that is the sole reality and their content. Whatever that consciousness decides "This is such and such" that it becomes, whether it is real or unreal. Such is the nature of consciousness.

This consciousness conceived of a body and it becomes aware of the body. It is self-awareness that becomes aware of the body, not the other way round. At the beginning of creation, there was nothing else and only consciousness was: and therefore the world-appearance arose in that consciousness like a dream. In whatever manner consciousness conceived the world to be, that alone it became. What else is this world? Since the world is nothing other than consciousness or Brahman, it is declared to be so by the scriptures.

Yet, like a frog in the blind well, foolish and ignorant people base their understanding on the experience of the moment and, on account of their perverse understanding, they are deluded into thinking that the body alone is the source of experience or awareness. But we have nothing to do with them. However intelligent a person may be, if he is unable to dispel one's doubts such a person is ignorant. If self-awareness is one of the characteristics of the physical body, then why does a corpse not experience anything?

The truth is the other way round. It is the consciousness of Brahman, the infinite consciousness, that appears as this universe—just as the dream-objects appear in your consciousness. Brahman is the infinite consciousness; he conceives of this dream-city which is the virāṭ or the cosmic person. This cosmic person is the creator Brahmā and is also of pure consciousness although it is known as this universe.

Whatever was conceived of in the dream-creation of Brahmā the creator alone is experienced here in that same manner. Thus the body has two states—the living and the dead. Even so this creation appears and disappears. It has no cause other than Brahman, hence it is none other than Brahman. Whether the body exists or does not exist, this consciousness experiences what it is aware of anywhere at any time, before and after 'death'. It is consciousness alone which conceives of 'the other world' and experiences it as such.

Such deluded experience does not cease until one resorts to the right means of liberation and attains awakening, when the mental conditioning ceases and the consciousness becomes unconditioned.

VASIṢṬHA said: VI.2:208

Whatever the infinite consciousness conceived of and whenever, that it then experienced. Even so boons and curses derive their power also from the infinite consciousness. It is because of the appropriate conception arising in consciousness that injunctions and prohibitions acquire their authority and their power.

It is because the embodied being here in this world could not comprehend what existed before the beginning of this creation, that it was said that non-existence alone was prior to that. However, existence and non-existence, creation and dissolution are like the opening and closing of the eyes of the infinite consciousness. Such is the very nature of the infinite consciousness that creation arises and ceases constantly, just as when you indulge in day-dreaming you build and dissolve your mental images in the twinkling of an eye. However, all these are but images that arise in the infinite consciousness. It does nothing at all.

Since the infinite consciousness is everywhere at all times, there are no barriers in it and it can give rise to any image anywhere at any time. Injunctions and prohibitions exist only for the preservation of the social structure here. But, since these are all established in consciousness, they are capable of yielding their fruits even after one departs from this world.

Brahman neither comes into being nor ceases to be. But when the subject-object relationship arises in it, then it is said to come into being: and the object is known as creation. When Brahman withdraws that relationship and exists in itself as itself, then it is said that Brahman exists as infinite space and supreme peace. These two (the existence and the non-existence of relationship) are natural to Brahman, just like movement and non-movement are natural to wind.

Old age, death, etc., as also the divisions of time, arise in the infinite consciousness again and again, even as images rise in your day-dream again and again. Even so have the herbs and the medicinal plants, as also the diverse objects, come into being in the three worlds.

The one infinite consciousness alone appears as this infinite diversity on account of the infinite (conscious) images that arise in it. However, in and as all this, it is the one Brahman alone that shines.

VI.2:209 VASIṢṬHA said:

You mentioned the case of one's friend and one's enemy praying for contrary results in a holy place. All these are determined by the infinite consciousness in the very beginning. The holiness of places and the conduct that earns merit enable one to acquire that merit in those places. Even if he has been a sinner, the load of his sin is either lightened or eliminated by the merit of the holy places. If, however, the weight of the sin is much less than the strength of the merit, then surely the sin is completely wiped out. If they are of equal strength, it is possible for two bodies to appear in the consciousness to work out both the merit and the demerit.

Whatever notions arose in the infinite consciousness and which exist in it determine the effects of merit and demerit. I, you and all this are all governed by the images that exist in the infinite consciousness, whether these images concern merit or otherwise.

The dying man thinks that he is dying and others are weeping for him. Even so do ideas of death and cremation, etc., arise in the others who are weeping for the dead relative. The dying man sees the world as it appears to him; but the others (the enemy who prayed for his death) think he is dead, and yet others (the friend who prayed for his welfare) consider that he has attained immortality. Thus both the prayers are satisfied. The three worlds are illusory products of delusion, but in it there are no divisions or contradictions. What is impossible in an illusion?

THE KING asked:

How can the formless merit and demerit give rise to a body?

VASIṢṬHA replied:

This universe is Brahman's dream-city: what is impossible in it? In a dream or while day-dreaming, one becomes a millionaire; even so, when the infinite consciousness begins to 'dream' one becomes a thousand (an army). Also, a thousand becomes one, as in deep sleep. Hence, it is not possible to say that something is impossible here, or to say that something happens here. Whatever is experienced is how it is experienced; hence, the knowers of truth see no contradictions or impossibilities in any of this. Such discussions concerning what is possible and what is impossible are meaningful only if they relate to a reality; but when even the world-appearance is only an illusion or a long dream, such discussions are meaningless. In a dream-like reality, the only touchstone is 'experience'; whatever is experienced is experienced as real. What exists here is in accordance with the image that arises in the infinite consciousness.

VASIṢṬHA continued: VI.2:210

I shall now tell you why a hundred moons do not appear in the sky when a hundred people contemplate and pray, 'May I be a moon'. All of them do not appear in this particular sky nor do they enter one particular moon. One person cannot enter the dream-city of another. Each one has his own dream-world and in that dream-world he becomes the moon. Even so it is with many men praying that they may all have a particular woman as wife. The fruit of such prayer is reflected in each one's consciousness which each one experiences as if it were real. Surely, all this is purely imaginary—and what is not possible for imagination?

Even so does one experience the fruits of one's charity, etc., in the other world. Such charity, etc., have formed an image in one's consciousness and consciousness itself imagines that in the other world it is experiencing the fruits of such charity. This is also the view of the wise men.

THE KING asked:

Lord, how does this body appear in the first place?

VASIṢṬHA replied:

What you have called the body does not exist in the eyes of the sage. It is only Brahman. Even so the word 'dream' used to illustrate the truth of the illusoriness of the world-appearance: there is no 'dream' in the infinite consciousness. There is neither a body nor a dream in it. There is neither a waking state, nor dream nor sleep. Whatever is is—it is void, it is OM. Enough of even such descriptions.

Between 'this' and 'that' is the body of consciousness: it is unity and diversity. Fullness (infinity) expands in infinity; and then the infinite alone exists as the world. It appears to be but it is not what it appears to be. Wherever consciousness conceives of creation, there creation seems to exist. The indivisible consciousness exists everywhere, and all that is also this creation. All this is the ever peaceful Brahman or infinite consciousness, which is also known as creation.

It cannot be otherwise. All else is ignorance and perversion. This is the experience of all in the world, this is the declaration of the scriptures and the vedas. When this truth is realised, that realisation itself becomes Brahman and this whole universe is realised as non-different from Brahman. Thus, my view is in conformity with experience and scriptural declaration. It is conducive to liberation here and now and hence it is the most appropriate one. When the truth concerning this tree of saṃsāra is clearly perceived, the realisation arises that 'I am the three worlds' and there is liberation.

The visible universe remains as it is, but ceases to be an object of consciousness; it merges in the infinite consciousness.

VI.2:211 RĀMA asked:

What are these siddhas (the perfected ones), sādhyas (celestials), yama (death), brahmā (creator), vidyādharas and divaukasas (celestials) and their own worlds?

VASIṢṬHA said:

Every night and every day, in front of you, behind you and above you, you see the worlds of these siddhas and others. You see them if you wish to see them, and you do not see them otherwise. If one does not practice the art of seeing them, they appear to be far away. These worlds, too, are subtle and supersensual (supernatural) and the whole space is full of them.

Just as this world is illusory and imaginary, even so are the worlds of the siddhas and celestials. By their psychic power, these worlds have been stabilised; even so you can make the world of your own imagination or fancy stable by intense contemplation. The siddhas or perfected ones have thus made their worlds stable; others find this difficult. This universe is filled with the infinite consciousness and the universe is whatever image the consciousness entertains within itself.

The universe has not been created by or out of something else: no such cause existed at the beginning of creation. It is whatever notion or image arises in consciousness. In one's own imagination a mountain arises though in truth there is no such mountain. Such is the nature of the world-appearance, too. Therefore, the knowers of this truth live here as if they were walking trees.

All these universes that appear in Brahman exist in it as non-different from it, just as the waves exist in the ocean non-different from it. Though this universe seems to have existed for a long time and though it seems to be a functional reality, still it is pure void and it is no more real than an imaginary city. Though people have experienced its existence, it does not exist: even as one sees one's own death in a dream. The unreal appears to be real. The reality and the unreality of the world are two aspects of the supreme being. Even the concept of supreme being is only a concept, not the truth. Let it all be this way or let the truth be different from all this. Where is the need to be confused and confounded? Abandon the pursuit of the fruits of actions. You are enlightened. Do not exert yourself in vain pursuit.

VI.2:212 VASIṢṬHA continued:

Brahman considers itself as the infinite space because Brahman is infinite consciousness. That infinite space itself is the cosmic person in whom this world exists; but all this is non-different from Brahman and hence all this is Brahman. This world-appearance is otherwise an illusion, though it is seen as a reality, even as water in the mirage is unreal and illusory though it seems to exist.

RĀMA asked:

Pray, tell me, when does Brahman not consider itself thus.

VASIṢṬHA said:

In Brahman, the infinite consciousness, the image of creation exists even now. However, though it is true that creation and non-creation exist in Brahman everywhere at all times, they do not exist independently of him—and hence from another point of view, they do not exist. Since this creation is (like movement and wind) non-different from Brahman, Brahman does not know it as an object. Therefore, creation is without beginning and without end and that is Brahman.

When you are not enlightened and when you experience an awakening by merely listening to these words, you experience an apparent duality or diversity in what is in fact non-dual Brahman. Nothing exists here and therefore there are no concepts of objects; there is nothing other than the self and the self does not conceive of an object. What appears to be the three worlds appears to be at all times, but it is the supremely peaceful Brahman in which there is no diversity at all. It is only as long as you are not fully enlightened that you experience apparent diversity. When you are fully enlightened, you will need neither scriptures nor instructions and you will not experience duality or diversity based on the notion of 'I'.

RĀMA asked:

What happens when the notion of 'I' arises in the supreme?

VASIṢṬHA replied:

When the 'I'-notion arises in the consciousness, the concept of infinite space arises with it, from this the time-space continuum and from this, division and diversity. Hence, there arise notions like 'I am here' which means 'I am not there'. When all these have arisen, the 'I' becomes aware of the subtle root-elements from which the world-appearance arises as also the world-appearance. Thus, from Brahman the infinite consciousness apparently comes into being that which is not-Brahman. However, this is only apparent and not real; in reality the infinite Brahman alone exists.

VASIṢṬHA continued: VI.2:213

Just as you questioned me just now, O Rāma, you did question me once before in a previous epoch. At that time, too, you were my disciple and I was your guru. I remember that dialogue clearly and I shall repeat it for you.

The DISCIPLE asked: Pray tell me, Lord at the end of the world-cycle, what is it that perishes and what is it that endures and does not so perish.

The PRECEPTOR said: My son, whatever is seen (the objects of perception) perishes, just as when you enter the deep sleep state, the dream-world perishes. All these worlds with their mountains and their directions perish utterly; even time and the activity, as also the world order, perish. All beings perish and even the space disappears because there is none that thinks of space or thinks in space. Even the gods like Brahmā the creator, Viṣṇu the protector and Rudra the redeemer cease to be; they do not exist even in name. What remains? Only the infinite consciousness, but even this is an inference based on the present experience.

The DISCIPLE asked: It has been said that the unreal does not come into being and that the real has no non-being: how does this happen and how does what is seen perish?

The PRECEPTOR said: My son, this does not perish and hence it is said that 'It is not seen'. It is said that the unreal has no being and the real has no non-being. That which does not exist at any time anywhere, is already non-being. How does it perish? What is permanent in the water seen in the mirage and what is permanent in illusion? Whatever is seen in this universe is an illusion, and why should not the illusion cease to be? Just as a dream comes to an end on waking up and the waking state comes to an end on going to sleep, all this world-appearance comes to an end. When one wakes up where does the dream-city go? Similarly one does not know where the world-appearance goes.

The DISCIPLE asked: Why does all this appear to be and why does that appearance cease to be?

The PRECEPTOR replied: It is the infinite consciousness alone that appears as all this—independent of it there is no world. Even while appearing to be all this, the infinite consciousness does not lose its own true nature or identity. Both appearance and non-appearance are aspects of consciousness, just as when your form is reflected in water, for instance, the reflection is temporary and your own form is not. Dreaming and dreamless sleep are aspects of one sleep; even so creation and dissolution are aspects of Brahman.

The DISCIPLE said: In a dream there is someone other than the dreamer (viz., pure consciousness which is not divided into the dreamer and the dream). Even so, is it possible that there is someone other than the perceiver of the world-illusion?

The PRECEPTOR said: That is so. Therefore, its real nature or form is not the world-appearance. Consciousness alone is and it illumines whatever is, but the appearance is experienced by another. Hence, it is the synthesis of contradictions. It does not illumine anything and it cannot even be said to be existence. It is the appearance in the infinite consciousness. How can there be 'real' and 'unreal' in the observer?

If it is said to be seen everywhere as all at all times, it can also be said that it is not seen as all everywhere at all times. It is the reality and it is the unreality at all times. It is the infinite consciousness. It does not perish and the other (the world-appearance) does not perish either. There is great sorrow only when the reality of the infinite consciousness, with its two aspects of creation and dissolution, is not realised: when it is thus realised there is great peace.

The Lord or the infinite consciousness alone is the pot, mountain, cloth, tree, grass, fire, the movable and the immovable—everything. The Lord is what is and what is not, the void, action, time, space and earth, existence and destruction, good and evil. There is nothing which the infinite consciousness is not. It is everything everywhere at all times; it is not anything anywhere at any time.

A blade of grass is the doer and the enjoyer; a pot is both the doer and the enjoyer; a piece of cloth is the doer and the enjoyer; sight is both the doer and the enjoyer; the mountain is both the doer and the enjoyer; man is the doer and the enjoyer—each one is the supreme Lord himself. In each of all these things, the Lord himself is the doer and the enjoyer or experiencer. For everything is Brahman who is beginningless and endless and the ordainer of everything. Hence, even creation and destruction are aspects of the one Lord or the infinite consciousness. Consciousness alone is both the doer and the experiencer of everything in everything. Hence, none here is the doer and the experiencer of anything, or the Lord is the doer and the experiencer of everything. Thus it is possible for everything (injunctions and prohibitions) to exist in the Lord and not to exist so in truth. All this is as all this is experienced by each one.

Thus did I instruct you, O Rāma. And thus have I told you all that is worth knowing. Remain established in the reality, in the state of enlightenment. Be free in nirvāṇa and rule the kingdom justly.

VASIṢṬHA said: VI.2:214

When the sage Vasiṣṭha thus concluded his teaching there was celestial music in the sky. There was a rain of flowers. Everyone in the assembly worshiped the sage with flowers.

Then king DAŚARATHA said: We have gained perfect knowledge. We rest in the supreme state. Our minds and our hearts have been utterly purified of all delusions and illusions, notions and perversions, by the illuminating teachings of the sage.

RĀMA said: By your grace, O lord among sages, my delusion has gone and I have attained the supreme state. I am now fully accomplished with my intelligence perfectly clear. I am freed of doubts. I rest in my own natural state as Brahman or in the knowledge of nirvāṇa. I shall do as you have said. There is nothing for me to gain by doing or by not doing anything. I have no friend or enemy. How can one realise all this except through your grace; how can a little boy cross the ocean without the help of a bridge or boat?

LAKṢMAṆA said: By the merit acquired by past births, we have heard the sage and are now rid of all doubts.

VIŚVĀMITRA said: It is as if we had bathed in a thousand sacred Gaṅgās (rivers).

NĀRADA said: We have heard what we have not heard either in heaven or on earth. Hence, we have been completely purified.

ŚATRUGHNA said: I have gained supreme peace and bliss.

After they had all spoken, the sage Vasiṣṭha said to the king: "At the conclusion of the recitation of a scripture, the holy ones should be worshiped. Hence, fulfil all the wishes of the brāhmaṇas. You will attain the fruits of this sacred undertaking." Then the king invited ten thousand brāhmaṇas from all over the country. He worshiped them. He fed them. He lavished gifts on them. Later, he adored the citizens, the servants, the poor and the crippled ones.

After that there was a great celebration in the capital, which included music concerts and dance performances, recitation of the vedas and other scriptures. Then all these artistes were entertained with food and drinks, and lavish gifts of clothes and jewels were bestowed upon them.

The enlightened king Daśaratha celebrated the successful completion of sage Vasiṣṭha's teaching for a whole week with a variety of entertainments and religious rites.

VI.2:215, 216 VĀLMĪKI said:

O Bharadvāja, thus did Rāma and others attain supreme knowledge and the state beyond sorrow. Even so, acquire this attitude and live as a liberated sage, free from doubt. Truly, by listening to this scripture you are already liberated; you are a jīvanmukta. Even a young boy listening to this attains self-knowledge. Even the ignorant ones, in whose hearts the bondage caused by cravings is strong and persistent, rise beyond the state of division by a study of this scripture that deals with liberation, even as young boys become mature men (non-boys). They will never again be involved in saṃsāra.

Even they who recite this scripture without understanding the meaning, they who write this (copy this) in a book, they who make someone read it or comment upon it, they attain great merit and enjoy life in heaven, and in the third birth attain liberation.

VĀLMĪKI said to king Ariṣṭanemi: Thus have I told you what Vasiṣṭha taught Rāma. By this path you will attain the truth. The KING said: Lord, by your grace I have crossed this saṃsāra. (To the messenger of the gods, the KING said:) You have been a true friend to me. You may now go. I shall contemplate the truth that I have thus heard.

The MESSENGER said to the celestial: I was supremely thrilled to hear all this. I shall now go to the abode of Indra.

The CELESTIAL said: I am truly blessed to hear all this from you, O messenger of the gods. Now you can go to Indra.

AGNIVEŚYA said to Kāruṇya: Thus did the celestial remain immersed in contemplation. Have you heard all this well? KĀRUṆYA replied: Surely. My delusion is gone. I shall now live a life of spontaneous non-volitional activity.

AGASTI said to Sutīkṣṇa: Thus did Agniveśya instruct his son Kāruṇya. Do not doubt this teaching, for he who doubts this perishes. SUTĪKṢṆA said: My ignorance has been dispelled and the lamp of knowledge has been kindled. I realise that all these objects of the world exist in the infinite consciousness like waves in the ocean. Hence, I shall live a life of spontaneous non-volitional activity. I am truly blessed. I salute you. For a disciple should adore and serve his guru by thought, word and deed. Lord, by your grace I have crossed this ocean of saṃsāra. I salute the supreme being, contemplating whom one realises that all this is indeed Brahman, the infinite consciousness. Salutations to the divine preceptor Vasiṣṭha.

OṂ TAT SAT— THE END

Index

human body and, 626, 630, 640
natural function and, 612
power of sight and, 484
prāṇa and, 356-357, 432
self-knowledge and, 500, 634
and suṣumṇā, 193
See also Solar energy (piṅgalā)
Suraghu, King, 281-285
Surrender, renunciation and, 399
Suruci (celestial nymph), 3
Surya, 397
Suṣumṇā nāḍī, 94, 193, 346
of Rāma, 486
Suṣupti mauna, 415
See also Silence
Sutīkṣṇa, Sage, 3, 725
Suvarṇa (color), 581
Suvarṇajaṭa, 108
Svabhāva (self-nature), 526
See also Self
Svarūpaṃ, 525
See also Self
Svasthah (I rest in the Self), 330

Takṣaka, 591
Tāmasa-tāmasa (dense and dull), 652-653
scripture and, 709
See also Births, types of; Impurity; Mind, purification of; Purity; Tamas
Tamas (darkness), 115, 201, 369, 375, 567
birth and, 653
cidābhāsa and, 324
and cosmic dissolution, 563
understanding and, 336
wisdom and, 530
See also Guṇas; Rajas; Satva
Tanmātras, 625
See also Element(s)
Taste, 48
Tatam, city of, 602
Teacher, enlightened. *See* Guru
Teja-dhāraṇā (fire contemplation), 581
See also Contemplation; Dhāraṇā
Thought
cessation of, 42, 57-58, 62, 91, 103, 134, 154, 175, 191, 212, 217, 218, 225, 243, 251, 257, 277, 289, 301, 320, 338, 340, 351, 363, 374-375, 383, 389-390, 399, 403-404, 415, 444-445, 460, 471, 478, 481, 515
and experience, 75, 86-87, 110-111, 129, 161, 208, 262-263, 273-274, 374, 386, 396, 444-445, 474, 493, 579, 652, 676
intelligence and, 87, 140, 213, 228, 329, 380, 381, 660
jīva and, 502-503, 553, 690-691
materialization of, 45, 48, 50, 52, 53, 61, 64, 81, 83, 92, 110, 117-119, 141, 151, 161-162, 183, 194, 274, 360-361, 363, 394-395, 397, 408, 411-412, 468, 471, 537, 559, 628, 644, 657, 676, 695
mind and, 44, 91, 110-111, 116-117, 129, 134, 161-162, 175, 214-215, 225, 228, 241, 257, 258, 269-270, 279, 286-287, 289, 301, 320, 496-497, 690-691
of no-mind, 504
power of, 515, 632, 656
prāṇa and, 301, 373
See also Consciousness; Mind; Perception
Time, 149, 313
and creation, 50, 60, 69, 88, 89, 160, 181, 186, 273, 308, 334, 386, 391, 407, 483, 495, 496, 498, 544-545, 633, 643, 714, 715
death and, 81, 149, 206, 333, 370-371, 558-559
divisions of, 119, 191, 242, 309, 319, 350, 396, 493, 567, 682, 692, 702, 703, 717
due, 92, 170, 192, 248, 318
illusion and, 706
jīva and, 502, 633
Lord Rāma on, 15-17
and meditation, 380, 543
Queen Līlā and, 60-61
and Sage Bhṛgu, 149-157
and seasons, 124, 557, 682
Self and, 102, 163, 214, 248, 296, 368, 407, 495
and world-cycle(s), 334, 346, 349, 351, 359, 377, 409, 451, 483, 498, 499, 504, 540, 546, 556, 558-559, 576
See also Existence, cycles of; Future; Past; Present
Touch, 48
Tranquility
and action, 151
awareness and, 660-661
creation and, 67
Lord Rudra (Śiva) and, 576
Self and, 664
self-enquiry and, 33, 142, 154, 179, 210-211, 244, 257, 540
wisdom and, 99-100, 178, 275, 279, 316, 353-354
Transcendent state. *See* Consciousness; Turīyātīta
Transformation, of body. *See* Body, transformation of
Transliteration, sanskrit, v
Tree, wishfulfilling, 236
Cūta, 346
and Indra, 497
Tretā Age, 359
See also Time, and world cycles
Trigarta, King of, 710